Computer Applications in Engineering and Management

Chapman & Hall/Distributed Computing and Intelligent Data Analytics Series

Series Editors: Niranjanamurthy M and Sudeshna Chakraborty

Machine learning and Optimization Models for Optimization in Cloud
Punit Gupta, Mayank Kumar Goyal, Sudeshna Chakraborty, Ahmed A Elngar

Computer Applications in Engineering and Management
Parveen Berwal, Jagjit Singh Dhatterwal, Kuldeep Singh Kaswan, Shashi Kant

Physics and Astrophysics: Glimpses of the Progress
Subal Kar

For more information about this series please visit:
https://www.routledge.com/Chapman-Hall-Distributed-Computing-and-Intelligent-Data-Analytics-Series/book-series/DCID

Computer Applications in Engineering and Management

Parveen Berwal
Jagjit Singh Dhatterwal
Kuldeep Singh Kaswan
Shashi Kant

CRC Press
Taylor & Francis Group
Boca Raton London New York

CRC Press is an Imprint of the
Taylor & Francis Group, an **informa** business

A CHAPMAN & HALL BOOK

First edition published 2022
by CRC Press
6000 Broken Sound Parkway NW, Suite 300, Boca Raton, FL 33487-2742

and by CRC Press
2 Park Square, Milton Park, Abingdon, Oxon, OX14 4RN

CRC Press is an imprint of Taylor & Francis Group, LLC

Library of Congress Cataloging-in-Publication Data
Names: Berwal, Parveen, author.
Title: Computer applications in engineering and management / Parveen Berwal, Jagjit Singh Dhatterwal, Kuldeep Singh Kaswan, Shashi Kant.
Description: First edition. | Boca Raton : Chapman & Hall/CRC Press, 2022. |
Series: Chapman & Hall/CRC distributed computing and intelligent data analytics series | Includes bibliographical references and index. |
Summary: "The book Computer Applications in Engineering and Management is about computer applications in Management, Electrical Engineering, Electronics Engineering and Civil Engineering. It covers the software tools for office automation, introduces the basic concepts of database management, and provides an overview about the concepts of data communication, internet, and e-commerce. Additionally, the book explains the principles of computing management used in construction of buildings in Civil Engineering and the role of computers in power grid automation in Electronics Engineering.
Features: Provides an insight to prospective research and application areas related to industry and technology Includes industry-based inputs Provides a hands-on approach for readers of the book to practice and assimilate learning. This book is primarily aimed at undergraduates and graduates in computer science, information technology, civil engineering, electronics and electrical engineering, management, academicians, and research scholars"—Provided by publisher.
Identifiers: LCCN 2021048779 (print) | LCCN 2021048780 (ebook) |
ISBN 9781032078823 (hbk) | ISBN 9781032228716 (pbk) | ISBN 9781003211938 (ebk)
Subjects: LCSH: Engineering—Data processing. | Business—Data processing.
Classification: LCC TA345 .B4824 2022 (print) | LCC TA345 (ebook) |
DDC 620.00285—dc23/eng/20220105
LC record available at https://lccn.loc.gov/2021048779

ISBN: 9781032078823 (hbk)
ISBN: 9781032228716 (pbk)
ISBN: 9781003211938 (ebk)

DOI: 10.1201/9781003211938

Typeset in Times
by codeMantra

Contents

     7.6.1.1 Setup...150
     7.6.1.2 Hardware Configuration...150
     7.6.1.3 Arduino Sketch Upload..150
     7.6.1.4 Calibration...150
     7.6.1.5 Load Monitoring and Data Capture..............................150
     7.6.1.6 Visual Observations...151
  7.7 Integrated Physiological Monitoring Status for the Evaluation
    of the Model between Emotional Exertion and Production for
    Road Construction...151
    7.7.1 Method...151
    7.7.2 Regression Models...152
     7.7.2.1 Signal Processing...152
  7.8 Evaluation of Low-Carbon Building Techniques for Simulating the
    Dynamic Response..152
    7.8.1 SD Model..153
  7.9 A Negative Emissions Building Adaptive, Context-Driven
    Evaluation Architecture..154
    7.9.1 Benchmarking for Building Energy Performance.......154
    7.9.2 Dynamic and Context-Driven Benchmarking..............155
    7.9.3 Framework Implementation.....................................156
  7.10 Optimum Windows Selecting Radiation-Based Modeling...........156
    7.10.1 Methods of the Model Development...........................157
    7.10.2 Model I...157
     7.10.2.1 Setup of Baseline Building Surface..............157
     7.10.2.2 Metric Calculation.......................................157
    7.10.3 Model II..158
     7.10.3.1 Window Subdivision....................................158
     7.10.3.2 Daylighting Simulation................................158
  7.11 Conclusion...159

Chapter 8 Circuit Simulation and Design...161

  8.1 Evaluation of TKK CTL Circuit Simulation Occurrences...........161
    8.1.1 Interconnect Modeling..162
    8.1.2 Linear MOR...162
    8.1.3 Micromodel Realization...163
    8.1.4 Module and Circuitry Block Behavioral Modeling.....163
  8.2 Outstanding Issues in Model Order Reduction...........................166
    8.2.1 Massively Coupled Systems......................................167
    8.2.2 Power Grid Modeled...167
  8.3 Projection-Based Framework...168
    8.3.1 Truncated Balanced Realizations..............................168
    8.3.2 PRIMA Projection Algorithm...................................169
    8.3.3 Input-Correlated TBR (PMTBR)..............................170
    8.3.4 Non-linear Positive Real Balancing..........................170
    8.3.5 Balancing of Nonlinear...170
    8.3.6 Model Reduction Truncation....................................171
  8.4 Efficient Activation of Electronic Component Models' Convolutional
    Neural Network Parameters...171
    8.4.1 Weight-Initialization Methods..................................172

Preface

This book presents the principles and techniques of managing engineering and construction of building from the initial conceptual phase, through design and construction, to completion. It emphasizes computing management during the early stages of development because the ability to influence the quality, cost, and schedule of a project can best be achieved during the early stages. Most books discuss computing management during construction, after the scope of work is fully defined, the budget is fixed, and the completion date is firm. It is then too late to make any significant adjustments to improve the quality, cost, or schedule of the project construction of management. Numerous tables and graphs are presented and discussed throughout this book to provide guidelines for the management of the three basic components of a project: scope, budget, and schedule.

Electronic Circuit Analysis and Design is intended as a core text in electronics for undergraduate electrical and computer engineering students. The purpose of the second edition of the book is to provide a foundation for analyzing and designing both analog and digital electronic circuits.

The majority of electronic circuits today are designed as integrated circuits (ICs), in which the entire circuit is fabricated on a single piece of semiconductor material. The IC may contain over a million semiconductor devices and other elements and may perform many complex functions. The microprocessor is an example of such a circuit. The ultimate objective is to understand the operation, characteristics, and limitations of these ICs.

Initially, discrete transistors are analyzed and designed. The complexity of the circuits studied is then increased. Eventually, the reader should be able to analyze and design the basic elements of ICs, such as digital logic gates.

This text is an introduction to the complex subject of electronic circuits. Therefore, more advanced material is not included. Specific technologies, such as gallium arsenide, which are used in special applications, are also not included, although reference may be made to a few specialized applications. Finally, the layout and fabrication of ICs are not covered, since these topics alone can warrant entire texts.

Authors

Dr. Kuldeep Singh Kaswan is presently working as an Associate Professor in the School of Computing Science & Engineering, Galgotias University, Uttar Pradesh, India. His contributions focus on BCI, Cyborg, and Data Sciences. His Academic degrees and 13 years of experience working with global Universities like, Amity University, Noida; Gautam Buddha University, Greater Noida; and PDM University, Bahadurgarh have made him more receptive and prominent in his domain. He received a Doctorate in Computer Science from Banasthali Vidyapith, Rajasthan and has obtained Master's Degree in Computer Science and Engineering from Choudhary Devi Lal University, Sirsa (Haryana). He has supervised many UG and PG projects of engineering students. He has supervised 2 Ph.D. graduates and presently is supervising 4 Ph.D. papers. He is also a Member of Computer Science Teacher Association (CSTA), New York, United States; International Association of Engineers (IAENG), Hong Kong; IACSIT (International Association of Computer Science and Information Technology, United States; professional member of Association of Computing Machinery, United States, and IEEE. He has a number of publications in International/National Journal and Conferences.

Dr. Jagjit Singh Dhatterwal is presently working as an Assistant Professor, Department of Computer Science & Application, PDM University, Haryana. He completed a Doctorate in Computer Science from Mewar University, Rajasthan, India and received a Master of Computer Application from Maharshi Dayanand University, Rohtak (Haryana). He has also worked with Maharishi Dayanand University, Rohtak, Haryana. He is also a Member of Computer Science Teacher Association (CSTA), New York, United States; International Association of Engineers (IAENG), Hong Kong; IACSIT (International Association of Computer Science and Information Technology, United States; professional member of Association of Computing Machinery, United States, IEEE; and Life member of Computer Society of India, India. His area of interest includes Artificial Intelligence, BCI, and Multi-Agents Technology. He has a number of publications in International/National Journals and Conferences.

Dr. Shashi Kant is associated with the Department of Management at Bule Hora University, Ethiopia, Horn of Africa. He holds a Master of Business Administration, UGC-NET, Master of Sociology, UGC-JRF, ANC-NIIT, and Ph.D. in Management from India. He has over 15 years of teaching and research experience in the field of Management and Marketing in India and Ethiopia. He has published several research papers in Scopus, reviewed national and international journals. He already published books on Strategic Management and Entrepreneurship and Perspectives of Marketing. He has taught several courses of management like information system, system analysis and design, strategic management, and entrepreneurship development from fundamental to advanced levels at higher educational institutions. His commitment and approach to teaching have been rewarded with the highest teaching evaluations an instructor can receive: in an institution particularly dedicated to outstanding teaching, he is consistently among the top 5% of all teaching staff.

He has held numerous previous administrative positions, including reviewer, and entrepreneurship trainer (Ministry of Skill Development, India). He has also been involved in developing and implementing UG and PG curriculums of strategic management and entrepreneurship development. His area of interest includes management, information system, strategic management, marketing, and entrepreneurship development.

 **Dr. Parveen Berwal** is Associate Professor of the Civil Engineering Department at Galgotia College of Engineering & Technology, Greater Noida. He is an experienced academician with over 10 years of versatile experience in the field of Civil engineering. He is M. Tech & Ph.D. in Civil Engineering. He has filed 3 patents in the field of civil engineering. He is also Session Chaired TEQIP sponsored conference in Government engineering college, Banswara (Rajasthan) 2018 & keynote Speaker in a webinar at GCET in 2020. He is having more than 20 publications in ESCI & Scopus Indexed and various International Journals and Conferences. He has successfully guided 20 PG students and various UG students. He has contributed to various prestigious Accreditations like NAAC, NBA, NIRF, and others. He is an active member of a professional society like IRED (New York), IAENG (Hong Kong). He is the reviewer of the American Journal of Civil Engineering. He has experience of around 10 years in teaching UG/PG students of Civil engineering, mentoring M. Tech thesis and projects in the area of highway construction, utilization of recycled aggregate, use of waste material in civil engineering.

1 Introduction of Management, Civil, Electrical and Electronic (MCEE) in Computers

1.1 INTRODUCTION

Many logistical and managerial tasks carried out in the office environment. The joint functions of an agency are preparing, distributing, editing, and reviewing information [1]. These works were done manually or with mechanical and electrical equipment before the invention of computers. The fundamental essence of an office has changed significantly in the past few decades. Automation of works using new techniques improves the overall skills of an office. Civil engineering experiments also require the development of complicated mathematical models to handle the large amount of data generated through a great number of repetitive experimental studies, thus offering a sensor modeling and simulation technology-wide platform. Theory and technology of Human–Computer Interaction is an important trend in computer applications, sound processing is text-friendly, graphical content, its image, and its comfort, its human–machine interface has been vastly improved, civil engineering sampling techniques have been an innovation [2]. CAD is one of the convincing and mature technologies, in which, using external CAD technical drawings, light transitions, surface décor, changes in dimensions, construction, and other environmental impacts can be detected by computer designing using animation techniques. CAD is a method of developing the responsive CAD system, the Optima 1 CAD system, the intelligent CAD system, and ultimately the implementation of integrated CAD interactive intelligence (III CAD) [3].

Coordination on the subject is also a significant aspect. The control and measurement equipment are provided to ensure a proper training workshop standard. Devices that are used regularly must be stable and resistant to harm. The appropriate entry to space seems to be another problem. The time of the research head and their team of an organization is reduced to regular working hours. This is not always practical to carry out experiments at home by students. Therefore, an effective way is needed to access the laboratories all day long. The use of interactive or remote laboratories enables connectivity throughout the research period. Moreover, when experiments are performed electronically, it can also reduce the possibility of contaminations to the patients involved in the research.. The experiments can be prepared and presented in the Internet. Thus, this approach enables many users to simultaneously use the remote laboratory [4].

From Very Large-Scale Integration (VLSI) aspects, the digital circuit and central processer unit have led to the development of digital design and machine planning technologies. In this respect too, logic gates are used. The traditional 5 V to low power CMOS can be built by utilizing various voltages (3.3, 2.5, 1.8 V). Use of CMOS technology is declining in traditional fields because of the problems such as increasing energy usage and leakage. Congestion due to storage of CMOS machines is another problem. Hence, many alternative technologies with high functionality, high integration frequency and non-volatility have been examined to deal with such problems. Meritor Crossbar with NAND—a mobile computer built on flash – has recently gained ground. The conversion of logical page numbers (LPNs) into actual page numbers is suggested to the Flash Translation Layer (FTL) owing to the limitation of deletion before writing. Because of the expenditure of hardware and power usage of the semiconducting material storage unit, there is a very small RAM in it. Computers have been extensively, used and innovation has been developed. We can design and produce electronic devices such as sensors with the help of nanotechnology, which can be used to

DOI: 10.1201/9781003211938-1

create smaller and faster computers. The increasing convergence of the transistor system means that high energy capacity and temperatures circuits have an enormous effect on the center of chip problems which lead to temperature hotspots. This influence will slow down existing speeds and generations of scaling. New methods are now used to eradicate this issue, and the methodology of machine learning (ML) is most helpful.

1.2 MANAGEMENT COMPUTING

1.2.1 Modes of Data Processing

The aforementioned types of information business processes are commonly used by organizations to improve their performance [5]. The programs involved in these programs are as follows:

Batch Processing
This method of processing allows the data to be clustered (in batch form) until they are analyzed on a serial basis, and regular reports are collected.

The batch may be a collection of offline purchase requisitions or purchases.

The package is handled at the defined frequency at a specified length of time and performed in a serial order for each transaction per batch.

The batch processing approach eliminates the computer system's idle time, so there is no operating interference to change work from one task to another.

It is the most suitable mode of treatment in many processes such as accounting or customer statements where information (records) is not required to be updated regularly. The drawbacks of batch production are as follows:

- It prevents timeliness in some cases.
- At every point, one job is waiting in line, and hence, the turning period often increases.
- It is impossible to have the optimum quality timetable.

1.2.2 Online Processing

Online computing is a kind of processing that results from data processing. It makes possible to spread an account's information immediately from the site of generation without sorting them first, thus improving the functionality of storage structures under the CPU. By entering a computer dialog, a user can initiate an inquiry request, and the user can collect updates on their inquiry in a fraction of a second [7].

This fact encourages consumers to carry out purchases one by one to verify that the action of the computer is right. The user also relies on all monitoring to control the device. Examples of online technologies are trading, bourses, inventory management, reporting construction process, and management of inventories.

1.2.3 Real-Time Processing

Real-time processing involves continuous input, process and output of data. Input production and response are so limited that physical activity can be monitored alone. Effective time management requires all facilities' ability to quickly share input (not regularly, as in batch processing) [8].

- Direct (online) connecting to central processor between input/output devices
- Response time is relatively rapid, allowing more contacts throughout the high-definition processing unit. The feature of data processing in real time that makes them truly distinct from the best-known batches and online retrieval devices is the direct response to receiving a letter.

Consequently, computer processing services are not necessarily Internet applications exclusively in real time. It can also have the following applications:

- Account balance inquires can be answered within seconds.
- An instant automatic credit check can be done, using which a sales manager can find information about sales trends.
- The original document for performance analysis can be updated online.
- An efficient schedule for reservations, banks, airlines, and airlines can also be made.
- Radar-related tools can be used for land signalized intersections, security, and ground automation.

1.2.4 DISTRIBUTED DATA PROCESSING

When multiple machines are used, distributed computing connects all the machines by creating a network among them using a computer system. Each control interface is usually chosen to handle the entire system for a specific workload. Databases must be built on many sites to function efficiently and used for numerical computation. The database is split into logical parts and stored somewhere. Users can easily access both physical and virtual databases from any site. Distributed information structures are the cornerstone of distributed database system (DDBS). This type is more useful for organizations having many branches in different locations over long distances. For its operational activities, each division retains information gathered from its homepage. Most of the output can be accomplished locally. A famous app is in banks where intelligent ends are fixed to a big machine in all subsidiaries at the headquarters. The components are transmitted to the master where they are saved [9].

1.2.5 BASIC FUNCTIONS OF DATA PROCESSING

The information collection shall, for certain purposes, be amended, modified, or documented to maximize its usefulness and significance. The below are the fundamental functions of every information processing [10]:

- **Origination:** Data analysis first involves generating the data to be collected. Generally speaking, the existence, form and content of the primary sources, such as order sales, orders etc.
- **Data capture:** Data must be recorded or collected in one way or another before data can be processed. The type of knowledge is used for input and storage, depending upon the industry and method adopt for data capturing. The data derived from source records in the form of papers and management documents can be:
  - Cravings
  - Automatic directory computers
  - Other machines supporting feedback understandable by the machine.
- **Sorting**
  When ordered in a linear sequence, management of documents is usually smoother. For example, they can be sorted in the following orders:
  - From high to low
  - From the oldest to the latest, and vice versa.
  "Sorting" means arranging hidden records in a sequential order.
- **Merging**
  This function lets you compile many files consecutively so that the files are already ordered. For instance, a new user file could be added to the current client master file in a magnetic disk with a label like a customer number.

- **Calculating**

  Numerical data manipulation is called calculation which is a common task for data analysis to obtain effective data. This is generally the most important part of the procedure since the results mostly occur throughout the manufacturing process.

- **Summarizing**

  Summarizing can be defined as a concise and practical reduction of the quantity of the data. The data are generally summarized in various forms such as charts and diagrams. There are a few graphs like column chart, bar chart, line chart, area chart etc., to view data from a view of several created machines [11].

- **Managing output results**

  Following details are needed, when data are recorded and essential:

  Following the conclusion of diverse statistics procedures, information, or results are to be distributed or transferred by:

  a.   The setup monitoring and diffusion of processed results.

  b.   Records such as draughts, invoices and reports are unrestricted.

  c.   The reclamation of a confident item or articles of well-preserved evidence user application.

  d.   An impression that comprises all features that the receivers use output i.e. the system covers evidence.

  e.   Interrelate and replication (transmission).

  This is a method that is continuous until the end user can use and additionally conveniently find the information from one place or operation to another. It is also necessary to copy or duplicate output records.

- **Storage**

  Finally, the results of data processing must be stored to make possible use of the document. This aspect is referred to as storage in Figure 1.1.

- **Data hierarchy**

  Below is the hierarchy of details in the ascending order of complexities:

Information structure consists of files and records. And so on, articles [13].

Bit: The word bit is the short form of binary digit. One of the dual terms 0 or 1 could be anticipated.

Byte: In a programming language, the basic knowledge unit is called a byte. An 8-bit mix normally saves a byte of data.

Field or object: One or several more bits of data of an area or data object contain data regarding an individual's personal properties.

Database: A record is a single person's list of fields.

File: A record collection is a disk. The description of a system file is much like the manual file in a repository.

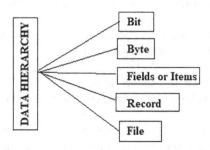

FIGURE 1.1   Data hierarchy.

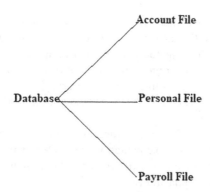

FIGURE 1.2   File record system.

Archive: A database includes all organizational archives arranged and incorporated for updating and collection of files as shown in Figure 1.2.

1.2.6   APPLICATION PORTFOLIO DEVELOPMENT

- IT-based application is a technology of the company's for collection of knowledge on expenditures by the enterprise. The knowledge is designed to demonstrate how these programs support an organization's mission and facilities, and how the expenditures are ultimately linked to expectations. The approach increases the capacity of policymakers to assess the possible impact of costs on the company's operation and technologies and the overall IT infrastructure. The application's asset allocation management aims to control the major corporate assets. In the tactics of the organization, average performance is key. The approach of portfolio honors the company's maturity [14].
- It also recognizes technological progress, and, given their full activities, the organization's application budget was included to look at future programs. The portfolio provides a mechanism for the organization of new projects within the context of enterprise strategy and evaluate a wider IT technology portfolio.
- This 1996 approach is based on the general policies, guidelines, and procedures needed for education decisions but with high applicability standards. The application portfolio
  - Shows similarities between corporate strategies and strategic initiatives.
  - Promotes identification of risk for application expenditure and contributes to the use of appropriate risk control methods;
  - Creates a structure for reporting corporate effectiveness;
  - Ensures that the whole IT infrastructure of a company is successfully incorporated.

1.2.7   CHARACTERISTICS OF PORTFOLIO-BASED IT MANAGEMENT

Management of the IT software maximizes the control process used to construct a specification. These experiences demonstrated the need to discuss the constraints of the process as well as extensive consultations with various stakeholders. The portfolio concept is based on management's philosophy that any big investment requires close monitoring to improve its value and shield it from threats to its integrity. The principle of traditional investment types—usually in portfolios, real estate, business papers, and inventories—is well known. The strategies allow policymakers not only to consider the whole range of investment, but also to take discrete investment into account [15].

The need for an equity investment is less understood, but not less important. Technological business investment requires large public funding; in a global networking world, they are also mission-critical and intertwined.

Request financing can be leveraged very easily if the portfolio is sufficient to meet evolving needs in markets and services. On the other hand, restrictive construction, unreasonable capabilities, productivity claims, and incompetence will undermine their value. Portfolio-based management control is a centralized evaluation of the success of the entire allocation continuum. This ensures that both the company's vast framework and its associated individual department's application portfolios are showing new ventures [16]. It sets out a framework in which

- Detailed decision-making information is accessible in light of an entity's operations.
- Application development and implementation are guided by the clear business needs of an organization to serve its citizens and fulfill its regulatory mandate. Tools for the administration of their statutory responsibilities.
- A comprehensive analytical mechanism is available for the determination of the best form of monitoring to conduct a project based on a quantitative risk study.
- Big projects are separated into equal, easier-to-use projects in any phase.
- Simply apply value without accepting the financing authorities' accompanying procedures.
- Portfolio-based IT is based on organizational knowledge about all instruments from the standpoint of an investment company. A wide range of decision-makers are responsible for this portfolio including ministry officials, specialist organization managers, and program managers. The experience is structured to identify trends, problems, and prospects and to analyze solutions to a company's total costs. In the program portfolio, information about an individual company is included:
  - Engineering and personnel capacity
  - Business- and corporate software development
  - Task, regulations, structures, and procedures within the company
  - Designed hardware, technologies, and physical network and operation
  - Other frameworks
  - Continuous
  - Cost of current and potential expenses and advantages
  - Difficulties and opportunities of the application.

1.2.8 MANAGEMENT OF DATA PROCESSING SYSTEMS IN BUSINESS ORGANIZATIONS

In a standard corporation, the measurement system can be very complex. Structural management is the key to the entire company's success. The management structure depends on the size and efficiency of the organization. Systems can occur so simply that one manager and even an entire organization involved in such contexts has retained. The information processing system is configured in a typical scenario:

1. Electronic data processing (EDP) chief
2. Software programming
3. Application for programmer
4. Controllers
5. Repair and maintenance engineers
6. Lists of management.

The data processing manager normally has the following duties:

1. Acquires new technology, including applications and hardware.
2. Same assessment.
3. Accomplishes approved innovations.

4. Provides EDP services in line with the requirements of the company's customers.
5. Adds new functionality and removes old functionality.
6. Implements new industry regulations and provides required interfaces for consumers.
7. Conducts resource accounting.
8. Maintains the system's functionality by inspection and remedial intervention in every collapse scenario.

1.2.9 COMPUTERIZED FINANCIAL ACCOUNTING SYSTEM (FAS)

The finance and accounting scheme is at the forefront of the whole supply chain. Like a traffic cop, he records financial documents or accounts. Financial planning is a process of capturing and handling all transactions within an institution involving operations affecting the financial standing of the corporation. The financial statements and the business balance sheet are prepared every year [16].

- **Why computerized FAS?**
  An organization's financing needs to be controlled, and computers are used to control this more efficiently. There is a considerable amount of quantitative accounting information obtained using the same instrument. The calculations are very simple and more accurate. Reports can be forwarded more quickly and occasionally [17].

1.2.10 COMPUTERIZED INVENTORY CONTROL SYSTEM

- **What is inventory?**
  - Inventory refers to the buffer inventories of the items used to minimize the harm caused by the company's non-accessible supplies.
  - Varying stocks of different commodities shall be retained based on use, cost, and other characteristics.
- **Why control inventory?**
  - In most businesses, stock accounts for total operating costs between 50% and 70%. Although keeping stocks is unavoidable, it should be remembered that the inventory is an idle resource that adds additional costs. The company's profitability will be reduced by excess stockpiles in Figure 1.3.
  - Inventories can also be tightly monitored and supervised. Stock objectives can also be controlled.

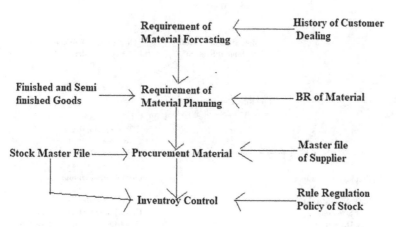

FIGURE 1.3 Inventory control and material management.

- It reduces the depletion of the consumer where necessary supplies cannot be used, and also reduces the total cost of products, covering the cost of sourcing, storage, and handling, in line with appropriate service requirements [18].
- Scope of quest inventory
- Supply preparation
- Supply-demand
- Goods receipt and testing
- Stocking machinery

1.2.11 COMPUTERIZED PAYROLL SYSTEM

The payroll system ensures that a precise and prompt calculation of pay is provided for each employee.

The payroll approach also generates essential inputs for financial reporting and accountability in Figure 1.4.

The system of payment is designed to calculate payments and manage documents [19].

1.2.12 COMPUTERIZED INVOICING SYSTEM

Billing is an integral part of a wide variety of procedures, including order scheduling and invoice processing. The issue with method is:

- Customer Receipts Ordering
- Customer Receipts Confirmation
- Control of order
- Invoice generation.

When the payment is made, the accounts payable method will take over [20]. The new invoice file was transformed into a deferred revenue system output in Figure 1.5.

1.2.12.1 Processing Steps

Consumer purchase orders are used in different formats in the computer system by fax in type of a request form. Applications are checked by checking product prices and customer credit ratings. Right instructions are saved in the order register.

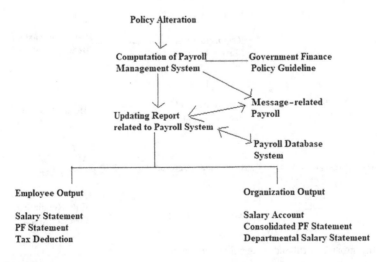

FIGURE 1.4   Payroll system.

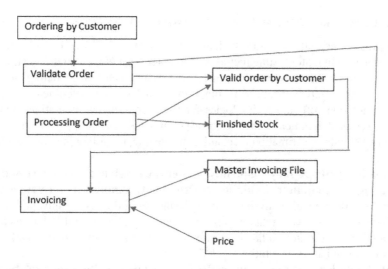

FIGURE 1.5 Invoicing system.

Transactions are performed by checking the functionality of goods from the finished inventory register. In this stage, three results are created: select list, slide, and sale booklet. After the order has been authorized, the relevant invoice will be created with reference to the expense master file. A checkbook is drawn up, and the required copy number is made during this phase. The most recent invoices will be transferred to the invoice master file.

1.3 CIVIL COMPUTING

Civil engineering is a professional engineering discipline that deals with the design, construction, and maintenance of physically and naturally built environments, including public works such as roads, bridges, canals, dams, airports, sewerage systems, pipelines, structural components of buildings, and railways.

A. **Strengthening being comprehensive and professional**

The creation of specific and interrelated irregularities extends from an construal of the objective world to the renovation of the objective world. To achieve structural reforms and societies, on the one hand, an analytically minded environment is expected, and the science and technologies are strategically divided; on the other hand, technologies have to be mixed so a lot of work alone cannot be solved. The development of modern and advanced technology thus infiltrates national life to prevent great disturbance or incomprehension.

B. **Infiltrate many components such as economic, social environment, and trade**

Engineering was the first complete reliability both in the past and in the present. Computer knowledge and technologies will also increase the complexities and costs of adapting to the progress of science and technology, which is a physically removing used in the computing technologies field, in the spirit of financial and cultural activity.

C. **Circulation in new products of modern science and technology**

After the development of an electric tube in 1904, it took just 42 years for the first unit to be opened in 1946. The dielectric transistor was designed to create a semiconductor for around 10 years. The integrated circuit interface only took less than 2 years to reach fine computer microprocessors. Ultra-fine computer development simulation software can be described as a coordinated performance in the fourth generation. Innovations and "device production" engineering is gradually giving room for technological development.

1.3.1 Computing Simulated Simulations Engineering Application

A computer virtual numerical simulation shall identify and integrate the core content frameworks of the system model and simulator testing methods. Computer technology that draws similar technical domains may use simulation system architecture. Systems and materials modeling and research are key civil engineering scientists. Numerical computing is included as a lifetime or validated instrument in new simulation software technologies for the promotion of simulations and computing technologies. A series of parameters and the corresponding text will now be dynamically generated for the interactive simulator estimation mechanics. In specific, the following are the advantages:

A. **Mathematical patterns may frequently answer the tough or impossible reality of civil engineering in a computer simulation environment, compositional relationship, etc.**

   Therefore, theoretical analysis of strength and durability is complicated in practice since many real component relationships are established, but several failure measures are also available. Each criterion has a certain size and, along with experimental outcomes, each requirement has a constitutional relationship.

B. **Virtual simulation software may model circumstances, alterations to the environment, and development of construction knowledge**

   We may, for example, conveniently evaluate performance with bridge or prototype construction tools to apply the properties of materials in several forms (including shapes, and combinations of steel) and calculate dynamic simulation.

1.3.2 Application of CAD System

Highly qualified technologies are also an attractive field for computers. He is a simulator expert, mostly based on a basic body of knowledge, an inference system, and user experience, and extra information for computer solving and analytical skills. The regular project typesetting is shown in Figure 1.6.

Information and knowledge storage experience is a static collection. A powerful knowledge base can very well articulate and store expertise in the body of knowledge. The machine of logic is

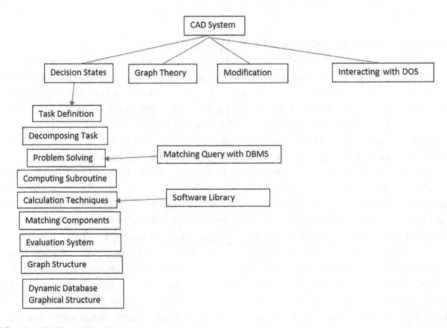

FIGURE 1.6   CAD system diagram.

an expert system technique used to improve parameter of problems. There is generally positive, cynical, and contradictory logic. The consequence of the reasoning process is based on the existing facts and rules, positive argument, and data orientation. The interpreter is a mechanism to answer questions of users in the thought process. Application in the context of reasoning is the context of complex information in the database to answer customer concerns such as why, how, and others. The graphical frame and the interface are peculiar to the technology expert system. They also culminate in the matured bounds, the CAD software kit is fused into the system, and the expert system is fully automated and intelligent.

1.4 ELECTRICAL COMPUTING

1.4.1 REMOTE CONTROL STRUCTURES

A. Direct control

Direct access means that you can interface with the hardware directly. The network system is shown in Figure 1.7. The server, infrastructure, and security witch computer control module are included in this framework. Both stages including the HTTP or the short Ethernet layer can be achieved by network modules.

Final control involves prompt completion of the necessary system procedures. One drawback is the minimal resources available from the built-in computer, which has two roles: the database and a process management system WWW (World Wide Web). A single control system is included with the 8-bit microcontroller and Ethernet controller. The entire user interface will be included in the programming memory chip as a static HTML script. The use of technology would have digital components that carry out all consumer experiences. JavaScript can be used for this purpose [3]. Another task for a microcontroller control unit is to the detriment of the presented structure solution. This paradigm is recommended for basic frameworks that need a direct response from customers. Please note, these services are only managed by a small number of users as shown in Figure 1.8.

B. Control via a dedicated server

As seen in Figure 1.8, the form extended from point A. The system has been connected to various online services specifically related to the control system.

The system offers all the advantages of direct control, including additional costs during deployment and operation. The dedicated server manages a web server's complicated websites. Meta description depends on the condition of the control system. Only the processor with a microcontroller performs certain required functionality on the computer. For the entire bandwidth of the user interface, a physical server is used. The server and control unit must be physically integrated. Due to the larger measurements of the server, the connection

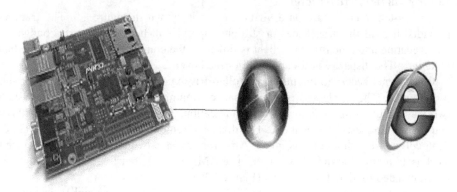

FIGURE 1.7 Structure of system in direct control.

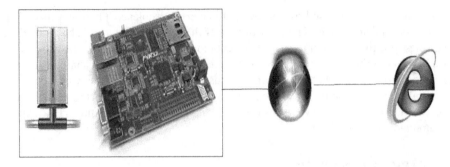

FIGURE 1.8 Structure of dedicated server.

FIGURE 1.9 Structure of virtual server.

is not always possible in terms of the controller height. It raises delays to link a device to a controller on long routes.

The wireless network assists in building and placing the history of the control strategy in a folder. All networking facilities, including that of the fixing and setup of the essential applications, may also be presented.

C. Control via the virtual server

The system architecture on a virtual server is shown in Figure 1.9. The framework provided has all the assistances of straight supervision, but delivers extra budgets during execution and amenity. The client is linked to the computing cloud as with dedicated machines. The disparity is not apparent for the buyer.

For Internet access to the microcontroller-driven controller, a network adapter should be mounted. The implanted computer can communicate with the computer system in two ways: request and continuous communication. The global solution is the Customer and Server Request-Answer mode. For this requirement, no regional static IP (Internet Protocol) address should be assigned. Any free server provided by an infrastructure network is an innovation in virtualization. The XML-RCP (Extensible Markup Language) is recommended for data transmission (Figure 1.10).

The method of data sharing is XML-RCP structured. It helps to simplify customer queries on the server. The driver specifies the suitable methods in the remote desktop: bring

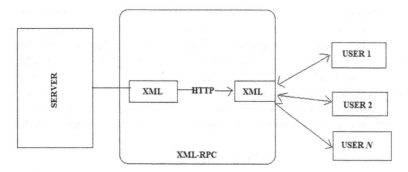

FIGURE 1.10   Data transfer using XML-RPC.

the service's current position into the virtual machine catalogue, and download running instructions.

A significant architecture requirement is the number of requests raised by the embedded device. To change nothing, an unnecessary entire network and server load may be generated in addition to the usual server monitoring for new duties. The lack of hardware contact will result in long questioning times.

D. Choosing the structure of remote control

To do the job, the code from B was used. It promotes direct customer experience with the technology and enables the expansion of modern control structures. As a different channel, a dedicated server was attached to the management system. A specialized node was used for NGW100 (Network Gateway) Atmel. The database is connected to the wireless serial device (Recommended Standard 232).

1.4.2   EXAMPLE OF REMOTE LABORATORY

A. Basic design goals

The protocol shall allow the user to directly interact with the object. The potential system flowchart is shown in Figure 1.10. The unit includes a temperature sensor and two electric motors: the radiator and the ventilator to refresh the destination. Both sections of the controller are included.

You will experiment automatically with an implemented two-state controller. The speed of command will modify hysteresis controller area fixed-point temperatures and width.

The aim was to create and implement an electronic system that enables remote control over the Internet. The remote control concentrates on the interaction of selected physical phenomena. In a lateral 30 cm cube, the minimal dimensions of the entire structure are compacted. The framework must help the designer to touch the object to monitor the implications of any parameter to change the object. The system should have an automatic operating mode to detect improvements in an object with a certain range of experimental parameters. The author proposed the calculation of temperature fluctuations based on modifications in the cooling mechanism during continuous heating of the object. Refreshment is forced to evaporate. HMI enables the user to manipulate objects conveniently. As a UI for the study, a web page was included. The object is seen on the map with temperature fluctuations. In an automatic or device protocol, the client may manage the object by a two-state monitor.

B. Proposed project

The test must communicate with other devices with the object directly. The proposed scheme was an experiment with the detector and an object with two elements: the cooling fan and the heater. Both elements are controlled by the pilot. The movement of the control object could take a long time—a first-order inertial object. An item was used as the aluminum radiator. It is possible to calculate the temperature of the product and to adjust the heating and cooling elements. The heating system has been permanently repaired without the possibility of a consumer exemption. The customer monitors the actual temperature. Connect a fan on a permanent heating system to or from record temperature fluctuations. The operator specifically controls the signal by adding three LEDs. You can change the status of your computer by tapping on the homepage. This is the manual mode. Two-state controllers were introduced in autonomous transmission. The control center is suitable for adjusting the set point temperatures and breadth of the hysteresis zone controller.

$$u(t) = \left\{ \begin{array}{l} \text{OFF when } e(t) > \dfrac{H}{2} \\ \text{ON when } e(t) < \dfrac{-H}{2} \end{array} \right\}$$

Legislation shall be implemented following Formula 1. If $y(t)$ increases after $x(t)$, plus half the amplitude of $H/2$, the fan is activated. The $y(t)$ is activated. If $y(t)$ decreases to less than half the parasite capacitance area at the fixed-point $x(t)$, the fan is turned off.

From the top of the floor, the module is linked. On a framework with THT (Through Hole Technology) assembled universal elements, the board is fully manually rendered. Device features: 1st outlet, 2nd micro regulator ATmega8L, 3rd standard ISP-6 programmable interface, 4th fan-free three pin connector, 5th fan, 6th thermistor, 7th, 8th radiator, 9th 3 pins accessible with 3,3V, 10th 3 voltage pins, 11th fast connector for the heater, 12th fan fast connector, 13th NGW100 connection with 0V connection, 10th NGW100 connection.

D. User interface

Only the application installation is needed for the application's UI (preferably Mozilla Firefox). JS and jQuery library maps generated the PHP, HTML, and JavaScript features. JS Charts shall be placed in the Id entity map field. JQuery's fundamental elements include keys, sliders, tabs, and columns. The verification class on the server-side checks all input results. A login string will normally contain digits with a lower potential length of three characters. The password can be a string with a minimum of four characters. You can log in through the device. The author's information, scheme certification, links, and sorting capacities or registration can be retrieved without sorting users.

1.5 ELECTRONIC COMPUTING

1.5.1 Detailed Study

Boolean Memory Crossbar Logic Circuit mapping methods enable the incorporation of massive multi-bit adder logic circuits. The aims of adding a CMOS crossbar are as follows:

- To use the perceptron crossbar to make massive logic circuits.
- To optimize region, time, and energy consumption.
- Peripheral CMOS architecture that functions as a control engine.

In this Boolean logic, a full-bit adder is proposed, and a simple logical operator is added.

A. Model of the mersister
- The model has two elevated (RH) and low conduction states (RL).
  The storage is shifted from one state to another when the voltage value is higher than Vth's voltage limit, or if it stays in the previous state. There is a need for two different states: medium to medium resistance (RESET) and high to low (SET).

B. Boolean logic working principle

Boolean logical architecture is applied to resolve the logical design using the sum of the material layout. The output f can be proficient by AND all NAND gates involving of several memory bars. Many input and output latches are available depending on the inputs and outputs.

The CMOS circuit required for the Crossbar portion of memory-based sense design is 7 states and discussed below:

- **INA**: Starting the RH memorandum as a whole. For this state, the RESET operation is necessary.
- **RIN**: In this state, it is essential to obtain inputs, SET, RESET, or copy operators.
- **CFM**: All state minterms configuration. Both bottom limits are simultaneously fitted for copying.
- **EVM**: Evaluate all the subtitles evaluated for the NAND service.
- **GER**: The outcome, this condition, and the process of AND will be generated.
- **INR**: Reversed result condition.
- **SOU**: Here the data for production and process are stored [7].

A storage device based on NAND was usually strongly condemned in various computer systems. It provides a more advantage over traditional hard drives in recognition of superior durability and shock tolerance. A flash drive cannot be incremented until the occupant block has been deleted. The deletion before the writing limit is the reason it occurs. The decrease in the volume of free pages faced with a lack of knowledge and waste treatment, and the impact on the shop is negative. The ability to store flash in the modern world is exponentially increased with minimum RAM. Map-processing methods are proposed to reduce the workload problem.

1.5.2 PERFORMANCE MODEL

1.5.2.1 Storage Access Time

A routing page cache is normally taken from an FTL page mapping to translate LPN into PPN with a limited RAM.

1.5.2.2 Waiting Time

The latency request consists of two components: disk access and waiting time. The cycle from check-in to check-out is the time of order. The operation I's latency is:

$$T_{\text{latency}}^i = T_{\text{wait}}^i + T_{\text{access}}^i$$

1) Mapping cache verification on embedded flash storage device

Now the new insane and his popular memory system are based on flash. The demand-based caching is Architecture. IoT has also started to make innovative changes to the integrated framework while constructing the new circuits. This control panel of the software is possible with the Electronic Application. The circuit breaker is an essential feature of the transmitting and supply mechanism. Online circuit breaker state monitoring can prevent errors that can lead to costly repair and loss of operation. The new version is now available [9].

However, the latest infrastructure for electronic circuits and architecture cannot meet the rising market opportunity for automation. There is no discussion of market time and lack of certainty [10]. The new version is now available. The circuit breaker is manually operated. However, overload and occasional heating information cannot be used in this inspection process.

This is now controlled using new automated IoT microcontroller technology, and various parameters are monitored continuously, including the power delivered, output pressure, and circuit breakers temperature. All outputs are supplied on the computer through VB software.

The 16/33-bit ARM7 microcontroller, incorporating 32, 64 kb microprocessor, is based on a real-time emulator and tracking aid in high memory encoding.

- **Microcontroller ARM 7**
  The LPC2148 microcontroller is built on 16/32-bit ARM7, which incorporates a 32, 642 kb microprocessor with integrated high-speed flash memory. Emulation and trace help.
- **LCD display**
  A simple and inexpensive way to screen text displays in embedded systems. Shows 6–20 characters display.
- **RF trans/receiver**
  His shirt is distant, cost-efficient, and productivity-enhanced.
- **Keypad**
  The array parameter can be modified.
- **Signal conditioning**
  A signal operation to be protected for the use of other circuits, called signal conditioning, in an appropriate manner.
  The array variable can be changed.
- **Temperature sensor**
  On this circuit, the thermometer is LM35. It includes three connectors: a pin (V_i), an input voltage pin (V_o), and a field pin (GND). If the weather is above the correct temperature, the water pump starts and gradually reduces the temperature.
- **Voltage transformer**
  The fundamental purpose of the power supply is to downgrade the transformer. The secondary converter is either connected to the phase or the ground, depending on the requirements. The second part has less wind or twist to act as a converter move.
- **Current transformer**
  The transformer's central principle is electrical power, but the main current function here has become a voltage level or current requirement.

  i. **Advantages**
     - Building low costs and energy efficiency
     - Real-time tracking
     - Computer repair software connection to the equipment

  ii. **Uses**
     This instrument can be used for the maintenance and monitoring of home appliances.
     A significant portion of the circuit is a microprocessor nowadays, and electricity needs mainly to be installed. Trying to reduce power supply is a standard approach to achieve poor power budgets, either by decreasing marginal software supply or by using dynamic stress scaling power-saving technology.
     Various techniques have been tested to solve this challenge. Digital and analog modems can be used to detect and save voltage situations. The Device Placement issue, nevertheless, faces two major problems, and the chip field and adjustment problem lie in its rear drawing.
     The second problem is the noise sensor that can consume a certain chip size, and it can be placed in the area where the sensor readings and voltage are to be monitored. The error occurs in that field.

It is also advantageous, based on a limited number of sensors, to predict the voltage circumstances at and far from the sensors. In recent years, machine learning has been used to address problems such as high-level synthesis, circuit control, and physical architecture. Both problems can be saved with the invention of a macho noise sensor voltage unit [12]. Requests have been made for the report.

1.6 CONCLUSION

The technology portfolio of an organization is a list of information about the company's IT application infrastructure expenditure. The plan for portfolios recognizes the growing strengths of firms. The portfolio concept is based on the theory of management, which entails closely controlling significant costs to enable them to be fully used and to reduce risks to their integrity. The portfolio is a liability for several policymakers, including department administrators, techniques organization heads, and project program managers. Financial accounting is a mean to assemble and development all activities in an organization, even events which effect the organization's financial position. The system is digitalized for accurate measurements and faster and more regular data production. Other computerized business systems include inventory accounting and payroll management. The system outputs include the list of boxes, packing glass, invoice, chief, and account manager. Computer technology has to a certain extent changed the traditional methods of analysis which have improved the efficiency of civil engineering. We anticipate that in the future, further advances can be achieved by computer-aided modeling and computer simulation technologies. Integrating digital, networking technology and a shared working environment has become an effective means for architectural design, construction, and research analysis. In civil engineering, computers are commonly used to provide the associated industries with specific long-term protection measures, which promotes the general growth of the industries. The project building proposal index foundation in the machine data map Embedded Systems with Web interface consent to control any entity in a modest custom. You need a web browser. The use of an expanded server and a micro-server controller structure provides programmers with several possibilities. The designer is exempt from various network protocol deployments. The modularity of the structure enables several tests to be prepared. A dedicated server is a common feature, whereas the controller is implemented separately. Embedded web interface systems allow easy control of any object. A dedicated server and a controller provide many possibilities for designers across the comprehensive framework. The designer is exempt from multiple protocol execution. By using Linux, several applications are available, including improved network connectivity. The dedicated server serves users' requests—these operations are not essential to execute. The control separation makes it possible to enhance the control object's reliability. In the case that the pilot is suspended, the operating system can continue to carry out its mission at last. During the evolution of old computers into the latest concepts, electronics was an important component. The application of the CMOS system to the Memristor Crossbar would undoubtedly have a few benefits concerning its scalability, which is the next thing in the smart world to scale up a wide circuit and automation. The NAND flash memory storage with a minimal mapping cache is introduced to address the storage problems without any cache miss. Batches of requests are re-ordered to optimize the waiting period. All use notifications are sent in real time in the new control center environment. And the details on the failure of the circuit will help to reduce the time.

2 Management Cost Computing

2.1 WEB-BASED BUILT COST PREDICTION INTEGRATED SYSTEM

In building a project's environmental assessments, cost estimates, cost-based budgeting, and financial monitoring not only play an important role but are also crucial to the final success of the project [21]. For businesses, it is vital in two ways to create and employ technologies that can anticipate failure in advance. First, for those (e.g., management, and authority) that are to prevent failures, such models, may be highly valuable as forecasting techniques. Second, such models can be valuable for assisting decision-makers in the assessment and selection of contractors of building companies. The budget estimate includes two ways, descriptive and analytical. The conventional technique of forecasting, which emphasizes the examination and forecasting of objects' nature, is often termed an instinctive approach of forecasting [22]. Appropriate studies of classification and modeling are usually predicted by specialists, the conjoint analysis and the probability distributions approach, etc. The prediction technique of specialists combines the technique of personal judgment, the technique of the meeting, and the storm of the brain. Quantitative predictions are intended to quantitatively anticipate the features of objects. It draws mostly on historical information and employs the science-based statistical equation to anticipate the number of targets attainable. The mathematical formula used to anticipate the quantity of an object exhibited was developed by integrating historical data with scientific methodologies. The quantitative approaches that are widely employed include statistical analysis, regression, and gray scale predictions. This study aims to utilize the artificial intelligence technique (RS-ANN) to combine Particle Swarm Optimization (PSO), Fuzzy Logic, and Neural networks (NN), to increase cost estimates and forecast precision. The Model Artificial Neural Neural Networks (NNs). RSANN integrates the advantages of rough sets with neural networks, rendering this model particularly relevant to the identification and implementation of potential remedies to complicated issues. In addition, this research proposes a new way to anticipate the construction costs of the building project through the integration of raw-set (RS) theories and artificial nervous networks (ANN) [23].

2.1.1 COST ANALYSIS BASED ON FCE AND RS PROJECT CONSTRUCTION

2.1.1.1 FCE Infrastructure Cost

The factors which influence infrastructure costs storage space, area, newly built objectives, conventional floor area, the quantity of story, higher level of the built environment, the type of window and door, the length of the story, category of the framework, type of basic principle, type of institutional set of stairs, short rigor, building structure, garage area, timeframe, understanding of project management, sports facilities, etc. The indices are then explained on a rough basis. Table 1 shows the table of the initial cost indices of the building project [24].

The project level of the management directly affects the construction cost of the enterprise in the construction projects. The project's level of management, though, is a generalized abstract term, it's hard to measure. Fast circuit enevelope (FCE) model for evaluating the product design level in this chapter. In areas such as the degree of the systems engineer, the position of the employees, the organizational, effective management, and the project control level, the level of managing projects is described.

One program manager would choose *A* as the assessment object for a construction firm and apply the above approach to assess and sort the overall qualities of applicants, then pick an overall

DOI: 10.1201/9781003211938-2

TABLE 2.1

Marking Table to Object A by an Expert

Index	Best	Better	Average Bad		Index	Best	Better	Average Bad	
u_1	1	1.5	0	0	u_2	3	1.5	0	0
u_3	0	2	0.5	0	$u_5 u_4$	0	0.5	2	0
u_5	3.5	1	0	0		3.5	1	0	0

prospect as project manager for an amazing matter. First of all, a team of selecting consisting of industry professionals and the judgment is carried out Table 2.1 shows a possibility as follows:

V of $u_1 \sim u_5$ the comment set to obtain a single factor evaluation matrix is:

A candidate's index weight is:

$$R^2 = \begin{vmatrix} 0.1600 & 0.8000 & 0.0400 & 0 \\ 0.8400 & 0.1600 & 0 & 0 \\ 0.1600 & 0.7600 & 0.800 & 0 \\ 0.8000 & 0.2000 & 0 & 0 \\ 0.6400 & 0.3600 & 0 & 0 \end{vmatrix}$$

$$A_1^1 = (0.0666, 0.0671, 0.0677, 0.0398, 0.0358)$$

Candidate A's fuzzy reliable monitoring vector may be found as:

$$B^1 = A^1 \cdot R^1 = (0.2904, 0.1960, 0.5076, 0.0048)$$

The argument is that 0.5076, an average, is a complete truly competitive procurement. A is the concept of optimum participation. Comparable management levels of other projects might be equally similar to the fuzzy complete evaluation outcomes [25].

2.1.2 THEORY OF ROUGH SETS

Pawlak created the first rough hypothesis (1982). The idea of rough sets [4] is predicated on an unparalleled technique of reasoning and the reduction of information. To analyze the data provided, the objects described by the same knowledge are indistinguishable and can be used to eliminate redundant characteristics affecting construction cost, optimize the significant advancements of capital expenditure understanding, illustrate the significance of various characteristics in the interpretation of organizational capabilities, optimize project management knowledge interpretation areas, and thus start preparing rapidly for the predictors of cost of the project. The building reducing costs method consists of two stages: a decrease in variables and values decrease elements.

As a crude set technique to numerical values, measurable features must be transformed into qualitative words. Although a continual measurement of an attribute, such as a floor space and standards layer area, is normally performed by experts based on the qualitative values, like low, medium, and high [26].

The outcomes of the initial indices, for example, are spread into Table 2.2. The indexes are 4° {0, 1, 2, 3}, {lower, lower, average, high}. For instance, performance measurement is split into four categories {0, 1, 2, 3}, which indicates {bad, average, good, best}. D is a choice attribute that is divided into three categories {0, 2, 2} that demonstrate the expense of constructing. U is the number of the building project.

TABLE 2.2

The Table of Real Performance Indexes

U	Floor Area	Purposes of Building	Standard Layer Area	Project Story Management Number Level		...	D
1	0	1	1	1	0		0
2	0	2	2	1	1		2
3	1	1	1	1	2		2
4	0	1	2	0	2		2
5	0	1	2	0	2		1
6	0	2	2	1	0		1
7	0	2	1	0	0		1
8	0	2	1	0	0		1
9	0	1	1	1	0		0
10	0	1	2	0	2		0
...	...	...	...	...	...	...	...

TABLE 2.3

The Prediction of Building Cost

Goal of the Building	Content
Building cost	Total height H_1
	Standard layer area H_2
	The type of structure H_3
	Project management level H_4
	Period H_5
	Basement area H_6

Using Table 2.1 to construct Table 2.3, the table with Table 2.3 reduces the actual index values. The investigation's rough analysis section utilizing the software we built at JAVA was carried out. The results of Table 2.3 reveal that the prediction index system of building costs was produced after rough analysis.

We have achieved a small reduction, as we can see $\{H_1, H_2, H_3, H_4, H_5, H_6\}$. Only six major criteria affect this modest cost reduction of construction works: total height H_1, standard layer area H_2, the type of structure H_3, project management level H_4, period H_5, and Basement area H_6.

2.1.3   ANN BASED ON PSO

Among the most widely-developed, artificial networks have now become the BP Genetic Algorithm. It has a three-layer feed-to-neural network, such as a layer of input, hidden neurons, and a layer of output. First of all, the control signal must spread to the concealed node. The concealing node output information is transmitted through the functionality activity into the output terminal [27]. The results are finally acquired for the independent variables. It helps to detect similarities between the data supplied, needs little, and produces a high level of forecast precision. These features make neural network technologies an alternative viable tool in terms of performance, flexibility, resilience, efficiency, and effectiveness to recognize, classify and predict building shown in Figure 2.1. Consequently, ANN might apply cost application areas requiring predictions. PSO, a social behavioral model of flocks of birds, is an optimization method. Its fundamental idea and strategies are contained in Ref. [6].

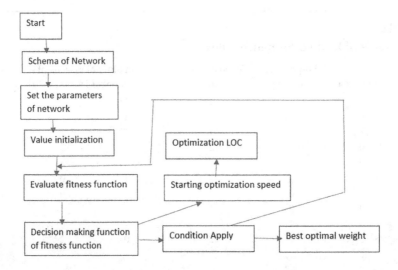

FIGURE 2.1   The network model for PSO.

TABLE 2.4
Comparison of Running Times Three XOR Problem Algorithms

Algorithm	Minimum Times	Maximum Times	Average Times
BP	4,444	5,891	5,214
GA	1,024	2,760	2,314
PSO	565	921	847

TABLE 2.5
Error Analysis of Three 200 Times Algorithm

Algorithm	Best	Worse	Average
BP	0.4466	0.9981	0.7794
GA	0.0182	0.4071	0.1872
PSO	0.0079	0.1208	0.2437

The PSO-based ANN demo diagram shows:

The ANN is assessed utilizing a regular BP network and a GA network based on PSO. Comparative network findings for three distinct perceptresses are presented in Tables 4 and 5. It can be shown from Tables 2.4 and 2.5 that PSO-based ANN is better suited to runtime and run-time faults. It may be inferred that the perceptron based on PSO is superior to the sigmoid function depending on BP [28].

2.1.4   CONCEPTUALIZATION OF INTERNET-BASED COST PREDICTION

- **Conceptual schema**

    The proposed web-based appropriate methodology forecasting issues include three major concerns: (1) Centralized information and knowledge base administration should be adopted by the minimum operational cost, (2) the system for worldwide and all-time access-the Internet connection-based web applications should be used, and (3) the platform for online calculations should be minimized in actual environments. As mentioned earlier, database management, the internet atmosphere, and the suggested cost prediction system were logically used. The system, as established via on-screen interaction buttons, can manage the important information held inside the database. Individuals can use the World Wide Web for access to the Web (WWW). For smart information mappings, the evolving neural learning system is utilized.

- **Neural network setup and simulation**

  In this field, 54 participants were obtained from the province of Guangdong as study samples for the inputs networks to predict building costs by making approximate use of the six qualities as an advanced forecasting development authentication process. An input layer, hidden neurons, and output level sportingly were 6-9-1 NN's communication network. The individuals numbered 200; 200 nanoparticles swarmed. Inertia w was 0.3 in gravity. The c_1 and c_2 parameters of speed were the same as 2.0. The top speed was 20 and the low speed was –20. The total simulation step was 500. Six terminals were in the activation function, five in the hidden layer, and one in the transfer function in the output nodes. The backpropagation was 0.01, with 0.001 expected. The MATLAB® 7.1 computer constructed the computational model. The EMS was averaged 3.25461 to 10–5 times, and just 0.405 seconds was the project implementation. The network error curves after initial training of 2,386 [29].

2.2 RESEARCH OF CORPORATE CREDIT-BASED COMPUTING

Concerning international economic integration and officially entering the WTO, major manufacturers face a rising number of issues while developing, and operational risk industries expand practically in the same percentages. Citizen of country companies is now confronting increasingly different issues. The credit risks are all growing, which leads to major credit risks to the listed firms, involving money damages, bad debt impairments, monetary policy and financial fraud, and other events. In this context, citizens of country companies should analyze carefully why they are doing good jobs and preventing credit risk and take prompt effective remedies. The company scale also expands as the number of borrowing firms in the Province of Anhui increases. There have been 24 firms in the Provincial of Anhui over the previous 5 years, a rise of 82.76%. The maximum total money supply of the firms mentioned is an increasing trend of 67.3% from a total of 16,426,000,000 shareholdings to 27,480,000,000 by the end of 2002; the gathered dollar amount of the real economy is 88,643,000,000 yuan by the end of 2002, which is an increasing trend of 5.66% to a total of 501,893,000,000 yuan by the end of 2007. Currently, the listed firms include almost all economic pillars and firms and play a more unique role in Anhui province's productivity expansion. There is a considerable increase in the standard of selected banks as the quantity and scale in Anhui rise. Now, however, the financial market growth of the Province of Anhui is still facing issues and weaknesses, particularly the unfairness of the circumstances and the polarization of the performances. The biggest operating earnings in the province accounted for 79.83% of the total gross income of the firms listed in the provinces in mid-2007, representing the 5 firms (Maanshan Iron and Steel Company, Conch Cement, Tongling Nonferrous Metal Company, Hoch Speed Anhui, and Jianghuai Company). There are 33 enterprises with a per-share income less than the provincial average; some firms suffer a massive loss. The creditworthiness assessment of the listed firm in the province of Anhui is so significant [30].

2.2.1 FINANCING DEALING

- **Risk assessment in credit**

  Credit is often considered as a credit. The characteristic of these investing standards is to pay for circumstances of reinstatement or to accept the terms of return as a responsibility:

and the explanation why the borrower grants loans is even though he is eligible to interest; the latter may borrow on account of an interest-payment promise. In other words, repayment is the fundamental definition of credits. The danger of creditworthiness, often referred to as the hazard of default, is the probability of damages for largest banking, investors, or other dealers as a result of the unwillingness or incompliance of borrower, commodities issuer, or dealers for several causes. For publicly listed firms with periods, the risk article is important.

- **Risk measuring**

  Each has its benefits when studying credit risk measuring methodologies, but each one of them is weak. Because many organizations are still adopting 5C statistical analysis, this approach still faces two key constancy and objectivity challenges. A different financial individual might use entirely different criteria for various assessment outcomes, and their assessments may readily be altered by the sentiments and external influences to analyze the differences. As a consequence, commercial banks progressively discontinued the quantitative examination of the 5C mechanical characterization in current history. No doubt there are insufficient necessary conditions for underdeveloped nations to use modern tools to undertake risk management practices. The stock data of publicly traded companies are necessary for many modern credit risk assessment models, but there are financial systems that are not excellent in the stock market, credit mechanisms have not yet been set up, and business statistics or bankruptcy have been seriously insufficient and are not sufficient for the use of its sophisticated measurement instrument on financial performance. The principal components assessment of this book is therefore the usual approach for assessing the financial risk of listed firms. The main component analytics (PCA) is often performed in six phases.

- **Profit margin**

  This paragraph selects 12 different factors from the dependent variable on the financial instrument, which indicate the sales and profits of liquid wealth, account foreseeable turnover, stock transforms, and net profit margin, operations capability, stock performance, and the economic expansion in revenue of the primary customer recognize economic development, current balance, rapid ratios, and investment recognize payment. The dividend yield and revenue need to reflect an economic development [31].

2.2.2 Regression Analysis of Principal Component Analysis

The primary component regression is a mathematical approach commonly employed in several areas, a few less of which replaces the underlying statistic with a more representational benchmark indicator. The thorough examination per major component analyses can not only minimize the effects of the different indices of varying sizes but also reduce correlations and overlaps in multi-indexes. In specifically, physical treatments have solved the problem of the goal weight. Generally, when the total significant level contributes to the given limit, we can pick only a few major elements as efficient frontier characteristics rather than the intended objective. Second, we may determine the overall values and rankings of the central ingredient. In reality, the procedure is therefore easy and intuitive. However, it is quite difficult and inconvenient to compute the main component individually so the use and improvement of this procedure are inhibited. SPSS, which extensively involves online descriptive statistics, can only compute the correlation matrix and cannot compute the primary ingredient. Therefore, the solution to the problem is disadvantageous. With the use of the Excel VBA macro application, it is effective to fix the highest importance calculation difficulty and complete the assessment. Users are thereby released from a manual setup with increased troubleshooting effectiveness.

The Macro program is a commanding set comprising VBA procedure code commands and instructions. In its development plan, Microsoft VBA is a common, computerized universal platform. When we develop a macro, we produce a concatenation of secure messaging. Excel VBA-based calculation steps and algorithms are as follows:

Step 1 is a selection of an index.

Step 2 is index standardization.

Step 3 is a calculation of the matrix of coefficient of correlation or Gaussian distribution.

Step 4 is to establish by computing explanatory and explained total variance the number of the main component.

Step 5 is the calculation of the principal component.

Step 6 is the full assessment calculation.

Step 7 is the output of the findings.

2.2.3 ANALYSIS OF CORPORATE CREDIT RISK

The internal economic situation of the province of Anhui is disadvantageous, being in the center of Smart country. The credit scoring for the listed firms in the province of Anhui is thus extremely significant. For shareholders, the credit of the firm is an ideal foundation.

Currently, a total of 56 firms are mentioned in Anhui, including Smart country's number 10. Over 61 inventories of machinery, textiles, cars, construction materials, energy, traffic, domestic appliances, metallurgical, computers, medicine, etc., are distributed by the 56 listed firms. All information on this page is derived from financial disclosures by the Citizen of country securities regulation committee of listed firms (SRC) [32].

From which to choose June 2007 to March 2008 four-quarter data of 46 listed firms, shown in Table 2. This research does not include Anhui Gujinggong B and Huangsha B, which have been multiple international equities in the Citizen of country and several companies in the short to medium term. Based on the specified index system indications, 46 listed businesses will examine their credit.

When computing using Descriptive statistics, five primary elements, Y_1, Y_2, Y_3, Y_4, and Y_5, might be provided. Up to 85.22% of the whole can be explained and better than before. The position of the essential aspects determining the standard deviation of the dependent data is illustrated in Table 2.4. Table 2.5 presents the inverse proportional formulation that the instructional process parameters are expressed using the central feature [33].

The first main category is defined by the return on capital on aggregate assets, profit/share, stakeholder rate and shareholders share, loads of 0.93, 0.84, 0.86, 0.63. The main component of the loading is the company's competitiveness, stability, and development capabilities. Since the return on assets ratio comprising net profits and losses indicates the financial performance of all assets, it is utilized to measure the financial performance of the undertaking in the utilization of all activities and also to determine the quality of the operational assets of the undertaking. And awareness leads should be limited because of the shareholder's shareholding ratio and the overall assets. The firm is not aggressively using financial leverage to increase the dimension model while its share of excess debt is too little, but it readily impairs the firm's capacity to stand action was taken, while it is too high. Since the return on assets ratio comprising net profits and losses indicates the financial performance of all assets, it is utilized to measure the financial performance of the undertaking in the utilization of all activities and also to determine the quality of the operational assets of the undertaking. And awareness leads should be limited because of the shareholder's shareholding ratio and the overall assets. The firm is not aggressively using financial leverage to increase the dimension model while its share of excess debt is too little, but it readily impairs the firm's capacity to stand action was taken, while it is too high. The two-factor theory is the Gross Margins and Account Receivable Rate, with loads in primary components at 0.85, 0.65, and the primary component is based on the company's revenue and operating capability. The premium differential pattern, which is the largest category and some of the sales of the company, is a perfect consequence of the sales volume as the basis for the rationality of the operating effectiveness of companies and the attempting to set prices which would help us to make a distinction to some large extend among both revenues and expenses. The cash conversion cycle indicates business processes and is a major part of the total management, impacting the short to medium-term liquidity of companies. The higher rate of inventory sales often signifies a decreased production occupation and better flexibility, so the merchandise may be transformed more quickly to cash or receivables. The improvement of the inventory employee turnover might thereby boost availability [34].

A binding force is the third primary aspect and 0.76 is the load. In transferring corporate assets to cash, it is frequently challenging to make capital assets with much more rebates and immaterial assets are also risky. Winding up and declining. Fixed ratio illustrates that the entire capital expenditures of companies cannot be easily realized. The long-term stability is a prudent indication.

The fourth main component is chosen by fast ratio, the load 0.66 reflecting solvency of companies, which indicates the critical ingredient. A fast ratio that directly reflects companies in their simple term's insolvency is a complement to today's ratio and is more straightforward and believable than the liquidity amount.

The fifth main component is determined by the rate of accounting turnover of 0.92 in the major ingredients. The main part indicates the business performance of the companies and the length of time necessary from the opportunity to access accountments for conversions and calculate the total periods during which trade receivables are turned into the next year's sales. If the rate of the circulatory system is insufficient, simple terms profitability of companies will be affected. Increased in a causal relationship with each corporation, the first principal component reflecting financial performance, financial stability, and emphasis on building, is the company that uses the first maximum likelihood to better ranking the firms using Anhui, Capitain, Wuhu Port, Feiya Anhui Low, ST Keyuan Worst as initial significant components of the coded firms: 46 coded firms.

The Wantong firm is a member of the shipping and warehouses business. It was published as "the top 100 Citizen of country companies in terms of investment relations," and obtained the 8th position, which suggests that the credit risk of the Company is minimal. Conch Concrete has been the top provider of cement and clinker in Asia, and its manufacturing and exports have been rated first in Smart country for 11 years. Today, the corporation's three new 10,000-ton cement clinker manufacturing plants reach the largest levels in the world's cement business. The port of Wuhu is a rail infrastructure sector with a total number of specialists on stock rated No 25, with the increasing trend being hopeful [35] (Tables 2.6 and 2.7).

The principal factors generated from the differentiated measurements mentioned above may not accurately represent the possible impact characteristics of the employee. To separate the low data measures retrieved is done, further improvements would be needed but adding the Repeating the

TABLE 2.6
The Situation of Principal Components Explaining the Total Variance of Original Variables

Principal Component	Total Variance	Variance Contribution	Accumulative Variance Contribution
1	4.05	33.78	33.78
2	2.11	17.57	51.35
3	1.86	15.51	66.86
4	1.20	10.00	76.86
5	1.00	8.36	85.22
6	0.61	5.07	90.29
7	0.42	3.47	93.75
8	0.34	2.84	96.60
9	0.18	1.50	98.10
10	0.13	1.06	99.16
11	0.09	0.71	99.87
12	0.02	0.13	100.00

TABLE 2.7
Factor Loading Matrix

Variables	Factor 1	Factor 2	Factor 3	Factor 4	Factor 5
ER	0.60	−0.61	0.20	0.32	−0.01
RRTA	0.93	0.12	−0.09	0.10	0.10
RE	−0.79	0.34	0.05	0.07	0.07
PSER	0.84	−0.07	0.03	0.16	0.12
WCR	0.24	0.36	−0.78	−0.19	−0.03
QR	0.02	0.29	−0.53	0.66	0.29
RRIS	0.63	0.29	−0.15	−0.64	−0.18
IRAR	0.24	0.65	0.55	0.07	−0.05
TRAR	0.03	−0.07	0.07	−0.37	0.92
RGP	0.39	0.85	0.02	0.18	0.00
GRRIS	0.86	−0.28	−0.11	−0.01	−0.07
FR	0.29	0.26	0.76	0.02	0.09

test would be much more risk mitigation indications that are not included in the above-mentioned action [36].

A cluster tree will be shown to apply the System Cluster Method for cluster analysis and 46 businesses will be classified into 3: Network ST Keyuan is a class, a class of which the Faster Speeds Wuhu Port, Leiming Scientific knowledge and Pharmacology and Conch Characteristics are the category where these businesses offer certain short-term financial stability economic benefits; the other corporations are a class, with no notable difference of the value systems of those indexes, which would include stockpile revenue, gross profit margin, or correct ratio. The findings are essentially the same for the main region detection.

2.3 EVALUATION OF INDUSTRIAL PARKS INDUSTRIAL TRANSFORMATIONS AND ENVIRONMENTAL

Given the steady deterioration of the ecological surroundings and increasing environmental problems, the use of raw resources free of the ecosystems and emittance to the ecosphere of a significant number of the later in the form of enormous cost has been difficult to accomplish in the Thermal Pollution Mode indicated in the conventional sequential industrial method. Some industrialized nations have shown how the sequence of "supplies—commodities—regenerated materials—recycled goods" is transformed from traditional economic growth to a polycyclic operation, which will contribute to a significant strain in the exploitation of energy and waste from the whole manufacturing to consuming processes.

Foreign academics identified a direct pathway for ecosystem services—Eco-Industrial Parks (EIPs) in a study on smart manufacturing in Fort Danmaikalun. Ecological industrial parks have been practiced worldwide since, with the construction of environmentally friendly Parks booming to practically all Western and some South-South East Asian developing countries. At least 40 EIPs were initiated by the United States till 2006. In Asia, Europe, South America, the Pacific Island, Africa, and elsewhere, more than 30 EIPs were developed in the remaining 60 EIP initiatives, of whatever kind. All these initiatives cover a range of sectors and have distinctive features.

At present, the ecosystem is increasingly unstable and the ecological climate has not yet continuously deteriorated effectively. Environmentally Parks will develop the conversion to third-generation communication parks from its economic and technical zones and high-tech office buildings specialized clustering of symbiotic manufacturing mainly builds on the idea of the circular economy through which economic gain and advantages constitute the core. This will develop into a type of Citizen of country society that supports the ecosystem and furnishings and equipment.

2.3.1 INDUSTRIAL TRANSFORMATION PATTERNS AND ENVIRONMENTAL PARKS REFORM

The citizens of the country's industrial zones are some comparatively separate places formed by the Citizen of the country financial reform program. They expose the outside world and impact the course of other places that have become binding sites of Smart country's economic growth. Citizens of country industrial buildings may be split into several types of parks, including financial and strategic special economic zones, increasing production industries, bonded areas, export-oriented, border trade, investment zones, and tourist destinations, depending on the nature of the enterprise. They have been a key driver of economic growth and exceptional regional development carriers in Smart country. Their progress also caused several difficulties at the same time.

- **Industrial parks transformation patterns**

    Its study indicates that thematic constructions may be regarded as communications infrastructure conditions for achieving the goals of the interested parties of the conventional office buildings. The use of technologies from the Small-World Network and the Scale-Free Network would acquire dynamic, advanced technologies for the change and reform of the surroundings.

    Students have noticed that many genuine networks have tiny world networks. Such a tiny world impact says the overall networking connection is tiny and straightforward. Such a tiny world impact says the overall networking connection is tiny and straightforward. A more stringent explanation is that if the average wavelength of a system increases by the logarithmic rate or is lower than the cluster growth speed, the cable network place impacts or the impacts of ultra-small worlds are predicted that a logarithmic is maintained at aggregate peak periods of the network. In keeping with the idea of small-word networks, the averaged space separation, which is significantly taller arbitrarily than the same number of communication connections and vertices, ought to be a more acceptable distributed generation design of industrial parks.

    In the present national distribution channel of business estates, particular emphasis should be devoted to this. It is not merely a numeric difference that their distinctive duty is. Some of Smart country's big manufacturing parks that are the scientific and political developmental zone at the state and local level play an essential role. They should conduct features of personality criticism in response to the environmental challenges, such as energy conservation and reducing pollution. Bak and others initially introduced the notion of self-organized criticality (SOC). Bak thought that the sands accumulating gradually would not influence sand as a whole because it was an addition, but that it may have a comparable oscillatory behavior, changing the morphology of the sand to a measure. Bak suggested a personal idea of containment, informed by this thought that focuses on a particular structure, with certain circumstances developing on its own. Utilizing the dissipating mechanism of kinematics, the following disturbance will finally lead to a response of various sizes and sizes to the distributions of the model equation. Although a better model for quantifying the actions used in environmental problems for business estates is not developed, the descriptive statistics of environmental impacts should show regional management according to different measuring equipment, which is in line with their non-scale natural environment. Thus, consideration should be given to business estates with varied growth opportunities in Smart country and the agricultural, and medicinal changes of the other business estates should subsequently be encouraged. It should also be emphasized that certain industrial parks' drawbacks cannot be eliminated by offering robustness for all industrial park systems [37].

- **Symbiotic effect formation in business parks**

  Symbiotic influence for manufacturing is the key to industrialized park' industrial change and social reforms. It can split symbiosis benefits into by-production impacts of interchange, cluster benefits, green impacts, and subsequent positive impacts. These four impacts may play roles in four ways that decrease or format producers' costs as a direct source of competitive advantage for business parks.

2.3.2 Technological Restructuring Assessment and Sustainability Reformation Updated by MATLAB Program Based on Analytic Hierarchy Process

In the process of transforming old industrial parks, three-stage models of optimization of economic evaluations based on recycling economic system might be utilized.

In combination with frequency and investment, the short-term physical and scale-free network technologies could be used in the establishment of a start with a full specification symbiotic relationship model of optimization; a model of game based on interest allocation of manufacturing symbiotic chains is essential to the stabilization of cooperative manufacturing chain models. It is also vital to introduce the addition of symbiosis industrial chains and promote eco-related linked companies. The comprehensive project of agricultural and medicinal changes has to be implemented in the field of continuous production to encourage ecosystem management modernization. The secondary aims of an index assessment Industries Transformation Mechanism and Ecological Park Improvement may be employed, primarily from the strategic economic effectiveness, for the construction of the third assessment index.

The Analytical Process of Hierarchy (AHP) approach is a systematic way of managing complicated choices. The AHP encourages individuals to decide one rather than to prescribe a "right" option. It was founded in the 1970s and since then it has been widely explored and improved by Thomas L. Saaty, based on mathematics and evolutionary physiology. The AHP provides a broad and efficient framework in which an issue may be structured and its aspects represented and measured. These elements are related to overarching objectives and possible solutions are evaluated. It is employed worldwide in a broad range of decision-making settings, in areas including administration, enterprise, manufacturing, health-conscious, and education.

A multi-target examination of the growth of manufacturing complexes assesses problems with qualitative and quantitative parameters. The MATLAB software-based AHP technique splits into many indicators for the assessment of metamorphosis in the eco-industrial park included. At the same level, certain wholly subjective judgments are stated and defined by calcium absorption with each indication contrasted to each other. It offers a systematic and successful way to measure the commercial conversions and the environmental reform of shopping centers in a whole way. The Industrial Transforming and Environment Transformation Indicator system consists, therefore, of a multi-level collection of parameters. Capacity analysis MATLAB is based on the evaluation of the specialists and calculates the weight of a matrix organizational structure through a kind of spatial discretization [38].

Consequently, the qualitative method seems to be more university-based, paired with the ability of MATLAB of specialists and simulation methods of determining weights. The tables set up several indicators for measuring architecture which include primary level: A; secondary: B_1–B_8 indicators; individualized index layer: C_{11}–C_{83} indicators; and then trigonometric functions created using a scale of 1–9 depending on the comparability of the objective layer. The primarily characterized and the mathematical equation ranking are computed using the proposed algorithm, which requires compromise yields results. Tables 2.8–2.11 shows the acronym for subcategories; the results are shown in Table 2.12. Thus, a large complex assessment, based on AHP's environmental-resource ability-dynamic program evaluation method and empowering of weights, upgrades the performance assessment of industrial park technological change and environmental reformation. The static and

TABLE 2.8
Acronym of Categories' Denomination

Denomination of Category	Acronym
First-Level Indicators (Object Hierarchy)	OH
Numbering for Object Hierarchy	NOH
Secondary Indicators (Rule Hierarchy)	RH
Numbering for Rule Hierarchy	NRH
Third Grade Indicators (Indicators Hierarchy)	IH
Numbering for Indicators Hierarchy	NIH
Indicators' Weights	IW

TABLE 2.9
First-Level Indicators

Object Hierarchy	OH
Evaluation of industrial transformations and environmental reform	A

TABLE 2.10
Secondary Indicators (Rule Hierarchy)

RH	NRH
Efficiency of economic development	B1
Situation environmental protection	B2
Regional energy saving	B3
Supervision of environmental protection	B4
The situation of capital market	B5
Science and technology education	B6
Manpower resource utilization	B7
Industrial agglomeration	B8
Efficiency of economic development	B1

TABLE 2.11
Comparison Matrix' Consistency Test

Comparison Matrix	CI	CR
A	0.0721	0.0511
B1	0.0193	0.0332
B2	0.0652	0.0693
B3	0.0046	0.0079
B4	0.0193	0.0332
B5	0.0000	0.0000
B6	0.0198	0.0220
B7	0.0853	0.0761
B8	0.0018	0.0032

TABLE 2.12
Indicators' Weights

IH	NIH	IW
GDP per capita	C11	0.0962
Fixed assets investment per capita	C12	0.0158
Total retailing of social consuming goods per capita	C13	0.0390
1/industrial wastewater discharge per square kilometer	C21	0.0095
1/industrial fumes emission per square kilometer	C22	0.0160
1/SO_2 emission quantity per square kilometer	C23	0.0294
1/industrial solid waste per square kilometer	C24	0.0041
1/annual water supply quantity per capita	C31	0.0041
1/power consumption of total output value unit area	C32	0.0134
1/energy consumption of total output value unit area	C33	0.0074
1/per break money for environmental pollution accident	C41	0.0107
Proportion of clean-process company	C42	0.0018
The number of sites for environmental monitoring per square kilometer	C43	0.0043
Asset-liability ratio	C51	0.0075
Hedging and proliferating ratios	C52	0.0075
Financial GDP per capita	C53	0.0226
The number of professional and technical personnel every 10,000 people	C63	0.1904
The proportion of educational expenditure account for expenditure	C61	0.0692
Proportion of the college teacher numbers every 10,000 people	C62	0.0316
The proportion of science expenditure account for expenditure	C64	0.1073
All labor productivity	C71	0.0480
Ratio of professional and technical person account for the total population	C72	0.0151
The number of people affected by college education each thousand	C73	0.0205
Average salary	C74	0.0032
Ratio of urban population account for total population	C75	0.0060
The proportion of the number of high-tech manufacturing employee	C81	0.1427
The proportion of the number of modern service industry employee	C82	0.0506
Profit of the state-owned and designed size non-state-owned enterprises per capita	C83	0.0269

dynamic manner of metamorphosis may be investigated and decisions may be taken from the views of authorities, parks management, synergistic business, and investment and manufacturing.

2.4   INTEGRATING FRAMEWORK BASED ON EMBEDDING EQUIPMENT MONITORING SYSTEMS

As greater and higher production technology is available, a controlling system is supported by the Manufacturing PC, PLC, and Relay (IPC). The IPC microcontroller, meanwhile, is programmed the resource-intensive, expensive, and highly reliable commercial Operating System. The built-in control system is the major computer control component. The integrated system, conducted with components communicating, is an implementation and HW/SW trimmed system. It is particularly suited for multi-faceted performance implementation, such as timeliness, consistency, durability, and resource utilization. This study is funded by the Third Program of the Shenzhen IT Institute (QN-08009) and the 11th Shenzhen IT Institute High Technology Fair Programme (GJH11-ZS005).

The present development of an integrated control scheme uses generic terminology and an atmosphere that makes it difficult for industry specialists to create their applications. Furthermore, at the system design stage, many of the challenges such as activities and non-performance have to be considered.

The integrated computer model (MIC) strategy solves these issues by increasing the size and utilization of the models. The technique involved in this method allows project management to use domain-specific communicative modeling language (DSML). DSML-based multiple-faceted models are developed and developed. An integrated circuit is a synthesis process, built dynamically by the models in the domain field. This methodology has been employed effectively in a variety of areas, including defense matters, automobile manufacturing, avionics, and chemical processes.

Karsai outlined the comprehensive embedded software model creation process. The most important aspects of this procedure are as follows:

1. **Concepts**: is a subjective abstraction, independent from that domain, and is understood in a particular data structure.
2. **Interpretation framework**: creates functional language modeling programming and tool application code.

We provide MIC in this article to the creation of software for the production of equipment control. The section provides an overview of MIC and then explains the software design of the advanced integrated program. Next, the prototype development cycle is shown in a basic example, indicating that the creation of an industry target context of modeling can assist integrated computer control construction.

2.4.1 Overview on MIC

Over a decade's MIC for integrated development process was created at Vanderbilt University, United States. In the problem domain, the primary advantages of this technique are as follows:

1. **The description permits the decomposition of the hierarchy**: The system is separated into components and covers several factors, for example, software, technology, and surroundings.
2. **Modularity is practicable**: Modeling in MIC encapsulate and explicitly specifies the interaction amongst interconnected elements.
3. **Software may be developed jointly with its related biological phenomenon**: Instead of artificial barriers, meta-models encapsulate a class of issues in a certain field. The graphical DSML facilitates the knowledge of the complete control unit for subject specialists, which helps in the appropriate understanding synthesis of model interpreters. Domain's designers can adjust modeling techniques and provide new software as exterior technology changes.

The MIC framework is Multi-graph architecture (MGA). As seen in Figure 2.2, MGA uses a two-stage estimation method [39].

The entire process of development covers the following:

1. **Meta-medialization**: Metaphysical acting is a role model UML/OCL-based meta-modeling languages in the metamodeling environment to express objects, characteristics, and interactions. With good programming language, meta-interpreters translate concepts to DSML.
2. **Medialization**: The systems are developed using DSML described in meta-level processes for a particular application. By assembling basic components, mathematical shapes may be produced.
3. **Maps**: Domain representations are mapped by an interpreter for the tool framework coding or relational database. As proven, this technique boosts the effectiveness of computing. Positive creations are implemented by programming with real code. A compiler is developed for the ordered sequence.

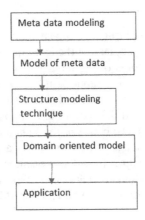

FIGURE 2.2 MIC method of system development.

The MIC-Model Architecture Difference (MDA) is the following: MIC focuses on domain particular modeling technologies and uses UML/OCL as a language of metamodeling, whereas MDA handles the applications of particular models and uses UML as a programming language explicitly.

2.4.2 System Architecture

It is essential to examine conceptual framework at a design site to construct the increased postmodern for the apparatus boundary condition.

The entire system has many subsystems or elements, i.e., data acquisition, data processing, guides leaders, alarm and reporting, communications, and others. The data-centered surroundings offer interoperability across subsystems. The Control Strategy Component includes specialized event control techniques, techniques, and rules. The system uses various control techniques to identify the behavior to take, such as triggering an alert mode, power feedback, logging, etc. The subsystem for statistical analysis does knowledge discovery; shows trends over time for various people, i.e., scientists and management; and gives practical perspective knowledge. The database maintains the fundamental data required by other interconnected elements and the clinical information produced. The real-time operating system (RTOS) provides the connection between software information systems. Communication constituent retorts to isolated appeal and convey data conferring to detailed etiquette. To maintain its timeliness for harsh verbal interaction synchronization or time-triggered congestion to be adaptable in video conferencing, asylum exhibition traffic applies its adaptability [40].

2.4.3 An Instance of MIC Systems Integration

The generic modeling environment (GME) is a field-specific tool in MIC modeling environments that may be modified according to meta-level specification. For GME to be productive in DSML development, an extensive understanding of the underlying field and memory configuration is required. Avionics application has been designed with extended system modeling language (ESML).

The signal payment invoice is critically important for the apparatus management system. A basic example of how MIC aids the full developing process is presented in this part for the creation of applications from the meta-level architecture for the signaling productive functioning. A core tool in MIC is the generic modeling. For equipment control system, signal process module is absolutely necessary. In this section, application development from meta-level construction for signal process module is described as a simple example to illustrate how MIC facilitates the whole development process. Consequently, the viability of building DSML for equipment control is indicated.

- **Meta-modeling**

    The Ability to contract Meta Structure, appearing in Objects, connections and characteristics, is expressed in the vocabulary of the consequence of the presence. The abstraction signaling objects is the atoms of the input voltage. The relationship is specified as the Conn datatypes and is adopted as Input Arm, PARAM, Specified Output Base is also acquired. The link between them is specified as the Conn variable. Multiple processing models exist the fundamental and the composite components. The composite part model may include Primitive Part models; however, the Fundamental Attributes or features can only include atoms and their linkages. The Signal Flow aspect and Parameters Aspects are different sides described. The Signal Flow Component is observable in the Primitive part, Compound, Input, and Output signals. Parameter Aspect displays the fundamental part, composite part, input arm, PARAM, and Output PARAM.

- **Domain construction model**

    DSML is constructed from the meta-model developed in semi-A with the ordered relationship. Domains architects may then build their applications with models. Here, the fast build process is illustrated using DSML by multiple application social human resources and a rudimentary model is produced. This program produces, stores, and visualizes a sequence of randomized database files.

    Based on the previous model additional model is developed. An FFT block is added. The original data and the transferred electronically are both sent to the presentation plot models.

- **Mapping**

    The modeling interpreters transfer it to the existing applications when the model is generated. The kernels incorporate programs dynamically defined by their information power distribution networks. The kernels enable data to be generated and spread among networks and offer a waste collection storage assignment system. The operation of the stream processing node is regulated by its scheduled features: trigger method and precedence. In this approach, after DSML has been created, the modeling interpreters may quickly produce an implementation leading name in this domain and create a deployable application that assists the complete project development and delegation of work. Moreover, as the needs alter with technological progress, the situational may be updated.

2.5 PROCESSING AND ANALYSIS AND MATHEMATICAL MODELING OF TWO-STAGE ESTIMATE METHOD

In the survey results, processing the usual measuring adjustments uses stochastic components as well as certain components commonly co-exist, but not only random mistakes but also certain systemic flaws. But the findings certainly contain systemic errors. The adapted outcome would be partial if it is omitted. When model mistakes are small, removing model errors does not have a substantial effect on the assessed cost of the characteristics based on random mistakes. If the model error is large, the model parameters will have a detrimental impact, which will also lead to incorrect results. Authentic experiences, dependent on a parameter set, are commonly thought to be represented by a function. The linear regression generally is supposed to be known as its linear function. The number of uncertain parameters is decreased to the issue and the observation is parameterized in this scenario. Numerous factors are hard to explain the findings adequately.

Following approaches to reduce or remove the model mistakes may be taken: To adjust the information using known systemic error compensation models, if the relationships between systemic errors and their components are linear, add a few repeatable characteristics. The statistical method can effectively reduce its effects. Another technique to decrease systemic mistakes is to adapt the questionnaire that used a set of cosine similarity information, rather than observations themselves.

Any double phase approach, for example, is utilized to cancel or substantially minimize the majority of the clock, ionosphere, and troposphere error in the GPS data management. The accuracy of localization is increased while some relevant device is compromised simultaneously.

There is not necessarily a linear connection in many situations. Development into more adaptable models is therefore necessary. In the 1980s, statisticians produced moderate models of regression consisting of a parametric portion and a non-parametric statistical half. Dealing with complex connections between data and anticipated variables offers some important benefits from parametric methods and provides relevant information. A lot of authors have debated this model. The semi-parametric extrapolation approach is presented in this chapter for assessing and developing an appropriate procedure to estimate statistical values and to concurrently remove model problems.

2.5.1 THE MATHEMATICAL MODEL

The standard test adaptation is

$$L_i = bx_i + \Delta_i \quad 1 \le i \quad n \tag{2.1}$$

where the model contains systemic faults and model errors are formed to distinguish systemic mistakes. Suppose L_i includes non-parametric answers $s\ t\ (i)$, $i=1, 2, n,$ Eq. (2.1) may then be re-scheduled as:

$$L_i = b\,x_i + st()_i + \Delta_i \quad 1 \le i \quad n \tag{2.2}$$

If $b_i=(b_{i1}, b_{i2}$-bit $p)$ is a non-random designing points vectors, $B=B\ (b\ b_{1,2}, ..., b_n)\ T$ has complete rank $(B)=p$, i.e., its components are completely separate, $x=x=x\ (x\ x_{1,2}, ..., x_p)\ T$ is an empirical probability vectors, $t_i \in D\ s()fu$ is the unknown smooth function of R_1, $s=($a sub set of $R_1)$ $(s\ s_{1,2}, ..., s_n)\ T$ is utilized for model channel estimation description. $\Delta=\Delta(\Delta_1, \Delta_2, ..., \Delta_n)^T$ is a random vector with uncorrelated error $E()\Delta=0$ and $D_\Delta=\sigma^2Q$, where σ^2 is the unit-weighted variance.

The error equation associated with Eq. (2.2) is

$$V = +- B\hat{x}\hat{s}\,L \tag{2.3}$$

where $\hat{x}$ and $\hat{s}$ denote the estimates of parametric x and non-parametric s, $V \in R^n$ is the residuals.

2.5.2 METHOD OF EVALUATION AND COMPLETION OF THE MODELING

The x and non-Parametric s parameters are estimated independently by two stages of estimation. More exactly, the two additional techniques may be developed.

Stage 1: For fixed x, let $\alpha=\underline{\quad}\ 1\ \Sigma n\ s\ t()_i$ and $\varepsilon_i=s\ t()_i-\alpha+\Delta_i.$ Then Eq. (2.2) can be

$$n \cdot i = 1$$

Written as

$$L_i = b\,x_i + + \alpha\,\varepsilon_i \tag{2.4}$$

To evaluate the axiom, we let $L=(L\ L_1, ..., L_n)\ T$, $1_n=(1, 1, 1)T$, $\hat{x}^*$ and $\hat{\alpha}^*$. Be the lowest x and α squares calculator.

The equation of error related to Eq. (2.4)

$$V_1 = B\hat{x} + 1_n\hat{\alpha} - L \tag{2.5}$$

We develop the Lagrange functional based on the common least square research methods:

$$\Phi = 1V_1^T P V_1 + 2\lambda_1^T \left(B\hat{x}^* + 1_n \hat{\alpha}^* -- LV_1 \right) \tag{2.6}$$

where $P = Q^{-1}$. The favorable symmetry is matrices, and the Lagrange constants is also a modulation index of measurements L, μ_1.

Using $\dfrac{\partial \Phi_1}{\partial V_1} = 0$, $\dfrac{\partial \Phi_1}{\partial \hat{x}^*} = 0$ and $\dfrac{\partial \Phi_1}{\partial \hat{x}^*} = 0$, we obtain

$$\lambda_1 = PV_1 \tag{2.7}$$

$$BT\lambda_1 = 0 \tag{2.8}$$

$$\lambda_1^T 1_n = 0 \tag{2.9}$$

Simply by calculation, the x-alternative (Eq. 2.5) and α-alternative (Eq. 2.10) is reduced to a minimal amount when x-alternatively to fulfill the x-alignment. This system of equations is generally exceedingly massive and cannot be solved directly or even in a practical way. This isn't essential, fortunately. One way is that Eq. (2.10) should be written again as a pair of numerical methods.

$$B^T PB\hat{x}^* + BP^T 1_n \hat{\alpha}^* - B^T PL = 0 \tag{2.11}$$

$$1_n^T PB\hat{x}^* + 1_n^T \quad 1_n \hat{\alpha}^* P - 1_n^T PL = 0 \tag{2.12}$$

From Eqs. (2.11) and (2.12), we obtain

$$\hat{x}^* = \left(B^T PB \right)^{-1} BPL^T \left(-1_n \hat{\alpha}^* \right) \tag{2.13}$$

$$\hat{\alpha}^* = \left(1_n^T P1_n \right)^{-1} 1_n^T P \left(L - B\hat{x}^* \right) \tag{2.14}$$

We could transition between Eqs. (2.13) and (2.14) and resolve x à la chamfered and α à la chambered. Sometimes an operation is called back-fitting. Synchronization can be quite slow in reality. A direct technique is an alternate strategy. With $d_n = 1$ $(T_n P - PB (B^T PB)^{-1} B P^T)1_n$, we have the first approximation, which replaces Eq. (2.13) with Eq. (2.14), $\hat{\alpha}^*$ of α

$$\hat{\alpha}^* = d_n^{-1T} P - PB_1 \left(\left(B^T PB \right)^{-1} BPL^T \right) \tag{2.15}$$

We get a first approximation by replacing Eq. (2.15) in Eq. (2.13). $\hat{x}^*$ of x

$$\hat{x}^* = \left(B^T PB \right)^{-1} BPL^T \left(-1_n \hat{\alpha}^* \right) \tag{2.16}$$

Stage 2: Replacing xæ pour into Eq. (2.2), is regarded to be a non-parametric model of extrapolation.

$$L_i - bx_i^{\hat{*}} = st()_i + \Delta_i \tag{2.17}$$

Therefore, $()s\, t_i$ can be estimated by the kernel method

$$ns\hat{t}()_i = \sum Ktt_h(i,j)\left(L_i - b\hat{x}_i^* \right) \tag{2.18}$$
$$j=1$$

where the strength of K_h () to an activation function K () to a kernel is related with the weight $h \Rightarrow 10$. For K (), the weight K_h () is defined as the asymmetrical activation functions, the K_h ()

$$K_h(t\,t') = K\,t((-t')\,/\,h)/h \qquad (2.19)$$

Substituting $()s\,\hat{t}\,i$ for $()s\,t_i$ in Eq. (2.2) gives

$$L_i = b\,x_i + s\,\hat{t}()_i + \Delta_i \qquad (2.20)$$

Its equation error is

$$V_2 = Bxs\,\hat{L}+\hat{\,}- \qquad (2.21)$$

We generate the Lagrange function based on the common least quadratic methods.

$$\Phi = 2V_2^T PV_2 + 2\lambda_2^T \left(Bxs\,L\hat{V}+--\hat{\,}2\right) \qquad (2.22)$$

$\partial\Phi^2=0$, and $\partial\Phi^2=0$, respectively.

Since $B^T\,PB$ is a positive matrix, we get the final estimate of x as

$$\hat{x} = \left(B^T PB\right)^{-1} BPL\,s^T(-\hat{\,}) \qquad (2.23)$$

Given Eq. (2.18), the final estimation is available

$$s\hat{t}() = \sum_{i=1} K_h(tt,i)\left(L_i - b\,\hat{x}_i\right) \qquad (2.24)$$

2.5.3   HAT MATRIX AND FITTED VALUES

If we now select that

$$\sim P = (I - W\,P) \qquad (2.25)$$

The weighting for parameter estimates Eq. (2.2) are complete column rank

$$\hat{x} = (B\,PBT \sim)-1\,B\,PLT \sim \qquad (2.26)$$

and

$$\hat{s} = W\,L\left(-B\hat{x}\right) \qquad (2.27)$$

where I have the matrix of identical n, and $W\,t$ ()=diag $(K_h\,(t,\,1),\,K_h\,(t,\,n))$.
  The most common squares for the data are

$$\hat{L} = B\hat{x} + \hat{s} = \hat{J}\,h\,L() \qquad (2.28)$$

with

$$J\,h() = W + \left(I - W\,B\,B\,PB\,BP\right)(T \sim)T \sim \qquad (2.29)$$

$J\,h$ () is normally called a hat matrix in the semi-parametric framework.

2.5.4 Selection of Frequency

As is known, the frequency variable h monitors the balance between fitness and smoothness, and the right h must be chosen.

The Residue Sum of Squares (RSS) of modeling is a prediction metric, as the discrepancy here between responsive measurement and its adequate or anticipated value is the residue:

$$e_i = -L\,\hat{L}_i \tag{2.30}$$

As a model selection, however, RSS is not sufficient. The difficulty is that L_i and other measurements are used by Lui to forecast L_i. This results in the shortest RSS paradigms, namely, the most autonomous prototypes, and the other variants as instances. Due to the assumption that L_i, as part of their predictor, appear to be ideal to RSS for the predictions result in a little amount of smoothness, which provides L_i a heavy strength. The solution to these problems is simplistic: utilize all of the data save one when forecasting L_i. Therefore, define $\hat{L}^{-i}$ $(t\ h_i)$, The semi-parametric approximation for extrapolation is used on the data but eliminated using $(t\ L_i, I)$. Then let the residue erased ith be $e()i = -L_i\,1 - i\ (t\ h_i)$. The expected square residual sum is calculated as (PRESS):

$$\mathrm{PRESS} = \sum_{i=1}^{n} e_{(i)}^2 \tag{2.31}$$

The Vulnerability Analysis approach separates the data into two separate systems, adapts the equations in a single set, and predicts the second tournament information. By utilizing only, the one fits for the first set. The approach of "leaving out a single person" is a means to prevent the wiggle response provided by RSS. The selection of h reduces PRESS.

It is not as hard to compute the PRESS criteria as it would seem. According to a crucial identity, you don't have to fit the models n times. Let J_{ii} $()$ H be the ith of the hat matrices $J\ h$ $()$ diagonally component. Then the removed residue is connected to the common residue by

$$L_i - \hat{L}^{-i}(t_i, h) = \left(L_i - \hat{L}_i\right) / \left(1 - J_{ii}(h)\right) \tag{2.32}$$

Thus, only conventional residues and diagonal features of the hat matrices are possible for the PRESS calculation.

2.5.5 Simulation Techniques

We contrasted the half-parametric technique with the common least quadratic technique for modification. For a moderately framework generated

$$L = + + Y\ S\Delta \tag{2.33}$$

where $Y = BX$, $X = [2, 3]T$, $B = (b_{ij})100 \times 2$, $b_{i1} = -+2\ i/20$, $b_{i2} = -+2\ (i/20)^2$, $S = (s_i)100 \times 1$, $s_i = 9\sin(t_i\pi)$, $t_i = i$ $/100$, $i = 1,200$. The observing error vector—bis is made up of the typical N $(0, 1)$ dispersed, 200 randomized data. The promising strategy reflects the genuine values Y, the screw figure represents L.

Select the matrices that are weighed P's a matrix of uniqueness. We derive the regression model that uses the mathematical expression

$$\hat{X} = \left(B^T\ PB^{-1}\right)B^T PL = \left(3 - 1,194, 3.3611\right)^T$$

The usual methodology may produce an inaccurate result if the model mistake leaves the model.

The quaternion kernels is used for the Eq. (2.33) $K\,t() = 15/16((1-t^2))^2\,I\,t(\leq 1)$.

2.6   DEVELOPMENT AND REALIZATION OF PARALLELISM REDUCED POWER PARALLEL E0 ALGORITHMS

Authentication systems are the key to extremely secretive and private communication. The customer information can be secured using cryptography of the payload packet in Bluetooth wireless communications. The payload is encrypted utilizing a stream cipher known as E0 which is resynced for all packages. There are three sections of the Stream Cipher System E0. One component is initialized (payload key creation), while the third portion is encoded and decrypted. The actual encrypted data strength might range from 8 to 128 bits. Then the original message will be decreased to the satisfactory strength with the usage of E0. For this polynomials module action, the Bluetooth system provides 17 distinct polynomials.

The study proposes a novel programmable LFSR architecture that may be planned and configured for implementing any one of these 17 polynomials stated before.

The suggested programmable LFSR achieved a reduction in energy usage utilizing the clock gating methodology. In mobile communications systems, the programmable architecture may, therefore, be employed efficiently.

2.6.1   DESCRIPTION OF E0 ALGORITHM

The E0 stream cipher, consisting of three components, is used to encrypt packet payloads in Bluetooth as shown in Figure 1. The first element is the payload generation that initializes the system. The second is that of the keystream generator, which creates the plaintext bits and employs four linear Shift Registers with outputs of the unencrypted sequencing or the randomized beginning number in the initialization process. The length L of the four LFSRs are 25, 31, 33, and 39 correspondingly. For activation of the LFSR, a starting value for four LFSRs and four bits for registers contents must be placed on the summing combinations. By employing the keystream generating itself, four inputs are obtained from the initial value of 132 bits. The criteria for input are the encrypting key and the 26 master clock bits and the 128-bit pseudo-random, the 48-bit Bluetooth address. The KC is changed into another KC key within the payload generator using the polynomial modular procedure explained in. This key's maximum effective size is established by the company and may be set to several eight, from 1 to 17.

After the encrypted data is produced, all bits are moved into LFSRs and start with the smallest bit. Then, the system is operating 200 cryptographic algorithms bits. The remaining 128 bits are returned as a start value of the four LFSRs in the keystream generation. The sequence diagram values are maintained. From this point on, in the principal dimension of the cipher, the generators construct a bitwise encrypting sequence using the sent received signal.

2.6.2   DESIGN FOR LOW-POWER CONSUMPTION

The CMOS circuit's power utilization is the combined transient and steady-state energy consumption. The constant energy demand resulting from the power dissipation relies mostly upon the chip size. It is quite little and can be overlooked in our context, which has an impact on dynamical power usage in the following equation. The engineering methods to reduce electricity use derive from the components in this calculation being minimized.

$$Pdyn = CL \cdot VDD2 \cdot fCLKeff \cdot psw$$

As additional doors are installed on the die, the chip CL loading impedance rises.

This leads us to immediately minimize energy consumption by decreasing the die size and minimizing the power factor. The low die-size limit and operational circumstances of the semiconductor tend to accurately predict these two characteristics. With a technology called sleep logic, the frequency of shifting PSW of the circuit may be minimized. Thus, the use of AND doors in the input of combining circuits eliminates unusual switching activities. Assume a constant voltage of the supply and a maximum frequency of switches in combinations, reducing the efficient reference signal fCLKeff circuit is the best alternative for low power architecture. This exponentially decreases electricity use. Clock gating is an excellent strategy to reduce the reference signal effectively. All data records and almost all control logical records are only timed in our architectures when a possible change in signal occurs. This resulted in a huge decrease in reduced consumption. This essentially disconnects segments of the circuit if not in use. Typical clock gate register that comprises a data latch and flip-flops. The D-latch is used to avoid flip-flops that create a register of bits in a shift register. Depending on the algorithms, the ideal bit-width of registers is employed. Reduced overall time complexity results from minimizing the number of memory components (of flop and latch consumption on the active clock edges is virtually the same) that are active at the same time. There are therefore b-bit statements separating all N-flops in the architecture. The quantity of information encoded n depends on the amount of computer memory N for the procedures and the bit depth b of the registers. The starting amount of n/b is the number of flip-flops within each register. The D-bit clock-gating latching is engaged at every stage.

It concludes that the optimum bit length of a technology is when this formula is minimized $b = \sqrt{N}$.

$$n(b) = \frac{N}{b} + b$$

$$\frac{dn}{db} = -\frac{N}{b^2} + 1$$

$$-\frac{N}{b^2} + 1 = 0$$

$$b = \sqrt{N}$$

With E0 algorithms, we are choosing to construct the appropriate quantity of flip-flops per registration in 5.6 lines.

2.6.3 Simultaneous Infinitely Customizable E0 Algorithm Low Power Structure

The programme is close to zero parallel algorithm E0. It may be noticed that The LFSR registers shift five bits every clock cycle. Only one register is timed using a clock gating mechanism simultaneously time. In addition, any combined circuits such as the final state machine must be installed in radix 5. The function inputs are picked bit from the registers, and in this picture, they are not depicted in full. To activate and deactivate the relevant inputs, the AND gates are employed. The finite machine's detail is displayed in 4.2. The key is stored in the registers during startup. The following clock cycle allows the EN1~EN8, in turn, to construct a final sequence number on the finite state machine. It takes nine cycles, then, to get a five-bit encrypting result after startup.

- **The use of finite state machine**

The keystream generating E0 used in Bluetooth corresponds to a combination generating with essentially four bits, indicated by $\sigma_i = (c_{t-1}, c_t)$ at time t, where $c_t = (c_t^1, c_t^0)$. Four linear modulation schemes are used for the complete enterprise $R_1, \ldots, R_4$ respectively. In cycle t, the three output bits of the four LFSR $x_t^i, i = 1, \ldots, 4$. The total as integers is added $y_t \in \{0, 4\}$ and is represented in the binary system. Let y_t^i identify its smallest point ($i = 1, 2, 3$). A 16-state machine releases one-bit c_t^0 from its condition $\sigma_t = (c_{t-1}, c_t)$ and simply updates the input σ_t by σ_{t+1}. T_1 and T_2 are nonlinear mappings that may be performed via XOR. Finally, the keystream z_t is obtained by XORing y_t^1 with c_t^0, that is, T_1 and T_2 are nonlinear mappings that may be performed via XOR.

More formally, by introducing two temporary bits $S_{t+1} = \left(S_{t+1}^1, S_{t+1}^0\right)$, the analytical method indirect terms amongst each clock S_{t+1} and c_{t+1} suffice to update c_t: the LFSR shift registers may be observed shifting five bits each clock cycle based on the aforesaid architecture. As illustrated at a single clock we can calculate s_{t+2} or c_{t+2}. If enough hardware is accessible, speed might easily be doubled by up to five if it is quite possible to enhance the output in this way.

2.6.4 Performance Assessment and Comparisons

- **FPGA and ASIC implementation**

The prototype was done in Verilog language based on the findings above RTL description. And the synthesizing proceeds with the Altera Corporation's QuartusII 6.0. A prototype based on Altera Cyclone EP1C12Q240C8 has been successfully checked. The performance is shown in Table 2.13.

The concept was created using Synopsys Design Complier for the 0.18 μm CMOS technology to assess its efficiency with more precision. The prototypes based on architecture have been synthesized, placed, and routed. Table 2.14 shows the prototype's operational findings.

In order to assess the power usage, the prototype utilizes Blast Rail from Magma. Table 2.15 illustrates the overall performance of the configuration.

Based on the results of the foregoing synthesis, we evaluate our approach with references for the two essential parameters, namely power consumption and throughput rate. The low wattage implementation of the E0 algorithms for gray code encoding. Table 2.16 displays the results.

TABLE 2.13
Leistung of the E0 Optimization Method on the FPGA

Maximum Frequency (MHz)	Logic Elements (LEs)	Throughput Rate (Mbit/s)
174	320	96

TABLE 2.14
E0 Algorithms Performances with ASIC

Maximum Frequency (MHz)	Area (μm²)	Throughput Rate (Mbit/s)
320	1,53,673	177

TABLE 2.15
E0 Algorithm's Power Consumption Performance

Leakage Consumption	Internal Consumption	Dynamic Consumption	Total Consumption
247.1 nw	87.8 μw	1.03 mw	1.11 mw

TABLE 2.16
The Comparison with Other Designs

Design	Power Consumption (MW)	Throughput Rate (Mbit/s)
Our design	1.11	177
Quality product	—	189
Functional analysis	1.30	90

The outcome has shown that our latency is the same, with just certain LFSR supported. Therefore, our design is more flexible, and our design has a lesser energy consumption than in terms of electricity usage. In particular, our design offers clear advantages over the performance.

2.7 CONCLUSION

The estimating and forecasting of construction projects are vital for the survival and growth of construction enterprises in the industry. The approach integrates the theory of crude collection with neural networks and forecasts construction costs. The outcomes from this work show the efficacy of the RS methodology as a preprocessing step of neural network input. The minimization of information technology is of considerable importance to the neural network, as it minimizes the curse of dimensionality problems and saves time. Industrial transformations and environmental reforms of environmental parks, power and data flow, management philosophy, and the domains of sustainable industrial research are obligated to enhance members' mutual interaction, institutional support, operating profitability, and effectiveness. The Graphic DSML system illustrates the benefit of this technology and is readily used for two signals industrial processes. In the quality construction area, the architecture of the control system is investigated. The modeling approach itself is in several situations an approximation of the genuine model at best and it is not simple to look for an appropriate model in the parametric family. If no convincing products are available, a possible expansion of the parametrical family can be seen in the family of semi-parametric regression analysis. Models for semi-parametric regression simplify complicated summary data sets.

3 Management Rule Mining Computing

3.1 ASSOCIATION RULES MINING ALGORITHMS

R. Agrawal et al. introduced the transactional database in 1993 mining associations that are widely used in pharmaceutical, biological, and commercial organizations. Since then, relationship regulations have gained much interest and many scientists have been working on them—static principles to dynamical principles, multi-lingual word standards to quantitative norms, etc. This document provides a high-level description of the methodologies and expansions of associational mining rules and we have also made some research ideas in the upcoming. Our discussions are organized into four subjects with a large body of literature: refining techniques for increasing the expansion of association principles and categorization concepts, research on factors such as aid and instruction, and implementation of new technologies [41].

3.1.1 BASIC PRINCIPLES OF ASSOCIATION RULES

Let $I = \{I\ i_i = 1, 2, m\}$ be a literal set, known as items. Let D be a set of transactions in which each T is a collection of elements $T \subseteq I$. A unique identification, termed TID, is connected with each transaction. We indicate that a test participant comprises X, several things in I, if $X \subseteq T$. An association rule is an implication of the form $X \Rightarrow Y$, where $X\ Y, \subset I,$ and $X \cap = \emptyset Y$. The rule $X \Rightarrow Y$ holds in the transaction set D with confidence c if $c\%$ of transactions in D that contain X and also Y. The rule $X \Rightarrow Y$ supports the transaction set D if $s\%$ of transactions in D contain $X \cup Y$.

The challenge of machine learning and data mining, given a collection of transactions D, is to produce all frequent patterns that have better support and trust than the maximum and minimal trust provided to the client.

3.1.2 RULES OF ASSOCIATION

The renowned association principles Apriori algorithm was found in 1994. Association's regulations have been more deeply investigated since then. There are two options for improving mining effectiveness algorithms: previous algorithms rather than prior methodologies. There is no prior optimization algorithm.

3.1.2.1 Improving the Algorithm to Increase Mining Efficiency

Apriori performed a really major role amongst the association mining algorithms, which had a big effect on the subsequent study. Apriori's fundamental rule is: The first iteration of the program only counts things to identify the big 1 object set. There are different phases of a succeeding passage, say pass k. First, the $Lk-1$ big array in the $(k-1)$ pass is utilized to produce the Ck array of candidates that used the Apriori-gen feature. The next step is to search the database and calculate the commitment to the Ck prospects. Until the huge k information set Ck is complete, the procedure will be terminated. Apriori can effectively extract principles from collections, but it takes a lot of time and is not too much effective. Several academics have since proposed better theory as a principle on the Apriori method. The approach is based on a thorough combined analysis of the data gathered in earlier runs, which enables needless rules on contestants to be removed. Manila et al. have provided sampling algorithms. This method was further enhanced submitted a hash-based DHP

DOI: 10.1201/9781003211938-3

method. This approach makes the candidate much smaller than prior approaches and particularly created two itemsets for the candidate. And generating smaller applicant sets helps us to efficiently reduce the size of the transaction database considerably earlier. Park created a parallel edition of the DHP in 1995, dubbed the Parallel Data Mining and sequential association rules (PDM). In 1996 Agrawal presented simultaneous mining techniques and provided three different approaches: Count Distribution, Network Configuration, and the methodology for Candidates' Apportionment, correspondingly, according to my association rules. Savasere and others have created partition methods that just continuously explore the database. The model was accurately monitored and improved.

The heuristic Apriori produces good results by a reduction in the size of the region proposals. However, it has certain inconveniences, for instance: when a great number of designs are present, it is expensive to manage a large pool of candidates [42].

And other algorithms do not exist with Apriori. M.J. Zaki and others presented a cluster-technical algorithm. The approach just scans the database once and costs 25% of Apriori to effectively identify all rules. The A-Closed method was submitted in 1999 by Nicolas et al. and used the closed itemset grid structure. This strategy is extremely useful for extensive and/or connected data and can decrease the cost of the algorithms by creating a small number of rules for associations without having to discover every common group of elements. Randomized algorithm creates a small set of association rules within the polynomial period. This approach has dealt with the problem of exponential computer resource usage for most algorithms like Apriori. FP-tree algorithms have been introduced to produce an effective FP-tree-based mining approach called FP-growth for extracting the entire collection of common patterns through pattern fragmentation growth. For mining both high and low frequent itemsets, the FP-growth method is efficient and adaptable, and it works well. The ant colony algorithm is a relatively recent technique that can produce more concise rules than the Apriori technique. In addition, the mathematical formulation is lowered.

3.1.2.2   Suggest New Algorithms to Enlarge the Classification Models

The Association Regulations concentrated first just on information relationships in feature representation; but, as time went on, investigators broadened the scope of their research, attempting to collect interesting input from a range of sources. These algorithms are instances of extended association rule mining, qualitative association rule mining, fudges classification methods, rare classifiers, and so on.

3.1.2.3   Rules of General Association

In 1995, Srikant et al. laid forth the broad laws of association, with components of all taxonomic levels. The form indicates a set of common principles of affiliation. $X \Rightarrow Y$, where $X \subset I$, $Y \subset I$, $X \cap Y = \varnothing$,

And no Y item is an offspring of any X item.

The generalized principles of an association incorporated taxonomy, allowing for the leaves and stems objects in the taxonomy in the Association Regulations. To improve the effectiveness of generalized mining association rules, Andras Myka et al. introduced a Prutax technique. Pretax performs better than previous techniques in order of magnitude. A shared, no-thing parallel machine suitable classification hierarchical rules for mining associations, and the parallel algorithm enhanced mining performance, was presented by Takahiko Shintani et al. Three algorithms were proposed: NPGM in terms of improving mining efficiency, NPGM in the form of HPGM in the form of HH-HPGM. Shiny Thomas et al. have numerous ways to formulate SQL queries apriori algorithm that generalizes items with their hierarchy and sequence pattern mining, according to the most commonly produced mining systems loosely interface with data stored in DBMSs.

3.1.2.4   Quantitative Association Rules

The quantifiable classification methods were proposed by Srikant R. et al. The rules governing quantitative associations are those with quantitative or categorical features. They considered it possible to map an issue for quantitative assembly procedures if all characteristics are categories or the qualitative attributes have just certain values. The APACS2 rules for quantitative relationship mining are suggested by Keith C.C. Chan et al. in very big databases. The methodology has the advantage of not having any frequently difficult to establish user-supplied criteria and it enables us to find both favorable and unfavorable rules for association. Ansaf Salleb-aouissi et al designed a methodology of quantitative association mining by genetic algorithms (GAs) dubbed QUANTMINER. In classification algorithms, this system can, therefore, dynamically discover "gut" intervals by maximizing support and trust. In 2007, they devised an approach to dynamically identify the limits of the qualities. It may continuously detect the limits of (quantitative) domains.

3.1.2.5 Fuzzy Association Rules

Fuzzy-automatic pattern analysis and classification system (F-APACS) was developed for mining fuzzy associations in 1997 by Keith C.C. Chan et al. To convey disclosed recurring patterns and exceptions, F-APACS utilizes language words. Linguistic representations are particularly useful when the rules found are submitted for assessment by human experts. The fugitive association rules imply that the qualitative characteristics are addressed by 'If X is A then Y is B.' X, Y are a collection of qualities, while A, B are fuzzy sets describing X and Y. The algorithms employed fluoridated technology for the regulations for mining associations were proposed in 1998 by Chan Man Kuok, et al., and the sharp border problem was resolved. In the extraction of fuzzy rules of associations, Hung-Pin Chiu et al. proposed CBFar algorithms, and this technique exceeds the Apriori-based fuzzy algorithm of mining regulations. The following strategy was applied: In 2008, P. Santhi Thilagam et al. suggested a technique employing a multi-objective evolutionary algorithm to identify and optimize fuzzy association rule mining [42].

3.1.2.6 Rare Association Rules

In applications of deep learning, the association rules of frequent articles were extensively examined. However, the desire for mining unusual things has increased in recent years like uncommon but costly products. Hyunyoon Yun presented RSAA for mining the rules of association for the rule discovery. In other words, The RSAA is better than Apriori and MSApriori because of the important rarity of scarce data linked to particular information, so rare data are conceived concurrently with the detailed information more often than the overall average frequencies in the collection. MBS and HBS are the two efficient ways for mining uncommon association rules. These two strategies extract the rules by just applying machine learning algorithms repeatedly, and they may also be used to quickly mine classification algorithms among frequent patterns with a maximum width.

3.1.2.7 Other Association Rules

There are other association rules in addition to the ones listed above, for example, mining numerical connection regulations, rules of simple association, maximal connectivity rules, and regulations for digitized records.

3.1.3 INTEGRATION AND CLASSIFICATION OF ASSOCIATION RULES

Bing Liu et al. suggest the inclusion of the matrix completion associations and the rule mining categorization. Integrating is done by concentrating on the mining of a special fraction of rules of assistance provider as rules of the classes. It needs to achieve the entire CARs package and to develop a CAR classifier. The classification constructed in this method is more precise than the grading system of state-of-the-art C4.5. Chapters presented in the GARC algorithm, which in the generation stage may filter out many candidate objects, thereby make the set produced by it far smaller than CBA. The RMR algorithm provided in the document eliminates an overlap by the suggested methodology. The result is a more effective classification between the rules in the classification by producing rules which do not share the learning items during training. There are a lot of books on rules of connection and categorization as it submitted the CARSVM model, integrating association rules and supporting vector machines; developed a model of differs depending on understandable, fluid-induced rules and meeting both efficiency criteria; study examined how predictive accuracy of CARM methods can have the effect of selecting ARM parameters. This describes various technologies that resume associative categorization rules using decision-making bodies. The classification method obtained incorporates the advantages of association classification with decision-making bodies and represents an important categorization than typical decision-making bodies [43].

3.1.4 PARAMETER RESEARCH SUCH AS SUPPORT AND TRUST

In association rules mining, minimum confidence plays a key role and the two parameters for extraction association rules are based on most traditional association rules mining algorithms. It has solved the challenge of establishing minimum frequent item sets supports if things are supported differently. The amount of association rule mining and big items obtained with the maximal constraints by the matrix factorization is similarly less than those using the minimal constraint. The study discussed in Ref. [40] suggested a matching mechanism as a replacement of trust. The rules obtained using the revised approach show that the precedents are highly correlated with those created by the aid-confidence framework when the rules were compared. The paper discussed in Ref. [41] has proposed two methods, MMS Stratify and MMS Cumulate, and enlarged in the existence of ontologies the scope of generalized association rules that allow for all kinds of multiple minimum customers supports. Offered an approach for identifying association rules that do not specify the current average support for an evolutionary algorithm [44].

3.2 APPLICATION TO BUILDING COOLANT CHARGE OF ROUGH SET THEORY AND FUZZY LS-SVM

The efforts have been made for heating, ventilation, and air conditioning (HVAC), due to substantial quantities of energy lost. In direction to progress the maneuver of HVAC structures, it is needed to have consistent optimization practices. Efficient heuristics are required to improve the functioning of HVAC systems. Precise forecast of the construction dynamic refrigeration demand is a key to optimum HVAC system control.

Estimating energy efficiency adequately in buildings is a difficult task. Various prediction processes, including the admission and Fourier techniques, the transfer feature approach, the artificial neural approach, the Monte-Carlo simulations technique, methods to filter Kalman, etc. have been implemented. While these techniques have to a certain degree reduced challenges in estimating and predicting air conditioning loads, there remain significant issues as yet. Support vector machine (SVM) addresses the lack of engineering experience inside the artificial neural network (ANN) framework. It provides a good solution for high dimensions, minimum error, and small samples. The last SVM square (LS-SVM) from standard SVM was produced. It replaces inequity limitations of standard SVM with equality limitations and replaces quadratic programming with a linear optimization framework. This decreases the difficulty of calculations, accelerates the resolution, and improves intervention capacity. Because the evidence released for the buildings load demand is not always precise and quantifiable but rather ambiguous and fragmentary, SVM does not communicate properly with knowledge on uncertainty and ambiguity. A hybrid proposed methodology consisting of a region-based element and an LS-SVM component is provided in this study to handle these difficulties. Our idea intends to take full advantage of Rough Set's strengths in the preview of vast data, removing superfluous data, and addressing the limitations of the SVM approach's sluggish computational efficiency. Without generating the parameters of the network from the dataset, LS-SVM can detect the geometric aspects of the higher dimensional space and can extract the optimum solution with minimal interaction. Particularly furious LS-SVM frequency prediction accuracy can set distinct membership according to historical data influence. It decreases the importance of the early data on the existing manufacturing process and enhances predictability in actual environments. The method was established for the refrigeration of load predictions, and the experimental findings suggest that the RST-based selection of functions and the Fuzzy LS-SVM-based predictors work well in aspects of calculation cost, computational efficiency, and effectiveness over other combinations [45].

3.2.1 BASIC PRINCIPLE OF RST AND FUZZY LS-SVM

Pawlak created a region-based theory to deal with unclear or imprecise ideas. The key notions of rough theories are the deduction of decisions or rules of categorization utilizing reducing information on the premise that the same categorization is maintained. Rough algebraic topology covers information described by management system tables. It consists of the following four-fold:

$$S = < U \, A \, V \, f, > \tag{3.1}$$

A is a limited, non-empty collection of qualities where U is a bounded set of objects known as the universal. $V = U_{a\,A}$, V_a is a domain of attribute a, and $f: U \times A \to V$ is the whole selection functional known as information factor $f \, x \, a \, (,) \in VA$, also seen as a decision table for the information system, assuming that $A = CUD$ and $C \cap D = \phi$,

where C is the set of characteristics of precondition and D is a set of attributes of decision.

In RST, the fundamental difference is made between items definitively categorized into a given category and objects which may be categorized. Objects are inseparable if represented by the same knowledge, with specific qualities. Let $P \subseteq A$ and $x \, x_{i,\,j} \in U$. Then x_i and x_j are indiscernible by the set of attributes in S if and only if (1) holds.

$$fxa(i,) = fxa(j,), \forall \in aB \tag{3.2}$$

A basic set is defined as a set of objects that are indistinguishable from certain properties. Thus, from $B \subseteq A$, we define the relationship of equivalency on U, called the relationship of indiscernibility, indicated by U/IND (B), The $U/\text{IND}(B)$ equivalency ratio generates S basic B sets that hold the B-indistinguishable objects.

Given $B \subseteq A$ and $x \subseteq U$, the B-lower BY^* of set Y and the B-upper BY^* is described as follows:

$$| \, |BY^* = \left\{ x \in U : []xU/\text{IND}()B \subseteq Y \right\} \tag{3.3}$$

$$| \, |\left(BY^* = \left\{ x \in U : []xU / \text{IND}()B \cap Y = \phi \right\} \right.$$

In addition, we can combine an index αB of approximations preciseness for each set with the properties B. $Y \in U$ as follows:

$$\alpha_B = |BY_*| / |BY^*| \tag{3.4}$$

where the representation of a set BY^* is shown as $|BY^*|$. Obviously $0 \leq \alpha_B \leq 1$, if $\alpha_B = 1$, then Y is, and is, concerning B; if it is $\alpha B < 1$, Y is concerning Be a rough set. Let $B \, Q$, class A, be the positive $U/\text{IND}(Q)$ categorization region for a collection of B characteristics.

The coefficient $\mu B(Q)$ shows the level of dependence between characteristics B and Q. It has already been demonstrated that it is possible to check that the correlation $\mu B(Q)$ modifies when certain attributes have been eliminated. This means the difference from $\intercal B(Q)$ to μB-$\{\alpha\}$, in other terms (Q). Essential part $\{\alpha\}$ is specified by a systematic pattern.

The characteristics $B \, BC$ (to) are reduced by attributes C, which fulfills the following terms: Let $S = (U, A, V, f)$ be the determination table

$$\gamma_B(D) = \gamma_C(D), \gamma_B(D) \neq \gamma_{B'}(DB) \forall' \subset B \tag{3.5}$$

A decrease in condition C is a subset that can differentiate decision-making classes with the same accuracy as C.

- **Vector support machine Fuzzy Least Square**
  A novel technique to regression is the Last Square Vector Support Machine (LS-SVM). If you are using LS-SVM to model the cooling load, you must choose first the output values. This work, therefore, takes historical values as characteristics for the input. The refrigerating load of the structure is selected as the objective function [46].

Data set for training $\{(x_1, y_1), (x_N, y_N)\}$ with $x_N x_N$—R_n input data and $y_N = R$ input. SVM transforms the original surroundings to a high-dimensional feature region and generates a linear return for operational dependence relations. The function regression is represented

$$y = f(x) = w^T \phi(x) + b \tag{3.6}$$

With ϕ (): $R^n \rightarrow R^{n\phi}$, the regression characteristics to be resolved are a function that maps the space input into a so-called larger dimensional vector space, w and b. This contradiction is met by LS-SVM regression estimates:

where the higher expected μ is continuous tuning. LS-loss SVM's function transforms inequality restrictions to governing equations and is distinct from the SVM standard. The equation Lagrange is presented as [47]:

Then, optimization can be transformed to:

$$\begin{bmatrix} 0 & \vec{I}^r \\ \vec{I} & \Omega + \gamma^{-1}I \end{bmatrix} \begin{bmatrix} b \\ \alpha \end{bmatrix} = \begin{bmatrix} 0 \\ y \end{bmatrix} \tag{3.7}$$

where equation is a square matrix. The elements of any function $k(x_i, x_j)$ satisfying Mercer's condition can be used as the kernel function. In this chapter, Gaussian function is also selected as the kernel function, whose expression is shown as follows:

where Δ^2 is symbol of width parameter of Gaussian kernel.

To replace the dot product, the formula can be written as:

$$\begin{bmatrix} \vec{I} & C \\ 0 & \vec{I}^r \end{bmatrix} \begin{bmatrix} \alpha \\ b \end{bmatrix} = \begin{bmatrix} y \\ y_0 \end{bmatrix} \tag{3.8}$$

The expression in the center figure in the subscripted symbol can be solved as follows:

Thus, the LS-SVM regression model is: Introduce an improved fuzzy LS-SVM model by formulating the classification problem as in this chapter, we introduce the improved fuzzy LS-SVM with the bilateral-weight method proposed, which formulated the classification problem as discussed later. Then the Lagrangian function can be constructed as: where equation as above is the Lagrangian function, we can get the following linear equation by simple substitutions. From the $2N+1$, we can drive unknown variables accordingly and we can obtain the following predictor.

3.2.2   RST- and Fuzzy-LS-SVM-Based Data Preparation

This article takes into account the hourly climatic data and the building refrigeration load from May to September. During the normal weather year, the SVM entry characteristics such as dry-bulb temperatures, air temperature, and sunlight strength are obtained from Guangzhou's climate information. DeST is used to determine the hourly water consumption of the apartment house that are considered to be the baseline values for comparisons with the forecast LS-SVM readings. Every day, data on the building's hourly outdoor temperature was sampled. Because structure sensible cooling data is usually collected with distortion, supervised learning is required to remove mistakes, and two generally used procedures are the thresholds test and building HVAC theory-based checking. Finally, the data should be standardized to enhance calculation performance [48].

- **LS-SVM Fuzzy design predictor**
    Rough set concept and fuzzy LS-SVM are utilized in this chapter to create predictive models for appropriate site data. In further depth, the algorithm is as follows:
    Step 1: With sampling, we first discern if the specimen characteristics are continuously extracted from the characteristic using rough set theory, thus we can obtain a small feature set which represents all ideas completely by reducing the characteristic.
    Step 2: Linear transformation algorithm converts the subscription of Fuzzy in terms of initial results based on the expert experiences.
    Step 3: Configure the fugitive LS-SVM algorithm; train the suggested energy demand using decreased particle characteristics as train and test; and modify the parameters β, α and b to these formulae. The forecast amount of refrigeration load z is thus:

$$z = \sum_{i=1}^{N} (\alpha_i + \beta_i) k(x_i, x_j) + b \qquad (3.9)$$

Step 4: Test the estimation transformation model together with the information recorded continuously.

3.2.3 COMPARATIVE ANALYSIS OF COOLING

BPNN, LSSVM, FLSSVM, and RS-FLSSVM are also analyzed in comparative analyses for the RS-FLSSVM prediction of building cooling loads. The July, August, and September data were utilized to find similarities and complexity based on the sensitive hourly refrigeration measurements as a sample group in May and June.

Three mistakes were employed for assessing the quality of its capacity to accommodate a wide variety of prediction research methods: relative mean bugs (RMEs), absolute average bugs (MAREs), and fundamental medium square bugs (RMSEs) [49].

Table 3.1 displays temperature levels variability measurements, and we can see that the RS-FLSSVM prediction was better than the two previous ones. A functionalized model of sparse representation and FLSSVM outperforms the other three predictor variables in general, exposing

TABLE 3.1

MLANN-AOSVR Evaluation Indices

Predictor	Evaluation Indices		
	RMERR%	MARERR%	RMSRERR%
BPNN	0.79	4.18	11.84
LSSVM	0.45	1.65	5.56
FLSSVM	0.42	1.36	4.47
RS-FLSSVM	0.37	1.24	3.29

that the crossbred model is the best predictor. When confronted with a variety of building environmental conditions, the hybridization figure showed high resilience.

3.3 AN EFFICIENT ALGORITHM FOR FEATURE EXTRACTION, DYNAMIC
LOAD BALANCING CLONAL GENETIC OPTIMIZATION TECHNIQUE

As the numbers of printed communications accessible on the Internet expand every day, efficient
text retrieving or screening have become vital in the organization and administration of numerous
information jobs. Text classification is an increasingly important method to handle this huge volume
of data. Data augmentation (FS) is usually used to minimize the complexity of data sets containing thousands of functions that could not be further processed. The classification of text is one of
the issues in which FS is vital. The computational complexity of the feature area is a big challenge
with the categorization; hence FS is the primary step in the categorization of texts. For optimization and productivity, FS is critical since it not only limits the dimensionality of the input set found
but reduces the potential biases hidden in the original interpersonal communication. FS often uses
selected measures for function words (TF), TF=IDF for log (N/DF), while n is the number of words
in a document, and DF is the number of processes including the focus term. The objective of the FS
approaches is to reduce the data size by deleting characteristics that are regarded as unimportant for
categorization. In this study, we offer a new FS algorithm named HCSGA. The proposed approach
is used for the text characteristics of the bag of words model whereby each location in the entry
vector correlates to a particular term in the actual document, and a document is viewed as a set of
words or phrases [50].

3.3.1 COMBINATORIAL OPTIMIZATION APPROACH

Many methodologies and machine learning approaches of combinatorial optimization have been
utilized for categorizing over the last few years. Three techniques include the central, horizontal,
and LDA/GSVD, meant to reduce the clustering data's dimensionality, utilized in the categorization
of text to reduce dimensions. A subgroup search technique for the issue of language categorization
is proposed based on ant colony optimization (ACO). Problems extracted features is provided to
choose the neural network classification. Holland created GAs that work on the combinatorial and
mixed the difficulty. It is straightforward to apply GA to the FS major issue: the chromosomal in
particular has one bit for each characteristic, and the bit value decides whether it is utilized in the
categorization. By employing the chromosome-specific function subset and utilizing the resultant
correctness to determine the fitness, the individual is assessed by learning analytics. In GA is to
discover a binary vector with an optimum matching feature for each bit. A "1" or a "0" indicates that
the function is either selected or discarded.

The objective is to locate the nucleotide sequence with the least ones to optimize the performance
of the classification. A GA, named Olex-GA for the introduction of rules-based text classification
is provided. In combination with numerous classification approaches, such as neural networks and
closest neighbors, for functional subsets, GA was utilized for exploring. GA may identify additional
properties concerning selecting functional subsets by searching for a quantitative coefficient vector
used to linearly transform the original features. The value of zero in this circumstance is equal to
the modal attribute omitted. Raymer et al. combined linear translations with explicit FS banners in
chromosomal and gave a benefit over the pure technique of modification.

The GA can produce an effective solution, but it can adhere to optimum solutions locally. Among
the most extensively used ways for artificial immune optimization (AIO) is the search and optimization algorithm. It is founded on the principle of clonal selection which describes the mounting of an
immune reaction when the B-cells detect the non-self-antigenic sequence. The CSA can improve
genetic variation in comparison to the related GA, to some extent prevent this immediately and have

a quicker rate. So, we propose to extract the advantages of GA and CSA, specifically GA for hybrid clonal selection. The tests show that the proposed HCSGA most often discovers subsets that achieve the highest precision, when compact function subsets are found, and that they perform at a greater speed than other conventional approaches [51].

3.3.2 HCSGA ALGORITHM

A broad explanation of the HCSGA algorithm is provided in this subdivision.

Assume a set of documents $D = \{d_1, d_2, ..., d_n\}$ and a set of classes $C = \{c_1, c_2, ..., c_m\}$, where one or more classifications are marked on each page. Moreover, each text has one or many words of a lexicon, general characteristics $W = \{w_1, w_2, ..., w_v\}$. For simplification, we solely take account of binary materials portrayed in documents that indicate which words appear and which do not exist as vectors of binary features. A text classification system usually consists of many key components, involving harvesting and several features. After the text documents have been pre-processed, the function extraction is utilized to turn the Functions Set text information (feature vector). For decreasing the data collecting dimension, FS is utilized. The effectiveness of knowledge gain subsets may be evaluated by performing an optimization procedure using the related decreased functional area and by analyzing the recognition performance. The highest probability subset is then produced as the suggested set of features to employ in the classification system's actual design. Figure 3.1 depicts this procedure [52].

The HCSGA algorithm begins by producing arbitrarily, in a given boundary for the issue, the starting populations (pop size) of anticorps. A binary string of bits is shown for each anticorpus that implies a possible solution. The user selects the length of the random value to achieve sufficient accuracy. The antibodies are assessed in proportionality to their sensitivities by an affinity measure and subsequently cloned. Antibodies and their clones are generated for a subpopulation. The duplicates are submitted to a process of hypermutation that reverses their propensity. The matured clones are then tested for the affinity's functionality and determined for survival by the best antibody of each subpopulation. The population of antimicrobials is improved by replacing the anticorps with the lowest randomly produced sensitivities. This substitution maintains the variety of the antikörper population so that it is possible to investigate the new fields of the search area. These operations are repeated until a criterion of termination has been achieved.

The major phases of the proposed algorithm for feature extraction are:

Step 1 (Initialization): Set terminating and algorithms like P_m, the current population of an antibody, and the α multiplier factor, for example. Random initialization of anticorps populations $A(0) = \{a_1(0), a_2(0),$ and $(0)\}$. Set the development $k=0$ at last.

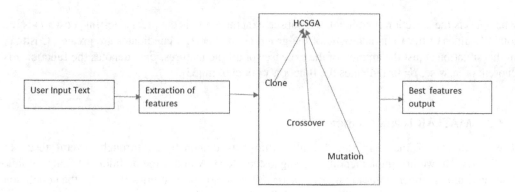

FIGURE 3.1 The algorithm for the identification of HCSGA parameters.

Step 2 (Affinity calculation): Determine starting affinity in the community.

Step 3 (Clonal operation): Calculate each antibody's clone scale q and utilize the replicating operations.

Where above equation in Step 1 is a dimension row vector. On the left-hand side is the clone of the antibody. We define where $f(a_i(k))$ is the affinity of the antibody, $a_i(k)$ is the multiplying factor, and round (.) is the operator that rounds its argument toward the closest integer. After the clone step, the population becomes:

Step 4 (Mutation operation). Since it is stated that affinity is maximized, conventional antibodies are classified ascending following their affinity. Then you can compute the appropriate likelihood of mutation of each immune response:

$$p_m^i = \frac{f(b_i(k))}{f_{max}(\cdot) - f_{min}(\cdot)} \tag{3.10}$$

where the above equation is the affinity of the antibody, max (.) is the maximum of affinity, and f_{min} (.) is the minimum of affinity. The mutations operation can be embodied as follows:

$$b_i(k) = b_i(k) + p_m^i \times \exp(-f(b_i(k))) \times N(0,1) \tag{3.11}$$

where $N(0, 1)$ is gauss variable, which means the value is 0 and mean square error equals 1 and $b_i(k)$ is the son antibody

Step 5 (Selection operation). In this step, the antibody population is updated, and the information exchanging among the antibody population is realized.

Step 6 (Determine the halt conditions). $k=+k\ 1$; Stop when stopping circumstances are met. If not, go back to Step 2.

In HCSGA, a binary dimensions m vector is used for each subset of characteristics. When a bit is 1, the feature is chosen. When the bit is 1 A value of 0 indicates the proper function is not selected. Recognition rate and expense are the two main parameters considered for designing an affinity function. This generates a large attraction value for anticorps with classification accuracy precision and cheap overall costs. By developing a single target affinity feature combining the two aims, we resolve the many criteria dilemmas. The high-affinity antibody is likely to remain in the following generation. We have developed a function of affinity as follows:

$$f(x) = \text{Accuracy}(x) - \frac{\beta \times \text{cost}(x)}{\text{Accuracy}(x) + 1} + \text{cost}_{max} \tag{3.12}$$

where $f(x)$ is the affection functional of x-subset, exactness x () is the precise testing, cost x () is the total of values of the x characteristic of the grouping, and cost_{max} candidates are greater. Costmax in this situation is just the amount of the expenses of all the features. $\beta=1$ denotes the function x is chosen; otherwise, $\beta=0r$ indicates the function x not chosen [53].

3.3.3 MATLAB IMPLEMENTATION

The usefulness of the suggested FS algorithm was demonstrated through several tests. In MATLAB 7.0, we are implementing the suggested HCSGA and three additional FS algorithms. The maximum number of iterations, MaxGen = 150, mutation probabilities $P_m=0.15$, the population size of an antibody (pop) size =100, and multiplier factor $\alpha=50$ were eventually modified by experimentation and eventually selected. The largest number of generations MaxGen = 150.

To make our assessment findings comparable in text classification assessments with the majority of the actively engaging, we have selected Reuters21566 as datasets. In the data set of Reuters-21566, The top ten courses, 5,218 training materials, and 2,126 exam materials are adopted. The largest class consists of 2,092 documents which fill 38.2%. There are 68 papers in the minimal class which occupy 1.13% of the training set.

We have utilized conventional recall and accuracy to evaluate the efficiency of text classification systems. Due to a classification CK, the recall is defined as the likelihood that this decision is chosen if a random material should be classed under CK. Analogically, accuracy is defined as the chance that this judgment is right if a random document is categorized as CK. Olex-GA for the ten most prevalent classes.

By evaluating accuracy and reminder, we observe that the HCSGA algorithm is in general higher than that of the other three different feature techniques. The average accuracy in the case of the figure for the ACO, GA, Olex-GA, and HCSGA is 82.8%, 79.9%, 84.3%, and 91.6%, respectively. The precision of every classification for HCSGA is higher than other techniques with perhaps the exception of classifications Methodology. This shows that the HCSGA algorithm typically performs with excellent accuracy. The ACOs, GA, Olex-GA, and QCGA median recall results are 85.6%, 82.3%, 90.6%, and 95.1% correspondingly. The HCSGA can categorize documents with a higher recognition ratio into the right category translating to accuracy. This shows that the HCSGA results in a superior ranking than the three other approaches.

3.4 CLONE PARTICLE SELECTION SWARM OPTIMIZING POWER DEMAND ESTIMATES BASED ON BP NEURAL NETWORK

A multifunction, nonlinear, dynamic network, with time uncertainties, is the socioeconomic system. The global economy enhances model parameters, such as setting up the straight line with time-variant characteristics and the linear model in part, although the outcome is not much met.

For these reasons, several enhancements have been developed, including the heuristic neural network, enhanced network object feed-forward model, and future penalization term function. However, the aforementioned solutions focus exclusively on network management gains and do not speed up network learning and enhance predictive accuracy. The algorithm of the particle swarm was utilized by literature for the introduction of the neural network particle swarm technique and the establishment of neural network properties and for achieving specific outcomes. But the basic particle swarm technique still exhibits rapid computational efficiency, such as a tendency to optimal local accuracy. The clone optimization approach in the innate immunity to enhance the swarm algorithm has been adopted to eliminate the aforementioned deficiencies, which incorporates the swarm method of the clone selection in the BP neural network and establishes the clone selection network architecture. The CSPSO-BP particle swarm method and the experimental analysis are conducted utilizing the defined model utilizing the yearly data of recent years.

3.4.1 ESTIMATION OF GENERATING CAPACITY

- **Selecting and pre-processing irrelevant information**
  Including GDP, national population, improvements in the fabrication shop, and so on are the parameters used in the following paragraphs. The yearly data for the years 1978–2005 are selected as a neural network training testing dataset. First of all, modify the logarithmic with the specified variables and then modify the difference. Data were utilized as network training from 1981 to 2000, whereas data from 2001 to 2005 were utilized as predictions testing.
- **Understand the location of the BP neural network**
  Enhance the neural BP networks by BP communication network in its formation based on the cloning selecting particle swarm method.

It is listed that the BP network (just a hidden layer) can do any complicated neural network until the extracted features of the three layers are adequate, which implies it may approximate the function with random precision, producing highly accurate licensing agreements. And the multi-hidden BP network fulfills the same job for multi-hidden layers. As the overall activation functions and connections are adequate, sophisticated nonlinear mappings may be easily performed.

- **Identification of neurons input and output layer**

  According to the following factors, neural network inputs, present real GDP, actual GDP prophase, demography, the generation sequencing industrial transition, and the industry neoclassical growth prophase may be determined. Consequently, the definite number of neurons in the input layer is five. The output layer has a neuron when the energy consumption is the sole interval estimate.

- **Selection of the transfer function**

  An essential aspect of the BP network is the reflection coefficient known as the kernel function. The role of transference should always be differentiated. The activation function is at frequency $[-1, 1]$, after data preprocessing, whereas the output sequence is at network interval $[0, 1]$. Thus, the middle layer neuron transmission function utilizes the S-tangent feature tension and the transfer feature of the output layer neuron employs the shape of the landscape function S—logarithmic feature.

- **The hidden layer and its neurons number determination**.

  The number of the hidden input layer is decided based on Kolmogorov theory. The theory of Swiss mathematicians indicates for any similarity measure $f: U_n \to {}_R{}^m, f x\,() = Y$. If U is the enclosed unit interval $[0, 1]$, a three-shot forward network can precisely realize f. The 1st layer of the network (input layer) has n processing units, the $2n + 1$ processing units have the middle layer (hidden layer), and the 3rd layer (activation function) has m stream processors. After identification of the intangible calculation k of the hidden layer components, contrast with the inferential statistics is simulated $(k - \delta\,\delta\delta, \text{k+}), \in N$.

The optimal hidden layer connections quantity of the neural network model is obtained by the sentencing process. The input layer nodes specifically known are 5, hence the buried layer nodes are 11 theoretical values. The resonant frequency of the activation functions is transient, whereas the neural number of neurons has a logical objective function and then the trials of errors, the results are presented in Figure 3.1. Various network training failures of hidden layer nodes are displayed in Table 3.2.

MSE is the mean square mistake in Table 3.1, while EPOCHS is the instructional time to start making the satisfactory malicious node in Table 1. It can be realized from Table 3.2, when the unseen nodes are 13, the network's excluded fault can be found after 86 exercise times, and the mean square error is 0.0227.

TABLE 3.2
Network Errors and Training Times

Hidden Nodes	MSE	EPOCHS
9	0.0253	169
10	0.0274	174
11	0.0262	146
12	0.0250	166
13	0.0227	86
14	0.0270	150
15	0.0260	176

3.4.2 THE ARTIFICIAL NEURAL NETWORK LEARNING PROCESS IS BASED ON THE SWARM ALGORITHM OF CLONE SELECTION (CSPSO-BP)

- **Parameters should be defined**: Assume the variables of knowledge in the swarm group $c_1 = c_2 = 2$, and 20 antibodies
- **Initialization**. Use and build nanoparticles as the BP neural network constants and sensitivities, the initial location random introduction (antibodies) nanoparticles x_i, and speed v_i, $I = 1, 2, N$ and $[-1, 1]$ value. In the meantime, the speed v_i of the portion is often controlled to prevent particles from being far from the search area between $[-V_{imax}, +v_{imax}]$. If the particles of V_{imax} are too big, the best solution will quickly be removed and, if it is too tiny, the local optimum can easily be dropped. It is therefore often thought $V_{imax} = cl_{imax}$, $0.1 \leq k \leq 1.0$ and the max iterative step$_{max}$ is 2,000.
- **Create cloning nanoparticles temporarily (antibodies).**

  Calculate the personalized greatest profit and globally extreme value of each existing component via equation.

$$F_i = 1/\exp(E_i) \tag{3.13}$$

- **The actual node k output and expectation.**

  Determine the ideal particle (antibody) depending on the attraction and memorize it to assess if it meets the requirements. If it meets the requirements, stop working and provide the results, else on to the next stage.

  New $N = 20$ antibody and produce new nanoparticles arbitrarily $M = \dfrac{N}{2}$ particles (antibodies).

  It is always hoped that these binding protein nanoparticles (antibodies) would be saved for the update process of the nanoparticles (antibodies) groups. But it is exceptionally hard to assure the variety of the particles (antisorps) if they too concentrate, which indicates a relatively frequent, but also easy to achieve local minimum that releases those particles (anticorps), which are of a negative affinity while keeping a decent development trend. This allows it to adopt a strategy to preserve variety based on a technique of concentrations that ensures that all nanoparticles (antibodies) have certain concentrations in the next again several at any affinity value. The ith thermal conductivity is as follows:

$$D(x_i) = 1 \Bigg/ \left\{ \sum_{i=1}^{N+M} \left| f(x_i) - f(x_j) \right| \right\} \quad i = 1, 2, \ldots, N + M \tag{3.14}$$

The following formula may be used to derive the probability formulation depending on particle (antibody) intensity:

$$P(x_i) = \frac{1/D(x_i)}{\sum\limits_{i=1}^{N+M} \left[1/D(x_i) \right]} = \frac{\sum\limits_{i=1}^{N+M} \left| f(x_i) - f(x_j) \right|}{\sum\limits_{i=1}^{N+M} \sum\limits_{j=1}^{N+M} \left| f(x_i) - f(x_j) \right|} \quad i = 1, 2, \ldots, N + M \tag{3.15}$$

where x_i and $f() \, x_i$, $i = 1, 2, N+M$

The more antibodies like the current iteration, the more likely the molecule is to be picked; it can be seen from the formula.

On the other hand, the lower the like of the ith, the higher the likelihood that I will be picked. This allows people with a low-affinity number to evolve, therefore the probabilistic selecting method ensures the diversification of the antibodies in principle.

Comprehend the likelihood of selection of newly created $N += M$ 30, formula (5) particles and sort them with $N+M$ particles (antibodies). N particles with higher values are chosen to produce a mature antibody group based on the magnitude of their likelihood.

- **Particle (antibody) update**. substitute the memory particles of the low-affinity value (Antibodies), create new particles (Antibodies) creation, and then jump to Step 2.

It implements the weight and thresholds network clone by selecting particles to the BP network method as the previous weight thresholds. Follow the BP method until an optimization problem is reached by the architecture, the resistance bands and model parameters are saved in the network, and results are calculated. The amount of the cached layer outputs and inputs of the BP neural network must be calculated according to the weights and threshold settings of the learning.

3.4.3 POWER DEMAND FORECAST

According to the yearly 1981–2005 data, the usage for model development of 1981–2000 is predicted by data from 2001 to 2005. For programming simulation analyzes, MATLAB 7.0 was utilized. The empirical study then started, taking into account the current real GDP, the actual prophetic GDP, population, present manufacturing structural transformation, and the industrial structural changes as the input from neural network models.

The new ff algorithm was used to build a BP neural network which had 13 hidden layer nodes and 1 neuron output in MATLAB 7.0, provided the cycle durations were 2000 and the learning rate was 0.001. Establish the weight of the network by the clone selecting particle swarm technique, then pick a sim to predict. At the same time, the normal neural BP network is employed to fit the same summary statistics, and outcomes are compared in Table 3.3.

Table 3.3 shows the results. The clone particular country for BP neural network particle swarm was improved in many respects comparable under BP neural network-based standards, such as the effectiveness of acquisition and forecasting precision, etc.

3.4.4 SERVICE BUILDING EMERGENCY MANAGEMENT SHARING PLATFORM

The technological trend within IT has made it feasible in recent years and then move toward service-oriented architectures (SOAs) and distributed systems. SOA is fundamentally a service group that communicates. SOA also covers the GIS domain, which includes several initiatives. This has brought forward a technological development from the self-contained, specialized, and interoperable GI services to a much more loosely linked and diffused architecture. Emergency management is a multidisciplinary approach designed to minimize the social and physical effects of such major catastrophes. It is, therefore, no surprise that IT is a vital instrument for enhancing disaster management communication and knowledge processing. The function of computer-to-computer communication in helping to provide this capacity is particularly relevant for Web Services and SOA. SOA is an interoperable, modular, uncompromising, self-containing, and self-describing sharing architecture with systems or services that communicate exclusively on clearly specified interfaces.

TABLE 3.3
Comparison of Two Algorithms

Model	Time(s)	Mean Absolute Error	Root Mean Square Error	Root Mean Square Error Rate
CSPS O-BP	15.6	156.8340	160.9708	0.0095
BP	52.6	691.6660	701.2059	0.0450

3.4.5 EMERGENCY MANAGEMENT

Accidents are usually classified by cause. For example, unconscious disasters such as earthquakes and landslides produce natural catastrophes. Technology disasters are typically produced by technological artifact design and management errors. The same may be used to describe other sorts of disasters. However, several similar traits are common to disasters:

- Devastation is a life, property, and livelihood danger
- Disasters are quick starting occurrences, i.e., when a catastrophe is obvious and the beginning of the catastrophe is relatively brief
- Incidents happen with an intensity that requires emergency reaction and external intervention
- In a relatively short amount of time after the catastrophe occurs, a bigger share of the direct damage is caused by a catastrophe.

The coordinated endeavor to eliminate and minimize the danger of disasters is concerned with emergency response. In emergency governance, there are four basic stages in the disaster response procedure: catastrophe mitigation, disaster preparedness, disaster response, and disaster recovery. In general, these periods can be classified into pre-and post-disaster periods. Pregnancy disaster prevention and preparation are processes that usually relate to efforts before a disaster. Post-disaster operations, on the other hand, are activities following a calamity. Disaster response and rehabilitation are the following steps.

3.4.6 ARCHITECTURE OF MESSAGING PROTOCOL

The structural features are depicted. WMS, WFS, and WFS services are required to access many sources. Evolution following topic data is possibly relevant for household damaging estimates:

- Info Agent is an Instant Messaging Customer that facilitates the easy communication, cooperation, and attendance management of the company built on the Jabber Instant Messaging Protocol.
- Satellite applications center Resource, which has developed a distinct organizational geographic database system.

One argument to utilize WFS information instead of WMS is that a WFS enables access to qualities that might be beneficial in the subsequent development of the program. Other significant data are as follows:

- Remotely sensed data picture, providing the application with background satellite imagery.
- Different geographical region location names, depending on provided geographical names.
- Besides mobile networks, the platform contains catalog services and two communications tools (a statistical area and transforming coordination service), which are essential for the applications)
- The catalogs system supplies the different theme mobile applications with information. Calculation of earthquake impacted regions is done by the area information agency.
- Adaptation of coordinate parameters into the specified reference coordinate system.

The purpose of including a professional and non-translation service is that, in geographical coordinates, the thematic data services give information that cannot be used for field statistics, and the co-ordinate transformation changes these coordinates into professional.

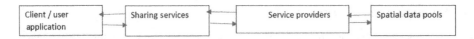

FIGURE 3.2 Disaster area image indicators selection tool.

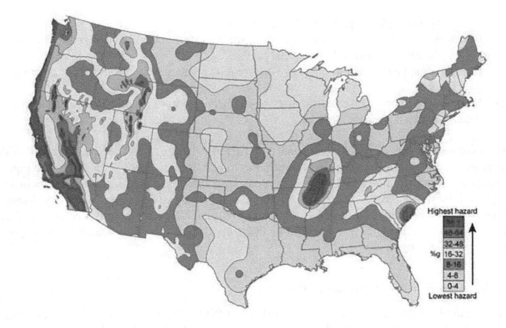

FIGURE 3.3 The architecture of messaging protocol.

3.4.6.1 Basic Components

The prototype was constructed utilizing a multi-client interface created in Java using ArcSDE software from ESRI. This client interaction conforms to the requirements of the proposed assurance model and incorporates cartography and database technology. The fundamental component perspective of the proposed approach is illustrated in Figure 3.2.

The consumer needs the information to be viewed from a distant sensor. Then the location or the year will be picked to get characteristics for picking relevant data and then visualizing the image data that indicate the region of interest.

In this catalog, the data used as source language and the target data are searched and selected. The original data in the scenarios are a certain layer of the affected region and target data might be data from satellite and aerial photos. Any kind of thematic data layer might be employed in theory, but these are the ones that can be utilized for our evaluation of earthquake losses. After selecting data, the client selects a variable for analytics to determine if statistics are to be per class as a whole.

3.4.6.2 Indicator Management

Includes explanation of what it symbolizes, how it is computed, cautions on its interpretations and its relevance as determined by the client (represented in weight), etc. Each indication declaration is maintained within the database. The customer may finally adjust some things or put more metadata to the indicators. You can pick each indication from many graphs and charts (e.g., traffic light, smiley, and speed meter) (Figure 3.3).

The value of the indicator is dependent on the geographical features of the mapping to the qualified specialist. When customers zoom in or out to a certain area of interest, performance standards for things within the disaster zone are updated.

TABLE 3.4
Map Quality Problems

Problems	%	Quality Problem Incidents Counted
Ambiguity	89	What is the average quality of the image displayed on your screen?
Inaccuracy	25	What image quality characteristics can be a problem according to the task defined for emergency management
Incompleteness	100	Positional accuracy looks problematic, but is it spatially heterogeneous?
Inconsistency	26	Inconsistent formatting or representation of the same elements
Resolution	92	How good is the positional accuracy of this specific object class?
Expert	86	What about the quality of the school building in particular?

TABLE 3.5
Assured Photograph IQ Metrics

Dimensions	Dataset	Band	Attribute Value	Object Instance
Accuracy	0.51	0.32	0.54	0.46
		0.19	0.62	0.38
Resolution	0.68	0.66	0.78	0.83
		0.88	0.88	0.83
		0.89	0.48	0.94
Completeness	0.67	0.53	0.59	0.74
		0.84	0.63	0.56
	0.62	0.76	0.36	0.64
		0.54	0.81	0.39
Consistency	0.79	0.86	0.88	0.77
		0.64	0.73	0.66

3.4.6.3 IQ Data Navigation

Quality information with the prototypes shown in the previous segment professionals may use different tools and features to expand their understanding of IQ. Table 3.4 outlines the potential of such a system through a variety of queries a customer could have on the IQ and the many tools the system provides to answer them.

The information about quality images is transmitted by indicators with different color interpretations (e.g., red, yellow, or green). Interactive thematic maps showing quality ratings for each instance of a feature or fundamental geometry can be used to convey primary outcome values. Using SOLAP operators, the data may then be trained directly on those maps for accessibility to another perspective of knowledge granularity. The data may, therefore, be typically processed on these mappings. Based on the product quality metrics are defined.

From Table 3.5 the prototype system displayed the IQ metric values of several layers for guaranteed pictures. This methodology also enables clients to investigate image quality following relevant indication hierarchies, in addition to the degrees of detail inside the image. For example, the customer examines the high-level indications first in the case of Figure 3.4.

He understands that "General Quality" has the lowest "internal quality" on average (i.e., yellow). Then he may look at its sub-indicators using "Internal Quality." He can ponder at this second-floor why the "Positional Accuracy" indication is merely average and then hydraulic on the "Positional Accuracy" for further details. He eventually reaches the final degree of details accessible in our prototype and perceives the "space resolution" as the difficulty. Then he may determine whether or not this feature of picture quality is significant for his application and then either internalize the rest of the unsureness or lessen it by, for example, searching for a different dataset.

FIGURE 3.4 Various quality of the image graphic presentations in emergency preparedness.

3.4.7 Component Design

The different architectural elements are shown in this section, in particular, the statistical offering, modeling and attributes, cataloging and customer support, and earthquake customers.

3.4.7.1 Quality Service

We have created a spatial data hazard quality measurement methodology and put the resultant technique into effect in a remote sensing system. To examine image preparedness for a specific field, we built an IQ Assessment tool to provide outcome measures on dashboards incorporated in a mapped interface as a service for the excellence of fitness assessments for emergency preparedness professionals.

3.4.7.2 Statistics Service

The statistical higher reliability implements the committee report on the WPS specifications (version 0.3.0) that is constantly changing and is being developed in the VB. Figure 3.5 illustrates a notional product offering and its interface.

The model is simplistic and has no technical parts of execution. Three activities are necessary for the OGC WPS specification: get capabilities, refer to the process, and run. The get capabilities action (usual for all OGC web services) allows customers to easily get information from the resource. Process identifies a particular process (operation) facilitated by a certain WPS. This procedure in statistical services has not (yet) been performed. The WPS-supported process can be invoked through the execution procedure, performing the specified high concentration.

3.4.7.3 Catalog Service

In our catalog, with Terra TerraCatalog, we are capable to store relevant data on temporal information and applications by implementing the specifications of the OGC Web Catalog Service. This applies, in particular, to support the CSW 2.0 catalog operations profile ISO 19115/19119. We utilized this process interface to build a customer that can retrieve metadata contained in the catalog to get access to the catalog via the Earthquake Client (and not the ordinary con terra client). Figure 3.6 shows a simple customer model.

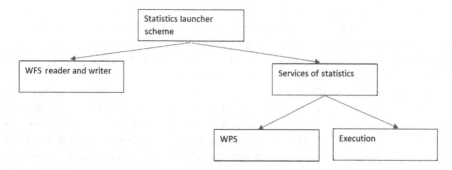

FIGURE 3.5 A statistical service models.

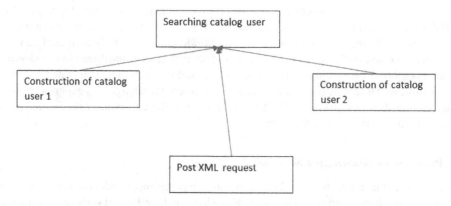

FIGURE 3.6 A customer paradigm for accessibility to catalog features.

Fundamentally, the client offers a rescue attempt that receives the title, container, and year characteristics. The customer can use HTTP for transport (Z39.50 protocol and Catalog of Web Services). This allows the customer to support two distinct protocol interfaces. We employ the CSWCatalogClient, which provides a protocol CSW binding for communication with the terraCatalog. The description of the data set and the URL of the service for the catalog is provided and the desired data set is picked in the customer forest fire. The URL is utilized for the statistical server request as the argument.

3.4.7.4 Earthquake Client Application

The customer was created with a geo-spatial designing and development solution for OGC distributed web services: Dynamic HTML (DHTML) and RedSpider Studio 3. In particular, the ASP "geotag" library enables simple access to distant services that fulfill OGC requirements. In Figure 3.6, users may utilize the getting system to zoom in or show an area, as seen in the photo. After choosing one year and phrases to hunt for burnt regions (only displayed) and the target data, a destroyed area statistical analysis will be created.

3.5 A CRIMINAL INVESTIGATION INTERACTIVE INTELLIGENT ANALYSIS

Intelligent Decision-Support Systems (IDSS) is a smart system engineering technique. Many IDSS do not give humans instinctive analytic capacity but depend on scenario assessment as an instrument to produce answers [1–9] instead. What cognitive tasks are we faced with? Who's wiser or cleverer: Is that a scientist, an engineer, or a manufacturer? A scientist? How to build a philosophy that is materialistic and academically powerful? What is intuition to learning? Can we build a new mechanism of intelligence interaction? All these concerns have been debated in recent years. Research hot zones. Mimicking the problem with human ability is one of artificial intelligence's fundamental and most essential tasks (AI). If the solution is not a pure reasoning process, it does not depend entirely on some formatters. The creation and assessment of factual reversal and development may be seen as establishing a collaborative relationship.

Academic achievements of IDSS in the last year's researchers originally intended computers to replace human intelligence, therefore gaining the decision-making power of research specialists and overcoming them. The limiting of field specialists, so that actual experts can attain the level. The smart research system (IIS) has, however, hindered systems management as a problem in computer science. But studies have been conducted (including the creation of the artificial neural network) and backpropagation does provide numerous new tools for developing IIS. No matter how much understanding and interpretation or uncertain reasoning is acquired, success in IIS is very low. The selection and efficient utilization of information is the key to building an IIS. "Effective usage" is if the system rule syncs with the real user thinking that is also the developmental difficulty of IIS. IDSS was remarkably successful in structured argumentation. However, there are too few examples of the set format. It has been shown that building a particularly technical and methodological experience and skill of people dealing with daily activities is non-linear in the identification and implementation of the system of an intelligent criminal investigation. The material and experience are not linear. Moreover, there is a difference between knowledge and experience. Research is inconsistent for different products. The first issue, then, is the consciousness of information and experience in crime management research.

3.5.1 PRINCIPLE OF KNOWLEDGE MAPPING

There are two fundamental intellectual ability constituents: experience (basic) and cognition. Learning can increase the intellect based on information. Knowledge is based on all sorts of cognitive activity in the field, but the information is not knowledge. Information is an intellectual "tool." You cannot achieve anything if you don't comprehend a goal. An essential intellectual ability to enhance information is learning ability. Intellectual engagement improves understanding in Figure 3.7.

The KMIP refers to a generic approach or criteria in the finding of knowledge. It is part of a principle of learning.

Definition 3.1

Let A be flipped perception and the amount of experience based on reasoning (Experience degree) $E\,x_A()$, then $EA()x = E_A^o()x + E_A^{no}()x$, where $E_A^o()x$ is an appropriate level of importance, $E_A^{no}()x$ is not-optimal, and experience degree $Ex_A() \to [0,1]$. The nature definition is as follows:

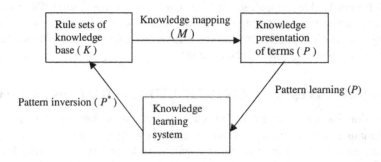

FIGURE 3.7   Structure of rule mapping knowledge.

1. If $Ex_A() = 1$, then with a maximal intuitive evaluation expertise degrees $E_A^{no}()x = 1$, $E_A^{no}()x = 0$. Therefore, the evaluation of intuition is optimization.
2. If $Ex_A() \in (0,1)$, then experience degree (experience level) with interval in (0, 1), for $\forall\ \theta \in$ (0, 1), IDSS with the θ-level of experience judgment.

In the non-optimal study of organizational learning, we have created the concept of the sub-optimal level, by which we may explain all factors in the flouted system, and decide if this is the basis for optimal experience, not optimum experience or border areas. The elements in one area might meanwhile be placed in multiple layers following the interval-optimum level.

3.5.2 INTERACTIVE INTELLIGENT ANALYSIS SYSTEMS

It must be operational to fulfill the approach that is based on a genuine criminal investigation to create the interactive intellectual system. The use of KMI in combination with intuition in the IDSS is therefore carried out in the ways discussed next.

3.5.2.1 Establishment of Cooperative Relational Database

Establish a criminal characteristics database, a criminal case understanding rule base, and linguistic variables, fluke related case resolution database on the computer. These three foundations are two distinct sources of knowledge that may be referred to as the cooperative relationship basis and connected organic entire. The Illegal Characteristics collection selects all typical data set for the characteristics of social crime. It is saved as a data warehouse on the computer. The criminal case knowledge and experience pick all typical social crime phrases. It is entered as IF AND THEN into the characteristic foundation. The intuitive, fluffy, relational basis of criminal cases identifies the events and adaptive procedures through which all criminal situations can be resolved. Practical reasoning learning chooses an examination of the different examples and is recorded in the form of interaction between person and machine.

The discussed debate shows that the KMI principle does indeed achieve a sort of reasoning and the manner this thinking ought to be in keeping with human thinking. Earlier IDSS research has endeavored to enable the computer, with the help of particular algorithms, to decide like human beings which were study objectives in this discipline. However, the findings were unsatisfactory. When making decisions on the real inquiry, investigators strive to discover the case-solving clues through intuition using specific and restricted facts. Previous research reveals that instinctive rationale for taking decisions is a similar infusion: they are the repetitive translations of nervous stimuli inherent in the human brain and is found in a definitive self-organizing and self-learning system when judging the disorderly information. Thus, by the use of the personality mechanism of the connection mapping, the first image of the structured goal is achieved. Thus, attain the well-ordered objective primary image by self-organizing progression of the affiliation plotting, that is, figure terminologies of numerous interactive matrixes, and invention the features of criminal features from in the section evidence, and then invention out the variety of opportunity of the criminal suspicious.

3.5.2.2 Intuitionistic Fuzzy Learning System

To generate an automated understanding of criminal facts from the information, we apply a new model-based method of intuition reasoning, developed on the current composition result of technological advances. The technique given below utilizes health product reasoning following current reasoning work on evidence. That is, intuition is modeled on the fluid reasons for proof and it is derived from the information it produces.

The objective of the IIAS presented in this article is the finding of an intuitionist, fluid set (IFS) of hypotheses based on intuitive experience that sustains the whole collection of data available. The hypothesis IFS can be defined as:

$$H_{\text{IFS}} = \left\{ h \in H : \exists \in s \, S, (\forall \in e \, E \, S, (\rightarrow e)) \wedge (S \rightarrow h) \right\}$$

where H is the IFS for any hypothesis (e.g., accident or murder), S is the space of crime's intuitive notion), and our tales in Example E is a collection of all the information found.

Cracks are the primary structure of a criminal intuition system: the hint and the personal belief that is the uniformity of both mappings and may generate suggestions for the suspicious types: the forming of expertise and the patterning of information. First, the mapping of information to be safe, and, second, the experimentation of suspected persons. The experiential indication denotes the confluence of intuitive knowledge and the like. The intuition learning system might therefore be established. The two mappings below shall mostly be established. $F_1 : S \rightarrow K$, $F_{\text{II}} : A \rightarrow I$. Notes: $S = \{s \, s_{1,2}, s_m\}$ is the total collect of the main clues, s_m ($m = 1, 2, g$) is the total collect of the specific clues, $K = \{k \, k_{1,2}, k_n\}$ k_j ($j = 1, 2, \ldots, n$) is the specific knowledge suspect-to- make-sure, $E = \{e \, e_{1,2}, e_u\}$ is the total collect of the experience clues, EU ($u = 1, 2, \ldots, r$) are the intuition clues, $I = \{I \, I_{1,2}, I_v\}$ is the total collect of the suspects, I_v $\{v = 1, 2, \ldots, 1\}$ are the specific suspects.

When we input a series of clues $W_i \subseteq W$, we accordingly get the output of the function of the two mappings: suspect-to-make-sure $k \, j \in K$ and suspect-to-make sure $I \, j \in I$.

We should partition the statistic clue grouping into the primary clue and experiences group before checking the properties of the two mappings.

If the information included is not consensual when a crime is identified, it is hard for computers to distinguish it. In such a situation, use the man–computer system to proceed with the decision to solve the problems and let the computers mechanically reason and identify the most useful hints. This is the transactions' faster function. When you enter several indications $E_0 = \{e_1, e_2, e_q\}$ while reading the computers, if $\varepsilon < \theta$ should be adjusted, here θ is the experience region value, $0 < \theta < 1$.

3.5.2.3 An Examples Reasoning Approach

The implementation of interactively insightful comment by the preceding investigative reasoning approach is shown by a specific criminal investigation scenario. Dialog is a mixture of wisdom thinking and experience thinking, specifically collaborative reasoning, drawn from medical law and social knowledge.

A combination of the output data shows that the killer may have an amour or affection for the dead.

The electronic display analysis system provides insights to the following:

- To check whether the dead handwrite the message in his pouch.
- To investigate who had a close relationship with the dead and before mortality.
- To learn about the murder of a victim, and the association of the deceased.
- To check to see whether one of her pals was handwritten on the message.

Research into this case shows that Wu (a married guy) was in close contact with the victim in the same neighborhood. His handwriting was on the note. And his parking place was unclear around the time of the killing. Wu was therefore seen as the primary suspect. And it was ultimately established that Wu had a case of adultery with Guo (the victim), and he killed Guo to hide the affair because of abortion failure.

The study these reveals that cooperative reasoning inside IIAS may influence the investigating expert to solve a crime, which suggests that the process of reasoning in the IIAS investigation is in line with reality.

3.6 CONCLUSION

The group has been governing mining for a generation and encapsulated the dispersed fruits and benefits and downsides of each approach on the ground. In various applications, different parts of classification algorithms are employed; they should be realistic to handle the practical difficulties by producing effective mining algorithms or association rules in a different environment. Models for cooling demand predictions should play a key part in the construction. They support, in particular, the optimum control systems for enhanced energy conservation. We construct an applicable forecasting system for the development of cooling load prediction, roughness components, and a fuzzy smallest SVM. A new system for text categorization dimensionality reduction, known as the GA of hybrid clonal expansion. The HCSGA shows the greatest outcome of these three approaches and also produces more precision even with a huge data set because with the lesser amount of features, it achieves higher performance. Next, create the clone selection swarm particle demand model for the neural network and pass the epidemiological investigation, and there were several benefits of the current design, such as quicker speed, better stability, and greater predictive precision. This is therefore a better model for demands for predictability. Critical problems in the performance of police prosecutions is to address by development of a system of interactively intelligent analysis. Identification must be the basis of the construction of the interactive intelligent analytic system, or this task is of little importance or worth. At the same time, the argumentation of information should be differentiated from the argument of intuition and experience. Conceptual thinking is changeable in different contexts.

4 Quality Learning Management Computing

4.1 PERFORMANCE MEASUREMENT USING PART OF THIS GROWING EVALUATION OF THE CLOUD-BASED EDUCATION

Initially, interconnected education delivered information to improve rural locations, but it is now moving at a breakneck speed. In 1999, there were just six institutions that offered networked courses. The Ministry of Education recognized 31 network educational institutions in 2005, the majority of which were essential institutes of liberal indoctrination and well-known universities.

Although computer-based programs have become more attractive, and remote education offers several substantial advantages, such as better visualization, greater personalization, faster access to other sources, and widespread engagement, networked communication has been widely known in many situations. There is a lower communication problem, which leads to more creativity and lowers costs. Students' writing skills should be improved since communication is an important ability to communicate online; further, students' lifelong learning skills should be improved since college courses should be accessible to graduate through their lives.

Improving student engagement in fewer populations of learners is a powerful technique of fostering an online community. Knowledge sharing created a feeling of togetherness among individual students, according to numerous studies. Though cost is crucial in instruction, the quality of teaching cannot be sacrificed to achieve the educational aim. The performance of asynchronous engagement in web-based videoconferencing among pre-service instructors was assessed. The routing protocol has three types of learning conversations: higher level, progressing, and lower level, with the findings indicating that higher level viewpoint taking was associated with the higher level conversation. Six scale questions have been introduced to analyze and increase the reliability of a distant learning program. Relevance, reflection, interaction, tutor and peer help, and interpreting are just a few examples.

Moodle has been utilized in business education, as well as in university education. However, according to their experience, the effectiveness of interconnected schooling is not assessed. The most noteworthy study is done on the sustainability of connected learning. They contrasted connected learning to in-classroom instruction and discussed the networked education's potential obstacles. They were concerned about infrastructural and environmental considerations but failed to include the connected education assessment technique. To facilitate connected education for technological advances, the college faculty built an online co-learning framework. The course administration system was built using Moodle. The standard of education in a co-learning environment is being evaluated based on course administrative experience, and the institution is striving to improve educational outcomes as co-learning progress.

4.1.1 QUALITY EVALUATION CRITERIA

Various parameters have been used to enhance the accuracy of interconnected communication with the co-learning platform, according to P. Taylor and D. Maor's six scales.

4.1.1.1 Relevance

The contents of the interconnected quality education must help the students' instructional behavior in terms of information interpretation, information processing, employee development, and

DOI: 10.1201/9781003211938-4

TABLE 4.1

Relevance Evaluation Form

Item	Low Relevant	Relevant	High Relevant
Information apperception	2	3	4
Knowledge acquirement	3	5	7
Skill enhancement	5	7	9
Talent development	6	8	10

developing talent to guarantee that internet co-learning is highly relevant to their working environment [54].

As stated in Table 4.1, a relevancy determination form is created. Significance is assessed on a scale of 1–10. Because skills and developing talents are so crucial to a student's business roles, the knowledge that is pertinent to these elements has a much higher worth. The value of applicability to information perception is poor because it does not enhance the technical specifications of the student. In this approach, the relevance of each website page is determined. The significance is derived as the total of the rankings of these pages when multiple pages are available.

Formally, vector V_s may be used to keep track of expert ratings for various characteristics. For instance, an expert can give a rating of 2 to knowledge comprehension because he or she believed the page was of low relevance in terms of information consciousness. He/she gave 5 and 7 for information acquisition and skill enhancement, and 10 for professional development since he/she thought the page was extremely significant to talent management. $V_s = 2,5,7,10$; $V_s = 2,5,7,10$; $V_s = 2,5,7,10$; $V_s = 2$. The Matrix may be used to keep all of the expert's relevant information [55].

$$
\begin{vmatrix} V_{s1} \end{vmatrix} \quad a_{11} \quad a_{12} \quad \ldots \quad a_{1c}
$$

$$
\begin{vmatrix} 2 \end{vmatrix} \quad a_{21} \quad a_{22} \quad \ldots \quad a_{2c}
$$

$$
M_r = \begin{vmatrix} V_s \end{vmatrix}
$$

$$
\begin{vmatrix} V_{s3} \end{vmatrix} = \begin{vmatrix} a_{31} & a_{32} & \ldots & a_{3c} \end{vmatrix}
$$

$$
| \ | = | \qquad |
$$

$$
|\ldots| = | \ \ldots \quad \ldots \quad \ldots \quad \ldots \ |
$$

$$
\begin{vmatrix} V_{sn} \end{vmatrix} \begin{Vmatrix} a_n & n_1 & a_2 & \ldots & a_{nc} \end{Vmatrix}
$$

where c denotes the number of relevant appraisal characteristics and a_{ij} is the value assigned by expert I to feature j. The professional level of the professionals in the disciplines relevant to the course is referred to as Vector V_e. The significance of each attribute is represented by the vector V. M_r and V_e may then be used to compute the significance value:

$$
\text{Relevance value} = M_r * \text{Vimportance} T * V_e.
$$

The greater the relevancy value of a new website, the greater the likelihood of improved educational success.

4.1.2 INTERPRETATION

We value interpretations by the survey since it is difficult to assess explicitly. To value the interpretations, perform the following measurements.

1. Attributes m to a potential of 100 or more group A students who used the learning system on an irregular basis.
2. As applicant group B, learners who may have never utilized the co-learning technologies but have other optimization techniques will randomly pick.
3. Randomly designate m individuals as application group C who have never used any system of studying.
4. Students must see and run a course's online page for several minutes and then offer to determine if the website is correctly understood. For each new website of the learning program, two or three significant features will be assessed.
5. The understanding can then be valued using the final average score.

The interpreted value for the service's usual users is represented by the value from group A. In practice, if the majority of group members place a high value on the internet publication's functioning, the web page either contains too much knowledge or its translation is poor.

The interpreting quality for potential customers in the learning system is represented by the number from group B. When pupils are unable to upgrade the game effectively, they will benefit from a user guide, online support, or even direct instruction. If the majority of group B members couldn't run the system without support from prominent leaders, the website would incur a significant range of information costs, and it would be urged that it be upgraded.

Group C is comparable to group B values; however, the value from group C shows the perception value of the web page for people outside the university (maybe from other academic institutions), whereas group B values reflect that these students within the university perceive the web page value. For group C material, it is worthwhile improving educational standards for those connected courses that will be given outside of the institution [56].

4.1.3 KNOWLEDGE ACTIONS ANALYTICAL PERFORMANCE EVALUATION

There was a time restriction for the students to finish the exercise and its tasks. The students should evaluate the course by class, study relevant materials from their books, provide knowledge, and examine how they may perform the job.

When they run into an issue, they may use the co-learning program's online support room to obtain immediate assistance. When accessible, a fellow student may be able to assist them. However, if they do not receive adequate assistance from the discussion forum, they may post their concern in the forum. The teacher will follow up on the discussion and give sufficient assistance for the student to complete their task.

Before delving into the specifics of the learning activities, the user's role should be determined to distinguish between the instructor and the pupil. The access activities to Linux will be automatically saved in the application of learning actions assessment, as illustrated in Figure 4.1 (LAA in Figure 4.1). For instance, when a student joins into the network, a credential checking message through IP address and certain messages are retrieved when search engine crawlers come on displays for pupils or teachers. On the other hand, these messages do not collect details on the responsibilities of users. The role should thus be identified using the log collected from the MySQL database

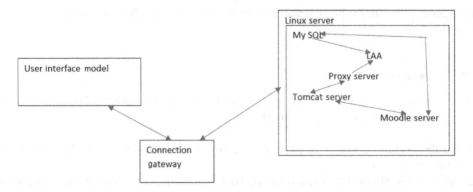

FIGURE 4.1   Evaluation of active learning in the co-learning world.

TABLE 4.2
Web Page Information in Action Messages

Time	IP Address	Message Type	Description
10:00:01 2008-9-1	192.168.15.3	Password Checking	URL for password checking
10:00:12 2008-9-1	192.168.15.3	Password Ok	URL for login welcome
10:00:25 2008-9-1	192.168.15.3	Learning interface fetching	URL for material loading
…	…	…	
10:01:02 2008-9-1	192.168.15.3	Note add page fetching	URL for note add

of the online grading system. The Mysql database task communications may be indicated and the web application responses can be provided as shown in Ref. [57].

4.1.4   REFLECTION EVALUATION

The assessment for the most important section of a course will be reviewed by a survey of practitioners and academics. However, a particular course may have several distinct web contents, and evaluating all of them before assessing a course's reflection value is impractical. The reflecting ratio of such websites may be assessed using processes highly evaluated.

The action message will comprise URL information, as presented in Table 4.2, and each line will have the individual new website location. Hyperlink's analysis algorithms may be utilized to search for all connections on a website page. To get the needed additional stability, students could use the hyperlink.

4.1.5   EVALUATION OF TUTOR SUPPORT

A tutor is available to teachers to give support in the current co-learning format. However, it is difficult to evaluate internet tutoring assistance. At first, we evaluate tutoring support just based on two criteria: the typical time required by the teacher to capture the action that must be taken by the student and the median time required for the tutor to react to that topic.

The tutor assistance assessment technique is depicted in Figure 4.2. There will be a thread that begins to look for problem-solving activities. When it detects such activities, it saves the current position in the MySQL system for future searches and then retrieves the cause of a problem's characteristics and position. It examines the following log to determine the tutor's closest action, which may record the problem is position, and the tutor's closest action, which response to the difficulty

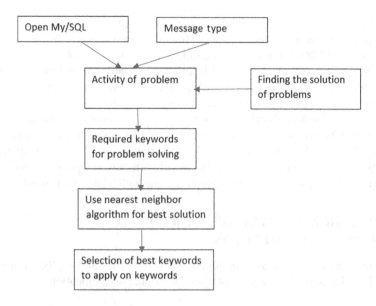

FIGURE 4.2 Structure of problem-solving.

using the same terms: the review of published difficulties (NoP), the time it takes for the tutor to gather difficulties, and how long it takes for the instructor to answer the trouble (T2R). The average time it takes for the instructor to record the problem that the student has submitted and then for the instructor to respond to the challenge may be determined as follows:

$$MT2C = \sum T2C/NoP, MT2R = \sum T2R / NoP.$$

MT2C measures how quickly a tutor will identify difficulties, whereas MT2R shows how quickly a tutor will provide a solution.

4.1.6 CASE STUDY AND DISCUSSION

Our college's program administration system now includes 26 courses and 2 contests. It has been in use for 3 branches and has already been utilized by over 300 respondents. The technology was well received by the students, and they are eager to submit their assignments on time via the electronic portal. The professors were pleased to see that the pupils were far more eager to study the material in class, and the final grade increased somewhat as a result of this improvement. Graduates from other disciplines, such as e-business and e-logistics administration, will be covered by the platform. Not just information technology but also computer programming, e-commerce, and computer technology will be covered in these classes. This system will also coordinate several research initiatives primarily carried out by students.

Instructors and learners can access the system through a portal. Following are the key features of the blended learning environment: Teachers upload teaching materials.

z Students acquire the necessary materials. Students submit their exercises and housework to the system. Teachers assess and grade the students' exercises and assignments. The course "Software Architecture and Modelling" have its home page. The course glossary, public content, calendar and events, level of knowledge, assessment, and more columns are available for approach shots.

The faculty began designing the architecture for a co-learning system after establishing a course administration system using Moodle. The co-learning system encompasses not only course administration but also the training route of students.

Such a system should improve students' critical reasoning skills, help students' instructional behavior, and promote teacher–student collaboration. The course management system makes the website available to students as a tool for navigating the course. To assure the quality of education, The Company's website contents, tools, and techniques should be significantly developed in the co-learning system. Support and cooperation of learners and lecturers are equally important, and a co-learning system is an economic mechanism for their connection.

The professional and non-approach are now employed in a school environment, where the internet is quite fast, and the teacher can acquire a variety of materials to foster commitment available on the internet. However, if we want to widen the definition to include the computer, the reporting progress will be greatly lowered; as a result, the facilities are now considering a solution to a problem. Educational technology might be done with this clearing technology if it succeeds [57].

4.2 INVESTIGATION ON AVERAGING GRAYSCALE BIOMETRIC AUTHENTICATION

Face recognition systems have grown ubiquitous in recent years and are becoming increasingly significant in the fields of protection, criminal investigation, communication and control, and emotional intimacy.

The widely used back-propagation communication system may theoretically be taught to detect facial access methods. However, even for a somewhat sized picture, the network may be extremely complicated and challenging to train. The number of inputs in the networks, for example, would be 10,000 if the image was 100×100 pixels. Neural networks are frequently used in the information processing step rather than the background subtraction step to minimize complications. The next chapter incorporates an average grayscale algorithm-based facial recognition system. Pre-processing of face photos, image segmentation using the mean Gaussian function, facial learning, facial recognition, and databases are the five components that make up the system. Average gray scaling is a supervised classification approach that can generate low-dimensional, neighborhood-preserving embedding of responsible for considerable and is used to reduce the dimension of data and the functions retrieved during the extraction procedure. A suggested technique outperforms the Eigenface algorithm in trials.

4.2.1 IMAGE PRE-PROCESSING

For the accompanying convolutional neural network, image pre-processing, such as Montenegrins and size standardization, is beneficial.

- **Grayscale transformation**

    The gray intensity of the location (x, y) is expressed using the function $f(x, y)$. The Gray-Scale translation is expressed as:

$$f(x, y) = 0.299 \times +r\,0.587 \times +g\,0.144 \times +b\,0.5$$

    The Red, Green, and blue components of the color picture pixel are represented by r, g, and b, respectively [58].
- **Standardization of image size**

    The data of the input pictures must be sent through the standardized procedure to define the number of the artificial neural activation function. The normalization in size of the face image is indicated in the following study:

$$RS = k * TS$$

    where RS is the physical value of the vehicle constraint, k is the fraction coefficient of the entire vehicle duplicate, and TS is the value restrained form the vehicle duplicate.

4.2.2 FEATURE VECTOR

- **Face feature vector**

  Numerous attributes may be utilized to define a human face; however, these selected features contain enormous amounts of data and multiple connected factors. Feature extraction, disambiguation, and feature extraction have all become more important as a result of processing these massive volumes of data. The following sections explain several conventional feature vector techniques for facial recognition software.

- **NMF algorithm**

  In the disciplines of text classification and spectroscopy predictive analytics, Refs [8–10] present a Nonnegative Matrix Factorization (NMF) technique for extracting the features and recognition. The following is a description of the non-negative Data Augmentation issue:

  Given a nonnegative matrix $A\ R \in m \times n$ and a positive integer $k < \min \{m\ n\}$, find nonnegative matrices $W \in R\ m \times k$ and $H \in R\ k \times n$ to minimize the functional

$$f(W,H) = \frac{1}{2}\|A - WH\|^2\ F$$

  where WH stands for a non-negative word embedding of A and is a rank at most k approximation decomposition. In reality, making the right selection about the value of k is essential, yet k is often problem-related to choose. This is an instance of how NMF can be used to depict different emotions.

  An ORL face image is 11,292 pixels in length and portrays a facial perspective of facial bodies. It is 256 images per frame. The picture becomes a vector of the facial in R^{10304} ($112 \times 92 = 10{,}304$) and the length of the facial vectors is too huge to build the kernel function A of sizes 10,304.

- **PCA techniques**

  Principal Component Analysis (PCA) is an ideal linear dimensionality reduction approach in terms of the reconstruction's mean squared error (MSE). PCA is the optimum polynomial strategy for compression of a set of high-dimensional vectors into a collection of lower dimensional vectors and then recreating the entire model in terms of least mean square error. It's a non-parametric approach, therefore the result is unique and unaffected by any assumptions about the statistical nature of the variables. The last two features, on the other hand, are viewed as both a strength and a disadvantage, because they are non-parametric, requiring no prior information included, and that PCA respiratory muscles frequently result in data loss. The constraints employed in the development of PCA limit its usefulness. These are the assumptions:

  Assumption of serial correlation. Assumption of Mean and Covariance's Statistical Importance [59]. Large variations are assumed to have significant dynamics.

- **Discrete Cosine transformation**

  The DCT is a way to split up a signal into its widely divergent frequencies. A DCT is a sum of cosine expressions at specific wavelengths that represents a succession of prime numbers many pieces of data.

  The DCT tries to re-arrange the info in the picture. Each transform parameter can be recorded individually after intensity variations without affecting compression performance. Illustrates how DCT may be used in image recognition. The original picture is (a), the image changed from (a) using the DCT method is (b), and the image changed from (b) using IDCT is (c).

  Using the DCT for application purposes has several benefits. The DCT's first major benefit is its simplicity. The DCT also has the benefit of having all real-valued elements in its basis vectors.

The spatial domain conversion, on the other hand, is somewhat complicated. Even though the Fast Discrete Cosine Transform (FDCT) has increased computation performance, the computation procedure is still lengthy.

4.2.3 INNOVATIVE VECTOR APPROACH

This work proposes a novel characteristic technique for defining a human face to tackle the challenges mentioned previously. The following is a detailed examination of this innovative approach.

- **Characteristic of grayscale**
  A gray (or gray) image is one in which only gray tones are employed. It may be explained that each pixel needs less knowledge to distinguish between these photographs and any other combined display. Today, a gray color has the same intensity of the red, green, and blue components in the spectrum of RGB, requiring just a single scale factor for each pixel, in contrast to the three intensities required for a full composite image. The color space brightness is frequently recorded as an eight-bit integer, resulting in 256 distinct shades of gray ranging from green to yellow. The difference between consecutive gray magnitudes is substantially better than the human eye's grayscale resolution capacity if the levels are uniformly spaced. As a result, for face detection, a grayscale picture is employed to characterize the face shape [60].
- **Average grayscale**
  When the entire reference model is utilized as the input vector for face identification, the recognition network becomes extremely complicated and tough to train. A 640×480 grayscale photograph, for example, consumes over 300 KB of storage. In the new image recognition methodology, the averaging of the grayscales was employed to minimize the supplied parameter width. The grayscale scales were classified according to the directions for the co-orientation in the following areas:
  - Horizontal grayscale average
  - Vertical grayscale average
- **Gray average human face vector**
  We assume a photograph is h, its breadth is w and the lined with gray averaged vector is avg[w], the light blue vectors are horizontally mean h [], and the value of the gray scale of a pixel of the gray scale image is $f(x,y)$, and $f(x\,y,) \in [0, 255]$.
  Therefore, the whole expression of the feature extracted from the image is:

$$\text{avg}[\ ]i = \sum_{y=0}^{h} f(i,y)\, i \in [0,w)$$

The horizontal average grayscale vector's value is

$$\text{ahg}[j] = \sum_{x=0}^{w} f(x,y)\, j \in [0,h)$$

As a result, the entire expression of feature extraction from a picture is:

$$p[j] = \text{avg}[j]\, j \in [0,h)$$

$$\left(\text{ahg}[j-h]\, j \in [h\,j,-+h\,w)\right)$$

- **Different human face vectors**

  The following examples of face coordinates using this approach are shown to demonstrate the viability of grayscale matrices for face detection.

  The facial vectors acquired by the same guy when seen from different perspectives: The left picture of each is the face picture, the center picture is the vectors of the man's vertically averaged grayscale, and the right picture is the vector of the very same man's horizontally averaged gray image. The face vectors derived by several males: Each picture's left picture is the face picture, the center picture is the left man's vector of horizontally averaged grayscale, and the right picture is the same left man's vector of horizontally averaged gray level.

  The face vectors reveal that the vector discriminating in the same person's face is extremely comparable, and, according to the face verticals, the vectors of the various people's faces are quite dissimilar.

  As a result, in a realistic facial expression recognition, the matrices mentioned above would be used to convey the face characteristic [61].

4.2.4 ALGORITHM ANALYSIS FEATURE EXTRACTION

- **The algorithm for feature extraction**

  The image recognition program's third stage is feature extraction processing. It's useful for the facial recognition that follows. During the extract treatment, we obtain the entire representation of Montenegrins using the already procedure described.

- **Complexity analysis**

  Back-propagation neural networks are utilized as the classifiers in this chapter to classify the aforementioned recognition. The widely used back-propagation computer program may theoretically be taught to detect facial photos directly. However, even for a somewhat sized picture, the network may be extremely complicated and challenging to train. During this procedure, we get the expression for the services to encourage as follows. The facial picture is the following size:

$$v = N \times M$$

where N is the photograph h value and M is the appearance w value. The feature extraction collected by our novel strategy is the following length:

$$f = v + N M$$

In the following experiments, for example, the functional vector size is:

$$fv = N + M = 100 + 100 = 200$$

In the succeeding trials, however, the height of the facial picture is:

$$v = N * M = 100 * 100 = 10,000$$

Therefore, it is difficult to quickly minimize the complexities of image recognition.

4.3 THE ACTIVE LEVELED INTEREST MANAGEMENT IN DISTRIBUTED VIRTUAL ENVIRONMENT

Zabele is finding a new technique by bringing active routing technology to the management of the interest (AIM). Distributed virtual environment (DVE) members interact in a proofread manner while Active Routers (ARs) control interest rather than servers by distributing subscriptions datagrams. The data transmission is regulated as connections are screened on ARs. We have created an AIM system, AIMNET, utilizing CBT, rather than SBT [source-based tree] by Zabele. The multi-cast tree can be administered easily and DVE may also be extended electronically, as fewer multiple addresses are used in this system. However, the study on AIM focuses on how the interaction between DVE items might be found and achieved. The correct amount of detail or communication periodicity according to with status and characteristics of the objects remained a novel issue. In this study, a system of active investment and consumption is proposed that combines leveled filtration with AIM [62].

4.3.1   AMINET

The ARs and hosts are structured in a CBT format as indicated and the root is the central AR. Each DVE application can individually create its own CBT.

Subscribers are maintaining subscription regions (SRs) and publishers are maintaining publishing territories to be compliant with HLA (PRs). As Virtual Interfaces (VIFs), the interconnections to other AR or hosts may be summed up for ARs and related information components. If the upstream AR is connected by a VIF, the downstream VIF is called. Alternatively, downstream VIF is termed. The SR of the VIF is the summary, direct or indirect, of hosts linked to this VIF.

The VIF SRs and other VIFs connected to this AR are successively merged and updated when the membership has been accepted from the downstream VIF.

AIM systems data packets are submitted by the hosts through their AR agents. If the datagram comes from AR_i 0, the datagraph is called D_{ik}, and PR is referred to by VIF_{ik}, which has $M+1$ VIFs (D_{ik}). The match function among D_{ik} and VIF_{ij} may be defined, 0 is as

$$\text{match}\left(D_{ik}, VIF_{ij}\right) = \left(j \neq k \wedge PR\left(D_{ik} \cap SR\, VIF(ij) \neq \varnothing\right)\right.$$

The findings of the matching function determine whether D_{ik} is delivered via VIF_{ij}. In the absence of one of the VIFs, a D_{ik} is rejected. It shows two instances of associated networks.

Data chart supply is content knowledge on the AIM system. No host or AR must know the condition of the sphere. You keep your own SRs and distribute and supply PRs using a sequence number. This non-status technique guarantees stability and adaptability.

4.3.2   LEVELED INTEREST MANAGEMENT

Many technologies in the DVE system separate items into levels and provide a variety of services to conserve infrastructure and related congestion. This would include LOD graphs, LOD motion, dead multi-threshold computation, stream contending method (DVE), the DVE radiative transfer model, the layered priority extension HLA, etc.

From the opinion of view of curiosity management, above that the techniques preserve Level of Interest (LOIs) between objects, to evaluate respondent interest in an issue and utilize it for communication information purposes while using the LOI. The ways to promote interest administration are grouped. Since these are the bottlenecks of the DVE capacity of the hosts and their network connection, the attention is mostly on how to decrease traffic loading and rendering times. System publishers must employ additional multicast addresses and networking devices to publish data copies at various levels.

These "mirror" systems give less information to subscribers but publishers publish more. In DVE, participants typically function simultaneously as subscribers and publishers, therefore leveling interest management is not very useful [63].

4.3.3 ACTIVE LEVELED INTEREST MANAGEMENT

ARs can manage and distribute datagrams in the AIM system to prevent communications from advertisers and consumers. If LOI in subscribers and ARs are expressed by a subscriber, we may enhance AIM to include active interest monitoring and analyze LOI and make leveled screening. This can further alleviate congestion strain and enhance manageability. Apart from what we described previously, there are some difficult threats in the proactive degree of interest monitoring. This section discusses the models and characteristics for assessing LOI, LOI calculation formulas, filtering techniques, and tasks. The evaluation factors for LOI are largely based upon motion and/or consciousness concepts such as location, size, exenteration, and speed in traditional interest administration. These measures assess LOI extremely well for a single participant in DVE. If the item is closer, slower, and more details should be viewed in front of a participant, for example. However, DVE has diverse sensory abilities and information propagation skills. The participants of Zhou's system broadcast and subscriptions at five distinct priority levels to imitate this status. Twenty-five communication connections are established following the partition. However, the number of divisions is determined by this procedure, and the division relates to requests. After it is decided, it is difficult to adjust.

If we see the SRs and the PRs of the objects as representing their capacity for sensing and communication, items with greater SRs and PRs are usually more objects, and more objects are noticed. In general, the spatially extensive radiation of meaning and knowledge stands for the acute SR and PR. And the capacity is the size. We can define functionality if we specify the collection of regions as regions. Region Volume: always R, R is the actual number specified. This process gave the area the volume performance was evaluated. In that case, SR (A) the object B's LOI is LOI(A), the object A's sR(A), and the object B's PR is SR(B), SR(A) the object's B's Radiation capability is both the object's A' capability portion that observes object B and the object A's information radiation capacities. If we refer to the result split by volume (SR (A) in volume (SR (A)) and volume (PR (B)) divided by volumes (A, B), P (A, B), the result would be connected to the LOI in a good light (A, B). Furthermore, there are LOI criteria from subscribers and publishers that stand for their state and functionality. We have termed the subscription leveled parameters (SLPs) of SLP (A) of object A, the publishing parameters of object B of PLP. (PLPs) of the SLP of SLP (A) are (B). If in SLP (A), SLP (A)1, SLP(A)2 there are I characteristics... A) i, j in PLP(B), PLP(A)1, PLP(A)2, etc., ... SLP (A)i. The parameters of i and j dimension are PLP (A)j, |SLP(A)| = I |PLP(B)| = j. PLP(A)j.

We commonly specify the range of LOI to be [0, 1] to be consistent with the Hardcopy consciousness assessment.

Limited variables may be indicated in their size, eccentricity, speed, role, and organization as well as any other character affecting LOI. It may be any PR or SR characteristic, or it may be standalone. We may use them to determine distances if the items are placed in leveraged parameters. Besides, if we express the capacity function to be geometrical, then when $SR(A)$, $PR(B)$ are static, the better $PerS(A,B)$ and $PerP(A,B)$ are, the quicker objects. We may use them for distance measurement too. In this concept, everything can be adequately covered in favorable exchange management. AR is the unit for LOI evaluation and leveled filtration in active interest management. SLPs for AR and VIF. 0 TO TO SLPs are called SLPs for Ari (VIF$_{ij}$). If AR$_i$ has m VIF downstairs and for a particular VIFI, it has 1 SLP (VIF$_{ij}$) and H$_{ij}$'s SLPs are SLP (VIF$_{ij}$), SLP (VIF$_{ij}$) (H$_{ij}$). SLPs also need to be combined and updated when the subscription is accepted by Ari. If we define a comparable to SR as the combined operations, VIF and AR may be defined as follows [64].

Datagram shall be provided over this VIF as long as communication of any hosts explicitly or implicitly through this VIF is necessary. At the same time, when leveling filters are carried out via VIF, we must make sure that LOI determined from the VIF SLPs is not less than any host LOI that connects directly or indirectly via this VIF. Members can acquire adequate information on this insurance. Any publishing B that corresponds to the publishing of particular LOI functions and combines operation B. We can establish that f is connected to the operations and that it cannot be operated. However, we can locate certain features *f* and procedures that comply with the afore-mentioned requirements. We may define an adequate combining operation in the following way for a monotone function *f*. For any *q*-size SLPs, SLP(A_1), SLP(A_2), and any integer *i*, $1 \leq i \leq q$, if SLP(A) = SLP(A_1) ∇ SLP(A_2), then AR must calculate be from membership A and publishing B both PerS (A, B) and PerP (A, B), such that SR and PR volumes should be brought into and published in a subscriber. Volume (SR (A)) has a negative relationship to LOI according to specification, if we mix A_1, A_2, ..., A_P *p* memberships.

Effective prevention programs management software can do leveled filtration with LOI according to all criteria. If the data graph content is prioritized, we may do personalized recommendations filtration details (DOCBF). If the datagram is regular, it can be filtered often (FBF). Only parts of the datagram required are included in the DOCBF. The FBF selects the datagram to be sent at a given frequency and discards the rest. In many situations, we can use one or both filtering methods. LOI should identify the function by application. We can't make sure that it's monotonous. We add an "I_" prefix to the attribute to f, if f__, we add an "I_" prefix for f f, or we add an "N_" prefix to this property. A leveled variable example is shown in Table 4.3. Since the DOCBF and FBF volume functions may be different, the volumes may have various properties.

Until this rule, the LOI function is single-toned, as long as no property has the "n_" prefix. After subscription approval, AR does not only merged SRs and updated them but merged SLPs and updated them as well. If AR decides to supply it through a given VIF, LOI will be evaluated and used when the data structure is authorized for leveling filters.

If LOI functionality is not a monotonous function, LOI is evaluated and filtered solely with VIFs linking hosts. The work of the other VIFs is comparable to the work of AIM.

The LOI function and the manner filters are carried out might also be seen by members as corporate lobbyists. So, it is automatically supported in AIM. In DVE, the participants' interests fluctuate continually over time, while the volume and the LOI function are rather consistent. In every registration, it is therefore essential to check them. We merely send out an LOI invitation if we wish to update them. Both DOCBF and FBF LOI subscribers are displayed in Table 4.4. And the intensity and LOI are allotted separately. If some elements stay constant in a new LOI membership, they may be omitted. The duty of the LOI "shutdown FBF and adjust the amplitude functionality of the DOCBF is presented in Table 4.4." As may be shown, abusers can demonstrate great expectation in the simplest computer program. This is the same way that navigation AR code in an existing installation is being ejected and used.

They don't require information from subscriptions if publications provide datagrams. You just transfer data graphs to your system. After the datagram is accepted on AR, it is necessary to know about filtering previously on other ARs. The correct filtering is determined according to the LOI. Therefore, in the subnet mask to capture LOI of DOCBF and FBF conducted two detailed DOCBF characteristics and FBF information is supplied.

TABLE 4.3
Level of Parameters

Type	Attributes	Value or Range
string	n_user agent	"bei.jia"
string	n_application	"e-classroom"
float	d_vol_DOCBF	10
float	d_vol_FBF	8
float	i_size	7
float	d_velocity	15

TABLE 4.4
LOI Subscription

Type	Attributes	Value or Range
	A Complete LOI Subscription	
String	volume_DOCBF	return spatial x*spatial y;
String	LOI_DOCBF	float temp f=max(PerS,PerP);
		if (0<temp f<= 0.2) {
		return 0.2;
		}
		else if (0.2<temp_f<=0.6){
		return 0.6;
		}
		else {
		return 1.0;
		}
String	volume_FBF	return size of(medium_set);
String	LOI_FBF	If (subscriber.n_application == publisher.n_application)
		return 1;
		return max (PerS, PerP);
	A Renew LOI Subscription	
String	Volume_DOCBF	return spatial_x * spatial_y*spatial_z;
String	LOI_FBF	return 1;

In short, the estimated LOI can either be reversible or irreversible inactive level interest's management platform, depending on various LOI functions. The procedure to analyze and the way to carry out filtering are defined instead of supplying LOI. Each subscription and posting pair might have distinct LOIs and filters. Thus, DVE participants have dynamic LOI and dynamic communication. The editors individually disseminate the datagram and there is no further cost for the editors. In addition, the balanced processing jobs on numerous ARs, which minimize bottlenecks are spread instead of a single server. Effective prevention program administration is more customizable and simpler to scale in comparison to older investment and consumption [65].

4.4 MONO-FACE EXTRACTION AND PARAMETERIZATION OF THE EYE CONTOUR

The identification of facial features based on images has gained increasing interest from scientists throughout the world. It has tight relationships with software engineering, applied mathematics, economics, physiology, etc., as a multidisciplinary research subject. The next generations can be used for human/computer user experience, intelligent systems, automated identification, and several other areas. Face observation, i.e., analyzing facial features and concerns is a significant technique in conventional medicine when it comes to the specific recommendation. Expressive is therefore exceedingly difficult to quantify mechanically. Too far, most documented facial expression approaches have been proposed for humans, while monkeys have been regularly utilized as experimental objects in medical sciences.

Emotion has relationships with sickness and illness, thus studying the origins of conflicting faces and looking for the appropriate therapeutic ways is quite essential. This kind of monkey can be utilized in biology since it is near to human beings and has similar reactions to the same treatments. To record in real-time the fluctuations in facial expression, photographs of monkey faces are taken and the frames are immediately processed by the computer. Based on the picture on the face of the chimpanzee, eye movements are identified and hence sentiments may be appraisal and development, such as eye and mouth boundaries.

Therefore, the research proposes an automatic way to extract the monkey facial shape, which is the pre-condition for the recognition of the mood of the monkey, and then parameters it. Our methods involve facial segmentation, facial standardization, eye outlines, and approximation of the eye contour.

4.4.1 FACE SEGMENTATION

For categorization, facial skin color is typically applied, hence a color model is developed based on example images. As luminosities influence skin color, color space YCbCr (YUV) is used since the luminosity value Y is independent of the Cb and Cr color values. The dimensions of the chimpanzee face are empirically determined from the photographs and the number of pixels Y, Cb, and Cr inside the image landmarks are utilized to make the color model statistically. Figure 4.1 displays CRs are within [124,149] ranges, and the color values of specimen monkeys are between [100,199]; the color patches within sampling monkeys are around 388,000, the CRs are within [110,139].

The 3D geometry of the input image can be described using Gaussian blend models to specify a more accurate color model. First, to train the characteristics of the Gaussian model of mixtures, we employ the EM method. Then, by calculating its probability using the following formula, it is determined if 1 pixel corresponds to the facial landmarks of the monkey's image:

$$p(x) = \alpha_1 g(x; \mu_1, \Sigma_1) + \alpha_2 g(x; \mu_2 \Sigma_2) + \alpha_3 g(x; \mu_3, \Sigma_3). \tag{4.5}$$

Each Gaussian model has its weighting value, center, and covariance matrix—α, μ, and Σ respectively.

The probability $p(x)$ demonstrates that the samples are closer to point x of the face area. The number of Gaussian mixture models are automatically allocated or mechanically calculated. We have tested the automated technique with 12 Gaussian mixture models as computed. The 12 Gaussian calculated model types are utilized to estimate the obtain sufficient appropriate audit evidence in YCbCr face areas. One spheroid symbolizes one Gaussian regression equation as indicated in Figure 4.3, and the center of each hemisphere is the greatest result in the relevant function, whereas the spatial resolution of each hemisphere is the dual minimum value of the correlation coefficients for diagonal information. Every pixel of an image is monitored and the image face region may be automatically recognized based on the color model developed. As Figure 4.3 shows, first-line images are monochrome monkey facial pictures, and second-row images are forming segmented regions, using a face-colored model of skin [66].

The approach based on a color model can partition the pixel with the colors in the probability distribution, but it can at the same time acquire some undesirable-colored areas. For example, the monkey's ears are of the same hue as the face, and dispersed pixels may occur in the image's areas. Through the next processes, segmentation findings continue to develop the recovered monkey facial.

Step 1: If there are more than four pixels of its 3×3 neighbors that are skin-colored, each skin-colored pixel is transformed into another skin-colored pixel, and the effects of monkey fur on the face are reduced.

Step 2: The dilation operations of mathematical functions are used to increase connection in the extracted face areas.

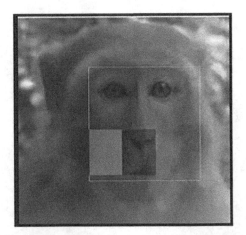

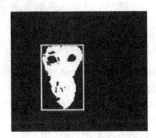

FIGURE 4.3 Face segmentation using a color model.

Step 3: Find the continuous area with the largest area and pick it from the gathered areas as the recovered monkey face.

Step 4: The extracting region of the monkey face is managed by templates of erosion and the face is then marked with a pyramid shape in the third row of Figure 4.3.

4.4.2 FACE NORMALIZATION

A monkey face may have several various positions, thus before expression recognition, the picture should be normalized. Standardization in the face comprises normalization of both size and movement. Regularization of the size is done according to the wide face of the monkey since when the mouth is opened the head might vary. The approximate two-eyed area may be placed by the human science of the monkey face after size standardization. Rotation normalizing utilizes the connected line between the two eye centers. The region of the eyes of the monkey and the rotation normalizing technique follows the following steps:

Step 1: Transform the color picture to a gray image and then take gray as the Otsu algorithm to dynamically activate the segmentation thresholds.

Stage 2: Split the gray image into real clusters of parameters, and white and black clusters will be shown.

Step 3: Remove small and identifiable black pieces and then use erosion and dilation procedures to transform the remaining black sections.

Step 4: Take the two huge and incessant black zones as monkey eyes, and the focus points of two eyes are allied by one line as shown above.

Step 5: Turn the line at one of its ends horizontally, and the rotated picture is a consequence of normalizing of rotational as demonstrated.

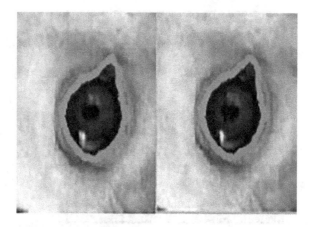

FIGURE 4.4   Extraction of the eye contour.

4.4.3   EYE CONTOUR EXTRACTION

The eye segment border is not relatively smooth; thus, it is not sufficiently suitable for the monkey eye contours. As a starting stance, points on the acquired limit and the Hough transform for the favorable circumstance, Model (e.g., snake model) is employed and the adjusted points are made to create the eye contours.

Similar to Figure 4.4, the first line shows the squares with the beginning points on the extracted eye boundary and the right side shows the corresponding corrected places after the ACM. Furthermore, the results indicate a comparable and smooth representation of the eye contouring developed.

4.4.4   PARAMETERIZATION OF THE EYE CONTOUR

Monkey eyes and weeks of treatment work in facial movements comparable, the length of the eyes generally exhibits little fluctuation, but two eyelid contours alter in their shape. This parameterizes and tests the contour features to discover whether there are any facial expressions like "ancient" and "reassuring." The inner and outer eyes which open to the greater may represent the sense of "fear," and the seemingly non-extracting form of the eye may show the feeling of "calmness" for these two forms of facial movements. We thus utilize the least polynomial approach to adapt the pixels on top and bottom contours to the polynomial curve. The large, expanded, and average open eyes are quantifiable with the polynomial component, and the corresponding equations are shown. We name this exponential quantity "curvature" in the eye, i.e., in our experiment, data on the curvature are gathered and analyzed.

Unlike humans, a monkey cannot remain in the investigation so that a sequence of photographs of monkey faces with shifting areas of the eye cannot be captured. Therefore, before measuring the deformations of the eyes, we are transforming the two separate photos with eye points. To produce a parabolic curve between the line's segments A and B, eye contours are rotated. Then we use one as the fundamental picture that transforms the other via translation and scaling. The eye's outlines are then transferred to make the corner B of the origins of the standard coordinate system more convenient for calculating the curve fitting. For the chest area of the furious expression, the solid curve indicates an adapted $f(x)$ function, whereas for the upper eyelid of calm expressions, the dotted curve represents an adapted $g(x)$ function. Of course, the absolute amount of the polynomial component $f(x)$ is bigger than $g(x)$, thus the curving of the patterns of the eyes may be employed to identify the expressions.

$$x = ax^2 + bx \tag{4.7}$$

$$x = cx^2 + dx$$

Within the range of $(m, 0)$, $f(x) > g(x)$, so

$$ax^2 + bx - cx^2 - dx > 0, x \in (m,0). \tag{4.8}$$

After transformation, there is

$$(a - cx) + b - d < 0, x \in (m,0). \tag{4.9}$$

For the intersection point A (m, n), there is always the equation $f(m) = g(m)$, so

$$am^2 + bm = cm^2 + dm. \tag{4.10}$$

After transformation, there is

$$(a - cm) + b - d = 0. \tag{4.11}$$

With Eqs. (4.11) to (4.8), there is

$$(a - cm) > (a - cx), x \in (m,0). \tag{4.12}$$

After transformation, there is

$$(a - cm)(-x) > 0, x \in (m,0). \tag{4.13}$$

Since $x > m$, we can conclude that

$$(a - c) < 0. \tag{4.14}$$

And finally, there is

$$a < c. \tag{4.15}$$

This indicates that a and c are both negative and that the relationship between the confidence intervals a and b is thus negative.

$$fabs()a > fabs()c. \tag{4.16}$$

The exact amount of the polynomial furious contour component is thus greater than that of a peaceful contour, which demonstrates that the curvature may be employed even in this case to characterize face emotion.

4.5 CONTAINER TERMINAL LOGISTICS SYSTEM MODELING AND SIMULATION STUDY

Since the 1970s, container shipping has become significantly easier and is still growing over the world. Given the current trends, the interprocess communication ratio of the entire general cargo is predicted to exceed 70% by 2015.

The increase in demand for container transit, the development in port size, and the increased number of variables for external insecurity are causing an increasingly serious problem in their administration for a large number of port authorities. Authors utilize simulations as a technique for such a large structure to enable some strategic choices that include too many diverse factors, which cannot be managed differently. It is broadly relevant in simulation and experimental successfully created for the Container Terminal Logistics System (CTLS).

The CTLS comprises principally of three subsystems, completing the operation of ship berthing, yard operations, and port transport. There is a lot of uncertainty in the CTLS, such as the anticipated time of arrival for ships, a dynamic system, and a set of discontinuous equations which are used to show dynamic characteristics. And a random new service is also the ship berthing subsystem.

As we are all aware, it is a component of worldwide research in CTLS modeling and simulation optimization in the field of heat and complex challenges. The main focus for project activities is how the numerical simulation is created. The first aspect of unpredictability factors is evaluated and the impact of the effectiveness of the port logistics network is analyzed. The different container logistic support subsystems are re-optimized to use a search engine information technologies subsidiary.

4.5.1 LOGISTICS SYSTEM MODELING TECHNOLOGY

4.5.1.1 Oversea Review

This section would demonstrate the content and technique of the research in CTLS modeling.

The CTLS modeling investigation ingredient can be synthesized as operational and managing technologies. Work: The resources allocation, the daily operating management, and the technology management system are given in this section.

Allotment of resources: A nonlinear optimization computer equation for container bridging programming was suggested and the best solution was developed using a branch-and-bound algorithm and heuristics method. Based on the study planning on the container bridges to achieve the shortest wait times for construction, the mathematical model has been developed and an algorithm of the branch and bind is built. The solution for the reduction of operating time was found by utilizing a branch-and-bound approach and greedy algorithm to investigate the landings and opening time of a single ship and the servicing state of the moving bridges.

Daily management: Mitsui Engineering & Shipbuilding Company develops the freight transportation simulation platform that may be utilized for day-to-day operations and managerial simulation. The main view is to improve container flows through very efficient operation. The particular part of the work: The major content relates to distributing in the courtyard of the storage system, concludes two parts, balances first of all the functional ability capacity and then connecting the load with boats, and lastly calculating the transport distance of the containers to be at least. The problem of an appropriate transportation management yard organization and the frequency response is introduced sequentially.

System of management technology: The basic technique for handling containers is separated in Rubber Tyred Gantry (RTG) Cranes, Railway Cranes the final two containers are more common in recent years, including moving Gantry, RTGC–EMC and automated cargo container terminals and straddle trucks.

Petri Net, artificial intelligence technologies and conceptual framework, is the major technology for simulation overseas.

Petri Net. Petri Net is an array of basic visuals that is a combined model. The container port is split into multiple container handling and transport operating spaces and various moving vehicles.

4.5.1.2 Technologies for Numerical Simulation

Non-focused simulation and models: The customized scheduling algorithm for the transport of freight was developed. The flex corporate gain, which is created using C++ for building, modeling, replicating, and analyzing the flexibility system and processes, is provided.

Specialized communications applications design and implementation: The process depicts for oil tanker movements containing containers, battleships, cars, yards, and managed structures, and users decide the system requirements for restrictions.

4.5.1.3 Models

Even if feature vectors are various, it is possible to split the theoretical foundation of the commonly eaten methodologies into operative research, cyborgs, and system simulations.

OR modeling methods used in describing the problem in general consist of integer enhancement, integer optimizations, queuing theories, model assessments of techniques, network flows, the theoretical framework of the game, data methods, and conventional enhancement, in which the prototype theories are branched and bound, the Lagrangian coefficients, the Be prototypes, all major in logistics activities. The distinction between the adjusting entries and the controlling quantity in CTLS as well as disturbance and output variable are particularly distinct in control theoretical basis on the processes engineering design technique.

A status vary should be monitored in detail by the number of containers on the yard and boat berthing, whereas systemic control strategy is based on the operating plan and the number of containers in the compartments, i.e., control quantities. The design of CTLS is therefore akin to designing an acceptable control choice for a distributed system that is consistent with system disruption in system output fluctuations. And the disturbance is probably a random or particular mode variable.

Furthermore, the system output is a means of transport between subsystems. CTLS control theory modeling is used to make usually constrained daily management choices, in particular in the case of linear hypotheses. The models are difficult to define if the system is unusually intricate, which is the most effective solution.

The simulation results modeling approach used for organizational behavior is a new area. To examine CTLS in the round, because the optimal relationship doesn't go out of the intricate system, the simulations are especially suitable for CTLS in all sorts of circumstances, which is large and hard to do the mathematical and computational examination.

4.5.1.4 Primary Coverage and Key Problem

The based on the analysis are accumulated in the system formulation phase and the key impact factors affecting the efficiency and productivity of any subsystems for the intent of developing a physical model are assessed; next, the system developed of any CTLS subsystem would be set up based on the Arena source code for the simulated world. The primary issues in this phase are:

How the resources input/output in the component border may be defined and described.

How the random factors and the effects of component performance are determined and identified and the parameter characteristics and statistical regulations of these factors are determined and how to construct subsystems, such as ship barges, yard management, and port transport.

The accompanying components comprise the layout for the terminal, resource plan, and work schedule for establishing the key functional components with a three-layer architecture.

Moreover, how to uncover the logical link between the specific functions is the logical relationship between the behavioral feature and the approach.

The essential problem in this phase is to determine the alphanumeric code and their numerical field, which affects subsystems' performance and the operative effectiveness indices.

4.5.2 VERIFICATION VALIDATION AND ACCREDITATION

4.5.2.1 Review

A wide variety of troubles such as spatial correlation, desktop computers, and software reliability, the productivity of simulation game machinery, and the accuracy of test results that were applied to the fitness of analysis and decision-making needs to be taken into account in the current research reliability evaluation above simulated system. The basis for dependability evaluation is verification, validation, and accreditation (VV&A).

The mathematical models used to test the mathematical models based on actual system data collecting are separated into three criteria. The verification is carried out under the following three situations.

No data from input or output: It is difficult to gather non-existing data in the actual system, so it is possible to generate data using a simulated template and to test the data with the Design of Experiments. The bilinear role models' model is built in model verification for the seabed mining detection for predicting the attribute values and is finally confirmed using the approach, compared with the expert's experience. A swine disease instance described in the foodservice business is also used for a multivariate regression because the inputs and output data are not real.

Just data output: To monitor the simulations and actual output data, statistical approaches are applied. The true and simulated output data are combined for verification and analysis of the simulator results utilizing statistical hypotheses.

Data from input and output: Monitoring simulations are used for validating and verifying models in this situation. In reality, the majority of data is not distributed in a regular way; therefore, resampling develops to further confirm the relationship among simulations and the actual data that focus simply, independent of the distributions, on the quantitative volume of information.

The modeling system for the production line of the corporation Ericsson in Sweden may be discovered in. The relationship between simulation and reality is investigated concerning colonial experience, then the ideal system is established yet the system is yet unchecked. This is why further study is necessary for the area of the VV & ACTLS approach.

While the study on VV & A is not very extensive whether the general production system or uncommon CTLS, the analyses of the simulation environment are thus complex and obstructing. To simulate the port logistical system, a true system model is required, but the difficulties in simulating these systems are also necessary.

4.5.2.2   Primary Coverage and Key Problem

The simulated approach is calibrated at this step of VV & A if the actual system is depicted appropriately using the model. The key difficulties are:

- How to test the CTLS simulation environment based on the DOD VV & A requirements.
- How to shape the subsystems such as arrange ship docking, yard process and conveyance in port.
- How to select the right static technique in terms of data nature and distributed processing feature, and the validity of the numerical simulation may be verified.

The way to evaluate the parameter thus by comparing the parameter variation trend among actuality and simulations is to make use of the experiment design technique and multiple regressions. It is essential to check that the difference here between actuality and the simulation is the authenticity of the simulated. And the other is to check the correctness of the simultaneous system by picking the correct static approach concerning data structure and distributed file characteristics.

4.5.3   Test and Design Screening Robust

4.5.3.1   Critical Screening Review

Screening may be characterized as a reasonably critical search procedure for a reasonably large number of criteria. In general, CTLS has several types of equipment and has relationships. This is why elements (also known as input variables) and the relationships amongst these relevant elements need to be examined to create the simulation environment for complicated CTLS.

Thus, the filtering IoT communication is typically a very important subject, including an element at one moment, Iterated Fractional Factorial Design (IFFD), SB, etc. The distinct methodologies are only defined if you examine the simulation process of the simulated models is smooth and monotonous. SB is particularly active if the optimization technique can produce a monadic recession.

Therefore the selection of broadcast examination expertise frequently is a very serious matter, which counting One factor at a Time (OAT), Iterated Fractional Factorial Design (IFFD), Sequential

Bifurcation (SB) and so on. Factor selection is highly important; there are still many obstacles. The research concentrates on the SB technique to filter complicated CTLS subsystem components.

4.5.3.2   Robust Review

Recommendations provided are sometimes referred to as risk assessment, originating from the technical writer Taguchi, who was responsible for the development of a stable automotive product line suited to changing market conditions. The design components are grouped into two types: changeable controls and factor interference. A modification of the interfering factors produces a steady value of regulated elements. If an external environment is fluently changing, the resilience of CTLS is a resolution that remains steadily steady, less costly, and more practical than optimum decisions. Because optimum interaction is in practice difficult to react to changes in the environment that have affected the weather, sea risk, aligned ships, breakdowns of the automobile, and upkeep of the road.

The risk of a catastrophe is slightly above abrupt heavy cost in the CTLS simulation, if the unexpected chance of external environmental variations is well above the specified amount. As managers cannot allow the useless cost, the regulated simulator variable should be changed. The range of controllable parameters is therefore specified and the system output variable within the robust strategy is constrained to a set value. In this project, the Taguchi idea is employed, without respect to the statistical approach as it is most appropriate to product design; however, there are more aspects and relationships involved in the sophisticated investigative system.

If the ideal solution is found in a certain atmosphere, the latent hypercube sample (LHS) is finally employed to evaluate the resilient degree of an ideal plan after changing environmental components, in which the stability of late-term analyses is carried out. Conversely, before the implementation of the project, the initial robust assessment is more simulated.

4.5.3.3   Screen Primary Coverage and Fundamental Problem

In this phase, the SB approach will be used to study key aspects that impact different subsystems' efficiency and productivity. The SB is that a relatively high multitude of factors is selected from the simulation model. The main problem is:

1. Whether factors can be screened efficiently in several voltage characteristics or any other screen methodology, SB can be used only in one output variable, while CTLS has many characteristics.
2. How the outcome after the SB end is verified and the irrelevant components checked, is if CTLS is described correctly.
3. The essential challenge is in this phase, the SB approach will be used to study key aspects that impact different components' efficiency and productivity.
4. The SB is that a relatively high range of factors is selected from the mathematical model.

The main problem is:

Importantly, the period, which calculates variations and establishes screen end regulations, shows how to select the length of each data and the mathematical space of a data and where the varied interactions of the component and the combined simulations would be halted.

4.5.3.4   Principal Reporting and Substantial Real Problem

The optimal proposal would be created in the last phase of the design approach by modifying the characteristic character of the principal factor of effect examined. The test data is created using the array center methodology to construct experiments, and the optimum parameter is eventually created by the response surface methodology models. The most important thing is:

How to achieve the controlling factor optimum value by using Arena's optimization program Opt-Quest.

Maximum likelihood is the way to identify the result. The optimum results in terms of KKT's contentment with the produced data are unequivocal If not one but many data, how to optimize the entire randomized system has been updated.

How the system correctness of events may determine that systems components are optimal.

How the robust value may be determined using the optimum value. The CTLS supervised learning methodology would apply if optimum design theory was combined with resilient design.

At this level, the key to designing an ideal solution for the complete CTLS is whether every subsystem is optimally designed. The other is how the robust value may be determined by the use of the optimum value.

4.6 LASERS SPEEDY PROTOTYPE DIGITIZED CONTOUR LINE MAPPING

Rapid Prototyping (RP) is built upon quantitative hard acceleration, computer graphics, technological, Electronic, and photonic computer-aided design. It was introduced in the late 1980s with new production technology. The considerable production adaptability of additive manufacturing. The complicated 3-D model of the CAD is translated rapidly and without fixture into a real prototype. Unlike the previous production technique, RP is a new technique based on the notion of "addition." The substance is gathered in the type of electronic knowledge, step by step and layer by layer, and the fast prototypes are termed digital forming.

Rapid manufacturing is often divided into lasers RP and micro-drop-based RP in two broader divisions. The three common processes include laser sintered (SLS), stereolithography, and creation of laminated objects (LOM). As seen in the picture. One, fast model programming processes should be followed:

Step 1: Computers generated is the manufacturer's 3-D CAD design.
Step 2: The layered program slices a 3-D CAD model with particular densities after the evaluation and alignment selection.
Step 3: The existing layers is controlled under severe acceleration with the laser light or government and legal nozzles.
Step 4: Worktable decreases with an absorption coefficient separation and the next material layer is produced. Repeat step 3 and step 4 until the CAD system is used to obtain a functional model of the part.
Step 5: Post-processing of the working prototype and according to customer need.

4.6.1 Principle Comparing of SLS, SL, and LOM

In Selected Plasma Spraying, powder ingredients are employed. The powder material examined by the light source is heated and consolidated under computer control.

Major depressive disorder breaks down at a film thickness and the next substance layer has been processed till a CAD system intention to use the technology of component is obtained.

The actual prototype with complicated forms is manufactured by SLS with the use of powder materials. Molding can take place using SLS wax, manufacturing polymers, metallic powdered, polyethylene powder, PA, and Pulver.

Stereolithography is utilized using liquid photosensitive resin (SL). Photopolymerization would occur quickly when the having fixed is UV-radiated and the substance moves from the fluid to the solid. Photosensitive resin SL is created based on the UV laser curing feature of the fluid photographic resin. SL is an SLS-like technique. Until a tangible prototype of the component is achieved, the UV lasers can scan liquid responsive resin layer after layer. In the SL, the hardened photocurable resin control depth is crucial to affect the correctness of the physical prototype's shape and dimensions.

In laminated object production, layered components are employed. The existing literature layer or other substance is sliced by a laser beam under hard acceleration. Whenever the contours of the probability population have been analyzed, the next new material layer is joined to the previous layer through a warming roller. The next layer of material is also reduced by infrared light. The surplus sheets are chopped to the squares by the laser pulse to remove the physical portion conveniently. Replay it until all CAD model elements have been cut. The extra material is removed after the LOM process and the intention to use technology is produced. Industrial designs, vacuum shapes, and bigger models are well suited to composite objects. The process concept of the manufacture of composite objects: The subsequent developments, marketing, and marketing of SLS, SL, and LOM have distinctive qualities.

The subsequent developments, marketing, and marketing of SLS, SL, and LOM have distinctive qualities. However, the toughness and accuracy of products due to their brief history and process restrictions are difficult to ignore. The demérits include SLS, SL, and LOM. Table 4.5 shows the pros and demerit points of SLS, SL, and LOM.

4.6.2 DIGITALIZED CONTOUR LINE SCANNING

Contour line (DCLS) is predicated on SLS, SL, and LOM variables and derivatives for the digitized contour line prototypes. The thermoplastic powder components in DCLS are employed and if heated to specific elevated temperatures, their thermoplastics characteristic would be removed. DCLS scans the actual physical layers all along the curved surface of the 2-D bridge when the laser light operates. The laser beam scanning material thermalizes and destroys the characteristic. The full powder mixture is cemented by ventilated oven or infrared hot plate when the tangible prototype's 3D shape has been scanned. The sintered part is finally split into the actual CAD prototype and surplus portion in two different halves.

DCLS digitally extracts 3-D contour geometry. CAD model contours line "0" and software line "1" for the remaining model. The flag data of "0" is provided to a laser-beam management system to scan the eye shadow and the remaining material to "1" is not analyzed by the program. The DCLS procedure is illustrated in Figure 4.5.

4.6.3 SCANNING OF LASER BEAM

A variety of possibilities are offered by DCLS materials. In DCls thermoplastics, the majority of powdery ingredients may be used. The scan by laser light is divided into two sections of powders and sintered into a heating furnace that provides the surface of the object DCLS with strong

TABLE 4.5

Advantages and Disadvantages of SLS, SL, and LOM

RP Process	Merits	Demerits
SLS	1. A wide range of SLS material possibilities 2. Do not need a system of support 3. Sintered into functioning pieces may be some materials	1. The low pace of treatment 2. Small roughness and poor product concentration
SL	1. High rates of use of material 2. High precision and product surface condition 3. The production of plastic components immediately	1. The low pace of treatment 2. Materials steep cost 3. Structure of support needed
LOM	1. High speed of treatment 2. High durability and comparatively low concentration 3. Appropriate for large modeling manufacture	1. LOM materials options are few and each layer's height cannot easily alter.

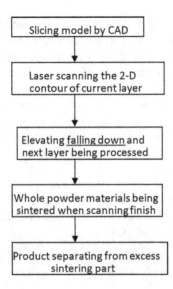

FIGURE 4.5   Process principle of DCLS.

structural quality. Only in the control points identified by lightning bolts are the system performances excellent.

In the DCLS case study, treated sand was employed. The process parameters $P=30$(W) and $v=0.007$ (m/s) are the appropriate experimental parameters, where P has laser power and v pulse frequency. CAD software has produced impeller and mold prototypes the functional model of the mold and the ultimate castings component of the mold.

4.7   USING WAVELET COEFFICIENT FITTING, 3D SURFACE TEXTURE SYNTHESIS

The synthesizing of textures has been a significant area of research in recent years. Current craftsmanship primarily constructs a new material that looks the same as the measurement flavor and the manufacturing process is like a kind of "creasing" procedure, which shows that the valuation of the new content now exceeds the cost of the textured samples rather than just a copy of the workpiece composites. The statistical techniques are based on several methodologies. The mathematical definition of texture is presented—the Julesz ensemble, the collection of all the pictures that share correct data. Texture may be synthesized from statistics on a mathematical basis by matching statistics. For collecting the Julesz ensemble, a Monte Carlo Simulation technique is suggested. Portilla and Simoncelli analyzed different pattern generation statistical techniques. In the setting of an overcrowded and complicated wavelet, they describe textured pictures by statistical characterization. The source material has now been broken down by Heeger and Bergen, using Laplacian and Steerable pyramids, to achieve various frequency layers. To depict sample texture, De Bonet employs multi-resolution photos and synthesizes the new texture with several attributes. Eros and Leung are a relatively easy approach, based on Markov's random field, which gives pixel value to a synthesis fabric by the comparison between both the sample and synthetic texture to the most comparable neighborhood. In many situations, it may provide realistic results, but the pace is poor. Wei and Levoy employ multifaceted pictures to describe the patterns of both the input and output samples, and they design a synthesis technique from lower resolution to the greater definition. Zalesny collects statistical characteristics comprising statistics of first order and demographics of correct result drawing on the idea of competition in the form of a typical clique of the example texture. Graphics are generated by imitating the sample texture statistics for the various sorts of cliques.

Bar-Joseph displays the text by employing wavelets to alter a structured signal. Different unique trees are created from the tree data structure by studying and testing the routes in the original tree. The new material is transformed inversely. Nevel gives the first features extraction technique for the sample material, then the first one (mean and histogram), then the subsequent one (correlation) Sample texture, and fake texture between each scale. The result is a synthetic texture with a reverse wavelet transformation. In recent years, theoretical guidance have been provided for the design and analysis by employing the admissibility, efficiency, and speed of sampling of texture samples. A novel approach for synthesizing textures is accessible in principle by pasting parts of the texture from the reference to the synthesized image.

The vision of making a study is typically about generating 2D texture pictures. However, the surface textures of the actual world include roughness geometries and different reflectance qualities. These texture surfaces are not similar to the 2D still texture, as their pictures can change significantly in lighting orientations. These curves compared are distinct from the 2D texture, as the light direction of the pictures can therefore change considerably. Since 3D three-dimensional surface texture can better portray the entity's edge detection than double lamination and may change with scene light and viewing perspectives, it is frequently utilized in virtual reality and videogames. A single 3D surface pattern creation frame is shown in this study, extended effectively to synthesize multi-dimensional surface abstractions. First, we are proposing a new 2D synthesization technique, which is based on a transforming wavelet, which may be expanded effectively to synthesize multi-dimensional surface representation. In contrast to earlier work, we suggest the new rapid project and made approach which, by first installing wavelet coefficients in overlapping textures, may eliminate joint seams when synthesizing the reverse waveforms to construct new graphics. In this photographic stereo (PS) three synthetic surface structure pictures yield subsurface gradients and albedo maps. The gradients mappings of the surface can be merged into a surface map (surface profile). New pictures of a Lambertian surface can be produced with albedo and height or gradient maps in arbitrary light directions.

The first is a new 2D texture generation technique based on wavelet transformation that may be used.

The other is to expand a multiple-to-multiple texture creation.

4.7.1 Use Wavelet Polynomial Approximation New Texture Fabrication

4.7.1.1 Discrete Wavelet Transform

The transformation frequency domain is a multi-resolution study representing picture fluctuations on many scales. A waveform is a function oscillated and filtered and has a component of zero. The calculation of the 2D signal discrete wavelet transform requires iterative filtration and subsampling as illustrated in Figure 4.6. Three detailed photos are available at each level. Following this, we refer to the pictures as LH (carrying power amplification horizontal information), HL (carrying frequency vertical information), and HH (containing diagonal information in high frequency). The discomposure also generates a different frequency info approximate picture, called LL. The transformation of the wavelet can break down the LL band recursively. Since the breakdown of the

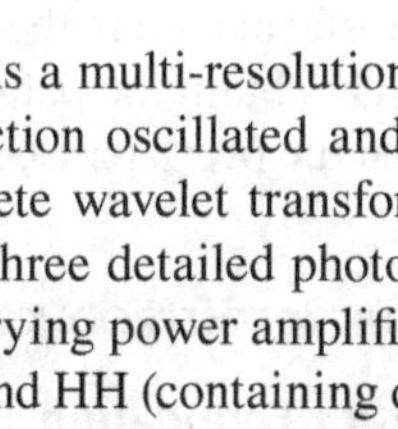

LL 2	HL 2	HL1
LH 2	HH 2	
LH1		HH1

FIGURE 4.6 Two-level wavelet decomposition.

wavelet of two levels produces six details of the pictures, all of the sub-band pictures are indicated by LH_1, HL_1, HH_2, HL_2, HH_2, and extra image approximations LL_2.

4.7.1.2   Use of the Wavelet Coefficient for the Novel Materials Synthesizing

In recent years, texture generation has become an important field of research. In the current art of making work, mainly a new fabric that appears identical to the sample texture is produced and the fabrication process is like a type of "growing" procedure, which indicates that now the value of the original fabric is greater than that of the textured samples and not just copy to the resulting fabric. Many methods are based on the statistical model. The specified sequence of texture is presented in the Julesz ensemble, the collection of all the pictures that share correct data. The algorithm takes into account the next two sub-images, which overlap each other in the same section. The overlaying of two parts of the short and mid should coincide in the architecture to produce the region overlapping to each other. There are K wavelet coefficients in the overlap areas provided the overlapping of the material is a vertical one. Then we fit in the single position on the image pixels. If otherwise, the measurement of the distance is mounted in perpendicular motion if the overlap component is horizontal.

We looked here at the very first sort of case and explained the particular method as continues to follow:

Input architecture development is often degraded by computers

Step 1: Modify the one-level waveform after four LL_1, LH_1, HL_1, and HH_1 comment sections have already been produced in the source texture.

Step 2: Enter the regions overlapped number K. Because of every overlap in the subpicture, determine the value of each fractal dimension effector.

Step 3: Determine the total orbital radius difference between the four subpictures for every pixel in the overlapping texture synthesis region. Every weight of the short and medium is the opposite fractal parameter. Decide the appropriate pixels of the covariance matrices given every line in the overlapping region according to the total value of the exhaustive weighted waveform.

Step 4: Select the set with an error criterion to regulate the fitting pixel of the covariance matrices. The component in the selecting set is the smallest succession of values of the sum of the actual number of the weighted waveform. The selection component in each line is randomly selected as the matching pixel.

Step 5: By using a reverse wavelet transformation in the overlap region of the four sub-images, the new texture of the synthesis may obtain the pattern of the creation procedure in (row) horizontal orientation is used when the overlap piece is horizontal.

4.7.2   3D Fabrication Machined Surface Reproduction and Reflecting

4.7.2.1   Gradient Method Mathematics Foundation

The mechanism of the gradient is predicated on a Lambertian method based. To produce fresh pictures under variable light directions, the Gradient method is using surface gradients and albedo maps produced from the photometric stereo approaches. The approach employs several photos as the input to extract pictures from the surface. The approach presents as a commodity the picture data matrices:

$$I = M_1 M_2 \tag{4.17}$$

Partial derivatives are where M_1 and M_2. M_1 is the matrices for the depiction of the surface we would want to retrieve. Therefore, by utilizing SVD we can resolve M_1 if we know M_2 and assume some reflection/lighting model. This category includes the gradient approach.

Thus, the operation of charcoal grilling may be stated as a product of M_1 and c vector representations for the desired direction of brightness:

$$i = M_1 c \qquad (4.18)$$

If T is a scale parameter, and I is an images vectors, $i_{1,2}$, it is a reflection coefficient.

- **Three themes synthesized of "a", "b," and "c" images are linearly combined.**
    We first capture three photographs of a material lit by a single screen respectively with a 0°, 90°, and 180° tilt angle. We call them "a" picture, "b" picture, and "c" picture. For further information, click [1,17–19,21].
    This is a scaled version of the pictures "a", "b" and "c." We may then display the generated pictures in an arbitrary light to create new backgrounds.

4.8   CONSOLIDATED BLOCK-BASED FEATURES EXTRACTION CUTTING ALGORITHMS

Image classification is a vital step in extracting image understanding and interpretation knowledge for form and location. Differentiation is usually a preparatory step for the identification of objects. Each object classification method has a strictly defined scope while machine vision is a tough problem. Today, segmented images are frequently used for the collection, annotating, analysis of images, and interpretation of images. The goal of the division of images is to organize images into image regions that will always correspond with different surfaces, entities, blobs, or geological zones. Regional signature and recovery were an active area of research in the recovery of images. A segment of images is an important step towards the acquisition of a regional signature. Without reliable segmentation, the signature form or resemblance is worthless. Segmenting techniques include Canny, local variation, advantage median-shift, and k-means. There are many different types of segmented procedures. All operators like the operator of canny use location feature to filter; therefore, they cannot guarantee a continual border restriction. The most common segmentation methodology is k-mean clustering for the construction of the closing border form signatures whose benefit is fast efficiency. Cut characterization is a new step forward in this subject, which is the spectral division application in the division of images. The picture segmentation technique is considered a graph partitioning issue. The Cut method maps the graph division segmentation issue. Any picture may be shown as a shot that resulted in an undirectional graph $G=(V, E)$, with the nodes in the character space being the points, and with each pair of nodes becoming an edge. A $G=(V, E)$ graph may then be separated by eliminating the edges linking the two segments into two distinct sets. As a weight of the deleted edges, the degree of discrepancy between the two parts is calculated.

$$\text{cut}(A, B) = \sum_{u \in A, v \in B} w(u, v). \qquad (4.19)$$

The best division of a graph is the one that maximizes the worth of the cuts. It is favorable to trim a limited collection of isolated nodes on the graph. Minimum cutting requirement Jianbo Shi suggested a new measure of disconnectedness among two groups to minimize unnecessary biases in dividing tiny collections of points. The prefabrication of the cut costs instead of looking at the share of net vertices and edges linking the two fractions and is called the Standardized Cut (N-cut) for the dissociative episode's measurement:

$$N\text{-cut}(A, B) = \frac{\text{cut}(A, B)}{\text{assoc}(A, V)} + \frac{\text{cut}(A, B)}{\text{assoc}(B, V)}. \qquad (4.20)$$

The above equation is the total connection from nodes in A to all the rest.

Similarly described are graph nodes and assoc(B, V). The N-cut is aimed at capturing the global visual impression, evaluating both the total differences between separate categories and total similarities across groups, as opposed to earlier clustering segmentation techniques. Since N-cut takes global and local knowledge as well as its resilience fully into consideration, it can achieve superior performance than earlier programming-based modeling approaches. The active issue of the study is now frequency segmentation with liking to N-cut.

4.8.1 BLOCK-BASED NORMALIZED CUT

Each graph's vertex is equal to a picture pixel. The N-Cut seems significantly attractive as it takes region categorization from a global view into account. It may be used to recognize the patterns and other domains, but it is not possible to obtain images online by examining small and large dataset because of the memory and communication overhead. The graph always describes an image with the image $(M*N)*(M*N)$ element number if the image's size is $M*N$ when an image is projected onto a network. This renders the unbelievable cost of computing meaningless. In addition, the results of the survey suggest that original N-cut algorithms are acceptable for non-textured images rather than textured images, because base unit clustered is a solitary pixel, which cannot contain information about the texturing.

We offer standardized block cutting based on an original standardized picture segmentation technique to enhance the speed. To increase performance, the aesthetic aspect of the basic unit for N-cut is to blend structure with color. We apply graded image gray as one of the regional feature values in conjunction with the probability curve for textured features to create a prejudicial transformation function.

We provide enhanced N-Cut algorithms not for one pixel, but for the picture to be turned into a graph, with an image block of 7×7 pixels. Each network node of the hypothesized N-Cut algorithm is an image block rather than a separate pixel. The weighting on each edge of the adjacent matrix W between node I and j is the product of a characteristic term equivalent to the similar.

Otherwise, $w_{ij}=0$, where $X(i)$ is node i's spatial position, and $F(i)$ is vector-based color node i. The $F(i)$ always reflects the pixel intensity of the associated pixel, when the algorithm is employed in the initial N-cut method. The $F(i)$ provides a visual vector of the appropriate picture blocks when performed to our block-based N-cut. Since the N-cut procedure consists of a grouping of adjoining pixels, the weight of the i and j nodes is 0 when the separation between them is greater than the r criterion. Because the block is uniform throughout N-cut fragmentation, we choose the integral images as the characteristic of the picture blocks. This is our suggested N-cut block algorithm.

1. Segment picture to several blocks of 7×7 pixels.
   - Construct the 72-dimensional gray vector color feature vector of the picture block.
   - Build picture block vector depth map, including averaged, variation, maximum, minimal amount, and pixel centroid weighted. Centroid pixel weighted is calculated via an enhanced image and standard normal convolution product.
   - Build a graph G with an image block vertex.
   - Computing the weighted eigenvector matrix W, which corresponds to blocks I and j, respectively, with the edge weight w_{ij}.
   - Compute the first m eigenvectors v_1, ..., v_m of the generalized eigenproblem $L_v = \lambda D_v$.
   - Let $V \in R^{n \times m}$ be the matrix containing the vectors $v_1, ..., v_m$ as columns.
   - For $i=1, ..., n$, let $y_i \in R^m$ be the vector corresponding to the i-th row of V.
   - Select the optimal parameters k and m.
   - Cluster the points $(y_i)_{i=1, n}$ in R^m with the k-means algorithm into clusters C_1, C_k.

4.8.2 Parameter Selection

The variables k and m and their influence are discussed in this section. Varied factors may yield different segmenting results. There are two types of result reporting of information, the first picture characteristics by grouping in the other manually. It is significantly more human-like. It may be concluded that the "optimal" k provided by the algorithm of a cluster may not always be the greatest professional pick.

The more m, the more and more impact we usually think, the more m, the more influence, and the less impact of them is more than the barrier. The overhead time of segmentation is 115 seconds when the bundle size is 7×7, k_3, m, and 10. The more rigorous and exact each characteristic with the greater m can be described, nevertheless, the discriminatory power will diminish if it is overflowing. As a result, when they are bigger than k, the greater m leads to inferior separation accuracy.

4.9 COMPOSING FRAMEWORK DEPENDS ON PARTICLE SWARM OPTIMIZATION SEMANTIC AND SYNTACTIC WEB SERVICE ELEMENT

The main characteristics of SOC (Service-Oriented Computing) are web service invention, service selection, and service structure and the service request is composed in terms of service formulation to incorporate a business feature that uses WSDL to achieve service feature, but WSDL lacks semantical recognition. W3C, consisting of Web and Web Semantics, hence proposes web semantics. To express web semantics that specifies Service Profile, Process Model, and Service Grounding as a web semantics service, you may also use OWL-S (Ontology Web Language for Services). Where, with services, Service Profile is comparable Yellow page describing servility and relationship properties; Process Model refers to the business process of service describing the manner of work of service; Service Business the basis for such process model is that the protocol, message structure, and other metadata are in touch with what service is described as. However, numerous services are provided by many business systems and they are distinct or comparable. The approach of service providers is very distinct, loose, and dynamic in nature. Many researchers have, therefore, suggested certain approaches to compute resources such as changes in service demand, intelligentsia, and QoS (Quality of Service). Services are a distributed computing methodology, and the major focus of service choice is on the recognition of semantics and QoS. We offered, nevertheless, a characteristic strategy of service composition among the distance relationship services and a specified trend and adaption formulation in computer science. First, we use separate criteria to distance services and establish a similarity between services to extract determinants of service quality, and then we create a mathematical model of composing consumer attitudes according to that form. Second, to optimize the model, we employ the Particle Swarm Optimization technique that effectively composes services and meets service demand need. Finally, we use Amazon services to carry out experiments: this is a nice outcome.

4.9.1 Weekends Service Web Feature Method of Composition

This web service is made up of customer inquiries, service responses, and UDDIs, and adopted by WSDLs (Web Services Description Language), to define the service function. SOAP (Simple Object Access Protocol). Semantics are nonetheless infused with WSDL, which enables web service semantics, i.e., web service semantics. To explain semantics, OWL-S-based ontology aims to provide services through semi-regulation and identification rules. In the meanwhile, web services have meanings themselves.

To measure feature distribution situation. The moment we suppose variable separately denote D dimensions feature vector of sws_i and sws_j. Denoting the distance between vectors, the average distance of service request and response is

$$A(a) = J_d(x) = \frac{1}{2} \sum_{i=1}^{c} P_i \sum_{j=1}^{c} P_j \frac{1}{n_i n_j} \sum_{k=1}^{n_i} \sum_{l=1}^{n_j} \delta\left(x_k^{(i)}, x_l^{(j)}\right) \qquad (4.21)$$

where c denotes SWS, s categories number, n_i denotes sws_i class's sample number, n_j denote sws_j class's sample number; p_i is sws_i class's probability, and P_j is sws_j class's probability, which can be defined

$$P_i = \frac{|\text{sws}_i|}{|\text{sws}_i| + |\text{sws}_j|}, P_j = \frac{|\text{sws}_j|}{|\text{sws}_i| + |\text{sws}_j|}$$

The equation denotes service request and response sample set number. The distance between two vectors adopts Euclidean distance to compute in the hyperspace. Simultaneously, we use m_i to denote the ith mean vector of the sample set

$$m_i = \frac{1}{n_i} \sum_{k=1}^{n_i} x_k^{(i)} \qquad (4.23)$$

Semantic web application selecting feature is a service optimization group [amount's $(D > d)$] characteristic of D dimensions. Therefore, we develop web service semantics evaluation metrics to improve the model and use the Particular Swarm algorithm.

where § 1, § 2 is P_i, P_j probabilities, we now utilize the Particle Swarm Approach to improve the y (10), which implies we utilize a much more fundamental strategy for improving the search, neural trace network training, semantic and fluctuating systems and control systems, etc. The present time is considered to be a swarm comprised of particles of m, the population of m, and the Particle Swarm Algorithm of m size; if considered to be $z_i = (Z_{I1}, ..., Z_{1D})$, ith ($I = 1, 2, ..., M$) vector of ith (D), the adaptive value of z_i is: The online search system integration character trait of all particles web service group; $p_g = (p_{g1}, p_{g2}, ..., p_{gd})$ so far is the search engine characteristic knowledge of the technology service group of all antiparticle search; $v_i = (v_{i1}, v_{i2}, ..., v_{id}, ..., v_{iD})$ is the molecule I flight speed, namely particle distance motion, yet the distance must be less than the Bhattacharyya distance; $p_i = (p_{i1}, p_{i2}, ... p_{i2}, ..., p_{iD})$ is $p_i = (p_{i1}, p_{i2}, ...)$.

Particles change speed and location at the moment of their iteration as follows:

$$vidk + 1 = wvidk + c\,r\,p11(id - zidk) + c\,r22(pgd - zidk) \qquad (4.29)$$

$$zidk + 1 = zidk + vidk + 1 \qquad (4.30)$$

Where

$i = 1, 2, ..., m, d = 1, 2, ..., D, k$ is iterations, w is inertia factor ($0.8 \leq w \leq 1$); $r_1, r_2 \in [0, 1]$, which keep diversity of population; c_1, c_2 is learning factor ($0.5 \leq c_1, c_2 \leq 1$) or acceleration factor.

Algorithm 4.1

Particle Swarm Algorithms improve the fundamental combination of Web Application semantics
1. Introducing a software platform semantically domain that can optimize a web service semantician region.
2. To pick μ and creation and innovation of a predefined threshold: Apple.
3. The $z_i(0)$ location of the nanoparticles (z_{i1}, z_{i2}, z_{iD}) is initialized, $i = 1, 2, n$ and the speed of each particles, $v_i(0) = (v_{i1}, v_{iD})$.
4. To test the z_i (0) beneficial consequences of each molecule and indicate: y_i (0); for ($k = 0$; $k < n$; k++).

{

According to $y_i^{(0)} = \max\left\{y_1^{(0)}, y_2^{(0)}, y_m^{(0)}\right\}$ seek global optimum $p_g^{(0)}$.

According to formula (9) update $v_i(k)$.

According to formula (10) update $z_i(k)$

}

5. To measure y's adaptive value and denote $y_i^{(k)}$, namely, $y_i^{(k)} = \max\left\{y_1^{(k)}, y_2^{(k)}, y_m^{(k)}\right\}$

6. To update $p_i^{(k)}$ and $p_g^{(k)}$;

7. if if$(((y^{(k-1)} - y^{(k)}/y^{(k)} > \varepsilon)$ and $(k\,N < \max)$ return (5); else exit.

4.10 CONCLUSION

Moodle has developed a course administration system. The cost is quite inexpensive as just Linux, Apache2, Php, and MySQL are utilized in the open-source program. There is now an online co-learning system established that focuses on students' learning paths. The parameters are provided for assessing the quality of education. The identification of faces is both a vital and hard technology. A new strategy was discussed in this chapter based on estimated gray size. To carry out the leverage of DVE, the active leveraged interest management system employs ARs. A LOD assessment model appropriate for several DVE objects is presented in this section and some intriguing challenges are discussed concerning active investment and consumption. Through studies with the joint transformation of data, we establish that effective prevention programs control may cut network traffic and further enhance DVE's adaptability. The superior and inferior eyelid outlines are then utilized to adapt the quadratic curve to the lower quadrated technique. For the choice of face emotions, such as furious or calm expression, the value of curving, and the significance level of the quadratic component.

5 Mas-Based Data Modeling in Civil Engineering

5.1 AUTONOMOUS SENSOR TAXONOMIES ASSESSMENT TO SUPPORT FIELD DATA COLLECTION WITH SIGNAL PROCESSING TECHNIQUES

For a series of appropriate DAQ tools, one crucial move is the development of a correct illustration scheme that will explain details on DAQ tools, which will provide the basis for the selection of acceptable tools. Many studies focus on the complex provision of functional schemes and conceptual frameworks for detectors and their properties, for example, Sensor ML and Onto Sensor. The object of these sensor conceptual frameworks, modeling sensations, and responsive forces are different [67].

5.1.1 INITIAL REQUIREMENTS FOR REPRESENTING DAQ TOOLS

We examined requirements and operational documentation for various types of DAQ tools to detect their common features that should be described to determine the initial demand for DAQ tool representations, e.g., 3D imaging sensor and automatic recognition sensor and location sensor. We evaluated a range of knowledge criteria found in three infrastructure projects collected through qualitative studies to find specific restrictions on the choice of DAQ instruments, such as tools' precision and ambient conditions under which the techniques are required to work. The first criterion of the DAQ Design is for the mechanical properties calculated by the DAQ instruments (e.g., temperature, moisture, symmetry, and situation). Second, the sense in which ground data are collected under various locational environments (e.g., weather, landscape, indoor, or outdoor), creating limitations on the accuracy of the DAQ instruments that also need to be interpreted [68]. For instance, the two standards for details such as "checking where steel pipes lie" and "checking where the delivery van lies" both involve coordinates. Considering that the stainless-steel pipes are in an enclosed container yard and the truck operates outdoors the relevant DAQ tools could vary entirely to catch the two information requirements. For example, a GPS can monitor the position of the delivery vehicle outside, but because of the indoor signal blocking that exists, it cannot detect the place of the concrete blocks. Consequently, it is essential to collect knowledge on the constraints under which DAQ tools run [69].

Third, requirements and methods of construction can generate different measuring capability restraints DAQ Instruments (e.g., consistency, consistency, and pixel density). For example, the PCI [91] sensitivity documentation defines the precast part length tolerance of 6 mm. Therefore, the relevant DAQ instruments must have the millimeter-level precision to acquire the knowledge prerequisite "to verify the length of the precast pier segment." If these restrictions are not considered, the selection of suitable DAQ instruments to satisfy a knowledge requirement can be misleading. In the representation scheme, details relating to the calculation capacity of DAQ instruments must be described. Fourth, a DAQ tool could have such preparation and implementation procedures for data (e.g., laser scanning identification and extraction process) (e.g., installing sensors). The case of arbitration should provide details about the transaction processing activities of DAQ tools and how to install such DAQ tools on-site to help project managers and employees deploy DAQ tools on construction sites. We determined and compared the sensor conceptual frameworks based on these four criteria, whether they can represent the specified needs. The following segment presents the specifics of this assessment [70].

DOI: 10.1201/9781003211938-5

5.1.2   Evaluation of Relevant Sensor Ontologies

A conceptual model is characterized as a "conceptual frameworks schema" [78] that consists of three parts: (1) concepts within an area, (2) the attributes and relationships between these definitions, and (3) constraints on the value of the property and agreements. The ontology includes a common language and a categorization in which the principles in a field can be defined and used in the analysis and management of the domain information. Many comprehensive schemes and conceptual frameworks for sensors and their characteristics were created. In the context of this paper, we have evaluated the conceptual frameworks of Transmitter ML, Onto Sensor, CSIRO, and SSN. Descriptions of these assessments are given in the following paragraphs [71]:

Sensor ML Ontology. Sensor ML establishes a basic model for the description and measuring of sensor systems [90]. Sensor ML is based on the process of inputs, outputs, variables, and procedures that translate inputs to outputs. The sensing ML method has two categories [90]: photocatalysis process related to sensor equipment such as the electrodes, actor, and filter; and non-physical activities referring to data acquisition activities without system characteristics including, among other things, function extraction, and data filtering [72].

The Sensor ML is a generalized data model that represents the key principles described in Sensor ML, sensor detail, database management, and sensor-generated calculations. It also identifies basic types of data, such as Quantities (e.g., a data type for a numerical point), Count (e.g., a type of data for an integer), Boolean (e.g., a data type for a Boolean expression), Category (i.e., a type of data for a values section of an approximation), and the Period of a type of data (i.e., a data type to represent time). These basic data categories help determine different components in DAQ tools, to assist reasoning with detector expected output and the specific information necessary to align technical specifications with DAQ techniques [73] (Table 5.1).

Onto Sensor Ontology. Onto Sensor aims to create a sensor repository for the collection and exploration of sensors [93]. It attempts to define the technical requirements of sensors in contrast to the ML Sensor, which takes the mechanism as the main term (see Table 5.2).

As Sensor concentrates on the description of physical components, it is not capable of representing complicated transaction processing chains (i.e., a sequence of data processing tasks). Onto Sensor specifies the measurement and class of model sensor performance and describes the functionality and the standardized characteristics of the sensors by the specification statement. These three dimensions allow users to search the information repositories of the sensor and identify the measurements that collect the appropriate form of data and have the necessary capacity (e.g., day/night operating capacity and temperature control functionality) [74].

CSIRO Sensor Ontology. The purpose of the CSIRO sensor conceptual model (hereinafter CSIRO) is not only to identify functionality and sensors but also to help search the sensing and their

TABLE 5.1
Foremost Perceptions in Sensor ML and Their Descriptions

Preception	Definition of Preception	Specimen
Physical process	Physical sensor devices	Laser scanner
Non-physical process	Mathematical operations without the involvement of physical components	Feature extraction
Capability properties	Characteristics of the sensor output	Accuracy, resolution etc.
Characteristic properties	Physical properties of sensor devices	Weight and size of the scanners, etc.
Phenomenon/observable property	The observable properties that can be measured by sensors	Geometric information of subjects' surfaces
System	A system which is composed of multiple physical and non-physical processes	Laser scanner+GPS for topographical site survey

TABLE 5.2
Foremost Perceptions in Onto Sensor and Their Descriptions

Preception	Definition of Preception	Illustration
Sensor	A sensor device	Total station
Platform	A physical device to which sensors are attached	Tripod
Measurand	The physical properties and quantities that can be measured by a sensor	The coordinates of the measured points
Capability description	The description of capabilities of sensors and platforms	Day/night operation, measurement time, etc.
Generic property	The properties of sensors, and has subclasses as (1) Supported Application and (2) Performance Property.	Supported Application: day/night operation Performance Property: measurement time=2s

TABLE 5.3
Foremost Perceptions in CSIRO and Their Descriptions

Preception	Definition of Preception	Illustration
Physical quality	The physical properties that can be measured by sensors	Temperature
Feature	Entities in the real world that are the target of sensing	The room where the temperature sensor is placed
Sensor	A sensor system that contains physical instruments and their associated measurement processes	Temperature sensor with its measurement process
Sensor grounding	Physical sensing instruments with their characteristics	A temperature sensor with its characteristics such as dimension, weight, operation conditions, etc.
Operation model	The processes by which a sensor performs its measurement	The process to measure the temperature
Model result	The properties of the results coming from the *OperationModel* class	Accuracy, latency, resolution, etc.

monitoring in a network system [72]. CSIRO describes a sensor device with three concepts: foundation of the instrument (i.e., the features of physical sensor instruments), operational processes (i.e., how a sensor is being measured), and performance of a product (i.e., the physical properties being measured by sensors). The main terms used in CSIRO are mentioned in Table 5.3 [75].

CSIRO describes the Outcome Class of the Framework to describe the styles and characteristics of the output voltage in consideration of matching among data requirements and DAQ instruments. CSIRO does not, however, have an expandable means of representing sensor measurement systems. The measuring capabilities of a sensor are determined using different characteristics (i.e., Accuracy, Latency, Range, and Resolution) in the Model Result class. If the additional measuring capacity (e.g., accuracy and frequency) is to be applied to CSIRO, internal changes must be made for the configuration of the Model Result Type that restricts the reusability of the scheme for distribution. CSIRO thus has a little capacity of describing the DAQ tool's calculation capability to fulfill the third criterion of the Framework Representation Scheme [76].

Semantic Sensor Network (SSN) ontology. Similar to the Sensor ML, the term Detector is used by my SSN to calculate and translate phenomena into an output value. Therefore, the sensor class may describe either functional embedded sensors or data acquisition tasks. Table 5.4 shows the main SSN definitions. To define the properties of sensors, SSN provides a systematic hierarchical organizational structure and quantification. Three classes show the characteristics of the detectors:

TABLE 5.4

Foremost Perceptions and Their Descriptions in SSN

Concept	Definition of Concept	Example
Sensor	The physical (e.g., sensor devices) or virtual instruments (e.g., signal transforming).	Accelerometer
Feature of interest	Entities in the real world that are the target of sensing.	The delivery truck where the accelerometer is attached
Observed property	The property of the feature of interest that is observed.	Acceleration
Process	A description of how sensors transform the observed property into the output value.	Measure the acceleration
Deployment	The deployment process of sensors.	Attach accelerometer
Platform	A physical object to carry sensors for measurement.	The delivery truck
Operation range	The environmental and power conditions under which a sensor is designed to operate.	Transmission range, power storage capacity, etc.
Measurement capability	A set of measurement properties of a sensor in a specific condition.	Accuracy, resolution, shift, etc.
Survival range	The environmental conditions within which a sensor works without causing damage.	Max temperature, minimum temperature, etc.

(1) Calculation Capacity defining sensor devices' measurement capability (e.g., precision, resolution); (2) Range of operation describing environmental temperature and energy circumstances in which the sensors can work; and (3) a survival range that shows the atmosphere in which the sensor operates without damaging the sensor (e.g., temperature limits of a sensor). The SSN model is very rich in hardware devices and sensor mechanisms of different classes. It meets DAQ scheme specifications in terms of knowledge collection regarding sensor capacities, performance data characteristics, and operating conditions [77].

5.1.3 COMPARISON OF SENSOR ONTOLOGIES FOR SUPPORTING THE MAPPING OF DAQ TOOLS TO FIELD DATA

The DAQ tool representation scheme describes the details about values measured, operating conditions, sensor measurement capability, process control tasks, and new optimization processes, etc. Following a critical analysis of data frameworks of the four ontologies, we found that this method needed would consist of a mixture of the four ontologies, and none of the ontologies can independently present all the information needed. The principles of data collection methods and data, sensor implementation, cannot be represented by the sensor. CSIRO does not have a corresponding class for deploying the template detector. The sensors ML and the Onto Sensor cannot identify the signaling target. To describe the DAQ tools' inputs and outputs, SSN does not specify the basic type of data (e.g., amount, number, and floating-point) [78].

The assessment results demonstrate that the alignment between the knowledge specifications and the DAQ tools cannot be used in its original form. In support of the mapping system, we have built a representation scheme by drawing on the core principles of the revised ontologies, which are detailed in a different publication. The scheme formed deals with the following themes: (1) procedure: information processing functions (for example data is transformed); (2) capacity: capacities of measurements which can be categorized into measuring functions; (3) sense: the perception involves signals instruments and input/output information; (4) Configuration: processes of deployment of applications (e.g., installation of sensors); and (5) Platform: physical or moving components, which have sensors connected to; (a) mobile or stationary element; The mobile and/or stationary cognitive component [79].

5.2 i-Con: GEOMETRICAL TOPOLOGY BASED ON A SEMIOTIC FOUNDATION FOR THE SEMANTIC REPRESENTATION OF PREFABRICATED STRUCTURES

The result of technical research and engineering is designed to allow for successful reasons for an explanation of architectural elements by project participants (e.g., BIM components, virtual 3D representations). Although i-Con is a language with a collection of definitions to manipulate the concept, they are compiled into logic to be evaluated. This logic is focused on contextual spatial reasoning [75] and regional connections geometry's general framework [80]. The representations (e.g., connection border-interior) of the i-Con are constructed by deriving formalities from a mere configuration theory, to preserve their consistency.

5.2.1 GRANULARITY

Granularity refers to the observation made by the investigator. The effective detection of the entities seen is attributed to the spectator's ability to identify the minimal costs in a granulated system. The constructs allow the viewer to activate their mental capacity for the perception of objects. Contracts (i.e., various light waves and stimulating lengths) allow a consistency or limit of the entity to be identified. The observation differentiates individuals in "the natural world" in the "bread" scale, performs cognitive processes to map visual representations to the focus that serves the function of the observation, and exploits them as necessary by cognitive processes [81].

The instance of granularity shows the importance of the purpose of the observer in interpreting definitions by linking the intention of the observation to interpret with the experienced interpretation. The observer sees distinctive and remarkable particles that describe perfect forms by the sensations. These forms are the conceptual scheme of the participant, which is the product of perceptual processes and correlates to the articulated meaning interpretation [79]. The analyst will deduce the necessary facts and situations from this cognitive reasoning method. This rationale relates to the perception of interpretation by the observer by sensory input, interaction with mental constructs, and concept analysis [82].

The intentions make the analyst neglect those facts that are not important for the understanding of a term in the structure of the description. Pierces epistemological categories of primacy, soundness, and thirdness, and the conceptual position (actually, epistemically, and deliberately) which derive from granularity in the chain of reasoning can be described by argumentation and understanding [96]. Initialism describes the first sensory perception. (e.g., black, and white color contrast, which defines the drawing's grains and forms). Second, the interaction between both the pictures, signs, forms, sounds, etc., experienced and the viewer is defined. Two or three natural beings or abstract forms are involved (e.g., a proposition that black triangle and an arrow to characterize valves in water pipe systems). Other logic types such as assumptions and ultrasounds require more steps to reach an inference from sensory perception, apart from the direct comparison. Third, this means that two or three real beings or abstract forms relate to traditions [83].

5.2.2 REASONING AND AFFORDANCES

Gibson [80] said that the experiences of the observers are affordances, not object characteristics. Accessories are invariant variations of variables, as perceived by computational agents. There is, therefore, a sensible explanation as an individual senses the sensory aspect that the object provides and observes this perception by a continuum of inference. To combine these with subjective impressions, the analyst uses semantic ideal templates of memory. These promotion opportunities are cognitive and behavioral constructs that are specific to the agent. The reasoning mechanism extends from inference, degradation, systematic, quantitative analysis to the analytical processes, involving inference and even kidnapping, that are more confined and stylized [84].

The choice or mixture of reasoning strategies of the agent depends on the desires and skill of the agent. In short, the comparison consists of the application of apparently analogous interactions by the agent to the current representation of knowledge and circumstances. Decomposition refers to the analysis of the object in its components by recognizing how it fits. The systemic approach is to perceive everything and the interaction of its components. Deduction means the use of a basic theory to deduce such facts. The theory of induction subsumes many facts, range of motion deviates a new hypothesis that describes several information that provides an overview of three stages in which the officer will encounter a final decision during the reasoning process (i.e., interpret the observed process). In the example, the investigator focuses on an opportunity to check his smooth front joints and to check the implementation requirements inside a structural frame (i.e., situational or context conditions). The observer, for example, can check that the hinge jamb is positioned at a minimum of three organically per door frame identical to the hinge jam and at the appropriate amounts. In a logical statement where the observation applies to the closing subject and the cause for its installation, the purpose of the observation may be described. The objective renders the object seen by the investigator for a certain reason. For example, Step One structure is an entrance to be built on the wall of stonework as seen in Figure 5.1 in step 2. The intention is necessary, to prevent contradictory interpretations, to connect the mechanical properties of the subject and the investigator. For example, if objects have the same morphology with various mathematical statuses (e.g., ontology axioms). The interpretations themselves have no inherent value, a material consistency status. The semantic ties of the interpretations are influenced by the intent of the agent, who lets the agent choose specific facts and situations for understanding. The "significance" of this function or agent refers to the degree of granularity or its provision, details, and circumstances of the case are included. Granularity is seen to lead to correct understanding by including sufficient detail and circumstance [85].

An assertion is that the negotiators have the capacity, through reasoning techniques, to come to conclusions, to relate partial knowledge from various documents (i.e., individual representations—opening, masonry wall, and detail) (e.g., provide for the spatial circumstances of the observing opening at least two or three wall connectors per jamb) and manipulate more the interpretation interactions (e.g., semantics) to produce other results. Examples include stonework wire and T-shaped connectors inappropriate anchor points.

5.2.3 REASONING ON VIRTUAL BUILDING COMPONENTS

The consistency of capabilities and the faculty of the good experience to effectively equate perceptions are challenges for the agent's ability. This facility is obtained through knowledgeable handling of symbols and learning interactions, which enable the agent to use the perception of solving, detailing, certifying, meaning, and the vicinity of items [69,75]. Cognitive skills, whose therapy belongs to psychology and organizational study, are inner sign manipulative talents and learned perceptions. The standard of functionalities can nevertheless be computed using mediating technology to simplify the interpretation, description, and recognition of objects [86].

In addition to the coarse or imperfect characteristics of elements' interpretations, for example, the cognitive agent's rationale on the virtual components (e.g., the combination of steel and the bridge column of a framework) may be rationalized. The importance of supporting the agent's logic is the inference of vital interactions, where uncertainty contributes to interpersonal disturbances in the depiction. (i.e., creating part functionality). The importance of rendering fine granularity is not necessary to express subjectivity for optimum visualization. Figure 5.3 illustrates the logic of the computational agent on virtual construction materials' logical neighborhoods. The argument in the instance is a sensory perception of the missing object, which persistently combines the object with the perfect mental scheme and helps to locate semantical of the state of the objects (e.g., details functionality of the connection) [87].

The intellectual geometrical optimization techniques to view structural elements simultaneously (i-Con) are images whose abstract language is a virtue. These photographs are characterized in terms of interpersonal relationships, parenthood, and connection. The symbolic word is an artificial

TABLE 5.5
i-Con's Representation Levels

Topological	Ontological	Semantic
Relation quality	Quality of material	Context
Independent of the indexed object	The existing thing or event: object, process, script history, prehensile identities	Quality of symbol
No mediation other than the cognitive structure		Natural or artificial conventions

programming language on three levels: (1) physical resemblance as it is the first reference to one or more of them, (2) ontological as in connections among individuals, particularly their connection to space, and (2) stemmatological as it distinguishes real and actual, as well as I physical resemblance as it is the first reference to one or more of them. Possible associations and arrangements, including proposals, defining the relationship between individuals and contexts [88].

i-Cons have freedom, making it independent in each case like it is for speech recognition syntax from the conceptual language. The description of the distribution degree in i-Cons is given in Table 5.5.

These levels are intended to classify the symbolism and promote the defined use of i-Con terminology connections. It has a significant meaning. Its problem structuring with operational rules in force. The images and symbolic significance of I-Con reinforce the logic of the educational context. Although cultural meanings are subjective, in essence, the heart of the representation of i-Con is like forms that maintain the quantitative direction indicated. A picture of i-Con, for example, is related to a well-established community definition that explores the rudimentary relationship of regions of an object with their physical environment or other entity where their borders cross. i-Con's imaging can be positioned in any location in a three-dimensional Euclidean space since the intent of i-Cons is to portray the language via any implementation in computer animation supporting three-dimensional images. The picture depicted by the i-Con imagery can be created and stimulated by 3D, i.e., rotation, cross-sectional, reflector, and refractive properties [89].

5.2.4 MEDIATION

The intended spatial reference of the i-Con imagery is given an explanatory interpretation through mediation. A mediation phase provides significance to the visual experiences and then to the picture or language. i-Con imagery seeks to resemble primitive cognitive true geometric structures, i.e., fundamental semantics that appear without additional actors, sign system relations, or numerical simulations. i-Con imagery, however, involves a minimal mediation to convey the physical reference's interpretations. I-Con images can be mediated by indexing, influencing, and linking an actual entity's i-Con terminology (e.g., attach the i-Con picture to every construction knowledge model structural piece). This deductibility states that the i-Con picture occurs by recognizing the real-world relationship between the objects.

To minimize conceptual agents' efforts for further communication, the i-Con similarly to the object should promote an evolving understanding of the underlying semantics of the i-Con picture. The more negotiation devices or systems being used, the more cognitive work is taken to support decisions, along with several or variations of reasoning processes [90].

5.3 A TECHNIQUE TO AUTOMATIC SEGMENTATION OF WORKERS' MEASURES FOR PSYCHOLOGICAL PROFILING

Successful testing fields of architecture include image recognition monitoring and monitoring for site data collection. Due to the growing frequency of security cameras on the worksite and the expense and easy-to-acquaint design of data gathering for these cameras, performance assessment, efficiency tracking, quality rules, and environmental perception tracking have been implemented. A view-based motion monitoring technique for the behavioral analysis of construction professionals, in general, was recently examined for security [90].

5.3.1 Data Collection

Three-dimensional collection data could be used as a source for information for the simulation of movement pathways and for identifying the human body variables unique to a given topic. The Humid repository [100], which was developed using a performance capture method based on the markings, is one of the publicly available movement repositories. The statistical solutions discussed in this work were collected using the Humid data on a treadmill with three various rates (1.0 mm −1, 1.5 m −1, and 2.0 mm −1), with two stable participants: one female and one male. Because the contribution of this project is the lower movement of the body, the only important marks on the spinal cord and limbs are seen in Figure 5.2. Open Sim is the basis for the simulation of the human skull [94]. No additional development kit features or simulation tools have been used. Human bearing is an almost periodical activity that can be separated in the position and swing of the two main bearing movements and, dependent on the used model, could further be classified into different subs-phases. In the initial contacts, loading responses, mid-positions, terminal postures, and pre-swing stages, the swing process consists of original, central, and peripheral swings. The interval of time for the full guide period of the respective leg is described by two sequential first-floor contacts of the same leg [91].

- **Feature Extraction**

     An image segmentation strategy is first required to obtain main advantages from the obtained model to detect high-dimensional data and increase prediction performance. In our sample, the effects of identification for raw data were imprecise. Therefore, the measurements of the kernel central ingredient (kernel PCA) were originally counted at 78 and reduced to 3. The PCA kernel is a valuable way for non-linear computing to calculate the kernel matrix (e.g., the computation matrix) and use the Eigen decomposition to playback results [73]. This system is thus useful for removing key structures that have huge eigen principles in the decomposed eigen vector space, as well as for duplicating non-linear statistics such as sign data. This means that mobilization in our previous research, including multiple sub-actions, can be effectively converted to a low-dimensional navigation [92].

5.3.2 Motion Classification

Action databases are divided into three behavior using the converted data sets in just three components (i.e., stepping up, working, and stepping down). Of the 25 loops, one was being used as a prototype, while the other 24 were used for test results, and the prototypes were thus graded. In other phrases, one loop of movement data sets was initially split into three data subsets, each of which was a prototype to calculate the similarities with classification algorithms. The DTW was used to measure the distance from and prototype to the three training samples thread; when the interval between two consecutive data sets was small, it was identical. The activities are ultimately marking the prototype with the shortest number from the data set; for instance, the data set classifies as step-up when it is the quickest route between a database and a step-up prototype of three parameters [93].

     Categorization errors, representing the percentage of wrongly categorized data sets, have been determined for output measurement by 25 times over-validation, i.e., of 25 cycles, each is an iterative process chosen in turn as a reference and validated for 24 cycles each time the iteration takes place. Validation data results indicate 76% of the overall accuracy of the classification method.

The findings also show that the precision of the movement data (e.g., the 13th cycle data set) as the model can be increased to up to 93%. In this context, individual behaviors must be recognized in motion data to choose a prototype. Therefore, individual workplace movements can be measured and used to find an optimum example to identify goal movement for the accurate measurement of construction professionals. This technique will also help solve a problem with motion differences that vary from person to person using precise samples of employees' motion to identify one's movements. The collection of the motion prototype will be facilitated because the number of staff on a single job is restricted and the scope of motion detection in the analysis is limited to previously specified movements (e.g., vital dangerous measures) such as moving a device and material up the ladder. The classification method proposed, therefore, has considerable potential to detect individual behavior robustly and systemically [94].

5.4 AN INTEGRATION FRAMEWORK FOR THE DECISIONS ON CONSTRUCTIONS USING CASE-BASED REASONING

A responsible party uses mountains of solutions that can be obtained from other programs following the mandate. For the decision-making of the building project, case-oriented thinking which is the method of addressing current issues, based on ideas from previous experience, is commonly used [95].

5.4.1 EXPERT SYSTEMS

One of the cognitive technologies is an immersive computer programmer, with decision, experience, laws or thumb, instincts, and other skills, to offer intelligent guidance on various tasks. Expert solutions for a wide range of any challenge which is currently resolved by using expert experience and pattern recognition method. Compared to a human expert, expert programs have many valuable features. It is constant, simple, documentable, accessible, and cheap.

There are two key elements of an expert system: the body of knowledge and the activation function. The basis of understanding is the compilation of decision-making data and laws. The deduction mechanism is the machine component of determining what facts and laws to implement to take decisions, shown in Figure 5.1 [96].

Case-based reasoning. Case-based reasoning is a method that addresses the problem using ideas from previous situations to resolve problems. The solution to a current problem is to find a related case and reuse it in new challenges. There are two key theories on case-based logic, that common problems have similar solutions, and after problems occur, they appear to occur again. It is commonly used in building projects such as building planning, decision-making, arranging, and expense calculations, where previous expertise and understanding as seen in Figure 5.2

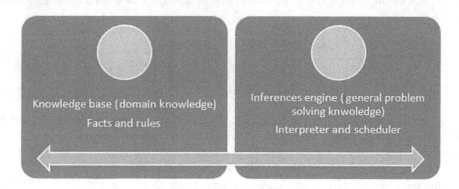

FIGURE 5.1   The structure of an expert system.

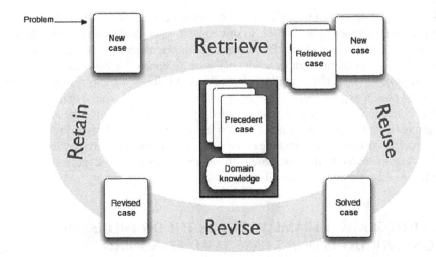

FIGURE 5.2   The case-based reasoning cycles [98].

must be considered. The following four mechanisms will explain case-based reasoning: the four REs [97].

- The most analogous case is RETRIEVE.
- REUSE the expertise to fix the dilemma in this situation.
- REVISE the solution suggested.
- RETAIN for the potential problem-solving portion of this training.

GA-CBR Model. In past research, case-based reasoning-cost frameworks using genes were suggested in the laboratory. A particular case can be constructed by weighing its attributes properly as a dependent variable (estimated target; expense, time, etc.).

$$C_i = X_{i1}W_1 + X_{i2}W_2 + \ldots + X_{ij}W_j$$

where
C_i is the dependent variable of ith case
X_{ij} is the value of a jth attribute of the ith case
W_j is the weight of jth attribute

When this relationship is expanded to an asset of general cases, it is described by the matrix formula below.

$$\begin{pmatrix} X_{11} & \ldots & X_{1j} \\ \vdots & \ddots & \vdots \\ X_{i1} & \ldots & X_{ij} \end{pmatrix} \times \begin{pmatrix} W_1 \\ \vdots \\ W_j \end{pmatrix} = \begin{pmatrix} C_1 \\ \vdots \\ C_i \end{pmatrix} \tag{5.1}$$

To make a range of weights from 0 to 1, assuming that all attributes and the dependent variable are normally distributed, they are converted to a standard cumulative distribution.
where
C_i is the dependent variable of ith case (standardization), $0 \le c_i \le 1$
X_{ij} is the value of jth attribute of ith case (standardization), $0 \le x_i \le 1$
W_j is the weight of jth attribute, $0 \le w_j \le 1$

Attribute weights are optimized to minimize the sum of the absolute value of the distance by genetic algorithms.

By using attributes and measurements, similar instances are retrieved from the index. The standard deviation of an objective case is determined by calculation.

Based on genetic algorithms, this approach can achieve accurate results. Calculating the time, therefore, is slower than other approaches, such as the technique of backpropagation and the study of many regressions [98].

5.4.2 Expert System Using Case-Based Reasoning

Different reviews on the expert method have been written over a long-time span. Nevertheless, few experiments have been done on the integration of intelligent machines and testimonials. The four-RE processes for case-based reasoning act as a mechanism for the inference mechanism in the expertise method suggested in this study. The expertise weighted and event repository shapes the information base. The collections of characteristics, which represent the expert's decision-making thinking, are contained in the expert system's body of knowledge. Moreover, prior cases involving difficulties and remedies are still contained in the system [99].

Process of the expert system using case-based reasoning. Figure 5.3 illustrates the expert method mechanism by case-based argumentation. User feedback constructing details on the user interface to resolve the present challenge. Similar incidents are extracted from the case library based on evidence-based weighs, and for this query, the approach of similar instances is proposed. The solutions suggested shall be amended and restored if appropriate. Lastly, in cases of potential conflict resolution, the response to the current problem is kept as the latest release. The case-based reasoning process is split into two key components of the optimization technique, and the operator communicates with a user experience with the expert system [100].

The closest neighbor would be developed by experts to implement expert expertise to the scheme. The choices would be dependent on the views of the specialist and his expertise. By using measured Euclidean distances as followed, the importance of attributes is determined.

$$d_i^{(w)} = \left[\sum_{j=1}^{n} w_j^2 \left(x_{pij} - x_{qij} \right)^2 \right]^{\frac{1}{2}} = \left(\sum_{j=1}^{n} w_j^2 x_{ij}^2 \right)^{\frac{1}{2}} \tag{5.2}$$

where

$d_i^{(w)}$ is the weighted Euclidean distance of the ith case

W_j is the weight of jth attribute

X_{pij} is the value of a jth attribute of the ith original case

X_{qij} is the value of a jth attribute of ith solution case

Attribute weights are optimized to minimize the sum of the weighted Euclidean distance by genetic algorithm. Through this process, expert knowledge is modeled as combinations of attribute weights. It is stored in a knowledge base and utilized for retrieving a similar case in case-based reasoning.

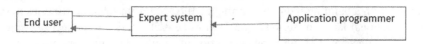

FIGURE 5.3 The process of the expert system using case-based reasoning method of calculating expert weight.

5.5 CONSTRUCTION AND SAFETY OF AN EMERGING EDUCATIONAL ENVIRONMENT THROUGH THE MERGER OF COMPETITIVE MATCHES AND 4D PLAN

To assess the feasibility of the study theory, an immersive multi-user virtual reality may be created and implemented for designers and site supervisors with an H & S preparation background. This involves the discovery and application in the other sectors and areas of study of advantageous learning methods [101].

5.5.1 STATE OF THE ART IN THE CONSTRUCTION INDUSTRY

The building has issues with the implementation and observation of approaches and practices to health and safety. Wong et al. [102] have carried out analytical research on building workforce patterns to forecast potential demands for preparation. Their work emphasizes the need for the building industry to be prepared to provide qualified employees the necessary work areas in a constantly evolving business environment. This ensures that providing enough preparation for these workers in a short time frame is the secret to this workforce management. The market looks to use 3D visualization development systems more fully developed and with greater emphasis on social media technologies [86]. With these established innovations, the engineering team seeks to use the technology to create data models that are appropriate for better clarification [102].

Rubin [95] examined the applications and the benefits of microprocessor training in engineering. The engineering engaged in the delivery of an immersive 3D environment has grown and sophisticated virtual environments are becoming more popular on the Internet. If such technologies grow, they offer more possibilities for expanding training on augmented reality in other fields.

In the building industry, numerous applications of new immersive 3D technologies have been investigated for the training of workers. Many of them were very basic design demos. There were also very ambitious learning platforms for other academic ventures that cross the borders of serious games and immersive learning.

Scope and personalization of the virtual environments are the major distinctions. This study explores alternative ways of creating the material of a simulated training system. Another distinction is that this research aims to extend the development of sites to allow various users to replicate their locations within the international arena and to produce a more precise site environment for their apprentices than conventional training instruments [103].

5.5.2 SERIOUS GAMES AND H&S TRAINING

The incorporation of technologies and techniques linked to video games in a more industrial context is becoming an enticing offer for others. Getchell et al. researched the integration of multiuser virtual and immersive media technology research methods [82]. Virtual experiences also influence the development of learning within organizations and how it can support employee training. This thesis aims to extend these frameworks to examine how technology can be used to create a teaching experience in the industry. The recent work in this area has concentrated on finding a basic training strategy for a crisis. We are aiming with this analysis to build a more modular toolkit. The use of a sandbox system in a severe competitive arena also must be stringently implemented. The 3D experience would automatically orient them to the desired learning outcomes by deliberately defining how users communicate with the game world. In the film sector, this becomes more popular and appears to suit naturally with a building industry training facility. Many up-job opportunities to merge the optimistic instructional facets of serious games with the 4/5D modeling project execution ability. By combining the concepts of 4D with the conception of simulated training environments, a deeper sense of truth in consumer minds is hoped for.

It has been shown that virtual prototyping of building operations is useful for construction works. This kind of virtual model appears to be a top-down company, concentrating on administration and scheduling. Will this be helpful if it were lower part centered? Through personalizing the platform and using it at all stages of training for workers, they may observe the site proactively and become conscious that they encounter possible challenges and problems in a secure atmosphere. The current study explores the incorporation of technology structures, particularly those in open-world technology, to find out how they can provide significant benefits to engineering workflows. The needs of a testing environment differ in terms of the required educational experience between fire suppression and building practice. Dugdale's tools saw users communicating in the same virtual world with their surroundings through a Microprocessor with different users.

The job is far more concentrated by building a designated environment for user testing or training. This allows the learning results to be organized into the basic lessons the curriculum wishes to teach. It looks like the setup of an early game. The suddenness of this interface framework makes it common for immediate tasks like learning. This strategy makes it possible to construct simulations quickly and effectively. The emphasis of substantial research in the framework acts as a teaching medium of serious games. This style of virtual learning's formal essence is often comparable to learning simulations or seminars, providing certain generalizability to development knowledge.

Nonlinear gameplay situations are beginning to be discussed in a building set for preparation. Even today's efforts remain rooted in architecture focused on scenarios. This indicates that the industry might benefit from a sandbox strategy if open-world design provides useful learning results to compare with a more oriented set of circumstances player.

5.5.3 SANDBOX ENVIRONMENTS AND MISSION HUBS

The main source of strength for creating the emerging virtual education world is famous computer games in the sandbox format including the Grand Theft Auto series. These types of games are normally organized around a quest center where players put content, thinking their audiences would enjoy. This hub is intended to provide a sense of plausibility in the world, enabling players to explore the broader ecosystem and to advance through the game, guiding players toward the specific objectives and encouraging the player to decide when to initiate this advancement. In the GTA sequence, this is done in the shape of an extensive town with a simulated population. The objective center also consists of a variety of game modes or story missions, with or without players. The aim will provide more condensed material than a complete mission to these unique game-playing components and to allow players to engage with the mission hub as a true setting and not to hinder development.

A set of circumstances framework offers an instant pathway to education from a pedagogical viewpoint. The atmosphere should be described to allow users to meet academic problems while entering. The experience architecture also enables users to increasingly enter the virtual world and to face tiered tasks based on the previously acquired skills. There are various and different problems to tackle in an emerging learning climate in the simulator style. Because of its open-plan layout, the atmosphere has a modified version and flow. If users engage with the world, a free wandering exploring feature as part of the learning process should be permitted. The setting should be personable in various ways: learning difficulties in the virtual space should not be sequential. Some drawbacks to the learning environment have grown around game elements. The traditional pedagogical foundation for the creation of such games generally has its roots in teaching. This adds to the layout of the game being limited by the kinds of games currently seen in classrooms, usually basic roles or much-focused demos. The way people view interactive technology suggests that this teaching and learning has a barrier to preventing a more playful approach by having the digital entertainment components involved and presenting instructional material as the scene of the play. In the building sector, the educational resources focusing on on-site management and health and security concerns also benefit from educational contexts.

The very essence of the business ensures that any comprehensive teaching method will often benefit from a construction or strategy context for planning and management. If a training tool helps visitors to discover safety and health hazards as they replicate a website accurately, the planner or the developer may explore the platform with the same tool. In this way, they may study their buildings and see issues that are less apparent than a 3D or 4/5D model of their site layout or entry. This chapter will look at architectural safety and security, human-centric architecture, immersive learning experiences, web tools, emerging technology, and 4D modeling as part of a way of building a virtual sandbox world, which reflects a building's existence. Instead of solely a set of circumstances learning effects, the teaching and learning of developing a virtual world focus upon the simulated space providing some of the learning results.

5.5.4 Design of the Virtual Environment

This chapter is based on the premise that a comprehensive and fully implemented virtual training facility offers more additional potential than a deliberately restricted virtual education situation. To do this, a comprehensive site in the virtual world needs to be developed. In this case, a true simulation of life was committed to ensuring that the simulated model is a fully open-world community. To do so, Morgan Ashur's decided to participate in a case study, and a comprehensive series of architectural drawings and a proposal were obtained. A fire escape schematic was collected in comparison to these. This is important for creating a replacement website since it contains existing buildings in the site architecture. These wooden shelters are necessary to make a living building feel but are not included in standard design schemes.

This "OpenSim" design has been used to restore this simulated platform, mainly because of the built-in feature supporting the interaction of several users with one another and the world. The construction plans and 3D models were introduced systematically into the setting. This model was then developed in several parts reflecting building processes, as in a more conventional 4D modeling instrument. Then these parts were clustered according to the task and their materials and their location were used to physically distinguish which constructs were part of the task. This enables the site to be connected to the timetable by constructing the setting in this way. The engineering "Holodeck" will make use of it. This is a mechanism in which the atmosphere in OpenSim can be modified with a good understanding from one world to another. The influence of the main diagonal that was in a standard 4D model is replicated with that. This engineering will be used to show how the site looks according to anywhere a simulator or scenario is required by connecting specific models to beginning and end dates for each job.

A variety of related training examples have been created to bring H&S learning to the community. These simulations demonstrate the possible use of this instrument by enabling trainees to communicate almost in the same way as on-site. The efficiency of learning environments can be tested by using predetermined simulations. The research situations are intended to model real-life experiences rather than a particular learning situation. In such a situation, the product means for the users are in line with a typical position in this context. It encourages users to work with the environment over time that enables them to achieve their given work rather than to optimize their "learning opportunities by putting the criteria of the position with the front center." This is critical because the objective is to enable them to engage with the world really or realistically. The collection of educational outcomes will inspire you to look through these tutorials but would make the world fake since a real site is not viewed in this way.

These simulations are considered smaller group activities with an educator available to assess the success of the technician. The users can also get input so their impressions can be documented. This allows you to assess the comparable success of both your preparation and your reactions. The disadvantage of this open educational process is that not all apprentices can explore all the accessible teaching methods in digital reality. It is expected that the dialogue with the apprentice community would help them to assess the performances of each other by constructing practice as a community exercise to make them understand why different individuals have different safety hazards.

A series of research sessions will be held to assess the test conditions concerning the training aspect of the project. Many users are simultaneously involved in the software. A direct session and a free session will be held to measure the global environment's opportunity to access information with its clients. The conference will focus on environmental interaction and interface topics and includes the use of established H&S teaching materials including orientation videos and toolbox discussions. A person representing the website masters can direct the learning world experience. This allows the collection of data on how responsive the world is to be manipulated. The free session consists of users performing tasks and allowing users to communicate without specific instructions with the environment. This is where the main feedback is gathered from the efficacy of the classroom environment. In the field of digital virtual environments, very few assessment systems exist [74]. Previous scholars have given attention to the fields of fully immersive assessment and provided some promising ideas to improve performance measures in the field under study. De Freitas's thesis provides a valuable basis for the implementation of input and assessment systems to be established in this chapter during the testing process of the study. This study hopes that as part of the suggestions, some of Augustin's approaches for individual qualifications are adopted where possible. By allowing users to dive into the world for a longer time, their actions can provide information about how people want to communicate with the app. This data would improve the emerging learning approaches used in the community. In the two test conditions, all experiments will be done. The results from the first filtering into the second picture and the post-match make a distinction between the goals and achievements.

5.6 COMMUNICATING DEVICES BASED ON AN INDEPENDENT LANDSLIDE MONITORING PROGRAM

Mudslides are seismic earth changes or pitfalls that can destroy civil structures seriously. Over the years, there have been reports of several deaths and microscopic cracks caused by landfall. Measuring and controlling future landslides is also crucial for human security and the protection of civil infrastructure. To track the activity of the slopes, human experts have mounted surveillance devices or manual examinations.

5.6.1 SLOPE FAILURE FORECASTING

So many techniques have been established for slope failure prediction [70]. A procedure based on the inverse speed of surface motion is used in this article. Fukuzono [76], who carried out massive experimental studies to model rain-induced landslides, introduced the principle of reverse velocity for the prediction of downhill collapse. Laboratory environments are known as typical of accelerated momentum charging creep environments. The evaluation of experimental data showed that the speed of divided into numerous and ground transformation can be compared to:

$$D^2x/dt^2 = A(dx/dt)^a \tag{5.3}$$

In the following equation, x is backward, d^2x/dt^2 is the acceleration, dx/dt is the speed, and A and α are variables based on the incline properties [77]. The experiments in the laboratory also showed that when the reverse speed function of time is calculated, the values of reverse speed are near zero as the ground rotation eye movements toward the last pitch failure. Designed graphically, the gradient failure time can be projected at the fact at which the drift line through values of reverse velocity crosses the abscissa axis. The equipment located should explain this association among speed and breakdown period as suggested by Fukuzono [76].

$$V^{-1} = \{A(\alpha-1)\}^{\frac{1}{\alpha-1}} \cdot \left(t_f - t\right)^{\frac{1}{\alpha-1}}, \tag{5.4}$$

__ where V^{-1} is the inverse velocity of surface displacement and t_f is the failure time. Depending on the values of α, the curve of inverse velocity is linear ($\alpha=2$), concave ($\alpha<2$) or convex ($\alpha>2$).

5.6.2 Autonomous Landslide Monitoring System

The landslide surveillance device aims to track dangerous pitch beginning movements. When the thermal expansion of the pre-failure path is observed, the system informs citizens automatically of potential disruptions. Suitable extracts from the determined pitch are collected continuously and can be used for exact pitch diagnosis. The risk monitoring device automatically adjusts the opposing speed and determines where and when natural hazards can be forecast. The specification of the implemented test system is presented. The device has two parts: a wireless sensor network and a server application.

Wireless sensor network. A system of wireless sensors has sensors, a processing board, and a three-axis motion sensor. To gather accelerometer sensors and to perform in-situ measurements of the observed incline, mobile application agents are incorporated into the wireless sensor network. A computer program is an independent and scalable software application that can perform a certain process without direct human interaction [103]. Software components communicate with the ability to respond to environmental conditions. To resolve difficult challenges virtual environments should work together. Several agents can simultaneously carry out time-consuming data processing and computational activities to improve the output of the machine, essential for tracking processes in real-time.

Three groups of computer programs are specified and included in each Mobile Sensor Network to provide a modular device design: a manager agent, a sensor multipack agent, and an evaluation agent. The Manager Agent facilitates coordination between the actors in the various sensor network and between the agents and the database. At a certain sampled intensity, the sensor multipack agent extracts acceleration data from the path and sends them to the analytic agent. The Sensor Sampler Agent also decides the sensor inclination, and if detected, records tilt adjustments. The analytical agent defines the motion of the node and thus reflects the deflections of the node's installation setting.

Radio links are important for coordination between the sensor network and the severe device. Since radio transmissions use a great deal of battery capacity, the number of data transmissions should be minimized. The Sensor Instrument Agent and the Observation Agent correspond to Agents located on another sensor network through with a common radio link with the management agency by transferring information to the Manager Agent and then transmitting them to the beneficiaries of other sensor nodes (managed by the Manager Agent) instead of numerous connections being created.

The Observation Agent passes an order to the management agent when a sensor node is in the movement to alert all the other modules and devices. As a direct outcome of an observed movement, the frequency response of each node is increased, and the server device begins to analyze the global pitch condition. The analytical agent also calculates the reverse momentum of the sensor network using the obtained acceleration data according to the procedure mentioned previously. The manager operator delivers the results to the server machine from the reverse speed review. The multi-agent architecture allows modern analytics to quickly expand the capabilities of the wireless sensor nodes.

Server system. The server framework enables people to interface with the network of wireless sensors. Data are saved by the registry system and comprehensive analyzes are carried out. In addition, where the results of the reverse metaheuristic techniques of each sensor network are not received by the server device, attempts are often made to create a connection with the sensor network. If it is not successful, domain operators would be aware of potential sensor dysfunction by email. The server can view all calculated data and data analysis findings through a Java-based script. Data requests can be submitted for viewing current geographic information to wireless nodes. The program also requires data plots to be saved in Pdf format.

5.6.3 LABORATORY TESTS

The efficiency of the experimental downhill control system will be validated by laboratory experiments. Machine agents' functional requirements are analyzed to assess the exactness of the inverse velocity system. A sand slope is subject to inundation to show the principle, leading to the ground movement (i.e., land sliding).

Laboratory test setup. The module's diameter is 42 cm. A sandpit with 45° inclined is constructed with a sand concentration of 1.56 g/cm³ and a sand-based ratio of 0.7; the void ratio defines how mussel shells are packaged. A sandy pitch is constructed with a 45° orientation and an overall sand-based density. A nullity ratio of 0.7 shows the sand being medium. On the top of the gradient floor, the developed prototype nodes S1 and S2 are mounted. The integrated agents are housed in every sensor network. A system of wireless sensors has sensors, a processing board, and three-axis motion sensor. To gather accelerometer sensor and to perform in-situ measurements of the measured incline, mobile applications agents are incorporated into wireless sensors. A computer program is an independent and scalable software application that can perform a certain process without direct human interaction [103]. Software components communicate with the ability to respond to changes in the external environment. To resolve difficult challenges virtual environments should work together. Several agents can simultaneously carry out time-consuming data processing and computational activities to improve the sample rates to be raised to 0.01 Hz immediately. The inverse speed values are measured and then sent to the database system for further processing and visualization, based on the momentum results. On the peak of the mountain, there is a crack in a total of 14 liters of spilled water that leads to a further uphill movement and a complete drainage problem.

5.7 A COMBINING FOR A TIME-EFFICIENT ASSESSMENT OF A SIMULATION STUDIO IN STRUCTURAL ENGINEERING: COLORED PETRI-NET AND MULTI-AGENTS

Computation is an important method for software development to measure and evaluate the effect of this complexity on the whole project [71]. Some professionals oppose simulations because the project is pushed into a set time frame and budget of the project. However, using a simulator remains straightforward to gain more and better knowledge to support a decision and improve its reliability [71]. This is shown by About Rizk's experiences in the simulator industry [68], for instances of complexity, demonstrates that the simulator is most efficient.

5.7.1 SIMULATION MODEL

The numerical simulation suggested is a subscription vehicle made up of combinations of a Petri-net probabilistic color model with a multi-agent model. A Petri-net model is based on the well-defined execution semanticist. The implementation of the CiSmo method model and its association with the modeling approach specializes in numerical simulation for infrastructure projects. Any agent's action is subjective, making the suggested framework a multi-target model.

CiSmo process model. It is involved in development projects [88]. Its structured model consists of building approaches that are closely related to object types rather than units. Each building approach describes several building projects and each operation involves various tasks. The building operations follow the architecture pattern of the listener and any operation is a listener of incidents and an event generator simultaneously. The "A3: build calcareous wall 11.5" activity, for example, includes the tasks "T1: construct" and "T2: make opportunities." The first functioning section was accepted for starting the task and the project measures are listened to (or waiting for): "activity A1: building calcareous walls 17.5 in one floor and every work environment" and "6 days have elapsed since the conclusion of operation A2, constructing RC walls 25.5 in the same floor in all working areas." When the operation is completed, the event "Cal cutaneous construction wall 11.5 on the floor is over" will be shot.

Deterministic colored Petri-net model. The method is described as the data set <P, T, W, M, C> where P is a set of places, T is a universal number of the manufacturing work from the data process, W is a finite set of arks that reflect precedent and arrangement inter-dependence between the tasks. The model is the amount of purchase integral part of the financial, development capital required, and transformation must meet the goal.

One token is consumed at each input point of a permitted transfer and one symbol is generated at each output point. In addition, any token has an associated token color, which the transformations will identify. It consists of four transformations of various types: phase, broken transformation, duration, and synchronized. The following how the systematic approach is mapped to a Petri-net system used in the preceding part.

A Petri-net is typically created for the system info, based on a collection of structured texture information. This network forms part of the project's implementation strategy in terms of assignments, instructions for workflows, and connections of dependence. Thus, modifications to process details, such as the modification of the part style construction system or the assignment of separate processing equipment to the mission, usher in a change Petri-net that is somewhat different from the previous one. This fact would help the subsequent simulation platform to construct first and only one international Petri-net, but also a dualist one.

Objective-driven multi-agent's model. The template is composed of four groups of agents; one project manager who has the color ID, one manager for the allocation of resources, one account executive, and a one-time delivery manager. The interactions of agents and interactive design are established [89]. Their environment is the petri-net that signifies the project implementation proposal. In addition, standard deployments of the agent characteristics are established and their specific behaviors, yet also sufficient for implementing and injecting the actions of a support assistant into a specification to incorporate the new goals. This turns the framework into an intuitive design. In the perspective of the systems engineer, the central device dispatcher is assessed for the transfer protection speech. The team should work with the resources administrators available to carry out the project through the required resource assignment manager. Managers for the distribution of resources are categorized by resource sort, name, and ID. Each template of simulations comprises a project manager who is allocated to a Petri-net, color, diverse organizational assignment managers, diverse organizational bosses, and timeshare supervisors.

5.7.2 SIMULATION FRAMEWORK

Our objective is to create a system that concurrently executes more than one mathematical model successfully. In addition to comparing these approaches with time, length, and resource use, the outcomes would then be various project timelines, the major elements of the architecture form.

Simulation engine. It is a parallel programming engine that uses an adaptive clock manager to speed up simulations. The beneficiary shall pull the flags out of the net that matches the color of the agent. It, therefore, manages correspondence between participants, so that all finished tokens are consumed, and new quantities produced. The symbols that are saved in the database system reflect the operation. The requisite information can be found on each token, such as related mission, date of creation, end date, resources allocated, and tracking of decision-making activities.

Agents' pool and IoC controller. The part of the pools would be where agents are protected and named during operation. Appeals are made using an IoC controller (inversion of control pattern).

The basic function of the IoC controller is to make the system interactive and maintain soft interactions between agents. According to their background, agents are reported with the IoC.

Global Petri-net. This network represents a union only within a numerical simulation of all other Petri networks (all the project implementation plans). After this step, there will be many positions in its preset or post-collection that may have upward of one transformation.

The assumption that a Petri-net maintains the current performance utilizing tokens maintains the execution sophistication quite relevant to the performance requirements of MOSAICA. In other words, only awaiting symbols (~20 tokens, that amount is assumed in the investigation) that reside in places are regulated in any clock period rather than searching at all net locations (~300 places for this test case) to retrieve all allowed transformations.

In addition, the universal Petri-net, the community of all networks, saves the running memory. It constructs only one net (<400, 400> from the testing ground registered) To illustrate more, the model can also differentiate between business planning rather than keeping several almost equivalent networks in the memory (in this trial case: 100 * <300, 300>).

The total variation stage also decreases the number of implementation cycles and controls required. In this scenario, the average stage size for operating an agent, i.e., 40 times quicker was 40 minutes instead of 1 minute. One hundred employees simultaneously shortened the stage size to 16 minutes, i.e., 16 times quicker, and one of the employees needed about 450,000 minutes to carry out the process.

5.8   CONCLUSION

A key move is to create a structured specification paradigm to explain knowledge relevant to DAQ tools and facilitate the visualization among research questions and DAQ tools to increase the importance of using DAQ technology to collect necessary field data from the construction projects.

This study developed intellectual geometrical topologies for mathematics analysis of construction elements (i-Con) based on a semiotic structure that enables the agent to monitor aspects, descriptions, and constructions in the i-Con language. Furthermore, i-Con usage is intended to reflect deliberate proposals by encoding results. The desired spatial reference of the construction elements would be better explained by this function as static pictorial imagery (e.g., BIM and 3D object parts), which are restricted to individual design perspectives.

The behaviors, without much human intervention and effort, can be calculated. The assessed data, therefore, have a tremendous ability to improve protection through input on the actions of employees and the determination of appropriate management methods for behavior change.

The new approach extends case-based reasoning to software experts, who can be referred to as "case-based development of technology." However, sustainability has left a great deal of space for change relative to current ones.

The primary focus of this research is on aspects such as 4D planning, emerging playing, and sandboxing. If an interface is provided which is easier to learn and communicate with, a greater amount of instruction can be provided for any person.

The significant benefit of the device is that it monitors the paste without prolonged human intervention relative to traditional avalanche control systems. In addition, the use of wireless sensor nodes avoids the costs of cable deployment and repair. According to the program agents' stability and inventiveness, the effective reduction of the calculated data is accomplished through resource efficiency.

The proposed method simulator multi-objective framework allowed for various overarching goal situations to be generated. MOSAICA has identified a wide variety of design approaches in milliseconds at the same time as the proposed analytical architecture.

6 Automated Building Information System in Civil

6.1 RECOVERY OF THE 3D STRUCTURE OF THE INEFFICIENTLY GENERATED INFRASTRUCTURE SCENERY

Most traditional depth perception procedures have used corner functionalities like those in the 3D regeneration phase, in particular, camera motion estimation; this is due to their cross-tabulation, allowing them to be more easily matched in various visual viewpoints [104], a foundational mission in the Motion Structuring (SfM) process. In non-textured situations such as clean building facades or roof constructions, corner locations are, unfortunately, not sufficiently available; this produces volatility in these procedures that might lead to project failures. Software businesses are obliged to double attempts in the preparation of export operations that have many views containing the identical interchange architecture. A conceptual platform is being developed to construct model views based on object-focused, verifiable, and repeatable informational subsystems, known as Semantic Exchange Module (SEM) components. We offer a set of SEM development criteria and a technique for providing SEM-based modeling representations. The effect of this chapter is highlighted by comparing current approaches with the new technique employing SEMs. This section presents a critical examination for the establishment of countable regulations on building standards that may be used in automation communications systems—BIM–based. It also discusses, for architects and scientists, the complexities of these conceptualizations and the management and advancement techniques of these systems.

Different methodologies were employed to enhance the importance of information exchanges established by the Industry Foundation Class (IFC) for defensible validation methodologies. In addition, the instruments and procedures necessary to fulfill such efforts will improve research requiring knowledge building. Building Information Modeling (BIM), which can lead to less disagreement and better coordination, is now mandated by many proprietors to be used for major infrastructure projects. However, they frequently don't know what BIM supplies and procedures to request, or how competent these technologies are for the partners with whom they seem to want to contract. The purpose of this investigation is to help facility owners to embrace and maturely deploy BIM procedures via assessment of their existing situation with BIM. It estimates the share of the owners who now require BIM, using a poll of property managers. Which standards for BIM deliverables are specified and if they are used for post-construction infrastructure upgrades. BIM has to be extended into the structure's quality assurance phase beyond 2–3 months of construction and operation, to streamline chores such as servicing and optimize its value for assigning resources. This leads to the wastage of building elements at the building maintenance phase, where they have most of their usefulness. The objective is to overcome the lack of communication between both the specialists involved in designing and building maintenance. It also concentrates on automated, two-way communications among computerized maintenance management system (CMMS) and BIM representations at the level of the databases.

6.1.1 BACKGROUND

A 3D reconstructing video grammar architecture consists of several different processes, involving data collecting that used a correct camera recording (e.g., single-, binocular-, or multi-camera rig),

DOI: 10.1201/9781003211938-6

feature identification, and aligning/monitoring (e.g., corner positions or straightening line). Since the paper's recommendations occur in the corresponding features and camera movements evaluation phases, the additional context for both procedures is only provided in this part.

In recent years, automated designs to match functions have been extensively investigated. The local district is characterized in multi-dimensional skill by most of the effective techniques developed for this reason [105]. The development of local, range image, and identifiers such as SIFT [131] and SURF [111] solved the challenge of matching feature points satisfactorily. However, a far lesser number of experiments have been done for line-feature finding compared to template matching, which makes this a challenge. The following were offered, by Schmidt and Zisserman [143]: (1) orthogonality geometric limits for small foundation equivalence line endpoints and (2) single flat served as powerful parameters families for huge foundation equivalence. This implementation involves established, not always accessible structural correlations among photos or feature vectors. The first set of feature point email exchanges are employed by the geometric features of Bay et al. [110] and the topological filters are employed to expand the variety of possible pairings. This approach, however, depends largely on color histograms from the immediate village of a portion that's particularly sensitive to light, point, and peripheral vision and the distances between the cameras and the item of concern. It developed a line-based approach based on the notion of segmentation techniques introduced in Lowe [131].

It generates a vector description for each connected component using the local image brightness. This procedure produces poorly for two vectors positioned within object borders when the item's backdrop varies from two views. The explanation is that for a rectangle pixel area surrounding a reference frame, the descriptors vector is created and consequently half-knowledge may modify in two distinct views for a certainly connected component at object borders (Figure 6.1). Comparable to the stepping to complement the features, a considerable study effort was made to locate movement with pointed characteristics although not much was done with the use of lines. It is even less necessary to use a mixed strategy (i.e., points and lines). Corresponding points enable a network of a polynomial function to be generated by geometric limitations [135].

Moreover, not enough relationships could be identified in badly constructed situations such as interior scenarios; so, these approaches are highly likely to struggle. Because line functionality is significant in most human-made contexts, this difficulty may be alleviated. Generally, line characteristics are utilized to generate a multifocal tensor to evaluate camera motion [109]. To increase the computer operational efficiency, Schindler et al. [144] utilized additional data from perpendicular disappearance orientations. Chandraker et al. [117] have provided a hypothesizing and testing methodology for the estimation of a movement of stereo equipment instantaneously from a connected component. This procedure eliminates calculations for enhanced performance and is thus only relevant when the estimated position of the camera placed in unfamiliar surroundings is determined. Pradeep and Lim [138] have merged the information given for points and lines to provide a minimum solution for dynamic brand tachometer performance. This technique generates a system of linear algebraic utilizing the restrictions imposed by two trifocal trigonometric functions and then resolves them using a direct quaternion-based solution strategy. In various phases, this strategy also employs assumptions to preserve the system's performance advantage.

The purpose is to introduce a technique that creates description vectors for rows and columns that take into account the particular scenario for object frontier lines. In addition, a new measurement for the calculation of the line segment prediction error is proposed. Even though this strategy is more computer-enhanced than the opposing strategy, it offers a rather more realistic prediction, the main objective of any existing documents [106].

For each of the identified lines, a descriptive vector must be built for each segment. The first step is to analyze the feature point alignment. The alignment of the local gradient can be found in all pixel resolution in the connected component:

$$\varepsilon = \tan^{-1}\left(dy/dx\right)$$

where ε is the gradients inclination; dy is the vertical gradients of the localized concentration, and dx is the horizontal gradients of the localized concentration. An essential aspect of the slope of the gradient is that the alignment of the reference line in 2D imaging is somewhat similar to that of a straight line. Therefore, an average cost for all images on the lines estimates the direction of the whole line [108].

After calculating the alignment, a line description with the SIFT-like technique is utilized. The community is divided into two categories split by the segment line for that purpose. For each pixel in these frames, the gradient magnitude and inclination will be determined. Then, by deducting the guideline from pixels gradient orientations, the comparative oriented quantities are determined. This allows predictive performance. The 25 values of reference images are utilized for orientation histograms in each window, summarizing the material over eight boxes encompassing 360° [110]. Moreover, the gradients and Gaussian-weighted circular windows of $\sigma = 1,5$ weigh on every comparative orientation value, as indicated in Lowe [132]. The gradient description matrix (GDM) idea is employed two times to take care of the varying lengths of parallel lines. (i.e., gray panes once and white curtains another time) For each L-segment, the length of each matrix is 16 µN, with N being the number of the pixels on L. Therefore, for each L-segment are two GDMs. The standard mean variation of the GDM-constructed vectors is identified and standardized to render the descriptors consistent with nonlinear lighting variations. The middle and standards vector of deviations are then combined to provide a 32-dimensional descriptor vector for each side of the straight line [109].

6.2 INNOVATIVE APPROACHES TO COMPUTERIZED CIVIL INFRASTRUCTURE SELECTING KEY IMAGE SEQUENCES

In recent times, video geometry has been regarded as an economical and convenient tool for 3D spatial perception, notably in the field of production [111]. The viability of video geometry has two main problems when that is used in structural design.

6.2.1 AUTOMATED KEY VIDEO FRAMES EXTRACTION: PROPOSED METHODOLOGY

The primary process of the hypothesized feature point method is illustrated in Figure 6.2. The following methods describe the technological specifics of the proposed algorithm:

Step 1: Low-quality video frame filtering. The process begins with the removal of images of poor quality. We compute the BluM and delete those with a BluM measurement less than the appropriate experimental criterion for the measurement of the integrity from each picture. That the very first picture is then recognized as the first important frame among all the other elevated pictures [112].

Step 2: Overlap and baseline filtering. When the first picture is chosen, a handful of subsequent pictures must be picked as the main picture possibilities. The primary requirements must provide adequate background and overlap between some of the applicants and the first global competence. To accomplish this purpose, we employ [113] correspondent ratio (2010).

Step 3: Degeneracy filtering. These possibilities also eliminate those leading to instances of degeneration and major camera parameter mistakes. To prevent degeneration, a common concept in computing GRIC ratings is proposed in Ref. [113].

Step 4: Selecting the next keyframe. The next stage is to choose the final contender from the rest of the pictures [114]. To this goal, we determine the proportion of inliers in the overall number of email exchanges after computing the foundational and homographic multipliers between applicants and the integrated circuit using RANSAC. Then the score for the final candidate may be calculated:

$$S_H = (1 - \sigma)\underline{S_f} - \underline{S_h}$$

where *SH* and SF are the fractions of wavelet coefficients and basic indices for the calculation of the homographs and σ is the confidence interval that shows the homogeneity of
feature distributions over the frames.

Step 5: Optimizing the number of keyframes. The distinction from the previous studies is
the optimization of the number of reference images retrieved necessary for usage in the 3D
restructuring process [115].

6.3 BIM-ENABLED BUILDING COMMISSIONING AND HANDOVER

Today, AECO has established far more strict requirements to ensure operating performance in the
fields of environmental, productivity, and safety when a project is transferred. The construction
commissioner is one of the industry's most important instruments for performance management.
The Commissioned Procedure, as described by ASHRAE Recommendation 0–2005, is a quality-
oriented procedure for the achievement, verification, and documentation of established targets and
parameters in terms of installation, system, and assembly performances [116].

6.3.1 THE COMMISSIONING PROCESS

Unless a new building or refurbishment is carried out, the certification process starts at the commencement of the project (while the designing or planned stage is in progress) and continued throughout
the development cycle of the facilities (through the Occupancy and Operation or Post-Construction
Phase). It involves particular actions to be performed at each step to ensure that design, training, and
technical compliance with the specifications of the Project Owner (OPR) [105]. Figure 6.1 shows the
certification process flow diagram with important activities stated at each stage. The flux diagram
serves as a basic guide and its argument applies during the whole construction commission, vintage-
inspired and refurbishment processes [117].

Current techniques typically focus entirely on the thread stage of the system assessment and try
to start a one-phase endeavor. The main difficulty with this strategy is that it offers you a chance to
evaluate the outcome of the products and detect any serious development problems before it is too late
and costly to alter. In contrast, Turkaslan-Bulbul and Akin's embedded commissioning method [118],
commissioning is described as an incorporated process of building deliveries that continuously checks
and confirms the design intentions throughout the life cycle of the structure. They determined that the
governance framework should be methodical and standardized to enhance the accuracy of construction
commencement. There should be no differences between distinct commissioning suppliers in test methodologies, assessment methodologies, and commission information. The production methods should be
supported by computing to decrease labor costs and inaccuracies in electronic documents. For various
stages of building assessment to be managed from planning through facility work, efficient commissioned technologies and documentation for architecture commissioners should be preserved on a digital
basis for data interchange reasons. Data created during the project's implementation should be ongoing,
providing further evaluation techniques over the various stages of the building product lifecycle [119].

6.3.2 BIM FOR THE CONSTRUCTION AND TRANSITION OF BUILDINGS

The following characteristics of BIM legitimize its adoption in certification and transfer processes
as a technique for the life cycle information technology:

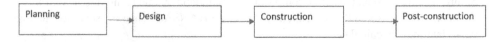

FIGURE 6.1   Non-BIM building commissioning workflow (Adapted from GSA 2005).

- BIM is extensive and abundant in information as all morphological and physiological characteristics of a structure are included [120].
- By output patterns protocols for communication, such as IPC, and other business techniques such as Extensible Markup Language, BIM may store, distribute, and decrypt messages via internal or external applications (XML) [121].
- BIM can conduct diverse, complicated building analyses and simulations economically and in standardized documents, producing meaningful findings.
- BIM covers all phases of the project cycles, and BIM can process the status of these stages to sequence and organize the operation [122].
- BIM fosters cooperation and communication amongst project teams as a single source of data for projects. During each step of licensing,
   1. key activities are performed,
   2. lead stakeholders are included,
   3. anticipated interactions between project teams, and
   4. standardized documents are completed.

In comparison to the non-BIM design and development process as shown in Figure 6.3, the BIM process gathers information collected in the BIM model(s), takes full advantage of the collaboration environment instigated by BIM and carries out design and development activities based on fully integrated dissemination of data between BIM and other institutional and outside implementations made possible by open data. As the project progresses substantially, installation information can be passed from stage to stage, therefore the BIM models are continually upgraded and continuously developing (Figure 6.2) [123].

6.4 SEMANIC INTERCHANGE MODULES CUSTOMIZABLE MODELS FOR THE PRECAST AND/OR PRE-STRESSED CONCRETE INDUSTRY (SEM)

A Model View is a qualifying portion of a building things scheme that gives an overview of the informational ideas required for an interchange of information on an Architecture/Engineering/Construction (AEC) and Facilities Management (FM) process [124]. If several components have been well divided, a module may be utilized again in all settings in which it may be utilized. These semantics communication modules are called SEMs.

6.4.1 SEMANTIC EXCHANGE MODULES (SEMs)

An SEM is a hierarchical module collection of items and connections necessary in each of the several BIM models of exchanges. There are two reasons for that: (1) enable BIM software developers to debug for import and export operations modularly, allowing for the testing of and certification of a single feature published to export or imported method artifacts under any given SEM, and reusing it to fulfill numerous export industries interchange models without any transformation and (2) enable numerous heterogeneity platforms, consumers, to identify an SEM and make it easier for both parties to automatically compile an Exchange MVD [125].

An SEM may be established by defining a bond to a series of IFC entities, characteristics, relationships, and operations and by connecting the appropriate information connected with the IFC

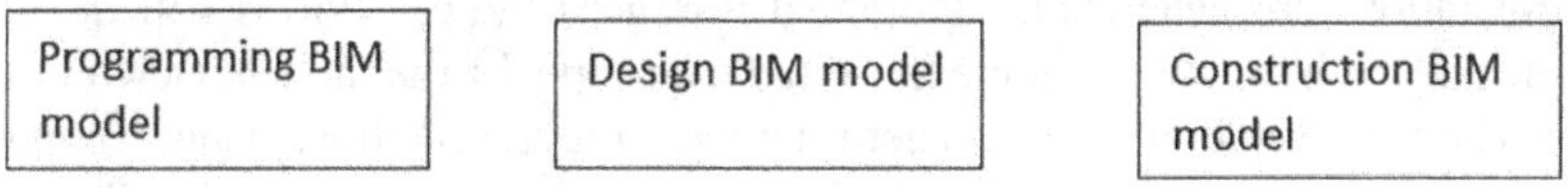

| Programming BIM model | Design BIM model | Construction BIM model |

FIGURE 6.2 BIM-enabled building commissioning workflow.

SEM specification with a set of native modeling techniques. The SEM provides the functions (techniques) required to successfully translate and integrate information between indigenous and the IFC structures with other techniques. SEMs may be used to construct a modeling view after extensive testing, comprised of an organized user to obtain feedback to describe all the content that the exchange apps support in combined. The two technologies create an interchange of dependable knowledge for speaking and listening by picking the same SEMs on their systems [126].

6.4.2 SEM LIBRARY STRUCTURE

SEMs are described as components that link objects dealing with a comparable aspect altogether. Geometry for instance is a SEMS set that addresses a comparable part of the model. Similarly, two SEMS families with substantially the same architecture are constructing element and architectural possible combinations, which make it easier for their relatives to execute or to reuse their architecture [127].

The SEM architecture defined in this study is arranged according to the following requirements:

1. These are aggregation units and hierarchies of IFC entities that do not limit combinatorial usage internal;
2. As permitted by its IFC authorization each SEM must identify all conceivable uses. This implies that its specification needs to be integratable into the prohibited sales are generated, capable of integration with both its predecessors and its subsequent SEM.

The first SEM library is created according to the aforesaid requirements. It aims to adhere to an open-ended philosophy. Once an SEM family is completely specified, it will be shut down, while the SEM library will be open to other SEM families for expansion. Figure 6.6 connects each of the huge boxes with a family of SEM. Each SEM family contains various details with comparable execution at their administrative level. Various measurement configurations indicate distinct meanings of the translation. The choices match DLLs which can be connected to a custom translation during execution. A list and explanations of existing SEMs may be obtained in Refs [128,140].

6.4.3 GENERATION OF SEM MODEL VIEW

Overview: In the industry, we identify the following four separate role categories: (1) the information modeler—the one who, together with the IFC template mappings, sets the SEM family for each domain, (2) the programmer of the program—who exports and imports the SEM structure into the native paradigm, (3) the BIM specialist—who is an expert in fields and understands the interchange needs and the model views, and (4) end-user—who operates on the company's BIM data [129].

The aim is to offer an explanation or demonstration of the concept of SEMs and construct a mathematical model perspective for the AEC/FM industry when it comes to the operating time of the BIM professional. As the case for applying for this study, a prefabricated concrete detailed planning model is used. The structural engineer requires a smooth transmission of data on one side to the prefabricated concrete certified technician and manufacturer on the other (the end-users). Ideally, interactions would be organized and the model perspectives specified by the BIM Expert would indeed be supported from the beginning of a project [130]. These may be carried out using a predetermined external connection. Alternatively, several of these desirable transactions might be continuously designed and maintained autonomously by the exchange parties. Based on SEMs, model representations are generated. Automated instances file creation is still in progress in the native scheme and we have at this moment limited the scope for the models view in the EXPRESS architecture. The future study involves generating model representations using computer programmers in indigenous programming languages. The objective is to illustrate that the architecture of modeling views may be modularized to form biodegradable compartments [131]. This requires a

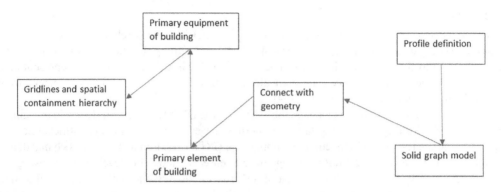

FIGURE 6.3 SEM library structure.

specific definition of how to interchange items of reinforced concrete models using IFC documents in Figure 6.3.

For instance, what IFC entity combinations should be utilized to represent the prefabricated particles? What can be the value of the properties? And what IFC interactions among companies are needed?

Take a look at a parking structure footing case. The design development model is used to validate the design by the designer, for the engineer's architectural project planning, for the landscape architect collaboration and identification of conflicts, as well as for the plant management to produce and sequence manufacturing Depending on product model and the amount of information necessary, there are numerous methods to describe that slab item by utilizing a designing the application architecture such as IFC. The focus is on the IFC data structure, and semanticized clarity of the relevant information of the interchange has to be provided while the amount of detail is increasing. The following can be given five distinct viewpoints of the same model the following [132]:

1. A basic boundaries description of the whole floor slab might be appropriate for conflict detection across several professions such as MEP or electricity.
2. Construction elements in the form of terminals and axes in a stick (analytical) architecture must be displayed for design and analysis needs. 3D geometry is not required, but interconnections and loads are necessary (static and live). The SEM library is expandable and an SEM family structure analysis will be added.
3. The sheet should be shown as a single hollow core board with precise dimensions, comparative arrangement, link details, and overlay characteristics for precast manufacturing 3.
4. The fourth situation is where both the parent plank and the welded steel boards, their overlay, washing, and any materials that are consolidated into the parental board are required. The shape of the parent plate must in this scenario be determined from the joining together of each component (and possibly stored).
5. There is no requirement for locations with different manufacturing and delivery sequences. However, it is of utmost necessity to count pieces and others such as construction sequenced and a project plan.

All five of the aforementioned situations may and may coexist with IFC. This demonstrates the complexity of IFC and its consistency because it covers a broad range of the AEC/FM domain. Successful exchange, therefore, need that an IFC (or any other) scheme is given a layer of special features. SEMs are designed to accurately supply such a layer. This means that users may pick and provide the pertinent information objects from schemas, their properties, and regulations that determine their potential SEM-based responses without having to bother about the fundamental IFC scheme [133].

6.4.3.1 Process

The procedure starts by completing the requirements for an SEM model exchange. We presume that already SEMs are enough to meet the criteria at this point, meaning that the breadth of the model view is limited to the extent of the study. The specified SEMs collections have a representation of the IFC scheme, which produces automatically an EXPRESS design file. Lexical checks from EXPRESS are provided as open sources [134].

The certification procedure involves the following: (1) the EXPRESS architecture file is scanned using the EXPRESS Engines; (2) the faults are notified based on the absent IFC entities, relationships, and characteristics; (3) for accurate mappings the EXPRESS architecture file is changed; and (4) processes 1–3 are continued until all bugs have been corrected. The developers are using the generated EXPRESS file as a legitimate part of the broader IFC scheme. The grammatical testing of the model view produced using SEMs is completed. The modeling representation is generated at this step by building the EXPRESS scheme programmatically and validating it for completion with parsers. The strategy may be mechanized by building a schema Generator to help generate the schema depending on user needs. The planned future functionality is an autonomous model interchange mechanism based on SEMs [135].

Test Cases: The definition of a modeling interchange for choc detection involves a basic description of the border of the floor plane. The SEM library contains the model view menu architecture. Let's suppose that the user picks the plate with B-Rep topology and prefabricated as a substance a high-level object. The modular SEMs inherited from this platform (building component) SEM are the shape, location and materials, and spatial confinement. It should be emphasized that for this particular scenario, the system generates the model representation in the EXPRESS scheme based upon the IFC mapping of SEMs [137].

This viewpoint may be generated in two alternative forms, namely B-rep and geometry extracted, in the IFC template. B-rep and geometric expansion have several uses. B-rep is a basic facial image and is used to calculate volumes and to find clashes. However, extrusion modeling is necessary for more complex operations like modification and parametric model advancement [137].

As regards model evolution and amount of sophistication, in comparison to the monolithic components in the prototype design, the comprehensive precast model should have all discrete pieces. Through individual prefabricated boards, connectors, and tops, conventional monolithic flooring plates are also changed with camber in situ. To produce contract document diagrams, material specifications, production drawings, and materials charts, the premaster needs a thorough model. The comprehensive model is provided to the designer and the manufacturing engineer for confirmation of the project design and mechanical reviews in the impact of remittances. Consultants are examining a comprehensive model with modifications necessary for joints and alignments of comparison with standard measurements, materials, surface treatments, and visible treatments. Building inspectors examine the structural stability model. Let us presume that the model view includes various dimensions, such as the prefabricated hole core boards, connectors, and toppings. Using the SEM framework, the user may define these [138].

The BIM-based coordinating activity is making a significant contribution to the industry in the light of a study [139]. In practice, the Main Contractor brings the prototypes from various subcontractors together again and monitors space coordinating across systems to prevent conflicts before real building begins. For this task, B-Rep geometry is enough. The subcontractor determines on building sequence and timeline at this or the previous date. The last scenario is such an application of the comprehensive manufacturing system. To complement the manufacture and supply of the precast part at the same time with many other design decisions, the precise precast model will be translated into the plant management platform [140]. Throughout these processes, project sequence is used so that the parts are created according to the order that they are constructed. These capabilities require the assignment of components to the manufacturing beds based on plant schedules and also to share the details. To transmit volumes of material and scheduling details down to the general contractors, part management systems can be coupled to enterprise budget management systems (ERPs). Manufacturing strategy provides all necessary elements to be supplied in schedule, as well as a technical description on the design, texture, material composition, classification and product packaging, performance requirements of conditioning, assembly and interconnection, concrete mixes, and complete forms, and elevating devices. The knowledge on whole core planks is therefore transmitted without geometric representation in a flat fashion. The essential qualities include dimensions, amount statistics, and concrete mix [141]. Further information on project assignment of precast/restressed concrete business security solutions may be found in Info [140].

6.4.4   FUTURE SCOPE

An effort is underway to establish a mapping of the SEMs offered to the indigenous database systems there. This effort entails developing interfaces that enable manufacturers of BIM software to integrate the SEM classes. SEM approach may be implemented at several phases of interoperable research successfully. Some of the submissions are identified in this [142]:

1. **Tool for documenting exchange requirements:** With SEMs as basic components, better exchange needs may be established immediately.
2. **Dynamic model exchanges:** The use of SEM libraries and subclasses are intended to automatically define manually the current job of IFC-mapping for modeling perspectives so that new generation viewpoints are created and interchange work time.
3. **Querying of exchange data:** SEM objects can make it easy to request interchange data for constructing model objects. This is a getting acquainted that still has to be checked.
4. **Testing and Certification:** The usage of specified and tested SEMs reduces the burden on model interchange verification and certification programs. Together with the SEM components, the regulations, requirements, and procedures are packed.

6.5   THE DIFFICULTY OF BUILDING REGULATIONS COMPUTERIZATION

Based upon the fact that the rational and interpretive capacity of the human brain is not like everything that is used in personal computers, the procedure of technology and automation presents a serious challenge to the AEC sector. Thankfully, current progress in the investigation and modulation of artificial intelligence (BIM) can give crucial solutions. The next paragraphs will look into some of the AI principles relevant to the AEC knowledge field [143].

6.5.1   NATURE OF HUMAN LANGUAGES

Different groups are quick to understand by youngsters, communicate any idea any adult could dream of, and conform to human respiration rates and short attention span [145]. This means that they have an unlimited expansion of phrases and a high range of sentences in a final language. They all mean that most concepts in a human language have an open number of meanings, therefore uncertainty and uncertainty are unavoidable. Numerous intellectuals spanning existence (e.g. Charles Sanders Peirce and Ludwig Wittgenstein) recognized uncertainty and decided that these are not linguistic flaws but vital qualities that allow them to communicate the diversity of phenomena and all the elements of the substances to be described by humans. For example, he stated that it is impossible, with perfect accuracy, to state any broad concept [145]: "The fundamental subject is simple to talk about with accuracy. Only often, all ambitions must be surrendered to confidence. It's just as simple to be sure. You just have to be ambiguous enough. There's no problem being quite specific and quite sure on a very small topic at once." This remark sums up the folly of any endeavor to establish a strongly symmetrical ontological but proposes two valuable alternative approaches: a categorization of the unstructured subject such as a vocabulary or nomenclature and tightly closed formal conceptions of barely delineated topics. They also ask how but whether such materials may be utilized as bridging between informal human language and concepts and programming languages that have been specified [144].

6.5.2 Modeling Languages

Specific language concepts were discussed and recommendations are made in computer systems throughout the second half of the 20th century. They were all beneficial for the treatment of some parts of communication, but none of them was suited for all parts of the mother tongue or even for a single comprehensive covering [145].

- **Statistics.** In the 1950s, Shannon's theory of communication and other statistical techniques were fashionable in theoretical and empirical aspects, but the computation and high capability of the early machines were not sufficient to handle the needed data quantities. By the end of the last century, computing power increased substantially and made them formidable in many different ways. They are strong in models of discoveries, but their shortcoming is that they lack the semantical understanding that can be translated to the actual world or other ways of computing [146].
- **Syntactic:** In the second half of the 20th century, grammatical studies were influenced by transformative grammar and associated methodologies, and a lot of theatrical and computer research has been generated and morphological frameworks, including all those competing with Chomsky as well others, can be adjusted to the outcome. Now, however, Chomsky's [116] thesis that syntactic is better examined without semantics is best shown and at the worst a diversion from a seamless integration linguistic modeling approach. ISO STEP is a notable example of this modeling in the building sector. The primary problems with the STEP system are that the modeling has been complicated and challenging to integrate, and that internet techniques may today be more economically substituted [147].
- **Logic:** In the 1970s, amongst many other things, the Carnap and Tarski philosophical research led to probability theory on superior memantine underpinnings and ways of argumentation than any rival approach. These approaches can only read phrases that have been expressed purposely in a notation that seems a natural language, but which is a syntactic version of the theoretical justification [148].
- **Lexical Semantics:** The lexical meanings deal with any grammatical, terminology, and organizational characteristics that might allow statements to differ in their meanings instead of constraining the speech into the modern form of formal logic. Linguistic sémantics are of better explanatory suitability and responsiveness than other approaches to more components of meaning. Its drawback is the absence of an established concept of "meaning," which may be connected with the world and computers of understanding [149].
- **W3C Semantic Web (SW):** Networking websites provide economic theories like extendable Markup Language (XML) and expandable Schema Definition Language (XSD), which replace SPFF and EXPRESS languages more efficiently. The drawback with languages, however, is that it cannot be extended to and restricted only to structures and does not provide genuine semántics for adding concepts, characteristics, and regulations. These restrictions have permitted the creation of the Web Language Ontology (OWL) as a syntax for the information in OWL-expressed taxonomy and the RDF (resource description framework)-XML. Especially with the information described in OWL, the database system is completely modular, completely transferable. OWL is a comprehensive internet and decentralized version of classic EXPRESS and SPFF ISO STEP techniques. OWL and RDF-XML are prospective future languages in development modeling Semantic Web

technologies. Your applicability for building specifications and regulations is nonetheless constrained [150].

- **Neural Network***:* Many scientists say that neuropsychology can help 1 day toward improved explanations of how people create natural language and understand it. This can well be accurate, but the amount that is understood about how brain functions can barely add to language theory and the application of knowledge. Networking is descriptive statistics that are the same as other statistical techniques, but they are unlike the real working of the sensory receptors. They are not very similar. Every technique is based on specific emerging technologies: mathematics statistics, grammatical rules, dictionary sizes, or neuron networks. Everyone overlooks the linguistic components that have not been changed for technology. However, language is intertwined perfectly with every part of life for people and does not stumble across barriers of various technology. The natural language has the highest strength and capability to communicate any sublanguage spanning from cookery instructions to inventories and numerical computations [151].

6.5.3 BUILDING CODES COMPUTABLE MODEL

The main objective of building standards is to collect, categorize, name, and define standards, events, and smart building characteristics to ensure the safety, efficient use of resources. Yet the unavoidable changes, growth, invention, progress, development, variety, and instability overwhelm their best place plans. These quick changes are far more disturbing for the frail conventional knowledge foundations in personal computers, which present issues for both inexperienced and seasoned engineers and experts. While accurate descriptions and requirements are necessary to resolve construction design challenges, several code sections are not properly defined and are very discretionary. Code regulations are also characterized by continual graduations and a variety of open exemptions make it hard for ideas learned through experiences to be fully accurately defined [152].

For almost centuries, the much more proposed model of rationale and ontologies was to build artificial intelligence in the categorization of Aristotle and its category system, Syllogisms [146]. The conceptual frameworks provide the basis of four phrase structures that tie each class of the predicated to some other classification: (1) Universal confirmatory. Each truss is a setting. (2) Particular confirmatory. Certain trusses are spatial frameworks. (3) Negative universality. No truss is a deep base. (4) Especially adverse. Some space frameworks are not bridging. Interesting enough has been Leibniz's effort in 1666 when he attempted to automate Aristotle's thought experiment with the creation of a computer model: The only way to fix our thinking is to render it as palpable as that of the mathematical, in such a way which makes us see our mistake at a moment. It is also important to understand the restrictions of all computing systems by specifying explicitly which parts of the requirements and rules cannot be digitized. The implementation of intelligent coding will drastically enhance existing design practices by streamlining accessibility to regulations and feedback controls. It is important, as mentioned in Leibniz, "Let us work without any more ado, to represent construction regulations and norms in a testable and adaptable model that adapts to and understands the special character of this regular inspection." By breaching the Charter and Specification requirements, materials and documentation data methodology modeling can be done to solve an insuperable obstacle [153].

The Smart Code is called a countable digital format for building regulations, which allows for automation control and control without changing the design but rather evaluates a design based on customizable object configurations, relationships, and characteristics. Smart codes use a design based on the rules and respond to instances where required documentation is inadequate or lacking, for such purposes as "PASS," "FAIL," or "WARNING," or "UNKNOWN." Several scientists have already reviewed the effect of the ontological method and somaticized web content, Yurchyshyna and Zarli [106], as the feasible computational framework for constructing codenames. The first research strategy comprises the following procedures for the formalization of conformity standards [106]: (1) the acquisition of information from texts of knowledge representation (e.g., XML and

RDF) of conformity requirement and (2) the representation of the prerequisites by the use of mathematical aptitude. Semantic mappings using industry-specific ontologies of legislation, and in respect of the reasonably prudent challenge standardization of the conformity standards. The somaticized web method, on the other hand, concentrates on an improved IFC model for employing logic theory literary elements such as in the somaticized website address.

The calculable representations of standards and regulations demand ontology for a particular purpose compatible with the generic metaphysics of the BIM standard (NBIMS). This ontology for this specific purpose must be able to deal with the exclusions and uncertainty in numerous parts of building regulation. In the recognition based, it is a key feature of these frameworks to organize items into groups and subdivisions. Though the majority of the codes are checked at the level of a single architectural piece, a lot of rules and logic start at the category level. Classification also helps to forecast constructing things once they have been categorized. In addition, classifications assist to consolidate and clarify inherited information. Thus, a system for linking current categorization tables with terminology, meanings, and code provisions will give crucial solutions. The Omni Class is a nice illustration for the manufacturing sector of generic (upper) ontologies.

In addition to ontologies for the test platform, the specific ontology should be built to cover the degree of depth for the Smart Codes knowable modeling. This specially modified taxonomy will serve a similar function in terms of cost estimates and software development fields as the Uni Format II categorization (ASTM E1557). In the United States, some version of XML is accessible for the International Codes Council. The vocabulary utilized in this model is based on the categorization system for Omni and the International Dictionary Framework (IFD). In conjunction with ICC, the dictionary is produced as part of the IFD project and is handled in the United States by the CSI.

6.6   AN EXPERIMENTAL PLATFORM FOR BUILDING INFORMATION RESEARCH

The methodology used to validate conformity with the technology for the Construction Operations building information. Coordination Model View was the complete construction model files to be ingested and copied by other software suppliers [124].

6.6.1   COMMON MODEL SERVER PLATFORM

The initial tools to test conformity with condition monitoring development theories with what was then the FM Handover MVD specifications were web-based inspection tools. An example of such a tool may be found nowadays. Bim Services is technology designed to automate transformations, monitoring procedures, filters, model combining, and monitoring and has later published publicly. Such productivity constraints may have been removed by succeeding dev kits of Bim Services not evaluated by the authors of this article. The open data model servers Project Bim Server was launched with the creation of the accessible Bim Services utility [112]. BIN Server is an open-source IFC model server (GNU GPLv3 license) that enables an affordable, accessible, expandable IFC exchange platform (import and export) for data exchanges using front end or distant backbone custom application interface, including SOAP, REST, and Java Client APIs. Bim Server offers a model merging engine that may use heterogeneous network priority criteria to integrate different model representations [154].

6.6.2   COMMON MODEL CHECKING ENGINE

The authors have created software quickly based on validation criteria of Schema Tron [129] and the plugin exporting mechanism of the Bim Server. Protocol Tron is a free XML-based quality standards language for defining claims that expand beyond the limitations common of the XSD

(XML schema) specification. Schema Tron supports the capabilities of XSLT 2.0 and XPATH 2.0 for advanced testing for connections among attributes in XML documents. Schema Tron offers living organism interpretations of rules supplementary to the programming specification of rules: e.g., the total of the square footage on the level may not exceed the net square footage. Extended Morphology Tron capabilities also enable the modeler to set up validation stages that may either run separately or be omitted when prior stages fail. The Scheme Tron specification also offers a standard XML validation meeting agenda, the Scheme Tron verification report vocabulary, in addition to a standardized regulations display (SVRL).

Schema Tron criteria for the sporting performance of COBie data on the life cycle periods described in the LaCie project have been created by the authors. The authors designed an SVRL exporting for Bim Server based on an individual constraint defined at the level of performance. The SVRL documentation is also given with a table export HTML. After three modifications, the verification report was prepared: (1) In-Memory COBie XML object retrieves the objective IFC model. (2) The Schema Tron rules shall be converted into an XSLT document in memory. (3) For the production of SVRL documents with the outcomes of the regulation verification from the COBie XML object created in step 1, the XSLT document created in step 2 shall be employed. The author control tool does not specifically address the automatic creation of recommendation systems from the Logically Centralized specifications, one of the prerequisites of a comprehensive testbed.

6.7 USE AMONG BUILDING OWNERS AND REQUIREMENTS

The quality of application among stake-holding entities varies greatly, given the evolution of BIM procedures and technologies. Owners need to be educated and knowledgeable of BIM's possibilities so that the stakeholders they seem to want to negotiate with may be selected and managed appropriately. Given that they will play a critical role in the future to reach a mature BIM specification, this study aims to examine the level of the Construction process amongst homeowners and to establish how the daily existence usage of BIMs may be improved [155].

6.7.1 BIM ADOPTION BY BUILDING OWNERS

Since 2000, in conjunction with the Structural Engineering Association of America (cMAA), the FMI, the leading supplier of management, consultancy, and wealth management for the AECO industry, has been conducting an annual report of property owners. In 2007, 35% of the owner questioned reported using the BIM for one or more initiatives and 12% reported using it for a 5-year timeframe or more. The owners questioned then stated that their lack of experience was the main obstacle to BIM adoption by the owners [123]. Forty-six percent of the proprietors polled said that BIM has utilized over 30% of their initiatives in a national survey of experts in the field and considered to be an increasingly high systems approach, and 41% believe that BIM had a favorable influence upon their plans (McGraw Hill Construction 2008). In a comparable poll that was out in 2009 on the perceived value of BIM, 38% said that a BIM-experienced customer has an advanced element affecting the success of the assets. Conversely, the responses from the industries indicated that it is the closing/start-up and F&E that have the least interest in which periods of life in a projected harvest the highest value from the use of BIM.

There are, thus, increasing BIM acceptance by Buildings Operators, but there are considerably more to benefit from the output of BIM for O&M, behind procurement, and build implementations [107]. More precisely, the utilization of sustainable depends on efforts to comprehend not just software programs, but the contract as well as what to specify concerning the supply. More precisely, in the university facilities section of owners, the acceptance of BIM is presently dependent upon efforts to recognize not only the software applications, but also the indenture and what to framework in relations of deliverables [141].

6.7.2 Potential Benefits of BIM to Owners

Managers can profit most by using the facility's modeling and its integrated understanding of the life cycle of the facility [125]. The same material is often examined while specifying, buying, installing, and finally making a transfer file. A more cooperative procedure can collect and record information once in the modeling and so reduce the duplication and work required throughout the development, build, and transfer phase. The automated development of inventories to complement the medical practice management technology of the operator is one important aim of employing a BIM for facility management (CMMS). Therefore, efforts may be reduced not just during the construction process, but it is also incredibly useful when transferring to eliminate the need for the information to be individually entered in another facility platform [126].

The approach also offers an enhanced technique for managing space assets and maintaining machinery after building. This is an important enhancement, as space assignments create the foundation for all CMMS statistics. For space management, BIM gives better accuracy about current environmental knowledge since identifiers and areas are automatically compared to the requirement to establish human files for each place in AutoCAD [126].

6.7.3 BIM Execution Trends among Building Owners

Several individuals have to start to dictate certain standards for BIM execution to guarantee that outputs are relevant for post-construction facilities managers. Many government organizations and private operators have created recommendations on BIM standards, contract supplements, and criteria for upgrading the efficiency of information transfer. The work of the Project Management Institute was perhaps most remarkable. In 2003, the chief architect's office of GSA's Public Building Services (PBS) created its "National 3D-4D BIM Programme" intending to require BIM to improve all the new projects done during the financial year 2006 as a means for refining proposal and structure quality and distribution. The publishing of several subsequent BIM guides covering a wide range of issues unique to GSA's specialized BIM support projects was following in years [154].

The Army Corps of Engineers Research and Development Center (ERDC) has also produced a BIM Roadmap 2006 addressing BIM's military and government work deployment methods [113]. Ultimately, the Homeland Security Administration joined forces with its publication in April 2010 of the VA BIM Guide. The handbook has 45 pages of the daily existence understanding of the company; approaches for deployment, roles, and duties of the individual players; sharing of images and prerequisites for the use of BIM; and an in-depth reasonable standard for modeling approaches and paper results.

The Consensus Documents 301: a BIM additional to deal with some of the legal consequences that might come from a shared model among multiple stakeholders, and responsibility for the model's integrity or correctness was drawn out by the AGC and Consensus DOCS consortium in June 2008. Shortly after that, the AIA published its E202 BIM Regulations for use in the design or building contracts utilized by BIM. The E202 refers to a comprehensive models table that describes the details required for each modeled object. The CD301 refers to an external BIM plan that allows the project team to create custom contracts to their specific depths. The other is that the E202 refers to a comprehensive model element table [119].

Two key trends have also emerged in connection with the increasing publishing by large building owners' associations of these master BIM guidelines, guidelines, and agreements. First, the need to notify the utilization of a certain project was enhanced and the CD301 BIM execution plan was the second redistribution of the media representation matrix to define the number of details necessary for each BIM item in the model. The VA is one of several owners that need such documentation to be used. They also use product packaging BIM control measures (BMPs) in the design and building stages in compliance with the purchasing strategy employed in this regard (Department of Veterans Affairs 2009). Many educational institutions were also in the vanguard of establishing these BIM implementation strategies. The BIM principles and regulations paper was produced at Indiana University in 2009, augmented in three construction templates with an implementation plan, an IPD Methodological Plan, and a BIM Property matrix. In October 2009, Pennsylvania State University produced a Project Execution Plan Guide shortly after the IU provided these publications. This guide explains a four-step process by which any management team that would like to apply BIM would prepare a thorough BIM execution budget for the organization. The most valuable item maybe was a summary of the many information types proposed for inclusion in a BIM implementation plan (BEP). These include performance targets and BIM goals, BIM project planning, BIM scope definitions, corporate roles and personnel, delivery strategy/contract, communications methodologies, technological infrastructure needs, quality control model processes, and building information references. Finally, Autodesk proposed its own BEP, the BIM Deployment Plan produced in 2010, as a "Revit-Centric Version." It mimics the IU template designed for the BIM implementation plan.

6.7.4 Perceived Difficulties in BIM Adoption for Owners

Facilities management is a "line of work that several areas to assure the operation of the customized version via the flow of technologies, sites, techniques, and methodologies," as per the IFMA, the International Facility Management Association [115]. The property owner cannot thus be considered one individual. Tragically, so when a term property owner is used, the trend is to affiliate the term including one section of the occupation fact is that the proprietor can be composed of a host of individuals who are all of their company that specializes in specific tasks and different priorities from the knowledge they provide. In terms of the availability of knowledge, the transfer procedure for owners has always been problematic. The change from physical media to electronic versions was an advantage, but the proprietor still has a considerable quantity of information to be disseminated to several parties involved. Standardization starts with the implementation of COBie and IFC standards but owners keep that information in many various forms, such as CAD, Word, Excel, and PDF as well as in GIS and BIM. This shows the difficulties that proprietors have when they are starting to use a new app because connectivity and compatibility have to flow from the acquired documents to the information-needed format. Suppliers attempt to satisfy these requirements but Implementation of BIM also depends on vendors' cooperation. Each area of the company will be focused on technological advancements. History shows that the first BIM was designed.

The building industry followed fast. Now the enterprise is starting to build the necessary technologies for integrating BIM into facility management [147]. In many situations, the information needed may be sent in a non-graphical format, eliminating the requirement for the owner to acquire instant skills and valuable advantages in BIM technologies. For example, it isn't necessary to use a table that recognizes the structure and the street address of a pump. However, the foundation of the location requirements is management and owners rely largely on spatial management to ensure practically all aspects of the handover files are organizationally utilized. A Space Manager should frequently do something on deliverables before distribution to offer this knowledge to program implementation. In CAD, the process usually includes the creation of a polyline around each area to identify room limits; however when BIM is used, it is no longer necessary.

The fact that capacity must be recorded based on certain space standards such as BOMA or the Facility Inventory Categorization Manual compounds issues for institutions (FICM). Owners only use extra procedures through technologies from third parties to give all participants access to the regional files with the necessity for space definition. It is also a problem to move data to CMMS systems. A 44-page paper concerning the migration of COBie data to Maximo was created in 2008 by the US Army Corps of Engines [136]. However, unlike GSA many companies are at the start of applying for models in their agreement and they have not yet found a skilled employee within the business to support this tool-based transformation for transferring data. In addition, the owner may not establish, despite the major effort, the document (type, amount, and format) requested by deliveries in one of the typical pieces described by Cotts et al. [115].

6.8 MAINTENANCE KNOWLEDGE A BIM DATABASES ENHANCED SERVICE

The AECO Company has demonstrated considerable interest in the use of BIM to manage facilities. There are appealing prospects to use BIM for facilities operations yet in the development process the use of BIM in building maintenance lags behind project management. A CMMS is the crucial component of the operational stage of a computerized master plan. Relevant information such as operator's information and machinery s parameter, which is required to properly operate a CMMS system, is required. The read and accessibility of this data reduce the operating time and unavailability. Data may be bidirectionally transmitted between BIM models and the CMMS system using procedures in the BIM database. A framework has been designed for the bi-directional flow of information between development and administration applications.

6.8.1 METHODOLOGY

As illustrated, the initial stage in this assessment is to investigate the objectives of facilities management and viable solutions. Existing FM software was reviewed and discussions with several management personnels were conducted. While certain difficulties may still exist with existing facility management (FM) software, particularly not even enough details for routine maintenance, this report is not at the heart of the article. The BIM model is added as characteristics to the relevant information by the FM program and other important details. Software document describes location ID, construction, room numbers, floor, describe, square feet, applicant, phone, etc. The following information is necessary. The end customer should include a descriptor, delivery of service, and phone and are not tied to models of BIM. Those three attributes are thus not taken into account for characteristics. Instead, the BIM model is created with different classifiers: the name of the manufacturer, the manufacturing phone number, hardware position, device reference number, and warranty expiry date. The BIM tool used is the Revit MEP as we have concentrated on the management of the MEP system. The Revit MEP capability is studied to keep the common characteristic, which can be used for many projects and transferred to an external system and to build Revit templates with maintained characteristics. Also studied were DB Link connectors that enable the export Revit data to an external database like Access. The suggested procedure is undertaken to automatically update material between Bim technology and FM software through a case study of an independent school.

6.8.2 CASE STUDY

The FM Communications System Administrator of major proprietors did a case study interview. The FM administrator said that they were gathering information from subcontractors and planners using an MS Excel file to feed the data into the CMMS using auto maid technology. For 14 years, the MS Excel format is utilized. Exporting data wasn't already an issue from the CMMS standpoint. This case study focuses on how to dynamically add the MS Excel file from the BIM model to CMMS software.

The first stage is to construct the Revit templates and exporting the information by adding the strength of the samples in Revit Model, after investigation of the current FM technology and conversations with FM personnel. The shareable parameters are utilized here since numerous projects and households can be exchanged, ODBC generated, and scheduled. The generated property may only be utilized with the present project but not shared with other projects when specific limitations are utilized. The attributes are more suited when common characteristics are configured to be utilized for several projects. Following the requirements of the end consumer the user can select different timetable types, a numerous subcategories timetable utilizing the common parameters defined. The template developed in Revit MEP may be saved as an MS Excel or may be transferred to ACCESS as an mdb file through DB People liked on the importing formats that the program can handle. Based on Data underlying the BIM Model 3D view can be computed quickly through DB Link. Any modifications made to the ACCESS can be immediately modified by changing the BIM model, as the mDb file can be converted back to a Revit model. Moreover, in the Application server, the users may bring different sections and additional attributes of the BIM model will be transmitted. Because we require some further details on the FM software that the current FM software that is utilized in a university should be modified in a database before importation into the FM computer system.

6.9 BUILDING INFORMATION MODEL SYSTEMS SEMIOTIC ANALYSIS

The study of and use of signals to express social significance is semiotics [108]. Systems using modeling techniques, therefore, constitute their core semiotic instruments for communicating among and exchanging information amongst computer programs. Semiotic concepts consequently have the potential to contribute to comprehending how information transmission is achieved by such architectural systems engineering.

6.9.1 A SEMI-CONTAINED APPROACH FOR DESCRIBING REPRESENTATIONS OF SPATIAL ANALYSIS

Because of their goal to influence technical choices, the creation of intelligible system components is not a simple undertaking. Systems must decrease the sophistication of engineering decision-making activities to allow people to readily grasp. Users also need to be able to match the system alternatives according to their decision-making conditions. Computer semiology is a strong way to study how constructing information management supports comprehension of a user in diverse settings. This is largely because the computer semantic framework can define the system construction and the environment within which the system uses the same set of ideas. I will offer an early analysis approach in this regard to define building computer systems. In addition to borrowing Andersen [108], the paradigm is principally created in the field of computer semiotics. Instead, it is extended.

The system was constructed with UML notation. The system consists of three primary components, each of which describes various semiotic processes. The first section is classified as "process"— and specifies the architecture of sign systems describing the user engagement process with the technology. Processing indicators are abstraction indications since they do not occur immediately inside the computer system. They are used to suitable dataset user-to-system interaction procedures. Each BIM system offers many methods of usage from a process point of view, allowing users to do multiple jobs. In turn, to complete a task, users must perform certain activities.

It is vital to recognize that the idea of form is therefore relatively distinct in computer semiotics from the idea of form recognized in the creation of a desktop application which is a compilation of sections that allow individuals to access data. Soundtracks of these two sign kinds comprise the computer semiotic system content. Indications can be either legal or illegal and can also, for example, be sent by sound or hepatic devices, not just too pictorial information. "Expression" is the last part of the structure. The term constituent is used to indicate how a given scene computer-readable has a complete comprehension of the user. Computer systems are based on images from the existent symbols and shapes. The user then interprets this combination together as a particular sign with a definite meaning. The meaning consists of what is called by Andersen [108] a "viewpoint"— a standpoint that is only seen passive, and a "participant standpoint," allowing users to participate with the system actively.

6.9.2 RESEARCH METHOD

I will study the user experience of enterprise resource systems to produce numerical simulations of commercial buildings—so-called 4D models—to highlight the potential of the methodological tool offered [130]. For example, Hartmann and Fischer [127], Mahalingam et al. highlighted the actual usage of visualizations of such building processes [132]. For example, I studied product Navis from Autodesk as a particular system for generating and using visualizations of building processes. The time locations based may be used in two separate settings at the start of the Navis operations. One option offers process viewing by linking 3D items, symbolizing building materials, to scheduled building operations, by providing the user's capability. The other method allows users to control and see the depiction of the building process. I reviewed several previously published guidance documents to direct the analyses of these two modes, which define distinct activities that users may do for the platform in each of the different mechanisms. I then picked several duties from these recommendations that I considered to be most significant in the three devices. After I outlined the activities required for these two tasks, I studied the management indications that enable these activities and the form signals that illustrate the task's intermediary and ultimate results. At the end of the study, I connected this content-based understanding of the basic with a representation of the end-stage system statements to the user given the usual difference between the contents and expressions. The next section describes two sample jobs in detail - one for the two approaches outlined previously.

6.9.3 Mode 1: Generating a 4D Model

Example Task connects a set of 3D model items to a timetable. According to the rules examined, this activity necessitates the introduction of "Selection Sets," entities that reflect a certain collection of 3D architectural elements in Navis works. Once these selected sets are made, this is another task that I did not explore in this restricted article—the collection objects may be connected by pressing the space bar of the game controller, while the mouse arrow is arranged with the subjects that reflect the planned activity. Over several of the columns indicate the individual building operation within the timetable. When you click on the modifier keys button, a dialogue box with textual symbols will appear, showing several possible activities. The user may now pick the "Attach Selection Set" phrase from the accessible strings in this menu. Also, this opens a new menu that allows the user to choose the final set of answers.

The results of the sociological analysis of this job for processes and substance domains are illustrated in Table 6.1. In current software systems, the table vividly demonstrates the cascading nature of handling and signals of form. The outcome of a sign indicating a performed action is generally a handed sign that users may use to commence the following action at the very same period. The field before and after the job is illustrated on the left. It is noticeable because after finishing the activity there is hardly any expressive feedback for the user which may also lead to incorrectly formed connections.

6.9.4 Mode 2: Dynamically Representing the Process Visualization

Example task—Analysis of a structural animated sequence interactively. Users are allowed to utilize the 4D system to animate the sequencing after the 4D model is created by associating 3D building constituent objects with scheduling operations. This animation may be controlled by users with many buttons. Users must enable the "play" option to launch the animations.

TABLE 6.1
GUI Analysis with the Semiotic Framework

Action	Sign Type
Right click activity	Handling form
Select—attach set	Handling form
Choose relevant selection set	Handling form

TABLE 6.2
GUI Analysis with the Semiotic Framework

Action	Sign Type
Right click activity	Handling form
Select—attach set	Handling form
Choose relevant selection set	Handling form

You may halt the animations using a "slow down" button at a certain point of interest. When one of the three switches is pressed, the buttons will alter their shape. Again, the two buttons demonstrate a cascade behavior since they are simultaneously exampling of indications of form and indications. Users can also manipulate the 3D model presented throughout the motion. This may be done using a multitude of management indications, to twist or slide the model's views, for example. A temporary handling indication is shown in the center of the major impact on the overall when the image is navigated, which indicates that a navigation operation is underway. Table 6.2 provides a more detailed overview of this work. Throughout and even before the tasks, the emotional scientific evidence shows considerable variations during and before the task accomplishment.

6.10   PHYSIOLOGICAL WORKER LOAD ASSESSMENT WITH EMBEDDED DEVICES

Provisional 2009 figures suggest that 816 deaths occurred in building accidents, a number which represents 19% of the total job-related mortality in all businesses. While low safety and effectiveness in development are two independent problems, they are highly affected by the physical state of building employees. General knowledge of building workers' physical capability and constraints can improve employees' efficiency and decrease injury potential [137].

6.10.1   METHODOLOGY

To assess the physical changes during the experiment, two different types of appropriate topics were used. One was a cardiac frequency monitor that monitored a fitness tracker at the pulse rate of the research chemist. The sensor consists of three pieces: a torso that delivers a signal and detects the heart rate, a band wristwatch that interacts electronically with the torso and saves the data, downloads cardiac data onto a local PC. A further sensor evaluated energy costs and was linked to the respondents' arms. Raw data has been sent to an internet system that provides feedback and electricity expenses. Both sensors have been off-shelf goods and before testing, there was no adjustment. The respondents in the test were required to explain their subjective sensations of systemic inflammation and weariness. Subsequently, paper-based assessments of Borg's CR-10 scale [114] with participants collecting ratings for perceived effort were undertaken. This instrument is a 10-point categorization measure to recognize the exercise after manual labor. The greater the rating of perceived exertion (RPE), the more effort the test taker perceives. The outcome of the embedded devices used is determined using four indices comprising mean cardiac rates, median energy prices, peak cardiac rates, and peak energy expenses.

Because of the differences in categorization for pharmacologic load owing to different indices, the authors presented a unique index to compare the physiological overall charge. Light labor, considerable labor, hard work, very hard work, and incredibly hard labor are given a range from 1 to 5. Then ranks are combined to indicate the total physiological charge level, described in several indices. The equation may be defined below

$$B_j = \underline{\Sigma R_{ij}}$$

For participant j, B_j is the average ranking of metabolic burden.

R_{ij} is the index I for test respondent j rankings of metabolic burden. The greater the B_j, the higher the physical total burden.

In conclusion, these findings are linked to the interviews and RPM of test participants to assess the effectively measuring the physiological burdens on building sites of the recommended wearable devices.

6.10.2 TEST DESCRIPTION

A test was devised to examine the physical environment of students throughout gardening jobs. The authors selected to try the masonry activities, partly because of the common over-effect injuries suffered by bricklayers that result in relaxation time from employment. In 2005, 75.4 of every 10,000 employees in the maçonery sector, the most in all the industries in the construction sector, had had back injury and disease. Table 6.3 shows the index range to evaluate physical load.

The civil engineering test was carried out in the University of South California civil engineering laboratory. Block of sand cement stonework was chosen to build 2.4 by 2.6 m walls. In one circuit of the wall, there have been six blocks and a total of thirteen courses. Each block had a width of 0.2 m, a length of 0.4 m, a height of 0.2 m, and a weight of around 7.5 kg. Often heavy building supplies such as cement steel mills need to be lifted, maneuvered, and handled repeatedly by bricklayers. The experiments were carried out on a moral compass in which the function of scaffolding was reproduced on building sites when the Wall was built above the head height. Research participants visited a camping trip to examine how plumbers truly operate at a masonry building plant in Los Angeles to generate true circumstances at construction projects. Construction companies were

TABLE 6.3
Index Range to Evaluate Physical Load

Index	Range	Work Load	Literature
Average heart rate	Up to 80	Light work	
	80–100	Moderate work	
	100–120	Heavy work	
	120–140	Very heavy work	
	Over 140	Extremely heavy work	
Average energy expenditure	Up to 2	Light work	
	2–4	Moderate work	
	4–7	Heavy work	
	7–9.5	Very heavy work	
Peak heart rate	Over 9.5	Extremely heavy work	
Peak energy expenditure	70–100	Light work	
	100–120	moderate work	
	120–140	Heavy work	
	140–170	Very heavy work	
	Over 170	Extremely heavy work	
	2.5–5	Light work	
	5–7.5	Moderate work	
	7.5–10	Heavy work	
	10–12.5	Very heavy work	
	Over 12.5	Extremely heavy work	

there to lead and give directions and experiences to the research respondents in Table 6.3. In the modern information technology (IT) environment, the commission procedure, specifications, and usual construction data exchange were examined. The characteristics and potential BIM use in the Information lifecycle were analyzed as a lifecycle information tool. This chapter study offered a novel technique to model perspectives based on SEM. The SEM-based technique, when completely applied, can cut the creation of model views, from the present 2–3 years, to that of the latest day. Modeling representations are built-in EXPRESS using an SEM library, and export/importation instances with SEM are automatically generated at run-time. The SEM-based approach has led to better flexible and modular, broad industrial process requirements converting static, and directory model representations into increased re-use of translators on exports and imports.

A building things generation is not viable without a clear and restricted model definition to be constructed. The extensive utilization of the computable MVD specification, which contains precise definitions of limitations and shared company norms, is thus a precondition for developing a full set of coverage standards.

Together with the results of the study, the competence of property owners in BIM is still in its adolescence. The report also found that even BIM owners do not use post-construction BIMs to maintain buildings. Similar barriers were identified by the participants in the publications including lack of comparability, incomprehension of the regulatory requirements, and a general lack of technical information needed to use BIM suppliers.

As we are aware, the usage of BIM technology increases in the built environment. This study showed that two-way knowledge may seamlessly be transferred between BIM technology and FM application using the methodology and case analysis mentioned. In addition, the storing of FM data in the BIM model can substitute for material lacking in existing FM technology, such as cuts and 3D work displays. For track maintenance, the contact details and the documentation of the contractor's equipment is easier to locate d.

A framework is developed to better define the qualities and opportunities of systems for intended consumers by system developers and designers. It may also assist technology managers and professionals determine why the usage of the system has failed in a particular situation.

For an invasive assessment of the physical burden of building workers with wearable sensors. To evaluate the psychometric properties of the individuals, two kinds of devices were installed; as the gardening, the operation was accomplished. To characterize the physiologic charge level of the work the output from the two sensors has been statistically examined. The whole physiological load was assessed by developing an index. The results have shown that the embedded systems presented were successful in the non-intrusive assessment of physiologic loads.

6.11 CONCLUSION

Vision-based techniques for infrastructural documenting in research groups acquire importance because of their reduced costs and accessibility. The usage of the standardized area between the reference line and its 2D image spaces projections to calculate a 3D minimum mean-square error makes it more accurate to rebuild than if a Distance measure here between line endings and their projections is employed to quantify images in the database error.

This chapter introduced a new approach for obtaining high-quality, interesting video stream frames. The input of the camera gram metric pipelines might be provided for the resulting important frames, to produce dense point clouds of civil infrastructure effectively. The approach presented automates the removal of blurry frames and the selection of a sequence of frames to optimize compute efficiency and reduce typical situations of degeneration.

7 Infrastructure Monitoring and Sustainable Building and Construction in Civil

7.1 A COMBINATION MODEL-FREE TECHNIQUE FOR FEASIBILITY STUDY DURING ONGOING INTELLIGENT BUILDING SURVEILLANCE

7.1.1 INTRODUCTION

Structural Health Monitoring (SHM) is an emerging technology of civil engineering study since it can avert structure breakdown disasters and reduce the cost of maintenance via timely identification. In recent decades, several huge constructions have been outfitted with sensors to detect environmental and structural features of response factors such as temperature, pressures, and wind velocity (such as acceleration and strain). However, it remains a problem to analyze this measuring data to evaluate the contextual factors. Ten approaches to information collection have been developed to tackle this difficulty. In general, these approaches are classified according to the existence of behavioral (physics-based) models in two class-based and model-free ways. Typically, statistical methods are costly to create. Moreover, although numerical simulations may correspond precisely to remarks, due to modeling and measurement errors, the correct representation of a component is not essential in the highest probability model [156]. Conversely, model-free approaches focus on analysis without the use of conductual models merely on observations. For inspection reasons, numerous non-destructive assessment approaches have been suggested, which cannot properly estimate fracture thickness. A new contact-less crack measurement approach is developed and tested in this work, based on computer vision and machine learning ideas. A deep perception is used to assess crack thickness in the methodology described. The current work here shows a cheap method that uses depth perception data to automatically identify and track the severity of potholes for both 2D classification and computer-aided diagnosis. The visual and physical characteristics of potholes and measurement of qualities (length, quantity, and depths) that are used to estimate pothole severity, a connection between the two methodologies is utilized to enhance identification results.

The current study additionally tackles the restrictions by offering a solution based on smartphones' recent popularity. The suggested approach collects data from all detected Wi-Fi access points (APs) in an interior setting utilizing the integrated Wi-Fi sensors in smartphones from the received signal strength indicator (RSSI). The RSSI values are compared to a series of known reference points, i.e., fingerprints that are previously collected and stored in a database.

Work also to analyze employee behavior by monitoring their everyday interrelationships with power using equipment in a workplace setting. In the case of nonintrusive monitoring of the power supply, and able to be compared is developed to analyze passenger's actions. The results of a 5-week period in which inhabitants of an office building are tracked everyday tasks and their tendencies of energy usage are discussed.

To study the association between physical strain and production, the research has used new developments in processing and communication technologies. Through statistical analysis which used the heart rate (HR) as a prediction of physical stress, the data gathered by physiologic status monitors were evaluated. Productivity and HR information was analyzed from seven individuals carrying out 4-hour simulated building work.

DOI: 10.1201/9781003211938-7

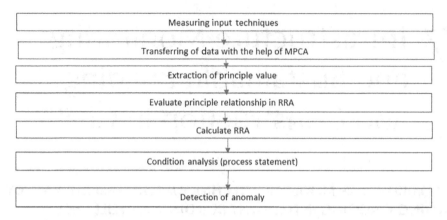

FIGURE 7.1   Flowchart of the hybrid model-free data interpretation approach.

Modeling mechanics model and analyze various building processes and compute their respective Time, Cost, and Environmental Impact (TCEI). The dynamical model of the system operates with a decisive system to choose between the ways of building and a selected project system for evaluation. To identify a construction approach that can best meet the three competing possible objectives as TCEI, both systems have been integrated into a case study of a motorway building project.

7.1.2   METHODOLOGY

In two phases, the novel technique evaluates the measuring data (Figure 7.1). The first stage is for the data gathered to be transformed into MPCA time sets of main components (PCs). It is performed with a fixed-fit window that moves to extract data sets through the measurements time-series data. The information in the windows is utilized to create a confidence interval and tackle linear transformation problems, so that the principal components may be analyzed statistically (eigenvectors). In the following stage, this time series is translated further with RRA. The basic premise underlying the second stage is that the relationships here between major components are modified when structural damage occurs. Due to these relationships, damage can be recognized over time by evaluation. In the second stage, the correlations among PCs are examined by utilizing a robust multiple regression to construct regression functions. The regression algorithms are then utilized for long-term structural monitoring to forecast the main component at one place using the known major component at another place [157].

If a discrepancy surpasses a predetermined threshold limit between the main components produced via regressive operations and the known values, harm will be identified. In the succeeding paragraphs, the effectiveness of the strategy is shown [158].

7.2   A NEW APPROACH TO NON-INTRUSIVE STREET LIGHTING LOAD MONITORING IN HOUSING DEVELOPMENTS

For both utilities and end-users, specific information on power use is crucial for managing the commodity price cycle effectively. Comprehensive geographical energy usage paper advances intelligent plans for future distributed generation expenditures and minimizes costs (Yu Yi-xin et al. 2008). The intelligent grid deals with some of the previously listed energy efficiency management requirements. A smart grid is an electrical network that tracks users' efforts to supply sustainable, cost-effective, and safe power [158].

7.2.1   LOAD MONITORING BACKGROUND

Various commercial power-measuring devices have been created to raise an understanding of energy use trends. The systems include construction/unit level metered methods such as the TED (The

Energy Detective, 2011) or "Kill-a-watt" or "Watts up?" These instruments include construction/ unit level measurement solutions (Electronic Educational Devices, 2011). This information may display the power usage of the devices on an LCD screen over time and in certain situations, it may be coupled (wired or wirelessly) to a computer and save the data. The usage of these technologies makes it feasible for every piece of equipment in a facility to measure the connection levels; the execution is, however, too costly. Construction/unit level monitoring sensors are a comparatively cheap approach in conjunction with NILM decomposition methods [159].

NILM employs total circuit level (main feed) voltage and present measurement to deduct specific loads of equipment. Different research initiatives have been undertaken over the last three decades to enhance the load monitoring mechanism on the device level. As devices may have comparable energy consumption characteristics, several empirical studies have used other measurements, such as reactive energy (Hart 1992) and power harmonics [160] to enhance pattern detecting of equipment. The use of the NINM for electrical comforts has more recently been researched, and practical advancements in the use of NILM as a communication channel have also been investigated in residential structures. The measurement of the historical power consumption in the circuit is dependent on the load state; however, owing to their various individual parts, some of the devices have different load characteristics. Many modern products in recent years have also used vertical electricity to manage electricity usage and to improve productivity, which led to non-linearity in tendencies of power use. Part of the research efforts, therefore, concentrated on these difficulties, for example [160].

Although substantial progress was achieved in the area of NILM, the implementation of this method is still extremely demanding in commercial properties especially to provide the power consumption at room level (as a criterion for the personalized power consumption of the residents of commercial properties). The near resemblance between the equipment in commercial properties, the challenge to decompose the power consumed for the equipment at every location and time-intensive personnel development are important hurdles to NILM in business premises.

7.2.2 Proposed Vision

Managerial functions in housing developments also need to recognize their human energy use to be encouraged to work on energy and resource efficiency. Therefore, in addition to timing and consumption level, the position of the consumer is significant for load monitoring systems in commercial structures. This research presents an alternate strategy using many datasets resources, sensing, and IFC modeling [161].

The usage of Building Information Modeling (BIM) has drastically expanded during the last few years. The BIM models consist of a building's virtual 3D geometry, whose elements include semantic data and relative placements. IFC models are interoperable models across various computer systems independently of the software applications employed.

To find located devices and features, this vision recommends using IFC representations. Decorative lighting, devices such as desktop and laptop computers, and HVAC systems are the key components of housing developments that play a leading role in energy usage. These are also the principal systems that offer utility and convenience to the passengers. Those characteristics are therefore the key topics of interest in the concept offered. Figure 7.2 shows the entire perspective. To transmit their demand over communications systems, equipment will be taught to utilize the sources of data for HVAC power consumption monitoring via information fusion, which will be utilized by IFC as well as the other buildings [162].

The major objective is the use of environmental sensors for load monitoring systems, by employing luminous intensity sensors (i.e., switching on/out the lights or decreasing the lights) to detect events and to correlate the strength with illumination platforms electricity consumption [163]. Similar to NILM, the incident is the intensity of light modification tagged for detection in the illumination operation of electrical view. In addition, broad trends in signal capturing would be employed

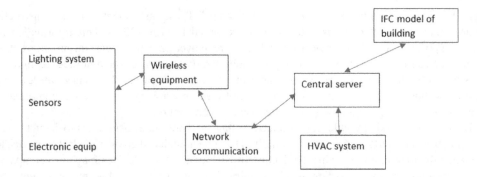

FIGURE 7.2 System architecture of the proposed vision for fusing data from multiple databases for load monitoring in commercial buildings.

to identify the occurrence and to relate events to the physical phenomena—changes in the number of incandescent fixtures utilized or light intensity decreasing. Furthermore, machine-learning algorithms would be implemented to train and correlate occurrences with energy use in a model for independent detection. Even though the detectors installed may be referred to and acted independently of IFC information provided through room numbers, more data may be provided by incorporating the building features of the IFC file such as room space, number of lamps, and kind of light bulb. To evaluate the properties of the collected signals for a training phase of autonomous identification and to evaluate the viability of utilizing light intensities sensing for non-intrusive lighting charge monitoring and the research of the demanding situations, an experimental investigation was conducted [164].

7.3 A NEW VISION-BASED TECHNIQUE TO CRACKING CHARACTERIZATION BY INTEGRATING KNOWLEDGE TO UNDERSTAND WITH STRUCTURAL EVALUATION

In the last two decades, relatively few research has committed itself to quantifying crack thickets using the deep learning method. In the latter two decades, imagery-based technologies have been implemented [165]. It has recently created a system designed for the collection, automatic post-earthquake architectural state evaluation, of maximum crack attributes such as longitude, orientations, and breadth. These characteristics have been provided as estimates of the reinforced concrete dimensions.

7.3.1 Crack Quantification

The complete break must be segregated from the backdrop to estimate a fracture width utilizing the suggested methodology. In this work, the entire crack from its surface is employed to extract crack through an adaptable crack-detection methodology [166].

7.3.1.1 The Proposed Approach

The segmented split was diluted by morphology dilution in the suggested methodology. The other pixels were the center lines of the fissures. The horizontal alignment of the fracture design in each pixel on the centroid must be recognized to quantify a crack thickness. For this purpose, the thin segmentation crack was associated with 35 kernels with the same orientation from 0 to 175.

The centering pixel is the perpendicular direction of the centerline in the kernel which matches the greatest correlation coefficient. The inclination of thicknesses was determined as the perpendicular orientation to the direction opposite observed. Next, the pixels for each centroid pixel were recorded in the longitudinal and transverse directions of the originating segmented crack which aligned with the relevant thickness's orientations. The hypotenuse was calculated using these two possible values and considering the thickness of the fracture in pixels. Finally, by recognizing the camera distance of the object and the focal length of the camera, the crack width was transformed into unit thickness [167].

7.3.1.2   Unit Length Conversion Using 3D Scene Reconstruction

The split sizes of n pixels may be translated into the given volume by the use of the standard pinhole video frames:

$$CS = (WD / FL)(SS / SR)(n)$$

If CS (mm) is the width of the crack that is seen in n pixels of the picture, the investigation team is WD (mm), the camera spatial resolution is FL (mm), the signal processing size is SS (mm), and the camera sensor sensitivity is SR (pixels) [168].

The estimated spatial resolution can be retrieved from the EXIF file, but the operating length should be specified. Usually, it's not always possible or feasible to measure the camera light intensity. The rebuilt 3D cloud and camera positions from the Motion Structure (SfM) issue are then employed to determine the tasks are handled and the focal length. To achieve this purpose, many photos of the item overlapped from various viewpoints are first collected. The SfM technique helps to increase a sparse 3D cetane number and view characteristics from multi-viewpoint views concurrently. This investigation is carried out using the SfM system established by Snavely et al. (2006). In this approach, in each image SIFT key dots are recognized and all pictures are compared. To eliminate outliers, the RANSAC algorithm is utilized. This combination is intended for recovering focal length, center, alignment, and radial lens distortions characteristics (two components are calculated for each view and corresponds to a 4th order construct for frequency region) and 3D scene structure. The capability of transferring is dubbed this great optimization procedure [169].

The SfM issue assesses the relative 3D point dimensions and the location of your camera. By understanding just how much video centers have shifted between only two approaches, 3D points and video places may be scaled. A plane is matched to the data models in the viewpoint of attention to determine the objective camera angular velocity. The RANSAC algorithm can be used to rule out the outer spots. The meeting between the camera orientations line running through the video center and the fitting planes may be found by extracting the equation from the installed plane. The distance to the camera center is calculated as the length of a sensor [179].

7.3.1.3   Perspective Error Compensation

The aforementioned strategy is feasible if the direction of the camera is perpendicular to a controlled object's plane. In case this plane isn't orthogonal to the alignment of the camera (i.e., the projector surface and the planes of the object are not simultaneous), there will be a perspective mistake. The camera orientation vectors, as well as the normal vectors of the optical layer, are required to combat the perspective distortion. The vectors for camera orientation were recovered using SfM, and a normal aircraft may be calculated using the RANSAC technique by mounting a plane to 3D locations that have been rebuilt and shown in the appropriate view. In longitudinal and transverse directions, for each centering pixel, the number of nodes matched with the associated thickness orientations should be tallied. Next, correction for the perspectives error is calculated for each constituent. The outcome of the two perspective-free elements is the fracture thickness for each centering pixel [170].

7.4   POTHOLE PROPERTIES MEASUREMENT THROUGH VISUAL 2D RECOGNITION AND 3D RECONSTRUCTION

Information gathering, processing, evaluation, and product creation of the road network (LTPP) concerns the coming decade's pavement efficiency program (LTPP) (FHWA 2009). Such procedures acknowledge the surface condition evaluation as a component requiring accurate measurements of an adequate standard for disturbances such as cracking, potholes, and slobbering [171].

7.4.1 Current Pavement Evaluation Technique

The sidewalk evaluation process may be split into three parts: (1) data gathering, (2) identifying and classifying distress, and (3) assessing distress. Currently, inspection machines replace traditional data collecting procedures swiftly. The data may be collected with a speed of up to 60 m/hour (96 km/hour) by these inspections' passenger vehicles with many sensors including the available Surface Sensors, optical sensors for measuring distance, profiling laser scanners, routing directional microphones, and proximity sensors for measuring ruggedness [172]. The two additional processes of distress categorization and evaluation remain mostly human despite the mechanization of the data collecting procedure.

Technical experts who recognize and measure the intensity of discomfort from the computer monitor are now individually analyzing the data gathered. This manual technique is laborious and might make the process non-systematic because of the enormous volume of data collected, which eventually affects the quality of the evaluation. For example, at the Georgian Transport Ministry, the state of its 18,000-km (29,000 km) midline highways has 60 full-time technicians (GDOT 2011). Although rules for the evaluation, manual recognition, and evaluation of asphalt discomfort are specified, technicians' expertise affects the final evaluation [173].

A 3D surface profiling is a computational technique of categorizing and assessing failure modes based on the use of time flight thermal cameras (Fugro Roadware 2011) or a piece of hybrid imaging equipment with a digital camera [174]. However, the total number of potholes observed does not indicate and calculate these professional software solutions. Pave measurements (2011) claims that 3D laser-scanner data is used to discover and evaluate potholes autonomously, while its effectiveness is neither proven nor proven. Furthermore, at the vehicle level, the costs of photogrammetry machines suffer from pixels that may impact the quality of the data.

7.4.1.1 Current Research State in the Detecting of Potholes

Recognition of Pothole may be classed as (1) computer-aided diagnostic method and (2) 2D vision-driven methodologies; (3). Pothole identification approach: thermal cameras or stereo visual process technologies are based upon a 3D reconstruction that may likewise be split into 3D points. Laser scanned collections of 3d points are either based on the 3D point time of the flights or on hybrid systems that use mobile devices to purchase laser-projected infrared lines (Chang et al. 2005, Li et al. 2010). The pricing of laser scanning technology remains nonetheless considerable at the environmental level and is determined by the precision of work by phenomena of the higher component. Furthermore, this research is focused mainly on 3D prediction accuracy, and no specific strategy is offered for classifying anxiety [175].

Stereovision-based surface modeling is yet another avenue of research for an integrated pavement evaluation (e.g., Wang 2004). Chang et al. (2005) employed a clustered method for calculating the severe and extensive size of potholes and used a 3D point cloud and Wang et al. (2009) provided a system in which depression and anxiety such as potholes could be identified, located, classified, and quantified. Both cameras require highly accurate alignment of stereo image processing technologies. The camera might affect human cancer cells and the quality of the resulting mechanical vibration of the vehicle speed [176].

Vibration-based approaches employ acceleration sensors, instead of "seeing" them with cameras, to "feel" the groundwater quality. The first assessment of pavement status based on the distortion approach is presented by Yu and Yu (2006). These technologies need limited storage, are economic, and may be utilized for computing in legitimate. However, the sensors react with the reaction of the car. Unless the vehicle state is corrected, the findings are not consistent. Moreover, the probability of wrongful convictions is still very high in existing methods (Eriksson et al. 2008) Bridge's connections were discovered as potholes, for instance, in some situations. In addition, this approach also does not indicate potholes that develop in the middle of traffic (which normally falls between the wheels of a vehicle) [177].

2d vision techniques include the identification, in color, of microprocessor (simulating) potholes larger than 2 ft (60 cm). However, these hypotheses are basic and do not represent genuine conditions of the pavement. A technique has previously been observed in photos for automatic 2D detection of bottles, including the segmentation of photos, the form, and the separation of textures and the last comparison of probable pothole texturing and healthier concrete surface [178]. A tiny, distributed region owing to the existence of a pothole and associated tiredness cracking is the texture achieved in the healthy paving area. Therefore, not properly portrayed is a healthy texture of the pavement. In addition, while this approach recognizes potholes, dispersed photos do not permit a methodical track of the number of potholes needed to measure seriousness. Koch and Brilakis provided an automatic pothole detecting approach for addressing the shortcomings of the aforementioned technique (2011b). A pothole is identified in this approach in a series of frames which allow the overall number of potholes to be calculated. In addition, during the duration of image sequences, appropriate, healthy sidewalk texture is gradually formed. The trial findings show 75% precision and 84% recognition precision in which the accuracy is the proportion of potholes that properly identified the ratio between potholes correctly, and the actual number of defects is the number of fractures and the rest. The results of a 2D viewing-based potholes classification are included in a single-camera 3D video-based rebuild to further improve the automatic potholes identification performance, providing the essential measurements (width, depth, and number) for the numerous successes.

7.4.2 SPARSE 3D

The procedure and technique data are shown in Figure 7.3. Originally, films taken with a High-Definition camera have been used to identify video potholes. At the same time, the same footage is utilized to recreate a sparse starting 3D. The occurrence of potholes is checked to limit the number of places incorrectly labeled as potholes based on 2D detection and 3D sparse

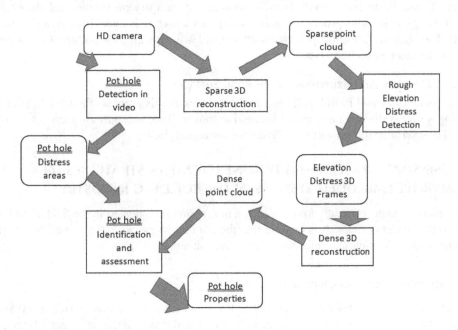

FIGURE 7.3 Proposed methodology.

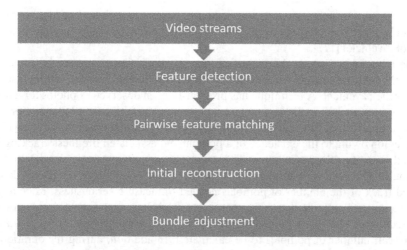

FIGURE 7.4   Spare 3D reconstruction pipeline.

reconstructing findings. Next, a thick reconstructing approach improves the results of the sparse 3D reconstruction [179].

7.4.2.1   2D Video Stream Potholes Recognition

Our technique expands on Koch and Brilakis' past work [180]. First, the bowl-shaped anxiety and depression with a darkening perimeter are recognized as the potholes (low intensity). In comparison with the normal tissue pavement, the interior texture of a pothole has more coarseness and roughness. The picture is broken down into distressed and non-stress zones by using these characteristics, a pothole and brightness distribution, a form-based cutoff based on three-way algorithms [189]. The shadow structure is computed from the lower intensities (darker shadow) areas of the pothole. The geometric characteristics of the skeleton are then estimated for the ellipse. The roughness within the pothole is contrasted with our number of classes which contains a good paving texture taken from numerous frames in the movie to distinguish between the stain/shadow on the road and potholes. Use the boot loader tracking process suggested [181] after a pothole is found to track it till this view goes off. The identification of the potholes is interrupted while tracking the pothole. Once a pothole is left, the detection of potholes is resumed.

7.4.2.2   3D Sparse Approximation of the Road Surfaces

The prior work discussed in Ref. [182] is a building block in this process (Figure 7.4). Initially, a streaming server is divided into several successive frames. Those images are then autonomously analyzed to determine the number of different measurement points.

7.5   ASSESSING INDOOR SMARTPHONE LOCATION STRATEGIES TO IMPROVE EMBEDDED SYSTEMS IN THE BUILDING INDUSTRY

The provision of context-friendly knowledge is a new notion investigated in the field of civil engineering over the last decades. It is thought that the building work can be improved by offering a technique to identify important information in a given situation [183].

7.5.1   METHODOLOGY AND OBJECTIVES

Indoor methodologies for positioning using the RSSI can typically be categorized as (1) inertial navigation based by locating the RSSI value to its length and manipulating its target, (2) proximity based on order to determine the position relative to the target in its immediate vicinity to points of reference, and (3) scene predicated on a match, done by trying to compare the R scene (Pradhan et al. 2009, Li and Becerik–Gerber 2011). In this chapter, the study applies the scene-oriented technique. The approach is not prone to errors connected with a technique of triangulation, which results from faulty modeling of the RSSI-distance connection in complicated construction sites when utilized in a mobile phone location solution. In addition, just a few APs are required for the scene-associated technique rather than a large volume of points of reference, as the approach technique requires less equipment and fewer intruders. The authors use the scene-compatibility approach as a transportable sensing and server computer to evaluate the smartphone or tablet for indoor positioning applications. Although the indoor Wi-Fi localization approach has been evaluated in earlier research, users are forced to transport Wi-Fi light bulbs, and position estimates are performed on a different platform requiring additional transfer of data, making it difficult to locate themselves. A notable potential disadvantage of the technology is that fingerprinting might be sensitive to environmental changes, and an extensive beginning of the project may be necessary. The researchers completely performed the test after one and a half months to evaluate the reliability of fingerprinting and the solution offered [184].

In the campus buildings, field testing was performed. In hallways all four levels of the building, the authors examined the accessibility of current Wi-Fi APs. The results revealed that at least five APs could be identified at all sites tested. Nevertheless, over 40% of identified APs had RSSI values below −85 and have been declared unreliable and so useless. The testbed is situated on a corner of the second floor of the building. It was around 300 m^2 in total, containing two big meeting rooms, a small lounge, and a corridor. A total of seven Wi-Fi APs, including five existing Wi-Fi APs with RSSI values exceeding −85 and two specially designed for the testing, could be identified. Mostly during the training period, a total of 13 fingerprints were gathered and a variety of 7 target sites were available during the authorization process. In both the learning and deployment phase, an iPhone 4 has been used through an application that can provide all detected Wi-Fi AP RSSI values in the area [185].

7.5.2 Findings KNN

7.5.2.1 Localization Performance

KNN classification performance is an indirect measurement of the solution's correctness. A greater reconnaissance rate for a specific k-value means that closer neighbors may be detected to target sites, which should result in greater reliability. The fact that most KNNs have been identified in the test shows that increasing the densities of fingerprints has a beneficial effect on the localization precision since the KNN of a target site forms a smaller polygon that includes the target site, culminating in less of a probable maximum inaccuracy [186].

7.6 ANALYZE THE IMPORTANCE OF INDOOR AIR QUALITY ON VARIATIONS OF ELECTRICITY USE IN HOUSING DEVELOPMENTS

Research [187] advocated adopting operating systems that enable environmental sustainability such as standing by modes to minimize the energy consumption of equipment. Power meters are also used to conduct a rudimentary audit of the usage of devices. These infrared thermometers gather or overall average measurements, which over an amount of time can be shown as volts, current, seemingly immediate energy, and existing and strength factors. Sadly, most traditional meters cannot develop patterns of use, as they are not intended to break down energy use by end-use [188]. While modern power meter models may break apart energy use, most traditional power metering cannot determine patterns of use since they are not meant to decompose power use by end-use [189]. Although modern power meter models may break up electricity use, they remain rather costly.

7.6.1 TEST BED DESCRIPTION

Load monitoring is much more significant if it is combined with actions of real-time occupants that influence the consumer footprint. In commercial buildings, several types of activities take place every day. For instance, photocopying, photocopying, chartering of cell phones, and the use of desk lighting and computers are instances of everyday work, including interactions with electronic components, and hence might affect energy usage. Visual observations may be utilized to derive patterns of the usage of appliances, documented tenant activity, and controlled electricity expenses. These groups are treated as a correlation to the influence of occupying activities on overall energy consumption in buildings. This study uses ocular measurements for tracking and recording the work of office inhabitants with ongoing monitoring of energy usage by workstations, smartphones, and printing [190].

7.6.1.1 Setup

Experiments were performed 5 days a week and 9 hours a day in a work area with 5 employees. In five machines identified with letters A to E, desktop activity was monitored. The project was conceived as a five-step procedure: device setting, sketch upload, calibrating, data collection, and visual monitoring [191].

7.6.1.2 Hardware Configuration

The load control was done with a breadboard, Arduino microcontroller, current, and voltage detectors as illustrated in Figure 7.5. Cooperation agreements were performed utilizing a loud monitor. AC-AC power adapter and a clip connected to the current transformer (CT) results showed significantly the load tracking set-up. The load measuring set-up is discussed in Ref. [192].

7.6.1.3 Arduino Sketch Upload

An Arduino sketch was published to the load monitoring device, an open-source code interoperable with the Arduino microcontroller. The Arduino program transforms raw data in numbers from the analog input to a serial monitor. The intelligent energy management system was set to estimate the true power, equivalent resistance, active power, square root average voltage (Vrms), and square root average current (Irms). All computations were carried out on the Arduino sketch computer potentiometer, coupled to a computer and the data logger to utilize the data. An analog input signal spanning 0 and 5v, the base tension of an Arduino microcontroller, was matched to the CT transmit antenna [193].

7.6.1.4 Calibration

The condition monitoring unit was validated with an off-shelf wattmeter to provide precise data. A two-step approach has been used to calibrate the voltage profile and voltage and to calibrate the current level. Standardization of the boost converter legitimizes the CT sensor phase, power adaptors, and ADC readings multiplex. The current and voltage calibrations were made to reflect household plug meters. Arduino software uses phase synchronization and high pass digital filters to prevent any offsets that might have a detrimental effect on findings [194].

7.6.1.5 Load Monitoring and Data Capture

The load monitoring requires that the equipment utilized by office occupants be extracted by signatures. All the equipment was pre-tested to determine their normal energy signatures with an off-shelf wattmeter. The next stage, once these signatures had been developed, was to analyze tendencies of utilization and remove signatures from different devices in use. The tenant workstations were modified with a proof-of-concept system composed of many standard components for data gathering, which collects the electricity consumption of the device every second. Figure 7.5 shows a basic monitoring device for expanding an existing user to evaluate the consumption of electrical

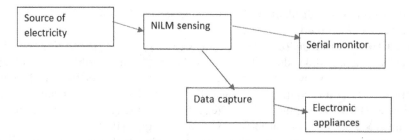

FIGURE 7.5 Load monitoring apparatus.

electricity graphically. For analytic reasons, each hour of satellite observations has been collected and preserved in a repository. Each entry in the data log of the serial monitor shows actual power, equivalent resistance, Vrms, and Irms, as illustrated in Figure 7.5.

7.6.1.6 Visual Observations

Complete visual actions of occupiers at workstations A, B, C, D, and E may be utilized to identify and make data comparisons generated by a load measuring system as a consequence, as visual observations were utilized. The occupants were kept secretly on their overall routines for 1 week. They were then observed for 2 weeks for the usage of office equipment. The usages of personal computers, computer screens, laptops, and printers were the common practices noticed for occupying devices [195].

7.7 INTEGRATED PHYSIOLOGICAL MONITORING STATUS FOR THE EVALUATION OF THE MODEL BETWEEN EMOTIONAL EXERTION AND PRODUCTION FOR ROAD CONSTRUCTION

Construction personnel has been continuously monitored only on inspections. However, ongoing progress in information, communications, and computer technology may be utilized to improve the construction industry's safety and efficiency performance. Although they have penetrated practically every part of people's lives, in particular industries, they lack a comparable level of infiltration [196].

7.7.1 Method

- **Participants.** The study included seven seemingly healthy subjects with minimal or non-experiencing expertise in warehouse management or construction projects (three male/four female), age 20.3 ± 1.25 years, height 1.70 ± 0.09 m, and weight of 65.8 ± 7.70 kg). All investigators were notified in writing of the study's possible dangers and notified about them. In addition, a questioning (modified from the PAR-Q) and a health history survey were performed to determine if reasonable regular exercise could be carried out for them without delay. Therefore, the paper distinguishes people having a history of cardiovascular illness (e.g., heart surgery, angina following exercise, high blood pressure due to exercise). The Institute Review Board at the University of Washington authorized the study to conduct an observational study [197].
- **Construction tasks and working conditions.** A prefabricated elevated deck comprising of concrete panels (20 ... 41 μ; 5 cm; 7 kg) and plastic supporting was utilized for the simulating building tasks for the trials. A two-step assembly technique (i.e., one support and two panel's positions) was intended for an incredibly low time commitment and readily executed by those with little or no building expertise. Contributors worked for four hours consuming working ages of 52 min with an essential pause of 16 min. Participants have

had the opportunity to drink as much water as necessary. But only during the middle break could they eat (i.e., 16 minutes) [198].

- **Productivity assessment.** To record investigations and evaluate productivity, a video camera has been deployed. Productivity, in particular, has been described as a work unit over an amount of time. A row of three configurations and four supporting was the unit of the final project. The time required to complete the specified management team was calculated in minutes. During non-simulated tasks (e.g., fastening toe guards), the time spent by participants inactivity was not considered to be working time [199].

- **PS Assessment.** In several laboratories and test subjects dealing with various occupational groups, such as the working population [200], the fabrication employees HR was effectively used and authenticated in the assessment PS process [201]; Nevertheless, several circumstances, such as environmental circumstances, health circumstances or the like, may impact HR without impacting parameter to assess (PS) without being concerned; sentimental activities or stress; dehydration; digestion; stimulants (e.g., coffee); and depressants. To regulate and reduce their effects, the following processes have been implemented:
  - Conditions of environment. During the trials, the ambient conditions remained steady.
  - Terms of health. The participants completed health history questionnaires permitted the selection of items that could not have affected cardiac activity. In addition, individuals were asked not to consume any medication within 2 hours of the test.
  - Activity of Emotion. The working circumstances and preparatory methods for subjects were meant to lessen mental stress.
  - Moisturizing. It provides drinking water and statements given to consume the amount of water they required; and digestion, stimulants, and depressant compounds. Two hours before the investigation, participants were directed not to take any stimulants or depressants, or meals. In addition, food was easily understandable in the laboratories.

7.7.2 REGRESSION MODELS

Various linear regression was created to assess the connection between the uncontrolled PS parameter and the dependency Productivity parameter (P). In the next sections, the technique for generating and analyzing the simulation is described [202].

7.7.2.1 Signal Processing

With varying reported frequencies, HR and P were monitored. The recording interval of P, in particular, was not consistent since it was equivalent to the amount of spending time completing a work unit, whereas the recording interval of HR was 1 second. P was therefore re-sampled at 1 second. However, the statistical analysis of the collected data at 1-second intervals was not practicable. In reality, when examined over such short times, R is often irrelevant as a PS index. Therefore, in the enormous margin of seconds the data was averaging at time intervals (TI's). There is no equivalent research to define a sufficient TI to the best of the author's knowledge. Therefore, the averaged characteristics were 8 TIs (i.e., 5, 10, 15, 20, 25, 30, 35, and 40 minutes) [203].

7.8 EVALUATION OF LOW-CARBON BUILDING TECHNIQUES FOR SIMULATING THE DYNAMIC RESPONSE

One of the main challenges of the construction project is the existence of several and competing aims (Burns et al., 1996). For the accomplishment of organizational goals, certain objectives must be maximized. Schedule, budget, health, and environmental sustainability might comprise these objectives, where their importance varies from event to event [206]. To identify the appropriate building materials, it is necessary to analyze the complexity of the changing operating conditions and their influence on the TCEI targets [204].

7.8.1 SD Model

The SD model is reworking cycle oriented and provides decision-makers response to changes in operating conditions and business targets to solve the above deficiencies. In direction to overcome the aforementioned deficiencies, the projected SD model practices redraft cycle and creates the executive mechanisms based on fluctuations in development circumstances, as well as the development goals (TCEI). The input of the SD model is supplied as the attributes of the operating conditions. The most workable CM is chosen under the effect of given constraints, based on stated decision-making principles. For the specified CM, TCEI is then computed. The CM choosing and TCEI computation are carried out by the SD model for each individual set of inputs. Figure 7.6 shows the flow diagram for the suggested SD model [205].

Two main subs such as decision-making and development procedures can be used to simulate the sophisticated structural components. The decision-making scheme replicates a decision-making mechanism's response to changes in management relies on, whereas the proposed network models program materials and activities and calculate TCEI activities. This report concentrated mostly on two systems integrations as well as system development specifics. Detailed information about the decision-making mechanism is beyond our investigation. However, the decision-making procedure will be explained so that the system dynamics (SD) model may be fully understood. The agent's decision-making algorithms are spread throughout the Vensim CM indications. As a choice of materials, procurement of materials, and stabilizing ingredient collection, there are three CM indications. Using CM indications, CM equivalents are built for various project circumstances. Every option consists of additive material, machinery, and stabilizing elements, which may be programmed in the model Vensim. The possibilities are presented through organized conversations with specialists from the road building sector. To impact materials, technology, and stabilization component selection for several reasonable options, experts were requested to measure the relative relevance of operational conditions. This knowledge was utilized largely to develop a framework of the sub-system for decision-making. A source of value creation information is gathered in addition to descriptive statistics from the interviews. The data were utilized in the project component to building equations [207].

The system incorporates the decision-making processes of the owners and agents under seven scenarios. To demonstrate changes in circumstances of the operation, in terms of their incidence reliability and validity levels, they have been defined. Interviews have achieved the probability of

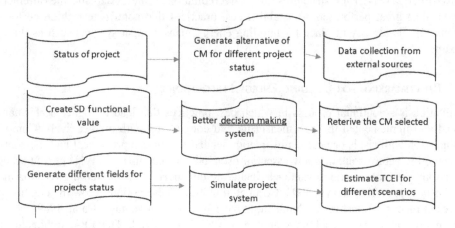

FIGURE 7.6   Flow chart for the proposed SD model.

seven conditions, while the effect values are indicated by the user or project decision-maker. The description of the probability and severity of a project allows quantifiable values to be assigned to changing situations. The input parameters were used to develop several equations and procedures for the performance of CM choices in Vensim since qualitative values would be used in formulae. The decision-making process is then carried out by IF-THEN, where the CM indication is an IF component, and the THEN element of construction is the chosen technique of development. Model is a combination of choice of materials, procurement of materials, and stabilizing of additional selections quantities, the CM Selection Control Unit is the most practical building function. If the contractor selects a construction technique under the requirements of the project, it is recorded into the system design. The choosing of CM is further broken down into components, which reflects the results of the agents' decision-making mechanism. Materials are employed as points in the network between both the enterprise and the decision-making system. The resource categories for each activity are entered into a simulator by utilizing the CM indications. Specific information is also accessible in MS Excel databases for the construction process, cost, and environmental consequences calculations concerning greenhouse gas (G HG) emissions for each operation such as material amounts, price of units, activities period, and fuel consumption. Using MS Excel, TCEI will be generated to input the result in the temperature sensors in the SD model project.

In terms of project time, project costs, and GHG items in the project model the TCEI computed under the impact of the project circumstances is shown. This knowledge is then matched with users' due date, cost, and GHG. To find the appropriateness of the chosen CM, the difference here between planned TCEI and TCEI is computed. The appropriateness of the designated CM is employed for maintaining the flow of the SD system with the reworking cycle. The rework cycle chooses whether to modify the present building approach or whether it is the preferred one that will be utilized in the project. The advancement rate of inflows and CMs requiring change are supplied with more project inputs and cumulatively accumulated progress of CM change is the result of decision-making. The feedback control system in the model is, therefore, realized. If the specified CM is for the user, the experiment terminates. If not, the intended appropriateness of the CM predetermined range or the maximum potential value specified by the user continues to be achieved during the simulations [208].

7.9   A NEGATIVE EMISSIONS BUILDING ADAPTIVE, CONTEXT-DRIVEN EVALUATION ARCHITECTURE

A large amount of energy made in the United States was used by the construction sector. Architects must address energy usage and CO_2 emissions throughout the design and planning stage to attain Zero-Net-Energy (ZNE) for structures soon. Accreditation is the systematic measurement procedure against great performers to establish best practices that contribute to high performance. Benchmarking is already in place for building energy measurement systems such as the Energy Star rating.

7.9.1   Benchmarking for Building Energy Performance

Accreditation is a continual process in which best practices that lead to higher performance are searched and implemented through measuring and comparison with market rivals (Camp 1989). In comparison with rivals or peer teams, recommended practice improvement and the continuous organization structure contain a few essential principles of incomparability. If proven successful, comparisons produce several advantages, including enhanced decision-making (BeathAm et al., 2004; Costa et al., 2006; Garvin 1993; Costa et al. 2006). These notions allow the creation of best practices in inner relationship development, to have a strategic advantage (Camp 1989).

The energy efficiency benchmark approach was also utilized. The EPA architectural label ENERGY STAR and LEED are now the most prominent energy efficiency assessment programs in building by DOE and the US Green Building Association. The program ENERGY STAR offers an environmental star rating of 1–100. The scoring system is calculated by comparing the power source of a property with a pair of structures. For instance, if the energy star score of a building is 50, it signifies that the energy efficiency of the structure is average. Seventy five or more buildings are certified as energy stars (ENERGY STAR 2011). CBECS collects energy utilization data for scoring purposes. Every 4 years, the US DOE conducts this poll. Using the data, several characteristics are used for determining the friendship group. These criteria have included the material properties of the structure, such as construction type, type, and weight, together with operating properties of the facility, comprising operating hours, number of employees, etc.

The LEED program calculates the energy efficiency of a building by measuring its energy management with the performances of a benchmark architecture, which is established by ACS 90.1-2007 for housing developments. Energy Star certification and energy efficiency comparison of related building types in nationwide structures for concrete institutions the average CBECS statistics are utilized (USGBC 2008).

Since the environmental impact is taken into consideration by the LEED certification, it is logical to anticipate that buildings certified by LEED show greater performance characteristics than the national median of the CBECS data set. A decrease in the energy requirements of buildings is the main motive of builders' green renovations (McGraw-Hill Construction 2010). Turner and Frankel (2008) discovered that LEED buildings demonstrate superior energy efficiency by comparing LEED-certified structures with non-LEED buildings. However, 25% of LEED structures have an energy rating system below 50, which is indicated in the assessment. These buildings have below overall energy consumption. A further result from this analysis is that the anticipated energy consumption of sandbox gameplay and the energy consumption use of a structure varies considerably. In the development or design phase, the actual energy utilization might be significantly greater than the projected figure. The results indicate the necessity, for comparison of the current and predicted usage of energy, to re-examine environmental quality variables and benchmarks systems.

7.9.2 Dynamic and Context-Driven Benchmarking

The existing energy efficiency measurements demonstrate a considerable discrepancy between the anticipated energy usage and actual energy consumption, as stated in the preceding section. There might be several reasons why the operational challenges, such as occupation or hours, development modification, transfer of understanding between the designers and end-user group, and kind of activity, are inconsistent (Turner and Frankel 2008; Newsham et al. 2009; Sabapathy et al. 2010).

This study concentrates on two problems and the kind of activities amongst those different assumedly reasons. First, several parameters that affect the metabolic rate are possibly missing in the existing system. For instance, power consumption may vary based on the sort of activity in which building occupants engaged, even across structures in that same area with much the same objectives, the same size, and operating time. Second, it may greatly influence energy utilization when structures are maintained. Maintenances of elements, such as temperatures, moisture, and illumination regulation, which contribute to electricity consumption throughout operating hours should, for instance, affect energy density. Moreover, there is another feature connected to energy usage that these elements are preserved beyond operating hours. Assessment of post-occupancy power consumption is informative to examine the aforementioned factors. The concept is that for the measurement of electricity usage, the kind of activities involved should be recognized. To better understand how electricity is spent both in time and beyond operational hours, the measurement should also be in near real-time or dynamically. The connection of knowledge on energy use to knowledge based on context helps to determine which variables impact performance characteristics. In the planning and design stages of the new home construction, the information may then be utilized for comparison. This approach is shown in Figure 7.7. There must first be several sensors, comprising temperature, energy, interior population, and behaviors, monitoring numerous

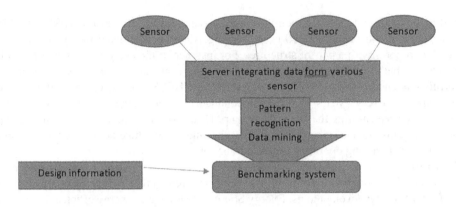

FIGURE 7.7   A benchmarking framework for ZNE buildings.

parameters. The sensor data should be put into a server that integrates all data. Some data processing abilities, such as information retrieval and image processing, must be used to find parameters
related to energy consumption. Then the information in the measuring system should be supplied to
compare electricity consumption. In the planning and design stages, the method is used to estimate
electricity consumption for building developments.

7.9.3   FRAMEWORK IMPLEMENTATION

The authors decided to examine and implement embedded sensors computer resources, interoperable with Johnson Controls Buildings Management System Metasys, to evaluate the architecture in
Figure 7.7. The purpose of the system is the collection of data in real-time and the identification of
variables impacting energy usage. LEED Gold School of International and Public Affairs, Florida
International University (FIU), has been chosen for the responsibility of setting standards.

In Miami IAP, Climate zone 1A and ASHRAE 90.-1-2004, Annex G, the SIPA-LEED engineers carried out an hourly baseline simulation utilizing the TM2 weather dataset. The background
assessment with the Energy Efficiency FINDER TARGET 64 from the Energy Efficiency spectrum
was performed. The standard says that, with accented with decorative levels, extremely effective
glass, an illumination design which is over 50.5% more effective, security cameras, and extremely
effective HVAC systems, SIPA is 33.1% more environmentally friendly than the Energy Star baseline. It also incorporates a tiny renewable array of Uni Flex lighting panels that use polycrystalline
silicon (thin film) technology to generate 38,700 kWh/year or just 4% of the annual energy supply
estimates of the structure.

Several detectors are now in the structure place. More detectors will also be put on the second
story of the structure, detecting different elements. The second level consists of both small and big
classrooms, a language laboratory, a center for social science technology, a computer laboratory,
postgraduate apartments, and support spaces. On the second level, the amenities assessed get direct
and indirect sunshine from the north, west, and south. Much of the sunshine from the west, though,
influences the second floor.

7.10   OPTIMUM WINDOWS SELECTING RADIATION-BASED MODELING

The intricacy of the spatial geometric model and insecurity of the windows systems integration
factors make it extremely difficult to compute manually illumination. The illumination techniques
of simulation were created based primarily on ray or radio-tracking techniques, offering flexibility
often impossible by other approaches (e.g., manual computations and models) (Heckbert 1990). The
survey by Reinhart and Fitz (2006) showed that 50% of lighting tools employed the Mardaljevic
verified radiance modeling tools (1995, 2000).

7.10.1 METHODS OF THE MODEL DEVELOPMENT

Figure 7.8 gives an overview of the structural model. The model's input comprised settings for simulations and creating a model. The settings for the simulation defined the times and sky types required for the simulation of daylight. The simulations may be performed annually or for a certain amount of time. The architectural model includes information concerning building geometry, construction surface reflections, and the window openings' materials and construction.

In Phase I, the model was used to assess window systems in preparatory order to identify various types of frames. As a basis for evaluating the natural lighting effectiveness of various window systems, a common household model was devised. The ranking of potential window support vector machine (SVM) and position would be based on the estimated volumes of lighting in Phase II. In each stage, the illumination values were calculated using three-phase methods. In phase II genetic algorithms (GA), the ideal window types and positions were determined.

7.10.2 MODEL I

To assess window application performance without requiring surface reflectivity measurements, a standardized baselines architectural model was constructed. During this phase, two metrics were calculated: (1) the concentration of sunlight around the surface and (2) the ratio of sunshine transferred to the total sunlight accessible.

7.10.2.1 Setup of Baseline Building Surface

Based on the windows to the building envelope and the wall area, the region of the systems was estimated. In the center of the wall was the doorway. Indoor transmittance was turned black (i.e., RGB values were zero). The space width (W) equals the space height (H). To assess the daylight distribution, the depth (D) of the space should be equivalent to the three heights (H). The three spaced subsections (wall, floor, and ceiling) divided each surface further (P1, P2, and P3). With the increasing distance from the window, the passive solar light dropped significantly (Bansal and Saxena 1979). Solitary simulations examined the utilization of a single control government.

7.10.2.2 Metric Calculation

For the calculation of light at a sensor site, Ward et al. (2011) employed the usual three-phase approach. In the Tregenza Sky subdivision, the s vector had a size of 146×1 with 146 panels (including ground). By utilizing genskyvec and gensky programs, vector s might be constructed. A Radiance-contribs software computed the V matrix (number of especially excel$\times 145$) and the D matrix (145×146). The transmission values between both the inner and outer surfaces of

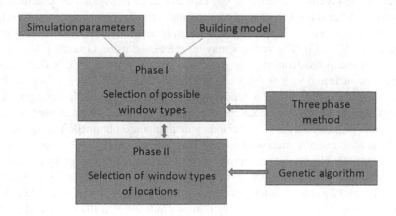

FIGURE 7.8 Overview of the model structure.

the window were demonstrated using a T matrix (145×145) on the entire bases of Klems BSDF. The BSDF matrix may be tested or simulated with the use of Window 6 or (Huizenga 2011) was entered in the T BSDF algorithm for radiance (Ward 2010). If a layered architecture contains an unobstructed view (e.g. light rack), dividing the vacuum surfaces into smaller regions should be employed to compute BSDFs in various parts (Ward et al. 2011). For a single platform, thus, many BSDFs were employed.

With a recursive process comparable to the binary search technique, the locations of the sensors in the benchmark construction have been added to the spatial surfaces (see the following function setup).

Function Setup (Point _1, Point_2)
If (the difference of illumination between point_1 and point_2 is larger than max. Diff)
Add a sesnsorpoint_3 point in the middle of point_1 and point_2:
    Setup point (point_1, point_3):
    Setup point (point_3, point_2):

7.10.3 MODEL II

Phase A featured (1) partition of the windows and (2) illumination reproduction in the principal stages. The lighting was computed using a revised three-phase approach (see Eq. (7.2), in Spanish). This approach divided the potential window surfaces into smaller pieces using a segmentation approach. The entire illuminance level E at a sensor theme was planned by outline of illuminance conveyed from patches that were engaged by windows. To choose window kinds and positions, a Genetic algorithm was employed.

$$E = \sum (V_i T_i) Ds \tag{7.1}$$

7.10.3.1 Window Subdivision

There were several spots at the bottom of a runtime environment. An integer number of patch regions can occupy a natural lighting technology. There may be just two neighboring patch portions in the area of the actual window. The window can have varied positions and dimensions by process occurs patching numbers.

$$Fi\left(x_{i1}, y_{i1}, x_{i2}, y_{i2}, h_i, w_i\right) < 0 \; ---\rightarrow \; gi\left(x_{i1}, y_{i1}, x_{i2}, y_{i2}\right) = hi\left(h_i, w_i, e_i\right) \tag{7.2}$$

7.10.3.2 Daylighting Simulation

Users have set up the potential location of the especial excel to assess the sustainability level of operable windows. After then, it was used to compute lightning using the improved three-phase approach. For each requirement in the future as given in equation, the control software was used to compute matrices V, D. (3). The vector s may be calculated using GreenSky Vec. The matrices V and s have been computed from time to time. The time frames of matrix Dare depend on the quantity of window surface divisions. Matrix T was taken from BSDF files, similar to Phase I. The location, dimensions, and materials of a winder system can be selected utilizing a genetic algorithm as a multidisciplinary issue (GAs). A crack measurement process was implemented in this investigation. First, pictures of the situation from various viewpoints are obtained. The sparse structure of the scene and the position, direction, and current handling for each picture may be established by resolving the SfM issue. The reading comprehension of the scene is achieved by expanding the scattered 3D representation of the scene. An algorithm for depth estimation is utilized to pull cracks off.

A new way of detecting and measuring potholes using a pointing device based on 2D recognition and 3D reconstruction. The preliminary early findings indicate that the suggested strategy would be applicable.

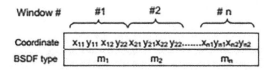

FIGURE 7.9 Chromosome representation.

With the highest error of 2.55 m, the method presented could determine the accuracy of indoor smartphone owners within 5 m, 97.1% of the time. The accuracy of the room level was 100%. The suggested approach can give a suitable degree of precision for users in different contextual scenarios, such as navigation systems. The approach is therefore available.

For estimations of electricity usage, both dynamic and standard modes of appliances have been calculated. Based on the results, people were not generally aware of how much electricity they could save or disconnect gadgets from sources of electricity. Second, it is the possibility to reduce energy through a change of behavior to provide occupants with information about their power consumption habits at coarse-grained layers. The first research of the association among physiological indicators and important performance measures in architecture (i.e. productivity) implies that new possibilities for project management and labor safety, productivity, and welfare have been presented for the construction sector. The physical demands surveillance system is now accessible in new fabric sensing technologies and wearable devices (PDMS). This approach may decrease physiological strain during workdays: HR at a certain activity level represents the entire strain of the work+environment. The link between higher HR and reduced employment will be straightforward; insecure workplace habits.

GA depiction of the chromosomal (see Figure 7.9)

7.11 CONCLUSION

The hybrids prototype appropriate statistical methodology, which includes two more benefits of Moving Principal Component Analysis (MPCA) and Robust Record Analysis (RRA), enables improved degradation diagnosis and reduces damage identification time for continual structural monitoring.

This chapter's study gives a perspective on an alternate technique to non-intrusive load surveillance of housing developments to give the tenants and management deconstructed power usage at room level. The possibility of utilizing light strength detectors was investigated in an experimental investigation to investigate the practicality of the strategy in non-intrusive illumination management. The results reveal that the cheap light intensity sensors are possible to perceive occurrences and relevant characteristics are economically recoverable for retraining machine learning algorithms. The consequence is a fluctuation in the illumination brightness.

The model findings showed that in determining the most practicable building approach the behavior of the SD model about typical and severe situations is consistent. In the CM selection of the models, changes in probability and corresponding weights of project circumstances were represented correctly. The approach results in better use of resources to develop environmentally friendly buildings under the effect of given constraints. In Phase I, without taking account of internal surface reflections, the characteristics of window systems were stressed. Phase II performed radiance-based sunlight simulations for the calculation of illumination. Based on the goals of evolutionary algorithms, the design characteristics, such as glass kinds and window systems, were determined. In the early stages of the construction design, when many factors were undetermined, the model would be very valuable.

8 Circuit Simulation and Design

8.1 EVALUATION OF TKK CTL CIRCUIT SIMULATION OCCURRENCES

This section summarizes TKK's Circuit Theory Laboratory's latest circuit simulation events (CTL). This chapter mainly cites the achievements of the national programs Improved Radio Frequency Simulation & Modulation (ARFSIM 2002–2003), Modern Broadcasting Equipment and Commission Report and Calculations (MOSAICS 2004–2005), and Precise Zero Defects Modes (AMAZE 2006–2008). The Finnish National Technology Agency, Nokia Organization, and AWR-APLAC Corporation supported all of these initiatives, and TKK CTL has had an average of 4.0–5.5 man-years. As a common medium for circuitry analyses and simulation processes used in these initiatives, the APLAC circuit simulations, and development tool was employed [209].

- **Transistor models**

  In ARFSIM, MOSAICS, and AMAZE programmers, the C-code specifications have been extended for several BJT, MESFET, and MOSFET semiconductors designs. APLAC also has the C-code conceptual model and the Philips SiMKit converter to make the construction of transistors modeling smoother. In empirical knowledge, a proposed policy has been suggested for MESFET main entrance partition according to the energies notion [210].

- Analysis methods: The following research methods were analyzed, created, and/or applied in APLAC MOSAICS and AMAZE initiatives even during ARFSIM: Programmers
  DC
    - Advances in speed/convergence related to industrial input
    - Non-monotone norm-reduction approach—piecewise approach algorithm
    - Techniques for nonlinear approximation and optimization
    - Techniques for homotropy
    - Hierarchical analysis in tandem AC
    - Slight enhancements truncation-error criterion for transient—event-based time-step monitoring
    - Transmission line care
    - Hierarchical analysis in tandem
    - C-code implementation optimization Harmonic Balance in Several Tone (HB)
    - Reducing memory use and maximum complexity—effective HB equation formulation
    - Non-monotone norm-reduction approaches with GMRES solver—inexact Newton method with GMRES solver
    - HB with transient assistance
    - Frequency mappings of many dimensions
    - Parallelization using threads—a collection of non-linearity component-model functions
- Linear interpolation—These are two sub heading point-GMRES preconditioners multi-grid approach and Large-signalss-small-signal.
- Large-signal—small-signal Envelope polynomial collocation/projection that starts on its own. MATLAB–APLAC model development of ODE-solver Time Domain with Endless Possibilities (FDTD) C-code integrating optimization of FDTD—Controller Co-simulation [210].
- EM/circuit modeling principal balance minimization

DOI: 10.1201/9781003211938-8

Let us divide down into more manageable parts the technique of Model Order Reducing (MOR):

- Model Integrate connection models (e.g., parasites of structure) employing EM simulations via huge RLC networks.
- Minimize the RLC network to get a low frequencies high bandwidth model with linear MOR (e.g., a series of leftovers and poles).
- Micromodel implementation: by creating an effective equivalent-circuit representation, relate the primarily refers to the transient simulation of the entire non-linear circuit.

8.1.1 INTERCONNECT MODELING

Multi-conductor propagation vanity topped with arabescato Carrara RC/RLC network system, tabular form bandwidth scattering specifications (based on calculation or EM simulation), and even 3D full-wave models can all be used to model interconnects. The number of operations, desired precision, available computing resources, and other factors all influence the choice of an appropriate interconnected model. The MOR system Pada-via-Lanczos was used to handle a dispersive inhomogeneous two-conductor transmission line (PVL). In conjunction, APLAC was used to introduce an Approximate of lumped elements RLC for the multi-conductor distribution system, as well as the evaluation of tabular form wavelength scattering parameters. While we have researched interconnect modeling, it has not been our primary focus; in most situations, we have used a given RLC netlist as our starting point for MOR [211].

8.1.2 LINEAR MOR

Various MOR techniques have been proposed in electrical engineering publications over the last 15 years. The first MOR methods could quantify linear circuits' single-input transmission mechanisms. In contrast, existing MOR methods can minimize massive RLC networks to the point that a reliable connection of significantly lower devices to theoretical calculations of the entire dynamic circuit is possible [212].

The following linear MOR approaches were compared and contrasted: Reduction via divided correlation transforms, asymptotic waveform evaluation (AWE), complicated intensity jumping (CFH), Pade-via-Lenclos (PVL), coordinate-transformed Arnoldi algorithm for both references, we employ the Syl, MPVL, Sy MPVL, and SyMPVL variants Passive Significantly decreased Macro modeling algorithm (PRIMA). "Most of these approaches were coded in a mixture of C, MATLAB, and APLAC input language," according to the researchers. The techniques were then used to limit many research RLC networks. The consequence in some cases was a transition feature that was identical to the original circuits. In certain cases, the outcome was a micro-model. Then, on both the initial and reduced circuits, CAAPA and boundary condition were employed by APLAC; exact techniques discovered were PRIMA and MPVL. PRIMA was investigated further based on this knowledge, and it was discovered that "PRIMA produced passive reduced-order micromodels for connectivity circuits with sufficient precision up to optical techniques." In the course of this work, efforts were made to construct a stop-over condition to cease PRIMA duplication. Immediately as quantitative precision was lost, development of active reduced-order models with the highest possible order was enabled. This effort, however, was futile: the decreased models' volatility could not be predicted depending on the characteristics of the vectors accessible during iterations. PRIMA has been incorporated in APLAC to simulate a huge asymmetric circuit using it as an intermediate pretreatment tool. Each wide RLC block is decreased with PRIMA as an N-port, resulting in document type poles specific to all N-port Y-parameters, as well as the telecommunications and information for each Y dimension, groups of chemicals. Let us underline that PRIMA is not a sequential MOR strategy; it is worth researching other novel ways too [213].

8.1.3 MICROMODEL REALIZATION

Diminished models must be connected to the whole dynamic circuitry. Time-domain simulations are therefore expressed as partial differential equations within the Fourier transform or as. This can be accomplished by substituting suitable micromodels for the reduced-order ones.

The majority of our scientific MOR work has been focused solely on this area: focus largely and entirely on micromodel realization. The micromodels are checked, interpreted coherently, and compared both technically and numerically in a systematic evaluation of nine frequency simulations decreased macro models. Diminished macro-models are classified into two categories:

Equivalent-circuit observations: using simple circuit elements, a SPICE, APLAC, or other netlist is developed. Then you can use almost any time-domain circuit simulator [214].

Time-varying micromodels are created by using time directly in the updating equations. This approach necessitates a change to the simulator's programming language in the majority of cases.

For both groups, we identified the most effective micromodels. Differential-equation micromodel (DEM) was the quickest on the whole. APLAC established the DEM wavelet coefficients during the project's development. In transient analysis, this night before going to bed micromodel is used. Another variant of DEM is used internally in other research approaches (DC, AC, HB, etc.); for example, in AC analysis, $s=j$ is introduced into related wavelength statements of Y-parameter.

The crucial point is that micromodel implementation has an important impact on time-dependent CPU time; for example, it might take much longer for confounding modeling to simulate than the non-linear circuit initial, unspecified amount circuit.

8.1.4 MODULE AND CIRCUITRY BLOCK BEHAVIORAL MODELING

Diminished models must be connected to the whole complex circuitry frequency simulations, which are therefore expressed as partial differential equations within the Fourier transform. This can be accomplished by substituting suitable micromodels for the reduced-order ones.

The majority of our scientific MOR work has been focused solely on this area: focus largely and entirely on micromodel realization. The micromodels are checked, interpreted coherently, and compared both technically and numerically in systematic comparisons for time simulations of nine decreased micromodels [215].

- **Modeling of RF technology**

  Because of rising operating speeds, the complexity of circuit, the granularity of implementations, and marketplace time modeling of microprocessor designs, RF/radiating elements are constantly changing. Analytical models for modern instruments are often impossible to develop. Numerical approaches such as the 3D EM simulator is accurate; however, it is a CPU-intensive computation. Logical patterns, on the other hand, are fast but unreliable over a large range of operations. Artificial Neural Networks (ANNs) have lately been shown to support urgent modeling requirements and quick and reliable ANN models for a wide variety of configurations have been developed. Our mission was to create a generator for commercial modeling and circuit designers who are not ANN specialists for manufacturing modeling programmers that are easy to use and don't want to move between different modeling software and simulators. To accomplish this, we first created a prototype of an ANN-model generator using APLAC's versatile input language. Later, we used the C language to introduce ANN Model Generator in APLAC. As a result, the qualified for some the same network simulator, Model parameters may be employed easily [215].

- **Multi-layer perceptron ANNs**

    In Radiofrequency successful model, the Multilayer Perceptron (MLP) is the most utilized ANN, although we also explored ANN's functional radial base. In our Neural Network Generation, a lot of MLP layers may be constructed, but let's concentrate on three MLPs that identify the appropriate mappings. Function for convenience and to demonstrate the good generalization theorem [216]:

$$E_{tr}(\mathbf{w}) = \sqrt{\frac{1}{N_{tr}N_o} \sum_{k=1}^{N_{tr}} \sum_{l=1}^{N_o} \left(\frac{\tilde{y}l(\mathbf{x}^k,\mathbf{w}) - y_l^k}{2} \right)^2}. \tag{8.1}$$

Where N_i, N_o, and N_h represent the number of inputs, outputs, and hidden-layer neurons, respectively; the above equation represents ANN inputs, outputs, and weights. Let $y=y(x)$ be an unknown, non-linear, multi-dimensional function to be approximated by the MLP mapping. Let $K=1,2, \ldots$ N_{tr} be an appropriate training set, N_{tr} being the number of samples, and the training-set inputs and outputs being scales in the range. Furthermore, let us define the normalized ANN training.

    The training of the ANN means minimizing E_{tr} (w) concerning weights, w, by optimization. The generalization capability of the trained ANN is evaluated by applying (Eq. 8.1) to an independent test set. $\{(x^k, y^k), k=1, 2, \ldots N_{te}\}$

    Figure 8.1 shows a schematic diagram of ANN-model creation (ANNModelGenerator) and ANN-model use (MODEL FILE, ANN Model, and ANNFunc). Strong and dotted lines are used to represent the mandatory and discretionary frames, accordingly. In the following five sections, the procedure of (most of) these frames is clarified [217].

- **ANN-structure selection**

    In ANN-based modeling, the number of covert layers and their neurons is challenging; a very basic, few weighted MLP structure does not have enough freedom to assess the problem, whereas a complicated MLP structure has led to the optimization of multiple values. ANNModelGenerator standard number of layers might be sufficient in many cases. In that buried layer the (optimistic) initial integer is $N_h=N_i+N_o$. The user may automatically enlarge the layering and circuits (see Figure 8.1) if necessary, by changing "Parameter values [218]."

- **Development of training/validation/test set**

    The initial part of the learning phase is the construction of training devices. The training-set file (MOSFET DC-biased Vg and Vds) and predicted outputs (e.g., MOSFET) drained presently Ids (Vgs, DVDs) from observations and measurements is contained in the auditor training (most ANN Model Generator input, Training Document in Figure 1).

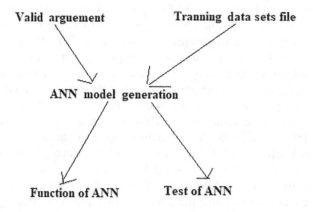

FIGURE 8.1 ANN-model generation and usage.

Overlearning, or oscillations curse of dimensionality to (noisy) training data, can occur if ANN training is continued for too long. As a result, by stopping early at the lowest random events received, an appropriate sampling collection may be used to prevent perspective contributes. Furthermore, after ANN instruction, the sweeping generalization potential of the ANN should be checked with an individual test collection. The optional confirmation file (VALID FILE) and test-set file (TEST FILE) should be built in such a way that all of their inputs, $x^k = (x_k, x_k, x_k)$, $k = 1, 2$, Nava, N_{te}, are placed within the area specified by the training-set inputs; otherwise, this data would be used for validating/testing the ANNs (non-guaranteed) [219].

- **Data scaling**

    Many heuristic approaches for developing ANN teaching have been proposed in the literature. The scalability of training examples is appropriate for ANN training because the times greater of input/output parameter values in standard RF/microwave simulation implementations are very unique from each other [220].

    Each ANN input or output, i.e., each column in the sequencing of training (and confirmation) is adjusted in the range [0, 1] before the particular ANN training. By design, regression analysis is employed; however, automated scaling (AUTO SCALE) is also possible which is concentrated in our study. In the automatic scaling procedure, a suitable proportional performance appraisal for each column is first determined, then the normal expressive form parameters are optimized such that the assessment evaluation is spread over the continuum as equally as feasible.

- **Tanning Optimization of ANN**

    There are ten optimization approaches in APLAC: Methods at a global level:
    - Simulated annealing – Genetic algorithm Methods dependent on gradients:
    - The steepest ascent
    - Gradient of conjugate
    Methods of direct search:
    - Nelder–Mead and Hooke–Jeeves
    - Searching in many directions other options include:
    - Random–Exhaustive quest–Minmax

    Both of these techniques can be applied to almost any (circuit) component to achieve any design objective. According to the intrinsic "ANNModelGenerator optimization techniques" C-code guide, all of the 10 approaches are also accessible to ANN training. To date, we have only integrated the Error Back Propagation (EBP) algorithm to gradient-based ANN management techniques for quick and efficient gradients assessment. The standard ANN Model Generation Optimization Methods are combined with verbs differentially with EBP and Hastens–Stiefel time to thoroughly specifications [221].

    Weight configuration is an essential aspect of ANN instruction. The weights are initialized at random this rudimentary approach will be modified in the coming within the region [0.25, 0.25].

    ANN Model Generator calculates the professional development error ETR (2). ANN learning was efficient if E_{tr} was less than 0.5%.

- **Validation and testing of ANN**

    ANNModelGenerator generates, by using (Eq. 8.1) at every 10th optimization curry, the standardized verification error Eva if the Validated FILE is supplied. The present Neural network is (only) preserved if Eva is lower than the actual one (the memory requirement being mainly determined by the, say, 50 ... 500 ANN weights, $w_{10}, w_{11}, \ldots, w_{NoNh}$). Whenever ANN workouts are complete (i.e., at the optimizing cycle optimum), an early stop point is the best ANN model with both the smallest Eva. If TEST FILE has been supplied, ANNModelGenerator calculates, after the Training phase, the standardized test error, E_{te}. If, say, $E_{te} \leq 1\%$, the adaptation power of the ANN is quite excellent [222].

- **Circuit simulation connection**

  Model of ANN file (MODEL FILE) is the end product of ANN training and includes information such as the ANN configuration, ANN weight values, and related statement Training/validating/test malfunctioning ANN circuits, computing ANN-training sections, and more.

  ANN Model (see Fig. 1), which reads in MODEL FILE and preserves the specifications, will link the qualified ANN model to APLAC circuit simulation. ANN-evaluation methods ANNFunc and ANNFuncD, which use the parameters stored in ANN Model, are used to calculate ANN outputs online (during circuit simulation). It is recommended that announced be used since the analytically quantified compounds are often returned. (i.e., "ALIdS/TOUVGS" and "ALIDS" "ALLIDS" "ALIds" "ANVds") To précis, in our method equally ANN-model generation and practice can be seam- lessly ended inside the similar circuit-simulation context: APLAC, in our technical context, for Newton–Raphson differential equation in controller design.

- **Modeling flow properties using Neural Networks**

  We've only recently begun to use Dynamic Neural Networks (DNNs) to research behavioral simulation of complex non-linear circuit blocks like Power Amplifiers (PAs). We designed and introduced a prototype version of DNN Model Generation using a combination of ANN Model Generator and APLAC intermediate language up to now. We put this tool to the test by creating DNN models for an inverting recorder and a 5 GHz PA. In an HB simulator, these DNN prototypes could be used to restore the current circuit board.

8.2   OUTSTANDING ISSUES IN MODEL ORDER REDUCTION

In several fields today, including the microelectronics design culture, model reduction algorithms are common techniques. Principal balance removal aims to replace a massive geographical system model with a lower dimensional model that shows comparable behavior, usually calculated in terms of intensity or time output responses. Models resulting from electromagnetic formulations of physical systems are often analyzed, approximated, and simulated using those techniques. Since all possible physical effects must be properly accounted for, the statistical formulation used to explain those systems often results in very high dimensionality. To allow approximation and confirmation of such structures, the order or dimension of these models must be reduced [2, 1].

The topic in order reduction of dynamic equations [20,18,4], which has received a lot of attention in recent years, has gotten a lot of attention. The report does not provide for a review of those approaches. We would limit the topic to problems arising from the reduction of linear processes due to capacity restrictions. Nonetheless, in the nonlinear case, this topic is also applicable because most non-linearity reducing methods are based on accuracy and attentiveness expansions or the sequencing of linear programming properly selected. While substantial advances have been achieved in the last generations, both in theory and in practice, there are far bigger obstacles aforementioned when fresh and fascinating implementations are examined to reduce the ordering.

Contemporary covariance matrix divisions may be separated into two categories: those using approximations and those using equilibrium procedures (sometimes also referred to as SVD-based). Krylova has been the most widely explored in the current development using space projecting techniques like PVL and PRIMA.

Although they have several known defects, their adaptability and constancy in dependability and precision make their incredible rates. The lack of a good methodology for problem-solving and ordering, as well as dependence on the originator, is among the most visible shortcomings. Formulation of the concept if after reducing inactivity is to be ensured. Alternative solutions, such as those from the TBR family, minimize the dependability and control of network cases based on a concept of dependability and are stated to offer optimization problem structures with easy a-posterior error boundary. Unfortunately, it is complicated to do so and costly to create and limits for its utility in small and medium-sized concerns. It has also developed hybrid strategies, which include some of the features of each tool form. Subsequently, a revolutionary methodology was developed to bridge the performance gap. The Poor Man's TBR is based on a segmentation approach that provides a suitable framework for cross bridging the two forms of methods, which includes the prominent Eigen's maneuverable domains and quantifiable measures computations. The method, however, is not without flaws, since it depends on the careful selection of sampling stations, which is a difficult task in general.

Despite their flaws, many of the techniques listed are currently in common use. Even then, some circumstances put current expertise in the field to the test. Consider the issue of minimizing massively coupled networks, which are systems with a huge number of ports. In surface, energy infrastructure, and rucksack parasite networks, such systems are common. Furthermore, the movement toward nano-scale measurements, combined with the frequency of activity, means that non-neglect able factors are becoming more significant. Electromagnetic forces must be taken into consideration in the simulations, which can result in enormously coupled issues. For such systems, simulation algorithms are unreliable since they depend on block iterations, where even the block includes a pair of ports. As a result, each block iteration raises the model's scale by the same sum as the number of ports, resulting in big models except with moderate reduction orders. When computation with such models is needed, this pattern is especially troublesome. TBR is less susceptible to the number of input ports because of its design. Regrettably, such structures are usually very massive. As a result, balance methods for reduction are inefficient [223].

New threats are also emerging, necessitating additional study. Include the issue of order reduction in probabilistic systems as an example. The amount of variation architecture models is increasingly being built on threshold value definitions. Process heterogeneity effects, as well as reliance on operational conditions, become extremely important at a higher frequency and nano-scale channel length and should be compensated for in the prototypes. For the most part, existing methods for dealing with such schemes are simple adaptations of basic order reduction algorithms [3, 12]. Taylor-series correlations, which are multidimensional moments in parameter-based definitions, are matched by projection-based techniques. Unfortunately, the expense of this procedure increases exponentially with the number of parameters, making it prohibitively costly unless the scale and hyper-parameters are minimal. It's also difficult to construct a projections space expecting minor perturbations all-around conceptual operating conditions: it's difficult to go beyond first-order, and it's unclear how to dial in precision. It's also difficult to sample the parameter space because it's unclear where explanatory variables should be placed in such a pervasive environment. Still, if knowledge on the input parameters target population is provided, sequences and template building can be applied.

8.2.1 Massively Coupled Systems

In such an invasive context explanation factors should be included. Although information of the accessible population input characteristics is supplied, sequencing and blueprints can be developed. As an example of the issues associated with significantly coupled structures, for power distribution, power grids are fairly regular networks that would protect the whole region of the chip. Because the electrical system is linked to all machines, sources of water, and substrates, those circuits will have hundreds of thousands, if not millions, of ports. Regrettably, this complicates the elimination mechanism much further [224].

8.2.2 Power Grid Modeled

The following findings are produced as an electricity supply is designed as an Operational amplifier and the suggested control mechanism is used: When C, Gn is the capacitance connection and lead matrices, Cv+Gv=Mu y=NT v, correspondingly (1) M np is an inputting matrix, Up is connected to the node voltage state vs. *nq*, where *n* is the total number of stages, indicates the number of inputs and *q* is the number of outcomes. The resonance frequency for television network PQ matrices is thus provided by $H(s) = N^T (G + sC) 1M$. Usually, combinations C and G are minimal, yet big. There is a large number of sensor networks in a contemporary power system. Nevertheless, there are extremely many sources and destination addresses. Consequently, it is too costly to approximate Eq. (1) directly utilizing it in a circuit simulator.

The objective of background subtraction is, in general, to identify a capacitive screen.

$$H_k(s) = N^{\wedge T} \left(\hat{G} + s\hat{C} \right)^{-1} M^{\wedge}$$

of size *k n*, with a state definition of $z = V T v k$ that precisely fits the underlying model's information behavior. However, *k n*, the fractional derivative approach, may not give the necessary decompression. This is conceivable because matrix multiplication *C* and *G* are scarce for main channels with a high majority of different orders (*n*). When there is increasing in synchronization with the majority of different participants in the corrective factor, the gains of reduction which be lost as *p* and *q* become larger [225].

8.3   PROJECTION-BASED FRAMEWORK

PRIMA, for example, provides a general-purpose, rigorous platform for deducing connectivity simulation algorithms, which has been shown to yield excellent acceleration in a variety of scenarios including on- and off-chip connectivity and manufacturing frameworks. They can be used to calculate specific approximate solutions to any of the *p q* matrix differential equation entrants in their most basic form. They are, however, most widely used to produce a single comparison to the entire machine transition operation. For example, the PRIMA method lowers a similar case by the following: (1) utilizing the Matrix *V* projections and function:

$$\hat{G} = V^T G V, M = V^T M, \hat{C} = V^T C V, \hat{N} = V^T N \tag{8.2}$$

In the standard approach of the block, Krylova sub-sections m (A, b)=span b, Ab, Am1b, A =G1C, and b=G1M are the ordinary selections. The significant relationship on investments V is employed orthogonally. The positive impact on investment *V* is constructed in blocks recursively, with each block being created using a back-orthogonal zing technique. The instances of the correction factor can be seen to approximate the moments of the initial formulation to a degree when these are built in the electromechanical energy. The smaller variation is, therefore, equivalent to the number of pairs times the amount of bandwidth. Also, dense are the simplified machinery matrices. In consequence, these techniques create two challenges when interfacing with networking with a wide range of interfaces. In the beginning, the cost of model computation corresponds to the number of inputs, *p*, or tales that specify inputs in the computations. The amount of column in patterns *V* in (3) is directly linked to *p*, as indicated (a direct result of the block construction procedure described). This indicates that construction models are prohibitive for systems with a large number of locations. Second, the size of the smaller model is equivalent, as described before and as shown by the graph. Although the cost of model design may be depreciated in subsequent experiments, the model's large scale is more troublesome because it has a direct impact on simulator price.

8.3.1   TRUNCATED BALANCED REALIZATIONS

Truncated Balanced Realization is an alternate class of reductions algorithms (TBR). By resolving the Lyapunov equations, the TBR algorithm first calculates the quantitative measurements and maneuverability Grampians, X, and Y.

$$GXC^T + CXG^T = MM^T,$$ (8.3)

$$G^TYC + C^TYG = N^TN$$ (8.4)

The template is then reduced by projecting it onto the domain associated with product XY's dominant eigenvalues. In TBR, XY's matrices are employed for specific intention and error control, which are also known as the discrete cosine transform (DCT) coefficients of Hankel. It provides a broad a-posteriori restriction on the TBR modeling original signal inaccuracy in the company setup:

$$\|H - H_k\| \le 2 \sum_{i=k+1}^{u} \sigma_i$$ (8.5)

The presence of such an error bound is a significant advantage of the TBR genetic algorithm, as simulation algorithms lack it. The model selection criterion, and thus the size of the proposed approach, should technically be achieved regardless of the number of outputs. In most challenges, however, there is an implicit dependency, especially in a massive bit combining connection, such as electricity grids (for additional discussion on the topic). In this circumstance, a useful reduction cannot be made. In addition, the answer for Lyapunov's X and Y equations required to derive computer-sensitive X and Y is only of critical significance for communication systems. A variety of methods and recommendations have been proposed to address this difficulty.

8.3.2 PRIMA PROJECTION ALGORITHM

The problem with regular projection algorithms such as PRIMA or multi-point projection systems, as previously mentioned, is that the models generated are relative to the number of routes. This limits their suitability to issues like electricity grids, where there are expected to be a vast number of network terminals. Given the number of ports, an important issue to consider is whether this limitation is intrinsic to the method or an outcome of the computing scheme selected. To put it another way, one would wonder whether effective modeling and simulation of an electricity network, designed as a massive RC mesh, really necessitates too much complex data. This topic is especially pertinent since it is widely maintained that to appropriately simulate a Circuit diagram, only a couple of poles are required. Although it is commonly accepted sometimes in cases, it is not ubiquitous. This is only an assumption.

Two newly formulated methods for solving the problems encountered by traditional MOR approaches are given in the following. The first approach is focused on analyzing the intensity value of device Instances because the latter is a "relatively cheap," predictively based version of the TBR class method.

Singular MOR values are decomposed (SVDMOR) to tackle the removal of large networks, such as transmission lines, the SVDMOR method has been developed. While this complexity of a simplified PRIMA modeling is proportionate immediately to the variety of stores in the circuit, SVDMOR theoretically solves this. Issue by shortening the device to any particular order using singular value decomposition (SVD) examination.

The fundamental theory behind SVDMOR is to presume that the different output signals have a high degree of similarity. SVDMOR also believes that structural device properties, as seen in matrices M and N, can be used to capture certain feedback correlations. An input–output correlation matrix, for example, can be used in the process.

Like the one given by the zero-order moment matrix SDC=NT G−1 M, which contains only DC information. Alternately, more complicated response correlations can be used such as frequency, a more genetic k –order moment, Sk=NT (G-1 C) k G−1 M or even combinations. Let K be the appropriate correlation matrix. If the basic correlation hypothesis holds, then K can be approximated by a low-rank matrix. This low-rank property can be revealed by computing the SVD of K,

K=UΣWT, where U and W are orthogonal matrices and Σ is the diagonal matrix containing the ordered singular values. Assuming correlation, there will be only a small number, $m \ll p+q$, of the dominant singular values.

8.3.3 INPUT-CORRELATED TBR (PMTBR)

A relation between wavelength significant phenomenon and approximation to truncated balanced realization inspired the PMTBR algorithm. The procedure is less computationally costly, but the growth of TBR continues with the degree of the estimate. The mechanics of the algorithms are comparable to that of multitasking. The column of the electromechanical energy is generated by selecting at various antenna intervals over a chosen particular frequency in a multi-point reasonable estimate. Producing sampling $z_i = (G + s_i C)^{-1} M, s_i = j\omega_i \left(\text{with } i = 1,2,\dots,P\right)$ are sampling points with a probability of P. The resulting wavelength equation can then be used to transform the original building into a regression equation. A similar technique is used in the PMTBR algorithm. The reference to TBR approaches is established by noticing that estimation is used. $\hat{X}$ to the Gramian X can be computed as:

$$\hat{X} = \sum_i w_i z_i z_i^H \tag{8.6}$$

8.3.4 NON-LINEAR POSITIVE REAL BALANCING

For passivity-preserving paradigm reduction, a good real balance for stability analysis is an appealing technique. The approach applies to passively linear systems. It incorporates the balancing technique's useful properties with the complacency principle. The above offers a specific pair of power mechanisms that must be balanced. The positive true singular values are shown by the balanced form of the energy functions. They assess the states' energetic significance. To achieve a fractional derivative structure, fewer essential states are removed. The reduced model would be passive if the full-order design was active. This chapter aims to broaden the scope of this approach to include passive nonlinear systems. A broad variety of applications, such as voltage stability assessment and system identification, are driving it. We employ a nonlinear balanced approach that was developed in conjunction with complacency theory. The assessment template's unique properties are the nation's variable positive characteristics that have the same significance as in the laminar regime; in other words, they compute the service's behavioral quality [226].

- Case of non-linear networks under these hypotheses—in this subsection we investigate a system (1):
    the x network is higher than expected, e.g., $r(x)=d(x)+dT(x)>0$, accessible from x_0; $x=$alternate from Y, where Y is a neighborhood of 0.
    Principle 1, however, does not compromise its applicability for the sake of uniformity. The non-linearity variant of the Kalman-Yakubovich-Popov lemma, which personifies the attribute of (strict) positive realness, supports Assumption 2. The presence of solutions to be implemented is guaranteed by the smooth surface presumed in the description of the method (1). While this condition may be eased, it is maintained for the sake of simplicity.

8.3.5 BALANCING OF NONLINEAR

In this section, assuming the following assumptions, a system (1) is taken into account:
- It is observed at zero-state at Y; there are both $S_a(x)$ and $S_r(x)$ and Y smoothness.

Observations 1–5 ensure that S_a and S_r are the minima and maximum cumulative distribution solutions of the formula, accordingly, for all x Y, as described in the following part. The treatment in

Scherpen is followed in the sequel. The job is to figure out how to transform coordinates. $z = \xi(x)$ this transforms the framework into a constructive, real-balanced state.

8.3.6 Model Reduction Truncation

Partition the state vector $\bar{z}$ into $\left[\bar{z}^{1^T}, \bar{z}^{2^T} \right]^T$, where $\bar{z}^1 = \left[\bar{z}_1 \ldots, \bar{z}_k \right]^T$ and $\bar{z}^2 = \left[\bar{z}_{k+1} \ldots, \bar{z}_n \right]^T$. Accordingly, the system can be partitioned into:

$$\bar{f}(\bar{z}) = \begin{bmatrix} \bar{f}_1\left(\bar{z}^1, \bar{z}^2\right) \\ \bar{f}_2\left(\bar{z}^1, \bar{z}^2\right) \end{bmatrix}, \bar{g}(\bar{z}) = \begin{bmatrix} \bar{g}_1\left(\bar{z}^1, \bar{z}^2\right) \\ \bar{g}_2\left(\bar{z}^1, \bar{z}^2\right) \end{bmatrix}, \bar{h}(\bar{z}) = \bar{h}\left(\bar{z}^1, \bar{z}^2\right), \bar{d}(\bar{z}) = \bar{d}\left(\bar{z}^1, \bar{z}^2\right).$$

According to the previous section, the energetic analysis of the state components tells that symbols in square bracket is less important than symbol in square bracket. Hence, to reduce the system, we truncate. The reduced system is described by the Hamilton–Jacobi equation is satisfied as follows:

$$\frac{\partial S_a}{\partial \bar{z}^1}\left(\bar{z}^1, 0\right) \bar{f}_1\left(\bar{z}^1, 0\right) + \frac{1}{2}\left(\frac{\partial S_a}{\partial \bar{z}^1}\left(\bar{z}^1, 0\right) \bar{g}_1\left(\bar{z}^1, 0\right) - \bar{h}^T\left(\bar{z}^1, 0\right) \right) \bar{r}^{-1}\left(\bar{z}^1, 0\right).$$

$$\left(\bar{g}_1^T\left(\bar{z}^1, 0\right) \frac{\partial^T S_a}{\partial \bar{z}^1}\left(\bar{z}^1, 0\right) - \bar{h}\left(\bar{z}^1, 0\right) \right) = 0$$

Substituting the required supply $S_r\ (z^{-1}, 0)$ from relation it is obtained that the required supply of the reduced system does not equal the reduced required supply unless an extra condition is fulfilled $F = 0$.

8.4 EFFICIENT ACTIVATION OF ELECTRONIC COMPONENT MODELS' CONVOLUTIONAL NEURAL NETWORK PARAMETERS

Because of growing operating speeds, circuit sophistication, implementation, the Wavelength modular modeling for computer-assisted design is experiencing changes in complexity and reduced time to the marketplace. ANNs have recently been shown to provide solutions to urgent computational problems experienced with traditional computational approaches (e.g., 3-D EM simulation) and mathematical models. For a variety of components, ANN-based models that are quick and accurate have been created.

Preparing or optimizing ANN weighting using specifications or, for instance, simulated outcomes of 3-D EM, is a critical part of ANN-based modeling. Some many mass methods for ANNs were developed and contrasted using classification problems. The optimum initial weights are, in several ways, calculated by the measuring device data set, and the choice of an initialization process determines the convergence of the optimization. The basis of these issues—approximation functionalities—varies substantially from, for instance, categorization difficulties with continuous information quantity and the traditionally non-linear system perfect representation techniques have not been systematically explored [227].

$$\tilde{y}_l\left(x, \mathbf{W}\right) = w_{l0} + \sum_{j=1}^{N_h} w_{lj} a \tanh\left(b \cdot \left(w_{j0} + \sum_{i=1}^{N_i} w_{ji} x_i \right) \right),$$

$$l = 1, 2, \ldots, N_0,$$

(8.7)

where N_i, N_h, and N_0 represent the number of inputs, hidden-layer neurons, and outputs, respectively

When the intakes, the activation functions (AFs), and the outcomes of N_i, N_h, and N_o are shown correspondingly, $x=(x_1, x_2, ..., x_{Ni})$, $\tilde{y}=(\tilde{y}_1,\tilde{y}_2,...,\tilde{y}_{No})$, and $w=(w_{10}, w_{11}, ... , w_{N_oN_h})$ represents ANN inputs, outputs, and weights, respectively. The function tanh (b_{vj}) is called the AF, where the parameters a and b determine the maxima and the steepness, respectively, is the induced normal field of the function. Let $y=y(x)$ be a known, nonlinear, multidimensional function to be approximated by the MLP mapping be an appropriate training set N_{tr} being the number of samples, and the training-set inputs and targets being scaled linearly in the range [−1, 1]. Furthermore, let us define the normalized training error as the training of the ANN means minimizing E_{tr} (w) concerning the weights, w, using a suitable optimization method in this work, Hestenes–Stiefel conjugate-gradient with EBP. The generalization capability of the rained ANN is evaluated by applying as above equation to an independent test set, to obtain the normalized test error E_{te} (w) [228].

8.4.1 Weight-Initialization Methods

To avoid premature convergence, the weighting factors was tried to introduce that are comparable to the optimum of E_{tr} (global). Learning methodologies can also be taken into account in more advanced strategies. The MLP parameters are initiated in several ways. The most frequent methodology used for ANN-based radio frequency components modeling is the redefined weight of the randomized real values from a Normal Distribution, which has a defined or flexible range. M1. The model was first proposed of uniform distribution (UD) with a predetermined space is one of the approaches explored in this study for a target for the treatment. M2. M2. Random UD start-up with ambient temperature and scalability of certain data inputs, and M3. UD randomized temperatures initiation and specific scaling of data inputs. Arbitrary UD initiation with variable differences and individualized instruction and expanding target training examples. Using M1, you put $a=b=1$ and w_{ji}, w_{lj}=lin, where, for instance, $c=1.0$. For AFs to be able to function in an almost linear boundary layer indicated by a maximum of the partial derivative max (TT) (TEN2THANH (v_j) / TEN2J), this heuristics initiation seeks to assure a certain local field (v_j) for the AFs. For the converging of optimization, this would have been beneficial since $\partial E_{tr}^2/\partial w_{ji} \sim \partial \tanh(v_j)/\partial v_j\, v_j$. Above this, in the transitional zone, its peak value is obtained. The weighting of the method, however, disregards the mean, x_i, and the sample variance of the input information, $\acute{S}x_i$, and, in the saturating regions, AFs can thus work, decelerating the performance analysis.

8.5 NON-LINEAR TRAJECTORY LINEAR TECHNIQUE IN CIRCUIT MODELING FOR A NON-LINEAR DIFFERENTIAL MATHEMATICAL MODEL

Many circuits used in a variety of fields are no longer just optical or analog. Made by mixing, these circuits are electrical and semiconductor devices that combine the two. The development of these vast circuits necessitates the use of software that can effectively model these circuits during the design and verification processes. In mixed-signal architectures, the digital component has had many multiple repeating sub-circuits. This might speed up the transient analysis by seeking to minimize these connections.

To do this, we may employ MOR techniques such as proper orthogonal decomposition (POD) focusing on the exponential or polynomial decrease. On the other hand, these approaches are mainly intended for strongly non-linear applications. This results in serial communication approaches which generally require very non-linear architecture becoming unsuccessful.

8.5.1 Linear Order Reduction Trajectory Piceways

In this part, we'll look at how the TPWL approach can be applied to a non-linearity differential-algebraic equation (DAE), which is used to explain a circuit's dynamical properties.

The input propagation matrices are the DAE framework we want to minimize, and $\tilde{u}$ is the circuit's assigned information.

$$\frac{d}{dt}\mathbf{q}(t,\mathbf{x}) + \mathbf{j}(t,\mathbf{x}) + \tilde{B}\tilde{\mathbf{u}}(t) = \mathbf{0}, \mathbf{x}(0) = \mathbf{x}_0$$

where q represents the contributions from capacitances and the inductances and j represents contributions from resistances.

TPWL operates by integrating the devices on a regular journey at certain intervals. The path should represent the whole irregular character of the system. Then, we minimize each domain controller and store the foundations of each locally reduced subdomain Si and use a nonlinear model reduction approach. With the assistance of the Si, we calculate a universally restricted subspace S. The S subdomain is then utilized in any dynamically linear structures. The average value of the decreased components regionally linearized provides the final TPWL building. A regular DAE time integrator will then solve the TPWL model. In the next part, we'll show you how to put the measures outlined above into practice.

8.5.2 Creating the Local Linearized Models

Creating the linearization tuples, and curves with different sources and/or initial values of the downside of traditional quantization approaches are that we can only be successful in this position if the strategies remain similar to the linearization tuple (LT), time, and solution space, around which we built the productivity and effectiveness. To address this limitation, the TPWL model is created by combining multiple linear system models. These LTs will be driven along a path that reflects the system's normal actions. As long as the approach remains true to one of the LT, we can be confident in the outcome. A standard scenario is depicted. In this scenario, we have constructed five LTs (x_0, x_4) along with path A and the related field of precision. (Shaded region) Even though they have several views (B) and presumably differing quantities, trajectories B and C are visible in the sphere of constancy (C). We may also be certain that we have a reasonable estimate of the original scheme as long as the trajectories remain in the precision zone. We would discuss a method in which the TPWL model selects as many LTs as are needed to achieve given reliability and as little as possible to obtain the optimum velocity. We'll need a workaround from the original model to get the LTs. However, we only need a solution with a low level of precision so it is sufficient if the LTs are similar to the same trajectory. Since we only need the LTs to stick close to the exact direction, we only need low precision. With this in perspective, we can see that selecting the LTs directly in the solution of a non-linear DAE is a smart idea.

The consistency of the current local mean difference, like that of a phase size controller, is determined by the potential LTs chosen. The explanation for this is that we use all regional input space we've generated along the pathway, including future ones, to calculate the global decreased search space. As a result, we can only make local accuracy predictions, so we pick a new LT using a basic technique. We realize that the final TPWL model is a variance of multiple reduced stability analysis structures from the description. By expanding all of the reducing linearized structures into the same significantly reduced spatial domain, we will construct the reduced linear system structures. The global diminished dimension is built by combining all of the locally diminished subspaces obtained during the linearized model's construction process. This is achieved in such a manner that the most influential sections of the locally reduced subspaces are represented in the regional diminished spatial domain. So, the real locally diminished dimensionality is a strong representation of the internationally diminished feature space.

Calculating many standard trajectories to construct a larger precision area is an extension of this technique. The more LTs we have, the more knowledge we'll need to save the TPWL model, and the more complicated the measurement methodology will be.

8.5.3 Create a Significantly Decreased Subspace

We must build the global reduced search space after we have generated p linear system structures and p connected locally reduced subspaces. Since we want a rapid integration from one consistency area to the next when solving the TPWL model, we need a globally reduced subspace. Transitioning from one local feature space to another would be far too complex if each local dimensionality had its own diminished search space.

Suppose there are p local reduction subspaces that are included: Pi Rn SOLUTION, $I=0, p$. The column Pi covers the ideal reduced dimensions of the i-th local structural equation schemes. As a consequence, a new framework can be built. Pal includes all the Pi's columns. Subsequently, $P=[P_1, P_p]$. The intersection is then calculated of all reduced feature space. Because P sections are often linear, and the sequence number is generally more than N, P is not a truly global projecting matrix. Since governing equations are the same, numerous Pi are far more probable to be the same. The sections among these Pi are hence particularly apparent in the matrices P. To get the most dominating P column, and therefore the least dominating part of the local reduction serving contains union, we utilize a singular decomposed (SVD) value of P=UV. Then U consists of the most dominating paragraphs of P and so on, of all Pi. As the globally decreased subdomain, we utilize the decreased search space that spans the first columns of U. A seamless transfer through one local machine to the next is possible, using this globally reduced subspace. Since summarizing, we arrive at Algorithm 8.1.

Algorithm 8.1 Creating the Global Reduced Subspace

1. Define $\tilde{P} = \left[P_1, \ldots, P_p \right]$.
2. Calculate the SVD of $\tilde{P}$. So $\tilde{P} = U\Sigma VH^{\mathrm{T}}$ with $U = \left[u_1, \ldots, u_n \right] \in \mathbb{R}^{n \times n}, \Sigma \in \mathbb{R}^{n \times rp}$ and $V \in \mathbb{R}^{rp \times rp}$.
3. Define P as $\left[u_1, \ldots, u_r \right]$.
4. Create the p local linearized reduced systems given as $C_{ir}\dot{\mathbf{y}} + G_{ir}\mathbf{y} + B_{ir}\mathbf{u}(t) = \mathbf{0}$ with $C_{ir} = P^{\mathrm{T}}C_iP, G_{ir} = P^{\mathrm{T}}G_iP$ and $B_{ir} = P^T B$

8.5.4 Creation of the TPWL Lowered the Weighted Principles Calculations

Now that we have locally generalized linear diminished structures that all lie in the same regional diminished spatial domain, we must merge them to get a worldwide TPWL model. This is accomplished by computing a linear combination of model parameters.

$$\sum_{i=0}^{p-1} w_i(\mathbf{y})\left(C_{ir}\dot{\mathbf{y}} + G_{ir}\mathbf{y} + B_{ir}\mathbf{u}(t) \right) = 0.$$

We have three LTs in this case, x_0, x_1, and x_2, as well as the accuracy field, which is represented by circles. The TPWL model has three potential trajectory stages. Since y_0 is just within x_1's accuracy range, the associated local framework should have the greatest impact on the TPWL model. As a result, we can pick $w_1 \approx 1$ and w_0, $w_2 \approx 0$. Looking at y_1, we can see that this point is in the accuracy area for both x_1 and x_2, so we can use both local versions. This implies that the weights can be chosen as follows: $w_1 + w_2 \approx 1$ and $w_3 \approx 0$. We have the following scenario for y_2: We should interrupt the simulation or at the very least issue an alert at this stage since the solution has abandoned all accuracy regions. Algorithm 8.2 describes a prototype for a weighting protocol.

Algorithm 8.2 Weighting Template

given p LTs $\left(t_{l_i}, \mathbf{y}_{l_i}\right), i = 0, \ldots, p-1$ and $b = 0$
for $i = 0$ to $p - 1$

if **y** lies in the accuracy region of the i-th LT

$0 \ll w_i \leq 1, b=1$

else

$0 \leq w_i \ll 1$

end

end

if $b=0$

Create warning

end

Such that $\sum_{i=0}^{p-1} w_i = 1$

We normalized these to obtain a symmetrical composite of the localized generalized linear reduction subsystems following computing the values. When we select the weights in the manner provided in the example, we receive a weighing plan according to the proximity, as shown in Algorithm 8.3.

Algorithm 8.3 Distance-Dependent Weights

Given actual state y, actual time t, p **LTs** $\left(t_{l_i}, \mathbf{y}_{l_i}\right)$ and α_y, $\alpha_t \geq 0$ with $\alpha_y + \alpha_t = 1$

1. For $i=0, \ldots, p-1$ compute $d_i = d_i = \alpha_y \| \mathbf{y} - \mathbf{y}_{l_i} \| + \alpha_t |t - t_{1_i}|$

2. For $i=0, \cdots, p-1$ calculate $\tilde{w}_i = e^{-\frac{d_i \beta}{m}}$ with $m = \min_{i=0,\ldots,p-1} d_i, \beta > 0$

3. Normalize the weights such that the given constraints hold $w_i = \frac{\tilde{w}_i}{s}$ with $s = \sum_{i=0}^{p-1} \tilde{w}_i$

There is also a generalized solution that calculates the weights using an estimate of the sliding mode control error rather than the size. This method is more difficult since we must calculate an approximation of the Hessian's of q and j, but it yields a more accurate TPWL model. To recap, we have made changes to the way LTs are selected. We have experimented with a variety of linear model order considerations given to see which one worked well. We have attempted to enhance the measurement process.

8.6 MOR FOR ANSYS VS ROM WORKSTATION MODEL ORDER REDUCING FOR MASSIVE SCALE ODE CIRCUITS

The diminishing size and increased integrated densities of Silicon Chips require the continuous development of cheaper and more sophisticated modeling methodologies and tactics in nano-electronics and microsystem technologies. The strategies for Setup Time Reducing (MOR) have been found to reduce both computational time and resources considerably. The reduction in parameterized and asynchronous DAE and mathematics models (PEA) is an active topic of research that moves from a reduced to the subscriber and regressive differential-algebraic (DAE) and partial dynamical symmetric (partial) equation systems (ODEs) PDAEs (differential equation) (PDAEs). There is also improvement in introducing reduced model orders. Practical MOR has advanced from instructional design and research to a range of sophisticated methodologies that may be used to extend industry modes such as ANSYS.

Inexpensive methodologies such as MATLAB or Wolfram may be used to build and evaluate novel MOR algorithms rapidly in today's era of the fast computer. The time required to execute the operating systems, such as C++, for the majority of industrial challenges. Such systems have improved outcomes, but the developer still needs more work and leadership abilities. This part seeks to quantitatively pick many MOR materials from the mentioned channels: ANSYS (M4A) MOR and ROM Workbench (RW). The first was designed as a complement to the German commercial finite element simulator ANSYS at Freiburg University. However, if the matrices of the nonlinear dynamical system are published in matrix market format, it may readily be connected with any circuit simulator. The regression analysis can be synchronized with the rest of the electronics with a reduction in Configure ODE/DAE in an electronic circuit or enable a simplified model to be used as a black box for a simulation. The Arnoldi block and the SOAR algorithm are used by M4A. RW has been produced in the European context project Objectives and constraints at the Polytechnic University of Bucharest in Romana as a MATLAB Libraries with multiple MOR approaches. It implements an Arnoldi-based PRIMA block. The COMMON European Project, which combines the work of key European semiconductor firms and institutions, will incorporate the two methodologies of Networking to build a technology protesting framework that meets today's half manufacturing industry demands. This comparison would illustrate how much in the industrial problem, MATLAB program would be used, and whether the main objective is changed to the build purpose.

- Arnoldi Algorithms

  In microsystem simulation, the spatial discretization of computational domain often results in a linear multiple-input–multiple-output ODE system of the form

  $$C \cdot \dot{\mathbf{X}} + G \cdot \mathbf{x} = B \cdot \mathbf{u}(t)$$
  $$\mathbf{y} = L^T \cdot \mathbf{x},$$
  (8.8)

  With initial condition, $x(0) = x_0$. Here, t is the time variable, $x(t) \epsilon R^n$ the state vector, $u(t)$ belongs to R^m the input excitation vector and $y(t)$ belongs to R^p the output measurement vector. G, C belonging to R^{n*n} are linear symmetric and sparse system matrices, and B belonging to R^{n*m} and L belonging to R^{n*p} are input and output distribution arrays, respectively. N is the dimension of the system and m and p are the number of inputs and outputs.

  Model order reduction is based on the projection of (1) onto some low-dimensional subspace. Most MOR methods generate two projection matrices V, W belongs to R^{n*v}, to construct a reduced system of the order v as

  $$C_r \cdot \mathbf{z} + G_r \cdot \mathbf{z} = B_r \cdot \mathbf{u}(t)$$
  $$\mathbf{y}_r = L_r^T \cdot \mathbf{z},$$
  (8.9)

  The ultimate goal of MOR is to find matrices V and W in such a way that $v \ll n$, while minimizing the error between the full and the reduced system in either time domain min $\|y - y_r\|$ or Laplace domain. Furthermore, the stability and passivity of the original system should be preserved. The Basic idea behind the Krylov-subspace based block-Arnoldi algorithm is to transfer into the implicit formulation

  $$A\dot{\mathbf{x}} = \mathbf{x} + R\mathbf{u}$$
  $$\mathbf{y} = L^T\mathbf{x},$$
  (8.10)

  with $A = -(G + s_o C)^{-1} C$, and $R = -(G + s_o C)^{-1} B$

  And to write down the transfer function in the frequency domain.

  $$H(s) = -L^T \left(I - (s - s_0)A\right)^{-1} R = \sum_{i=0}^{\infty} m_i (s - s_0)^i$$
  (8.11)

  where $m_i = -L^T A^i B$ is called the i-th moment around s_0. One aims to find a reduced system whose transfer function $H_r(s)$ will have the same moment as $H(s)$ up to degree v. However, due to numerical instabilities, the moments are not computed explicitly, but via the right-sided Krylov subspace Kr (A, R, p):=span (R, AR, A^2 R, A^{p-1} R). Block Arnoldi algorithm generates a single orthonormal basis W for K_r (A, R, p) and the system is reduced by the projection to

$$A_r \dot{z} = z + R_r u$$

$$y_r = L_r^T z,$$

(8.12)

The order of the above equation is $v = p \cdot m$. The property of the Krylov subspace is such that the first v moments are identical.

As the reduced system, in the above equation, is not necessarily passive, two alternatives to the "classical" block-Arnoldi have been suggested: PRIMA algorithm.

8.6.1 ALGORITHM OF PRIMA

The PRIMA algorithm was established in 1998 to assure the inactivity of the system. The passively macro modeling algorithm significantly reduced for interconnection stands for passively macro modeling algorithm substantially less interconnect. X utilized with the specified projections (1), meaning Cr=XT CX, Gr=XT GX, Br=XT Br=XT L. XT L, is utilized. It is observed that the contentment of the relative shares is preserved if C is a positive dump truck and if the first n transitional times of the main and the decreased subsystems are unbalanced. A PRIMA implementation that employs $X_k = [x_{km} + 1 \ldots x(k+1)]m$ is present in Algorithm 1.

8.6.2 FREUND'S ARNOLDI

Vectors that are almost absolutely proportional with other vectors in the span of the orthogonal variable should be omitted, according to Freund. He refers to this form of vector elimination as depreciation. Although there is a block framework noticeable for frequency division multiplexing (of d_m output structures, his algorithm is projectile). Instead of orthonormal blocks, the model computes member vectors, with each vector containing one or more orthogonal frames, $\hat{v}_k$, that satisfies

$$\|\hat{v}_k\| < \text{DTOL},$$

(8.13)

DTOL is omitted for any acceptable threshold. As a result, the number of variables the number of matrices per n-dimensional block m might be less than or comparable to block m 1.

8.6.3 COMPARISON BETWEEN BOTH ALGORITHMS

We say that Algorithms 8.1 and 8.2 produce identical results. Freund's Arnoldi was, in other words, PRIMA deflated. We are now going to demonstrate that this is right.

To prove that both procedures have precise results is comparable to establishing that $X = V$ (V is the n-dimensional foundation for Algorithm 8.2), i.e., both approaches take into account the same universe and that it holds V.

It states that the columns of V do form the desired Krylov space with oropharyngeal cancers, which is the desired consequence of the Arnoldi algorithm for several beginning variables. The positive impact on investment for both architectures will be referred to as V in the following.

$$q(v_j, \tau, \varphi) = \left(1 - \sum_{i=\tau}^{\varphi} v_i v_i^T \right) g(v_j),$$

(8.14)

8.7   CIRCUIT SIMULATION DEPUTY TRANSIENT SENSITIVITY ANALYSIS

The result of the chance to make temporal differences through an electric motor (power) is a common quantity in circuit analysis, and when combined over time, it represents the overall power dispersed. Another time and frequency domain challenge is determining the point in time where an unknown or an expression reaches a certain amount. This may be the point at which coordination between digital circuits and then another simulation method is needed in professionals.

The adjoint approach in dynamic simulation can be defined as a matrix multiplication of the circuit coefficients with a meticulously crafted function that, by its very existence, is a linear combination of the logic coefficients with a meticulously crafted variable. In a comparable DAE, a defuzzification plan is imperative (and for which a proper initial value has to be determined). The method was established for solving the nonlinear. The system has been analyzed in a more mathematical formalism for more general DAEs.

The implementation of circuit formulas to nonlinear DAEs was studied in greater depth. The challenge of locating suitable origins in reducing errors in analog circuits has some interesting applications. When it comes to size issues, though, there are a few things to keep in mind (in which for instance the physical area of a capacitor has to be taken into account), it indicates that transistor dimensions, in particular, produce terminology that needs further analysis. The influence of the associated DAE's index is seen here.

Aside from optimizing, adjoint structures are useful for evaluating optimum fractional derivative structures, which include a wide range of methods. The equations actually can be subjected to a transfer function modeling procedure since the adjoint structures are dimensional.

We'll go into how to measure hypersensitivity reliably and effectively.

8.7.1 Transient Analyzes of Sensitivity

Equation (8.1) is an algebraic expression of difference, utilized for the modeling DAE of the behavior of any circuit over time. The state vector $x(t)$ RN describes the node currents and voltages from voltage sources and inductors in Modified Nodal Analysis (MNA), whereas j and q are vector parameters defining the present and charges behavior (capacitance) or flux behavior (transformers). S is integrated with all sources (t)

$$\frac{d}{dt}\left[q(x(t))\right] + j\left(x(t)\right) = s(t). \tag{8.15}$$

At $t=0$, DC solutions $x\mathrm{DC}$ fulfills the improved guess

$$j\left(x\mathrm{DC}\right) = s(0). \tag{8.16}$$

Application of finite element laplace transform t_n and $t_n+1=t_n+\Delta t$ enables to calculate x_n+1 as approximation at t_{n+1}:

$$\underline{1}\left[q\left(x^{n+1}\right)q\left(x^n\right)\right] + j\left(x^{n+1}\right)\quad s(t\Delta t_{n+1}) = 0 \tag{8.17}$$

A Newton–Raphson procedure involves the coefficient matrix $Y = {}^1 C + G$, in which $C = \partial q/\partial x$ and $G = \partial j/\partial x$. Making explicit that the equations and their solution depend on a parameter $p \in R^P$, we will write

$$\frac{d}{dt}\left[q\left(x(t,p),p\right)\right] + j\left(x(t,p),p\right)\quad s(t,p). \tag{8.18}$$

By adjusting these parameters, it is possible to optimize the behavior of required functionality. The sensitivity of $x(t, p)$ concerning p is denoted by $\hat{x}(t,p)\partial x(t,p)/\partial p = \left(\partial x_i(t,p)/\partial p_j\right) RN^{\times P}$, and similarly for $\hat{x}_{\mathrm{DC}}(p)$. After solving (3), and saving the LU-decomposition of the matrix $Y = LU$, the sensitivity $\hat{x}^{n+1}(p)\hat{x}\left(t_{n+1},p\right)$ may be calculated by recursion of the vector f requires $O(PN^2)$ operations for the last term in addition to O(PN) evaluations for the term. For simplicity, we assume full matrices. Solving the system requires an additional O(PN²) operation.

A more general basic observation function is denoted by $F(x(t, p), p)$, which belongs to R^F from which other observation functions can be obtained:

$$\mathbf{G}(\mathbf{x}(\mathbf{p}), \mathbf{p}) = \int_0^T \mathbf{F}(x(t, \mathbf{p}), \mathbf{p}) dt. \tag{8.19}$$

If can be determined rather cheaply, the main emphasis in sensitivity analysis is in the efficient calculation or even in sufficiently calculating the inner product. This is a direct forward analysis.

Where a library for analyzing q, j, or s does not require conceptual distinction, a synchronous limitless distinction would be used instead (at the expense of two extra assessments for each amount) $\frac{dq}{dp} \approx \frac{q(p + \Delta p) - q(p - \Delta p)}{2\Delta p}$. This indicates that the resulting combination will have an inaccuracy at each inner point (assuming this discretization error is dominant). A q à la parallelogram rule starts to add up to O(p‖2/future)leading to p‖=o(future) if a q à la trapezoidal is required and permanent sensitivity errors are not sought o(fast). In the next sequence, (backward) Deputy Products and applications are now considered. We distinguish w.r.t. p and divide the outcome by a function— just (t)RF (Translating))

$$0 = \int_0^T \lambda^*(t) \left[\frac{d}{dt} \frac{d\mathbf{q}}{d\mathbf{p}} + \frac{d\mathbf{j}}{d\mathbf{p}} - \frac{\partial \mathbf{s}}{\partial \mathbf{p}} \right] dt \tag{8.20}$$

8.8   COMPONENT REPLACEMENTS ELECTRICITY CIRCUITS COMPONENT REDUCING INDEX

Electrical circuit simulation is a popular method for testing experimental electrical circuits before making a prototype. It's critical, particularly in semiconductor manufacturing, to be able to simulate the behavior of a circuit quickly and accurately. However, in this case, the circuits typically contain millions of components. As a result, the simulation model can become challenging due to the problem in sheer scale.

Methods for the circuit modeling include MNA, load/flux oriented MNA (MNA C/F), and the lacking in detail Tableau Approach. To build a system of relationships, Kirchhoff's laws and basic contacts are used. The mathematics defines the desired attributes of the circuit, such as frequency and voltage.

This scheme is known as "Differential-Algebraic-Equation" because it includes both differential and algebraic relations (DAE). One well-known issue with DAEs is that to differentiate between particular solutions or differential equations, in addition to seeming mathematical relationships, they might have so-called secret limitations, which can only be found. Provided certain principal components of the system, these DAEs are considered to have index 2 in circuit simulation. This higher index has many negative consequences in the analytical scheme of DAEs, such as lack of precision and excessive computation. Small phase sizes and challenges in computing appropriate initial values recent methods and references therein attempt to lower the index of DAEs to increase numerical behavior. Numerical rank inferences and time-consuming algebraic representations of the equations are usually used in these approaches. These modifications become too expensive to be useful, particularly for large-scale circuit equations.

The secret constraints in the MNA and MNA c/f can be calculated, and it has been shown that they can be achieved without algebraic modifications of the circuit coefficients by only using knowledge found in the circuit topology. Until now, the information collected in this manner has primarily been used to calculate consistent control parameters for system identification of the circuit equations, which must satisfy both hidden and explicit constraints. A definition known as minimal expansion, as seen, has commonly been used to incorporate hidden restrictions into the implementation phase.

The DAE obtained in this manner has an index of 1, while certain schemes that arise in reality may have an index of 2. The issue with this approach is that adding implicit restrictions to the equation increases the range of parameters. We'll tackle topological analysis in a somewhat different way, focusing on index reduction. It will be shown that secret constraints can be incorporated into channel calculations while maintaining Equation shape: MNA or MNA c/f. In this recommended strategy, the conclusions of the molecular dynamics correlation coefficients will be employed at a circuit compressor inlet. The main advantage though is that the whole circuit equation does not need a computational modification, but it changes the circuit itself. Therefore, a proteomic methodology for the circuit structure evaluation would be necessary before the practical simulation and to replace newly discovered elements with these components to form a circuit indicated in the index 1 DAE.

The benefit of this approach is that after the preprocessing, no more algebraic conversions have to be achieved, but the netlist, i.e., the list covering all structure- and section related data, itself is changed. The modified netlist will then be interpreted using the same modeling software as the initial netlist, as long as the simulation tools are capable of handling the new components. Since the current netlist generates index 1 circuit formulas, the transition process is frequently quicker and more precise than in the index 2 examples. Typically, the linear systems that result from discretization are better conditioned. Furthermore, obtaining a set of consistent initial values for the index 1 case is much simpler. The only additional expense is a one-time preprocessing phase, and the calculations can be integrated using existing tools.

Here, we'll go over the basics of the element substitution methodology and point out certain limitations to its use. We show a numerical example of the approach being used to evaluate a NAND gateway connection.

8.8.1 Element Replacement

We are going to deal with circuits consisting of overall resistors, two-term condensers, and condensers. This performance and perceived loudness are assumed to be regionally and individually of time. This implies that a module is made of CV cycles that are department grooves consisting of capacitors or supply voltage, and the resulting output of connector cuts that are sections that consist only of inducers and electrical accessories are the main characteristics of a conductor.

$$jc = \frac{d}{dt}qC(u_C) = C(u_C)\frac{d}{dt}u_C, \quad u_L = \frac{d}{dt}\phi L(jL) = L(jL)\frac{d}{dt}jL.$$

Here the above equation denotes voltage and current across the respective element, q_c denotes charge of capacitance and null value of flux in an inductance. The charge-voltage- and flux-current-relations $q_c(u_c)$ and null $L(jL)$ are assumed to be strictly monotonous such that as above equation are positive for all arguments.

For frequencies and impedances not present in these constructions, the tight "locally controlled two-term feature" limitation can be reduced. Secret restrictions arising from special circuit parameter choices and regulated sources that do not meet the criteria would not be included. The number of the circuit formulas is assumed to be less than 2 under these conditions.

Orientation can be selected for each loop and cutset. It provides a more comprehensive overview of these mechanisms. Loops of input voltages and cutsets of voltage dividers are usually not permitted because they can cause calculations to be inaccurate. The measures required to perform an index reduction would be easily evident as we extract functions for the secret restrictions. The number of inductance and capacitance and power switches in the loop is given by n_c^{loop} and n_c^{loop}, separately. The following is how the CV loop's implicit restriction can be construed:

- Denote the voltages across capacitances in the loop by $u_{C,k}^{\text{loop}}, k = 1 \ldots n_C^{\text{loop}}$.
- Denote the source voltages by $v_k^{\text{loop}}, k = 1 \ldots n_V^{\text{loop}}$.

- For every element in the loop, the constant is 1 if the element is oriented in the same way as the loop and -1 otherwise
- Kirchhoff's voltage law over that loop states that

$$\sum_{k=1}^{n_C^{loop}} \alpha_{C,k} u_{C,k}^{loop} + \sum_{k=1}^{n_V^{loop}} \alpha_{V,k} v_k^{loop} = 0.$$

- The derivative of the above equation holds as well

8.8.2 NUMERICAL QPSIM

What is the source of the following example? It's a NAND gate research circuit that was first discovered. The charge/flux-centered MNA circuit equations were set up with QPSIM 3, a PSIM expansion, cf., to the charge/flux oriented MNA formulations.

LEVEL B substitution circuits were used to model the MOSFETs. Vibrational but locally owned and operated capacitances are used in these replacement versions. We refer to Refs [15, 3] for more details and requirements. Displays the sensor readings utilized and the analog output comparing methodology. RADAU5 was used to calculate the comparison approach, with an index decrease for sensitivity configurations of 1015, since this was the highest possible tolerance level. To achieve a DAE of index 1, the circuit was subjected to the element substitution protocol. To calculate capacitance currents, seven voltage sources must be inserted into the operation. The number of unknowns in the c/f MNA system has been increasing between 29 and 36. For embedding power sources, QPSIM uses the form of MNA c/f equation, which only permits undetermined magnetic fields from all of these publications while ignoring the node capabilities of the implanted node, which only implants seven dependent variables rather than the 14 specified in Remark 3. RADAU5 as well as DASPK3.1, a version of DASSL, have been used to calculate approximations. Different tolerances ranging from 103 to 1012 were used for the numerical integration. Figure 3 depicts the obtained accuracies of the node potential at #1 i.e., an Intel Pentium portable PC with 1.4 GHz and 1 GB of RAM, both the output and a computer cost are. The picture brightness difference between the responsibility compliance and the precedent solutions is called 'error' at 0.1 ns.

8.9 USE OF 2D NON-UNIFORM QUICK FOURIER PROCESS TRANSFORMATIONS TECHNOLOGY TO ANALYZE THE MICRO-STRIP INSULATED CIRCUITRY

Microstrip discontinuity classification is a critical role in microstrip circuit computer-aided design (CAD). Interdisciplinary study, the technique of spatial analysis, time and frequencies domain, and the technique of boundary conditions are some of the methods for modeling divergences that have been established.

The Moment Method (MoM) provides the basis for the evaluation of microstrip circuits. As the capabilities of renewable progressively grow and there are many memberships needed to increase surface power density on the conductor, the analysis of the MoM matrix elements consumes the majority of the Central Processing Unit (CPU) time. Two-dimensional discrete fast Fourier transformations are used to compute the MoM matrix components (2D-SW). But the grid layout in this technique is confined to standardization. Because electromagnetic field varies fast across micro-rand borders, homogeneous matrices for analysis of a given micro-rand circuitry are ineffective. As a result, time local discretization is needed for effective analysis of the entire circuit. The currents are extended by a weighted sum of the current distributions of the first few resonance frequencies of the circuit to reduce the number of uncertainties. However, fine discrete and massive 2D fast Fourier transforms (FFT) resounding mode qualities still have to be found.

A 2D non-uniform rapid Fourier transform (2D NUFFT) is featured in this piece, is established for slot antenna circuit analysis, and is incorporated into the same classification approach (SDA). While each subsection must be a rectangle, the mesh arrangement for the micro strip circuit can become very versatile.

8.9.1 NUFFT Algorithm

The FFT is a quick methodology for computational transformations for the discerning Fourier system that includes several implications in, but not limited to, electric power and mechanical technology. It requires a uniform distribution of the displays on the monitor.

A non-uniform sample point in higher dimensional space is estimated by the NUFFT with a finite non-zero parameter approximation of the observed homogeneous Fourier foundation.

Take into consideration concise summary, which has performance data that are not evenly distributed.The incoming and destination information elements are N_f and N_a, respectively, and the input series f_k may be evenly or inequitably spaced.

To test Eq. 1 with linear antenna s_p, the NUFFT uses a total of measured nonlinear functions patterns in the area of s_p model appropriate at $q+1$ to estimate each $e^{jks}p$ as follows:

$$e^{jks_p} \approx \varphi_k^{-1} \sum_{l=-\frac{q}{2}}^{\frac{q}{2}} \gamma l(s_p) e^{j\left(v_p+l-\frac{q}{2}-1\right)2\pi\frac{k}{mN_f}} \tag{8.21}$$

The accuracy factors are normalization constant as the above equation is chosen to minimize the error of approximation in the square sense. Here q is an even positive integer and $m>=2$ is an index indicating the over sampling rate of the approximation. The sampling points of the complex exponentials on the right-hand side of the above equation collocate with those of a regular FFT with size $mN_f >= 2N_f$. A larger value of m improves accuracy.

8.9.2 2D NUFFT Algorithm

In the 2D NUFFT algorithm, the cross is a non-uniform sample point (x_t, y_s), $-\pi \leq x_t \leq \pi$ and $-\pi \leq y_s \leq p_i$, and the circles and large black dots are $(q+1) * (q+1)$ uniformly oversampled grid points (X_i, Y_i), which are called the square neighborhood of (x_t, y_s) therein. We are going to evaluate the following 2D Fourier transform:

$$D_{st} = \sum_{m=-\frac{M}{2}}^{\frac{M}{2}-1} \sum_{n=-\frac{N}{2}}^{\frac{N}{2}-1} G_{mn} e^{jmx_t} e^{jny_s} \tag{8.22}$$

where D_{st} and G_{mn} are finite complex sequences and M and N are even integers. In a similar manner as in the NUFFT whereas above equation denotes the integers nearest to the required symbol respectively. The accuracy factors j_m are chosen to minimize the error in the above equation in the least square sense.

Substituting equation yields the calculation of the above equation and can be performed by regular 2D FFT of size CM*CN. Similar to the above equation, the interpolated coefficients r_{pg} can be obtained by two sets of $(Q+1)^2$ NUFFT coefficients, the square neighborhood.

8.10 A FILTER DESIGN FRAMEWORK WITH MULTI-CRITERIA OPTIMIZATION BASED ON A GENETIC ALGORITHM

Continuous period filters are extensively used purposeful blocks, from modest anti-aliasing filters earlier analog-to-digital converters (ADCs) to high-spec channel-select filters in unified RF transceivers. Filter architecture is difficult, particularly when the system must satisfy a variety of requirements. There are several CAD tools for PID controller, but the majority of them is focused on classical governing equations, which only satisfy criteria for magnitude or step responses. In a cascade application of the filter, this chapter suggests a new approach for deriving filter digital filters that consider not just the requirements of increase and progress but also the duration of the extension, rise, and settlement, as well as the amount of the quad's ultimate strength.

8.10.1 Traditional Quantitative Measurements

The review concentrates on the most difficult step in filter design: the abstraction of the filter Fourier transform, also known as an approximation. Traditional quantitative measurements such as Butterworth, Chebyshev, and Cauer, which are commonly available in filter design applications, only satisfy gain or step specifications. Additional functional requirements, such as peak overshoot, rise- and settling-time, and/or application characteristics, such as the spread of same-type part values, biquads quality attributes, adjustability, and so on, usually require filters. This problem is solved with our CAD method, which takes into account many parameters. The approach begins with the structure that has been suggested. The transfer function with n complicated pole pairs defines a general consistent filtration system. Next, all behavioral properties— the magnitude, phase, and step response—are expressed in symbolic form as well.

8.10.2 Multicriteria Optimization Function Design

The pass-band of an ideal stabilized filter has unified negative and zero frequency resolution severity, the transition band has zero severity, the phase is linear, and the step-response is fast with low undershoot. With unavoidable defects, an actual analog filter calculates the observable traits (some of) described above. No typical estimate can manage both relevance and step needs, much alone more limitations (e.g., peak over-shoot, constancy factor value, etc.), such that the foregoing criteria are satisfied by a multi-objective output signal. In the setting given in the resolution, a sequence quadratic computing (SQP), the technique of optimizing the first stages to such a matched filter were obtained. The weighting challenge of multi-target modeling was:

$$F = Wpb\sigma pb + Wtb\sigma tb + Wsb\sigma sb + Wlp\sigma lp + Wlp\sigma Q + Wlp\sigma t \tag{8.23}$$

where Wpb is the proportion on b and pass the impact of technological reaction, Wtb is the frequency on transitional band significance reaction, WSb is the frequency-on-frequency response scaling function the weight of the linear phase deviation, and WQ is the strength on the price center frequency is the strength on the exceed cost. The graphical response areas σ_{pb}, σ_{tb}, σ_{sb} measure the eccentricity from supreme extent response for a lowpass filter in the pass, transition and stop-band:

10d of the asshole. In the phase μt reaction, one may infer, in a similar way, the symbolic representations of the departure from the Wlp, the difference between the weights and the loading axis. The best assumption for the optimization of multi-criteria is a customer mandatory skill. The input is a collection of data obtained from the bandpass Da, passband angled frequency (too many), stopband attenuator, and passband angle frequencies (too many), by use of an additional margin approximation. The features are computed by examination of the winning parts mostly during multi-criteria optimization problems. The rippling and corner frequencies are, for example, in the passband.

$$\omega \le |pk|, \quad d_a = -20\log\left(\max|H(j\omega)t| - \min|H(j\omega)|\right)$$

$$\omega_p \ge \max|pk|, \quad H(j\omega_p) = \min|H(j\omega)| \tag{8.24}$$

where pk is the differential equation pole. The stop-band attenuator and stop-band-angle fundamental characteristics in the slowdown are calculated.

8.10.3 MULTICRITERIA OPTIMIZATION GENETIC ALGORITHM

In our system, a population's chromosomes Ci is made up of a series of N which was before equations and 5 weighting factors (see Eq. (8.4)). N_v elements are found on the chromosome, where $N_v = N + 5$.

$$C_i = [P_i W_i]^t,$$ (8.25)

The SQP algorithm specifies the coordinates of the current poles p_k and zeros z_k for the genetically modified P_i and W_i, minimizing the objective function (4). The quantitative estimates of the appropriate FOPID controller are contrasted to the requirements S. The deviations are collected in an absolute error, which is used to assess the fitness role of chromosomes C_i. (See Figure 8.2)

$$E_i = [\varepsilon_{li} \varepsilon_{Ni}]^t$$ (8.26)

The aim is to get at least one chromosome with filter parameters that are similar enough to the requirements; the time of the optimization process is determined by the tolerances (limit error) defined by the customer. There are six steps to the continuous evolutionary algorithms:

Create the genetic algorithm—Since the population is made up of N_p chromosomes, the algorithm creates an NpxNv collection of random values. In a folder, the matrix is held. All parameters are standardized and have three-digit accuracy, taking constant values between 0 and 1 (the range of a uniform random number generator).

Natural Selection—The error vector (11) is obtained from the transfer function correlated with each chromosome. They are classified from cheapest to most expensive, based on an order of importance among the E_i elements (11). Only the top N_k chromosome from each individual is retained for copulation; the selection rate, which is set by the consumer, determines the value of N_k.

Pairing—The coupling pool is made up of the N_k most fit genes, with two fathers and mothers pairing at the chance. Every couple has two children who have some common features from both parents. Hence, both the parents and their descendants live to see the next generation.

Mating—Using the Radcliff method, the descendants are produced as a mixture of the parents.

Mutations—The genetic variation, which is set by the user, determines the range of parameters that will be mutations. The product of the gene sequence (Np 1) and the number of mutations (NV) yields the total number of bacteria. Following that, a random procedure is used to choose the location (row and column numbers in the community matrices) of the variables to be mutated. A mutated parameter is turned into a new value that is also created at variance.

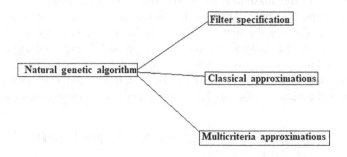

FIGURE 8.2 Multicriteria optimization.

The next generation is derived from all of the prototype steps and stored in a separate archive. The algorithm protocol is replicated before one of the three points mentioned below occurs: (1) a solution is discovered, (2) the population median stays stable for many decades (no evolution), and (3) the process meets the user-specified total amount of iterations NG. The genetic algorithm protocol requires the following input data: the size of population N_p, number of generations NG, selection, and mutation rates. At each stage, the critical features are saved: the average of errors, the demographic average, and the mean expense. The algorithm is written in C++ and uses SQL and the Paradox database.

8.11 TECHNIQUE OF THERMALLY NETWORKING IN HEAVY MACHINERY CONSTRUCTION

The thermal network (TNM) process is based on the substitution of a circuit made up of arbitrary 3D shape, thermal strength, abilities, and heating coils. The heat streams in this network are the same, and the terminal options are equivalent to degrees. Electrical circuit software should be used to achieve a solution since mathematical formulas are identical. The main benefit of thermal neural networks is their quick computation time: large model steady-state computations can be completed in a matter of seconds. As a result, the TNM is well suited for parameter studies and has grown in popularity as a method for software engineering. The construction of the node, in general, the transformation from actual geometry to a network-based model, is a flaw in TNM. This disadvantage can be overcome by using a hierarchical modeling approach and interchangeable library components that have ready-to-use descriptions of the entire device.

Ventilation is a critical effect that can be patterned using TNM technology. We developed the idea of ventilation networks for complicated models of power devices with different storage containers, which allows a systematic study of mass transfer combined with TNM. The hierarchical TNM approach, which includes ventilation networks, is described in this article, along with its implementation in actual design situations.

8.11.1 THERMAL NETWORKS CONCEPT

Figure 8.3 shows the basic mathematical objects replaced by thermal network architecture, for example, with an encased train operator carrying electric current I. Thermal power losses are produced by the current, which are carried through the conductor (in metal) and the insulating material and dissipated by thermionic emission. A portion of the produced heat may be deposited in the capacitance C of the conductive material (used for the transient computations only). Specific

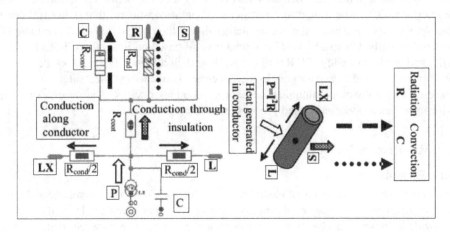

FIGURE 8.3   Thermal network model of a coated conductor.

formulas for calculating the circuit elements corresponding to convection R_{conv} and radiation R_{rad} are presented in this chapter. Other network components (R_{cond}, R_{coat}, C, P) have more descriptions and formulations used.

The convectional temperature difference is represented as:

$$R_{conv} = \frac{1}{\alpha_{conv} A_{conv}} \qquad (8.27)$$

α_{conv} and surface properties A_{conv} convection parameter. The α_{conv} computation is based on the notion of resemblance, which involves an assessment of Nusselt (Nu), Grasshof (ttr), Prandtl (Pr), and Reynold Distinctive Numbers (Re). You can use the understanding fundamental connection:

$$\alpha_{conv} = \frac{Nu \cdot \lambda_{fluid}}{l_{ch}} \qquad (8.28)$$

where λ_{fluid} consists of results of the electrical properties of the liquid and l_{ch}, e.g., vertical plate height or horizontally cylindrical diameter. For the forced convection with c_1 and n_1 parameters, the Nusselt index is determined:

$$Nu = c_1 (ttrPr)^{n1} \qquad (8.29)$$

whereas with coefficient c_2 and n_2 induced thermal expansion:

$$Nu = c_2 (RePr)^{n2} \qquad (8.30)$$

For a typical prognostic marker, the values of explanatory variables c_1, n_1, c_2, n_2 are experimental results achieved. The temperature depends on products ttrPr, RePr, and fluid. For turbulent and laminar models in various liquids, the constructed convection resists can be employed (Air, SF_6, oil, H_2O).

8.11.2 Hierarchical Thermal Networks Approach

It takes a long time to create a thermal network for a complicated system. We implemented the idea of hierarchical thermal networks to make it simpler and quicker. We construct networks using a hierarchical approach that includes not only primitive elements that describe elementary particles such as resistors and sources but also models of whole components. The channel arrangement of a conductor includes five thermal resistances, one capacitive coupling, for instance, and one source. The pins contribute to a thermal conduciveness (L, LX), a condensation (c), radiation (R), and an outside interface (O) can be joined to construct a different constituent that is the full conductors (S). The Network model depicts the encapsulating driver the current "covered conductors" function (referred to as the CN gICYL1). This model was all based on irradiation (RRA1), circulation (RCO1/2), and the loss of eddy (PI2R1) of the walls and circulation. The network depicted can be enveloped in and utilized at greater tiers in the "integrated conductors" element.

We use up to 5 network communication tiers for complex devices. The decentralized method makes for improved model control and product reusability.

8.11.3 Modeling of Ventilation

8.11.3.1 Formulation

Modular transmission lines, levels of electrically isolated air Controlling displays, and equipment are examples of air-insulated electrical power system systems that provide holes in the outside walls which provide for more natural airflow. A compartment containing heat sources usually has at least one inlet and one outlet for air exchange.

8.11.3.2 Ventilation Networks

Nonlinear dynamic channels describing respiratory mass flows can be generated using the formula (8.12). The reference to electric circuits is used in the case of ventilation connections, much as it is in the case of thermal networks: the electromotive force expresses the mass transfer m, while the stress difference p is the voltages. This illustrates a ventilating problem that requires an infrastructure investigation.

The primary objective of the circulating channels is to obtain oxygen transfer levels that may be employed in the ventilator resistance of the thermal networks. The following improvement steps were considered:

- Assume that the transmembrane temperature in the thermal network has an exact value.
- Construct the variational breathing system, using known temperatures to measure the values of rectifier diodes S and differential pressure p between all opening and according.
- Find the velocity of R_v resistors using the flow rate values obtained from the combustion system. Address the spectral channel in new nodal temperature values.
- Examine the variations between the current nodal temperatures and the equivalent values used in step 2's simulations. Stop iterations if the deviations are minimal enough; otherwise, proceed to step 2.

In the case of actual ventilation issues, a few iteration steps are usually enough to accomplish convergence (nodal temperature variations of less than 0.1 K).

8.11.3.3 Structural Thermal Network

It depicts an instance of a complicated power unit. We calculated steady-state temperatures along the transmission line using a structural thermal network method. It shows the deviations between mathematical calculations and measurements for most calculated points in the 3 K scale. The developed model can simulate mass and heat-transfer phenomenon and has been used to investigate various breathing options.

8.12 HIERARCHICAL MIXED MULTI-RATING IN CIRCUIT SIMULATION

8.12.1 MODULAR MODELING

Most big electrical circuits are modularly manufactured. Multiple different of multiple purposes are generated autonomously or fused from a database. To integrate an image criterion of psychology in a complicated design, each module must have locations where it may link up to its surroundings. For this reason, a portion of its constituents is referred to as "pins." These pins alone enable current flow beyond the border of the subcircuit.

Each module is identified by a¨-to-each integer and the pin voltage is introduced by the vector jP'. We also agree to leave the machine at the stations. As a result, the pin flows may be translated to the subcircuit's respective nodes. $ne\lambda \times nP\lambda$ described by the extra incident matrices $AP\lambda \in \{0, 1\}$, where ne and $nP\lambda \ll ne\lambda$ are the set of neurons and pins, correspondingly in the λth subcircuit. Charges guided MNA generates networking formulae of the following sort for basic portions, i.e., constituents that do not contain other subcircuits' categorizations:

Each subcircuit may be thought of as a black box feature with a certain number of terminals from the outside. As a result, it can be seen in a more complicated subcircuit. In this way, a centralized circuit architecture is developed. However, in the following, we will look at circuits made up of r subcircuits that can be represented using (1). This interpretation can be achieved in a hierarchical design by spreading out the hierarchical arrangement of the subcircuits. First, we'll go through certain methods for coupling r subcircuits.

The most versatile approach is to use a master circuit that also serves as network infrastructure. The only components are nM master nodes and r subcircuit instantiations. The incidence matrix can be used to define the master's topology as the pin currents exit the subcircuits and flow through the master nodes.

$$A_M = \left(A_{z_1},\ldots,A_{z_r}\right),$$

with $AZ_\lambda \in \{0, -1\}$ assembling the pin currents of the λth subcircuit. Kirchoff's current law, applied to the master nodes yields since the slaves are connected to the master's degree nodes, the necessary nodal impedances must match, system (1,2) with $\lambda = 1, \ldots, r$ determines the slaves' quantities $e_\lambda, j_{L\lambda}, j_{V\lambda}, q_\lambda, \Phi_\lambda$, i. e. node potentials, currents through inductors and voltage sources, charges and fluxes, and the pin currents $j_{P\lambda}$ as well as the master's node potentials e_M.

8.12.2 COMPATIBILITY OF MASTER NODES

The shorts to the leading nodes (2b) and the others pins of the subcircuits (3). dc voltage pathways with a zero-voltage drop. As a result, the two methods are upward compatible, as each virtual input voltage may be applied to the range of power supply of a single balance of the ecosystem.

The master circuit and community network method have model equations that can be published as quantitative differential equations (DAE): The terminal possibilities and current flow in yµ are transistors and power switches (and pin weather systems), correspondingly in xµ with the charges/ streams and next with the couplings currants (or network state possibilities); we exclude temporal dependence based on the good reasoning.

We will adhere to the peer-to-peer system and the maestro circuit remedy for the following paragraphs. The pin vibrations in circuitry simulations that support multilevel control circuits are not required particularly as extra unknown factors. They organically derive from the matrices polynomials that depict the interior architecture and the contributions of the excessive dependence to the master circuitry. We shall, however, take them as possible difficulties for reasons to be discussed later.

8.12.3 INDEX PROPERTIES

Several r subcircuit models (4a) are coupled by the network equations. We demand the following if we limit ourselves to index-1 problems:

(C1) Index 1 is assigned to the total scheme (with respect to $x_1, \ldots, x_r, x_{ext}$).
(C2) With x_{ext} = was data, all systems describe index-1 systems concerning x.

We know from that (C2) holds if neither CV-loops nor LI-cutsets are present in the sub-circuits. It's worth noting that the simulated voltage sources are known as current sources in this sense, providing the current w. Following these lines, we will prove that (C1) holds if the total circuit contains no capacitor loops, voltage sources, or virtual voltage sources.

8.12.4 HIERARCHICAL MIXED MULTI-RATE

Hierarchical mixed multi-rate appears to be the most realistic solution for a multi-rate system that can work with an infinite number of operation levels. The key principle is to nest composite measures and subsequent segments and sub in such a way that only a two-level extended Kalman scheme is used at any given time. At each integration time point, each configuration has one of two states: active or inactive. If the most recent company was subsequently at which an estimate is visible is past the present one, a component is sleeping. The set of non-sleeping subsystems is divided into two subsets: those that suggest a broad individual operate independently and those that require a specific measure. The previous is known as latent, while the latter are known as effective. Although

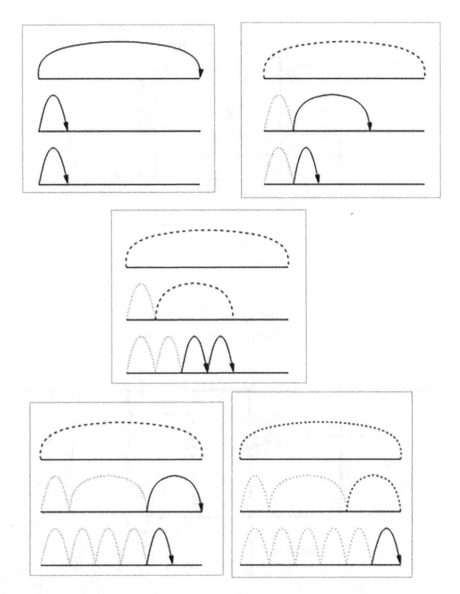

FIGURE 8.4 Hierarchical mixed multi-rate blocks.

this method can decompose the collection of not sleeping structures, it requires a compound stage. Otherwise, subsequent microsteps are carried out. Via high-density, the sleeping subsystems contribute to the existing phase (Figure 8.4).

8.13 AUTOMATIC PARTITIONING FOR MULTI-RATE METHODS

DAEs of the following form are often used to model analog electrical circuits: MNA is used to create the vector-valued quantities q, j, which represent the contributions and currents in the network model. The state vector $x(t)$ R_d, which is dependent on the time variable t, describes nodal voltage levels by output power elements such as voltage sources and inductors. The transient analysis is a typical analysis that quantifies the resolution $x(t)$ of this nonlinear DAE forgiven original conditions over the time interval $[0, T]$. Sections of electrical circuits also exhibit multi-rate behavior, which means that certain parameters differ limited in comparison to others.

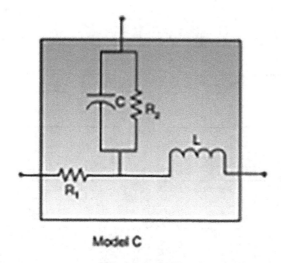

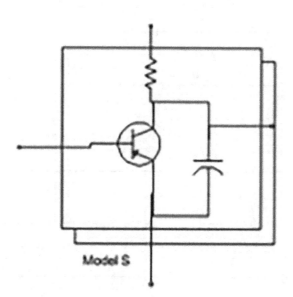

FIGURE 8.5   Circuit diagram.

Figure 8.5 shows a two-dimensional scalable circuit with M N inverters and M 2N nodal voltages as an example. The subcircuits are linked by linear filters that have been selected such that only three subcircuits are involved and nearly disentangled from the others. This ownership implies that the error vector's form resembles that of an iceberg, as seen in the right-hand side of Figure 1.

8.14   MULTI-RATE TRANSIENT ALGORITHM

8.14.1   THE DAE SYSTEM

The partitioning should be correctly selected for DAEs to make it workable as well. In addition, if the consistency and indexing are retained, it is a desirable characteristic. That's not generally the case in actuality.

- **BDF algorithms Combination**

  Multirate approaches participate both part by means of diverse time-steps H and h. The multi-rate factor is used in circuits with multi-rate behavior, such as in the previous case.

  On both the coarse and polished grids, we use the Backward Differentiation Formula (BDF) Compound-Fast algorithm [8, 7] describes this technique. It divides the circuit model into two parts: slow and fast. Each iteration begins with a broad compound stage that integrates the entire method. During the Newton method, the active component is calm. After that, only the fast component is integrated (or "fined"), with interpolated values replacing the associated slow application parameters. It is seen that if both components are loosely coupled and the active component is globally stable, this is a mathematically stable arrangement.

- **Automatic partitioning**

  This section introduces several separating architectures. Following that, it is shown how these methods can be used creatively. Ultimately, certain problems of deployment are addressed.

8.14.2 THE OPTIMAL PARTITION

An 0-1 software of exponential complexity is the ultimate method to optimize the issue (8). It is simply impossible to consider all feasible index set transformations. As a result, we can rely on simplifications, such as determining the optimum, only for all size k sub-sets modifications. The difficulty of the procedure is then calculated $E(dk)$.

8.15 PARTITIONING ALGORITHMS

The system practices have been examined by us:

- The first sort attempts to solve by only taking into account the extended Kalman factor m, which is estimated by $\hat{m}$ from. It is assumed that H_{new} only depends on $BL\hat{e}$, which is the compound step's latent discretization error calculation After that, the latent element with the highest local error element is identified. $\hat{e}_i$ and should be refined such that m^ becomes larger. Also, the active element which has the smallest $\hat{e}_i$ is determined 1. The most effective dormant component and the most active latent element are chosen. The optimum transformation is then achieved by comparing all four potential transformations of these two discovered components to their respective approximate speed-up variables. The transformation with the highest approximate speed-up factor is generated iteratively before convergence. To begin, this algorithm requires an initial guess. It may be the previous partition, a partition calculated by a different algorithm, or a partition defined by the user.
- When the predicted local error satisfies, all nodes become refined.
- Another method calls the absolute criteria.

  The user specifies the level of tolerance TOL such that the local error meets the requirements.
- A fourth method uses the local error vector to calculate the required stepsizes per component $\hat{e}$. It finds the greatest difference between the stepsizes. This difference is then used to divide the machine into two parts: quick and slow.

8.16 DYNAMICALLY CHANGING PARTITIONING

Multi-rate cannot be used for a static partition in wireless circuits, for example. Then thermodynamic splitting procedures [2, 4] that can follow the moving active component are needed. This implies that during the multi-rate time-integration, the partitions should be modified. Since repartitioning are expensive, changing the partition during the improvement is not permitted. As a result, repartitioning will only happen right after the compounding process or right after the refining phase. The three following options are available:

- Using the calculated error vector at the coarse grid, the partitions are modified immediately after the compounded phase. The partitions are revised shortly after the refining process, which includes the use of the refined time-active grid's errors.
- After performing a single rate phase, the error vector is used to repartition. Since the active component of the coarse error vector in method A is not reliable, methods B and C are best suited for stepsize regulation and relaxation of the Newton mechanism. Nonetheless, method A was used for the numerical tests in the following section because it is better at detecting discriminant analysis wake-ups. Figure 8.8 depicts a hybrid of these techniques. Method A is used with the caveat that only latent elements can be transferred to the refinement section. The number of repartitioning is minimized by retaining the old partition for an acceptable speed-up factor S.
- The Multirate Algorithm's Consequences the latest multi-rate algorithm is also affected by hierarchical segmentation. So, there's the issue of storage. Conceivably, each node will now have its time points. It is difficult to store the strategies and time-grids in a regular sequence because the lengths of these moments would vary with each unit. Furthermore, there is an activation issue for the wake-up fast nodes that were sluggish during the previous composite stage in multistep methods. Returning to one-step processes, such as Euler Backward, will minimize the productivity achieved. For the latest optimization phase using upgraded data, we use the previous coarse-grid quadratic formula as a predictor quadratic formula. The calculated acceleration factor can also be used to determine if the next step will be a compound or single rate step, which is a pleasant feature of dynamical partitioning. This is, in reality, an advantage of the Compound-Fast process in Figure 8.6.

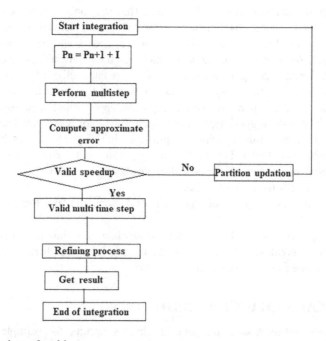

FIGURE 8.6 Flowchart of multi-rate.

8.17 SIMULATION OF QUASIPERIODIC SIGNALS VIA WARPED MPDAEs USING HOUBEN'S APPROACH

Circuit components commonly create oscillating impulses of highly separated time frames in broadcast operations, for example, the amplitude of elevated oscillations can change quite slowly. A schematic diagram of the circuit must be resolved with the associated time-based system of an algebraic mathematical model (DAEs). As rapid oscillations restrict the phase-in time and the entire period is defined by the slow time, simulation is expensive. A multidimensional signal model creates a distinct method, which assigns its vectors to each geological timescale. The corresponding method of multi-rate differential equation mathematical model (MPDAEs) was proposed, which yields an accurate simulation of strictly reference signal signals. The method was generalized by Narayan and Roychowdhury for both amplitude-modulated (AM) and frequency-modulated (FM) signals. As a result, a system of twisted MPDAEs emerges, with the selection of a suitable local frequency feature critical to the multidimensional model's performance. Unnecessary oscillations in the multivariable result from rash decisions.

8.17.1 MULTIDIMENSIONAL MODEL

The mathematical model of electronic circuits yields a structure of DAEs. We examine a set of elements.

$$\frac{d\mathbf{q}(x)}{dt} = \mathbf{f}\Big(\mathbf{b}(t), x(t)\Big), \qquad \begin{aligned} \mathbf{x} &: \mathbb{R} \to \mathbb{R}^k, \quad \mathbf{q} : \mathbb{R}^k \to \mathbb{R}^k, \\ \mathbf{b} &: \mathbb{R} \to \mathbb{R}^l, \quad \mathbf{f} : \mathbb{R}^l \times \mathbb{R}^k \to \mathbb{R}^k \end{aligned} \qquad (8.31)$$

where x denotes undefined branch currents and node voltages. We presume that the input signals b that have been predetermined differ steadily. The solution x, on the other hand, must include high-frequency oscillations whose magnitude and phase are steadily modified through the impulses of input. The indicators x, therefore, extend across a wide variety of periods. Consequently, the resolution of the DAEs (1) requires several time stages, making a temporary evaluation ineffectual.

8.17.2 HOUBEN'S METHOD

A priori, an appropriate local frequencies method for effectively expressing the signals is unclear. Unwanted oscillations in the multiversion file systems (MVFs) are caused by inappropriate choices, as seen in. The minimization dilemma was proposed by Houben.

$$s(t_1) := \int_0^1 \left\| \frac{\partial \mathbf{q}(\hat{\mathbf{x}})}{\partial t_1}(t_1, u) \right\|^2 du \to \min. \quad \text{for each} \quad t_1 \geq 0 \qquad (8.32)$$

$\|\cdot\|$ using the Euclidean norm. As a result, oscillatory behavior is minimized by minimizing the incomplete derivative's effect on the slow time scale. As a result, a subsequent optimization process allows for computational simulations of comparatively broad phase sizes. A required condition for an optimization process is implied by demand (8): with the Euclidean inner product $\langle \cdot, \cdot \rangle$. The unexplained local frequency function can be eliminated using this formula. As a result, solving partial differential issues on a slow time scale is possible. In addition, the condition is the same as the orthogonality connection.

8.18 CONCLUSION

In this chapter, we offer a new method of modulation process and the existence and sustainability of the chaotic fractional-order system. The experimental modeling of this nonlinear systems system is demonstrated by the use of the chain ship circuit form. Since fractional differential equations potential in numerous scientific domains, such as rheology, diffusive transmission, communication systems, electromagnetism theory, complex systems' quantic development, colored noise, etc., have been identified. It is shown that differential equations give a superior tool for memory mapping and inheritance of numerous phenomena in comparison to traditional well-known modeling. Furthermore, the construction of the circuit may practically test the chaotic properties of chaotic systems, encourage chaos, and encourage future use of technology. Then there has been an increasing interest in engineering applications in the circuit execution of chaotic systems. In particular, circuit constructions are particularly crucial for these fractional-order convergences.

9 Computational Electromagnetics

9.1 FINITE INTEGRATION TECHNIQUES RF & MICROWAVE SIMULATIONS — FROM INDIVIDUAL TO SYSTEM ARCHITECTURE

The Finite Integration Technique, for brief FIT (finite integration technique) was primary projected nearly 30 years ago, as a technique for the replication of electromagnetic arenas and of numerous attached problems. The main principle was that the integral structure of Maxwell's equations should rather be used for the approximation. This initial insight was right and has many analytical, algorithmic, and computational benefits. Furthermore, in a traditionally different approach, the Finite Element analysis lately seemed to predominate the same perspective. The finite integration technique (FIT) was first presented to overcome Maxwell's Calculations of frequency response. The first algorithms in their mode was able to remove all false modes efficiently, while just 10 years later, a solution to this problem could be sought for other approaches like the finite element method (FEM).

FIT was presented for the first time in an eddy existing situation 1 year after the first chapter (1978), followed by (for a few reasons) the expansion of FIT to FDTD-like plans, along with an enhancement of the rf-z coordination system (1980) and rectangular meshes implementation (1987), stable sub-grading algorithm non-orthogonal grid implementation (including triangular fillings), Model order decrease combined with the FIT (2000).

Around 1980, the FIT expanded rapid renown in the worldwide accelerator physics community. This is the start of the MAFIA cooperation, which brings together universities, research institutions, accelerated workshops with the purpose of developing a 'MAXWell's Equation Solutions with an Obligations In relation Algorithm' as an FIA technology package to address electromagnetism problems.

This consortium, which has lasted 10 years, has been spread to (and used extensively in) testing facilities in 26 countries by absolute electromagnetic, thermal, and monitoring applications.

Possibly three variables lead to the effectiveness of the FIT. First, it is a sound theoretical algorithm, which showed, inter alia, stability, the geometry of arithmetically calculated modes, energy efficiency, and charge preservation early on. Second, it is not only true in the intensity but also in the time sector, which enables very broad or very complex structures to be simulated. This applies to a lot of mesh forms, finally [229].

9.1.1 THE MINIMUM TECHNIQUE FOR ALGEBRAIC INTEGRATION

FIT generates precise quadratic formulations to Maxwell to ensure that the physical features of the areas in the universe are distinct and lead to a particular system. Electromagnetic polarities are allocated on the edges of the grid faces (the main grid) in the System of equations and related content equations, from persisting to disconnecting the power stages space and electromagnet at the margins and magnetism circulations on the characteristics of second networks ("dual grid").

It does not just utilize intrinsically free levels, i.e., polarities and streaming, and does not merely produce field components (as in FDTD). The matrix structure of the Maxwell equations to be written very elegantly but also has significant computational and numbered algorithmic effects. Measurable quantities often have an integral type, the electrical field force, for example, and cannot be determined directly but by an electro tension intermediate along an extremely short line.

The problems in coordination frameworks or tetrahedral meshes [230].

DOI: 10.1201/9781003211938-9

FIGURE 9.1   Mesh types for a coaxial connector.

9.1.2   State of the Art

The area of Microwave frequency modeling has a wide range: numerous devices (filtration, connections, antenna, cavities...), each of them having the special capability of post-processing; variety in mechanical stability and level of detailed information (for example, rounded sections, thin layers, tiny details in otherwise structural components, intricate forms) see in Figure 9.1.

Though no one approach can solve any challenge, FIT is possibly the 3D numeric method with a broad range of approximation needs because of its simplicity. In this segment, some will be addressed [231].

9.1.3   Discretization Mesh Types

The structure must be spatial, and temporal quantized before mitigating an electromagnetic problem, i.e., a mesh of fractional order must be converted into structures geometries. One of the key elements of FIT is the "translated" in a particular mesh of Maxwell equations (2D or 3D). The tetrahedra, hexahedral, and conforming hexahedral matrices seem to be the most frequent meshes of linearisation (Figure 9.2).

Tetrahedral meshes have the benefit of ensuring that curved surfaces are well approximated. The only drawback is that such a mesh is not suitable for time-domains: The corresponding matrix multiplication (for any number method) can be solved in frequency-domains efficiently but are ineffective for time-domain algorithms because of their non-diagonal properties. It must be emphasized, finally, that tetrahedral numerical solution is not a trivial operation.

The traditional hexahedral triangles have the benefit that all time- and often-domain algorithms can be implemented quickly. They result in very memory and computer-efficient algorithms in the time domain. Even with very difficult geometric shapes, the numerical solution is simple. The principal drawback of the classic hexahedral mesh is the imitation of the pathway on curved surfs and often serious effects upon solution accuracy, as well as its extension over the whole computer domain if a similar technique is desired in a small area of the system [232].

Luckily, remedies for these two drawbacks are available The PERFECT BOUNDARY (PBA) is one of the most utilized, which preserves every advantage of the Cartesian ordered grid and enables precise simulation of its rounded parameters.

The enhancement of PBA geometry makes the use of a much coarser mesh with the same exactness as to the steps in the estimation. Figure. 9.2 demonstrates the evolution of an independent

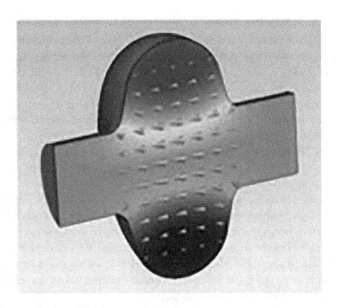

FIGURE 9.2 Eigen frequencies changes with the volume of air in the discretizing mesh for conventional cavities.

structure with the number of mesh cells. In the PBA mesh, 20,000 mesh cells are adequate for the accuracy (<0.1%), of 1.277 GHz for a speed, although more than 500,000 mesh cells are essential for the escalating matrix.

The Thin-Sheet Technique (TST) PBA extension enables precise computational simulation of thin-level structures, for example, the curved patch-antenna array for Figure 9.2. (Which is difficult to mesh with any numerical method.)

The current sub-gridding methodology is an invention that enables the local finesse of the cartesian coordinate system in countries with high field variations or with finer geometric information. There is a significant reduction in the total numbers of mesh cells and the computer time (Fig. 6). The PBA§R and TSTTM algorithms allow for much more precise geometry classification in each simplified cell. Please note: In contrast to the most known sub grating methods, the one applied in CST MWS ensured reliability and thus prevented a detrimental impact on the precision of the data [233].

Each problem is subject to a form of mesh that is appropriate in terms of memory specifications and the precision of the geometry approximation, according to its dimensions and constantly exploring. The disposal of various types of mesh processors will significantly improve the performance of RF component modeling in a simple simulation model.

9.1.4 DOMAIN'S COMPUTATIONS OF TRANSMISSION AND RECEPTION

The FIT method is not merely a periodicity, opposed to widespread assumption. To name a few optimizer forms, it gives overt and implied frequencies (broad, adaptive control, reductions in sequence) and phase modulation.

Luckily, remedies for these two drawbacks are available The Complete Boundaries (PBA) is one of the most utilized, which preserves every advantage of the Cartesian ordered grid and enables precise simulation of its rounded parameters.

The enhancement of PBA geometry makes the use of a much coarser mesh with the same exactness as to the steps in the estimation. It demonstrates the development of an independent structure with the number of mesh cells. Thus, with altogether separate algorithms you also can solve one single problem. This allows by far the most effective algorithm for the moment process of the building construction (computing time and storage needs), but also provides separate outcomes for cross-checks in the validation and development, and testing phases.

The Second touchdown is the optimal solution for the requirement to produce broadband out-comes since they produce broadband results in one single pass. The comprehensive 3D simulations of a 30-meter airplane, with a flat wave at 500 MHz, illustrates the use for standard time. Although quite high (9 million cells), it takes a few hours to simulate the FIT/PBA domain method on a com-mon PC. This dilemma would be too large for a domain solution on a volume basis [234].

Even TD solvers are required if the approximation requires predetermined or complex time signaling. Examples include Ultra-Wideband Antenna Applications (UWB) or Time Domain Reflectometry (TDR).

On the other hand, FD-resolvers can be most effective where small structures need narrow-band or one-frequency results for both numbers and the electrical scale or when periodic border condi-tions are desired in non-null phase changes.

The frequency selective surfaces are an example of the latter (FSS). They contain a large number (exponential in theory) of equivalent cells, such that only a single unit cell can be represented in the first approximation (periodic boundary conditions). Figure 9.3 illustrates this surface: a metal surface with broken rings in the form of frequently positioned slots designed to simulate is just one repetitive part. The landscape is illuminated by a waveguide with distinct incidents. In the graph of reflecting and transmissions in Figure 9.3 to the correct, the discriminating feature of frequencies is obvious (here, around 9.8 GHz and around 19 Gaz).

High-resonance architectures are often thought to work for FD only since it has a lengthy time to oscillate graphics in the technological improvements systems, which also makes it especially lengthy for TD simulations. However, when using time signals with signal processing techniques, including autoregressive filters, the condition will adjust again for the benefit of TD methods. In addition, if wideband results in an FD solution are (relatively) required, the frequency range requires "intelligent" sampling, otherwise main frequency targets such as resonant frequency could be just It could not occur with a strategy TD ignored. The widely known asymptotic waveforms analysis may be employed for linear interpolation between recorded resonant frequencies in a speedier approxi-mation of bandwidth. In the case of a complex frequency behavior, the AWE approach extrapolates around every individual estimated signal frequency but may collapse [235].

For example, Figure 9.3 shows the shape of an EMC problem: a thin slot aperture repeating. The methodology emphasizes resonance from the S-parameter map. The wear glasses solver and the

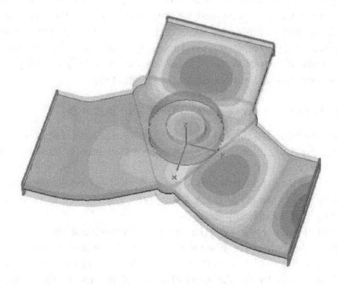

FIGURE 9.3   Electromotive force within the circulatory structure comprising a gyro-tropical ferrite sub-stance in the center.

frequency domain ability to solve (combined with an auto-regressive filtering method) (combined with an efficient automatic generation wipe) were employed. Funny enough, the frequency solution is the fastest for this problem: It took 8 minutes on a regular PC to achieve this precision, although the spatial frequency ability to solve needed longer than 1 hour.

Another tool that may be more effective for purposes: the model order decrease (MOR). This is the case with the classic RF filter seen in Fig. 10: the previous program has a very large value of 130,000 owing to its fine network. This is simplified by MOR to a device of just about 1,000 unknowns which can be resolved on a regular PC in approximately 1 minute [236].

Meshing itself is only half of the equation: in tandem with automated optimization and maximum quantification, full performance can be achieved. The new research was conducted into the development of automated mesh, based on the expert method that takes the geometry as well as its physicochemical parameters into account. The latest trend is to merge the expert method and the conventional automated mesh adaptation.

9.2   DESIGN AND SIMULATION

The effective evaluation is one of the key "factors" for design and simulation precision. Real materials are most commonly complex, anisotropic, or have varying characteristics. Anisotropic, degradation, and scattering materials of different scatter action forms are available in FIT (Debye 1st, and 2nd order, Lorentz, gyro tropical). The more complex systems such as plasma devices or combiners are stimulated by these devices. In Figure 9.4, the electrical field inside a circulating framework (in the center is a gyro tropical substance cylinder) [237]. The magnetic moment of the ferrite component, followed by a high-frequency time field simulation, was achieved through a FIT-dependent magnetic materials computation. The influence of the circulator is obvious.

Recent issues about EMC/EMI and emerging methods in medical research demand more and more simulations including body models for human beings. These are very uniform, contain several different diffraction materials, and usually include a wide fine mesh. It depicts a model human head subjected to cell telephone radiation. A time/domain approximation was used because the model was reasonably large (FD would have required too much memory). In Figure 9.4 you can see the defined absorption rate (SAR) in the brain (b).

Though 3D field simulation is well suited for replicating complicated structures and structures, it would be ineffective to simulate complete systems: computational effort would be too massive to achieve the required precision. A hybrid solution is essential for such implementations. In such a design setting, FIT was completely implemented, which randomly combines numerical methods: one can quickly, for instance, combine three-dimensional blocks with a flat solution instrument, empirical solutions or process matching techniques; or practically every other strategy deserving

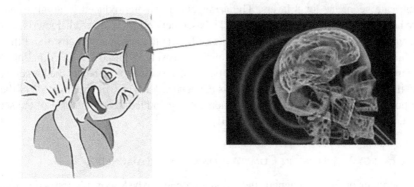

FIGURE 9.4   EMI human skeleton analysis: EMI: (a) Smartphone humanoid skull. (b) High diffusion rate (SAR) on the eye height inside this skull. Light-gray shades exhibit massive SAR regions.

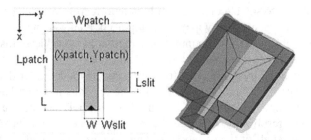

FIGURE 9.5 Circuit-3D EM issue co-simulation andco-optimization: impedance bandwidth array with wide bandwidth.

of porting an aspect. Above all, this flexible approach to architecture enables interaction with other advanced systems and reduces the dependency on single proprietary technology [238].

For instance, Figure 9.4 shows a patch antenna block scheme with a feeding network. The feeder network includes both lumped circuit components (amplifiers, resists, condensers, etc.) and virtual blocks from 2D microstrips using a geometric area simulation.

A complete 3D solver is generated for the antenna array itself see in Figure 9.5. The cumulativefar-field of the two patches can be computed after the optimization of the controller gains to ensure a fair fit with the frequency of operation [239].

9.2.1 SPECIFIC APPLICATION CATEGORIES AND CURRENT PROSPECTS

The demands of today's market are being steadily increased in the context of graphical representation: the use of operational frequencies is growing, and current methods are becoming difficult to implement, the sophistication of the system is increasing each year in Figure 9.6.

Of course, in the traditional fields of industrial applications, radiofrequency electric modeling today continues to be required: filters, connectors, lead systems, antennas. Application characteristics of this field are that the prototypes become much more extensive and include highly effective computer and memory architectures see in Figure 9.6.

Field simulations are now being implemented for domains where only circuit optimization algorithms have been needed until recently: PCBs, integrated circuit components, etc... This is because circuit design methods fail partially as the signal frequency of embedded systems increases. Figure 9.7 shows this example: 10 GHz, at a very high frequency, of surface waves in a padlock. The results in the field were easily evident and no circuit simulator would catch them [240].

A further example of a challenging issue is shown in Figure 9.7 in the whole architecture and 3D image of a tiny portion of a PCB. A very tiny feature extraction mesh of up to 10mesh pixels is used to construct intricate geometry for 8 layers. The arrangement was reproduced in ahigh-frequency crass talking here between parallel pairs on a 24-CPU IT-based network. Two more characteristics have eventually been visible in recent years, but not least. The first is that electromagnetism and thermal, electromechanical, or fluid dynamical technologies are extensively required for coordinating difficulties. Second, the incorporation of the present electrolytic capacitors electromagnet by the longer wavelengths Second, the integration into huge flows of models (Cadence, Advisor Animations, etc.) of the electrical charge components of electromagnetism simulation software added to the outcome of the sector which the most recent circuit designs cannot include [241].

9.2.2 THE ENERGY VIEWPOINT IN COMPUTATIONAL ELECTROMAGNETICS

Reading a dissertation on Electromagnetic induction is probably to be Maxwell's first series of calculations

$$\text{curl } h - \partial_t d = j \tag{9.1}$$

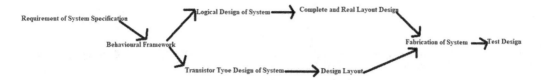

FIGURE 9.6   Surface currents on an IC package at 10 GHz.

FIGURE 9.7   IBM's PCB architecture. (a) 3D layout. (b) Schematic perceive. The left figure displays also a possible structural division that simulates every piece with another CPU.

$$\operatorname{curl} e + \partial_t b = 0 \tag{9.2}$$

$$\operatorname{div} b = 0 \tag{9.3}$$

$$\operatorname{div} d = \rho^Q \tag{9.4}$$

A series of socially constructed forms connections supplemented

$$b = \mu h, d = \varepsilon e, j = \sigma e \tag{9.5}$$

The first set is universal (still valid), and the second set includes any relationship that should be 'closed' and resolvable. In this manner, electromagnetic induction is seen as a series of domains that have a partial differential equation (PDE) and socially constructed connections because of the development of spatial and temporal. There is no space for energy requirements in this environment [242].

However, certain energy-related concepts could be incorporated forward in the same document. For example, magnetic energy is generally known as a b or h feature (or even both). Various materials, from the simplistic medium (vacuum) and from the ground up to more advanced materials can be perceived: linear, anisotropic, non-lipoidal, etc. Not long, however, since the meanings easily become very complicated and go beyond the meaning of a general monograph see in Figure 9.8.

Thus, the traditional explanations of the principle of electricity and magnetism give the idea that energetic Components are usual techniques toxic chemicals, peripherals, and are difficult to use. However, the laws of thermodynamics are general and must therefore be valid for electromagnetism. Maxwell's equations suggest much still about the preservation of electromagnetic energy, but they do so in a manner that prevents the difference in energy fluxes from being distorted. In addition, classical theory explanations leave problems such as • what are the state variables in an electrical system unresolved?

- How is commonly defined electrical or magnetic energy?
- What are the possible dissipating mechanisms?
- How does electricity now become an electromagnetic point in time?
- How can electromagnetic radiation become other energy forms?

Such deficiencies are especially impeding when dealing with problems such as the combination of local electrical powers (energy conversion), magnetic hysteresis (energetic dissipation), or general

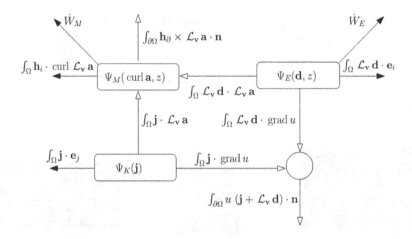

FIGURE 9.8   Energy flow diagram.

capacitor (both). For such questions, it is very sensible to provide an electromagnetic philosophy where aspects of energy are considered from the beginning to the end.

Since experimental research in these areas and expertise of how energy is behaving in electromagnetic fields, it has finally become clear and comprehensive. In a way, that creates electricity and magnetism concept, quite unexpectedly. The electromagnetism is represented in the form of a flow diagram. It offers more than the traditional theory facts and answers to the above questions. The continuity equation can be defined directly in arbitrary configurations since they are expressed in an analytical equation instead of a series of PDEs. Finally, the energy-dependent principle introduces surgical principles that explain concerns such as modeling of hysteresis and offer several clues about how linking terms and specifications in decreased order models can be handled consistently [243].

- Flow chart for electricity

    The hypothesis of energy-dependent electromagnetic is presently being a democratic framework. More details may be found in. The picture in the Euclidean Space of the power diagram. Three related energy stores each with a random vector are seen in the diagram. The status variables are both the power potential of the magnetic vector and the electrical real-valued function u and the electric charges, i.e., the electrical pressure and initial concentration j. The status parameters are two gravitational [244].

    The magnetization in the a-reservoir is which is additive around the domain Ú Based on magnetic density Ú SIE, is the function of the curl inhibition and perhaps even of one or more other non-electromagnetic amounts (e.g., the pressure), as defined by the unspecified vector z generically. The d reservoir also contains electricity $-E(d, z)$. U tank is now empty.

- Equations of sustainability

    Since the probability distribution is major system parameters, the limit requirements suggested by data - interpretation can vary flexibly, following the kind of argumentation of a variation. When defining energy consumption in indicates how efficiently, initially the total of all factor values equals all production flowing and, from the other hand, the differentiating connects the system is implemented for mathematical electrolyte materials functions, the energy variability in the picture is achieved utilizing two statements. Sustainability coefficients are derived locally by using the cognitive matrix multiplication of Fractional calculus and the arbitrary time variables of the differential equation. $v\ x$, $x=a, d, j, u$, playing the role of the variations δx. The Euler-Lagrange equations obtained this way are

9.3 NEWTON AND NEWTONIAN APPROXIMATION REFLECT THE INCREASE WITH THE APPROACH OF DIAGONAL FINAL INTEGRATIONS

FIT is usually used in conjunction with a perpendicular, sprung grid pair that results in sparser linear algebra matrices and greater computational simulation performance than unstructured grids.

In this article, we demonstrate that the use of the Newton method to linearize a non-linear field dilemma does not have these positive algebraic properties. We analyze the causes and devise a Newton approach to solve this. For chosen research models, in which case it is advised that the estimated Functional monomer over the actual Newton's method is favored and in which case the approach is not proposed. For contrast, the classical following approximation approach is used [245].

9.3.1 DISCRETIZATION OF THE MAXWELL EQUATIONS

FIT is a discretization method for vectorial partial differential equations, first proposed in 1977 for discretizing the Maxwell equations. The dis- creation process is carried out on a primary-dual, staggered grid complex $(tt,\tilde{t})$ (Figure 1a). The considered degrees of freedom are global ones, such as electric voltages $\hat{e}_p$ along primary edges L_p, magnetic fluxes b_p through primary faces A_p or magnetic voltages h_p along with dual

9.3.2 ASSEMBLING OF A MATRIX OF ORGANIZATIONAL NORMS

In FIT, the assembly of the linear material matrices is efficiently organized as a loop over the primary faces. In more complicated cases, however, it is more convenient to assemble material matrices element by element by introducing a local numbering at the level of a single material cell V_e. Let the number of primary faces and the number of primary edges be n_{pf}, and the matrix Q_e be $a+* \; n_{pf} -$ matrix for selecting a local vector associated with cell V_e from the corresponding global vector [246].

The primary face areas and the lengths of the parts of the dual edges inside the primary cell are collected in the 6*6 diagonal matrices S_e and L_e, respectively. With these notations, the local reluctivity matrix is computed by With V_e the reluctivity of the material in the cell e, and the global reluctivity matrix is assembled by

$$M_V = \sum_e Q_e^T M_{V,e} Q_e \qquad (9.5)$$

9.3.3 NEWTON METHOD

9.3.3.1 Iteration Scheme

Similarly, as for the chord reluctivity matrix M_v, the differential reluctivity matrix can be assembled cell per cell: The cell differential reluctivity matrices M_{vd}, we are computed by differentiating concerning the fluxes at the local faces: Where above equation follows from evaluating the material features. According to the local numbering depicted in the square of the magnitude of the magnetic flux density in cell e can be determined by averaging the x, y, and z components:

The square root of this value is used to determine the working point on the nonlinear features. The differentiation of leads to the 1-by-6 vector in the total device matrix is not vertex and no symmetrical, so the second concept is also not symmetrical. The explanation is that in the content mixtures that catalog FIT in the Petrov-Galerkin family of techniques, various form functions are joined: The reactivity matrix takes fluxes into account, which are discreetly distinguished by some primary facet positions and voltages, described along two arches. Despite the nonsymmetry, as monotonous increases in the applied material properties, it is possible to see a significant positive difference in the reluctance matrix. A Krylov curved spacetime solver for addressing the resultant

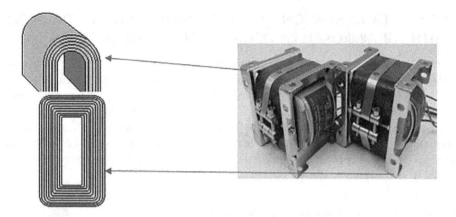

FIGURE 9.9   Double C-core configuration (a) Geometry.

magnetization problem non-symmetric subsystems such as the BiCG (BiCGStab) technique have to be applied (9.7). The only algebraic preliminary conditions are algebraic methods, such as incomplete LU fabrication (ILU) for instance, rather than linear algebra maximum likelihood estimation technology. The non-diagonal nature of the reluctance matrix represents a connection between directions simultaneously [247]. This is an integral property as seen in the hand calculations to take the bridge into account and ensure the consistency of the Newton system in the second-order see in Figure 9.9.

9.3.4   C-MAGNET CORE

A basic test model was used to compare Newton and Newton preschool methods. The C-core comprises a single-wire rotor that generates a magnetic stream through to the iron cube, as well as an external core and revolving positioned perpendicularly to the nonlinear piece of iron (Figure 9.9). To implement a near straightforward flux through into the non - linearity part of the tube, the kinematic viscosity of the C-core is taken up to 106. The present on the spindles is variable in size and is selected to strongly overwhelm the variation component.

9.4   DISCHARGE MODELLING OF A DECISIONS RELATED TECHNIQUES FIXED SUPPORT

Many electromagnetic instruments have two relatively moving components. Normally it is possible to simulate a relative position by re-meshing the entire geometry or just part of it for each displaced position. However, there are two separate mailings in this paper at a similar gui, eliminating the need to replenish and reducing the computer time.

A transient model integrating the "multi - dimensional with a magnetic wave is simulated to model the complex behavior of the control module [248].

A tumbling method is used in this article to account for non - linearity motion. The Decisions Related Technique.

9.4.1   ELECTROMAGNETIC MODEL

A linear hybrid stairs motor that uses the concept of reticence is the studied linear actuator. PASIM Direktantriebe [PASIM] is developed and commercialized and is affected by many factors where intellectual rigor mapping is essential. The set and spinning electrical engine of the linear 3D actuators (Fig. 1) was thoroughly modeled independently with the aid of the commercialized set of EM

Studio [CST]. The continuous ensure the consistency is used to discretize the electromotive force components.

The two apertures are fixed in the middle of the air pressure to a vibrating structure. The stationary bracket (rail) is composed of solid iron, whereas the movable frame sections are built of layered iron. The bipolar pitching is made up of one single tooth and one rail slot. With only one mesh cell, the design is discreet in z. The results are therefore excluded from the FIT model inside the real Smart nation. C++ codes the solution to the two components can be connected and the electromagnetic model can be connected to a modeling method.

In this manner, the actuator action can be fully modeled by measuring the force produced and the effect of force on the relative location of the armatures [249]. The specification of the magneto-quasistatic vector is discrete by the FIT

Potential integrated along primary edges a read:

$$\tilde{C}M_v C\hat{a} + M_\sigma \frac{d\hat{\mathbf{a}}}{dt} = \hat{\hat{\mathbf{j}}}_s - \tilde{C}M_v \hat{\hat{\mathbf{b}}}_r \qquad (9.6)$$

Where C and C bar represents the discrete curl matrices at the primary and dual grid respectively, j_s is the current applied in the coils, o_r is the remanence of the permanent magnets integrated over primary facets, M_v is the reluctivity matrix and M(submission) is the conductivity matrix.

9.4.2 MECHANICAL MODEL

The displacement of the moving part obeys:

$$m\frac{d^2x}{dt^2} + c\frac{dx}{dt} + kx = F_x \qquad (9.7)$$

Where the first term is related to the inertia of the moving armature, the second term represents the friction force and the third is the spring force. Here, m is the mass of the moving armature, c is the mechanical damping coefficient and k is the spring coefficient. F_x is the magnetic force in the x-direction which is obtained by integrating the Maxwell Stress Tensor on a surface that encloses the mobile armature.

9.5 ELECTROSTATIC ON-CHIP MODELS BASED ON DUAL INDEFINITE INTEGRATED TECHNIQUE, REDUCED-ORDER

The running frequency is raised by the diminishing of on-chip machines and according to Moore law. Here the literary work expresses a great deal of concern in calculating on-chip interconnected frequency-based properties and sensitive components. In general, a schematic diagram is still seen as too complicated to be a practical alternative to the microprocessor development of system components. However, comparisons with each other verify the authenticity of some other recent method. That is why a major obstacle to continue progressing in the last 30 generations was the higher frequencies modeling (> 5GHz) of interconnection and on-chip passives, announced by the International Technology Roadmap for semi-conductors.

The aim of this paper was for the CAD environment and for existing electronic systems engineering (EDA) architectures to be presented with methods for speeding up numerical electromagnetic simulated passive on-chip compounds. The study conducted on the European projects FP5/IST Code star and FP6/IST/STREP/Chameleon RF culminated in these strategies. In these projects, several research systems, including passive compounds, were developed, manufactured, and identified by experimental results. A common example of such frameworks is the spiral inductor described in Fig.1 that is used to verify many modeling and simulation methods and techniques that were formed during the time of works see Figure 9.10.

FIGURE 9.10   A typical on-chip component.

9.5.1   THE NUMERICAL METHOD

The implementation of ALLROM and the Very Quick Approximation (VFS) [3] approach leads to the identification modeled automated system:

- The configuration of the grid is continuously refined to the minimum orthogonal grid until the sensitivity and ability are sufficiently reliable extracted.
- The computer scope shall be progressively expanded for virtual boundary calibration before the impedance is adequately retrieved.
- The wavelength network of circuit functions was analyzed using the grid after the method of refinement and enlargement

$Z(\omega) = R(\omega) + j\omega L(\omega)$ and $Y(\omega) = Z(\omega)^{-1} = G(\omega) + j\omega C(\omega)$ is calculated by FIT in a minimum range of frequency measurements that solve the Maxwell equations.

The optimum order of the portable increasing percentage models and their SPICE resonant frequency is obtained and calculated in the spectral domain until the results are like the previously calculated Y(to); (B) The scatter specifications S(o) for a series of test structures are determined and compared to the parameters based on results from the SPICE simulations in the frequency domain, (A).

Below is how this methodology reaches an optimal balance between resolution error and the appropriate computational power [250].

- **dFIT grids measurement**

  The multiplying of strengths R and C matrix for multilateral semiconductor switches is developed from the concept 3D major factor in determining of the static electricity distribution semiconduction framework, the integrated electromagnetic field dispersion in isolators. Apparently, the scalar significant problems must be fixed by two basic 3D Laplace problems with Dirichlet boundaries. However, the uniqueness of cargo delivery at the discontinuities of transmission lines is not a simple job in such problems. It was well known that capacity versus discretion convergence is relatively slow because of these elementary particles. First-order FDM, FIT, FEM, or BEM according to the most frequently-used Galerkin shape or collocation. Our increased method is suitable for Finite Integrations – FIT pseudo dielectrics and hence does not require a green function. Besides upgrading FIT, the company has the name it, a dual Obligations in relation technique that accommodates charges. Two times on the ground, one with the principal grids and the other with the supplementary doubled grids, is a fundamental principle of it. dFIT is the combining quantitative analytics secondary and tertiary approaches to the static resource problem.

9.6 APPROACHES FOR EMI FILTER INTEGRATING APPROXIMATE SIMULTANEOUS CAPACITY

One of the main objectives in the development of EMI filters is to enhance the higher frequency properties of these filters. To do this, specific technologies must be established, including the EPC and analogous series inductance (ESL) mechanisms, since the significant losses are growing. The paper's main aim is therefore to improve and analyze the efficiency of various technologies that reduce EPCs. The chapter is conducted using the Maxwell Q2D Extractor quantitative assessment tool which can provide the lumped per-unit-length measurements at the end of the quantitative analysis method. Geometric form inductance suggested. The EPC is calculated for the four different primary winding and the coupled windings.

A low-pass filter is the given meaning of an EMI filter. Analyze and model the combined L-C setup carefully to construct a negative indications filter. The L-C flat structure incorporated is made up of exchanging conductor, electron mobility, insulation, and ferrites which create an overarching framework with a terminal feature that is like those of the substantial assistance. Figure 1 showed the explosive vision of an interconnected L-C structure. The combined L-C population at the end of an insulating substratum with directly embedded conductor field winding on both sides and thus results in a sufficiently powerful structure. The corresponding incorporated capacitance and inductance are achieved. The same configuration can be designed to equal the four endpoints A, B, C, and D of the combined L-C Resonator that have been appropriately connected with the L-C resonance, parallel oscillator, or low pass filter. The EMI filtering includes the L-C limited configuration where the inputs are AD and the outputs are the CD.

Figure 9.11 shows the diagram illustrating the integrated EMI filter configuration. Figure 9.12 shows the explosive picture of the biological phenomenon.

To obtain high performance and high output power, current integrated L-C techniques and optimization techniques were primarily designed for the application of high-frequency power components. Because the features and specifications for semiconductor devices in EMI filters vary, specific technologies for EMI filter implementation need to be created see Figure 9.13.

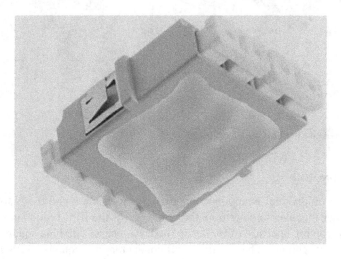

FIGURE 9.11 The integrated LC structure.

FIGURE 9.12   EPC of two coupled windings.

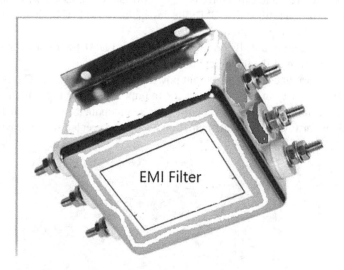

FIGURE 9.13   CM-Agitation Simplified circuitry.

9.6.1   EPC Technology

The EPC of the four individual wrapping complexes was measured with the A soft Maxwell Field Solver -2D Cylinder modules to determine the efficiency of the EPC reduction technologies. The bridge of a half revolving aperture of the ferrite nodes appears. The blue squares are the sparing winding conductivity sections. The lengths of all conductors are equal to 1.2×0.3 mm. Table 9.1

TABLE 9.1

Properties of Material for Simulation

Materials	Ferrite	Air	Copper	Kapton	Ceramic
E_r	12	1	1	3.6	84

TABLE 9.2

Calculated EPCs of Four Structures

Structure	(A)	(B)	(C)	(D)
EPC (pF)	93.6	23.81	10.3	10.7

gives the relative allow ability of the components used in the simulations. A 2D workspace was regarded to carry out computer modeling. For each framework, the quantization mesh contains around 20,000 linear rectangular components.

In the existing construction, there are two six spins per depth, levels, and rotations. The initial structure of the deal specifically an articulating, delicate L-C twist revolving of copper, a concrete layer, and a dense winding of copper. The second layer of winding is a standard winding of copper foils. The isolation Kapton density of 0.1 mm here between revolving layers. The arrangement is identical unless the thickness of the caption is raised to 0.5 mm. In the structure, Kapton is replaced by air. It shows the configuration of the revolving design. The cumulative number of revolving surfaces is raised to four, and hence the rotation speed per surface is decreased to three to ensure non-overlapping stator winding.

The corresponding capacity is determined described by the equation in the case of the constant current propagation along with the wrapping range. $C_e = 2W_E V^{-2}$, where W_E.

The retained capacity of the electrical field is V and the termination wrapping voltage is V. Table 9.2 shows the estimation results. The EPC of more than nine orders of magnitude smaller than the configuration in the original version of the planned phased revolving configuration.

9.6.1.1 EPC of Coupled Windings

The EPC of a single winding is the measurement capability in Table 9.2. There are two shunt-connected currents for the common-mode (CM) chokes, so there is an improvement in the overall equivalent mechanical wind capacity. Figure 9.14 shows the analogous circuit with two field winding combined with wrapping capacity.

The analogous circuit can be streamlined to Figure 9.15 under high-frequency stimulation.

The connection wrapping capacity is equivalent to Ce=C1+C2+C3. The wrapping capabilities of each circuit are C1 and C2, and behind them are C3 structural capacity. The EPC of the CM

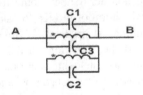

FIGURE 9.14 Composition of the integrated EMI filter.

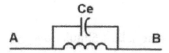

FIGURE 9.15   Integrated EMI filter physical structure.

choking is hence the quantity of at minimum one EPC winding. FEA mathematical models with a planar CM coil, with a graduated roller arrangement for each roller coil. The CM excitation is 28,237 pF for EPC calculation. The field winding of CM squeezes can be interlaced Generated by mutual inductance to lower the enhanced EPC. The two windings may be consecutively considered as a single electrostatic wrapping under typical modes of excitation. Therefore, the overall equivalent.

The winding capacity shall be equal to the single wrapping structural capacity. It demonstrates a structure that combines phased winding techniques with interlaced winding strategies. The estimated equal winding capacity is only 8 pF for the same product and geometry variables.

9.7   METHOD OF EM WAVE DISPERSION APPLIED TO BUFFERED BLOCK FORWARD BACKWARD (BBFB)

In the field of computer electromagnetics, the issue of wave dispersion calculation is important. There exists various method from dependable but inefficient exponential strategies to very accurate but processor-heavy, full-wave approaches to resolve similar situations. This paper explains the Buffered Block Future Backward Method (BFBB) originally used to effectively compute dispersal from perfectly conductive systems. We define the issue of the dispersion of uniform dielectric bodies utilizing a coupling of the EFIE theorem. While dispersion from an ideally conductive object can be characterized by a single integrated equation, which depicts fields outside the disperser, dispersing Simultaneous integrating electrical field calculations with equations both for internal and external charges are generated by a homogeneous dielectric material. The integrated solutions will be reduced by using the situation systems with the right basis and application requirements. This translates to a numerical solution that has to be addressed for unknown frequency and amplitude of functions.

$$ZJ = V \tag{9.8}$$

Z is a dense matrix of the NXN complex. J and V are column longitudinal vectors N. These equations are solved with direct matrix reversal for artifacts small in terms of wavelength. We must use iterative approaches for larger artifacts.

Iterative Solvers

Due to their prohibitive scale, the matrix value indicating by using the Moments Method can indeed be resolved by direct reversal. Instead, iterative solutions are used to consecutively build solution J. A very thorough description of incremental approaches is available in Golub and van Loan. Iterative solvers, stagnant and non-permanent, come in two major groups. Non-stationary approaches generally are based Specification of the Krylov sub-space matrix. The most common non-stationary solutions are the combination gradient (CG) technique and its derivatives like the Generalized Minimum Rest (GMRES). The functions of these algorithms are fully described by Peterson, Ray, and Mittra for solving for incident electromagnetic dispersion applications. For example, Gauss-Seidel, Jacobi, Successive Overrelaxation and Rotational symmetry Successive Overrelaxation are stationary. The two last are changes to the Gauss-Seidel basic method.

The block implementations of these implementations are taken directly from the traditional fixed algorithms. We note that, because of their uncertain convergence characteristics, stationary computations were not traditionally preferred to solve problems in electromagnetic radiation. However, West and Sturm demonstrated that they could outperform non-stationary solvers in the situations where these algorithms converge. But they observed that the traditional stationary strategies can differ in applications where there is a great deal of scattering potential. The benefit of non-stationary architectures is that the geometry of the dispersive body is much less influenced. In certain cases, non-stationary processes converge, even as the number of different dispersions decreases at a far slowest rate.

9.7.1 INTEGRAL COUPLED ELECTRIC FIELD EQUATIONS FOR HOMOGENEITY DIELECTRIC SYSTEMS

The output waveform formulates the issue of dispersion from an insulated substance combined electrostatic potential. These parameters can be determined the equation embraces the theory of surface correlation and represents the fields of vector potential and F inside and outside the scatterer. These possibilities are published for the magnetosphere incidental (electromotive force) and the electrical field of vaguely related energy the electromagnetic voltage so-called K. The Differential Equation applicability and the N pulse-based technique produce outcomes.

$$\begin{bmatrix} A & B \\ C & D \end{bmatrix} \begin{bmatrix} j \\ k \end{bmatrix} = \begin{bmatrix} E \\ O \end{bmatrix} \tag{9.9}$$

Each of A, B, C, D is a $N*N$ matrix. To best describe the forward-backward method we explicitly rewrite the equation illustrating the matrix entries

$$\begin{bmatrix} A_{11} & A_{12} & A_{13} & \dots & A_{1N} & B_{11} & B_{12} & B_{13} & \dots & B_{1N} \\ A_{21} & A_{22} & A_{23} & \dots & A_{2N} & B_{21} & B_{22} & B_{23} & \dots & B_{2N} \\ \vdots & \vdots & \vdots & \vdots & \vdots & \vdots & \vdots & \vdots & \vdots & \vdots \\ A_{N1} & A_{N2} & A_{N3} & \dots & A_{NN} & B_{N1} & B_{N2} & B_{N3} & \dots & B_{NN} \\ C_{11} & C_{12} & C_{13} & \dots & C_{1N} & D_{11} & D_{12} & D_{13} & \dots & D_{1N} \\ C_{21} & C_{22} & C_{23} & \dots & C_{2N} & D_{21} & D_{22} & D_{23} & \dots & D_{2N} \\ \vdots & \vdots & \vdots & \vdots & \vdots & \vdots & \vdots & \vdots & \vdots & \vdots \\ C_{N1} & C_{N2} & C_{N3} & \dots & C_{NN} & D_{N1} & D_{N2} & D_{N3} & \dots & D_{NN} \end{bmatrix} \begin{bmatrix} j_1 \\ j_2 \\ \vdots \\ j_N \\ k_1 \\ k_2 \\ \vdots \\ k_N \end{bmatrix} = \begin{bmatrix} E_1 \\ E_2 \\ \vdots \\ E_N \\ 0 \\ 0 \\ \vdots \\ 0 \end{bmatrix}$$

$$\tag{9.10}$$

The unknowns can be re-arranged to sequentially run through the unknowns in each domain $j_1, k_1, j_2, k_2, \dots, j_n, k_n$ rather than first running through the unknown electric current amplitudes $j_1, j_2, \dots j_n$ and then the magnetic current amplitudes $k_1, k_2, \dots k_n$. This trivial re-arrangement yields

$$\begin{bmatrix} A_{11} & B_{11} & A_{12} & B_{12} & A_{13} & B_{13} & \dots & A_{1N} & B_{1N} \\ C_{11} & D_{11} & C_{12} & D_{12} & C_{13} & D_{13} & \dots & C_{1N} & D_{1N} \\ A_{21} & B_{21} & A_{22} & B_{22} & A_{23} & B_{23} & \dots & A_{2N} & B_{2N} \\ C_{21} & D_{21} & C_{22} & D_{22} & C_{23} & D_{23} & \dots & C_{2N} & B_{2N} \\ \vdots & \vdots & \vdots & \vdots & \vdots & \vdots & \vdots & \vdots & \vdots \\ A_{N1} & B_{N1} & A_{N2} & B_{N2} & A_{N3} & B_{N3} & \dots & A_{NN} & B_{NN} \\ C_{N1} & D_{N1} & C_{N2} & B_{N2} & C_{N3} & D_{N3} & \dots & C_{NN} & D_{NN} \end{bmatrix} \begin{bmatrix} j_1 \\ k_1 \\ j_2 \\ k_2 \\ \vdots \\ j_N \\ k_N \end{bmatrix} = \begin{bmatrix} E_1 \\ 0 \\ E_2 \\ 0 \\ \vdots \\ E_N \\ 0 \end{bmatrix} \tag{9.11}$$

Where negation Z_{mn} contains the interactions between all basic functions in groups m and n. A forward-backward solver finds a global solution by solving a sequence of problems, each one describing the surface current in one grouping. By 'marching' the currents forward and backward from group to group a solution can be found in a manner that can be more efficient than using other iterative solvers. A block forward-backward proceeds by a variation on the block successive over-relaxation method is introduced and applied to the case of scattering from perfectly conducting objects. Rather than solving for the unknowns in each group individually, the interactions with neighboring groups are included to suppress spurious diffraction effects that would otherwise arise and cause the solution to diverge. Specifically, the following equation describes the forward sweep of the BBFB scheme: In the forward sweep group $m+1$ acts as a buffer zone for group m. $Bm+1$ is a dummy unknown used to temporarily compute the unknowns in group $m+1$ to allow them.

9.8   FINITE ELEMENT ASYMMETRIC CONNECTIVITY AND ELECTROQUASISTIC FIELD SIMULATIONS BOUNDARY INTEGRAL METHODS

In this topic, temporary formulations are pre-submitted under the electro-quasistatic assumption (E QS) that excludes the magnetic flux density partial derivatives under initiation legislation. This simulation can be conducted to analyze technological instruments with minimal electromagnetic seismic wave consequences and a much higher intensity of electrical energy than gravitational fields. These requirements are usually appropriate for high or microelectronic systems. Electro-quasistatic calculations already have been described in the time region, using depreciation systems of approximation. The methods simulate inhomogeneous and nonlinear material comfortability. The perceived loudness approaches however have in common the need to connect the approximation domain, meaning that design parameters on the boundaries of the sphere must be given. This is a clear drawback of such techniques, in simulating high-voltage self-standing devices for which the electric far-field cannot precisely be modeled in common initial conditions. This problem is addressed in this article by the asymmetrical combination of FEM and BEM. For particular, asymmetrical BEM or FEM-BEM formulations have been offered for the resolution of oscillating flow field problems to resolve the hurdles in ferromagnetic materials or to compute eddy flowing current difficulties.

9.8.1   Electro-Quasistatic Field Domains Compression

9.8.1.1   Electro-Quasistatic Fields of Transition

Entering in the equations of Maxwell the electro-quasistatic assumption=0 in the equation=$B(r)$ ϕ (r, t) Exists to calculate the resultant electromagnetic current of irroration via E (r, t)=grad ϕ (r, t). As a result, the Fourier transform, along with Faraday's law, describes electro-quasistatic fields

$$-\text{div}\left(\left(k(\phi,r)+\varepsilon(r)\partial_t\right)\ \text{grad}\ \ \phi(r,t)\right)=0.$$

The electrical conductivity is known as β, whereas electromagnetic permeability is known as m. The suitability of dielectric permittivity for application areas depends on the electrical field and hence on the energy μ's governance capacity.

9.8.2   Model Finite Element Problem

Since a Finite-Element approach will conveniently take into consideration the inhomogeneous electric essential for effectively and field-force based electronic properties, whereas the border-element method can include the mechanical amplification state, the computer domain is broken down appropriately, see Figure 1. In Ω_{FEM}, $\varepsilon=\varepsilon$ (r) as well as $\kappa=\kappa$ (ϕ, r) are valid, Whereas in Ω_{BEM} $E=E_0$ as well $k=0$ holds. In the following, the dependence of the position vector r, as well as the time t, are omitted. With these conditions, the model problem is defined in the unbounded domain $\Omega=\Omega_{\text{FEM}}$ U T_c U Ω_{BEM} with the interface boundary T_c. The normal vector on the boundary symbol as the above equation is assumed to be directed from the domain Ω_{FEM} to the domain Ω_{BEM}.

9.8.3 Boundary-Element Formulation

The solution of the above equation in Ω_{BEM} can be formulated based on Kirchhoff's representation formula,

$$\partial_t \varphi(\mathbf{r}) = \int_{\Gamma_c} \gamma_0'^{\text{ext}} \frac{1}{4\pi|\mathbf{r}-\mathbf{r}'|} \gamma_1'^{\text{ext}} \partial_t \varphi(\mathbf{r}')d\Gamma' - \int_{\Gamma_c} \gamma_1'^{\text{ext}} \frac{1}{4\pi|\mathbf{r}-\mathbf{r}'|} \gamma_0'^{\text{ext}} \partial_t \varphi(\mathbf{r}')d\Gamma' \qquad (9.12)$$

Considering the time derivative which occurs in the above equation. Application of the exterior trace operator and the operator of the exterior co-normal derivative, respectively, as above equation results in a system of boundary integral equations

$$\begin{pmatrix} \gamma_0^{\text{ext}} & \partial_t \varphi \\ \gamma_1^{\text{ext}} & \partial_t \varphi \end{pmatrix} = \begin{pmatrix} \frac{1}{2}I + \mathcal{K} & -\mathcal{V} \\ -\mathcal{D} & \frac{1}{2}I - \mathcal{K}' \end{pmatrix} \begin{pmatrix} \gamma_0^{\text{ext}} & \partial_t \varphi \\ \gamma_1^{\text{ext}} & \partial_t \varphi \end{pmatrix} \qquad (9.13)$$

With the factor ½ for points on the smooth boundary as above e equation. The single-layer potential operator V, the hypersingular integral operator $\mathcal{D}$, and the double-layer potential operator K and its adjoint K', respectively, are used. The identity operator is denoted by

9.8.4 Symmetric FEM-BEM Coupling

9.8.4.1 Continuous Formulation

The BEM formulation as an above equation can be coupled to the finite-element formulation by expressing symbol as below equation by the second boundary integral equation of the system and applying the interface conditions as equation expresses the normal continuity of the total (conduction+displacement) current density. According to the as above equation, substituting and inserting as above equation yields the variational equation.

9.9 HYSTERESIS PRICE MODELING COMPUTER ERRORS

Electromagnetic excitement generators are valuable in technological applications. Their architecture starts with the spread of the gravitational flux (period and location) necessary to get the desirable outcomes. However, this behavior relies on the ferromagnetic materials of the aiming reticule, requiring a material model including the phenomena of hysteresis.

The Preisach hysteresis model provides a decent rate between computer performance and the results reliability for technological applications. A paramagnetic material is dipoles (hysters) with the magnetic conduct of a rectangular hysteresis cycle, according to the classically known Preisach model. These el-mentary operators are divided by the pre-selection function P (a, b) concerning their up-and-down values (a, b) and the modeling material is defined. The superimposition of hysteron inputs is calculated for magnetization (model output). In the Preisach triangle, the material development can thus be followed $(H_{sba}+H_s)$, H_s

The saturated magnetic field. This evolution is equal to a continuous series of steps in the Price triumph between positive and negative hydrate regions, which rely on all preceding strong magnetic values H the line of stages (model input).

The analysis or quantitative approximations can be used to detect Preisach functions.

The Preisach function may be computed in the first situation by identifying variables for these probability distribution functions (e.g., factored-Lorentzian or lognormal-Gaudis; Unpredictable modeling errors are present when the assumed distribution mechanism is not genuinely warranted. The figurative approach includes a phase function specified for the meshed triangle Preisach and may use a small collection of experimental results.

Modeling errors may be intrinsic pattern errours, experimental errors (for example, calculation noise), or intrinsic computational errors (according to Preisach's hysteresis theory). In whatever electromagnetic field calculation, it uses, the computational errors in device parameter recognition affect model accuracy. You presume that the Preisach function is numerically defined, begin with a group of experimental FORCs (first-order reverse curves) obtained with a vibrating sample magnetometer Bank cards, metro passes, memory, and disk drives (VSM 7304 LakeShore). The quantity of FORCs enforces the number of neurons on the Preisach triangle mesh. By determining the maximum magnetism and the current phases that set the border and mesh of the Preisex triangle, the fundamental effects of the test are managed. Preisach numerics are then employed in the mathematical computation by overlaying each cell's contributions, either by employing sequence-substitution techniques or integration from Everett (identified in FORCs by solving the optimization problem). Each procedure is subject to significant statistical mistakes. The influence of these observational and number mistakes is demonstrated for different magnetization histories.

9.9.1 Experimental Evidence Produced Computer Mistakes

To eliminate these errors, the paper concentrates on the uses of artificial intelligence of the classic Preisach recognition method, but it might be from the testing results utilized that these issues are caused. The test FORCs are obtained using a materials comparison for electronic applications. Magnetometer (VSM): banking cards, card entry tapes, and cassette tapes. In such instances, the Preisach scalar model should be used, but the results still apply to every practical system.

The experimental procedure uses a small (4×4) mm^2 sample crackled into the airfield between the VSM's two poles. Parallel to the sample surface, the applying gravitational force is regulated and evaluated by a Hall sensor by the current that flows through electromagnetically monitored bobbins. For every field value, the magnetic moment is calculated. The whole measurement process is automated and the needed sequence of class labels is determined before the experiment with a specialization computer system that supports the VSM. FORCs start with affirmative concentrations estimate. The field is decreased to the point of departure of the first FORC and is then elevated to the first FORC. The testing is done for the next FORC, where the magnitude of the magnetic force is less the almost steady fluctuation of the magnetic field employs the necessary field phase. The measured parameters influence the model's identification. For magnetic storage material, a proper satellite duration magnetosphere value is generally high and requires many forms. Our analyses demonstrate that 80 FORCs have a greater sensitivity to numerical errors than with 40 FORCs: the division number on the disk sample of the algebraic method matrix to be solved is nc = 1020 vs. nc = 287 for 40 FORCs. Simultaneously, Equipment mistakes have a larger impact on the setting of each applied magnetic field value if the area phase is less.

The second issue is that the reptation effect is present, and the VSM yoke saturation [Fio04] influences the calculation of forces. Five successive cycles show the relative average increase of the reverse chart value, which would 0.4% for the region be of saturated of the bank sampling card and 11.3% for low negative magnetization, depending upon the magnetism stage. One alternative may be to standardize the value of each FORC before the recognition is performed. The noise of the instruments can also influence the exactness of experimental results for tiny samples of a low magnetic moment. Smoothing for FORCs will boost numerical identity but adjusts the curves for mathematical entropy. Figure 1, for illustration, displays combining nearby dots with a sample of the electromagnetic bridge toll (4×4) mm^2 of the total low-pass filters. Soccer 2 reduces the local maxima of the Preisach functional for raw research observations and Figure 3 for the original dataset. The distributed form shows that the mathematical characteristic Preisach is more trustworthy than an analysis of distribution.

9.9.2 NUMERICAL ERRORS

The identity presumes that the feature Preisach is identical in every cell of the bonded hexagon. This value is determined using either an accurate mathematical optimization problem or a knowledgeable person (e.g., Gaussian rotations) for simultaneous substitution such that FORC's quantities are minimum (less than 100) for an efficacious computing model. The Preisach feature necessary or appropriate slight variations between the two solving scheme methods (10–12, percent in just six cells). By double implementation, the Instead of Preisach, the usage of the Everett operator minimizes mistakes. If uncertainty is quantified, a satisfactory solution might be reached by applying Prisach support vectors to every cell of the Preisach meshes triangles. A local phenomenon is created in mathematical shapes as in the local maximum.

9.9.3 TESTING OF PREISACH MODEL ACCURACY

The computational approximation takes place in the various histories of the magnetic field decided to apply: the development of asymmetrical first order periods (with static and dynamic field steps) and the development of the as- and descending curves of various order. Figures 4, 5, and 6 display the analytical and numbering curves of a sample of a permanent magnet bank card. The model precision, as in electric field calculations in hysteretic magnetic instruments, is adequate for a scientific objective. There may be major mistakes in the reversing points of the oscillation cycle where The duration of the magnetic fields is changeable and Magnetic attributes (model output) of the Preisach Triangle Geometry must be adjusted (see Figure 5). It is easy to create changeable geometry, but it might be costly on a computational basis.

The displacement curves inaccuracies are bigger, especially in hard magnetically building materials, starting with near-compressive magnetosphere levels. The explanation is because the amplitude of the primary repetition phase is big and two FORC are somewhat different from points that have the magnetic field values like the series resistance. At the same time, the application of the same field phase creates very near to each other FORCs that are influenced by the reputation phenomena for the threshold voltage. The result is that the number of FORCs is not as significant as the distribution: the FORC start points must be around equidistant with magnetic moment values. This constraint unexpectedly leads to a harder experimental design (a variable field step) and a non-uniform Preisach triangle mesh. These disadvantages may therefore be solved if a specific program were made more accurate.

9.10 CONCLUSION

Perhaps the most dynamical incident electromagnetic stimulating approach, the FITs is now 30 years old. Because of its potential to tackle electromagnetism issues in the spatial and temporal fields as well as its diversity of materials properties and remarkable mathematical effectiveness and precision, FIT has been utilized in simulating a broad range of devices, ranging from DC to THz globally. The primary accomplishment in the time field has been to introduce the Absolute Boundaries Approximations, which enables for exact modeling of curved lines while retaining all the benefits of time-domain techniques. In addition, the theoretical underpinning of Finite integration methodologies has contributed to important shifts in views for other mathematical analyses, such as the Numerical Simulation procedure, in the previous decade. Electromagnetism's electricity description is not only a reform. It offers major advances in the economics of the system and is particularly a stronger relationship with the thermodynamics fundamental concepts. The objective of this work was for parameter estimation to evaluate the advantages of the energy-oriented paradigm. We showed that the controls are produced in a way immediately utilizable by the convex analyses and numerical simulation approach. In addition, the physical comprehension of all phrases is apparent. This helps to define coupling terms in the modeling of several physics and offers useful criteria for identifying parameters.

10 Mathematical and Computational Methods

10.1 MANIFOLD MAPPING FOR MULTILEVEL OPTIMIZATION

Space projection is a technique used by basic substitute models to minimize calculation time in demand improvement procedures. Specific and time-intensive space mappings use both precise (but less) and less precise models. The initial space-mapping protocol coincides with the correct pre-conditioning of the course (precise) model to speed up the process for optimizing its fine (precise) model. As a defect correction process, the incremental technique used in the optimization of space can be subdued and the calculation method can be performed accordingly. We demonstrate the general lack of right treatment and (also) left preconditioning. The result is better to space mapping or "manifold mapping [251]."

10.1.1 OPTIMIZING FINE AND ROUGH MODELING

- **The optimization problem**

    The integer programming requirements described in the parameter are autonomous. The regression model shows the amount that describes the behavior of the studied events. The Y set is the target set.

    The response variable depends not just on t but also on parameter supervision. The disparity here between y_i and the (t_i, x) measurements may be the consequence of, for example, measuring errors or the algebraic representation being inadequate. Simulations describing existence appear to be sophisticated in varied temperatures. Spatial maps make use of the mix of accessibility and precision of less complicated technologies. Thus, the finer and the rough models are distinguished [252].

- **The fine model**

    The fine model response is denoted by $f(x)$ denotes R^m with x belongs to X subset of R^n the fine model control variable. The set $f(X)$ subset of R^m represents the fine model reachable aims. Notice that, with $n < m$, $F(X)$ is an n-dimensional manifold in the Y subset of R^m. The fine model is assumed to be accurate but expensive to evaluate. For the optimization problem, a fine model cost function $\|f(x) - y\|$ should be minimized [253].

$$X^* = \arg\min_{x \in X} \|f(x) - y\| \qquad (10.1)$$

    A design problem, characterized by the model $f(x)$, the aim y belongs to Y, and the space of possible controls X subset of R^n, is a reachable design if the equality $f(x^*) = y$ can be achieved for some x^* belongs to X.

- **The coarse model**

    The coarse model is denoted by $c(z)$ belongs to R^m, with z belongs to Z subset R^n, the coarse model control variable. This model is assumed to be cheap to evaluate but less accurate than the fine model.

    The set $c(Z)$, $\subset$ of R^m, is the set of coarse models reachable aims coarse model. For the coarse model have cost function $\|c(z) - Y\|$ and we denoted its minimizer by z^*,

$$\mathbf{Z}^* = \arg\min_{\mathbf{z} \in Z} \|\mathbf{c(z)} - \mathbf{y}\| \qquad (10.2)$$

DOI: 10.1201/9781003211938-10

- **The space-mapping function**

  The similarity or discrepancy between the response of the two models is expressed by the misalignment function $r(z,x) = \|c(z) - f(x)\|$. For a given x belong to X, it is useful to know which z belongs to Z yields the smallest discrepancy. Therefore, the space-mapping function p: X subset of R^n implies Z subset of R^n is introduced.

- **Perfect mapping**

  To identify the cases where the accurate solution x^* is related with the less accurate solution z^* by the space mapping function, a space-mapping function p is called a prefect mapping iff $z^* = p(x^*)$.

  We notice that perfection is not a property of the space-mapping function alone, but it also depends on the data y considered. Space mapping function can be perfect for one data set but imperfect for a different one, and if a design is reachable, a space mapping is always perfect irrespective of the coarse model used.

- **Primal and dual space-mapping solutions**

  Many architecture based on spatial mapping can be identified in the literature [1, 2], which can be of two types: the primary and the two-fold. The primary approach to space mapping aims to resolve the reduction issue.

$$S v = f(x) + S(v - c(Z))$$

Where S is rank n's m-matrix. A maximum range m-matrix S through a good portion of rank n is possible, while the rest of rank m-n can be selected. We maintain the last part of the identification because of the supposed similarities among versions f and c [254].

So we propose the following algorithm, where the optional right-preconditioner p bar: X implies Z

Is it still an arbitrary non-singular operator, which can be adapted to the problem? Often, we will simply take p bar$=I$, the identity.

$$\mathbf{X}_{k+1} = \arg\min_{\mathbf{x} \in X} \left\| \mathbf{c}\left(\bar{\mathbf{p}}(\mathbf{X})\right) - \mathbf{c}\left(\bar{\mathbf{p}}(\mathbf{X}_k)\right) + \right.$$

$$\left. \left[U_c \Sigma_c \Sigma_f^\dagger U_f^T + \left(I - U_c U_c^T\right)\left(I - U_f U_f^T\right) \right] \left\|\left(\mathbf{f}(\mathbf{X}_k) - \mathbf{y}\right)\right\| \right. \tag{10.3}$$

The above equation denotes the pseudo-inverse of sigma base f. It can be shown as the above equation is asymptotically equivalent to this, and the fact that as an above equation, makes that, under convergence to x bar, the fixed point is a local optimum of the fine model minimization.

As analysis and conditions for convergence of manifold mapping are found to make the algorithm more robust for ill-conditional models, regularization can be used for utilizing the generalized singular value decomposition. Notice that the singular value decomposition is applied to relatively small matrices so that the time for its computation is negligible. Reports showing results of the manifold mapping technique for problems from practice can be found [255].

10.2   MULTILATERAL OPTIMIZED ELECTROMAGNETIC DEVICES SOFTWARE PROGRAM

In the advancement of integrated circuit technologies, resistive, capacitive, and deductive approach parasite effects are very critical and in the global circuitry design of buildings, need attention. These are the amounts rarely analytically calculated since we mostly work with dynamic geometries of multi-routing. Optimizing the route located within the integrated architecture will lead to reduced coupling effects in compliance with the imposed constraints.

Because of the high number of architecture material properties, stochastic optimization approaches were historically employed based on genetic algorithms (GA). The first approach proposed was to use a simple GA in which the partial goals are limited to a single global fitness value.

The only disadvantage of this approach is that, while the global fitness feature declines during the optimum development process, specific goals rise significantly.

A first attempt was made by the quantitative approach of weighting to minimize this disadvantage. To properly choose weighting values, it needs some previous knowledge of the behavior of partial targets. In general, this is very hard to achieve. Therefore, an algorithm will be the appropriate solution that takes account, without background experience, of the input from partial objective behavior during the optimization problem and the overall fitness behavior. The response consists of a multi-target optimal architecture optimization method on Strength Pareto Evolutionary Algorithm (SPEA).

10.2.1 Optimum Multi-objective Designing Elitist

The optimization of several conflicting goals concurrently involves several commercial obstacles. Generally, there is no ideal solution, but several alternatives. Such approaches are ideal in the broader sense that they do not need any other approaches in the search area where all goals are considered. They are called ideal solutions from Pareto. The Pareto optimization principle can be defined as follows arithmetically.

Consideration of m parameters (decision variables) and n goals to create a multi-objective reduction issue: Both decision vectors that no other vector of decision dominates are considered non-dominated or optimal Pareto. Sometimes the Pareto optimum set is of particular interest to be found or approximated, primarily to obtain further understanding of the problem and awareness of al-dominate solutions. Evolutionary algorithms (EA) seem particularly appropriate for this challenge as they parallelize and use the similarity of responses by crossover to produce several solutions [256].

The technique is based on the optimization computation of Pareto (SPEA). This algorithm expressly preserves an established community P. elitism. This population preserves a variety of non-dominated approaches that can be sought before a simulation begins. New non-dominated solutions are correlated at each generation with current external populations and the corresponding non-dominated solutions are maintained. In the expectation that the populace will be influenced by positive regions within the quest space, the SPEA not only conserves the elite but also uses these elites to partake in genetic operational activities along with today's population.

10.2.2 The MOOP Integrated Software Package

Created as an optimized SPEA software kit, MOOP has been written in C# language. It is the first version of SPEA.

The program uses a numeric analysis package, which is designed as an external component library, to evaluate the optimal solution. Figure 10.1 shows the kit flowchart.

The boundary conditions are stored in a file to improve usability, and MOOP provides new features, opened, and saved.

Upon completion of the optimization, the patient would be able to see the latest generation tables, all external community values, the completion time, the minimum and optimum values of

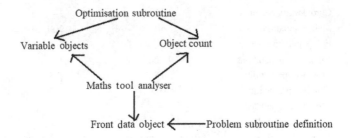

FIGURE 10.1 Software package diagram MOOP.

all targets, and a solution. The solution presented is the shortest exercise system worldwide. The results are calculated in a file type Excel Spreadsheets [257].

10.2.3   SPEA Algorithm

To reduce the component levels of resistance among their terminals, the SPEA algorithm has been created for the optimization of the form of the satisfying functioning resistance. The resistor consists of eight terminals, showing the large fragments of white bullets. The optimized design problem includes 28 partial lenses (complete interference across each temporal couple) and eight building elements in the dark-skinned node y positions. The parabolic approximations shall be employed to assess y co-ordinating the vertices in the enclosing segment by modifying one "moving" node's y professional and none mostly during the program.

For the entire geometry, the component residual stresses of the original geometry have been calculated using 204 risk and uncertainties recognizing the copper strength of uniform thickness. The residual stresses of the original form of the resistance are assumed to be providing direction with greater relevance to the shape and performance (unit values). Then you will see FSUM=28 as the sum of all goals for the beginning phase.

The simulation examples are successfully detected using an ordinary GA that seeks to minimize the general target function as recommended to highlight the effectiveness of the suggested optimization technique. For optimal architecture algorithms, Table 10.1 presents the location factor.

Table 2 shows the effects using ordinary GA, while in Figure 4, the corresponding optimum resistor form is seen. It should be noted that the total amount drops to FSUM=24,98, meaning a global 11% cut. The few partial resistors, for example, R58 and R68 with a factor of 0,6, are significantly reduced. Despite these very positive performances, there are two R12 and R45 resistors with a strong increase of 1.48, whereas another 8 resistors with small displacements are also decreased [258].

The simplest GA optimum architecture algorithm is, therefore, suitable to optimize the global process as predicted, but the changes in the partial objective are not considered. This fact is a significant downside for the actual category of applications.

The understanding of the outcomes at the end of the method of optimization depends very much on the needs of the customer using MOOP optimal design tools. The cumulative reduction of the total values of objectives is, of course, a general measure of a decrease in objectives, but this metric is not applicable for partial targets during the optimization phase as it was shown in the case of single GA.

TABLE 10.1
The Optimal Design Algorithm Settings

	GA	SPEA
Chromosome length	32	–
Main population size	40	200
Ext. population size	–	150
Number of generations	1,000	100
Crossover probability	0.8	0.8
Mutation probability	0.05	0.1
Crossover parameter	–	2
Mutation parameter	–	2
Total running time	7 hours 44 minutes	33 hours 43 minutes

10.3 MULTI-OBJECTIVE OPTIMIZATION OF THE DESIGN OF UNITARY ESBT DEVICES

The main points of the configuration of control devices for high-power and high implementations are state voltage, decay, and switching failure. Applications requiring high currents and high frequencies would eliminate both natural convection and power losses for substantial changes in the performance of DC-DC converter applications. Emitter switching bipolar transistor (ESBT) is a revolutionary control system particularly suited to high-power and high-frequency applications. ESBT is a revolutionary transformer switching device. An ESBT architecture critical variable is the optoelectronic structure of the collector region:

- It characterizes the peak energy bearable through the off-state,
- It describes the current that flows in it during the system into the system and the transmission loss during the start-up period.

The above requirements are based on the thickness of the collector area and the accumulation of doping in the Location. It should be noted that conductivity is closely linked to current density. To achieve an optimum architecture for organizational output compensation, a multi-objective problem statement is required [259].

10.3.1 THE ESBT CONNECTED WITH MOSFET DEVICE

ESBT is composed of bipolar junction transistor (BJT) large electrical energy and MOSFET low voltage power connected in cascade link (see Figure 1). The incorporation of the MOSFET within the BJT's emitter fingertips is a monolithic approach (see Figure 10.2). A family of instruments with a constant switching frequency have been developed that can achieve high voltage (up to 1.9 kV) and retain low forwarding current. A MOSFET switching coupled with the BJT transmitter in combination is used for controlling the bipolar transformer in a switched capacitor circuit. Indeed, as the MOSFET is shut down, the BJT's emitter current is cut off at once and the entire collection current is then transferred Foundation train station. The polarizing semiconductor is thus quickly disconnected because of the fast load reduction from the foundation and the collection. This allows BJT to work at a very higher frequency (up to 200 kHz). In many applications, such as installation of electrical delivery, this unit is useful [260].

The form MO Direct is an enhancement of the DIRECT algorithm multi-objective case. The following three operations are used as a method:

- Lipschitz constant estimate
- Option of domain sub-region opportunity
- Subdivision of a domain

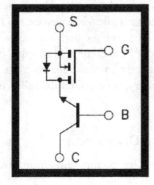 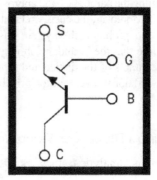

FIGURE 10.2 MultiDIRECT optimization algorithm.

The choice of possible optimality is dependent on Lipschitz constant approximation for the optimization problem in the domain's partitions. To determine the value of the optimization problem, this partition is constructed by sampling hyper rectangles at their centers. The estimate of the Lipschitz variable, therefore, means that hyper rectangles are possible to choose from in the partitions for further profiling which makes good use of the domestic and global searching estimate and in a broad domain achieves a quasi-global approach. Hyper rectangles for samples in the inner program of Algorithm 1 are chosen if they have a large field, high release from custody constants, and a strong function value in their center. The following description can functionally be given in one parameter for the single complaint.

10.4 FAST OPTIMUM OPTIMIZATION OF THE CONSTRUCTION OF A SEMI-CONDUCTOR RELATED TO ENERGY TRANSPORTATION

In both the engineering and analytical mathematics industries, substantial interest in optimum control for semi-conductor architecture was generated. A key objective of the optimal placement is to increase the current flowing over such connections, by slightly modifying the system filtering profiles for defined supply voltage. In addition to the conventional black-box approach of optimization, the adjoint method previously introduced in optimized semiconducting design that, in general, requires numerous methods for solving the advanced model has high calculation costs and produces good results by dramatically reducing computational complexity. The adjunct calculus includes a single run from the (non-linear) forecast model and a solution of the (linear) dedicated method, regardless of the dimensions of a space parameter, to evaluate an entire gradient vector of the management-approved.

In recent years, the applications of semiconductor equipment, on the other hand, have been examined by various models ranging from computational modeling such as the Freundlich isotherm to macroscopic models, such as hydrodynamics, normal drift-diffusion, and tracking devices [261].

We suggested and evaluated the assistant approach based on the model of drift propagation. In this case, a variable of control was considered for the doping profile which enters the state equations as a source term. In the meantime, the Energy Transport paradigm was generalized to the same solution.

In contrast to the drift-diffusion, which is predicated on the assumption of adsorption movement, the battery discharge method also takes into consideration the temperature distribution linked to electron flows through the semiconducting crystal; as the semiconductor devices are continuously miniaturized, such effects can no longer be ignored if the physical definition of the equipment is to be improved.

The dimensional-free stationary energy (ET) model for load carrier systems in a microelectronics in a limited area $\Omega \subset R^d$, $d = 1, 2, 3$, in a unique case and with the use of dual equilibrium parameters $w = (w_1 = (\mu - V)/T, w_2 = -1/T)$, is specified by the subsequent stability equations for the electron density and the energy, united to the Poisson equation for the electrostatic potential V.

I_1 is the carrier flux density, mew is the chemical potential, T is the temperature, $C(x)$ is the doping concentration. Assuming the parabolic band approximation one has for the electron density $N(w, V) = (-1/w_2)^{3/2} \exp(w_1 - w_2 V)$. Moreover, the energy relaxation term is given is scaled energy relaxation time.

To get a well-posed problem, the system has to be supplemented with appropriate boundary conditions. We assume that the boundary ohm symbol of the domain ohm splits into disjoint parts models the Ohmic contacts of the device and represents the insulating parts of the boundary. Let v denote the unit outward normal vector along the boundary, we consider the following mixed boundary conditions.

10.4.1 THE OPTIMUM DILEMMA OF MODELING AND DEVELOPMENT

To introduce a functional analytic framework, we consider the following minimization problem:

$$\min_D F_r(w, V, W) \tag{10.4}$$

With the admissible domain

$$D = \left\{ (w, V, W) \in H^1(\Omega)^2 \times \left(H^1(\Omega) \cap L^\infty(\Omega) \right) \times L^2(\Omega) \quad \text{satisfying} \quad (1)-(2),(7) \right\}$$

And functional of the type

10.4.2   FAST TECHNIQUE FOR OPTIMIZATION AND QUANTITATIVE MODELING

The partial differentiation in the adjoining structures indicates that the Gummel iteration offers a rapid iterative optimization algorithm. This prevents the complete resolution of the ET scheme, but only the continuum equations and their assistants need to be fixed.

One resolves first with given V, then the concatenated equations of continuation for w_1 and w_2 with a certain V. In consequence, for the specific V and W_1 and W_2 perspective, the combination assistant problem is resolved LaGrange variables μ_1 μ_2. Finally, an optimum equation shall be used for a regression phase toward the architecture variable W. In truth, a more vibration variable S can be used to view this iteration as a descending algorithm [262].

10.5   EXTENDED HYDRODYNAMICAL MODELS FOR CHARGE TRANSPORT IN SI

A classification of the operating conditions of modern electronic equipment demands a more precise physical model of charge separation in semiconductor materials, as manifestations cannot be represented by the conventional drift-dissemination or energy models in the context of very large and changing rapidly energy fields. This has contributed to the creation of new models called hydrodynamic systems. These are normally obtained by appropriate truncation processes from the limitless structure of current Boltzmann transport equations. But, due to the ad hoc handling of the closed issue, most of them suffered a significant theoretical disadvantage. These disadvantages have recently been solved by an adversarial timeframe dependent on extended periods of conservation of energy. This approach makes approximation probability distributions, known as the Maximum Entropy Probability Distributions, from which the closure strategy is implemented mechanically.

In inflow modeling, only two scalar and two vector phases in the distributions of electron probabilities are frequent: quantities of concentration, medium power, and speed and energy diffusion. These instances are the unique physically meaningful scalar and vector moments. In cases where there are very high or very increasingly variable areas; however, certain models may struggle, and a larger number of times may be necessary to describe the physical condition properly.

In this document, we build models that randomly distinguish and differentiate the indirect vector periods. The principal challenge in constructing these models is the reversal of the constraint relationships that can, however, be dealt with by efficient measurement guesstimates. The electron carrier's problem in Si is considered, but the designs can easily be generalized to other semi-conductors. A non-parabolic reconstruction is used to handle the electromagnetic radiation in the charge carriers, the Kane dissipation connection, and all key diffusion processes of phoned electrons are processed. We aim to examine at least from the perspective of volume silicone how the number of times influences the outcome. Transport of electron in Si, the Boltzmann semi-classical equation

We consider the case of silicon unipolar devices for which the charge transport is due to the electrons in the six equivalent valleys around the six minima of the conduction band. We assume that, for those electrons, the relation between the energy and the quasi-wave vector k, both measured from the bottom of the valley, is given by the Kane dispersion relation

$$\varepsilon(k)\left[1 + \alpha\varepsilon(k)\right] = \frac{\hbar^2 k^2}{2m^*}, \quad \mathbf{k} \in \mathbb{R}^3 \tag{10.5}$$

which involves a parameter called the non-parabolicity factor, while m^* is the electron effective mass. In the semi-classical kinetic approach, the charge transport is described by the Boltzmann equation, which reads

$$\frac{\partial f}{\partial t} + \upsilon^2(\mathbf{k})\frac{\partial f}{\partial x^i} - \frac{qE^i}{\hbar}\frac{\partial f}{\partial k^i} = c[f] \tag{10.6}$$

where $f(x, k, t)$ is the electron distribution function, v is the electron group velocity related to the energy by $v = 1/h$ is the planck reduced constant, q is the absolute value of the electron charge, and $C[f]$, the collision term, represents the effects due to scatterings with phonons and impurities. The electric field E is calculated by solving the Poisson equation for the electric potential null

$$\mathbf{E} = -\nabla_x\phi, \quad \nabla_x(\in \nabla_x\phi) = -q(N_+ - N_- - n) \tag{10.7}$$

N_+ and N_-, respectively, being the donor and acceptor densities the dielectric constant and in the electron number density, the equations constitute the Boltzmann–Poisson system that is the basic semi-classical model of electron transport in semiconductors.

As $C[f]$ reflects the various scattering mechanisms the electrons undergo in a semiconductor. Some of them leave the electrons in the same valley as they are before the collision, while other scatterings can drive the electrons into the different valleys according to suitable selection rules. In the non-degenerate case, the form of $C[f]$ is

$$c[f] = \int_{\mathbb{R}^3} \Big[w(\mathbf{k}',\mathbf{k})f(\mathbf{x},\mathbf{k}',t) - w(\mathbf{k}',\mathbf{k})f(\mathbf{x},\mathbf{k},t) \Big] d\mathbf{k}',$$

where $w(k, k')$ represents the sum of the various electron scattering rates from a state with wave vector k to one with wave vector k'. We take into account the following scattering mechanisms for silicon. Electron- Acoustical phonon intravalley scattering for which the transition rate, in its elastic approximation, with as above equation acoustical intravalley scattering kernel coefficient and Dirac function, b Electron – phonon intervalley scattering, for which there are six contributions Where alpha runs over the three g1, g2, g3 and the three f1, f2, f3 intervalley scatterings, k alpha are the correspondent optical or acoustical intervalley scattering kernel co-efficient and the occupation number of phonons with frequency w alpha, K_B and T_L respectively being the Boltzmaan constant and the lattice temperature.

10.6 CONCERNING THE DEVELOPMENT OF A 3D MESH PROJECT FOCUSED UPON DELAUNAY

One common challenge in technology, referring to the number of limits, a quantitative simulation to a normal system of equations or a coupled group has to be found and the ordinary solution to the problem begins by disclosing the domain in basic volumes. This paper focuses on mesh production for solving field incidents in subjective VLSI frameworks. We presume that consistency or consistency cannot simply minimize the dilemma to a lower level, such that the problem area is inherently three-dimensional. We also presume the statistical methodology chosen a three-dimensional discretization (e.g., the finite element analysis) is needed (as opposed to a surface-discretization). Surveys are conducted for post-processing. This study describes the mesh generation centered on strategies from mesh generation literature has focused on Delaunay. The key benefits of these methods are guaranteeing the accuracy of the resultant meshes and, equally importantly, the usefulness of the mesh. A further benefit is that mesh calculation is practically efficient. Mesh calculations are generally much easier than approaching the computational problems following them. Figure 1 shows an example mesh created by our execution [263].

Although the ideas of the Delaunay-based meshing process are familiar, it is a huge challenge to incorporate a mesh converter of this kind. In addition to coding the topologic of 3D simple (tetrahedra in our case) manipulation tough, the methodology must be resilient against floating-point errors. Furthermore, the principle of meshing process based in Delaunay enables a quick mesh production using only business activities, and this is not insignificant to use.

10.6.1 DELAUNAY REFINEMENT

Our mesh generation implements the Customers' increasing mesh refining conventional method. Space limits preclude us from taking the system and its theory fully into consideration, so we must direct the reader to literature.

The quantitative simulation to a normal system of equations or a coupled group has to be found sub-section, sub-section, and tetrahedron division. $\beta(t)$ refers to the circumradius-to-shortest-cutting ratio of an octahedron. In addition, the constant B is "the maximum performance of rectangular prism" and should be chosen for more than 2. The input of the algorithm is confined exclusively to a small bit linear complexity (PLC) $\pi/2$.

This includes dihedral and is based on cross vantage points. There is no clear limit in our case of VLSI architectures. In cases in which minor input angles are inevitable, the reminder is that the offending angles are switched off and the original structure may be somewhat modified, but in some cases, the modified domains should have meshed independently.

10.6.2 DELAUNAY TETRAMERIZATION

The tetrahedron (translated DT) of Delaunay is a key data structure that is kept by a mesh generator and has an alternate name for the Map projects but uses the "3d" or "2d" beginning in situations of misunderstanding. The DT has been constructed in steps: we start with a simple DT (one single tetrahedron), which is altered in understanding by the use of beginning parameters for the meshes. The DT's mathematics approaches are very important.

For the progressive insertion of dots, we employ the Bowyer–Watson method. The investigations report in principle the so-called Bowyer-Watson polymer (the tetrahedra union which has p on its perimeter) supplied it is introduced by point p in the DT (which may be seen as the calculation of the polyhedra in) (t). The main idea of the proposed is then emptied and a new tetrahedron is produced between both the p and the triangular shape triangles (its component structural wood would be detached from the mesh). In theory, the DT is thought to be the one trying to adapt.

10.6.3 PREDICTIONS OF GEOMETRICAL TOPOLOGY

The mesh generator relies on mathematical probabilities under which basic decisions are made. Geometric sequences link up topological knowledge (how elements are linked) to geometric data (where elements are physically located). Reducing to a minimum the number of mathematical constants provides the greatest opportunity to make our method resilient and comprehensive degenerations.

Two separate iterators are needed. Indicates the degree of 4 dots in 3d space is described by one definition, ORIENT3D. Provided the 4 points in 3D space, a further parameter, INSPHERE, a fifth point deceits inside or outside the restricting sphere of those four points. The sign of a determinant may be calculated by all predicates. These double counterparts of predicates are not used for the algorithm.

It is essential and adequate to exclude all degenerations from the geometry postulates to specifically classify the Delaunay tetrahedrons. This implies that the relevant causal factors may be positive or negative, but never necessarily null.

We use the complexity simulations (SoS) approach developed by Edelsbrunner and Mu cke to introduce non-degeneration. However, with all geometric predicates to be tested, the SoS approach will be extremely inefficient since it depends on accurate calculation. We thus compute the sign of the essential for each prediction we eventually meet without the need for a representational disruption exercised by SoS. We exclusively utilize SoS if there is the detection of deterioration.

We depend on the Shewchuk responsive graphics processing proposition library to calculate routine indications of determinants. In the case of SoS, we have introduced a module that can perform symbolic modifications required, to pass accurate floating-point math to the GNU multi-accuracy library. We (physically) disturb marginally the implanted points to reduce the probability of degenerations. Therefore, the SoS-Module can only be used in operation in a limited fraction of the instances, with negligible reliability. As most optimizations referred to are not commendable, they can be overlooked (at least in our case).

10.6.4 Coordinates Mesh Data-Structures

To develop the real data constructs for the mesh device, a reasonable amount of research was required. The reliability of the algorithm depends much on getting the right data structures. Here you can get a rundown of the object forms handled by the mesh generation. This summary is an essential tool to comprehend the algorithm.

A node object that includes the physical x, y, z-coordinates of the point is assigned to each point embedded in the mesh. The node's address is used for the SoS system as the disturbance table. For other things (sub-segments, sub facets, tetrahedral, etc.), refer to the position of the base station via a pointer. Each sub-section entity reports a series of sub-facet-objects (their 'wings') which are arbitrarily big. A set of (top two) tetrahedral is recorded on every surface. These sub-facets comprise three sub-facets (a pointer can be null in case a neighbor does not exist). Each tetrahedron also has four points against its neighbors.

A sub-facet preserves the direction of each adjacent subface in premature convergence by preserving the neighbor's edge number. Likewise, a tetrahedron saves each opposing tetrahedron's orientation by keeping its face but by keeping its face amount this face's orientation. Note, however, that the local topological investigation focused on node comparisons will easily obtain such details.

10.6.5 Detached Refining Elements

In the last mesh, each subface is concerned with different tetrahedrons (assuming the subface is not at the boundary of the mesh). But a subface will be separated from its two theoretically bordering tetrahedra throughout patch refining.

We maintain as far as possible the sub facets on the tetrahedra. Thus, we inspect each side of each altered tetrahedron while adding a point in the mesh (reconfiguring the 3-dimensional DTs to/or 2-dimensional DTs) and see if this suits some subface that is separated. If such a sub-facet is found, we only bind it to the tetrahedron. A hash table would be introduced as the table to connect subface and tetrahedra. Indexing is performed with the collection of three-node indicators.

To link sub-sections to sub-facets, a similar procedure is used. We specifically bind tetrahedra to our implementations.

10.6.6 Splitting Encroached Elements

During the phase of refinement, such comment thread and sub-facets may be invaded [7,10] and invaded before the corresponding sub-section or sub-fact is divided (notice that certain other splits can also cause the subface to vanish from the meshes).

Subfacets which are (probably) intruded are kept in a list. When another subface (this happens when points are inserted) is attacked, we add that to the list as well. That's the result injection rectangular prism used for Bowyer–Watson insertion, which includes just those components that may be impacted by the insertion point. The number of elements to be incorporated in the predatory list is then restricted to the point district.

The actual predatory test is postponed until components are retrieved from the invasion list: if we choose a predominantly random predatory surface, we choose one from the predatory list, and we verify whether the sub-face is still present and if it is still predominantly intrusive. It is important to say that the strategy is equivalent for sub-segments.

10.6.7 Representation of Globalized Facets

On each side of the PLC, a separate (2d) Delaunay triangulation must be maintained, but not vice-versa, in 2d DT as well as globalized 3d DT, all nodes embedded therein. Each DT is fully implemented with 3D predicates. A subsidiary node has defined some distances from the face plane, and the domain is used to add a parameter to the set of our 3D postulates.

Most 2d DT operators are easy changes to the related 3d DT operations. However, in 2d DT we delete sub-facets for productivity on the outside of the facet. Via a restricted triangulation of the Delaunay (CDT), the boundary of a facet is then established. Since these borders are several continuous borders, (2d) the Bowyer–Watson inserting scheme is still applicable and is preserved incompatibility with only a few modest changes.

10.6.8 Dynamically Modified Bookkeeping

We record whether this is in or out of the domains to mesh perfectly for each rectangular prism and that information is dynamically modified. Wherever the boundary of a dodecahedron is undefined, its region is labeled as "unknown."

If the area of a tetrahedrally μ is not "unknown," we can be confident we have the right area. Otherwise, we step right through the mesh to some point at the end, counting the number of crossed walls. If we go through the mesh border, or if we find a hyperbolic paraboloid with a known region, we can rebuild the area knowledge from τ.

After a question, we document the zone details with T, and recurrently with its neighbors to refine potential queries.

It states that the definition of the area in which a tetrahedron is situated is adequately described only at STEP 3, as in this case, no tetrahedron can penetrate the wall of the domains if any subface is unimpeded and ensured that it is part of the mesh. Unfortunately, in this phase only we need the area details. In the shattering of fine tetrahedral only the material properties on the realm within must be considered, as exterior refinement will be ruinous. Notice that the region is always bounded by a broad cuboid in the framework of the physical VLSI structure. In that case, it is very easy to determine the tetrahedron region. If you analyze a pattern in bits, though, various forms of geometry will easily be achieved.

10.6.9 Point Set Location

The dodecahedron in which a certain point sits is often determined. For instance, when excruciating a tetrahedron τ_1, we want to addition a node into the tetrahedron τ_2 comprising the circumcenter of τ_1. For example, A linear walk is used to find a tetrahedron comprising a given point or point location.

In proportion to the number of tetrahedrons visited, a longitudinal walk costs time and is the main trick in keeping the initial tétrahrone mathematically close to the final tetrahedron. In the case of splitting a scraggy tetrahedron, an obvious applicant for the initial tetrahedron is of course the scraggy one, and fortunately, in practice, with this optimal one detects that the quantity of intermediate tetrahedra visited is usually below a small constant. It is vital to make a point in other scenarios. If the subface f is separated, for example, we must determine the tetrahedron of circumcenter f (since we have to put a node within). We do not have a straight-forward original tetrahedron because it is not guaranteed to be tightly bound to a tetrahedron (it is intruded because it is probably not connected). To remedy this, we record a rectangular prism near each separated subface (the most currently connected tetrahedron, essentially), so that we can proceed with this tetrahedron. Of course, it will "drift further" from this tetrahedron, when a surface is detached (through other insertions), but experience reveals that it always takes roughly constant time to locate the point. The effect of wandering is instinctively limited as all mesh operations for external efficiency purposes are engineered to be centralized to the greatest extent possible.

We will need points in multiple directions, i.e., the opportunity to locate the surface where there is a certain point. The operation is identical to the above, except that 2d does not have components on the outside of the domain. A linear walk will thus stop on the edge of the domains abruptly. In such cases, we scan the surface on which the dimensional walking ends for a more broadness first. This search is supposed to be very cheap (practice proves that) because we already conclude that the initial surface is near the target surfaced.

10.7 NON-LINEAR POSSIBLE ISSUE COUPLING FETI/BETI SOLVERS IN (UN) CONSTRAINED CONDITIONS

Available for the use of huge area calculations on parallel computers are domain decomposition methods (DD), such as the traditional end FETI techniques, FETI Multiple Primal FETI (FETI-DP) techniques, and Limit-Deposit Regulated Domains (BDDC). The numerical simulation gold medal is processed on each subdomain, including its boundaries, independently under the traditional FETI approach. Lagrange thresholds enhance the global consistency through the frameworks, resulting in a saddle point issue that can be solved recursively through its double question. The solution can be conveniently calculated from the Lagrange multipliers. The method of iterations is nothing but a propagandized thread iteration of conjugate gradient (PCG).

A careful selection of the different propositions is necessary to achieve a quick process. For the instance that the constants of the primary elliptic fractional differential equation (PDE) are endless in each subdomain, quasi-optimal preconditioners are accessible. For the instance that the constants of the primary elliptic fractional differential equation (PDE) are endless in each subdomain, quasi-optimal preconditioners are accessible. It has been proven that the criteria are equivalent to $(1+\log(H/h))^2$, where h is the mesh size and H is also the mean dimension. In particular, when springing over subdomain connections in coefficients, the preconditions are high. The usage of conventional Dirichlet and Neumann solvers is required for the iteration of the PCG subspace. In conclusion, its overall smoothness, increased application, moderate complexity, durability, and ultimate parallel computer adaptability are certainly the fundamental achievements of the FETI, FETI-DP, and BDDC approaches. The Toselli and Widlund monograph is a detailed guideline for the domain biodegradation process, FETI, and FETI-DP. We are discussing the following.

$$\mathrm{div}\Big(v\big(x,|\nabla u(x)|\big)\nabla u(x)\Big) = f(x)$$

The border element tears and interconnects (BETI) methods as the counterpart border element of the FETI methods and the combined FETI/BETI methods have previously been implemented by Langer and Steinbach. The BETI approach uses FETI operators' boundary integral analogs. Many of the abovementioned FETI properties remain true for BETI methods, owing to spectral arguments. In addition, techniques have been developed which are inaccurate and sparse in detail.

The benefits of both discretization techniques can be gained by coupling boundary elements and numerical simulation discretizations. For instance, the Finite Element Method (FEM) can more efficiently handle the origin and discontinuities in electromagnetics than the Boundary Element Method (BEM), while BEM can be used efficiently for the handling of unfettered domains, mechanical components, and air regions. We refer to the symmetrical connection of finite and limit components and for the construction of accumulated Solvers of depreciating employing this approach of linkage.

In this contribution, we employ coupling techniques of FETI/BETI to resolve possible nonlinear problems as three components are combined in non-linear energy foods. In this involvement, we use attached FETI/BETI approaches to explain nonlinear probable hitches as they seem in nonlinear magnetostatics in two dimensions.

For the case that a coefficient v is unchanged in the subdomains, assuming a bounded system with Dirichlet conservation equations, we give an analysis of the Coupled FETI/BETI Methods.

The present researchers have been researched to solve the inverse equations (1) in a limited domain using FETI/BETI approaches. We provide an overview of the key topics. The continuum of Jacobi matrix in non-linearity sub-domains, especially where there are antimatter particles in the solution, could be significantly varying if the Newton method is applied to the global formula. In a typically magnetostatic model dilemma, we suggest a special requirement for overcoming these challenges and showing their good numbering action.

Unlimited domains are covered in Section 4. We demonstrate how BETI operators alter and produce such analytical outcomes. Until now, we can only prove an unsatisfactory state figure, while the output of the numerical experiment is far more positive.

10.8   A HIERARCHY PRE-CONDITIONER IN ELECTROMAGNETIC ELECTRICITY COUPLED BE-FE

Numerical field calculations of 3-dimensional issues play a vital role in the formulation of electromagnetic devices. To get information on the conduct of modules in an early stage of development, effective optimizer principles are required. Spatial discretization is achieved by using the BEM and the FEM process on both sides. Edge components are the basis of spatial interpolation. Fine discrete problems contribute to massive equation schemes. With a block adaptive cross approximation (ACA), the BEM part is solved with asymmetrically total optimum difficulty. The key costs are then incurred by the FEM component of the main problems. An effective requirement for the large sparse FE matrix is studied in this paper.

BE-FE coupling can lead to a multiplication of connected subdomains for complex structures. The discrete space around the boundary data can then be expanded to take account of the freedom levels that refer to the boundary information. The Galperin BEM was mentioned as well. The edge collocation approach mentioned considers certain levels of freedom in this work. Discretization then results in a normal set of non-symmetric equations, which is iteratively resolved, consisting of coarse FE matrices and compact BE equations. A preconditioner must be built, because of the ill-conditioning of the FE matrix.

The sparse FE structure was faced with various hierarchical definition approaches. In addition, a non-recursive algorithm has been developed which combines the absorption of the Cholesky block with the approximate similar level and the drop of the product. In this study, the effectiveness of the different propositions is demonstrated in solving the BE-FE puzzle.

For this, a portion of the BE-FE coupling fuel is replicated, and multiplication linked fields are used. By the procedure described and two other capacitive coupling conceptual frameworks the FE rigidity matrix will be conditioned from birth. This results in an assessment of the preconditions.

10.8.1   BAND LINEAR SYSTEMS SOLUTION IN VSLI MODEL REDUCTION

- **Band linear systems efficient solvers**
  The first codes in LAPACK for factorizing band matrices are reviewed in this section. Then we suggest two new versions that can achieve greater productivity. In LAPACK, we use the xPBTRF band matrix Cholesky routine to demonstrate this. The LU matrices permutation is subject to the same changes.

10.9 MOESP ALGORITHM FOR CONVERTING ONE-DIMENSIONAL MAXWELL EQUATION INTO A LINEAR SYSTEM

In general, the techniques of device recognition are often established within the field of the automated trolley to decide the best model of a particular data set encountered (in the context of the input-output ratio). 1-D Maxwell equation is transformed into a set of state-space equations using MOESP process, which is a affiliate of subspace arrangement identification intimate of processes. The concept can be helpful when simulating VLSI interconnectedness. The results of VLSI interconnectedness are calculated primarily using the Maxwell equations solution for chip geometries. The RLC parasites are made with the Maxwell formulas approach. Finally, techniques of principal balance reductions are used to reduce the linear structure dimensions of these circuits. In this analysis, 1-D Maxwell is directly transformed into a small-scale SISO structure without using any algorithm for state estimation. Therefore, a decreased order of the principal balance affect concentration can also be found. But let us use a common mathematical problem to demonstrate the usage and process information before grappling with the Maxwell equations.

10.9.1 Definition of the Problem

A general nth order ordinary differential equation (ODE) is known to describe the fundamental elements and the implementing information of the MOESP algorithm. For this case, we also show numerical results in the article. The procedure is then used in component PDE and the Maxwell equations more precisely.

10.9.2 MOESP Algorithm

The dual biodegradation of Regression Quantization (RQ) is often used to generate the Zero Data Matrix upper-right block. A vector can be decomposed with linear quantization (LQ) like, the real LQ decomposition is calculated by transposing the RQ matrix breakdown.

The following equation for L_{22} can be obtained using orthogonal conditions in the input-output spaces

$$O_k X_0 Q_2 = L_{22} \tag{10.8}$$

X_0 is the original state where O_k is the expanded observability matrix. If the L_{22} matrix is taken by our SVD, the machine element of the MOESP algorithm is based on the eigenvalues of the L_{22} equation and the extended observability matrix can be defined as the last identity.

10.9.3 Maxwell Equation

Consider a single-dimensional space in which the x dimension varies only. Suppose there is just a z part in the electromagnetic field. We can write a 1-D Numerical method with the laws of Faraday and Ampere.

The source component is utilized to the node of the computer-0th domain and the data is captured in the 50. The FDTD technique is utilized after deregistration for extracting u_k and y_k input data. The particular value circulation of the L_{22} matrix and the inventive and appraised yields are in Figure 10.3. Here are two distinct characteristics. First, a sine curve, and second, an increment. For exponentially supply functions, the MOESP method works more accurately. The predicted order n for both situations is selected as 2.

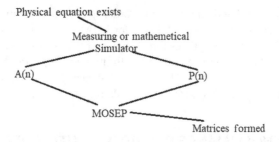

Physical equation exists

Measuring or mathemetical
Simulator

A(n)   P(n)

MOSEP

Matrices formed

FIGURE 10.3   Framework of MOSEP.

10.10   TRANSIENT NOISE ANALYSIS ADAPTIVE METHODS

Transient analyzes often take place without taking into consideration noise effects. But this is no longer necessary because of the parasite damage. The growing convergence size, high clock speeds, and low voltages of supply trigger lower transceiver ratios. In certain implementations, the noise mostly affects device behavior, such that linear Analysis of noise, i.e. modeling of temporal noisy processes, no longer becomes sufficient. Here we are concerned both with the thermal noise of resistance and with the shot sound of semi-conductors, modeled on external additive sources or Multiplying Gaussian background noise impulses shunt in conjunction with the noise-free components.

The thermal noise of resistors with R resistance is due to electron thermal movement and is explained by the theorem of Nyquist. Therefore, additive noise modeling the corresponding current, when Boltzmann's parameter, and in Gaussian, it is a standard white noise phase. Owing to the distinctive design of the threads due to the fundamental load, the shooting sounds of the pin joints are modeled by amplification of the cacophony. In case the vibration current from p_n connection is defined by the Stochastic Yellow Regulation Covers the $I = g\,(u)$ characteristic depends on the voltage u.

The regular white noise method is Gaussian once more and the elementary charge is q_i. Kirchhoff's current law is combined with characteristics of the elements and with the charging formulation a stochastic differential-algebraic equation (SDAE) is generated for the vectors $q(x)$ comprises of dynamical circular component consisting of loads and streams and x is an indeterminate frequency response vector with various intensity elements intensities in the branch. The word $f(x, t)$ identifies the influence of the static component, $gr\,(x, t)$ indicates the strength of the rhythm noise source, and kami is an isolated, Gaussian white noise source ξ m-dimensional vector. Therefore, a vast range of calculations and noise sources must be addressed. The noise frequencies $gr\,(x, t)$ is minor compared to the other amounts.

10.10.1   ADAPTIVE NUMERICAL METHODS

The step size must be modified by an effective integration. We have modifications of existing SDE schemes implicitly (drifting) in the determinism section and expressly in the SDAE's stochastic section (mixing). Designing a strategy to satisfy the SDAE restrictions at present is the key notion to adapt established SDE approaches to a Probability distribution (2).

The two-phase backward distinguishing formula (BDF2) and the trapezoidal rules take stochastic analogs into account, where only the increments in the Viennese driving mechanism are used to disregard the diffusion portion. Such methods are called Maruyama multi-step methods, similarly to the Euler Maruyama scheme. The BDF2 Maruyama variable phase size system for the SDAE (2) takes its shape while the steps are constant).

In the stochastic case, probabilistic case, and order 1/2. More structural detail is needed to correctly formulate the stochastic trapezoidal rule for SDAEs. The stochastic trapeze rule for the so-called inherent SDE (2), which regulates the elements of the dynamic system, should be implicitly implemented. One option is to differentiate the limitations, requiring a clear awareness of the restrictions or an R projector along in A. The discreet balances $\ell = 1,..., N$, suggest the right limitations and implement the intrinsic SDE graphing calculator.

10.11 EFFICIENT PERFORMANCE IN GRID ARCHITECTURES WITH DISTRIBUTED SOFTWARE ACTIVITIES

The grid framework adds a vision of current hardware and software components, coordinating the allocation of resources and resolving problems in diverse, multi-institutional digital organizations. Grid frameworks now evolve in an open grid service architecture (OGSA) which streamlines all the resources you find in a grid application. The infrastructure is a service-focused one. There are two standards for the OGSA execution: Open Grid Services Infrastructure (OGSI), launched by the IBM team in 2003, and the Globus Alliance (GLOBS) implemented the Web Service Mechanism (WSRF), [OASIS], in 2004. WSRF aims to re-facture all the principles in the OGSI system to be more compatible with today's web applications so that the tooling of web services is not changed.

The Globus program is expected the most favorite grid toolkit implemented by IBM, HP, and so on.

WSRF.NET, a free source application of Virginia University WSRF, for Windows systems under the.NET platform is another interesting grid tool kit. A remote taken to execute service has been created with the help and support of a Message queue service based on WS-Notification systems for vulnerability detection and packet forwarding between Windows-based computers in the framework of the grid. We have built a complex planning framework based on Master Worker's Paradigm [MWWIS] in the WSRF.NET grid to research the effectiveness of carrying out a series of loose, grid-conscious activities.

10.11.1 Implementation Paradigm for Professional for a Series of Projects

For the creation of distributed systems, the Master–Worker (MW) paradigm (also referred to as Master–Slave) was commonly used. Two processes typically are available in the MW model: master and employees. The master algorithm defines the duties to the employees considering their dependence. Normally, employees do most computer work only by doing certain functions. The MW model has demonstrated its efficiency in creating apps with various degrees of parallel level of detail (grain size) and is especially useful where there is little dependence between functions. Our work aims to show how viable the MW model is when performing a series of in a grid configuration, jobs are inadequately combined. To achieve this, we have developed and deployed the modeling references Grid Implementing utilizing the WSRF.NET framework with one Gigabit Ether-Net switch on a local social network made up of 18 PC nodes (Pentium IV 2 GHz, 80 GB HDD, 512 MB RAM). With Windows XP, each node runs the .NET platform, providing the grid structure necessary for experimenting. For the test, we have used an acyclic task dependency graph (TDG) generically parallel application representing a pair of G's $= (V, E)$ where V is a collection of triangles that satisfy the assignments on the chart, and E is the set of directed borders that indicate the preceding connections. Only at the commencement and the conclusion of tasks is communication between operations and open purchasing necessary. The network connections are only completely truthful messaging among master and staff that convey the requirements and parameters of the worker's techniques used for the master's program to integrate tightly tasks with unrestricted resources. The algorithms on the diagram are simple loop activities, and the particle size is measured from the systematic sample (pit count) and stored as a time-out from the diagram node. The determining layer thickness of the jobs (compute costs) is not required for the professional method and is solely utilized in software conduct scientific knowledge.

The test drawings were made off again and placed in disk files for each task including its implementation requirements (string structure and operations), all preceding tasks (raising activities), and a listing of all assessment methods (child tasks). At WSRF Grid Solutions, the masters and subcontractor components are constructed and distributed on different grid nodes. A TDG execution order is received from the application server from the Master Services and the tasks are shared out to all worker resources which are available and which are held at the worker nodes of the grid.

At least one program is published in the operator road network (do Task ()) which the master's supplier calls for a worker to distribute it to. A multi-operation guía such as the digraph () feature is provided by the professional Grid Service to be called by the client for the dispersed implementation of the TDG program. The customer's program is a basic C# software with a graphical user interface that collects and sends different task requirements (vector length and process) to the master's application system do graph ().

10.11.2 IMPLEMENTATION OF WORKER MODEL

The dominant preserves a lean of all available workers (AW), a lean of all running workers (RW) and progressions the established TDG, generating a lean of ready tasks (RT) and a list of waiting tasks (WT). If he has no parents or all his parents have already performed, a mission is ready to do. The distributed implementation of a TDG is performed as a loop in the main service provider thread that operates across all tasks.

The required employee list is reviewed in this loop and, if the list is not empty, an employee is identified; the original link will wait for a worker. The main thread scans the list of remarkable improvements when an existing worker is chosen and, if that list is not complete, a ready job is chosen.

The main thread introduces an additional thread at this stage of implementation. The loops are returned to the available staff lists. The auxiliary process calls the worker service's chosen do Task () function with the job control variables before the function is returned, updates the employees' list and the pending activities, and exits list. Each task is invoked in a new thread to be performed simultaneously, while the regularly programmed remains to be dispersed and checks for pending activities. When this queue is null, and the set of items is empty, the thread waiting will wait for a job to be finished; since all Awaiting Tasks List and Workers List (WT) is void, the TDG will perform all jobs, the final run-time is calculated, and the full time is returned to the customer. Until this work is finished, the main thread will be opened before the task is completed.

The actual content eliminates the WW list employees and the RT list functions. The supplementary threading pumps the employees on the AW list into the RT list and transmits assignments from the WT list. All the lists listed above are reciprocal vectors, where the threaded and supplementary threads are accessible. All of C#' clubs are implemented thread-safe activities.

10.12 CONCLUSION

Concerning optimal semiconductors architecture related to energy transfer, a rapid optimization approach was developed and validated in this chapter. An examination of the development of the aim indicates the effectiveness of the technique, as with few repetitions the minimum is attained. Since only two systems of the elliptic component ordinary differential equation need to be solved in each repetition, the computational effort per iteration is comparable to successive lines of the Gummel type per step. The overall speed of the one-dimensional arithmetic testing method is already very promising. Left-wing pretreatment enhances standard space mapping because the exact optimum is delivered with the same spatial mapping procedure computational efficiency. The program MOOP, which has been developed by the authors, is a multi-objective optimum design package. A numerical example outlines the benefits of the novel optimization criterion compared to the common GA. The approach is useful and useful for applications that throughout the objective function need to check the partial objective development. The software program enables the connection with external solvers that are helpful for optimum process applications in a broad variety of electromagnetic fields. The multi-target technique was effective in guiding the design of devices. The sample might also constitute the basis for future scaling of the power device into greater voltages of disintegration.

11 Basic Chipper Design in Electronic Computing

11.1 ON THE TESTING OF A DIFFERENTIALLY STIMULATED ENGINE

The DC motor action equations were established using foundation-mental electrical and mechanical laws.

$$V_f = r_f i_f + L_{ff} \frac{d}{dt} i_f \tag{11.1}$$

$$V_a = r_a i_a + L_{aa} \frac{d}{dt} i_a + L_{af} i_f \omega_r \tag{11.2}$$

$$J \frac{d}{dt} \omega_r + T_L = L_{af} i_f i_a \tag{11.3}$$

$$\frac{d}{dt} \theta_r = \omega_r \tag{11.4}$$

Table 11.1 provides notation for parameter values. When we evaluated experimental effects from various transient and stable states, the activity coefficients in Eqs. (11.1)–(11.4) were determined [264].

11.1.1 Torque Model

A various loading torque framework is characterized for this implementation. It is to increase the efficiency of the locked loop design that this model should be proposed. Let's suggest a load torque state equation.

$$\frac{d}{dt} T_L = K_0 \omega_r + K_1 T_L \tag{11.5}$$

where the present is the armature and the electromagnetic torque we are respectively construed as system input and output.

An observational test was performed to define parameters in Eq. (11.5). During the test, a steady current of 0.46 A was added to the field winding. It is obvious that the image of the destination under these assumptions is transformed into a linear time consistent definition. The frame connections are essentially fitted with a random collection. A FIFO technique was utilized to get experimental spatiotemporal parameters in the coherent message [2,3]. It includes an ATmega8 microprocessor for video recombination in the laboratory arrangement used to identify parameters in linear combination (1,6), for which, a hall effect sensor for calculating the armatures current of Nana Electronics SHR-100, a Pepperl Fuchs incremental encoder for controlling the velocity of the rider, a custom-made PWM H-b exploratory set-up diagram can be found in for parametric recognition. Furthermore, reference includes the microcontroller source software for pseudo-random definition. We also used MATLAB for the portable data analysis once we have received transient observational evidence. The prediction–error method is used specifically to measure the status equation's numerical variant. The load torque quantities K_0 and K_1 can be described by comparing them to the equivalent online document [265].

DOI: 10.1201/9781003211938-11

TABLE 11.1

Variables and Parameters

θ_r	Rotor position
ω_r	Rotor speed
i_a	Armature current
i_f (0.46 A)	Field current
V_f	Field voltage
V_a	Armature voltage
r_f (309.52 Ω)	Field resistance
R_a (6.615 Ω)	Armature resistance
L_{aa} (0.0645 H)	Armature inductance
L_{ff} (14.215 H)	Field inductance
L_{af} (1.7686 H)	Mutual inductance
J (0.0038 kg/m²)	Inertia
T_L	Load torque
K_0 (0.20907), K_1 (−9.8297)	Coefficients of load torque

11.1.2 Polynomial Representation

Nonlinear dynamic behavior is often found in physical systems. However, under certain circumstances, a linear time-invariant resentment may be regarded. It is a DC motor that is supplied by a continuous source with a primary winding. The minimal order polynomial continuous and discrete model can be obtained by replacement of the numerical parameters defined where Eq. (11.7) is the transition time and Eq. (11.8) is the discreet time equation outputs. It is clear the subsequent explanation for the state $x = \left[\theta_r\omega_r i_a T_L\right]^T$ the output to be measured and the input of the system. State Eq. (11.7) follows order polynomial parameters. Similarly, a power supply that maintains a field currently constant at 0.46 A is expected to provide the field winding. That is why the time visibility of the field winding should not be used. Section 4 extensive experiments would demonstrate that like a productive experimental or control rule, the nominal model incorporates the fundamental dynamic characteristic properties of a system [266]. A modulator shall be used to solve parameterized complexity, i.e.,

$$x_I(k+1) = x_I(k) + e(k) = x_I(k) + y(k) - r(k) \tag{11.6}$$

If x_I is the vector of integrator status, r is the converts solar energy, and y & r are the managed performances.

11.1.3 Non-linear Observatory

On the other side, when there is a pulse with modulation (PWM) H-bridge adapter in the experimental installation any noise is switched. Furthermore, some issues concerning the building abnormality of the exponential encoders render rotor speed measurements unreliable. To prevent these problems, an innovative nonlinear observatory is implemented to evaluate the rotor rpm, the current of the frame, and even the torque of load. A regular order polynomial discrete observation can also be written as a computational complexity approximation.

The win for the observer K_e is an outputting error-related 4×1 continuous variable. As mentioned in the next paragraph, you want Pole to be calculated essentially by setting the time constants you like. A typical K_e gain process is implemented when the collection of desired poles is collected. The Scilab/Scicos pool control is also useful to calculate this increase. In this specific case, improvements have been selected to make the optimal poles for observers [267].

It is necessary to note that the rotor location is the only difference operator to be determined for the implementation of a closed-loop system in accordance. The State Input is based on the state variables given by the observational precisely defined observer (including the load torque). Robust current and electromagnetic torque were only tested to indicate the load torque model off-line.

11.1.4 PREDICTIVE MODEL CONTROLLER

A pole positioning strategy is used to measure the model predictive benefits. The tension of the actuator $u(k) = V_a(k)$ the accompanying standard public feedback is now established

$$u(k) = -\begin{bmatrix} K_I K \end{bmatrix}\begin{bmatrix} x_I(k) \\ x(k) \end{bmatrix} \tag{11.7}$$

where K_I benefits from the variable fundamental status and K is the vectors of gain related to the initial system status variable x. The gains are based on a normal procedure. You can also use the MATLAB command position to calculate gains. On the other side, the connection between that s-plane pole that has a certain equivalent resistance and the subsequent z-plane pole is well established [268].

$$z_{1,2,3,4,5} = 0.998001998, 0.99801997, 0.998001996, 0.998001995, 0.998001994$$

thus the corresponding controller gains become

$$\begin{bmatrix} K_I, K \end{bmatrix} = [0.000168, 1.2288494, -0.6467532, -4.021708, -2.4009498] \tag{11.8}$$

11.1.5 DIGITAL POSITIONING ROTOR

A specification is applied to measure the rotor location. This hardware/software architecture contains many components. One is the Pepperl Fuchs encoder physically connected to the engine shaft. The third is the real-time program that measures the digital positioning of the rotor utilizing the electronic circuits given. The other is an ATmega8535 microcontroller-based signal processing system. The whole rotor displacement measurement system electronic diagram, a 16-bit binary count that describes the rotor location is given in the microcontroller. The Scilab/Scicos-source software codes the algorithm for interpreting the 16-bit binary count. This equation that appears in the algorithm is composed of the accompanying decimal system value multiplication each bit (1 or 0). When the data are applied, the rotor direction is measured decimally [269].

11.1.6 DC MOTOR POWER CONVERTER

The MOSFET H-Bridge Converter was developed and implemented for Pulse Width Modulation. This type of power system is usually used to drive DC motors, where bi-directional controlling of velocity/position is required. State feedback determines and calculates the quantitative score of the induction generator. This value is transferred to one of the analog data processing cards by the real-time software.

11.2 MASH DIGITAL DELTA-SIGMA MODULATOR WITH MULTI-MODULI

11.2.1 MASH ARCHITECTURES

The geometry of the lth order MASH Digital Delta–Sigma Modulator (DDSM). It includes oscillators for first-order error feedback modulator (EFM1). [xÈn] and [yÈn] are digital words in the input n_0-bit and the feedback m-bit. They have a friendship.

11.2.2   FRACTIONAL-N MODULATION SCHEME

The static frequency divider is controlled with the standard Delta-sigma modeling transfer function, mean/y, in a fractional-N modulation scheme. The objective is to prove that in an MM-MASH, mean/y is only influenced by the first stage EFM1, M_1, quantized module and is separate from other phases. This being so, the precision of the optical delta-sigma modulator cannot be affected by the multi-modular framework. It is also an appropriate delta-sigma modulator for digital applications. Available for proof:

11.2.3   THE MASH DDSM

The series of the MASH modulator is dependent on the product of all the quantizer modules. It must be shown. The term for the lth series duration of MASH DDSM is where h is a specification for making N the least common multiple of each stage of Ni's sampling frequency.

Furthermore, if C_1 and C_2 have complied with the following two conditions:

1. X and M_1 are numbers of co-prime
2. FM_1, M_2, and $M_1\,g$ are numbers for co-prime.

11.3   SENSORLESS PM-DRIVE ASPECTS

A dynamic multiple physical operation is still the design concept phase for contemporary, cost-effective magnetic motors, as seen in Figure 11.1. A system of several proposed prototypes, based on computational, professional simulation software, must be examined in terms of achieving both high performance and basic maneuverability of the motor. Several complex experiments are carried out of mechanical machines, electric power converter, and a software-based control system to check the required output behavior [270].

Moreover, it is possible to simulate the entire driving mechanism in advance by including simple control features in the circuit method. A more detailed overview of the 4, 5-kW synchronous generator and the electric motor with the control filter is presented in Figure 11.2, where the usual inner configuration of a ferromagnetic material and the control module DC-link condensers is evident [271].

- **Sensorless control mode**. The induction motors engine functions as a current source inverter-controlled system in vector control mode that uses continued current modulation. Therefore, it is important to accurately understand the rotor location. The

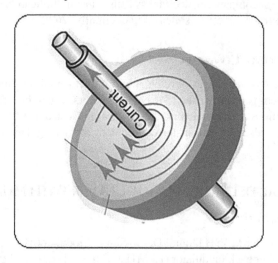

FIGURE 11.1   Multi-physical design process of drives.

FIGURE 11.2   Interior construction of magnet machine.

machine's reaction to the arbitrary injection of standardized test signals could be processed to accomplish this by requiring specific anisotropic characteristics on the rotor machines. The program for the induction motors is adjusted to the hardware system seen in Figure 11.2.

- **Nonlinear motor model**. Fortunately, the functional implementation of the routing protocol is achieved within the fixed rotor reference scheme (d, q), as the quantities of the electric stator in the stable functioning condition are consistent. Thus, the purely descriptive for stator voltage and flux connection are typically developed in (d, q) the motor rotation framework.

11.3.1   TESTING OF POWER SIGNALS

Inside the energy stack application-specific integrated circuit (ASIC), the received signal test impulses are overlaid and typically accompanied to create the respective spatial vectors. The reference voltage section you required u_s and u_{sq}. The present signals are indeed almost coupled in the d-direction of the approximation relationship (d_0, q_0) [272].

11.4   MICRO-ACCELEROMETER SILICONE RESONANT TECHNOLOGY RELIES ON ELECTROMAGNETIC ROBUSTNESS

11.4.1   OPERATING PRINCIPLE

The resonant activity tracker principle is made up of the double-ended tuning fork (DETF), condenser, sensor, proof volume, and movements. AC voltages with DC bias, DETF is connected to the base and DC voltages are attached to the fixed brushing electrodes of the motoring condensers, which include the electrode of the detecting captain. Every beam of DETF vibrates 180ι out of alignment on the horizontal direction, with its normal frequency, to cancel the compressive force at the end if accelerations don't occur. Via Interface Circuits, sensor condensers can sense DETF vibration frequency. As acceleration occurs, the evidence mass moved by inertial force closes or moves away from the DETF electrode and increases the distance between sensor condensers. The electrostatic force inducing an additionally electrically charged rigidity between electrical contacts causes the change in frequency with the acceleration of DETF resonance. Therefore, it is possible to calculate acceleration by sensing the frequency range of DETF.

11.4.2 THEORY ANALYSIS UNFOLDED BEAMS

The structural integrity of a portion of the scaffolding is analyzed. It has a four-folded suspension spring, which not only supports the evidentiary weight but also allows movement flexibly on the x-axis. V_{d2} is a DC voltage for the evidence mass, a clamping GND beam is connected to the DETF, and a VC sin't/V_{d1} DC voltage for driving voltage is attached. Inertial power, humidity power, elasticity pressure, electromagnetic pressing, and detecting energies are the influences on the compressed beam. The oscillating beams are a mathematical formula of dynamics [273].

11.4.3 STRUCTURE OF SENSOR DESIGN

The sensitivity of the accelerometer influences its accuracy specifically. The key feature of this model of the sensor structure is to specify appropriate structure dimensions to increase sensitivity while structural stability is ensured. With the above equations, the sensor sensitivity is measured at various dimensions of the structure, moving or sensing voltages. The vibrating beam is 500 μm long and 5 μm wide. The diameter of the sensor is 25 μm. The AC amplitude of the driver is 1 with 15 V DC. The pliable beams are U-shaped. It demonstrates how selectivity and the detecting voltage interact with a capacitor distance of 3 μm, a folded beam is 450 μm in length, and a sensor diameter of 6 μm. It shows the sensitivity difference of condenser gap distance where the plied beam has a length of 450 μm and a width of 6 μm and a 16 V switching frequency. When the sensor impedance is 17 or 18 V, we can see the sensor sensitivity is 70 or 250 Hz/g. The sensor is manufactured by dissolved processing in bulk-silicones and SEM images of the sensor chip can be seen in Figure 11.3.

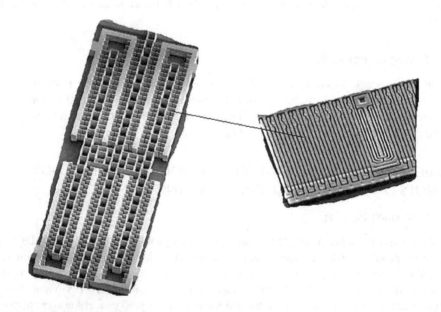

FIGURE 11.3   Structure of sensor design.

11.5   INNOVATIVE DUAL-PULSE AMPLIFIER DRIVER EXTENDED MEMS SWITCH DURABILITY USE

11.5.1   DIELECTRIC TUNNELING CHARGING

Typical touch-sensitive membranes switching usually demand a voltage of 30–50 V, which is very high in a dielectric layer of 100 MV/m. In this situation, charges may be carried by dielectric tunneling and stuck within the oxide material through a mechanism analogous to that of emissions of Pseudopotential with thin insulation films, which are progressively proportionate to the electrical field to the charging substance collected. Throughout switching ON, charges will be accrued on the exterior of the dielectric or even on the bulk of the substratum meanwhile the recombination period for these charges can be very extensive and there is a deficiency of transmission path to drain off the stuck charges. The switching is locked into the ON condition if the imprisoned cargo reaches a particular criterion that is adequate to retain membranes on the insulating plate even without the involvement of a power source.

The integrated charges additionally affect the pull-in and V_{po} voltages of the system. Pull in the V_{pi} potential is the voltage minimum that must surpass the pull-in pressure so that the induced electrostatic force reaches that of the pull-in membranes and closes the change. When the switch is off, owing to the slight difference between membrane and electrodes, the electric field would be stronger. Consequently, the switching is only activated when the power to be used is lower than the squeeze potential, V_{po} [274].

The loads trapped in the dielectric layer measure the distribution of the electric field and hence the electrostatic force produced. If the actuation voltage is positive, because of the strong electrical field over the divide the charge carriers will tunnel into the dielectric layer. The trapping charges themselves produce electrostatic strength and increase the net electrostatic strength between chromosomes and electrodes. This eliminates the external force/voltage wanted to pull the membranes of the change. The net impact of the positively charged injecting is thus a negative change of the C-V turn.

11.5.2   DIELECTRIC CHARGING MATHEMATICAL MODEL

Each operation cycle may be modeled on electrostatic charge:

$$Q_C = \sum_{J=1,2} Q_J \times \left(1 - \exp\left(-\left(t_{on} + t_{eJ}\right)/\tau_{CJ}\right)\right) \tag{11.9}$$

11.5.3   EQUIVALENT CIRCUIT MODEL

A SPICE model was introduced by Yuan et al. to study the dielectric charges using a more dynamic actuation reference voltage by using two RC sub-circuits to represent the dialectic charged and discharge comportments. The two sets of RC traffic reflect, the two trapped organisms with separate time constants of charging and discharge. The charging of both the C_1 and C_2 condensers is represented. The two condensers were mounted to match precisely the loading and release time constants with the resistors. RC_1 and RD_1 represent constants of loading and unloading time for J_1, RC_2, and RD_2 the time parameters loading and unloading for J_2 are represented. Circuit diodes have been used for the direct flow of charges. By adding the charges collected on the unit capacitors, the regulations that affect contained in the dielectric can be retrieved (C_1 and C_2).

11.5.4   DUAL-PULSE ACTUATION SIGNAL

The time parameters loading and unloading for J_2 are represented. Circuit diodes have been used for the direct flow of charges. By adding the charges collected on the unit transistors, the regulations that affect contained in the dielectric can be retrieved (C_1 and C_2).

The flexibility of execution is a major benefit of this strategy. A simple low-pass RC filter following the peak voltage source will easily control the proposed actuation Voltage Curve. It is easy to implement a MEMS transition via an analog circuit instead of using an active component such as an active component microcontroller and sensing circuit. Certainly, with a specific MEMS, switch the RC value needs to be carefully adjusted such that the switch functions properly and doesn't affect the delay of the switch. As shown in the figure, this novel actuation voltage further decreases the dielectric charging.

11.6 OPTIMAL CONTROL OF FULL ENVELOPE HELICOPTER

11.6.1 MANUAL CONTROL OF HELICOPTER

The pilot's job is tougher than an aircraft pilot because it is strongly interconnected with the helicopter's temporal and longitudinal movement. Three collective, cyclical, and tail pedals should be controlled by the pilot at the same time. The altitude can be adjusted mainly by the mutual controller pilot. The pilot will adjust the angle of the main rotor blades via cyclic controls, allowing longitudinal and transverse movement. The orientation of the tail rotor blades is adjusted with the foot pedals such that movement is performed. Any error may cause the platform to collapse. In this article, the controller gains are maintained to the desired values thanks to optimal control methods. The contributions in this analysis are described as "$a_1 = b_1$;" &0tr.

11.6.2 COORDINATE FRAMES AND TRANSFORMATIONS

In principle, the movement of the helicopter, body fixing, and ground fixed frames is shown in the image sequences. The body framework is affected by force, moments, and other consequences. The source of the body's fixed structure is the center of gravity and the fuselage swings. In this image, x is horizontal and y demonstrates lateral movement, and z is up/down. x points to the North, y points to the East, and z points to the middle of the World within the above coordinate system. For calculating lateral displacement, earth frame terminology is needed.

11.6.3 MOTION DYNAMIC EQUATIONS

Even while operating on a helicopter, the platforms as customized do not move two locations. Two forms of action may occur: translational and rotating. They describe direction changes and move around in an axis.

11.6.4 KINEMATIC EQUATIONS

Kinematic equations must be used to represent the helicopter movement about earth-fixed frames. For the film industry, the body-earth-fixed frame relationship is the following: x_E; y_E; z_E determines a helicopter's location concerning an earth-fixed framework.

11.6.5 FORCE AND MOMENTS ACTING ON HELICOPTER

The strength and moment consequences must be considered to reflect the helicopter movement.

The helicopter can be designed by integrating five sub-systems—the main-rotor, the fuselage, the empennage, the tail-rotor, and the engine. For the definition of magnitude and phase consequences, the tail, gravity, and drag consequences on the main rotor were generated [275].

11.6.6 TRIMMING AND LINEARIZATION

Certain operative points can be normalized using the non-linearity Cartesian coordinates. Eight trim checkpoints (0, 20, 40, 60, 80, 100, 120, and 140 knots) were used to improve the model's

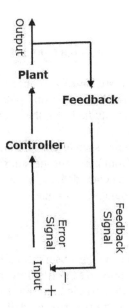

FIGURE 11.4   Block diagram of the controller.

consistency. First, if translational and rotational deceleration is zero; trim requirements are achieved. It adjusts conditions up to a stable state value of ϕ; &; a_1 and b_1 in our ideal flight status.

11.6.7   CONTROLLER DESIGN

Fully accessible insecure automobiles must be synchronized and closely monitored (Figure 11.4).

11.6.8   MICROCONTROLLER FOR FEEDBACK LINEARIZATION

Comprehensive strengthening control approach tries to lower the outcome index (J) in which "x" shows assertions, "u," "Q," and "R" matrix which contribute,

$$J = \frac{1}{2} \int_0^\infty \left(xQx^T + uRu^T \right) dt \qquad (11.10)$$

Bryson's law is used for deciding suitable weighting matrices. The weights of this law are determined in opposition to the measure of the maximal input/state accessible.

11.6.9   STATE INTEGRATOR

Complete state response controller gives satisfactory results. However, controllers govern the state values of the complex system to zero. Errors between the benchmark and real status should be taken into consideration when monitoring the helicopter.

11.7   ACCURATE MOTOR INDUCTION PARAMETER EVALUATION

The efficiency and voltage coefficients on the grading plate indicate specific differences in volume produced by computations of nominal frequency and voltage induction engines supplied with conventional electric engines. The plate data for ratings is generally rounding and specifications are established. Therefore, discrepancies from the assessed data on the plates are not unexpected [276].

11.7.1 Power Balance

- Only three stage inductive motors (motor operation) are studied for the current power condition and equivalent resistance.
- The motor and the voltage stream are entirely balanced.
- The voltages and currents are only stable for a sinusoidal shape.
- Only the basic wave properties are studied with the electromagnetic field.

Non-linearities are not taken into accounts such as concentration and the deep bar effect.

The algorithms of this piece vary from person-to-person stage analog circuits. This analog circuit considers the stator, rotor ohm, and center defects into account; therefore, the termination current must be distinguished from electromagnetic torque.

11.7.2 Parameters Determination

The following presents a compilation, using observational evidence, of parameter equations and estimates. The findings seen all apply to scientific information derived from normal motors of 50 Hz. The empirical evidence in this article cannot ultimately be disclosed. The statistical solution applicable to the estimate is, however, provided. However, results obtained can be estimated with reasonable precision for engines with any mechanical ability and numbers of switching states.

11.7.2.1 Core Loss Measurements or Estimate

If an actual motor produces the findings of testing, core inefficiencies can be avoided by differentiating core and frictional inefficiencies. And according to IEEE Standard 122, nominal voltage and marginal amplitude are referred to in $P_{c,0}$ no key losses of loading. No-load test is supposed to be conducted at the synchronous motor ($s\,D\,0$), if there are no calculation effects, no-load contact forces can be measured on the analytical data of an engine with a specific minimal mechanical force, P_m, N, and a certain quantity, p.

$$\log_{10}\left(\frac{P_{c,0}}{P_c'}\right) = k_{c[p]}\log_{10}\left(\frac{P_m,N}{P_m'}\right) + d_{c[p]} \tag{11.11}$$

11.7.2.2 Measurement or Estimation of Friction Losses

The tensile stresses, $P_{f,0}$ of a specific actual engine, can also be calculated from a no-load test ($s\,0$). In the absence of observations, analytical evidence will predict no loss of frequency of load,

$$\log_{10}\left(\frac{P_{f,0}}{P_f'}\right) = k_{f[p]}\log_{10}\left(\frac{P_m,N}{P_m'}\right) + d_{f[p]} \tag{11.12}$$

11.7.2.3 Stray-Load Loss Calculation

The minimal loss of stray load is possible

$$P_{stray,N} = a_{stray}P_{m,N} \tag{11.13}$$

IEEE will receive astray specification

11.7.2.4 Stator Resistance Estimation

Trying to apply the power dynamic to the nominal operating point, the stator resistance can be measured. Nominal limitation of liability from the mechanically rated maximum output, P_m, N

$$P_{f,N} = P_{f,0} \left(\frac{\Omega_{m,N}}{\Omega_{m,0}} \right)^{a_f+1} \tag{11.14}$$

11.8 SQUIRREL CAGE ROTOR BARS BROKEN—SIMULATION MODELS

The amplification computer's squirrel cage is used as a multi-phase winding with fast spins. The reciprocating air of N_r bars and two end rings rather than a wounded frame and connects the bars at it from both extremities, as seen in Figure 11.5. At the end of the circular are fins forcing air traffic into the adhesive layer of the machinery.

A completely perfectly straight squirrel cage is to be produced in the manufacturing facility. However, tolerances of manufacture and technical uncertainty lead to uniform densities. These abnormalities create uneven rotor bars and ring contact resistance—the so-called asymmetric information of electric rotors.

- Shrink troughs and gaps in the product on the bar or ending rings
- Improper chains and end rings joints
- Start of service, the mechanism is not developed for
- Machine thermal exhaust
- Elevated temperatures specular highlights, triggering cracking

The computer topology discussed is constructed on Modelica, a multi-physical structures' acausal object modeled language. Generic physical bundles for electrical, mechanical, thermal, control, and logical modules are collected in the Model Standard Library (MSL). The kit equipment includes versions of electric trim devices based on the calculations of textbooks. The three-step induction devices are based upon the principle of space lasers and a complete symmetry between the stator and rotor winding. Therefore, the MSL can't be used to model electromagnetic asymmetric information of the rotor.

11.8.1 MODEL OF STATOR WINDING

The operational amplifier is supposed to be entirely symmetrical in the following. Furthermore, the amount of debt of the stator is limited to three. The space vector equation can be entered in this case as

$$V_{s[i]} = R_s I_{s[i]} + L_{s\sigma} \frac{dI_{s[i]}}{dt} + \sum_{j=1}^{3} L_{sm[i,j]} \frac{dI_{s[j]}}{dt} + \sum_{j=1}^{N_r} \frac{dL_{sr[i,j]} I_{r[j]}}{dt}, \tag{11.15}$$

FIGURE 11.5 Framework of induction motor.

11.8.2 Model of Rotor Winding

The Nr rotor bars may be considered a very effective number of field winding equivalent to the curved arrangement in the squirrel cage. The direction of the spinning rotor force can be articulated

$$L_{rr[i,j]} = L_0 \xi_r^2 \cos\left[\frac{(i-j)2\pi}{N_r}\right] \qquad (11.16)$$

11.8.3 Rotor Faults

An electric rotor disproportion causes the interference of the rotor bar current and the rotor magnetic properties motivation force's essential pulse (magneto motive force, MMF). Therefore, concerning a particular rotor reference framework, the basic rotor MMF can be rotted away into and the forward-reverse rotor moving wave. The forward wave reflects the dominant magnetosphere, and the electromagnetic rotor discrepancy results in the reverse phase.

11.8.4 Investigated Machine

The results investigated include an 18.5 kW four-pole built-in configuration with 40 armature winding. Tests were conducted out on marginal load torque, line-to-line nominally tension (400 V), and nominal amplitude (50 Hz). When the electromagnetic abnormalities were examined experimentally, a rotor's bar was separated by melting a perforation in the aluminum section of the rotor as shown in Figure 11.6.

11.9 LARGE CHIPPER DRIVE MANY DESIGNS

For smashing stumps and producing pine needles, paper mills use chippers. The drives used are ratings between many 100 kW and 2 MW for such requirements. Chipper drives are generally not continually driven, so the instinctive reflex load is only stripped of a trunk. Afterward, the next trunk appears after a time of no-load service. The strong load bursts that also reach twice the face torque result in a high motor current, which results in large voltage drops on the power supply. During the impulse load or start service following the legislation, such voltage declines cannot be surpassed, based on the current set-up. When the grouchy drive was still and any other portions of the trunk were left, it would be a crucial prerequisite to restart the whole drive. Two drive models are examined to take suitable steps to prevent this reaction. A slip ring rotor amplification system

FIGURE 11.6 Induction motor lab.

FIGURE 11.7 Squirrel cage motor.

and a rheostat are shown first on the voltage regulator. Second, the machine with a wound rotor is contrasted to a speed-regulated inductor (see Figure 11.7).

11.9.1 ROTOR RHEOSTAT SLIP RING ENGINE

Unless a motor has been provided by an amplifier, the low locked rotor amplitude of the induction machine induces high starting currents. Easy steps can be taken for a slip ring engine to minimize starting pressures and increase torque-speed function. The increased speed feature reduces the load impulses' Motor weather systems and pressure gradients respond since kinetic energy produces a portion of the loading impulsive energy. The ensuing load impetus includes systems and the associated power factor is homogenized. The disadvantage of induction motor engines is the worsening productivity due to the increase in brush particle deposition in the motor because of the extra loss of the external rotor rings and a high abrasion of the brooches. The dust from the pins increases the probability of mechanical damage.

An acceleration converter topology with a squirreling cages engine may be used rather than a slip ring engine with extra rotor resistance values [277].

11.10 MACROCELL LOCATION: FLOW GUIDED BY A FORCE

- The annual growth of the semi-driving industry has increased exponentially in recent years. The increasing use and demand amongst users of electronic equipment have meant that better and faster management strategies are required. In fulfilling these requirements, the designers are pressed to the brink, jugging the strength and output limitations of ever-declining circuits. EDA (Electronic Product Automation) techniques are used to help designers achieve their goals to help them simplify the development process entirely or partly. The positioning aspect is one of these essential backend methods. The challenge of positioning is essential to find a position to achieve as many or more of the placement goals for any of the cells in a circuit. The two key targets for today's fixed die designs to be met by any placement method are
- Unlimited overlapping
- Fit into the defined placement location.
- Other goals can include vaginal discharge reduction, congestion, location, runtime, etc. The optimum solution would meet all the conditions stated. It is far from feasible to reach such a solution and even the easiest cell location-related problems are characterized as

NP-hard. The outcome that a successful positioning is not achieved will lead to a slower and/or smaller chip or an unrollable design. It would take time and resources to either change the positioning or restructure the concept at a later date.

11.10.1 PLACEMENT TOOLS

There are several traditional cell positioning resources available in the EDA group both education-ally and professionally. Several of them can position cells in mixed modes, i.e., designs that both include regular panels and batteries, but only certain tools for placing macrocells are available. This is because systematic mapping is used until recently to control most configurations. Recent improvements to designs containing Makro-based designs like computer memory or IP blocks (Intellectual Property) have also resulted in microeconomic structures on top of the architecture methodology to overcome fabrication costs. While failover clustering tools can manage macros, these tools do not position cells in the greatest advantage of macros in models with a plurality of macros that include a specialized massive Mimo capturer.

11.10.2 STANDARD CELLS VERSUS MACRO-CELLS

Placement of the cellular system is not as simple as normal positioning of the cell. The cells are of a reasonable temperature in normal cell placement and are limited to the rows where they have been placed. These restrictions permit positioning tooling for regular cell positions to be more accurate and routing services to be allocated. Macrocells have no such limitations, on the other hand. They could be of any length, width, and format (the most common sources, while rectangular, are L, T, and U) and are not limited to a single placement position. Consequently, it can be much difficult to choose a suitable position for macro-cells as the combinations of places are unlimited. Similarly, unwelcome restrictions in finding placements can result from the various cell forms. This can lead to detrimental effects like costly calculations and slower runtime.

11.10.3 FORCE DIRECTED GRAPH DRAWING ALGORITHMS

Graphic design algorithm concerns primarily nodes without any size or shape, but careful consideration is required in cell placement cell sizes. A recent publication presents methods of changing graph-drawing algorithms to add node dimensions. The key purpose of this work was specific techniques for graph drawings and the parameters used for chart drawings.

Vertices should not be overlapped

- Edges should not be overlapped

    The first condition refers specifically to this work since the purpose of the placement method is to achieve a non-overlapping positioning. The second requirement still applies, since it appears to combine cells directly linked, but if routing is permitted over a cell, it may be too conservative. The node alignment is constant and could be replicated or rotated, one of the drawbacks of the work.

    A visually pleasant chart of increasing speed and flexibility is the main goal of the FR algorithm. Having followed Eades' work, both attractiveness and repulsive forces are both used in the FR algorithm, but it takes it one step further, stating that attractiveness only forces for adjacent nodes are computed while repulsive forces are measured for all nodes in the graph. Looking at the parameters of FR, two key points are taken into account in drawing diagrams.

- Edge-connected vertices can be drawn close together.
- Not too close to one another should be drawn vertex shader.

11.11 SURFACE ROUGHNESS SCATTERING IN MOS STRUCTURES

11.11.1 Associated Scattering Potentials

There are two key sources for the dispersal surface dispersal impacting the movement of the carrier of the load according to Ando's point:

- Wavefunctions fluctuation attributable to interface physical "measures." $T/1$
- Potential energy changes due to the interactions with Coulomb.

The results of "change in energy potential" are further known as

- A change in picture capacity.
- IP charges are generated $T/2$
- Carrier density fluctuation of charge

As the "measures" on the interface disturb the surface potential and hence influence the Wave functions, its values, and so on, the first key cause of dispersion is apparent, and wave functions derive from the two surfaces: perturbed and uninterrupted. This wave function transition is spread across the substratum depth.

11.11.2 Relative Strength of the Scattering Potentials

The SR's reduced mobility can be measured using the above four dispersing potentials until the testing framework is formulated. Next, the relative value of each potential dispersion is assessed. Figure 11.3 is an assembly of SR mobility findings with the consequences and the cumulative impact of individual dispersion terms.

11.11.3 Remote Surface Roughness Scattering

The "Remote Surface Roughness" (RSR) spreading is another dispersion process that is closely similar to SR scattering. Charging carriers in channels will disperse their impulses through means of the remote interaction with the gate/insulator software for ultra-thin-oxide structured MOS tires. The second interface, that is the gate/oxide interface, does not smoothly differ from the perfect plane, like the oxide/substrate interface. The degree of roughness at both interfaces depends on the steering system of the system.

11.12 A NEW HYBRID RECURRING MIXED FREQUENCY DOMAIN EQUALIZER FOR DIGITAL COMMUNICATIONS

Equalization of the canals is an important strategy for trying to compensate inter-symbol Ferris in a diffraction communication channel, for the non-linearity of amplification operations, and the sound emitted in the device. Linear equalizers seldom do very well on deep spectrum zero or non-linear streams. Researchers have shown that non-linear equalizers have higher efficiency than linear equalizers in applications with non-linearity channel disturbances. Even the Analysis Solutions Late winner cannot efficiently restore the distorted signals if the canal is non-linear or if nonlinear channel distortions are too severe to be ignored. Since neural networks (NNs) can carry out complicated projection between both the inputs and the output and can construct decision-making regions with non-linear boundaries, a wide range of non-linear equalization channels has succeeded. NNs are explained by the fact that the limits of the optimized decision areas are in most situations strongly nonlinear and that non-linear classification is required, even on linear channels. This is justified. Latest proposals have been made for effective adaptive equalization on an NN basis for automated communication networks. In the literature different ANN Architectures like MLP, an RBF, etc. were suggested and numerous novel frameworks as well as effective training algorithms. Furthermore, the selection of the structure for an ANN equalizer was always a problem since a less complex structure can be deployed with very large-scale integration (VLSI) and digital signal processing (DSP) chips, etc., in real-time, and it can be used more effectively with traditional applications such as time-varied channel systems, optical recording media, etc.

11.12.1 PROPOSED HYBRID RECURRENT NEURAL EQUALIZER

A spatial domain transformation unit with real value is tumbled the recurrent neural network (RNN) component is seen in Figure 12.1 after the presentation. Applying the converted signaling energy standardization technology, a weighted total of all the normalized signals is assessed for its final result from the developed system. A new concept centered on the replication of the channel output error given the standard backpropagation algorithm was created to change the relation weights of this converters structure. The transforming block requires no weight adaptation because the RNN module consists of fixed weights, but the link weights need to be updated using the regular Real Time Recurrent Learning (RTRL) aligners, which enable the error determination of RNN nodes. However, the BP algorithm can't explicitly achieve this approximation due to the transform block's location near the output end. Thus, the last exit error spreads across the network here.

11.12.2 HYBRID NEURAL TRAINING ALGORITHM TRAINING

The configuration suggested is a composition of RNN module nr different nodes with external nx inputs and a transform block. Phase by step, the strengths of the computer program as described below have been updated.

11.13 INTEGRATION OF CROSSED CUBE INTERCONNECTION NETWORKS

The Hypercube designs are closely combined with the binary cube network's multicore processing. In parallel computing, computers focused on the configuration of hypercubes have achieved widely accepted recognition. Many global-based machines were recently developed and placed on the market. The hypercube provides the opportunity to approximate the overhead minimal most connecting networks, of a rich connectivity configuration with wide belt distance, an exponential length, easy routing and data broadcasting, a recursive layout that is normal in dividing and conquering applications. Benefits have been suggested to boost its properties and computing ability given the popularity of hyperbolic geometry. A good hypercube, the crosses cube was introduced and preliminary experiments have shown that a crossed cube retains much of the hypercube's appealing qualities, most notably, by a factor of 2 (1, 2, 4, 6, 8, 11, 15) in circumference. This means that while data connectivity is a big problem, the crucible cube offers hyperbolic geometry benefits. Data transport costs are well recognized in parallel architectural computational expenses. Also relevant is comparative analysis on cross-cube and other networking with links and discusses the advantages they offer. Heterogeneous calculation of algorithms across various architectural capabilities, the configuration of VLSI circuits, and the translation of logical data structures to machine memories, the problems with integrating one interconnected transmission network into the other are quite significant.

11.13.1 EMBEDDING COMPLETE BINARY TREES

This report explains our intention to incorporate a CB_n binary prediction model in a crossed cubic XQ_n with advanced control modules. The system is based on the in order category to insert CB_n into

XQ$_n$ in a conventional onward way. The encoding is made of the maximum tree structure Algorithm Embedding (ECBT).

Algorithm ECBT

1. Start.
2. Mark the whole binary tree nodes using random permutation based on an inorder traversal
3. Map each node in the crossing cube with the appropriate binary sequence to each node in a maximum binary tree
4. Finish.

11.13.2 EMBEDDING CYCLES

Consider the dilemma of determining the cycle nodes of the crossing cube XQ$_n$ in a series C_{2n} with $2n$ nodes to ensure their adjacence. Now that there are two neighboring nodes in the cycle, their image should be neighboring in the crosses cube by any element I were 1 picture I picture n. We can see this uploading as a series of measurements crossed by neighboring nodes.

11.14 FAULT-TOLERANT SOFTWARE: A TECHNIQUE THAT HAS A COMPONENT

Increased sophistication of core functionality is added to fault tolerance mechanisms for sensitive and expedition technologies. Additional sophistication will adversely impact the trustworthiness of activity on the critical path or critical systems device by the use of the controller software for detection process, controls, exception handling, and redundancy/diversity and inclusion.

One approach to minimize this complication is that the additional bridge problems be separated and modularized from the true function.

Several methods were developed at the architecture and programming stage to separate feature and non-functional elements. Computer level solutions, such as IFTC, CR, and MOP protocol-based metal objects, have demonstrated that reliability problems can be applied irrespective of practical demands. In the developing field of AOP&D, the modular application of bridge issues is supported by the same degree of freedom.

The change rate (ROC) of data or signals may be applied by activating appropriate preservation techniques to recognize inaccurate situations that help to tolerate and prevent errors. ROC-based error detection and recovery plausibility controls are presented in the context of executable claims.

11.14.1 ROC DETECTION APPROACH AND RECOVERY BASED ON BELIEVABILITY

Error detection is the fundamental step to implement every method of fault tolerance. Running affirmations are usually used as a tool for error detection. Change rate (ROC)-based provided data plausibility tests can be used to detect any incorrect conditions leading to failure. Though Hiller has discussed the ROC-based executable affirmations, these restrictions are accompanied by changes in the transition probabilities, but without a time limit. However, in a given time frame as affirmed by Clegg, the true rate of change should apply. There are more opportunities for misclassification of things without knowing a time limit.

11.14.2 ASPECT-ORIENTED EXCEPTION HANDLING PATTERNS

Exception management was used to enforce software high availability through forwarding downward error retrieval mechanisms as the main mechanism. It offers an easy way to structure applications to handle misconditions.

The authors examined the shortcomings that mainstream programs such as JAVA, ADA, C# had in their exception management systems. Exception coding is linked to standard code in their experience. This impedes both usual and exceptional handling of software development and recycling. We, therefore, suggest simplified aspects-based models track, spot errors, raise exceptions, and use a static aspect weaver to handle exceptional conditions. These trends will contribute to a stable and reliable device fault tolerance dependent on aspects. The following design notes were used to express design trends directed toward the aspect.

11.14.3 ERROR COMPONENT OF IDENTIFICATION AND EXCLUSION

Fehler identification and exceptions are anchors in the implementation of any technique for fault tolerance. This feature senses defects and lends exceptions to the scope, input, and output. For each form of fault tolerance event, the GenThrowErrExcept unifies NormalClass with three specifications.

- **RangeErrPc.** The context method () just points to this join. It begins with advice to search for errors of range sort before the context method is executed (). In the event, the statements are not true or the behavioral limitation is not fulfilled, the exception Ra-neErrExc is created.
- **InputErrPc.** This adds contextMethod () to scoped more with contextMethod () input arguments (). It starts with a bit of advice before checking the valid input before the context process is executed. If the input is not real, InputErrExc is elevated.
- **OutputErrPc.** The context method () added to this connection with results as the context method () performance (). It needs to initiate a recommendation after the implementation of the context system to verify the valid performance. If the output is not correct, OutputErrExc is increased.

11.15   AN ADAPTATION UNCERTAIN AUDIO MULTIBIOMETRIC SYSTEM

Increased sophistication of core functionality is added to fault tolerance mechanisms for sensitive and expedition technologies. Additional sophistication will adversely impact the trustworthiness of activity on the critical path or critical systems device by the use of the controller software for detection process, controls, exception handling, and redundancy/diversity and inclusion.

One approach to minimize this complication is that the additional bridge problems be separated and modularized from the true function.

Several methods were developed at the architecture and programming stage to separate feature and non-functional elements. The fusion solution to the biometric system is one of the solutions to solve these limitations.

Several investigations have been documented using lip knowledge for image classification. Likewise, the form and loudness characteristics from a lip of a person are utilized in a gadget identification of the speaker. The use of geometric parameters such as the speaker's height, breadth, and mouth angle was also examined. To recognize pixels, such as the Discrete Cosine Transformation (DCT), in addition to lip contour parameters, personal recognition criteria were also explored.

11.15.1 SUPPORT VECTOR MACHINE CLASSIFIER

The safe virtual machine (SVM)-classifier of the simplistic form, dimensional, and distinguishable case is the ideal hyperplane to optimize the distance from the nearest exercise data point known as support vectors.

The resolution of a linearly discrete instance is given as follows. Consider a problem of separating the set of exercise vectors belonging to two distinct classes.

11.15.2   Visual Front-End Subsystem

The SVM-classifier of the simplistic form, dimensional, and distinguishable case is the ideal hyperplane to optimize the length from the nearest exercise data point known as support vectors.

The linear separate case approach is provided as follows: Consider a question of dividing the number of available routes into two distinct groups, our storage contains 22,200 pictures with a total capacity of 64 pixels for 37 people. Each person used 60 captured images (including ten images per sequence).

11.15.3   Front-End Subsystem Audio Component

Predicted Nonlinear Encoding is a domain-frequency approach approximating a spoken sample in a common distribution of previously mentioned samples. The number of quadratic variations here between real and linear specimens is calculated to minimize a special collection of prediction coefficients. Also shown are the parameter values used in each point of the experiment. There are 14 cepstrum coefficients for a series of feature vectors calculated from each window.

11.16   HARDWARE VIRTUALIZATION DESIGN AND IMPLEMENTATION USING A PURELY HARDWARE-ASSISTED VMM

Cloud computing is a strategy to use hardware power effectively. A virtual machine monitor is a component used to execute a virtualization software (VMM), also known as a hypervisor. A VMM governs the simultaneous operation on a separate hardware unit of several operating systems. It's a thin layer of tech that offers an abstraction from the virtual machine. The approximation is similar to actual hardware in such a way that applications written for the system will operate in the VM without modification. The VMM is known as the host and each OS running above the VMM is a guest. The VMM offers direct power over a whole physical machine for each Guest OS (processor, memory, and all peripheral devices).

11.16.1   Hardware Virtualization

Until major hardware vendors had recently created architectural extensions supporting virtualization, it struggled to fulfill the 86 processor architecture classical virtualization standards. Intel VT codenamed Vanderpool and advance micro devices (AMD) SVM codenamed Pacifica are the corresponding Intel and AMD technologies.

11.16.2   86 Architectural Limitations

The 86 technologies do not follow the standardized standards for enterprise applications for the Popek & Goldberg in their original form. Responsive instructions are named in a virtualized environment and need the power to be turned over to the VMM. The VM may be stuck with restricted orders to transfer access to the VMM. If all-important commands are favored, then the architecture of the processor is said to be virtualized. In 8,617 guidelines breach this fundamental requirement.

11.16.3   AMD SVM Architectural Extensions

The AMD SVM architecture is an array of hardware extensions to 86 directly developed to make virtual machine systems effective. The AMD SVM is configured to quickly link guest operating systems to the host VMM worldwide. World Switch corresponds to the process of host-guest switching.

Significant characteristics of the SVM involve interception of specified instructions or activities in the guests, external exposure to memoir security, interrupt management support, remote interrupt service, the Guest/Host tagged TLB, and Nested Paging to minimize Virtual machines overhead. SVM can interrupt specified directions and events.

11.16.4 THE HARDWARE-ASSISTED VIRTUAL MACHINE MONITOR

The HVMM that we use in best performance analyses depends on the AMD SVM virtual machine hardware acceleration. This is based on a pro-type VMM open source called Kaneda's Tiny Virtual Machine Monitor (TVMM).

The TVMM has the following components and is a basic VMM designed for educational and verifying purposes. The specific tasks needed to begin the processor modifications for AMD SVM are performed. It builds a single VM effectively and then starts a skeletal Guest OS in the VM.

With the following additional features, our HVMM is an expanded TVMM variant. Multiple guest operating systems can be managed. It builds several virtual machines with various guest operating systems. The framework also provides round-robin planning for the guests one after the other.

11.16.5 HVMM DESIGN

A few critical steps are necessary to get the HVMM going.

Initialization of the SVM by INITIALIZE SVM is the first step (). ENABLE SVM () and SETUP HYPERVISOR are called (). Initialization of unique SVM flags, including EFER.SVME with the required values is done by ENABLE SVM (). Host Save Area (HOST SAVE PA), which is a secure space that can be managed by the VMM alone, is assigned and set up by SETUP HYPERVISER ().

The final method is to operate the HVMM by the HYPERVISOR CORE function ().

11.17 PREDICTION OF QUALITY OF METRICS-DRIVEN SOFTWARE WITHOUT FAULT DATA

Tomorrow's computer software is getting more complicated, and shortly their coding lines will cross millions or billions. Such large-scale applications face exceptional information consistency challenges. Different definitions of software development can be made dependent on lesser composition views:

- **Transcendental point of view**: Instead of observable features, performance can be defined in abstract ways, and when the product appears, consumers can consider performance.
- **Value-based view**: The value it offers determines performance and whether it is attractive, consumers opt to pay the technology. Consumer view: The user's degree of comfort with his/her desires is quality. Fabrication perspective: the consistency and application of these specifications can enhance process standards.
- **Product perspective**: This consistency view reflects on the features of quality attributes.
  As software systems get more complicated and perceptions of the quality of our people are rising, in a quality system development we must balance this customer satisfaction. Three classes of operations, listed below, include a precision machining project:
- **Planning quality:** It identifies quality objectives, selects quality assurance (QA) tasks, and selects measurement systems for enhancement. QA activities performance and fault management: selected QA activities will be carried out and the faults identified will be eliminated.

Measuring, evaluating, and enhancing quality: Activities for quality assessment begin in conjunction with the QA activities.

Computer verification is one of the best recognized QA software practices. Besides program review, there are several alternate QA methods including evaluation, requirement specification, tolerance to faults, and defect prevention. Unbiased customer satisfaction evaluation is conducted based on quality engineering method measuring data gathered. Quality evaluation approaches are quantitative data analysis models and more accurate than personal decisions typically emphasized. They can be classified into two classes, which are comprehensive and product-specific models:

- **Widespread models:** In widespread models, project or product-specific statistics are not used and industrialized statistics contribute to approximately evaluate product output. The three subsections are categorized:
- **Styles in general:** A rough content assessment is available. Similar consistency calculations are used in different product categories.
- **Dynamic model prototypes:** Dynamic model graphs show the pattern inconsistency overall goods over time. Commodity simulations: in comparison to the generic models, product-specific data is used in these modeling techniques.
- **Semi-customized versions:** These models add historical details on all products from past launches of the same product rather than the profile.
- **Observation-driven simulations:** These models only use current project data, and accuracy is measured based on current project measurements.
- **Predictive model-driven measurement:** These model "the following that software and output are predicted.

11.17.1 CLUSTERING

This section includes previous information on cluster analysis and clustering approaches used in our scientific investigations.

11.17.1.1 Clustering Basics

Clustering is an unattended way of studying. Clustering does not use class labels and aims to find the relationship between functions as classifications are trained. Clustering procedures may be used by using similitude scales or ranges to group the modules with identical measurements. Analyzing the cluster consists of four fundamental steps: the collection of features, the selection of algorithms, the validation cluster, and the description of results. Clustering algorithms are not easily classified. Berlin has defined a categorization.

11.17.2 CLUSTERING ALGORITHMS

11.17.2.1 K-Means

K-means is a clustering algorithm based on the center and center algorithms are more effective than clustering algorithms based on similarities. In the beginning segment, clusters are adjusted with arbitrary occurrences and in the reiteration segment, in-stances are allocated to clusters rendering to the distances added among the centroid of the cluster and the occurrence. This process of iteration continues until the cluster modifications do not happen. The collection of the number of nodes, k, as a model parameter is one downside of the K-metal algorithm. The Bayesian Information Criteria (BIC) or Akaike Information Criteria (AIC) measures have been developed for optimization by Pelleg and Moore to resolve this problem. k, x-means need k_{min} and k_{max} values instead of selecting a single cluster number. The algorithm begins at a value of k_m and if necessary, adds centroids. The BIC or Schwarz criteria is used to divide many centers into two, thus creating new centers. The ultimate center set is the highest score.

11.18 HETEROGENEOUS EMBEDDED SOFTWARE COMPUTING MODELS

11.18.1 EMBEDDED SYSTEMS

Wearable sensors are specially designed systems normally integrated into larger systems that provide this device with a dedicated service. The equipment developer offers a functional software application for most embedded devices, and end-users have little access to modifying the system applications. The operating device, for example, is the product of consumer electronics (such as cell phones, PDAs, and microwaves), transportation process control, plant control, and defense mechanisms.

The features of embedded systems that distinguish them from other digital systems are defined: functioning as a single. Incorporated structures execute a certain role on many occasions. The time is reactive and true. Many embedded systems are reactive systems, particularly in the control domain, which must constantly respond to environmental changes and without delay meet time constraints.

Compressed tightly. Embedded devices have near specification metric restrictions. For instance, embedded systems must have minimal construction costs, have compact size factors, and have low power consumption, especially for portable devices, have to satisfy real-time specifications, have to be secure and steady, with a limited term on the market. The aforementioned are common establishing organizational: special hardware module (ASIC); customizable microprocessor; information and coding storage systems; A/D, I/O, and D/A devices; linking bus; etc. ASIC technologies and a heterogeneous system.

Hardware synthesis techniques have historically been used to improve efficiency (logic syntheses and behavior synthesis). The fact that Embedded Systems use more technology, however, is insufficient for synthesizing hardware. Hardware synthesis approaches often concentrate on the creation of a single hardware chip where heterogeneous designs are used for more embedded systems. The challenges of embedded systems motivate the need for more effective tools and methodologies of design. System-Level Design is a system for addressing these complications and allowing SoC designs.

11.19   SYSTEM-LEVEL DESIGN AND DEVELOPMENT

System-level development addresses the problems of the homogenous embedded software design. In system-level design, the nuances of system-level development are handled:

1 The controller is programmed at the highest refinement (system level).
2 With the use of the automated design approach to step up the design process.
3 Reuse of industrial design elements (IP), as far as practicable.

The purpose is to include system-level needs for the user interface by transforming the need into a sequence of accomplishments. For instance, a more abstract design approach reduces the quantity and effectiveness of the developer's components. This change in architecture includes methods and techniques and automatic methods to encourage the development of higher different levels of abstraction.

11.19.1   SYSTEM-LEVEL DESIGN APPROACHES

The development of hardware/software, defined clearly on platforms and performance, depends on components are three major systems approaches.

Professional and none (also called machine crystallization) hardware/software is a top-down approach. The device behavior begins and creates the process structure. It is done by incorporating implementing information progressively into the specification.

Designs are focused on platforms. The device behavior is mapped to the network infrastructure dependent on platforms, in which you will see an example of platform architecture.

Bottom-up is a piece of equipment method. The wrappers between these modules are mounted to assemble informative information modules. An example is defined as a piece of equipment architecture.

11.20 CO-DESIGN OF HARDWARE/SOFTWARE

The co-design of equipment can be described as cooperation equipment/software designs to achieve device levels (features & limitations) through the use of equipment/software synergy. Although implementing hardware offers increased performance, technology is cost-efficient and more scalable than software. The option between development tools in co-design is a compromise between different parameters such as efficiency, cost, and flexibility. It depicts the movement of a co-design framework of traditional equipment.

The following operations are generally co-designed with electronics: development and verification of specifications and models.

11.20.1 SPECIFICATION AND MODELING

This is the first step in the co-design approach. During specified steps, device activity at the system level is recorded. It offers specifications and modeling information, like economic models.

11.20.2 DESIGN AND REFINEMENT

To turn a requirement into architecture, the planning process implements a step-wise optimization methodology. The next development steps are described by Niemann and O'Nils as assigning of tasks, an estimate of cost, allocation, partitioning of equipment, programming, and co-synthesis. Nieman categorizes as co-synthesis various design steps: information propagation, refined specification, hardware synthesis, and synthesis of software.

11.20.3 VALIDATION

Confirmation is colloquially defined as the process by which the design is right, at various abstractions. The founder is the verification of hardware/software programs. Co-validation approaches are formal and simulator verification. Contrast is given in the co-simulation processes.

11.21 MODELING AND SPECIFICATION

The specifications are the start of the co-design technique when the author specifies the specification for the device without defining the implementation. Device parameters are captured in languages. Modeling is the mechanism by which requirements are conceived and refined. A model differs from the system specifying vocabulary. A model is a mathematical terminology describing the optimal device behavior, while a particular language captures it in a specific format. In several languages, a prototype can be collected and a language catches several models. Two systems specifications are approached, consistent modeling, which uses a standard language to define a retrosynthesis, and a homogenous modeling framework that uses specific Hardware Languages (e.g., VDHL) and software. Two methods are used for system definitions.

11.21.1 COMPUTATION MODELS

A computer simulation describes the system's actions in an abstraction detailed definition. The Computer Model (MOC) can best include concurrent behavior, sequential actions, and methods of communication. Co-design systems use computer templates to formally reflect a structure. Several computer models were created to describe heterogeneous structures.

11.21.1.1   Model of Finite State Machines (FSM)

Several Stages are included in the FSM model, a collection of constants, an input, and the ability to work independently with a next-generation functional. A collection of statements and the input value is defined as a mechanism that can initiate a transfer from one state to the next. For modeling control-flow-controlled structures, FSMs are also used. The only drawback of FSMs is the gradual increase in the number of states because of the loss of leadership and competence as machine complexity increases. Research has suggested many derivatives of the classical FSM to overcome the shortcomings of the classic FSM. These are some of the modifications below. SOLAR is built on the Enhanced FSM (EFSM) model that is capable of supplying port hierarchy and competition. SOLAR also advocates connectivity principles of high level, including networks and global variables. It is used in influence system communication to describe high-level principles and is primarily adapted for propagation applications. This paradigm offers an intermediary format for the system-level computerization of equipment architectures.

Hierarchy competition FSM (HCFSM) overcomes the disadvantages of FSMs by dividing States into a variety of sections. These sub-states can simultaneously interact via instance variables. This improves the hierarchy and competitiveness of HCFSMs. Statecharts is the graphic official language of the HCFSM MOC machine. The receiver responds to the sender's post immediately on the implementing corrective in informed decision-making. The model HCFSM is developed for regulators in legitimate.

The *Codesign Finite State Machine* (CFSM) [16,17] is designed for software and hardware, adding to the basic FSM competition and complication. It is used extensively for modeling flow-controlled systems. The basic interaction between CFSMs is called occurrences and the system's behavior is described as event sequences. CFSMs are widely utilized to transfer heightened language used to catch CFSMs in intermediate methods in co-design systems.

11.21.1.2   Discrete-Event Systems

The availability of separate contemporaneous occurrences transforms an object-oriented architecture from one circumstance into another. An event is known as an instant action that has a date stamp for the occurrences. Occurrences are grouped worldwide because of their date of delivery. A signal is called the incident sequence and the main communication interface method. Typique for simulating hardware is object-oriented calculation. For example, Verilog and VHDL employ Dynamical Events modeling as a core computer model. Modeling discreet cases is expensive as all occurrences have to be classified by the number plate.

11.21.1.3   Petri Nets Simulation

For simulation applications, Petri nets are commonly used. Petri networks consist of locations, resources, and transformations in which tokens have been deposited. Tokens are generated and consumed by shooting a transfer. Petri Nets support competition and are synchronized, but they lack hierarchical modeling capabilities. Therefore, because of its lack of structure, Petri Nets can be challenging to use in designing complex structures. In response to the lack of authority, combinations of Petri Nets are devised. For instance, Dittrich has proposed Hierarchical Petri Nets (HPN). In addition to preserving big Petri Net functionality like competence and intermittent, HPNs support hierarchical functions. As the underlying construct, HPNs are using Bipartite directed graphs. Since they endorse competition and hierarchy, HPNs are ideal for the simulation of complicated systems.

11.21.1.4   Data Flow Graphs

Systems are defined with a direct diagram of the Markov decision process (DFG), in which inputs, outputs, and procedures are represented by nodes (actors), and the edges represent data paths between nodes. Data Flow is used mostly to moderate applications governed by the data flow. Only when the operators are available, simulations are performed. An unlimited FIFO buffering scheme allows connectivity between procedures. The Data Flow model supports hierarchy since node structures or a different Data Flow are dynamic. In the literature, several variants of data flow diagrams such as Synchronous Data Flow (SDF) and Asynchronous Data Flow (ADF) were proposed. The SDF consumes a fixed number of coins, while the ADF consumes a variable number of tokens. A summary of data flow patterns and differences is given by Lee.

11.21.1.5 Sync/Reactive Modeling

Synchronization modeling is built on the presumption simultaneously that outcomes are created instantaneously after parameters are postponed. In the simulation of reactive real-time processes, sequential simulations are used. Two models for modeling reactive real-time systems are listed in Cortes: multifunctional clocked recurring systems (MCRS) that are suitable for data, which dominant real-time systems and state-based formalities, appropriate for re-time control-dominated. Synchronization dialects like Esterel are used to capture a contemporaneous computing model.

11.21.1.6 Heterogeneous Models

Heterogeneous components represent the characteristics of various computational models. There are two types of heterogeneous models.

Languages include a heterogeneous model to facilitate data modeling and power. Affirmative and descriptive linguistics such as lisp and prolog are two examples of programming languages. Declarations are performed in the same order defined in the description in high-level languages. On the other hand, the execution order in propositional environments is not expressly defined, since the executing order is built on a series of logical rules or features. Most of the languages do not have different constructions to set the state when using the computer programs for simulation.

11.22 A DIFFERENTIAL DIAGRAM FOR REFLECTING PETRINE OBJECT RECOGNITION

During their product life cycle, most current object-oriented mechanisms can evolve. Think, for example, about mobile ad-hoc networks, tech adaptability, business requirements, etc. Appropriate Tata global beverages and tools are needed to design energetic discrete-event structures. Sadly, the very well formalities for object-oriented structures, such as traditional Petri networks, do not include the normal expression of any improvement in the configuration of the system. A typical solution involves functional features of the polluting environment with evolutionary specifics. It hinders the review, reuse, and repair of the device. Reflective Petri nets have recently been designed and applied to hierarchical business processes as a basis for complex discrete occurrence systems. They are based on two conceptual layers of a transparent design. The accomplished smooth isolation of functionality and development results in an easy formal model of systems with high dynamism that can retain the analytical capacity of traditional Petri networks. The Reflecting Petri networking approach is intended to achieve a good balance among articulation and analysis capabilities, by rigorously applying concepts of contemplation in one centralized Petri net context, as compared with another complex extension of Petri net in the last decade that developed a new (hybrid) framework.

11.22.1 WN's Basic Notions

Institutionalism in the two layers of the reflection layout (meta- and base-)—the Colored Petri Nets (CPNs) and the expansions are well-formed nets (WNs). However, of the commonplace transition networks. This choice has been advantageous for two major factors: first, concerning the classical Petri net transformation, the compliance of the Reflective Petri net Nets can be formally stated; second, the symbolic state concept characteristic of WN enables the recognition of similar basic level transformations to be made effective. WNs preserve the expressive ability of the CPN, though using powerful analysis algorithms, are distinguished by formal syntax. Not every function that can be referred to by the reader in this section is presented informally and focuses on the concept of conceptual marking. WNs include transformation priority thresholds and antagonist arcs, as opposed to CPNs. These characteristics promote formalism and support the transactional implementation of improved navigation.

11.22.2 REFLECTIVE PETRI NETS LAYOUT

The Reflective Petri network is based on a two-layer amendment in the bill. First, a Petri net (P/T net with precedence and inhibition arcs), which is a developing system (PN base level), while the main house, known as the conception net, comprises of a high-level PETRI network, which depicts advancements at the base level (meta-program, according to the reflection).

The meta-level functions on a base-level leader called filmmaker, formally established in a colorful branding. The earliest forms are used for monitoring (introspection) and manipulation (intercession) of the foundation PN by the meta-program. Modifications to redefinition are reflected at the base level at the end of a Meta computation (shift-down).

At some base level transition in the state, the concept is explicitly triggered (shift up). A strategic approach is then chosen based on whether a particular situation is reached in the base level and/or external (meta-level simulation) happenings. The opportunity to define arbitrary collection criteria improves the transparent interface functionality. Another high-level Petri network node, which somehow resembles a clear meta-layer that implements base-level deep thinking and intercession, is the reflective structure. The architecture has a set structure, which consists of transformations of higher priority. Intercession is conducted in a small, total series of low-level operations (the Evolutionary Interface): adding/removing nodes and arcs, changing transformation objectives (structural changes) (state changes). When one procedure of this kind is not performed, the meta-program is resumed as a whole and any modifications caused in the meantime are discarded. An example of an error is trying to uninstall a node not yet occurring the evolutionary techniques have a transactional interpretation, in other words. Following a successful approach, improvements are mirrored in the Petri network at the base stage.

11.22.3 HANDLING STATE TRANSITION

Particularly, the recently developed government meanings explain the excruciatingly long performances of a reflective Petri net but have two clear disadvantages that affect productivity and performance. First of all, the idea of state is highly repetitive and includes a metaphor that defines the operational aspects of the system. Second, there is no way to recognize the analogous requirements of the process developments. The last issue is a crucial one: it is also necessary for all strategies dependent on state-space examination for the opportunity to know finitude and close connections (strictly related to the ability to collect comparisons). Identifying an emerging system's comparability is difficult. The normal level can return to its original condition after a sequence of transformations (state). More often than not, the system's inner dynamics will lead to comparable environments. The dilemma is solved by the conceptual notions of branding, which is unique to WN, and the legitimation of the base level on a Meta level.

The modeler will specify a logical class Place, Tran division on his/her needs, which may be different from totally separated partitions (implicitly) adopted when the basic meta PN is set.

11.23 THE DYNAMIC PHILOSOPHERS EXAMPLE

A variant of a very well-known fast food philosophies dilemma, which introduces high creativity, has been tested in the (symbolic) state-transition semantics of reflecting Petri nets. This edition fulfills the minimum specifications: First, there are two intellectuals on the bench.

A philosopher can only eat when the adjacent forks, one of which is the property of the philosophy, are concurrently picked up.

A philosopher on the table has the following two abilities, each of which requires the possessed fork at the moment.

You should ask an external partner to enter the table, share their work with him. If there are three philosophies at a minimum on the table, he/she will leave the table.

Each philosophical goes for his or her fork. The base level net Petri reflecting the initial state. The practical elements are defined in-depth, while the dynamic characteristics (transitions $invite_i$, $leave_i$) are only outlined, thereby making the model as straightforward as possible. Any request/leave attempts trigger the situation that applies two separate techniques.

11.24   USE OF REAL-TIME HARDWARE XILINX EMBEDDED SYSTEM GRAPHICS PROCESSING SYSTEM CO-SIMULATION

In automotive purposes and everyday life, video processing and computer auditory memory become progressively important. In general, video editing uses tasks with some very significant computational requirements. The regular processors and computers can do these activities or computers linked to computer networks. However, it is not always the appropriate technique, which is why advanced, DSP or field-programmable gate arrays (FPGA) hardware approaches are normally used in embedded systems [2,3]. Xilinx device generator offers a high graphic design of the Simulink framework for the creation of the hardware system. The Granite Counter enhances the standard HDL framework and includes graphical components to prevent the need for a comprehensive understanding of plexic languages. Simulink's visual language allows the infrastructure to be abstracted via blocks and parts in device generation. This minimizes the time between system identification variations and hardware deployments. The application also supports hardware reproduction and electronics confirmations from within the hardware co-simulation setting. In comparison with the HDL technique, this paradigm offers better hardware confirmation and execution. Something that is much more cost-effective than other methods is the simulation and hardware-in-the-circulation approach. The ability to design a control system streamlined way as an integrated system in real-time improves the creative process significantly.

11.24.1   Xilinx System Generators Design and Analysis for FPGA Implementation

Effective, fast-track development and testing involve a hardware design platform design creation framework. Used methods are MATLAB R2007a with Math Works Simulink, DSP System Generator 10.1, and Xilinx ISE 10.1. Although the Xilinx ISE 10.1 base program is not used explicitly, it is necessary since the system blocks are applied in the context. The System Generator environment provides direct interfaces between the Xilinx FPGAs line and the Simulator. Moreover, many cost-effective production boards are available commercially and can be used for the development of applications.

MATLAB is an interactive digital calculation program that simplifies linear algebra routine implementations. The MATLAB commands given enable powerful procedures to be carried out. A further MATLAB Toolbox is used for the modeling, simulation, and analysis of complex structures in a graphical interface is Simulink. The software helps the development of modular and hierarchical models that offer the advantage of designing a complex, philosophically simplified system architecture.

11.24.2   Hardware Description Language (HDL) Modules

Due to the low degree of abstraction in the HDL environment, the situation changes with the more complicated design.

The Integrated Software Environment (ISE) of Xilinx is an efficient, context architecture environment used to execute System Generator blocks. ISE includes several HDL-written software modules that are designed, captured, simulated, and implemented digitally in a CPLD or FPGA device. The summary of these modules builds netlist files that are the input to the framework for execution. The logic architecture is translated to a physical file that can be accessed on the target computer after the generation of these files.

- **Converting of RGB to YCbCr Color Space**

Video and image quality from one image pixel to the must be converted in several applications. Pictures and motion pictures (video) have been used to reproduce color within an image in many binary images like RGB, YCrCb, HSI, and others. Each of them has its combination of advantages and drawbacks. RGB, for example, is usually used to meet the most stringent requirements for maintaining ultimate color reliability. The composition of the bold colors the color that may be seen in the imaging lens may reflect (Red—R, Blue–B, and Green–G). In truth, our automated human vehicle developed for green and red bands, but not as responsive to blue changes, cannot show the human eye in the different color stripes. Investigators have produced additional vectors (and sample spaces) for minimizing the frequency and/or throughput of a display adapter, which lower the amount and maintain better quality images in blue understanding inside the system. Furthermore, human eyesight is more concerned with changes in luminance (black, white, or gray) than with color change (changes from one color or another with the same brightness).

Consequently, several video techniques support colors (chromatin) to sample the color image in full monochrome resolution (light). In color space systems such as YCrCb, where Y signifies the luminousness data and Cr and Cb are color alteration signals that characterize the chrominance data. This subsample is often suitable for the space color. All Y samples, save for any other color, are utilized in these patterns. The sample is termed 4:2:2 in these frameworks. For each sample of 4 Y, the 4:2:2 methods and techniques mean 2 Cr and 2 Cb. Due to the advantages of capacity reduction, multiple color storage encodings are employed on several video devices. Compatibility between any of these devices also implies that the system translates the output of a streaming server into the input image necessary in a certain color space to enter the subsequent device. For example, turning RGB videos on a TV monitor from a VGA card into YCrCb is a suitable example to translate color space (Figure 11.8). In other words, when a recorded system such as a YCrCb DVD player and videos are converted to RGB for displaying driving, the reverse manner is also quite common. Also common is the other way.

11.24.3   YCBCR COLOR MODEL

The YCbCr color scheme is also part of the transmission spectrum of colors. The color components in the color image are segregated from the brightness. Element (Y) is light and homomorphic knowledge is maintained as two color differential components. Color constituent Cb signifies the variance among the blue constituent and an orientation value and the color integral Cr signifies the alteration between the red constituent and a reference value.

FIGURE 11.8   RGB and YCbCr.

$$\begin{bmatrix} Y \\ Cb \\ Cr \end{bmatrix} = \begin{bmatrix} 0.299 & 0.587 & 0.114 \\ -0.169 & -0.331 & 0.5 \\ 0.5 & -0.419 & -0.081 \end{bmatrix} * \begin{bmatrix} R \\ G \\ B \end{bmatrix} + \begin{bmatrix} 16 \\ 128 \\ 128 \end{bmatrix}$$

Figure 11.8 demonstrates that the RGB color model is converted to a YCbCr color image with the MATLAB rgb2ycbcr method.

11.25 CONCLUSION

The digital delta modulation MASH is a new construction that utilizes the multi-modules (MM-MASH). In each level of the EFM1, this approach uses several modules. The multi-module structure has been demonstrated to be appropriate, as the outputs of the MASH modulator depend solely upon and independently of the quantity of the first stage EFM1 module. Details are calculated for each stage's sampling frequency of the EFM1 and all MASH DDSM. To provide the highest modulator duration, there are two criteria. The outcome is a lengthier sequencing architecture and hence improved operating voltage. Different considerations should be considered in the design of induction motor drives for reduced maintenance. First, concerning the (d, q) nomenclature, the strong sensing capacity of test signals necessitates various differential inductances. It is necessary to limit the effects of saturation on this behavior. The anisotropic inductive characteristics should be considerably varied to increase the production of the torque due to torque impedance. This boosts the useful torque of the engines to 15%, for example, by a positive d-axis current. Moreover, other adverse reactions, such as torque grip, ripple torque, non-sinusoidal no-load voltage patterns, and inefficiencies, there are specific values to restrict the efficacy of such innovative urges that are deteriorating. Therefore, a strategy for linking electromechanical mechanisms probability distribution with closely connected external circuits is useful with voltage waveform, electromagnetic interference, and other losses. The impacts of acoustic impedance on process growth are shown in this technique.

12 Demographic and Principles of Electronic Computing

12.1 DIFFERENTIATION USING NEURAL NETWORKS AND LINEAR REGRESSION BASED ON PERCEPTION AND TRAFFIC

The color that may be seen in the imaging lens may reflect (Red––R, Blue–B, and Green–G). In truth, our automated human vehicle developed for green and red banding, but not as responsive to blue alteration, cannot show the human eye in the different color stripes. Investigators have produced additional vectors (and sampling areas) for minimizing the frequency and/or throughput of a display adapter, which lower the amount and maintain better quality images in blue understanding inside the system. Furthermore, human eyesight is a system that affects luminance (black, white, or gray) than discoloration (changes from one color or another with the same brightness). Although the costs of operating a big imaging system such as this are significant, it is necessary to implement it since it enables real-time traffic situations to be simulated. Detailed traffic data information, for instance, vehicle type speed and number of cars on the route, can also be provided. In the process of quantifying road congestion degrees, the requirements of traffic cameras with image recognition capability. An image recognition approach is now being employed for the identification of the level of blockage utilizing the Occupancy Ratio (OR) approach. The results of the present procedures are, according to a study, incompatible with passenger impressions. On the other extreme, our observations observed a significant increase in effectiveness that can result in a successful intersection control contender with a highly trained neural network employing velocity and vehicular traffic [279].

12.1.1 The Road Traffic Congestion Estimation

For each form of data collected, a variety of techniques for estimating traffic congestion levels were explored. Set and mobile sensors are two kinds of sensors that may be used to help extract traffic data. The data was gathered using cell phones in the analysis, and the neural network method was used to analyze it. It employed cell dwell time (CDT). It provides rough estimates of trip time and a time when a mobile telephone is linked to the ground station. Similar problems were employed, using data from the real surveillance cameras. Data from surveillance cameras were developed to measure overcrowding by the use of fluctuating reasoning and a hidden Markov model. In our investigation, we have applied neural network approaches and forecast more precision. In the investigations, the density of traffic and the speeds of roads were taken into consideration. Our technique relies on multiple discreet bandwidth utilization, although works have employed fluffy logic to evaluate continuously and six discreet network congestions.

According to the study time, velocity, quantity, customer satisfaction, and the interglacial periods in road signs that delayed motorcycling are the major components that were used to establish congestion charges threshold in several nations. Our study investigated if additional factors, such as road shape, the times of day, and any day of this week, have been affecting road congestion. The overcrowding degrees that we evaluated were limited to three categories according to the review: moderate, heavy, and jammed. This has been needed and appropriate.

DOI: 10.1201/9781003211938-12

12.1.2 COLLECTION OF DATA SETS TOOLS AND TECHNIQUES

Mobility data was gathered by surveillance cameras each time. Streaming video analysis was conducted to establish the speed of the automobile (km/h) and the amount of traffic (cars/min). The collected photographs and relevant details were then shown to respondents, who were then asked to rate the levels of traffic congestion. We required a significant number of samples to guarantee that the density levels calculated were compatible with road users' perceptions. The views of road users were gathered through a web-based survey [280].

Figure 12.1 shows the online poll that we have designed to collect the congestion level estimates of individual users on the photo provided. On the left side of the web-based poll, respondents were able to pick from a large number of camera locations located in congested locations of Phuket.

12.1.3 DATA CLASSIFICATION

A neural network's design is made up of three-node layers: one input layer, one hidden layer, and one output layer, all of which are connected, as seen in Figure 12.2. The weight of each node in the neural network model will be adjusted to represent the trends of the training datasets.

In the input layer, the characteristics of input data include (a) day of the week (DW): Monday through Sunday, (b) time of day in terms of minute of the day (MT), (c) vehicle velocity (SP) in km/h, and (d) traffic volume (VOL) in cars/min. As seen in Figure 12.2, the input layer is made up of 10

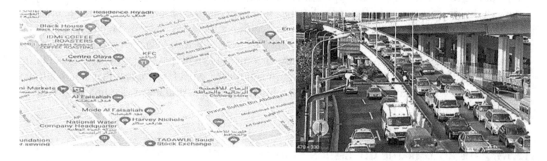

FIGURE 12.1   Traffic image congestion level.

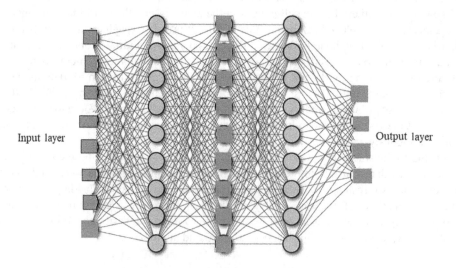

FIGURE 12.2   Learned neural network model.

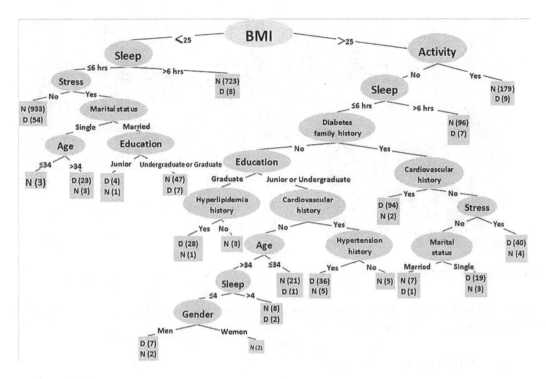

FIGURE 12.3 J48 decision tree.

nodes. Due to its nominal status, the day of the week variable produced seven parameter triangles. The intended congestion level (CL), as determined by the participants, is the output layer.

In classification and estimation, decision trees are often used. It's an easy but effective way of representing information. Decision trees generate templates that are depicted as a tree structure. The class of the examples is shown by a leaf node. As seen in Figure 12.3, the examples are classified by ordering the root of the tree from the root node. Percent 21.3 Decision tree algorithm illustrates a supervised technique for categorization. The J48 Algorithm is used by Weka, which is an adjustment of the algorithm C4.5 of the Decision Tree. J48 is a C4.5 and the latest version, significantly upgraded [280].

The interaction between pace and concentration level in the current BMA system was studied further. The clear differentiation of each congestion stage is separated in Figure 12.4, particularly for light or heavy transport. The speed ranges of the three BMA congestion stages, on the other hand, mostly overlap [281].

12.2   RDF AN ONTOLOGICAL MOBILE MALWARE STRING ARCHITECTURAL DESIGN: TESTING AND ASSESSMENT

According to the X-Force 2008 Trend and Threat Survey, web server weaknesses accounted for over at the end of 2008, 54% of all vulnerabilities were identified and 74% still did not have a remedy provided by the seller. To store data permanently, web apps must communicate with a database in any way. Establishing requests that modify or extract data contained in the database is how this communication is carried out.

Lawbreakers may modify SQL queries and tamper with data, extract data in the database, or take control of the database system by inserting punctuation marks or instructions into the database. As a result, the main problem in this chapter is that user feedback on a server that performs the SQL

FIGURE 12.4 Traffic control system.

query can be disproved. Client-side validation is used by many software developers to prevent users from entering escape characters [282].

12.2.1 DATA VALIDATION PROCESS

Standardization ensures that a bespoke application operates on secure, precise, and useable information in terms of protections for web applications. Validation rules are used to ensure the data entered into the web-based framework is right, relevant, and safe. The laws can be applied using an information oxford dictionary automatic feature or by including clear software validation reasoning; following are the two core standards of statistical analysis:

1. Evidence the validation standards with the greater control of comprehending backgrounds should be considered in the database schema;
2. Hazardous meta-character escapes, often in data access elements, can be carried out shortly before the data is saved. Verification via webserver, customer side verification, multiple verifications, and performs are only a few of the common validation approaches that web developers have introduced to better maintain data integrity. More information on these methods can be found in our previous work [283].

12.2.2 NDVS DESIGN

We introduce a new appropriate data framework built on Web semántic techniques to mitigate security issues at the application layer and to protect the database framework even when input validation modules are bypassed. The Resource Description Framework (RDF) and annotation for elements of web pages, interceptor, RDF extractor, RDF parser, and data validator are seen in Figure 12.5 as components of the data validation service architecture.

12.2.3 FUNCTIONAL OVERVIEW

The following procedures are followed:

- Using RDFa annotation1 to define all relevant data in a web application to use an ontology and then have the end-user fill out an (X) HTML form.

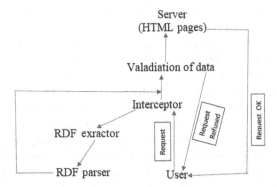

FIGURE 12.5   Framework of NDVS.

- Before the controlled high the webserver program for execution, the armored vehicle portion intercepted communications per HTTP request at the server-side.
- Use the online RDFa extractor to retrieve RDFa annotations from RDFa ontology terminology.
- Using the validator variable to ensure that all user inputs are correct.
- Where the check is successful, this request is transmitted to the guidelines for the design of the MySQL database; if the check is wrong, the application is refused.

12.2.4   OVERVIEW OF THE FRAMEWORK ARCHITECTURE

Figure 12.5 depicts an RDFa ontology-based structure. This system is made up of five parts:

- **New website components RDFa3 code snippets**: URI is a sort of URL, which may be used for the classification of any resources, not only websites. Universal resource identification is a URL (human, book, and an author property).

  It is important to mention that there are technologies that can be added to current XHTML Web Pages for the conversion of RDF/XML data (and other formats like N3, in the future). As a consequence, the annotated XHTML static web pages will become breezy. One of these resources is RDF2RDFa Converter.
- **HTTP interceptor:** It handles server-client-to-client HTTP requests. It intercepts, checks that HTTP requests in the given directories of the web server, HTTP requests are accessible, then RDF extractor is called.
- **RDF extractor:** The distillation is used to remove the RDFa annotations from the(X) HTML new website and build the RDF ontology shown in the following tables. The unanticipated fault in the RDFa Distiller is caused by a missing tag or quotation mark. As a consequence, you may register missing tags and save your code as .xhtmL via the browser W3 Validator services located at validator.w3.org. As a syntactic confirmation is needed instead of a user interface, an RDFa distiller was designed. It should be noted that the extractor has various caching difficulties. In several RDF representation forms including RDF/XML, 6 Turtles, and N triples, we are using the pyRdfa5 distillery to produce RDF triples from an RDFa or SVG Tiny 1.2 (X) HTML. RDFa7 is a special process that may be downloaded free of charge.
- **RDF parser:** In the preparations for verification, the kind of input and its parameters retrieved. The purpose of this parsing is to work within the interception interfaces, allowing RDF to handle HTTP answers supplied to customers. RDF-parser reads and translates RDF files into RDF data. It was checked and is expected to run on various Online Windows versions. Note that the RDF parser understands both RDF and RDF data structures. We

develop our parser for the validation process, which examines the inputs and character-istics. The decoder is compatible with the existing N-Triples10 and Notation 311 formats, based on Turtle language's syntax. The processor operates well based on trials against entirely random conceptualizations and existing wide taxonomies.

- **Validator:** The certificate authority employs user inputs to verify the information, once the specification has been extracted using the RDFa extractor. The validation process exam-ines to verify if a user's input is validated to match its attributions (e.g., weight, kind of data, maximum length) since it has been utilized but if the result contains code or letters peculiar to it). In case of inconsistencies, the search for authenticity of material would fail. The data validator complies with the rules to decide if the assessment is successful or fails. The site content is instantly transmitted to the operating system, provided the scientifically supported is acceptable. The network interface is refused if it fails.
- **RDF parser:** It retrieves input types and verification arguments. The data validator utilizes the information entered to verify the information when the definition is generated using the RDFa extraction. Since utilized, the testing phase attempts to check if the user's input value fulfills the characteristics criteria (such as weight, data type, minimum length, and if the value includes code or special characters). If there are differences, the investigation for the authenticity of material would fail. The data certificate authority complies with the criteria that decide whether the assessment crashes and burns the next stage in the operation. The site contents are instantly forwarded to the executing process if the pen testing is successful.

```
<FORM NAME=EmployeeForm ACTION=emp_add.jsp METHOD=post>
             <h2>Add Employee Record</h2>
<B><I>Employee Number: <br>(1 to 6 characters)</I></B>
              <INPUT TYPE=text NAME=EMPNO>
             <BR><B><I>First Name:</I></B>
        <INPUT TYPE=text NAME=FNM VALUE=First Name>
             <BR><B><I>Last Name: </I></B>
        <INPUT TYPE=text NAME=LNME VALUE=Last Name>
        <INPUT TYPE=submit NAME=Submit VALUE=Add>
                        </FORM>
```

12.3 IDENTIFICATION OF VEHICLE MOVING MOVEMENT'S ROAD CONGESTION CONCENTRATIONS: COMPARATIVE AMONG ARTIFICIAL NEURAL NETWORK AND DATA MINING ALGORITHMS

Actual traffic reports are crucial to overcrowded and overcrowded places such as Bangkok, or even scattered and rural places during a lengthy period of vacations. Pedestrians not able to do so don't pick the optimal routes and might be detained for hours on a plane. These reports can be created with the automated congestion proposed algorithm. Such notifications are possible. Several business and public sector programs for collecting network activity for the ITS were suggested and accepted. Our research shows that the majority of the effort is focused on the limited application of stationary sensors such as sequence and sophisticated functional image processing video recorder. The price of such installations is nonetheless quite significant because of the high expenditures of equipment, installation, and repair. In addition, the permanent detectors in some nations are sensitive to harsh weather. Moreover, the installation of permanent sensors to guard all highways in big cities is either practicable or practically feasible. A more expensive and broader range of technology is thus needed to collect traffic data [284].

Recently, remote sensors, often called test cars, have been developed as a free solution for improving availability and accuracy without requiring expensive infrastructure expenditure to permanent sensors. Mobile detectors are used for both GPS and cellular applications. GPS-based sensors that employ cell network information as traffic monitors are correspondingly known as GPS-based and cell-based sensors.

Due to a large number of cellular telephones and their associated infrastructure, mobile sensors are presently in use, at low cost. According to current statistics, Thailand's overall cellular income is expected to exceed 90% in 2009. On the contrary, GPS-based devices are far more efficient at identifying the position of vehicles, enabling very exact driver behavior information. More recently the advancement of GPS management is achieved through cellular telephones such as the Apple iPhone and several other mobile phones.

12.3.1 Empirical Evidence Gathering

Data from many popular Pattaya roads and also as Sukhumvit, Silom, and Sathorn were acquired. GPS phrases for GPRMC were derived from the date, time, latitude, longitude, and speed of the vehicle using a notebook connected to a USB GPS unit. A video camera mounted on the dashboard of a demonstration car captured photographs of road traffic conditions. Within 3 hours, our car traveled 30 km through congested urban areas [285].

12.3.1.1 Balancing Class Distributions

We recorded vehicle movement patterns per minute from 13:00 to 15:45 in our experiment. The first four instances were skipped because MVt and AMVt calculations focus on previous cascading calculations. As a consequence, 162 incidences have occurred: 52 cases of jam traffic, 74 in busy traffic, and just 36 in intermediate traffic. As points out, a class disparity will lead to lower accuracy among data mining students. Where there is a class imbalance, classification models prefer to estimate the dominant class. The dominant class in this situation was heavy traffic, while the majority classes, the traffic groups of light and heavy, were also crucial. To prevent the dilemma, we needed to align the classifier performance.

12.3.2 Data Classifications

The classification model was trained and evaluated using the preprocessed data collection. There were five characteristics in our data collection. MV3t—2, MV3t—1, and MV3t were the first three attributes, which were three successive simple moving rotational speeds that reflected the traveling sequence. AMV3t, the average velocity of the associated traveling sequence, was the fourth parameter. The final characteristic was Level, which represented the level of congestion as determined by human ratings. We chose the J48 algorithm, a well-known decision tree algorithm in the WEKA scheme, to produce a decision tree model to define the Level, in addition to the artificial neural network (ANN) algorithm that we used to make relations with previous work. In WEKA, the Multilayer-Perceptron was chosen for ANN. The University of Waikato developed WEKA, a machine learning program. It's a series of data mining–related machine learning algorithms. The model's target parameter was set to Level. Ten-fold cross-validation was selected as the test choice [286].

12.3.3 Sparely Populated Shared Memory Encoding Data to Be Used

An SDM is used as the foundation for navigating a robot based on sequences of views in this subject. The robot preserves collected images it captures from the pathways during the training process and during automation. If it performs the identical pathways, it will be possible to rectify view correspondence faults as set out in Refs. [6,8]. Kanerva said the SDM is suitable for storing binary vector sequences and has thoroughly discussed this probability.

Kanerva shows that the model's properties hold for arbitrary binary vectors. However, in certain cases, data is not random but rather skewed against those points. This problem is already stated by Rao and Fuentes, but they do not provide a solution. Black or white photographs, for example, are uncommon in the world of images. The authors suggest reducing the issue by altering the memory's configuration to provide more memory positions near where they're required, or by using dissimilar addressing methods. However, this only addresses part of the problem, and in some situations, it can cause the model's property to disappear [287].

12.3.4 Sparse Distributed Memories

An SDM can be implemented in several ways. It has two main arrays: one holds the descriptions of the positions and the other holds the data. The same vector as addressing may be utilized in the auto-associative results of the software presented in the below information at the same time, resulting in the need for just one sequence. According to Kanerva, the application-specific area is much less than the number of addresses.

"Hard places" refers to the real locations that occur. This is a theory condition as well as a functional limit. On the one side, using current popular technologies, it is impossible to deal with, say, 21,000 places. The features of memory, on the other hand, are a product of its sparsity.

12.3.5 Binary Codes and Distances

Each bit performance is derived by its position in the Natural Binary Code (NBC). 01 isn't identical to 10. This characteristic means that the HD does not correspond to the binary difference between two NBC integers.

Table 12.1 shows the HDs of all 3-bit binaries. This amount is not the same as the whole distance as observed (AD). The HD might increase when the AD rises. It has nine adverse situations whereby the HD decreases while the initial value can be increased or, at the very least, retained. The problem is that PGM photos are evaluated in the usage of the Natural Binary Code, which represents different values by locating the bits. Consequently, due to the numerous factors utilized to decode and analyze information within the storage, the effectiveness of the SDM might be affected [288].

12.3.6 Binary Code

As said at the moment, with 256 gray patches, it is difficult to identify the most unfavorable binary code, so that one may use the representative government of the NBC and the peculiarities of the

TABLE 12.1
Hamming Distance Bits

	000	001	010	011	100	101	110	111
000	0	1	1	2	1	2	2	3
001		0	2	1	2	1	3	2
010			0	1	2	3	1	2
011				0	3	2	2	1
100					0	1	1	2
101						0	2	1
110							0	1
111								0

TABLE 12.2
Binary Coding Value

Decimal	Sum-Code
0	0000
1	0001
2	0011
3	0111
4	1111

SDM. Only by lowering the number of separate bits to one and employing a total value can unwanted transformations be avoided. As a result, only five separate gray levels can be used with four bits, as seen in Table 12.2. There are nine gray levels visible while using eight bits, and so on. Working with an HD equal to the AD can only be done this way.

12.4   A SUGGESTION FOR THE INTEGRATION OF ARTIFICIAL AND FORMAL LOGIC

Philosophical reasoning will lead to a major improvement in software effectiveness and consistency as part of the challenge—Mathematics solutions, for example, Critical Type Theory [1,2], designs huge software systems. This study aims to study the link between the theory of the construction type and the neural networks in a type-based structure by illustrating how two distinct networks may be used. The following are some of the advantages of the application interface suggested:

The creation of a formally constructed and provable software framework in the realm of ANNs do not necessitate precise mathematical arithmetic. The development of a formally formulated and provable software framework in the realm of ANNs do not require the programmer to perform extensive mathematical analysis.

Under the constraints of the simulation network architecture, the derived framework may evolve to meet changing expected requirements [289].

12.4.1   CONCEPTUAL LOGIC THEORY

- Productive Type Theory is theoretical probabilistic reasoning on Descriptive Mathematical, in which assumptions must be supported on an explanation of the asserted theorem or assertion. In other words, evidence of inconsistency is not allowed. As a result, proofs in Productive Type Theory may be thought of as algorithms for generating examples of the proposition in question. The assertion also serves as a data type description or, at a higher level, a prototype implementation for the algorithm.
- Each logical proposition is followed by its proof object in Constructive Type Theory, resulting in a pair of values known as a Judgment. The evidence item p bears witness to proposition P, and the judgment is generally written in the form p:P.
- Constructive Type Theory assigns four laws to each logical connective.
- Introduction Elimination Formation (syntax).
- Calculation (simplification).

12.4.2   STRUCTURE OF PROTOTYPE

The purpose is to apply and implement the techniques that have been created under the framework of productive type theory. The process of derivation is thus a tool to change the significance of the template. A short comment to excerpt: implied a kind of signatures, [A] indicated a set of type A objects and [>indicated a philosophical understanding before resolving its implications (in Haskell, the main meaning) (i.e., a function type)].

Finally, parentheses are employed to indicate the aggregation of results or to show how the operations of a subset of their sentence set are performed (partial application of functions). The initial stage of the prototypes only included the principles for the channel and its constituents, and the functions it constructs. The following are represented in the Language script.

```
data NeuralNet = NN {arch:: Net_Arch, fun::Net_Func,
                     layer_nodes:: Layers}
               | ENN
```

where

```
        type Net_Arch = Array Edge Weight
        type Weight = Maybe Weight_Function
        type Weight_Function = Param -> Output -> Input
        type Edge = (Vertex, Vertex)
        type Vertex = Int
        type Layers = [[Vertex]]
        type Net_Func = [Node]
```

A neural network is specified as a Net Architectural property, a Net Func node list, and a layer organizational list of its agencies (Lays) above (if this applies to the particular network). The topology is specified as a 2D weight system maintained on the edge of networks.

12.4.3 A Feedforward Neural Network

The first step in creating a new network implementation algorithm is to use Productive Type Theory principles to come up with a solution. We believe that a standard Neural Network Architecture has been derivated for this study to emphasize how The ANNs concept is possible in combination with such a derivative prototype. We do not pretend to have a straightforward explanation, but rather that once completed, it can be used as the foundation for an electronic machine capable of detecting and correcting algorithmic errors using provided explanations of the dilemma. The prototype's various functions are described as a result of the network's construction.

12.4.4 The Dover Tides Predict

A method for evaluating data regarding the current flows and tidal conditions within Dover Harbour in Kent, United Kingdom, is needed. The key issue is the system's sophistication, which includes the tides and current flow structure, which has proven to be challenging to model and forecast. This project aims to make tidal level estimates based on a collection of historical measurements obtained by a set of sensing devices in the harbor. The data collection included hourly observations of six variables thought to influence tide dynamics. The tide, air, and sea levels; ambient pressure; and wind speed and direction are all factors to consider.

12.5 A PORTFOLIO MANAGEMENT CLUSTERING APPLICATION

The Markowitz portfolio allocation and the parametric asset allocations are the two main types of investment portfolio approaches. Provided the same risk ratio, an effective investment returns at the optimum border of Markowitz a greater return than other strategies. Because of forecast mistakes and shareholder value noise, it is impossible to precisely compute two elements of the Markowitz assessment, assets forecast and correlations for correlations. So many methods for increasing or preventing the effect of error and noise on investments have been proposed in the literature. To boost the estimation method of multivariate conditional variance–covariance matrix, for example, merge the return-based and range-based measurements of volatility. On the other hand, one should use parameter-free assignments to avoid estimation bias. Researchers have discussed the so-called 1/N law, or evenly weighted investing approach, in literary works. A simple market with independent and uncorrelated properties suggested that the 1/N rule should be optimal. Properties, on the other hand, are rarely independent of one another, particularly in large repositories. Standard asset distributions can therefore be insufficient for an effective investment portfolio [290].

12.5.1 THE OPTIMIZATION PROBLEM

The optimizing problem aims to find the best clustering partition, which is a combination of the best sections. $c_1, c_2, \ldots c_G$ The optimal strategy should have a higher Standard deviation in the study than strategies calculated with other agglomeration trends with the same G cluster number. The classification problem's optimizing goal can be expressed in terms:

$$\max_{c} SR = \frac{\bar{r}_p - \bar{r}_f}{\sigma_p} \tag{12.1}$$

where SR represents the sharp ratio, C denotes the optimal partition set, r_p is the average return of the portfolio, r_f refers to the risk-free return, and submission p is a measure of the portfolio risk over the evaluation period.

12.5.2 THE MARKOWITZ MVP ALLOCATION

At the Markowitz effective frontier, the MVP is considered to be the best portfolio with the lowest volatility. The cluster participant weights, and perhaps even the cluster portfolios load, are typically computed using quadratic programming: where w denotes either the cluster portfolio weights vector w_g or cluster member weights vector $w_{g,s}$; sigma denotes the variance-covariance matrix of the cluster portfolios or the cluster members. The lambda is set at 0 for a minimum variance portfolio.

12.5.3 THE REVISED ALLOCATION FOR TOBIN TANGENCY

Third, Tobin's Tangency portfolio will be expanded. An analytical solution may be used to represent the allotment, while commercial properties are permitted. The terminals portfolio in this situation is a point of intersection investment based on the inventories of cluster points of intersection that are built by utilizing the membership of the clustered as the inputs to the assignment of tangences. The allocation of the point of intersection investment is as continues to follow. The third distribution is Tobin's Tangency portfolio expansion. Short sales are permitted, and the allocation can be represented using an empirical solution. The terminals portfolio in this case is a point of intersection portfolio dependent on cluster point of intersection portfolios, which are built using cluster representatives as tangency selection inputs. The following is a summary of the point of intersection portfolio allocation:

12.6 A MULTI-TARGET STRATEGY TO AN OPTIMUM MANAGEMENT STRATEGY IN AN IMS-QSE

Companies have adopted new strategic principles as the modern industrial context has evolved and market demand has increased. In this sense, several organizations saw the introduction of international standards relating to various management systems as a true need and a realistic goal. Integration of the three parameters relating to performance, protection, and the environment, collectively, can be considered a worldwide phenomenon. However, the main challenge of implementing such a method is that all three management systems were proposed independently, but combining them is not an easy feat since they have similar and confusing processes. As a result, if they are implemented without regard for their interactivity, many flaws in duplicate management processes proposed by the three principles (e.g., written protocols, testing, control types, and so on) may be found. As a result, scholars and practitioners have been drawn to the idea of going to propose an international standard including the QSE management system of quality, production, and environmental management practices. These studies looked at the convergence of the three schemes from a variety of perspectives, mostly concerning the concept of performance requirements [291].

12.6.1   New Process-Based Approach

This section summarizes the current process-based strategy to incorporate an integrated framework for quality, safety, and environmental management. Three interlinked considerations are the main focus of this approach: risk management to maximize coherence and coordination among the three methods, procedure cooperation and communication strategy among operations, and management system to guarantee the global economy monitoring and harmonization as continuous learning. It shows the proposed approach that encompasses the entire PDCA (Plan, Do, Check, Act) system at several stages. The assumption is that these processes should be divided into three phases. The first is the preparation stage, the second is the completion stage and the third is the control and action process. In the next paragraphs these three phases can be further described:

12.6.1.1   Planning Phase

This process is divided into six steps: the first involves establishing both efficiency, protection, and environmental goals based on stakeholder criteria and aspirations (i.e. customers, employees, population, and environment). In the second, we'll use each method to implement all of these goals. The third step entails analyzing each procedure about the pre-set goals identified in the previous step to determine potential causes of danger and expectations that may hinder the effectiveness to meet the objectives. Each defined risk must be assessed in terms of possible effects in each management field in the fourth phase. We must identify a QSE management strategy in the fifth phase to incorporate chosen therapies as corrective and preventative measures to minimize the amounts of threats currently defined and increase the performance of the In this regard, the interaction here between management styles areas must be understood; after all, some acts might aid specific administration sectors while being destructive to others. In the sixth phase, ultimately, verifying the appropriate implementation of the QSE strategic plan involves the development of an adequate reporting plan. This phase will incorporate the chosen therapies using the QSE management strategy and the transaction-made monitoring plan developed during the implementation stage. It's worth noting that we'll need to identify effective scheduling to maximize resources and achieve the goals more quickly.

The phase of Checking and Acting if they do phase is completed, this phase will complete the economic integration by assessing the feasibility of various decisions and adjusting them in three phases. In the first, we would test all of the previously identified metrics to assess the efficacy of chosen therapies and calculate the degree to which goals have been met. We must sum the metrics of each goal for this purpose. A rebalancing of the organizational design would be made in the second phase to meet unmet goals. Since some of the original assigned goals cannot be met, to achieve them, several of the tendencies to expand need to be updated; in this sense, the later phases of the process (i.e., goal revision) should be recommended to lead to sustained development.

12.6.2 QUALITY PROTECTION SYSTEMS

The bow tie approach is a widely used deterministic methodology developed by shell for modeling and evaluating the unwavering quality of massive protection systems. The basic idea behind this strategy is to create a bow tie reflecting the whole circumstance with each perceived danger R_i [also known as a top event (TE)], The first section refers to the scheme's left half, which depicts a phylogenetic tree outlining all potential causes of the problem (TE). These occurrences can be divided into two categories: the activator events (IE), which are the primary triggers of the TE, and the unintended or vital events (IndE and CE), which are the IE's causes. The design of the left portion is done from the top down (from TE to IndE and CE).

12.7 GEOSPATIAL TOPOGRAPHICAL RELATIONSHIPS FOR INFINITE-DIMENSIONAL CIRCULAR SPACES

Humans make comprehensive use of contextual markers to clarify the truth and make spatial thinking more effective. Spatial reasoning is the method of gathering knowledge about objects in space and their relationships by calculation, analysis, or inference and using it to draw conclusive results about the entities' relations. The exploitation of quantitative spatial entities is the foundation of quantitative verbal skills. Path relations, distance relations, and topographic interaction have all been listed as forms of visual features between geographical objects. Topological relations are functional relations that are retained whether space is rotated or scaled indefinitely.

12.7.1 QUALITATIVE SPATIAL REASONING

Manipulating quality geospatial relationships which are supported by structural tables makes it possible to deduce current geographical data in qualitative spatial reasoning. Geographical Information Systems (GIS) allow users to submit information about geographic anomalies and store that information. The requested spatial association must be derived from the available data if it is not directly contained in the database. The inference method necessitates the discovery of connections that can be used to create an inference path between the two subjects. The compositional procedure combines two contiguous pathways to establish a third geographical connection. A composition table combines a series of inference rules for determining the outcome of a particular composition process. The typically people that can occur between the objects in the analysis must be established before characterization tables can be defined.

12.7.2 DIRECTION SPATIAL RELATIONS

An object's position is determined by directional relations about each other. To identify an alignment [3,5], two aberrations and a fixed frame of reference are required (typically the North Pole). In terms of ideology or objects such as North or South with a matching approved area, the cardinal orientations may be expressed numerically at the degree (0.45) or subjectively.

12.7.3 DISTANCE SPATIAL RELATIONS

Distances are numerical values measured from known positions of two points in some reference system or estimated by measurements. Using Euclidean geometry and Cartesian coordinates, the most often used concept of distance can be obtained. It refers to how long the shortest travel route in a two-dimensional Cartesian system (one straight line) connecting two locations, also known as the Euclidean distance (13). A series of numerical variables must match the subjective distance given by an interval. It is easy to utilize the near (VC), near (C), far (F) and very distant (VF) qualitative measurements to characterize degrees from the nearest item [292].

12.8 GEOGRAPHICAL NEIGHBORS FOR TOPOGRAPHICAL SPATIAL OBJECTS: THE MULTIPLE SCALES SPHERICAL MULTIDIMENSIONAL SPACE INSTANCE

The necessity to understand spatial links between various items within a geographical location depends upon their relevance in establishing topological spatial interactions. The study under discussion here is related to a topographical semantical relationship that connects a geography item with a circular spatially extended point (CSEP). A CSEP is a region-like object with a command post and regions the reference point's area (see Figure 12.6).

12.8.1 NEIGHBORHOOD CONCEPTUALIZATION STATISTICS: MODEL SNAPSHOT

In time, the location, direction, shape, and scale of the topographical phenomena may change. A qualitative change occurred if the topology connection of one item to another item is altered by deformation. For spatiotemporal cognition in the geographical environment, modifications in the model of topographical relationships are significant as they identify the most significant factors and allow significant changes in forecasts (based on inference).

Nodes reflect spatial connections in a mathematical neighborhood graph, and edges connect related relations. Different conceptions of similarities result in various graphs containing the same set of relationships. Typically, conceptual relationship graphs are constructed to reflect conceivable transformations from one connection to another in situations of continuous change. These diagrams help narrow down the search space when searching for new possibilities.

12.9 MULTI-AGENT EXPLORATION INSIDE STRUCTURAL COLLAPSES

Consider the following scenario: structures have collapsed, main roads are impassable, and the newly developed network and electricity have broken. Within 48 hours, the flood victims must be saved. Human rescue workers must make fast choices and risk their lives to bring victims to safety. They must confirm the victims' whereabouts and status. They can also determine the structural integrity as soon as possible so that medics and paramedics can reach the crisis area and rescue victims. Many of these activities are often carried out by humans and professional dogs, and they are also carried out in very difficult and risky situations. Officials of some disasters discover that even specialized search and rescue dogs are unable to climb through any of the debris. Furthermore, the dog's sense of smell was harmed by the dusty air. Robots, on the other hand, maybe sent into environments that are structurally deficient or polluted, that are unsafe for humans, or search and rescue dogs to navigate.

As a result, specialized teams are needed at a variety of affected locations to find victims under the wreckage, evacuate them, and provide initial emergency care. Emergency crews should be equipped with enough mountain rescue robots to enhance their results. This robot must collect important information from both patients and the environment. These robotics aims to gather

FIGURE 12.6   Circular extended point.

FIGURE 12.7 Infrared sensors.

such information more quickly and precisely than assistance personnel and to fit in locations where men might.

12.9.1 CONVERSION TO THE SIMULATED WORLD

Simulations are often used to promote development in the field of mobile robotics discovery strategies because they are considerably less expensive and make for much quicker and more scalable testing than actual robots. Modeling the USAR scenario, particularly pancake collapses, is also not very realistic. As a result, we map the physical world to a virtual one. We define three main elements created for the simulation to be able to translate the real world to the virtual world: The world model, the robot model, and the configuration interface are also used see in Figure 12.7.

- **World model**: We defined the virtual world based on a review of several emergency site photographs and firefighter accounts. The basis for calculating success is described by the US Department of Homeland Security's Urban Water rescue robot's effectiveness guideline published.
- **Simulation model**: The simulation model is divided into equal size small squares. For defined 2D processes that shape structures, several frame lengths can be provided.
- **Robot model**: we have chosen Millibots as the most suitable robot for this activity. We will create this mechanical system and then send it to the simulated world in our bounding box to execute multiple algorithms of exploration. The robot is supposed to maneuver through a variety of search fields that are dense, cluttered, and constrained. Obstacle avoidance strategies are the normal alternative for motion in such a setting. In this respect, this thesis defines several detection schemes. A ring of eight simulation Infrared (IR) sensors spaced 45° apart is mounted on all simulated robots. The current sensors' beam (45 cones) covers neighboring grid cells around the agent, and an IR range analysis offers information about unused or filled volumes in the area surrounded by the beam (45 cones). Each robot has a vision of eight cells in its immediate neighborhood, it has been assumed. Cells may be either sterile or filled. If the chosen cell is empty, mobile agents can also only move one cell in either direction. With their fitted simulated gyroscope, they are aware of their direction, such as North. We also believe they can track stuck victims based on their heat (body temperature) and CO_2 fingerprint (Table 12.3).

12.9.2 SIMULATED AGENT TASKS

In this part, we describe the features and tasks of our simulated agents. Inside the grid cell simulated world, our modeled robots have two major tasks to complete:

a. They are responsible for building searching regions for the creation of life-safe voids. They stroll randomly to look for individuals, utilizing the algorithm ANT. Your trip across the landscape will be recorded and labeled as roads, with undiscovered cells designated later as barriers.

TABLE 12.3
Fuzzy Rule

Input	Fuzzy Rule	Output
θ_{NE}	**IF** $\alpha \in \{+23 \cdots +45 \cdots +67\}$	**THEN** agent moves north east
θ_N	**IF** $\alpha \in \{+68 \cdots +90 \cdots +112\}$	**THEN** agent moves north
θ_{NW}	**IF** $\alpha \in \{+113 \cdots +135 \cdots +157\}$	**THEN** agent moves north west
θ_E	**IF** $\alpha \in \{-22 \cdots 0 \cdots +22\}$	**THEN** agent moves move east
θ_{SE}	**IF** $\alpha \in \{-23 \cdots -45 \cdots -67\}$	**THEN** agent moves south east
θ_S	**IF** $\alpha \in \{-68 \cdots -90 \cdots -112\}$	**THEN** agent moves south
θ_{SW}	**IF** $\alpha \in \{-113 \cdots -135 \cdots -157\}$	**THEN** agent moves south west
θ_W	**IF** $\alpha \in \{-158 \cdots -180 \cdots +158\}$	**THEN** agent moves west

b. They are utilized for the evaluation of the effectiveness of searching robots modeling different exploratory methods within the simulator. Our simulation tries to emulate robots on a sensory basis.

In this system, we have only built one type of robot: millions. As a consequence, only a robotic size (80 mm) is present and only one cell may pass each step. SENSOR-SET, including IR, gyroscopic, and NIDR simulation detectors, is included in any formulated robot. The SENSOR-SET can be reconfigured by the operator. Furthermore, we can send various numbers of robots into the virtual search area, ranging from one to a hundred. One of the most often used random discovery methods is the ANT algorithm.

12.9.3   2D Search Field Simulated

The key aim of every testbed is to make it easier to try out and evaluate ideas that have potential in the real world. As previously stated, there are confined voids bound by narrow waterways within architectural collapse. The most difficult parts of exploring robots are these life-safe voids. To find victims, search robots must navigate the entire labyrinth of barriers and debris, and the right exploration strategy must ensure that the total victim detection period is as short as possible.

Our virtual agents can create different 2D simulated environments by executing Ant Brownian movement. The following statement is provided in this section: The predictor of a search field has an analytical method. Use the index to differentiate between these generated test fields. The simulated development is divided into similarly sized L-square cells. In this situation, the grid size was chosen to L 100 mm.

The victim(s) are placed at random within an empty area to create a life-safe void. We may alter the number of casualties and robots, as well as the simulation model, by following the steps outlined above. All of the agents' routes will be called highways, while unchanged free cells will be classified barriers. In this case, there might be several routes to the victim, but the victim's just one. This allows us to provide a wide range of protection and enhancement inside an unused space by continually using our ANT algorithm. An open area with tightly stated complexities specified by its Euclidean distance is a factor in the advantage of such a Searching Fields Generation.

12.10   DIAGNOSIS COMMUNICATION STYLE BY THE USE OF CONCEPTS OF THE NEURO-FUZZY, EVOLUTIONARY ALGORITHMS, AND QUANTUM MECHANICS

Due to a large number of process factors and continuous interconnectivity, principally the relevant information technology in a machinery environment is situational and insufficient.

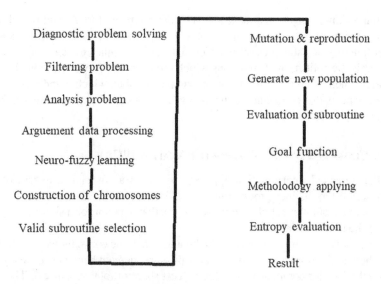

FIGURE 12.8 Framework optimization problem.

The fundamental law of the solution describes in Figure 12.8.

Computer diagnostics variables may be explained through a probability distribution with a fuzzy set characterization by "fuzzification" in terms of a particular fuzzy membership function. Superior links between the support encourage of activity are established by fluctuating legislation, i.e., varied operating circumstances, vibration, precision, safe loading, and workload. In reality, traditional instruments address this problem by using a large number of sensors or by developing specialized sensors. This method raises costs while lowering efficiency. Higher analysis efficiency at lower criteria for definiteness of inputs will efficiently compensate for this unfavorable situation.

12.10.1 NEURO-FUZZY NETWORK MODULE

The suggested technique is focused on estimating the parameters of the diagnosed device. By comparing the calculated specifications to the nominal system's a priori predicted values, fault detection and recognition can be performed.

The remaining strata to do the divisions were removed and analog signals left the machine. With the ideal output in consideration, the inaccuracy of the initial output is computed. At the final exit, the desired signal is unchanged and equals "one." We may build the modular framework after studying trigger constructs based on the initial concept. The regulations in such a scheme can be ordered in any order. The modified fuzzy c-means clustering algorithm is used to evaluate input fuzzy sets at the start of the simulation analysis. The backpropagation algorithm then fine-tunes all parameters.

12.11 THE NEW MEASURE OF ROBUST PRINCIPAL COMPONENT ANALYSIS

When a vast number of variables are evaluated, certain practical issues occur in data mining. This is usually attributed to the fact that the same knowledge can be measured by several variables. The one of variables can be printed as a nearby linear grouping of the other variables, and the amount of linked variables will rise when the number of variables increase. To do a trustworthy analysis it is vital to reduce redundancy by developing a new assortment of factors that determine the fundamental properties of the data. Principal Component Analysis (PCA) is a way to condense huge numbers of parameters, which represent the majority in the shipping box, into a lower proportion of linear relationships. A new group of discrete wavelet dimensions to define the dispersion of a range of n points inside the p-dimensional environment is the core premise of PCA, and sampling deviations from the specific points decrease in line of complexity. A primary module scrutiny focused on dropping the dimensionality of a statistics set in order to describe as much evidence as conceivable. The first major factor is the collection of functions which represents its most variation. The next biggest variation is determined using the primary or secondary variable, which is independent of the first. For all the main aspects that contribute to the own vector pattern of the covariances, this procedure will be continued.

12.11.1   THE CLASSICAL PRINCIPAL COMPONENT ANALYSIS (PCA)

The PCA is the statistical interpretation approach that uses a covariance matrix of the original variables to describe the distinct group framework. The method is useful for expressing several variables using a much smaller set of composite factors that account for a significant portion of the variance within the initial variables.

The discoveries have a strong influence on the breakdown of the conventional covariance matrix S. If there are outliers in the original variable p, the k primary element becomes unsteady. Outliers are usually put into the k major component with the biggest share of total variance S. The strongly connected data supplied by n 100 and p 3 are represented by an independent study of the predicted values

Below is the second instance of PCA typical of the floral clustering methods. There are three classes of flowers; red color for Red Hisbiscus, purple color for Linum Narbonense, and yellow color for Oxalis Pes-Caprae. Vectors extract color functions and define object picture characteristics. Figure 12.9 shows these blooms.

12.12   THE EFFECTS OF DEMOGRAPHICS DIFFERENTIATIONS ON AUTHORSHIP IDENTIFICATION

Blogs are amongst the most important ways for people to contribute to the material on the internet. There are several classifications of blogs, each with its text, publication technique, and even readership. The most well-known genre is the personal blog, or web diary, in which the author shares his emotions, displays his imagination, and communicates with others more quickly than emails or other forms of communication. There are also some focused or oriented blogs, such as news blogs, news websites, and educational blogs that concentrate on a particular topic. The group of personal blogs is the subject of our investigation. We choose one of the most well-known personal blog pages, "LiveJournal". LiveJournal is that has a network of millions of people who share their own ongoing personal diaries on the internet.

Since users may be anonymous and inaccessible in cyberspace, the abuse of online communications is increasing. This promotes harmful activity and the dissemination of illicit material. The need to authenticate such texts is growing in importance, necessitating the development of new strategies that can catch the identical regardless of the IP address or any other potentially false content. Authorship

FIGURE 12.9   Colorful flowers.

attribution is a successful approach for finding the sender of an unidentified communication by simulation. Authorship identification is a decent resolution and able to realize the author of unidentified communication via modeling the stylistic features of preceding known posts of the author.

Authorship recognition in blogs is motivated by a variety of factors and presents a variety of challenges. The ability to identify the author of unidentified blog posts may come in handy in a variety of situations. This involves online protection, where extracting the habits of writers who may interact in several blog sites under various identities is beneficial. The job, however, comes with its own set of difficulties. One of the most important considerations of authorship attribution is the huge number of authors. Scaling current solutions with the large, and growing, several writers is a unique problem. Furthermore, several variables such as text length, number of posts per blogger, and type of writers play important roles and influence the success of the testing phase.

12.12.1 FEATURE

The collection of functionalities is a critical issue in classification tasks. We used the Linguistic Inquiry Word Count, the MRC Psycholinguistic index, and a selection of lexical items in our research. That feature sets chosen to have a psychology foundation and are considered to be compatible with the author's style and/or personality. The characteristics of diary text are better captured using our curated feature sets because they contain a lot of emotions, online responsibilities, and ideas. The 88 LIWC features that were chosen are divided into four categories:

- Typical linguistic characteristics (e.g., total word count, word per sentence, pronouns, punctuations, articles, and time).
- Psychological characteristics (e.g., affect, cognition, biological processes).
- Characteristics with personal interests (e.g., work, sports, religion, sexuality), assents (e.g., accepts, ok), fillers (e.g., err, umm).
- Non-fluencies (e.g., I mean, you know) are examples of paralinguistic characteristics.

12.12.2 FRAMEWORK

The framework's architecture and experiments for recognizing blog post writers are described in this section. The extraction process transforms each post to wavelet coefficients representing the respective risk compensation after capturing the data corpus from the site. This transforms the input data from a text documents space to space with able to highlight. The previously submitted vectors were first grouped into classes based on three parameters: post length, number of contributors, and number of posts per blogger. The classification algorithm manipulates each category separately. In our framework, Support Vector Machines (SVM) has been chosen as the machine learning algorithm. SVM is one of the most effective algorithms in this field.

12.13 ANONYMOUS ID ASSIGNMENT AND OPT-OUT

The anonymity of correspondence is critical in a variety of applications. Health care, company, e-voting, schooling, online search, telecommunications, and other industries are among them.

Assume a consumer has reverted on their loans. This knowledge would be useful to banks as a whole. However, a bank that has made loans to a financially stable borrower would want the customer's identity to be exchanged with other banks but do not want to compromise itself by disclosing its (the bank's) name. The use and sharing of medical data are subject to stringent data protection laws. Health centers do not want to share details about a person's DNA sequence or medical records, but they do want to support one another figure out how medications and DNA sequence interact.

As e-voting becomes more common, questions about privacy must be answered. Anonymity, comprehensiveness, consistency, and uniqueness are all characteristics that must be guaranteed by the e-voting scheme. Endpoints in mobile networks, likewise, require dynamic IDs to keep their static IDs private. The dining cryptographers (DC) dilemma is an example of unconditionally stable confidentiality. It helps every diner to anonymously pick up the meal tab for the group.

Assigning IDs to nodes within the network is one way to have secrecy so no node knows what ID is allocated to a particular node. In this article, we define and test those procedures. The implementation of these protocols to distributed data mining is then defined (DDM).

DDM tackles privacy concerns in a way that protects the privacy of mined data (PPDM). Considering the explicit reference (SS) of the information retrieval operator: at the end of the computation, each node presents a value in a scalable atmosphere. SS's a hazard to collusion. The basis of the secured cycle sum (PCSS) method is illustrating how networks may divide their value into configurable portions in a secured amount, each of which is transported across a different safe sum circuit or cycle. If no network has identical neighboring nodes two times in a row, privacy for cooperation is achieved. And if crystal collaborates to find someone's worth, then that value is concealed as important as the overall of vertices that collaborate is below a particular threshold. You use SS and a requirement for a fully linked network, but data is forwarded to regions in a tree-like way for every round of the algorithm. Encryption is a regular technique for the confidentiality of PPDM, as demonstrated for a long time. However, there are times when a node is concerned that its worth will be identified by others. If a node has confidential or strategic details, it will refuse to engage in the mining computational because it believes it would be damaged. Alternatively, a node may believe that attendance breaks or oversteps a limited amount of research. Finally, if an abnormality is important to a node, others will determine who contributed and might also approximate it. Even if fewer knot(s) participate, or rather if a restricted number of knots contribute too much to the total, or if a few knots are contributing too little, the likelihood of disclosure of the estimate of confidential communications exists.

12.13.1   AIDA-D – DECENTRALIZED ANONYMOUS ALGORITHM

Unlike AIDA-H, AIDA-D does not depend on EDHCs. AIDA-D is similar to AIDA-H in concept, but it requires a reasonably obtainable network and uses a broadcasting procedure in the second stage, which will be more effective than AIDA-H. AIDA-D has multiple rounds, each with two moves, and much like AIDA-H. I'd like to make a couple of remarks about both these architectures. For starters, both algorithms use the same method for selecting a slot around. As a result, regardless of the algorithm we use, the number of individual IDs selected in every round is the same, as is the number of rounds needed. Second, all implementations have a non-zero chance of pushing indefinitely. If network entities select the same slot in every round, this can occur.

12.13.2   PERFORMANCE ANALYSIS

For each round, AIDA selects the amount of M slots (node number) at randomness from the N-size slot list, until a unique anonymous ID is available for each node. Unfortunately, as many as the M nodes can crash at random, every node can use the same slot in an immediate release round at unpredictable intervals.

In around, it's an amazing question how many nodes obtain a certain ID. The probability of AIDA in one round and the number of distinct IDs in one round are determined because M is a set of cells that requires an anonymously and N is the length of the AIDA slots list (or number of IDs).

12.14   OPTIMIZED *K*-MEANS ALGORITHM FOR CLUSTERING OF BIOLOGICAL DATA

Technologies of scientific data acquisition have improved to produce a massive aggregate of genetic information through several sources of data. As new data creation technologies such as DNA

Microarrays, the economic expansion of scientific databases has increased. As a result, using traditional database analysis methods to derive valuable information from them is virtually impossible. Successful mining techniques are critical for extracting latent data from large datasets.

Cluster analysis, as described in, is a common data analysis technique that has a broad range of applications. The method of dividing a given group of objects into non-overlapping clusters is known as clustering. This is achieved in such a manner that clustering is the method that is identical in terms of their attributes, whereas objects in separate categories vary significantly in terms of their attributes. Clustering biological data aids in the discovery of curious patterns and intrinsic groupings in the data.

For several functional uses, the k-means algorithm suggested is useful in generating clusters. However, the original k-means algorithm has a lower computational cost, particularly for huge datasets. Furthermore, dependent on the randomized selection of initial centroids, this algorithm produces various types of clusters.

12.14.1 k-Means Clustering Algorithm

This section defines the original k-means similarity measures. The goal is to partition the data gathering into k numbers, with k pre-determined. There are two parts: the first includes the definition of k centroids for each cluster. The second part consists of two parts. The next step is to compare every point with the nearest center in the provided data set. Using geometry, the distance among data items and the center is calculated. The first step is over, since all points are discovered in particular groupings, and the early categorization has been reached. At this step, we have to re-calculate the updated Euclidean distance because new items might make the cluster centroids change. Once k new centers have been found, we'll need to establish a new binding even between data sets and the network and sharing centroid, resulting in a loop. The k centroids can change location in a step-by-step manner for this loop. It will ultimately come to a point where the centroids will no longer shift. This represents the clustering procedure's trustworthy brand.

12.14.2 Computational Complexity

Since the longest amount needed here is for calculating the distances across each piece of data and all other relevant data in the set D, phase 1 of the improved algorithm demands a computation time of $O.n2/$ for locating the initial centroids. The centroids are determined several times before the algorithm converges in the original k-means algorithm, and the pieces of information are allocated to the closest centroids even before the algorithm converges. This requires $O.nkl/$, where n represents the total of data sets, k is the number of packets, and l is the number of samples since the pieces of information are fully redistributed based on the current centroids. Any data points stay in their cluster, while others migrate to other clusters regarding the relative distances from the new and existing centroid. If a piece of data remains in the cluster, $O.l/$ is required; otherwise, $O.k/$ is required. For each iteration of the algorithm, the number of data points traveling away from their cluster reduces. Considering that half of the data points leave their clusters, $O.nk=2/$ is needed. As a result, the overall expense of this step of the algorithm is $O.nk/$ rather than $O.nkl/$. Since k is much less than n, the total time complexity of the improved algorithm (Algorithm 2) is $O.n2/$.

12.15 THE LÉVY METHOD AND APPLICABILITY TO FINANCING ORNSTEIN–UHLENBECK PROCESSES

Empirical experiments have also shown that, according to the popular Black–Scholes model, variance is not constant. The logarithmic government provided is, therefore, fatter than the usual distribution suggests. Strong kurtosis and negative skewness are two characteristics of logarithmic returns. The expectation of continuous uncertainty cannot account for these facts. Fluctuations follow a stochastic pattern. The result implies dynamics can be a good fit for predicting fluctuations. The stock exchange values fluctuate freely, as, like many other real assets, price differences are visible in the short term, but the demand for the commodity is adjusted over time. Prices are moving towards the pace of the asset's output expense [1,2] introduces stochastic variance models that are motivated by Levy cycles. The Bates system is easier, but leaps and stochastic variance are separate from this model. Jumps and stochastic volatility are linked in the BNS model. A Brownian motion can be used to model particle motion. The particle does not stop after shifting direction after a collision but continues to travel at a slower rate. Brownian motion cannot be distinguished anywhere. Uhlenbeck and Ornstein (1930) suggested the Ornstein–Uhlenbeck method to develop the Brownian motion model.

12.15.1 ORNSTEIN-UHLENBECK PROCESSES

Uhlenbeck and Ornstein (1930) suggested the Ornstein–Uhlenbeck method as an alternative to Molecular diffusion. A Concentration gradient with drift, which is a Levy process, drove this procedure.

OU Brownian motion with a process: The solution to the stochastic differential equation, X $D.X_t/t_0$, can be represented as a one-dimensional Gaussian OU operation, $X D.X_t/t_0$.

$$dY_t = -\lambda Y_t dt + \sigma dW_t$$

If X_t is the interest rate at time t and m is a reference value for the rate, Y_t is a unique strong Markov solution.

12.16   A NEW TERRITORY COVERING CATEGORIZATION FOR AERIAL PICTURES: THE COMBINATION OF EXTENDED RELIANCE TREE-HMM AND UNCONTROLLED SEGMENTED

Land Cover Classification (LCC) in high-resolution aerial photography is a crucial remote sensing application. It entails using a series of known patterns to distinguish natural objects in an elevated aerial photograph. The aim of labeling each pixel with the subsequent texture in the most generalized form of aerial photographs, where the image includes multiple regions with various patterns, is to mark each pixel with the subsequent terrain. The segmentation method is used in the marking procedure, but instead of segmenting the image into various regions, it assigns each area to one of the natural object patterns.

In the LCC dilemma, obtaining pixel-level identification is a major challenge. In reality, recognizing a relatively large image is simpler than recognizing a single pixel. In particular, pixel-wise image classification approaches are rarely appropriate for solving problems encountered in remote sensing applications. They produce an unpleasant salt and pepper effect.

Recent studies explicitly demonstrate the benefits of combining multispectral characteristics using differentiation classification approaches and, as a result, relying on image regions rather than pixels.

To model, the contextual relations between labels, more advanced methods use a family of Markov models. Genuine 2D-Markov modeling of contextual data, on the other hand, is an iterative method that takes time.

Fair complexity methods, on the other hand, define each pixel by taking into account its neighbors, typically by computing a resemblance measure (likelihood probability, for example) on square windows centered at the pixels in question. The following are some of the disadvantages of those approaches:

- They use square screens, which can lead to a preference for rectangular areas. In addition, corner pixels are farther apart than most pixels. Because of the used model or measurement nature, adopting non-square windows is typically unaffordable.
- The wider the aperture, the better the chance of a right identification. A large window, on the other hand, can penalize small regions. In certain cases, a tradeoff is made.
- Since a static threshold value is used, the window size is too small for the classification purpose of all image pixels and too large for edge preservation, so the classification of frontier pixels is skewed by the inclusion of neighboring points.

We introduce a scheme in this paper that overwhelms the previous challenges by adding the following:

- Unsupervised segmentation is used to accomplish segmentation, which preserves area edges even though the image is over-segmented.
- Using stochastic supervised learning, each area is defined. On windows of various sizes and shapes fixed at the pixels in question, possibility likelihood can be calculated.
- An auto-adaptive distance dependent on the perceived pixel location towards area edges is computed to determine window size and shape.
- We expanded the Dependencies Tree-hidden Markov model (DT-HMM) to allow likelihood probability calculation on non-rectangular windows by having four-dimensional requirements instead of two, and when working with explanatory variable, using the central pixel as root instead of the upper-left pixel.

12.16.1 EXTENDED DEPENDENCY TREE-HIDDEN MARKOV MODELS

For texture simulation and differentiation, Markov models (Markov Random Fields, Hidden Markov Fields, Hidden Markov Models, and Hidden Markov Trees) have been used widely and effectively. This is owing to their aim of understanding spatial dependencies as well as noise absorption. Their efficiency, however, is highly dependent on the proposed scheme: true 2D models produce better results but have a much higher computational cost. In general, the more complicated the model is, the better the results.

Nonetheless, some methods recommend linear models like HMM for numerical complexity purposes, even if such a model is not suitable for this double data. More complex methods depend on 2D structures with simplifying assumptions. One simplifying assumption used in DT-HMM yields good results with a noticeable influence: one location (pixel) can rely on either the horizontally or vertically counterpart, but not both at the same time.

The need to quantify likelihood probability on non-rectangular-shaped windows of various sizes, as well as the need to use the central pixel (to be labeled) as the dependence tree root since the root displays more connections with neighbors than other pixels, inspired the expansion of DT-HMM in this work.

12.16.2 CLASSIFICATION SCHEME

We use the scheme represented to create a class map of a given aerial picture. Each move is presented in the subsequent sections.

- Real image
- Computation of window size
- Maximum computing probability
    a. Pre-classified image (combine and map)
    b. Image segmented (combine and map)

12.16.3 Image Unsupervised Segmentation

Until we can identify the picture pixels, we must first conduct an unsupervised segmentation process that meets the following criteria:

The edges of the image are maintained. We may have over-segmentation but not under-segmentation since pixels in the same area must belong to the same natural individual object. This move is a pre-processing step that will take you through the remainder of the classification stage.

The EDISON scheme, which we use in this study, produces an unsupervised differentiation that has been shown to yield good results. It shows an example of an increased aerial picture (50 cm per pixel) and the subsequent unmonitored segmentation using the EDISON method.

12.16.4 Window Size Computation

Since the texture is not a local phenomenon, we remember a pixel's surroundings when classifying it. To put it another way, we'll calculate the probability of the data within a window based on the pixel in question. For both pixels, most methods use a square window with a fixed dimension. A compromise is normally made between using a large enough window to properly identify the central pixel and a small enough window to protect the region's edges.

In this part, we suggest that the window size be computed dynamically to enable our device to handle a large volume of data without misrepresenting area borders. The wider the frame, the more the pixel to classify is from the area boundary, while edge pixels are categorized without regard for their surroundings.

As a result, the window size is selected so that pixels inside the window correspond to the same area based on an unsupervised view surrounded by white.

The shape and height of the window are determined by a single parameter. The maximal Euclidean interval between neighbors and the central pixel s is represented by rays.

The pre-segmented image is used to calculate this parameter. Its value is the biggest number that can be used to ensure that all pixels in the display contribute to the same area.

12.16.5 Pre-Classification Photograph

In possible to allocate pixels to a category it is likely that the EDT-HMM window of every class of a particular substance will be observed. The pixel is then assigned to the class which optimizes this chance.

After a learning procedure on mono-class aerial photographs, the parameters of the EDT-HMM corresponding to each natural object class are collected. We used the traditional RGB color space to reflect each pixel. We use k-Means cluster analysis on pixels of mono-class images of the classification model to partition the image pixels into N sub-classes to approximate the specifications of the DT-HMM for each class. The parameters of N Gaussian functions are then obtained. These parameters function as the EDT-initialization. HMM's the photographer's final specifications are then extracted through an iterative process as defined.

12.16.6 Classification Correction

The resultant classification report illustrates and this so salt and black pepper effect despite the final procedures. This is because many helpers, particularly near borders, have difficulties differentiating themselves. To do so, we propose that the photons from the same location are merged into the same natural object class (as decided by an unattended segmentation), with a focus on the innermost pixels in an image that were labeled using bigger apertures.

12.17   CONCLUSION

We examined current verification methodologies in this chapter and took into account their advantages, weaknesses, and restrictions. We have also compared the methodologies, methods, and tools that exist. We have unveiled a novel certificate authority to overcome the deficiency and avoid validation concerns. This idea of community is a five-piece real-time conceptual model: RDF annotations for new website resources, an interceptor, an RDF extractor, an RDF parser, and a data validation. The study used the techniques and decisions of the ANN to define the levels of congestion in traffic autonomously. The achievement in the nodes combinations 10–11–3 of an ANN precision of 94.99% with a 0.1583 average radius root, based on driver's perceptions. The input weighted priority was vehicle speed (km/h), the volume of traffic (car/min), daytime day of the week and. J48's precision of 95.80% and the average root squared of 0.1515 are 97 nodes with a decision tree size of 59. The rotational speed property is the base node. This implies it is the main element to measure the type of the machine learning algorithm of road transport bottlenecks.

13 Rehabilitation Computing in Electronic Computing

13.1 APPLYING VIEW MODELS IN SOA

The introduction of Service Oriented Architecture (SOA) is a significant development in evolving distributed networks, as it allows various organizations to collaborate while maintaining their independence in terms of platforms and deployment languages. Existing legacy networks should be wrapped in services, allowing for a smooth transition to SOA and expansion with existing platforms, which can be expanded by launching additional products.

Service engineering entails collaboration between a variety of tools and participants, not just for front-end market applications but also for back-end design—which is built on specifications for managing processes and ontologies, keeping smart service archives up to date, finding applications dynamically, and ensuring protection. As a result, these structures become very complicated, requiring collaboration from a variety of stakeholders to create and maintain them; as a result, design description must be achieved at both a high and low degree of abstraction, displaying more or less information. For example, a network administrator requires knowledge of all subsystem configurations, while a project manager only requires knowledge of system separation and dependency to plan activities. They all include device specifications from the perspectives that are relevant to them, such as the ability to identify, create, or review applications, as well as administer and fund the corresponding programs [292].

13.1.1 VIEW MODELS

One of the most important aspects of software creation is correctly defining design such that it is recognized by all parties and encompasses all of the program's issues. Due to the application's complexity, several model types are needed, as we can see by using the traditional Unified Modeling Language (UML). These models contribute to the representation of the system from the perspectives of different stakeholders in its advancement; as a result, several views of the system are created, each of which plays an important role in its definition and documenting. Furthermore, some features can be tracked from one model to another to ensure continuity, demonstrating a tight correspondence between the different forms of graphs within or without views.

The Three-Level ANSI-SPARC Architecture, which defines views that characterize the portion of the database that applies to a specific user, was an earlier use of viewpoints for data modeling. Philippe Kruchten's "4 1" View Model, which is general and not tied to a specific notation, but can be used, for example, with UML models, is a traditional and good technique for technology systems. Network Engineering Institute (SEI) came up with another model that is mostly used for recording software architecture.

There is also a framework called "Suggested Practice for Architectural Representation of Information-intensive Systems," which was first introduced as IEEE Std 1471–2000 and then as ISO/IEC 42010:2007 for representing software. It defines view-related principles and partnerships, as well as the conceptual definition [293].

Views, which are made up of templates, are used to arrange the data. It further defines the system's owners, each of which has a different set of interests. To build views, the definition first chooses the perspectives of interest, then specifies the presented stakeholders and addresses questions for each of them. Methods for generating templates are developed for each perspective, allowing the device views to be realized.

There are view formats devoted to more complex architectures, such as the ISO-adopted Reference Model for Open Distributed Processing (RM-ODP). Concerning SOA, some tactics try to detention precise essentials linked to commercial analysis, commercial progressions, service description and detection, quality features, taking into account all the latent stakeholders; are the examples of view models devoted to SOA structures. The following are some of the advantages of SOA systems:

- Modeling SOA in the business of Service Views.
- BDC is an acronym that stands for Business Development Corporation—three distinct points of view: View-Based Modeling Framework (VbMF) for Business Analysis, Composition, and Design —designed to bring process-driven SOA and meta-modeling together.
- The OASIS SOA Reference Architecture is a set of guidelines that describes how to construct a service-oriented architecture. A three-way perspective model: Each of the three books, Business through Services, Realizing SOA, and Owning SOA, includes several models depicted in UML diagrams.

The 4 C 1 View model is composed of: the Logical View (representing structural components, degrees of abstraction, and separation of concerns), the Process View (treating relationship patterns and concurrency), and the Logical View (representing structural elements, levels of abstraction, and separation of concerns), the Production View (outlining the degradation of software applications on sensor servers, such as computers or processors); the Physical View (highlighting the redistribution of software applications on network machines, such as computers or processors); the Scenarios View (outlining the redistribution of software applications on physical nodes, such as computers or processors); and the Possibilities View (highlighting the distribution of software applications on network machines, such as processors or processing units) (describing use cases and considered the one view, because they make the connections between the other four views). This model has been extended to the LD-CAST method.

LD- CAST's use cases include Business Service Details—providing information about business services to the Guest Business Service Management, demanding and tracking professional services to authorized End-Users Business Analytics, allowing the simulation and publication of complex business procedures, the operations of which can be carried out by Web applications; it is linked to the Business Process (BP) Designer.

Ontology Management designs and manages ontologies, making them accessible to Information Engineers.

13.1.2 APPLYING THE "4 C 1" VIEW MODEL

The 4 C 1 View model is composed of: the Logical View (able to represent structural members, levels of differentiation, and differentiation of worries); the Process View (treating social interactions and synchronization); the Development View (showing the dissolution of subsystems used in the development platform); and the Physical View (highlighting the deployment of software products on sensor servers). This model, as extended to the LD-CAST method, is depicted in Figure 13.1.

Following are the key use cases that LD-CAST supports: Business Service Details—providing information about business services to the Guest Business Service Management, demanding and tracking business services to authorized End-Users BP Management, allowing the simulation and publication of complex business procedures, the operations of which can be carried out by Internet services; it is linked to the BP Designer.

Ontology Management designs and manages ontologies, making them accessible to Information Engineers [294].

FIGURE 13.1   4C 1 view model.

Web Service Management entails registering and posting Web resources, which only the Service Provider Administrator can handle.

Monitor Business Support Applications—the Service Provider Clerk is in charge of providing facilities that require manual operations.

Security Management—the LD-CAST Manager is responsible for ensuring the system's security and credibility. Performance Monitoring—the LD-CAST Operator is also responsible for overseeing client and system performance.

The conceptual view identifies three levels of abstraction that refer to market resources and their translation to various technologies. The BP is the most relevant term at the top level; it is a process that is connected with a business service that can make it compiled code; it belongs to the Modeling Layer and is articulated in a vocabulary that business technology providers can understand. These procedures must be translated into functional BPs to be automated. Due to the late linking of Web resources imposed by the LD-CAST flexibility condition, there are currently two levels of execution. First and foremost, obtains an Abstract Workflow—a collection of abstract resources that refer to company operations but provide technical information to generate a Concrete Workflow automatically; the Abstract Execution Layer is where it resides. Then, on the Concrete Implementation Layer, one creates a Concrete Workflow—a workflow in which each conceptual service is substituted with a corresponding Web service.

The Creation Theory explain how LD-CAST is partitioned into the following subsystems:

LD-CAST BP Solid modeling—accessed by the Process Management Designer for specifying process models.

Knowledge Engineers use Ontology Management to construct the reference market ontology.

Management of Concrete Resources—Service Provider Administrators provide access to a Web service directory as well as support for recognizing and distributing information.

Process Execution Management (PEM) is the act of establishing and implementing concrete Business Process Execution Language (BPEL) workflows.

Search and Discovery (S&D) is the method of finding a semantic match between a collection of accessible Web resources and the abstract services that lead to a BP.

Promoting an enterprise information system for authentication is important for security.

Performance Monitoring—providing a centralized monitoring console for the execution of services and the operation of sub-systems applying scenarios and performing business operations, the Process View explains the relationship between subsystems, actors, and groups. In the BS Management case, for example, the End-User initiates communication between the Run-Time Portal, PEM, and S&D subsystems. When an End-User chooses a process for the desired business operation, the system allows him to choose one of the available implementations of conceptual Web services discovered by S&D; this specification is then used by PEM to produce the concrete workflow and initiate the process, which will be supervised by the applicant and occasionally aided by a Network Operator. Clerks are responsible for half-manual tasks.

The Physical View highlights LD-regional CAST's delivery, which includes a Core of the above-mentioned subsystems, as well as State Agencies (responsible for payment and local administration of consumers accessing Critical services) and Network Operators (which provide services that will be orchestrated by LD-CAST Core). The Core subsystems are also distributed through three architectures: Modeling Platform—contains everything you need to get the system up and running, including Ontology Management, BP Modeler, and Concrete Resource Management are three tools that can help you manage your BPs. Execution Platform—incorporating Run Time Portal, Process Execution Analysis, and Searching and Discovery Administration Platform— for handling users and regulating the quality of system activity using Scalability and Reliability Monitoring sub-components [295].

13.1.3 Applying SOA Specific Models

13.1.3.1 Service Views

The Service Views model, which is specific for SOA, comprises nine views, each of which is represented at two levels: conceptual and physical; their match onboard leadership structure varies depending on the request. There is also Quality of Service (QoS) and Quality of Management (QoM) qualities, which cut through both perspectives and represent two main perspectives: the customer and the supplier. There are no specifics of how templates are defined.

The Enterprise View, which develops the Use Case View from the "4 1" View Model for directly implementing process instrumentation, groups use cases, situations, and business operations. There are four additional views devoted to services: Exploration, Configuration, Activation, and Invoking, all of which are well-suited to the LD-CAST definition. The Discovery View describes the late linking of services in our given scenario, as well as the fact that they are identified by existing matching between both the descriptions of process operations and those of documented Web applications, all chosen from Business Ontology. The Application View illustrates the use of common technology for domestic and foreign Web services, such as SOAP and WSDL, as well as basic details provided in service contracts, such as price and timely delivery. The Conversion View is not needed for existing service providers, but it is useful for fitting dynamic web input types to the inputs of services invoked by a specific concrete configuration, as well as matching system outputs to the presentation of results shown by End-Users via the portal. The use of BPEL4WS (BP Execution Terminology for Web Services) for creating and executing processes on the Active BPEL Engine distinguishes the Invocation View [296].

The "4 + 1" View model has good correlations for Component, Data, and Infrastructure Views, as well as Growth, Logical, and Physical views and was included in Version 3.1. Due to the problems often faced in evaluating facilities, such as versioning requirements, payment models, designed to simulate a heavy load, and reward practices, Test View makes a fascinating contribution. The work processes specifically specified for testing the implementation of Execution and Modeling frameworks in LD-CAST should be described in this separate view. Other qualities listed in the Service Windows model were also taken into account for validation: security, reliability, availability, usability, and efficiency.

Monitoring is an important problem for an SOA system, according to the Service View model. Manageability was addressed in our research study using the Run-Time Portal (by End-Users and Provider Clerks) and Performance Management to track and trace the execution of services (by the LD-CAST Administrator). Furthermore, one of the most significant goals in the implementation period was to make an ideal, which included creating new processes for professional services, reporting new web services, and categorizing systems and online services.

State Authorities and Government Agencies constantly adding the ontology incorporating the multiple languages content of the LD-CAST Portal.

Many of the element product displays are used in the Unified Network Display. However, to explain how LD-CAST fine aggregate products from several e-government providers into additional technologies, more information is needed. The ambiguity arises from the fact that pre-arranged providers are not restricted, but the availability is elastic, such as to meet a specific end-user requirement [297].

13.1.4 Useful Elements from Other View Models

13.1.4.1 RM-ODP, the Perspectives for Distributed Processing

For the following viewpoints, the RM-ODP paradigm describes definitions and languages:

Entrepreneurship (describing the organization objectives and BPs) Data (as it relates to information management)—one of LD-unique CAST's features is the use of regional ontologies that are projected into an offers delicious ontology.

Mathematical (presenting the system components and their interfaces) Engineering (detailing relationships between modules)—SOA, with permanently bound internal Internet services and permanently bound operational environments, is defined by this view in LD-CAST.

Technological advancements (describing the choices made for the implementation) The Innovation point is needed for our case study because it captures fascinations that aren't captured by other view models. LD-CAST offers the following technology options: JEM (JBoss Enterprise Middleware) was used to introduce the Run Time Portal; ADOeGov was used to model the BP Modeler, and Ontology Management was built on the PEM subsystem contains an ActiveBPEL driver, and the Security subsystem uses Shibboleth's enterprise information solution [298].

13.1.4.2 The SEI Viewpoint Model: "Views and Beyond"

The SEI model, dubbed "views and beyond" by others, is based on the principle that the number of viewpoints used to record architecture should not be set, but rather determined following the framework. Module, Component-and-Connector, and Allocation are the three display styles available. A language specification describing the key design methods can be created for each of them. The views are the types that have been implemented to the mentioned method, and they can be recorded in more or less depth depending on the needs of major shareholders.

The Work assignment format, from the Allocation view type, leads to a view that is useful and was not present in other models for our case study. Even though it can be paired with Integration or Module decomposed views for small projects, it is extremely useful in our case, particularly for stakeholders involved in funding and managing. The company and management team need specific details about the work assignment similar to different types of framework engineers and maintenance personnel. The European Community's project officer still needs some information on this viewpoint [299].

13.2 INDEPENDENT AND CENTRALIZED OPPORTUNITIES TO SHOWCASE ACTUATOR NETWORK OPTIMUM WORTH REMEMBERING

The incorporation of wireless connectivity into the Sensor Actuator Network (SAN) sparked new studies in the areas of network structure and strategic strategies to network setup. Two structures are considered when implementing Wireless Sensor Actuator Network (WSAN) in an automated process application: heating process and decentralized structure. The Heating, Ventilation, and Air Conditioning (HVAC) system is an example of WSAN implementation.

Sensors in a central network calculate the surrounding environment and relay their data to the network's base. The data is processed at the heart, which then makes decisions about actuators. After that, the command would be sent to the transducers. No network node, such as a sensor or an actuator, has the power to make decisions. They are simply subordinating to the middle and must obey orders. Two topology forms distinguish the central structure. Tanenbaum refers to the first as the Star model, while Elazar refers to it as the Center-Periphery model. The relational topology is the second topology. Figure 13.2 depicts which components of the device model are housed inside the core, namely the sensor and actuator.

A routing algorithm is required to create direct connections between nodes to build an autonomous network with the above requirements. A Sequential Location Routing Algorithm (SCAR) is designed for Wireless Sensor Actuator Network (WSAN). The automated system has two advantages:

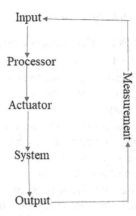

FIGURE 13.2   Central wireless sensor actuator system.

lower electricity generation and greater reproducibility. The concern is how much the detector should test the control parameters or what the sampling rate should be for interpreting the reference voltage. This chapter describes a method for determining the best sample size for future WSAN growth. Furthermore, it demonstrates how, in contrast to the central network, the autonomous network is capable of dealing with optimization [300].

In a centralized server, each sensor regularly sends its calculated parameter, while in an autonomous network, the sensor decides when to send the information to its corresponding rotor. In the On–off control system, for example, the sensor compares the calculated function to the amount of the limitation and sends a warning to the appropriate actuator if it exceeds them. The detectors are independent in this way when they choose when to transmit a message. Based on the data sent from sensors and perhaps other parameters from other nodes, the actuators make their own decision. The actuators, in particular, are in charge of the control tasks. Actuators, in this context, are also autonomous entities. What portion of the control structure is located wherein node is depicted? The processing device is isolated and put in the actuator as a part of the decision-maker (controller).

13.2.1   SAMPLE FREQUENCY CALCULATION

Wireless networking in industrial automation is difficult to implement, one of the issues that arise is the system's real-time capability. The dependent variable is measured and stored in a digital control system. The sampling interval is determined by the system time constant, which determines the system's normal frequency. The frequency response should be greater than or equal to the machine's normal frequency, according to Nyquist-sampling Shannon's theorem. The survey frequency should ideally be 10 times higher. Before the next sample comes, the sampled vector should be transmitted and stored over the sampling period. If you can't complete the control task within the organization's objectives, it means that the management system can't keep up with the changes in the system, which can lead to instability. The signal will be similar to the continuous signal structure and the frequency range will have a higher resolution if you use a high sampling frequency. It is possible to raise the sampling frequency as much as necessary in a wired network.

Growing the sampling rate in a wireless network generates further message transfers and networking devices, which has other effects such as increased challenge-response latency and higher network electricity generation. On the other hand, the propagation delay time can cause system uncertainty. The sample number may be impacted by the number of transmitting nodes or the electricity generation of the node.

The system is believed to have a first-order transfer function, and its Differential equation is defined by $H(s)$, which is represented setpoint value is Y_0, and the limit values are Y_{hc} and Y_{lc}, all of which are equal distances from Y_0. As an actuator, an on–off relay is used. The equation calculates the actuator on–off amplitude in phase space [301].

13.2.2 AUTONOMOUS NETWORK

Wireless networking in factory applications is difficult to implement. One of the issues that arise is the system's real-time capability. The dependent variable is measured and stored in a digital control system. The total current is determined by the system time variable, which determines the system's normal frequency. The frequency response should be greater than twice the machine's normal frequency, according to Nyquist-sampling Shannon's theorem. The survey frequency should ideally be 10 times higher. Before the next sample comes, the sampled vector should be distributed and stored over the sampling period. If you can't complete the control task within the organization's objectives.

13.3 WI-FI POINT-TO-POINT LINKS: PERFORMANCE ASPECTS OF IEEE 802.11

Wi-Fi [Wireless local area network (LAN)] is a wireless networking system that has been gaining popularity as a way to supplement conventional wired networks. Wi-Fi has been used in both ad hoc and network mode, for networking in temporary circumstances such as conferences and workshops. An AP (Access Point) is used in this case to enable Wi-Fi devices to communicate with a wired LAN through a switch/router. In this way, a cell is shaped, which is a WLAN centered on the AP. In the context of a PAN, a WPAN (Wireless Personal Area Network) emerges (Personal Area Network). Indoors and outdoors, directional and omnidirectional antennas are used for point-to-point and point-to-multipoint setups. Wi-Fi is based on the IEEE 802.11a, 802.11b, and 802.11g protocols, which use microwaves in the 2.4 and 5 GHz frequency ranges. IEEE 802.11b and 802.11g, which use 13 channels in the 2,400–2,485 MHz frequency range and allow nominal transmission speeds of 11 and 54 Mbps, are used both indoors and outdoors in ETSI countries. IEEE 802.11 allows for nominal transmission speeds of up to 54 Mbps. It has four channels in the 5,150–5,250 MHz and 5,150–5,250 MHz bands for domestic environments in most European countries. It is accessible in maximum European nations for indoor claims through four stations in both the 5,150–5,250 MHz and the 5,250–5,350 MHz frequency bands. In the same nations, 11 shows are available for both indoors and outdoors in the 5,470–5,725 MHz frequency bands. Since the 2.4 GHz band is being more widely used, resulting in higher interferences, the 5 GHz band, despite its slower consumption and smaller distances, is becoming more appealing. The medium access control in the standards listed is CSMA/CA (Carrier Sense Multiple Access with Collision Avoidance). The 802.11 architecture has been thoroughly investigated, with a successful transmission rate efficiency review. In 11 Mbps point-to-point connections, an optimal factor of 0.42 was found for the effective transfer rate, resulting in a 4.6 Mbps effective transfer rate. There are studies on Wi-Fi efficiency in indoor crowded conditions with major transaction involves barriers.

The conversations were conducted over interference-free networks. The WEP (Wireless Equivalent Privacy) encryption was turned off. Since the APs were so close by, no higher power levels were needed. The current study's findings were unaffected by the AP emitted power level.

The laboratory setup was used for both forms of tests, Exp-A and Exp-B. The WAN Killer program was available for 7-echo user data protocol (UDP) traffic injection (OSI level 4). The default packet size of 1,500 bytes was chosen. The PC (Personal Computer) with IP 192.168.0.1 was the source of the traffic, with the PC with IP 192.168.0.5 as the destination. The round trip time of ICMP (Internet Control Message Protocol) packets (OSI level 3) between PCs with IPs 192.168.0.2 and 192.168.0.6 was used to calculate latency. Via the same two PCs, percentage packet loss was calculated for various ICMP packet sizes (32 and 2,048 bytes). In addition, using the Iperf program, measurements for Network devices and UDP communication were made, allowing network output results to be registered. Transmission control protocol (TCP) bandwidth was achieved for a TCP link. UDP throughput, jitter, and percentage loss of datagrams are calculated for a UDP

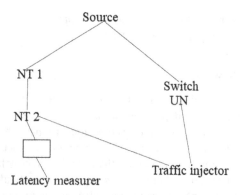

FIGURE 13.3   Laboratory setup.

interaction with a given bandwidth parameter. TCP and UDP datagrams with a resolution of 1,470 bytes were used. For TCP and UDP, a window size of 8 Kbytes and a buffer size of the same value were used. A configuration scheme close to that seen in Figure 13.3 was used, with the exception that only two PCs were used. The Iperf server had an IP of 192.168.0.2, while the Iperf client had an IP of 192.168.0.6. Jitter was continually calculated by the server, as defined by RTP (Real-Time Protocol) in RFC 1889. It can be thought of as the smooth mean of variations between sequential transit times. File transfer protocol (FTP) calculations were also conducted using this scheme, with FTP server and client programs mounted on PCs with IP addresses of 192.168.0.2 and 192.168.0.6, respectively [301].

To conduct the TCP, UDP, and FTP checks, batch command files were developed. The findings were collected in batch mode and saved to the client PC disk as text files. Each accompanying PC had a second Ethernet network adapter to allow remote control with an external switch from the official University network.

13.4   UNDERGROUND TELECOMMUNICATIONS SYSTEM THAT IS BASED ON A SUBNET TRANSFER SCHEME

Simplex communications networks use the subway track circuit to relay information from the surface command center to the train in standard subway established written. Wireless information exchange train control systems are seeing rapid growth as a result of the widespread use of wireless technologies. That is, a continuous duplex link between the train and the ground control system can be developed using radio stations installed on the train and adjacent to the track [302].

Moving WLANs pose a problem since they need wireless connections to heterogeneous networks as well as seamless handoff without disassociation when traveling. The APs connect mobile devices to infrastructure, and the devices' subsequent prerequisite is to have dependable service with high QOS. The mobile entity is a unit called a subnet that consists of not just one but several units that are connected by networks and move rapidly as a whole.

One of the most critical aspects of providing a streamlined service is mobility control. Many researchers have proposed technologies in this field, the most significant of which is IP-based mobility, such as Mobile IP (MIP) and Cellular IP (CIP). There are several MIP-based implementations, such as Mobile Regional Registration (MIP-RR), Hierarchical Mobile IP (HMIP), and others. Paging Mobile IP (PMIP), for example, is proposed with various focuses. None of them, however, is a suitable option for roaming a large number of terminals through a subnet. And when all mobile nodes (MNs) roam together from one AP to the next, these technologies can handle all of the massive connection handoffs in a short amount of time. When we have a lot of handovers, we get what's known as handover power.

The above restrictions point to the creation of a new roaming scheme that treats all machines in heterogeneous networks as a subnet. The main concerns are ensuring that mobile subnets have consistent and high-speed data connections regardless of their location. The current initiative is a network layer (L3) scheme that can accommodate high-speed subnet roaming (over 50 km/h). Traditional Mobile IP only allows for one hop between both the MN and the tunnel exit, while the modern scheme allows for multiple hops [303].

13.4.1 Principle of Subnet Handover Scheme

We suggested and engineered a subnet handover scheme based on the loosely coupled concept that enables a group of MNs to roam through various types of wireless networks at high speeds while maintaining smooth networking and high-speed communication.

The network structure and mobile subnets, which include multiple MNs and an STA (Station), are seen in Figure 13.4. The subnets travel quickly in this situation, maintaining high-speed duplex connectivity with the fixed network F net. M net1 and M net2, two mobile subnets with separate topologies, are Ethernet and cellular ad-hoc, however. M net1 and M net2 bind to the AP through STA1 and STA2, separately, and then interact with networks in the F net, which is divided into subnetworks.

We need to handle the inter-network changeover of M-net since it can link to separate AP of various subnets via STA as it moves.

A subnet roaming system based on expanded mobile IP is proposed. In a sensor network, how to roam the cell network. By going via STA, AP, international agent, and home agent, the node MN binds the distant node RN in the F net, and the path from the tunnel outlet to MN is more than one hop. The program's key concept is to use a home administrator, an international agent, an inter-network filtering agent, recycled tunneling, and an STA/AP gateway to incorporate multiple hops handheld IP.

- We can overcome the constraint of single-node roaming by expanding the mobile IP protocol, allowing all nodes in a subnet to switch concurrently while maintaining duplex telecommunications. The below are the specifics:
- The STA has two IP addresses, one for mobile and the other for Ethernet, and each MN in the M net has a set IP address.
- The STA and AP are elevated to network layer computers to just provide portal capabilities. Any node in M net will send data packets to any node in F net, and vice versa.
- As the mobile subnet passes, a MAC algorithm known as Well-time is used to determine the cause time when the STA and M nets are in the same network. The STA then moves on to the next AP. As M net switches networks, the STA receives its CoA, and the routing agent on the AP sends login credentials to the international agent FA or the home agent HA, depending on the current location, to keep the route discovery from F net to M-net.
- For large MNs, a recycled tunnel model is used to prevent creating a tunnel for each MN individually. To control the tunnel's reuse, a references count is added. When an MN binds to an RN, the count is increased by one and decreased by one in the opposite direction. The tunnel can be removed only if the reference count reaches zero. Based on the state of the M

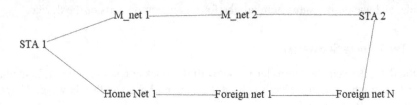

FIGURE 13.4   Principle of subnet handover scheme.

net, the HA determines how to handle the packets. HA will capture all packets sent to M net and forward them to M net's new FA if M net is not in the home network.

- The STA collects data packets from FA whose target hardware's MAC address is the same as its own or a default gateway and then extracts the L2 header to examine the Ipv6 header. The IP data packets would be summarized into Ethernet data packets and sent to MN if the source IP address is the IP address of one of the nodes in M net (e.g., node MN). The packet sent to F net, on the other hand, will be intercepted by STA via the External monitor and reassembled.

13.4.2 Gateway Model on L3 STA

The STA of a cellular subnet, a wireless networking system, and the MNs in the M net that links to STA is viewed as traveling entity known as STAPC. STA provides connections to MNs for nodes in the F net. It depicts the situation in which a mobile subnet approaches one of F net's regions. Packets sent from PC2 to STAPC are handled via STA's wireless port and then sent to their destination by the Ethernet port. Data is sent to PC2 via STA, then to wireless media via its wireless port, and eventually to PC2 via F net routing [304].

13.4.3 The Reused Tunnel Model

- The reused tunnel model eliminates the need to build a tunnel for each MN. The tunnels are maintained by the replicated model as MNs are moved.
- Tunnel construction, which involves both physical and virtual construction. In the condition depicted mobile node A joins the international network. After obtaining A's particulars, the foreign agent will submit a request message to HA. Following that, HA handles the request message and establishes a connection with the FA. A reference counter is also specified for each tunnel, which counts the number of processed requests. When the registration is complete, the counter is incremented by one.
- As cell node B connects to a foreign network for the first time. The STA then moves on to the next AP. As M net switches networks, the STA receives its CoA, and the routing agent on the AP sends login credentials to the international agent FA or the homes agent HA, depending on the current location, to keep the route discovery from F net to M-net.
- For large MNs, a recycled tunnel model is used to prevent creating a tunnel for each MN individually. To control the tunnel's reuse, a references count is implemented. When an MN binds to an RN, the count is increased and decreased by one in the opposite direction. The tunnel can be removed only if the reference count reaches zero. When B switches to a different network, the reference is reduced in the same way. The tunnel would be removed if the relation is 0.

13.4.4 The Subnet-Based Communication System

We developed and implemented a new light rail coordination system based on the subnet handover program developed above. As depicted in the Vehicle module, the racetrack subsystem, central control module, and wandering subsystem are the four main components of the device.

13.4.5 The Vehicle Subsystem

To send the data, the vehicle controller works with the trackside subsystems. It is made up of two different STAs mounted in the driver's cabs at the station's head and tail, however. Ethernet is used to coordinate with the two STAs.

13.4.6 THE CENTRAL CONTROL SUBSYSTEM

- **Wireless networking servers, networking devices, and routers are all part of the central response framework**: The subway information system's wireless connectivity server is a hierarchical monitoring and control device. Routers are used to link the trackside wireless AP with the provided satellite, and key switches are used to connect the racetrack wireless AP with the supporting initiatives. The wireless transmission server has the topography of the whole device, as well as the position APs that are installed next to the track, and the following are its important features: Management of radio frequency (RF). The wireless connectivity server will simply be assigned the RF operating status of each AP and check the real-time status of electromagnetic radiation of each AP to ensure optimum device efficiency.
- **The strategy on security**: Multi-identifier-dependent authentication identities, such as 802.1, WEB authentication, MAC, and SSID, are given when the vehicle controller connects to the racetrack wireless network. All STAS will switch between any APs without replenishment.
- **Network administration**: The wireless network setup can be completed entirely on the contact server. For example, all APs and vehicle subsystems, namely wireless spectrum, wireless protection, access authentication, and handover handling, should be accessible and maintained.
- **Detection of intrusion**: The wireless communication server will detect and trace the unlawful violation by cooperating with the trackside APs. Around the same time, the illicit data source can be filtered and warning information can be recorded to the customer. The server may also take automated countermeasures, such as adjusting the ratio control.

13.4.7 THE ROAMING SUBSYSTEM

The traveling subsystem necessitates the collaboration of the STA, AP, home agent, and international agencies. The connection to the input devices, which are defined in Section 44.3, is already present in our implementation of the STA and AP. The modern coordination system's process is depicted in the MN (M-node) of the mobile subnet that establishes a connection with STA after the device is initialized. The transmission of data will begin after STA completes the registration to FA or HA via AP and notifies the M node that the connection is ready [305].

13.5 PROMESPAR: A MAXIMUM PERFORMANCE PROMES REGIONS ATMOSPHERE MODELING RESULTS

Climate change caused by human activity is one of the issues that scientific science is currently focusing on. This is attributed to the great uncertainty of the mechanisms influencing the climate, as well as the danger posed by the real economic and environmental consequences that exist in many parts of the world. It was once thought that the seas will be able to contain the contaminants released from anthropogenic activities; nevertheless, maritime pollution is now undeniable. And more recently, the notion that humans might cause global warming was a theory with no scientific backing. However, experts have come to a general agreement on the facts of climate change impacts and the need for more information on what will happen in the upcoming years.

We use computational computers to predict the environment, which reproduces the major processes in the five kinds of environment: the atmosphere, hydrosphere, geosphere, and biosphere, as well as the mass and energy balance among them. The models' outputs are calculated and compared to observable characteristics of the atmosphere over the last few decades. Once the climate model's consistency standard is determined to be right, we use it to model future climate changes based on varying models caused by human activity greenhouse gas, and aerosol pollution. We may conclude the possible effect of climate change generated by such a hypothesis based on this knowledge.

The invention of elevated and computer vision is inherently connected to the tradition of weather prediction.

Indeed, scientists now have the potential to work with longer simulations, improve spatial precision, and so on, due to the parallel processing of weather prediction models [306].

13.5.1 THE REGIONAL ATMOSPHERIC MODEL PROMES

PROMES is a nationwide atmospheric computational model that is used for weather forecasting as well as meteorological and climate analysis. It was first identified by the MOMAC (Modelización para el Medio Ambiente el Clima) research group at the University of Castilla-La Mancha (UCLM) and the Completeness University of Madrid (UCM). It's a hydrostatic constrained model with vertical coordinates of sigma levels and horizontal dimensions of Lambert conic projection. The variables are arranged spatially according to the Arakawa-C grid. The research area is divided into vertical columns, with each column subdivided into many tiers. As a result, the state of the atmosphere is described in a finite number of parallel organized in a mesh at any given time. Based on this, the PROMES model employs a split–explicit time integration scheme. Based on their traditional time scale, the various terms of the rudimentary equations that control atmospheric dynamics are combined with time measures. The terms are solved using measured number based on finite differences. The gravity waves terms are solved using a reverse process, while the advection terms are solved using a cubic spline upstream form. For lateral propagation, a fourth-order explicit system is used. Analyses of data from the Digital Elevation Model are used to change the necessary lateral boundary values. The approach mentioned is used to vertically interpolate the wide-scale parameters to model levels. In a contour band follows, the model variables are relaxed to the external input [307].

PROMES is a nationwide atmospheric computational model that is used for weather prediction as well as meteorological and climate analysis. PROMES was first identified in by the MOMAC (Modelizacin para el Medio Ambient y el Clima) research group at the University of Castilla-La Mancha (UCLM) and the Complutense University of Madrid (UCM). It's a hydrostatic constrained model with the vertical coordinate of sigma levels and vertical dimensions of Lambert conic projection. The variables are arranged spatially according to the Arakawa-C grid. The research area is divided into concrete slats, with each column subdivided into many tiers. As a result, the state of the atmosphere is described in a finite number of parallel organized in a mesh at any given time (Figure 13.5).

Based on this, the PROMES model employs a split–explicit template matching system. Based on their traditional time-scale, the various terms of the rudimentary equations that control atmosphere dynamics are combined with time measures. The terms are solved using measured by the number based on finite disparities. The gravity waves terms are solved using a reverse process, while the advection terms are solved using a square meter downstream form. For lateral propagation, a fourth-order specific system is used. Analyses of data from the Digital Elevation Model are used to change the necessary lateral computed conditions. The approach mentioned is used to vertically interpolate the wide-scale parameters to model levels. The model variables are relaxed to the exterior data in a contour band following.

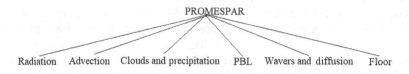

FIGURE 13.5   Structure PROMES code.

13.6   DECREASED LINUX ADAPTER FOR DOLPHINS' SCI
AND DX TRANSPARENT CONNECTIVITY

Computational capacity has always been a limited resource, and forecasts indicate that this will continue to be the case shortly. Around the same time as computing efficiency improves, the need for more processing capacity rises.

CPUs, as the central part of a computer machine, have become more efficient by increasing the sampling rate until currently. Parallelism, in the form of increased cores per die, is now used to improve performance. The next stage of parallelism, in terms of hardware, is the grouping of single computers into a cluster. Historically, the single computers in these clusters—known as nodes—are linked by Ethernet in one of its forms. The TCP/IP stack is the most common protocol used on top of Ethernet in terms of applications. With highly communicative applications running on the cluster, the network is increasingly becoming the restricting factor for overall cluster efficiency [308].

As a result, there are two issues to deal with:

- Gigabit Ethernet networking hardware is too sluggish for a variety of applications; 10 Gigabit Ethernet is only in the early stages and is very costly.
- TCP/IP, on the other hand, is a protocol suite optimized for networking in wide-area networks, with complex routing protocols and the ability to deal with even significant packet loss, among other things. Clusters are not well suited to it. To address these issues and allow for smoother connectivity (both in terms of network bandwidth), there are primarily two main approaches:
- The use of high-speed networks, each with its low-level programming interface (API), with the majority supplying a POSIX socket API application and others providing an IP interface. InfiniBand, Myrinet, QsNet, Scalable Coherent Interface (SCI), and Dolphin DX are examples of these networks. An IP GUI for Dolphin DX was introduced.
- Retaining the Ethernet hardware when removing the software layers TCP, UDP, and often IP. SCTP is an example of a substitution protocol (Stream Control Transmission Protocol), TIPC, DCCP (Datagram Congestion Control Protocol), UDP-Lite, and AoE (ATA over Ethernet) (Transparent Interprocess Communication Protocol).
- The above-mentioned TIPC was originally designed at Ericsson for the telecommunications industry, but it has certain characteristics that make it suitable for high-performance computing (HPC) with clusters, such as a networking architecture that supports failover mechanisms and the possibility of less overhead when communicating information within a cluster. The Kerrighed project uses TIPC as its transport layer of choice for kernel-to-kernel connectivity. It can't currently use high-speed networks like InfiniBand, SCI, or DX because they don't have an Ethernet port. After all, TIPC doesn't have a specialized "bearer," which acts as an adapter layer between TIPC and a native network interface.
- Describes a first approach to enabling TIPC to use elevated networks, focusing on ETHOS, a Wired driver designed using Operating systems UDP sockets to send and receive information. As a result, nearly all high-speed interconnects are directly supported by ETHOS. In comparison to Gigabit Ethernet, measurements of ETHOS on top of SCI and InfiniBand indicate considerably greater bandwidth and reduced cost.

13.6.1   DOLPHIN'S HIGH-SPEED INTERCONNECTS

We choose to abandon connectivity with other high-speed connections to reduce connectivity latency any further and instead use the Message Queue Interface, the next lower program layer available in the Dolphin Express stack. ETHOM (ETHernet over Message-Queue driver) uses this interface to provide an Ethernet interface for SCI and Dolphin DX hardware. As a result, in addition to the TCP/UDP-Sockets already supported by the Dolphin software stack, ETHOM provides an

Ethernet gateway for the SCI and Dolphin DX interconnects, allowing interface bonding, bridging, and another layer 2 kernel capabilities, as well as (IP-) Routing. Furthermore, by using its Ethernet bearer, TIPC can utilize these two network technologies.

13.6.2 SCALABLE COHERENT INTERFACE (SCI)

The Versatile Cohesive Interfaces is a well-known interconnect technology for clear memory access and/or I/O read/write communication. It combines (parts of) the physical address spaces of devices connected into a single global main memory, allowing memory to be exported and imported transparently way via controlled input/output (PIO) transfers or directly via direct memory access (DMA) transfers. The norm supports cache coherency between nodes, but not through I/O interfaces like PCI. Since each host adapter transfers packets among its multiple connections, the nodes are linked in multifaceted torus configurations without the use of a central switch. Remote store latencies start at 220 ns with a maximum bandwidth of 334 MiB/s per channel in the latest SCI hardware generation (D352).

13.6.3 DOLPHIN DX

The Dolphin DX serial interfaces are built on the Sophisticated Switching Interface protocols (ASI). As a result, it couples distributed machines' buses and memory areas, but it is optimized for PCI Express rather than consistent memory coupling. In addition, unlike SCI, it does not use decentralized swapping; instead, all nodes are connected to a single switch. Present devices have 10 ports and can be scaled to meet the needs.

In terms of programmers, DX has many of the same capabilities as SCI, such as opaque PIO and DMA connections to direct outward and re-mote interrupt. This allows it to be integrated with the same tech stack for SCI and to use the same APIs. On both PIO and DMA transitions, DX has greatly outperformed SCI. At 64 bytes transfer rate, the latency to store 4 bytes to remote memory is 40 ns, when the bandwidth is already 1.397 GiB/s.

13.6.4 DOLPHIN SOFTWARE STACK

The SISCI API is the most simple and effective way of using SCI or DX as a high-speed interconnect. The SISCI operating system has the ability to share application software. It enables user-space access to the features of the SCI and DX interconnects and comprises of a user-space shared library, which communicates with the SISCI kernel driver via IOCtl () operations to generate and export interposes communication segments, map remote memory segments to the main memory of the calling process, send and wait for local interrupts, and perform DMA transfers from and to remote memory segments. These means enable processes running on multiple machines to construct general, globally dispersed interposes communication regions and speak and read data from and to there either by PIO or DMA operations. Synchronizing can be achieved via shared memory or via mobile bursts.

To achieve optimum transmission efficiency, data exchange needs to be aligned to acceptable SCI packet and acceptance level (16, 64, and 128 bytes), and remote read procedures should be prevented except for very limited data volumes.

SISCI does not have the means to transfer messages between operations except for reading to any shared program memory and synchronizing by either message passing or remote interrupts. Pocket is a word that is used to describe a group of people. Therefore, centered on this main memory framework, Dolphin supplies a thin programming interface for communications via message queues (MBox/Msq). It allows users to create uni-directional channels of communication between devices that can be controlled through simple send () and recv () operations. This software layer takes care of synchronization, information gathering, error correction, and so forth and provides various optimized protocols for small, moderate, and large sample sizes.

It is also the foundation for Dolphin's Super Sockets, which in the data plane offer a Berkeley API compatible sockets functionality via lib k supers

13.7   ARCHITECTURE OF ETHOM

We installed a light coating of abstraction under the Ethernet protocol to tie together the two realms of Ethernet-based applications and Dolphin's increased channels. This layer transfers Ethernet images to the SCI Response Queues, which are the Dolphin device stack's highest packet forwarding layer. In comparison to ETHOS, we forego connectivity with other high-speed connectors in exchange for improved efficiency at the expense of increased device load. SCI or DX cards, at the most basic level, actually communicate information to peer points.

13.7.1   CONFIGURATION

ETHOM is programmed in three stages: compilation time, loading time, and driver run time. A common structure is very static for simplicity's sake; the number of participants in the network and their ETHOM host id to SCI node IDs mapping must be defined at compile time. The ETHOM host id must be transmitted as a parameter at load time, enabling one binary to be used by all nodes within the network. For the sender's hand, immediate purging after each call to send msg () is an option, as is dynamic voting for the receiving line. A transmit timeout can be defined, telling the kernel when to drop a packet after a certain amount of time has passed. The Ethernet protocol is now configured and ready to use using the parameters listed above. With ifconfig, you can delegate the IP address, MTU, and other options at runtime. At run time, all module parameters defined at load time may be modified.

13.7.2   CONNECTION ESTABLISHMENT

After downloading the operator, each node creates two single-direction contact points for each peer sensor node, (e.g., 14 message queues on each node in case of 7 peer nodes). The regional and peer node numbers are used to generate message queue IDs.

$$\text{ID}_{\text{Receive Queue}} D \# hosts \sim peer\, C\, local\ \text{ID}_{\text{Send Queue}} D \# hosts \sim local\, C\, peer$$

They'll be sure to be special in the cluster this way.

Two threads are launched for each peer node (14 threads in the case of 7 peers), one attempting to bind the local send to the distant receive queue and the other waiting for a link on the local retrieve queue. When the first of the thread waiting on local receive queues completes its contact, it becomes the main queue, polling all associated receive streams. All other submit and receiving threads stop working as soon as their link is created, essentially decreasing the number of threads left to one.

13.7.3   COMMUNICATION PHASE

The process of exchanging files between various nodes in a network is depicted: A request on ETHOM host 1 on the left sends data to a request on ETHOM host 4 on the right via a TCP socket.

I'm sending it. The kernel network stack receives data from a request on host 1 that writes to a TCP socket attached to a receiver on host 4. If required, the kernel breaks it into packets that match under the previously defined MTU (Fragmentation) and endows each packet with a wired header. By calling ETHOM's ethom tx () module, this newly built Ethernet frame is transferred to it.

- **Receiving:** The data is immediately transferred to the messaging queue's data space in system memory by the Dolphin equipment as it arrives on host 4; no interruption is called to announce the presence of data. As previously said, a thread is initiated by calling the function ethom rx thread action (), which polls the obtained message queue either statically or not. This thread retrieves data immediately after it arrives by having called Dolphin's recv msg () function and passing it to ethom rx (). Dev alloc skb () is used to assign a skb structure in ethom rx (), and parameters like dev, protocol, and ip summed are set such that the device level above ETHOM recognizes the skb. With netif rx, the Ethernet frame is transferred upwards (). The IP packets are reconstructed from multiple Ethernet frames (if they were previously splintered), the IP and TCP headers are taken off again, and the user data is sent to its ultimate stop, the program on host 4.

13.8 DYSLIPIDEMIA EFFECT ON A FUNDAMENTAL ARCHITECTURAL CHARACTERISTIC MEDIATED DILATION FROM PHOTOGRAPHIC PLETHYSMOGRAPHY

One of the most common causes of cardiovascular disease (CVD) is atherosclerosis. Atherosclerosis can be caused by many causes, including smoking, elevated blood pressure, diabetes, and a high cholesterol level in the blood (dyslipidemia). As a result, an index that can measure coronary heart disease using endothelial cell dysfunction would be useful for early detection.

13.8.1 Vascular Endothelial Dysfunction

Since atherosclerosis induces a malfunction in the activity of endothelium cells, assessing endothelial dysfunction is critical for early detection. The vascular wall is made up of three layers: the Intima, which is the closest to the light output and is caused by blood flow; the Media, which is the furthest away from the lumen and is not affected by blood flow; and the Endothelium, which is the furthest away from the lumen and Cardiomyocytes are found in the second layer (Media), and Adventitia is found in the third layer. Endothelial cells are found in the Intima, the cardiovascular wall's internal surface. Cellular membranes are important in a variety of vascular functions because of their strategic position (contact with blood), such as regulating thrombosis with their antibiotics and preventing blood clots. Antithrombotic surface, leukocyte, and platelet interactions with the vessel wall, and vessel tone and growth control.

Endothelium-derived soothing (such as Nitric Oxide—NO) and constricting stimuli are balanced by the endothelium to preserve vascular equilibrium. The vasculature is vulnerable to vascular constriction, leukocyte compliance, platelet release, mitogenesis, pro-oxidation, thrombosis, compromised coagulation, artery inflammatory, and arteriosclerosis when this equilibrium is disrupted. Flow-mediated dilation (FMD) assessment is a reliable way to assess vascular permeability. The capacity of the venous system to consciously its tone and monitor blood flow in addition to acute or pharmacologic stimulation is assessed using this methodology.

13.8.2 Flow-Mediated Dilation

A sphygmomanometric collar is used in this procedure to occlude blood supply in (usually) the brachial artery (BA) by inflating the cuff to supra systolic pressure, inducing ischemia in the lower arm. As a result, the vessels far below ischemia dilate in a self-regulating manner. After 4–5 minutes of occlusion, the strain is abruptly lifted, causing reactive hyperemia and shear tension on the blocked BA's inner wall (Intima). The BA is then distended as a result of the activation of vasodilators. High-resolution longitudinal ultrasound B-mode scans are used to determine the BA's diameter. Since a variety of factors affect FMD (such as temperature, food, medicines, and sympathetic stimuli), subjects must fast for at least 8 hours without using any vasoactive medications for at least four half-lives, caffeine, high-fat diets, vitamin C, or nicotine, and then be observed in a temperature-controlled room.

Unfortunately, the latter approach is costly due to the machinery used, which is vulnerable to mistakes and necessitates the use of an expert operator.

Photoplethysmography (PPG) has recently been introduced as another non-invasive process. PPG is a signal that reflects pressure waves produced by pulmonary arterial artery activity as a result of muscle contractions. A photoelectric probe is used to track dynamic blood volume variations caused by pulses.

Active blood capacity fluctuations due to the beats are perceived by a photoelectrical probe located on the fingertip (finger PPG) or ear lobes, amongst other sites. Owing to the expansion of the heart ventricle, blood flow increases during systole, reducing light diffusion through the peripheral vasculature, and vice versa during diastole.

Following a 4-minute brachial artery occlusion, PPG pulse amplification changes due to circulation dilation in the forefinger are reported (PPG-FMD). PPG is caused by occlusion because it represents interstitial fluid variations in the microvascular bed of tissue. Obesity, diabetes, asthma, and hypercholesterolemia were the risk factors studied. Taking into account the impact of such risk factors, it was discovered that except for participants who have had more than a health risk, PPG-AC curves evenly resembled US-FMD responses (good correlation). The current thesis focuses solely on one risk factor: dyslipidemia, and the next sections examine how well this specific potential risk influences PPG-FMD data.

13.8.3 DATA ACQUISITION

The raw information was obtained from Universiti Kebangsaan Malaysia (UKM). Average temp, food, drink, caffeine, and sympathetic stimulation all trigger vascular circulation vasodilation, so each participant followed a stringent diet protocol before the procedure. Data collection occurs in three stages: before occlusion, after occlusion, and after cuff deflation.

13.9 TWO-DIMENSIONAL ELECTRIC RESISTANCE STUDY OF THE GENERALIZED SOLUTIONS

Alberto Pedro Calderon, an Argentine mathematician, posed an intriguing in-verse question for the Electrical Imbalance Formula.

$$\operatorname{div}(\sigma \operatorname{grad} u) = 0,$$

The Inhomogeneous Laplace equation or the Poisson equation are other names for this equation. The dielectric constant is denoted by and the electrical current is denoted by. Electrical Impedance Tomography is a term used in technical domains to describe this inverse challenge.

It's essentially a Dirichlet principle component problem in which the values of the possible u are given in a system elements T of some domain, and the aim is to approach the dielectric function within using the values of u in that boundary T.

Many researchers paid close attention to the two-dimensional case of the Calderon dilemma (named after A. P. Calderon), and they understood it almost instantly. That the mathematical methods used to arrive at a solution were anything but simple. Indeed, theoretical models looking for an analytic approach to the Calderon problem are difficult to come by in the literature reviewed. The majority of them are focused on a variety of intriguing numerical techniques. Nonetheless, the images acquired using such methods do not, in certain ways, have the necessary resolution to be considered useful diagnostic tools.

The use of a broad range of analysis methods to the Electrical Impedance Spectroscopy issue is an alternative to strictly numerical methods for solving the issue (48.1), Consider a collection of conductivity functions and compare their corresponding solutions u; valued in the domain boundary points with experimentally obtained results, iterating this process until the error can be called minimal.

Nonetheless, the computational difficulty of solving (48.1) without using numerical analysis prompted many experts to believe that obtaining exact solutions in analytic form was difficult except for the linear case of (exception done for the constant case). This viewpoint prevailed until Kari Astala and Lassi Paivarinta of Finland provided the solution for the three or four cases of the Calderon problem by applying the Electromagnetic Imbalance Equation (48.1) to a Vekua equation. This means that they not only noticed the one-to-one correspondence between the equations of such Vekua equations and the double case of (48.1), but they also proved that this correspondence guarantees the presence and uniqueness of the Calderon specific task in the plane.

13.10   BIO-APPLICATION OF A LARGE-FIELD PHOTOLUMINESCENCE MICROSCOPY FOR THE CELL/SURFACE INVESTIGATION AND THE EFFECTS OF TGF-3, HCL AND BSA/HCL IN THE BONE MONOLAYER CELL SEPARATION TESTING

In vivo, molecules bind to other cells or the underlying plasma membrane (extracellular matrix, ECM) environment, while in vitro, they adhere to a substrate or a wall. Any structure and function and pathological processes are influenced by the association of bone cells with their underlying ECM system. Integrins, which are capable of transducing messages from the ECM to the cells, mediate such contacts and lead to cell proliferation, division, and complex protein synthesis. Spectrophotometer analysis and immunofluorescence are used to evaluate which receptors are concerned. Bone morphogenetic proteins (BMPs), Mullerian inhibiting agents, nodal, activating, inhibins, and TGF-$\beta 3$ are all members of the TGF-3 superfamily. These proteins are involved in a wide range of processes, from growth to disease. TGF-3 is a cytokine that is formed by a variety of cells in our bodies, including osteoblasts, keratinocytes, and others. TGF-1, 2, and 3 are three isomers of this cytokine that function in a paracrine or autocrine manner in mammals. TGF-3 may have a positive or negative effect on cell function, based on the physiological status of the target cell and its surroundings. It induces a drop in multiplication when fibroblasts are grown in monolayers in the presence of epidermal growth factor. When these cells are grown in a semi-solid medium; however, TGF-3 helps them to mature. TGF-1, 2, and 3 exert their effects through several signaling channels, as do all TGF-3 superfamily proteins. The activation of cellular processes is caused by interactions between ligands and receptors on the cell surface. The TGF-3 receptor complex is composed of type I and type II serine-threonine kinase receptors. These bind to type III, also recognized as beta glycan, a third captor. The TGF-3 abilities and limitations to this cell proteoglycan. Signal transduction is activated when it is presented to the type I/II receptor complex. This beta glycan was shown to act as a dual modulator of TGF-3 action, which is interesting. TGF-3 signaling is inhibited by the liquid solution of this enzyme, which is no longer bound to the cell membrane.

There are many methods for enhancing tissue regeneration, but the easiest way of stimulating cells to proliferate, divide, and regenerate is to add growth factors to the transformation site. Direct application of growth factors, in general, has no impact so because growth factor diffuses rapidly away from the site of restoration. This is a challenge that can be overcome by using a bioabsorbable scaffold to deliver a regulated release of a protein called at the site of action over a long period. Cell behaviors are mediated by growth factors in responding to environmental cues. They can be developed in a variety of ways and have a variety of effects, including autocrine, paracrine, juxtacrine, and renal. Growth factors play a role in growth, progress, day-to-day management, mobilized intentionally or recklessly interfere, and injury, among other things. If the growth factor gene is introduced into the cells at the reconstruction site and causes the cells to contain growth factors, tissue reconstruction can be accomplished. To convince recovery, bone cells should be removed from the recipient (bone marrow/connective tissue), extended in tissue culture, subjected to bioactive factors, mixed with the scaffold, and then injected into the donor site.

The effect of TGF- β3 and its carries on cell attachment was investigated using trypsinization. Dilutions are deposited into the three rows of a 12 well plate to determine the optimal dilution for plating cells. TGF-"3 was given enough time to affect cell cultures by growing them for at least 2 days before the attached test. The 1 in 3 titration was selected for this assay because it was confluent by day 3. A solution of HCl (4 mM), BSA (1 mg/ml), and purified water was prepared to reconstruct the vile containing TGF-"3. To investigate the effect of TGF-"3, HCl, HCl/BSA, and bone cell only as a guide on cell removal, trypsin was applied to four classes of cultivated bone cells with four separate solutions, including TGF-"3, HCl, HCl/BSA, and bones cell only as a control. TGF-"3 is carried by HCl and HCl/BSA solutions, so they were used. This procedure was carried out again for groups A, B, C, and D. The rate at which cells detach from the surface is critical, and it was possible to identify which group (A, B, C, or D) disconnected faster. To investigate the effect of TGF-"3, HCl, HCl/BSA, and bone cell only as a guide on cell attachment, trypsin was applied to three classes of cultured bone cells with four separate solutions, namely, TGF-"3, HCl, HCl/BSA, and bones cell only as a guide.

13.11 IMPLEMENTATION OF A NOVEL, BROAD FIELD OPTICAL ABSORPTION MICROSCOPE IN TGF-3, BSA/HCL CULTIVATED HUMAN BONE CELL MONOLAYERS AND MICROENCAPSULATION CHARACTERISTICS

Surface Plasmon Resonance (SPR) occurs as a result of an electrode and a resistor when p-polarized light reaches the conductor at a certain angle, causing free electrons to oscillate. The attachment of microbial species to the metalized layer will cause changes in the SPR excitation angle, which are proportional to the index of refraction and thickness of the molecular structure. Surface Plasmon devices are thus highly useful for calculating molecular thickness on substances down to the sub-nanometric level. However, the Kretschmann design is used in the normal surface Plasmon microscope. Surface Plasmons disperse and disperse in this setup, lowering picture quality. The spectrum of excitation angles also limits the objective lens, resulting in regular surface Plasmon microscopes with an average lateral resolution of around 20 m.

A completely new WSPR method has been developed to allow for the analysis of contemporary observers at sub-nanometer vertical and lateral resolutions. The procedure of thrilling surface Plasmon's differs significantly between the traditional surface Plasmon microscope and the recently evolved WSPR device (SPs). A mirror covered with a simple gold layer is commonly used to excite SPs in a typical SPs-based method, but in the WSPR system, SPs were excited on thin coverslips coated with a 50 nm thick gold layer using a higher optical diameter lens. By examining mobile phone interactions and device interfaces for a deeper understanding of the concepts in cell guidance, we hope to show the possible biomedical applications of this modern innovation. The physical associations among cells and ECM proteins that affect cell structure and function can be studied using these photographs. Integrin's bind the ECM protein to the membrane, causing cell surface binding and bond strength reactions, which were also studied using WSPR pictures. WSPR imaging of cellular cultivated bone tissue on protein-shaped polymers could reveal previously unknown specifics of integrin and ECM response to changing requirements, and thus gene material up-regulation in treated cells replication during wound healing.

Regenerative medicine is a growing discipline in medicine that combines biology and biomedical engineering concepts intending to create a functional tissue replacement that will preserve human tissue function. And the fact that soft tissues regenerate, bone healing has degenerative characteristics, and there is normally no scar after healing. The renovating process starts as soon as the fracture is bridged by fresh bone. Different stimuli, such as growth factors, distraction osteogenesis, and endothelial cells, can influence bone recovery. TGF-"3 is a cytokine released by a variety of cell types in the body that affects a variety of cell functions such as differentiating, stimulating mesenchymal stem cell (MSC) formation, acting as a chemotactic factor, and promoting bone cells and

ECM product secretion. This section aimed to look into the effects of TGF-3 and its dose carriers HCl and BSA/HCl on MG63 bone cell monolayer wound repair.

13.11.1 CELL CULTURE

In Dulbecco Eagle Environment, MG63 bone cells were grown in regular 25 cm^2 culture flasks with a 1:5 cell suspension (50,000 cell/mL) (DMEM, SIGMA). Cells were incubated at 37°C for days until being separated when they reached cells were cultured.

13.11.2 SP SUBSTRATE PREPARATION

A prefabricated glass slide (0.18 mm thick and 22 mm diameter) was stamp styled with fibronectin protein using a 50 m stamp, which was coated with 48 nm silver on top of 1 nm chromium (for greater adherence). The MG63 bone cells were then plated on the substrate. The substrates were dehydrated in serial ethanol after the cells were fixed and imaged using a light microscope. The substrate was then placed in the WSPR microscope's sample holder and imaged further.

13.11.3 WOUND HEALING

Bones cells were cultivated in Dulbecco's Modified Eagle Medium (DMEM, from SIGMA), a low-glucose culture medium containing L-glutamine (4 mM), Amoxicillin (5 mL), Amphotericin or a fungi zone (1 mL), HEPES buffered liquid culture, and fetal calf serum (50 mL). The bone cells were grown and bathed in pure culture in culture flasks. The cells clumped together at the bottom of the culture flasks to form a sheet. A discarded lengthy plastics pipette was used to create a burn. The tip of the flask was angled downwards so that it could be inserted. The wound was then generated by drawing the tip over the cells on the cultured surface. The scratch marks helped with alignment during photography, and a new wound was added at a 90° angle to the original scratch, with pictures taken at the cross points. As a result, the same points were recorded every time, resulting in more precise results for the study.

To assess the time limit for fracture healing in the injured models, a "test trial" was conducted. Another experiment on fracture healing using NIH/3T3 fibroblast monolayers found that wound closure could be achieved after 300 minutes. Cell monolayers were wounded with "the corner of a sheet of Mylar film that is widely used in paper documents" in their research. After 300 minutes, the wound was fully closed with an average scratch of 300 m, which is three or four times larger than cell widths. Because full wound closure was not reached during our "test trial" with TGF-"3, the time frame for our experiment was extended to 30 hours, with data collected every 5 hours.

The wound closure property of TGF-"3 and its dosage carriers, HCl and BSA/HCl, were investigated and contrasted in this in vitro study. In TC grade culture flasks, the wound healing reaction was studied by forming a wound (with an average scratch width of 300 10–30 m SD, 1:7–5 m SEM) on a confluent monolayer of MG63 human bone cells. Following wounding, colonies were set to 50 ng/mL TGF-"3 in 4 mM HCl and 1 mg/mL BSA, as well as purified water. The same approach was used to cultivate a cell monolayer with no growth factor as a control, as well as HCl/BSA and HCl only solutions. After that, the culture flasks were placed inside the artificial womb, and the wound diameter was imaged and calculated every 5 hours for a total of 30 hours. The gap between both the wound edges was measured using Image J software. The distances between both the intersections of the lines with the brush border were calculated. Six vertical lines at semi-random known points were drawn and the distances between the intersections of the lines with the brush border were calculated. For each image, an image processing consisted of a set of six wound width measurements. The wound was fully covered in some photographs, but there were also some holes where cells had traveled over to cover the wounds in others. Readings of the holes were also taken into consideration in these circumstances. Six different sets of photos were taken along the marked line for each file. This necessitated the use of two averages. The average wound width inside a picture was the first average. The sum of the "wound diameter ratios" for each of the liquid cultures was the second. For 30 hours, measurements were taken every 5 hours. The median wound diameter was plotted versus. For each image, an image processing consisted of a set of six wound width measurements. The wound was fully covered in some photographs, but there were also some holes where cells had moved over to cover the wound in others. Readings of the holes were also taken into account in these circumstances. Six different sets of pictures were taken all along the marker line for each file. This necessitated the use of multiple categories. The average wound width inside a picture was the first median. The average of the "wound diameter ratios" in each of the liquid cultures was the second. For 30 hours, samples were recorded every 5 hours. The average wound diameter was plotted versus.

13.12 SPEECH REHABILITATION METHODS FOR LARYNGECTOMIES PATIENTS

The voicing of speech is based on amplified lung exhalation flowing through the larynx, where a taut glottis produces a changing pitch excitation that then resounds through the vocal tract, nasal cavity, and out of the face. The sparking, tongue, and lip locations within the genital, dental, and nasal cavities play critical roles in defining speech sounds; they are collectively referred to as speech signal oscillators.

"The larynx is the second most common source for cancer in the upper aerodigestive tract," according to Corey, who goes on to say that "Laryngeal cancers account for about 1.2 percent of all current cancer doctors in the United State governments." According to SEER data from the National Cancer Institute, there were about four cases of laryngeal cancer per 100,000 between 1973 and 2000. Squamous cell carcinoma (SCC) is the most prevalent histopathologic diagnosis, responsible for over 95% of all laryngeal malignancies, according to Corey. The main therapies for these cancers are surgery, radiation, or a combination of the two. Even though organ safety protocols and conservation laryngeal surgery are now available, patients with advanced or chronic SCC of the larynx still have a laryngectomy. In certain cases, patients who have had a total laryngectomy have lost their glottis as well as their capacity to pass lung exhalation into the vocal tract. Patients who have had a partial laryngectomy, on the other hand, can also have the ability to regulate lung exhalation through the vocal tract. About the lack of their glottis, all sets of patients maintain the capacity to modulate their vocal tract and therefore can whisper by regulating lung exhalation (or anything similar). In other words, they regulate the majority of the speech-making machinery. As a result, in this chapter, the novel method is to recreate natural speech from the sound generated by the remaining speech articulators. However, since the fastball glottis is absent, this quest is effectively one of regenerating vocal speech from (pitch-less) whispers. There are some speech therapy approaches available, including esophageal speech, transesophageal puncture (TEP), and the electrolarynx; however, each has flaws ranging from learning disabilities to clumsy use and increased infection danger. Furthermore, they all contain speech that is repetitive or monotonous at best. Concentrating on the electrolarynx, which is the most commonly used voice therapy method by laryngectomies, recent attempts have been made to improve the accuracy of the resulting speech by reducing context and radiated device noise and simplifying its use (i.e. producing a hands-free variant). Despite such efforts, no successful approach for resolving the mechanically sounding (robotized) induced voice feature has been published. By comparison, the novel speech processing technique explored in this chapter aims to achieve higher quality speech with a more natural tone, based in part on our previous work in. It uses a modified code excited linear prediction (CELP) codec to analyze, adjust, and recreate the missing elements in whispered speech. The suggested device operates in live time or near-real-time to recreate normal speech from whispers.

13.12.1 ESOPHAGEAL SPEECH

In this process, the patient is taught to evacuate air through the esophagus rather than the lungs. To retain an esophageal opening, the tongue must be rubbed against the corner of the mouth during this operation.

Esophageal speech may produce a harsh, low-pitched voice with sufficient volume for conversation in small groups and silent environments. Few extraordinary esophagus speakers can have enough mobility and dynamic vocal range to mimic a natural voice, but others are unable to learn this form of speech recovery. Esophageal speech is surprisingly intelligible, despite being difficult to understand and sometimes sounding unnatural. Just 6% of overall laryngectomy patients produce functional esophageal expression, according to a report (Although five times as many do use or attempt to use it). The actual state of esophageal expression is that tracheesophageal puncture operations and electro larynxes have completely eclipsed it.

13.12.2 TRACHEESOPHAGEAL PUNCTURE (TEP)

TEP is a surgical procedure that can improve the quality of speech of people who have undergone a complete laryngectomy and are breathing through a stoma. The TEP operation makes a small opening in the digestive tract and trachea to reconnect them. When the stoma is temporarily shut down, this is equipped with a one-way valve to allow air from the lungs to reach the mouth via the trachea.

Various clinical and scientific trials have been conducted since the adoption of the TEP technique in 1980, ranging from technique changes to studies of speech content and ease of processing. While speech-language physicians consider TEP speech to be the best approach in terms of consistency, just about 30% of post-laryngectomies patients use this laryngeal expression form.

The fairly decent directly toxic comparison to other voice treatment strategies, as well as the high survival rate of maintaining usable voice with minimal instruction, are the main elements of effective, whereas the daily treatment of the prosthetic limb by the patient, recurrent leakage of the prosthetic limb over time, and the resulting need for reconstruction by the physician (including invasive surgery) are the major drawbacks. In addition, the implant is clumsy to use and poses a risk of disease.

13.12.3 ELECTRO LARYNX

The electrolarynx is a razor-thin device that resonates with the vocal tract by being squeezed against the side of the throat. The collar and intra-oral electro larynx are the two forms of an electrolarynx, with the former being the most common among laryngectomies. During phonation, the hand-holding instrument is held against the neck near the former glottis to send a ringing pulse into the oral and esophageal cavities by an electron-mechanical vibrator incorporated into the device. The vocal cavity resonates as a result of the sound source being absorbed thru the neck membranes. By moving articulators like the lips, jaws, tongue, jaw, and velum, the user attenuates this vibration to produce voice.

While some pioneering figures have a hand trigger to adjust pitch, electrolarynx speech is automatic sounding and repetitive. The electrolarynx is one of the simpler types of speech therapy, as well as being more efficient for communicating in certain cases. Even though the esophageal and transesophageal expression is popular in voice rehabilitation, electrolarynx phonation is the most widely used procedure, with more than 55% of post-laryngectomies patients using it. In general, these methods have one flaw: they emit unnaturally monotonous "robotized" expressions. By comparison, the method described and attempts to improve speech content by analyzing, modifying, and reconstructing speech using a modified CELP codec.

13.12.4 WHISPERED AND PHONATED SPEECH

Whispered voice, rather than usually phonated (pitched) speech, is the key area of research into speech recovery for laryngectomy patients because they can often generate whispering speech with little effort, especially partial total thyroidectomy patients.

Whispers (or "still whispers") are made by naturally speaking people to minimize detectability in a comfortable environment, such as a library. They're made without the use of vocal fold vibrations. Whispers from laryngectomies people have similar characteristics (although some patients may be capable of partial phonation). The lack of essential pitch and harmonics is caused by the loss of vocal cord vibration. Exhaling slowly can be defined as the cause of stimulation in whispers that used a source filtering template, with the structure of the pharynx modified so that the voice box does not vibrate. Whispers are therefore generated by intermittent electric dipole circulation.

13.12.5 SPEECH REGENERATION

A CELP codec is used in this chapter's approach to making whisper voice sound very much like completely phonated speech. CELP selects excitation from a code word of zero-mean Gaussian strings, which are then formed by an LTP (long-term prediction) filter to express the campaign speech pitch essential. CELP is among the most common analysis-by-synthesis LPC (power spectrum coding) schemes, particularly for low-bit-rate coding.

Line spectral pairs (LSPs) are used to express the resonance properties of an integrated tube representation of the human vocal tract in most CELP codecs, where linear prediction correlations are converted into LSPs. The model has two states that characterize the auditory system as being completely open or fully closed at the glottis. Since the human glottis opens and closes quickly during everyday conversation, the real resonances are right in the middle of the two extremes (and this can be seen in any analysis of speech LSPs). However, since the glottis does not oscillate during muttered voice, this model no longer stands true, and the LSP model must be marginally adjusted. Since changing the frequency of lines will trigger unintended peak forming by closing the distance between two irrelevant pairs, it's critical to choose the pair of lines that corresponds to probable formants. As previously stated, this can be accomplished by selecting the three thinnest LSP pairs, which function well when the signal has fine peaks. But, as amplitude bandwidth utilization expand (as they do in muttered speech), the difference between the corresponding LSPs increases, the selection of the narrowest LSP pairs can fail to locate the correct formant positions, especially for syllables. While describing an improved LSP-based approach, the enhancement protocol is updated to function efficiently on both whispering vowel sounds and phonetic symbols.

13.13 INVESTIGATION OF GLASS MICROPIPETTE TIP MICROSTRUCTURES AND GIGA-SEAL EFFECTS

The patch-clamp methodology has been successfully used to study cellular ion channels. The practice is accomplished of sensing streams flowing in/out of the cell concluded a single ion network at peak resolution. The dysfunction of ion channels has now been shown to be the cause of a variety of diseases. The patch-clamp system can be used to study the operation of different ion channels under various physical and chemical stimulations, as well as cell communications, and these experiments can help one better understand the fundamentals of cells. Patch clamping involves isolating a patch of membranes from the extracellular environment with a glass Pasteur pipette to record the current running into the region. Glass micropipettes with a tip diameter of 1–2 m are created by heating and pulling small glass capillaries. After that, the capillary tubes are backfilled with an electrical conductor and rubbed against a surface of cells. A soft suction is applied to the pipette's backend to increase the sealing state. In the enzyme immobilization setup, there are different attributes: monitoring electrodes within the pipette and a buffer solution in the bath solution, as shown in A resistive element seal between both the crystal and the membrane patch is done to avoid single cell membrane current flow of the order of a few Pico Amperes. The increased resistance seal decreases current flow between the metal conductors, finishes the membrane patch's electrical separation, and lowers recording current noise. The seal is known as a giga-seal because its thermal conductivity is in the gig ohm range.

The physical–biological processes underlying giga-seal formation are still unknown, which may be due to the large number of various factors that play a role in giga-seal forming, such as capillary tube and cell surface neatness, tip surface roughness, tip geometrical, biocompatibility of the patch site, material type, test tube crystal type, tip size, maintenance of healthy ions in the solution, gentle going to approach of the capillary tube to the plasma membrane, skill, and patience.

This study aims to enhance patch tightening sealing tolerance and increase the number of giga-seals acquired. The effect of the surface roughness of glass micropipettes on seal formation was investigated in this study. Pipettes' tips were photographed and recovered. The roughness of the surface is determined.

13.13.1 3D Reconstruction of Micropipette Tip

The boron carbide micro peristaltic pumps used in the experiments had an average width of 1.5 mm and an internal surface of 0.86 mm (BF150-86-10 Sutter Instrument). With a raging micropipette puller rig, they were heated and removed. The computer was programmed to make pipettes with a tip diameter of about 1:5 m. The pipette tip was 3D reconstructed using high-resolution magnetic resonance microscope (SEM) images. Stereo vision technologies, in which the same neighborhood of an object is scanned from distinct viewpoints by tilting the item with a camera, have been commonly used to predict the multiple configurations of an artifact about the fixed optic axis Measurements were performed from two perspectives in this method. Surface features at various heights have varying energy dissipation, and depth can be determined by calculating the parallax shift of surfaces from their original position in the first picture to their current location in the second image. 2D paired points in two SEM images obtained from two angles between 5° and 10° away from the norm are used to calculate 3D points. It depicts the SEM setup, spinning angle, and forecasted coordination $P_1(X_1, Y)$, $P_2(X_1, Y)$ (X_2, Y).

13.13.2 Effect of Canned Cycles on Drilled Whole Quality

Digging is one of the most ancient and widespread used machining processes, accounting for roughly a third of all stainless-steel operations. The relative movement of a cutting tool called a drill or drill bit is used to generate or enlarge a round hole in a workpiece. Different drilling methods are used, including material deposition, deep hole dredging, and peck drilling. The scale, resistance, and surface finish required, as well as the manufacturing specifications and the equipment required to do the job, all influencing the drilling method chosen. The performance of holes drilled is influenced by several factors. Cutting circumstances (cutting speed and feed rate) and cutting layouts are the most evident (tool material, diameter, and geometry). As a result, the majority of previous research has focused on these factors. Notwithstanding, a few scientists have looked into the impact of other factors: Pirtini and Lazoglu looked into cutting force, Nouari, List, Girot, and Gehin looked into tool wear, and Bono and Ni looked into thermal distortion. However, their consideration of the subject was short, and their results were incomplete. As a result, the impact of a packaged process on the surface quality complete of drilled holes should be investigated further; whole performance should not be sacrificed in the name of productivity increases.

13.13.3 Drilling Canned Cycle

A canned loop is a collection of computer activities that are started by a single piece of code. The coding serves as a workaround to make the software easier to use. For computer-controlled control

(CNC) mining operations, a variety of primed processes are used, with the microprocessor packed cycle (G73), spot digging packed cycle (G81), and deep hole packed cycle (G83) being the three most common options. The following subsections provide a concise overview of these activities.

For drilling a substance that tends to yield stringy chips, a microprocessor canned cycle is being used. To put it another way, the chips form from around the tool and are harder to shake. By partially recanting the tool throughout a drilling process, G73 can be used to split the chips out of the cavity.

For regular drilling, a canned spot hydraulic fracturing period is used. The instrument would plunge to the whole's edge and quickly withdraw. From point R to point Z, drilling is done.

13.14   AQUA BASE STERLING SILVER SLURRY MICRO MACHINING PIECES

Micro-electromechanical system (MEMS) modules can be used in a variety of applications, and their materials have grown in popularity in recent years. Metals have some advantages over other new MEMS products. One of the metallic components with excellent oxidation and tribological resistant properties is 316-L corrosion resistant. Many micro-fabrication processes have recently emerged to cover a broad variety of materials and implementations. Microsystem Technology (MST) is one of the most widely used methods for fabricating micro components with dimensions ranging from nanometers to millimeters. X-ray Lithography is a traditional micro-manufacturing process that can be used to fabricate polymer-based and semiconductor components. Micro electro-discharge machining (EDM) and laser micromachining are two other manufacturing technologies that have a wide variety of components in micro materials. Laser micro machine tools create devices with rough edges, while EDM is limited to electronic circuits. Changes and technology are a technique for fabricating micro components out of metals. Because of its sluggish metal deposition speed, changes and technology have trouble manufacturing micro-modules with a diameter >0.5 mm.

Micro metal injection molding (MIM) is a technique for fabricating micro parts from a broad variety of materials formed from MIM. Soft lithography is a modern advanced machining method that has only been used for a few years. It has been effectively used in the manufacture of free-standing micro-machine parts made of metals and ceramics. The kind of mound inserts used is the key distinction between surface modification and MIM. The soft mound inserts used in metal casting are normally polydimethylsiloxane (PDMS) molds. Rigid mound inserts, on the other hand, are often found in MIM. Powder-binder slurries are a very powerful way to fill soft molds due to soft mound inserts (PDMS). As a result, the binder must be deliberately chosen to be properly discarded before the sintering. During sintering, the incomplete combustion binder tends to increase carbon and decreases steel tensile strength. At different substrate temperatures and weather systems, stainless steel sections have been effectively sintered. The physical behavior of sintered components is improved as the speed was increased.

13.14.1   SU-8 MASTER MOLDS AND THEIR NEGATIVE REPLICAS

SU-8 2075 [MicroChem, USA] was used to make ultra-thick micro molds in this research. UV light in the range of 320–420 nm can be used to image SU-8. SU-8 structures with depths ranging from a few microns to over 1 mm were created using UV mass spectroscopy. Previous papers go into great depth about the fabrication process; casting SU-8 resist onto a 4 in. Silicon wafer and soft baked it at 65°C for 2 hours, accompanied by 95°C for 34 hours, was the first step in the fabrication process. The Canon PLA-501 FA UV-mask right to freedom of religion was used for the illumination. Following that, the wafer was subjected to a post-experiment bake and growth in EC solvent. The following are the steps involved in replicating soft mold (PDMS) inserts: (a) A 10:1 weight ratio of PDMS raw material (DOW Sylgard Silicone) and sintering temperature was added; (b) the solution was put in a sealed container to eliminate any embedded booms; (c) the elution buffer solution was poured into SU-8 molds and sterilized again, and (d) the PDMS was cured in a 90°C oven. The SEM images of the SU-8 and PDMS micro mold cavity.

13.14.2 PREPARING STAINLESS STEEL SLURRY

316-L stainless material, dispersant, binder, and purified water are used to make a carbon steel metal sludge. In this study, 81.7% powder 5 m 316-L carbon steel material (Sandvik Osprey Ltd., UK) was used. A percentage of 65.5 Fe, 18.5 Cr, 11.6 Ni, 2.3 Mo, 1.4 Mn, and other minor elements are used in the chemical properties provided by the retailer. The molecular mass is 1.9, 3.4, and 5:8 m for D10, D50, and D90, however (supplier). Duramax B-1000 (Rohm and Hass, USA) is an ammonium salt of acrylic homopolymer that is used as an extraction solvent for a variety of ceramic and metal powders in this study. The binder is a combination of an aqueous emulsion of acrylic polymer Duramax B-1000 and B-1007 (Chesham Speciality Ingredients Limited, UK). The slurry is made in the following manner:

- The dispersant and purified water are combined in a specimen tube using a UV spectrophotometer for 5 minutes.
- Stainless steel powder is added into the mixture is shaken using a magnetic stirrer for 20–30 minutes to adequately distribute the powder.
- The binder is added and then the whole substance is stirred again for 15 minutes.
- The slurry is degassed by means of blankness to eliminate the foams formed through mixing and dispensed onto the micro gear soft mold.
- To fill the soft molds, the lined mold is vacuumed, and the remaining slurry on the top of the mold cavity is cleaned with a razor to hold the designs smooth.

13.14.3 DE-BINDING AND SINTERING

In this, two separate sintering environments were investigated: (a) de-binding and sintered metal were done in one continuous loop in a rotary kiln with a complex flow of developing oxidizing environment of 90% Nitrogen and 10% Hydrogen and (b) de-binding was done in a combustion chamber with nitrogen environment and sintered metal was done in a plasma environment. In both cases, the de-binding rate was increased to 1.2°C/minutes before 700°C was reached and sustained for 1 hour. During the sintering point, the heating rate is reduced to 5°C/minutes before the sintering temperature is reached. This study looked at four different sintering temperatures. For both situations, the sintering holding time was reduced to 1.5 hours.

13.15 EXPLANATION OF THE VOXEL-BASED ELEMENT FOR ELECTRONIC PROPERTIES

Mechanical components' functions are often the product of novel material configurations and complicated geometry. This is particularly true in the automotive and aviation industries for increased materials. Graded parts are a more environmentally friendly alternative to today's plastic materials. "Functional gradation is the regulated and repeatable modification of a material's microstructure to determine the component's physical phenomena. The goal is to see how the microstructure changes over time in at least one temporal position". Several seemingly conflicting properties are found in the component, both of which help the component's posterior function.

Despite this, only one kind of substance is used. The hardness and damping behavior of a module, for example, can be described using the module's cross-section. This term occurs during the production process. The aim of the cooperative research center Transregio 30 (CRC/TR TRR30) is to investigate graded structures and their manufacturing operation.

A flanged steel shaft is used as a demonstrator of a part with key activities in the results described. Within the CRC's study, the flanged steel shaft is manufactured in a three-step process. A steel cylinder is locally heated (a) with the aid of an induction coil, and then converted into a flanged steel shaft via a two-step deformation process. Steps (b) and (c), which are tool-independent, and phase (c), which is tool-dependent, make up the reshape method.

A five-step framework was built for the preparation of production processes for products with key activities:

- **Overview of the component**: It is necessary to map the module's graded property into a CAD model for this phase. A voxel model is built from this CAD model. Each volume unit (voxel) can be connected to component property data. To make the input of property data easier, interpolation techniques are used. The manufacturing system preparation is based on the improved component outline.

- **Specification of install applications**: Using the improved component model, the construction manager specifies the manufacturing operations. Heuristics, cognition, and an inference engine can be used to support the manufacturing engineer in the future. Production technology is calculated for each constructional purpose. An expert system aids in the decision-making process. An information base and the previously listed inference engine make up the expert method. The information base is made up of a database and an ontology that stores all of the information about manufacturing technology and their associated manufacturing roles, as well as their interdependencies. The production functions and innovations that have been established are then mapped onto a phenotypic framework.

- **Replication of the processing chain**: In a continuity matrix, processing technologies are compared to one another. This study yields highly consistent industrial technology variations. Process chains are built using compatible technology variations. A process chain is a series of manufacturing systems in which a manufacturing system is allocated to each manufacturing role. Under the process chain optimization, the specified process chains are tested to be capable of producing the operational graded portion.

- **Process chain optimization**: Empirical models are used to explain the relationships between production technologies and product properties. In the optimization process, the models of each technology are merged and used. The estimated values of each production technology are calibrated concerning the desired product properties using multi-objective optimization. Finally, the whole process chain is optimized using hierarchical optimization. All of the coherent process chains are subjected to optimization. Only the process chains that are appropriate for producing the graded part are moved on to the next specification level.

- **Process chain specification**: The optimization process generates process chains that can produce the graded products most efficiently. The optimized parameter values of the chosen manufacturing systems are defined in the process chains. A specification technique is used in this case to allow the definition of the method and resources. This provides a fully-funded concept for a manufacturing method for producing a part with graded properties. This term serves as the foundation for the implementation of the manufacturing method in the areas of production resource planning, shop floor planning, and inventory.

13.15.1 Procedure Model

A process model for the definition of functionally graded elements was developed and the phases of element classification are depicted. The fluted steel shaft bystander is used to illustrate each step in the upcoming sections.

13.15.2 Component Construction

The part is initially created in a 3D CAD framework. The CAD model is then shipped to the next level of production. There is no distinction between the descriptions of conventional and graded elements in this step.

13.16   CONTRAST-ENHANCED EVALUATION OF PIPELINES APPLICATIONS DRIFT FLUX ESTIMATES

Multi-parametric research entails a comprehensive review of numerous studies on drift flux models on both vertically and horizontally pipes. Zuber was the first to construct drift flux models in 1965. The Drift flux models are used in particle transfer forecasting models using Smoothed Particle Dynamics (CFD). To reflect slip among fluid phases, a drift flux model is used. The idea behind the Drift Flux models, according to Brethour and Hirt, is that the relative motion between other components can be defined as a continuum instead of by small components. The whole method is seen well and, in a system, with no distinct exclusive or definite consideration paid to the elements or components individually. It's only used to analyze soil erosion, fluidized beds, or other stream issues surrounding linear movement (interaction) among processes dominated by buoyancy and fluid drag forces. Kinematic Shocks or Expansion Waves allow the relative flow to travel in a slip pattern, which is primarily induced by turbulent fluid motion assisted by environmental forces such as internal lateral pressure produced by interfacial tension of a liquid in a balanced high-temperature environment. When transporting a viscoplastic slurry or paste, the condition is similar to that of a viscoplastic slurry or paste.

Applications vary from simplistic elements like bubbles and slug particles to more nuance and subtly devastating effects like pipeline degradation and the associated wear rate. Drift Flux models take into account the varying concentrations and dimensions of the volume concentration of particles that are thought to be constantly slipping; in other words, it assumes the constant velocity relative motion between and inside the fluids or fluid/particle or fluid/particle/pipe wall due to the gravitational and/or gravitational fields.

13.16.1   Application to a Vertical Pipe Considering the Buoyancy Effect

After their invention in the 1960s, Drift Flux models have proved to be extremely suitable for a wide range of engineering issues. This flexibility is extremely useful in predicting planned and predicted engineering problems, as well as analyzing root because analysis after a failure has occurred. The importance of doing a complete parametric study of different flow flux systems could be overstated.

13.16.2   Drift Flux Models as Applied to Wear Rate in Horizontal Pipelines

The impact of sliding speed on the interfaces between the volume fraction of objects submerged in a transportation fluid and the internal walls of a pipeline was investigated in this case. The Eulerian spectrum modeling approach, the particles equation of motion, and the spatial interpolation equation, on the other hand, is thoroughly discussed here.

13.16.3   The Continuous Model

The behavior of fluid flow trends in a discrete process is defined by this model. The boundary conditions for conservation of mass, as well as expression patterns for an SST turbulence, are used in this process. Tian believes the boundary conditions in CFD model equations are essentially dependent on fluid mechanics, which reflects mathematical assertions of physics' boundary conditions. The idea that such steps must be preserved in a specific amount, known as a porous medium, led to the creation of these rules.

13.16.4   Particle Equation of Motion

Two hypotheses were used to arrive at this formula.

1. There is no interaction with the fine materials.
2. Particle motion has a negligible effect on the fluid-flowing fluid and can be ignored.

13.17 CONDITION MONITORING FREQUENCIES INFLUENCE THE EFFECTIVENESS OF MANUFACTURING INDUSTRIES

Manufacturing processes deteriorate over time as a result of use and age. Maintenance may recover the operating state of manufacturing machinery after accidents or maintain it by reducing the chances of breakdowns in reliability assessment. Repair work unscheduled downtime, on the other hand, improves resource consumption and system uncertainty, adversely impacting key efficiency indicators like work in progress (WIP) and cycle time. Although there is a large body of literature on replacement management and design, the relationships between project management and the efficiency of manufacturing systems have received little attention. Some standards have been suggested in particular for continuously determining maintenance behavior based on system state. However, in real-life situations, most of these methods are very difficult to implement. Instead, several simple estimated queuing models are used in this paper to evaluate the effect of preventive maintenance intervals on lean manufacturing efficiency, with a particular emphasis on WIP. This is made to demonstrate how the level of preventive maintenance, whether chosen arbitrarily or to reduce maintenance costs, may hurt WIP and cycle time, necessitating trade-off decisions.

13.17.1 Economic Optimization of Preventive Maintenance Schedule

Condition monitoring that restores the body to its normal state (as good as new) is useful in systems that are subject to wear and thus have an increasing failure rate (IFR). The issue of assessing the preventive repair time TP then occurs. This is normally chosen by construction administrators to comply with any external condition (such as machinery vendor orders or quality control department guidelines) or, all too frequently, is determined randomly. When it comes to TP optimization, a repair expense risk mitigation strategy is commonly used. Many regulations exist in this regard, the majority of which fall into two categories: age reduction policies and periodic replacement policies. A device is often replaced at failure, or at time TP if it has not failed up to time TP, according to the age reduction scheme.

13.17.2 Queuing Models for Unreliable Machines

The queuing principle allows for fast evaluation of the most important production system output indicators. In contrast to discrete events complex computer models, analytical queuing models have generally applicable outcomes and specifically display the function of the affecting parameters. The latter, on the other hand, are much more versatile and stronger, but they take a long time to develop and verify. Even though a variety of scheduling schemes for insecure servers have been established for a long time, the majority of them is focused on the accumulation of exponentially spread time to failure (i.e., continuous failure rate) and only fixes preemptive disruptions, such as power outages, breakdowns, for example, or non-preventive maintenance, such as routine maintenance. This precludes the use of simplistic queuing models to simplify maintenance policies since all types of interruptions must be modeled. Furthermore, the continuous failure rate assumption makes the templates inappropriate for examining preventive maintenance strategies, which are only useful when a system's failure rate is increasing due to gradual wear and degradation. Furthermore, owing to the complexities of production interruptions, selecting the right clustering method can be challenging. It proposes an effective way to deal with this end. They differentiate between precautionary and non-preemptive interruptions at first. Preemptive disruptions are unplanned and can happen at any moment during the production of a task, inflating the average process time in comparison to the natural process time. Non-preemptive disruptions, on the other hand, are usually planned and can be delayed until the job processing is finished. They then differentiate among chase and moment disruptions. Only if WIP is present in the machine or is indirectly triggered by the existence of WIP will run-based disruptions occur. Breakage of a tool, for example, may only happen while the system is handling a component. Distractions dependent on time, on the other hand, will happen even though there is no work in progress. Failures or out-of-spec inputs, for example, and outages, however, are examples of run-based and time-based preemptive interruptions. Setups and proactive repairs, for example, are also examples of run-based and time-based non-preemptive disruptions.

Finally, they assign state-induced or commodity events to be sub-cases of non-preemptive events that occur during a run (i.e., a state-induced event is an interruption deriving from a change of state of the machine such as a warm-up period when the machine passes from standby to working conditions). We're involved in run-based pre-emptive incidents (i.e., breakdowns) and time-based non-preemptive events in this study, according to this classification (i.e. preventive maintenance.).

Provides a more detailed classification of M/M/1, M/G/1, and G/G/1 queuing models, relating to run-based or time-based disruptions when uptime is extracted significantly; however, here we only would use for queues of Poulet arrivals and basic service processes in standard application servers (M/G/1), which best suits the scope of this article. Given the lack of clear queuing models that expressly provide both preemptive and non-preemptive disruptions for insecure servers with Weibull spread increasing rate of failure, we adapt two estimated queuing models from the publications in this paper to investigate the effect of maintenance policy on system efficiency. The models are used to approximate average WIP at the workspace when the preventive duration TP is modified, equate the TP moderate contribution to a maximum WIP, if any, to the value corresponding to the reduced maintenance cost per unit time, and calculate the overall effect of adjusting TP on device WI.

13.18 ON THE NUMBER OF THIN-WALL GRINDING INSTABILITY PREDICTIONS

The production method in aerospace is gradually reducing the use of joints by fabricating components as a single monolithic component. Due to its flexibility and high sliding distance in generating parts in ideal lengths, machine tools are a very popular activity in production. Parts made from machined aluminum or titanium blocks include aircraft wing panels, fuselage sections, turbine blades, and jet engine compressors. Weight considerations force the construction of much thinner parts as a result of the environmental issues and the general need for higher performance. There is normally a physical requirement that the machining process parts must meet to ensure the accuracy of the manufactured surfaces. To ensure that this is followed, machined components are routinely inspected before being approved for use. Parts that fail this test are either discarded or exposed to extensive manual labor to eliminate the surface finish.

Milling involves feeding the workpiece into a revolving tool with one or two teeth, which allows for a very high "Depth of Cut" (MRR). The substance is removed from the workpiece in the form of tiny individual "chips" by the dentition.

13.19 RISK MANAGEMENT OF ERP SMES INFRASTRUCTURE DEVELOPMENT

The industry landscape is rapidly evolving. Globalization, market competitiveness, technical sophistication, and growing consumer orientation are all obstacles that businesses face today. Companies must expand their product portfolios, minimize time-to-market, shorten product life cycles, and deliver high-quality goods with faster response, reduced prices, and more customization to meet market demands. Companies rely on their core competencies and partner with other organizations with similar expertise and capabilities. Collaboration has become a mainstream theme and success driver in today's enterprise and market practice. Businesses that want to step closer to a fully collaborative model must change their BPs and procedures. Companies must now disclose the sensitive in-house details that they previously fiercely secured with their manufacturers, dealers, and consumers. In addition, business functions must improve their ability to produce and transmit timely and reliable data. Companies are constantly using Enterprise Resource Planning (ERP) systems to achieve these goals. Order administration, procurement, human resources, financial processes, and delivery with external vendors and consumers are all linked into a closely interconnected environment with common data and accountability as ERP systems are efficiently applied. ERP systems offer smooth synchronization of data as it flows through a company. They deliver on this pledge by incorporating information and evidence-based systems within and through an organization's functional areas, as well as allowing data to be shared across organizational boundaries. The advantages of implementing such a structure are many, starting with the most basic, such as cost savings, efficiency enhancement, and improved efficiency, and include increased customer experience, better resource allocation, improved decision-making and preparation, and organizational empowerment. As a result, economic metrics can be improved, which eventually leads to increased business performance.

Despite the numerous advantages of ERP schemes, statistics indicate that just 30% of previous ERP implementations were successful. Many ERP implementations are complex, to say the least; long and over budget, are dismissed before fulfillment, or fail to meet their market goals even after a year. The ERP project must be closely monitored and the risks associated with the programs must be correctly measured to achieve the expected benefits. The management of an ERP project is a difficult challenge for any organization, but it is particularly difficult for SMEs who lack the necessary capital, skills, and ERP project expertise. Even with substantial time and capital expenditure, there is no certainty of a positive result. Several structured technologies, processes, and procedures have been developed to assist businesses in properly managing their IT programs, but they are often too common for ERP applications. Big organizations are also required to use consultancy, project management, analyze situations, and risk management approaches (RAMs). SMEs have very different needs, operational conditions, logistics fulfillment, and financial resources than major corporations. Targeted control measures are required in this context to assist SMEs with their ERP project.

13.19.1 Main Characteristics of ERP Projects

The disparity between being an ERP project and a basic software project is significant. The majority of development programs are focused on creating a software framework. However, an ERP project is made up of interconnected information frameworks, enterprise processes, and process reengineering. The integrated design of ERP software implementations is a significant distinction between ERP projects and conventional IT projects. To integrate the program with the business operations, an ERP software kit requires a combination of BP changes and software setup. The primary focus of an ERP deployment has turned away from technological research and scripting and toward BP architecture, business-focused software configuration, and legacy data clean-up.

Owing to the vast number of changes it introduces to an organization, an ERP initiative can also be regarded as an organizational transformation project. Many businesses implement ERP solutions without thoroughly comprehending the consequences for their business or the importance of ensuring that the framework is compatible with overall corporate objectives and strategies. Broken programs or weak processes whose reasoning clashes with corporate priorities are the product of this hasty strategy. Often, businesses do not realize the full value of the ERP scheme because they are not organized properly to reap the benefits. Many organizations who want to incorporate an ERP scheme get into problems because the organization isn't ready for incorporation and the different divisions within it have competing goals and priorities.

13.19.2 Risk Factors

ERP ventures that include the whole company are a new type of management problem. The management methods for these projects can vary significantly from those used for standard IT projects. For any scale of business, an ERP project is a large and costly undertaking; however, the risks are greater for SMEs, as cost overruns during execution will place financial pressure on the company and have a significant effect on its success. SMEs also have a lower risk of returning from a botched ERP deployment than big corporations. The most common cause of IT project loss is that software engineers struggle to adequately evaluate and handle the risks that their tasks entail. Furthermore, most project managers see risk management processes as additional labor and cost, because they are often eliminated when a project's timeline falls. Budget overruns, time overruns, project cancellations, weak business efficiency, insufficient system functionality and flexibility, low organizational process fit, low user experience, low degree of alignment and versatility, low strategic target fit, and accounting practices are the major risk effects for SMEs.

ERP threats can be categorized in a variety of ways (for example, Organizational, business-related, technical, entrepreneurial, contractual, and financial risks are defined as the six key dimensions of ERP implementation risks. The context in which the framework is implemented creates organizational risk. The business-related vulnerability stems from the internal and external continuity of the enterprise's comment models, artifacts, and procedures. The operating system, database system, client/server infrastructure, and network are all examples of data processing technology that are needed to run the ERP system. The entrepreneurial or administrative risk stems from the owner or manager's management team's mindset, while contractual risk stems from relationships with investors, and financial risk stems from cash-flow issues, such as the failure to pay licensing fees or upgrade costs.

13.20   RISK MANAGEMENT TOOLS

The RAM determines the most important risks and their likelihood in the sense of the enterprise. The risk list for this analysis was generated using Vilpola's risk list. The danger list is made up of 63 statements or queries about ERP collection, execution, and use.

13.20.1   Risk Analysis Method

The main goal is to recognize ERP threats that arise from the corporation's facts, so workers from all levels of the organization were questioned and examined. In close collaboration with company staff, the corporation risk list was developed. On a scale of one to five, the risk is assessed by measuring the likelihood and impact of each risk. Numbered one denotes a very low likelihood and consequence, while number five denotes a very high likelihood and disastrous effect. The risk aggregation was then used as a risk importance measure. It's determined by multiplying the effect's meaning by the probability's meaning.

13.20.2   Characteristics Analysis Method

The requirements data analysis (CAM) guarantees that an IT project's various priorities, content, and implementation methods are manageable and reliable. The CAM's output is a suggestion on how to break down a big and complicated IT project, such as an ERP project, into manageable subprojects. The CAM ERP project management factors are also significant. The main goal is to determine the scale of the ERP project that the case companies can handle. CAM also makes guidelines on the management elements that should be prioritized to effectively handle ERP projects (overall project management, integration management, project scope management, time management, expense management, etc.). Quality assurance, human resource management (HRM), operational processes, risk management, and purchasing management are also examples of management. The concerns are either positive or negative claims whose suitability to the project would be assessed (0 blame, not valid, 5 exactly right; N/A, not sure). The tool was created as a Microsoft Excel file with automated tabulation based on decision rule sets. The effect can also be effectively connected.

13.20.3   PRODUCT DATA MANAGEMENT

Blast cleaning software is designed by Company A, which also produces automatic blast cleaning devices and robotics. Company A does not have an ERP scheme, but it is considering implementing one shortly. Internal and external, the need for a new ERP system has grown as a result of issues with the existing IT system. Customer relationship (CRM), product data management (PDM), purchase and order management, and product lifetime management are also part of the company's current IT structure, which is built on Excel. The current system's challenge is managing hundreds of various Excel, Word, and AutoCAD document variants and combinations. Company A's goal is to implement an ERP structure that aids production capacity planning and management, allowing scheduling and resource distribution for various projects to be prepared in advance before they begin. Furthermore, the current system would facilitate the procurement process and provide warehouse and stock storage features.

The company's core people have been added to the risk list, and the risks' consequences and likelihood have been measured. The most serious risks in the ERP selection process are miscommunication between an ERP provider and a customer, an ERP scheme that isn't scalable enough, and the lack of definition of special company-specific ERP requirements. The following are the most important threats during the ERP installation phase: a company's project manager is not a full-time PM, data migration from the old to new ERP system is challenging, ERP system synchronization with other IT systems cause's difficulties, and an ERP provider is not dedicated enough to the company's ERP system implementation. The following are the most important threats during the ERP implementation phase: An ERP system does not help a company's operations and the ERP provider has no plans to upgrade the system in the future.

In the RAM performance, the most important considerations in each process (selection, execution, and use) are determined by the company's decision on which ERP system and ERP supplier are used. The most important considerations are those relating to an ERP system's mechanical and practical aspects, as well as those relating to the system's supplier. Even though company A has less staff, the scarcity of resources, qualifications and experience, and other personnel-related considerations have not been identified as possible threats in this study.

HRM, according to CAM, is the management/leadership area that reaches the essential level. In its ERP project management, Company A should pay particular attention to this aspect. Several other management/leadership areas, such as "communications management," "pursue management," and "project management," are also accessible. "The overall mission," "Integration management," "Project scope management," and "Quality management are also important. Just "Cost control," "Time management," and "Risk management' are simply below vital. Lifestyle factors associated with staff planning and growing personnel expertise and experience, according to CAM, demand more from management, even though they are not rated among the most possible risk factors by RAM. Based on the CAM, it is possible to conclude that company A has a thorough view of the ERP project's costs, time spent on it, and technological and organizational risks.

13.20.4   ERP

Company B specializes in steel, paper, chemistry, and ship production machinery and equipment, as well as difficult sheet metal work, welding, and heavy metalwork. Offshore machinery and ship propellers are also produced by the firm. Around 150 people work for company B. The ERP project at Company B is in the selection process. The company's existing IT solutions are nearing the end of their useful lives, and it will need to invest in a decent ERP system. Several ERP vendors have been contacted by the company. The business created a tentative criteria description, which is similar to a demand list, and used it to narrow down prospective ERP vendors to two alternatives. The firm has also employed several IT contractors.

The risk list has been packed with key business personnel, and the risks' consequences and likelihood have been measured. The most significant risks during the ERP procurement process are choosing an ERP solution that is a bad compromise for all stakeholders, selecting an ineffective general contractor or project team, misinterpretations between an ERP provider and an organization, and selecting an ineffective ERP system. The following are the most important threats in the ERP installation phase: normal business disrupts ERP project operations, ERP project disrupts normal business, ERP project is late, Software setup and testing are slow, and an ERP system isn't used in a systematic way. The following are the most important threats during the ERP implementation phase: An ERP method that is not used consistently, and only a portion of the ERP system is used. The conduct, expertise, and IT experience of the staff (including project manager/team and top management level) are the most important factors in the RAM performance. Company B is also concerned with how the proposed ERP system will affect the company's current operations, as well as how the normal operations will impede the ERP project's development.

"Communications strategy," according to CAM, is the management/leadership area that reaches the essential stage. Company B should pay particular attention to the talent, experience, and competence of its employees. Furthermore, "Human capital management" and "Quality management" are at an all-time high. To effectively execute an ERP project, the organization should focus on these three management/leadership considerations.

13.21 SLEEPING IN THE ECONOMIC CLASS AIRCRAFT CUSTOMER SITTING POSITION ANALYSIS

People are finding it easier to fly by plane, thanks to the availability of low-cost flights and the willingness of airlines to accommodate people of all ages and skills. Before flying, health issues may arise as a result of anxiety and lack of understanding with airport departure procedures, while problems may arise during the flight as a result of the meals available onboard, discrepancies in the cabin's environmental factors (pressure, ventilation, moisture content, and vibrations), the risk of cross-infection from fellow passengers, seat position, and posture ado. Differences in geographic locations and family dinners will exacerbate these issues, affecting an individual's wellbeing long after they arrive at their final destination. Traveling by air, particularly over long distances, is not normal human activity. During the flight, many people feel mental and emotional pain, as well as stress. Excessive tension can make passengers offensive, overreact, and even put their health in jeopardy.

Today's commuter places a high value on comfort. The comfort of aircraft passengers is determined by a variety of factors, including the atmosphere in which they fly. Seat comfort is a qualitative problem since the final decision is made by the consumer, and customer reviews are focused on their personal experiences with the seat. The seated passenger on an airplane plays a critical role in meeting passenger satisfaction needs. The seat is a significant part of the vehicle since it is where the occupant spends the majority of his or her time while flying. Since the aviation market is intensely competitive, airlines strive to increase the number of seats available. People on the plane's boarding room are often severely restricted as a result of this, particularly in economy class. We defined subjective and quantitative measurements to study sleeping in a sitting position of economy class airline passengers in this article.

13.21.1 Aircraft Seat

One of the most critical aspects of ride comfort is the seat. Seatbelt extender aspects must be observed and accounted for in the demand for health. The two least desirable characteristics of charter and economy class are "seat comfort' and "leg space'.

The Civil Aviation Authority (CAA) is the governing body in charge of aircraft seat spacing safety rules. The rules are based on the reliability of aircraft seating in the event of a collision and the convenience with which passengers should be evacuated in the event of a disaster. In airplanes, there are three types of seat positions: windshield, aisle, and separated. One of the toughest features of economy air travel is the sense of being surrounded by travelers sitting in the center of three or more seat rows.

The bubble is a seat concept developed by InNova. The design's breakthrough is to move hand luggage beneath the seat, removing the need for overhead compartments and thereby increasing the passenger's sense of room by increasing the tunnel effect. The ICON seating system was created by B/E Aerospace. The passenger will sleep in a variety of positions thanks to the shifting seat board, like back and side sleeper. Leg support in a side sleep position can be provided by adjusting the side support wings on the seatback. Passengers in ICON seating have complete control of their convenience and personal space.

The pneumatic mattresses comfort device for aircraft seats was established by a Swiss firm. Traditional foams have been replaced by air-filled chambers in the current design. Passengers will tailor the seat's compressed air to their preferences, ranging from hard when sitting upright to mild when comfortable to gentle when completely flat.

13.21.2   RELATIONSHIP OF SUBJECTIVE METHOD TO COMFORT AND DISCOMFORT

Seat makers have chosen to focus on subjective assessments as the primary measure of protection from unfairness due to a lack of validated objective indicators. Seat manufacturers devised in-depth subjective assessment procedures, which included highly structured survey questions. In the survey questions, passengers are asked to attribute their dissatisfaction to a particular seat area. Subjective ratings are produced by the questionnaires, which usually have numeric scales (e.g., one very unpleasant to ten very comfortable) and are converted into evaluation requirement gathering. A well-designed questionnaire is important because it provides researchers with a tool with which to test hypotheses.

The tractor seat comfort was measured using a ten-point scale in the analysis. From technology and biomechanical standpoint, the job is to project the most suitable method of assessing and selecting tractor seats. To investigate the relationship between spine and back pain, used a visual analog scale to measure local discomfort. To gain average scores of relaxations and pain for the entire body, a visual body mapping analog scale is used.

13.21.3   OBSERVATION ON SLEEPING POSTURE

The key goal of the study is to learn more about sleeping in a sitting position and the sleeping activity of seated economy class passengers on long-haul flights. The study was carried out on a long-distance flight from Amsterdam, the Netherlands, to Kuala Lumpur, Malaysia. The journey took 12 hours to complete. The re-searcher recorded the passengers' activities within his visual range. In the study, fifteen people were chosen, eight of whom were female and seven of whom were male. The participants ranged in age from 19 to 62 years old. The average age of the participants was 28 years old.

Seven separate sleeping positions were established based on the observation findings. A ground policy on sleeping conduct of economy class passengers in a sitting posture was developed after observation on a long-haul flight.

There are four general sitting positions and one free sitting position in the sleeping position protocol. The procedure for sleeping in a sitting posture is as follows:

- Stand in a neutral place
- Sit in a neutral place on the bench

Using a pillow

- With pillow (between arms and chest) (without a pillow) assisted with hand (between arms and chest)
- Torso sitting posture (head in diagonal with backrest) with cushion without a cushion (head at an angle to the backrest) as perpendicular to backrest (head lying on headrest)

13.21.4 OBJECTIVE ANALYSIS ON SITTING POSTURE WHILE SLEEPING

The objective method aims to quantify and verify the sleeping in sitting procedure, which is dependent on evaluation. A low-cost aircraft cabin simulator was used to perform the objective study.

The low-cost plane cabin simulation is a testing ground created for a European initiative called SEAT (Smart technologies for Stress-free Air Travel). Via the incorporation of cabin structures with interactive features, the SEAT project seeks to create a new radical solution. We developed and installed the aircraft cabin simulator from the ground up. A small-scale cabin-like research area, an inventory area, a simulation section, and a control section make up the simulator. There is an economy class section, a business class section, a galley, and a lavatory in the aircraft cabin.

The experiment was carried out separately for each individual. The experiment protocol and regulations were explained to the subject before the experiment. The person sat in the adjusted seat for 30 seconds while interpreting the ten seating positions from the protocol. When the subject indicated that he or she was in the right sitting posture, the calculation began. A microcontroller was used to quantify each location. The stance measurement was done with a force-sensitive resistor (FSR). It depicts the experimental setup for detecting seated human posture.

13.22   CONCLUSION

A standard laboratory setting allowing systemic assessments of performances of accessible wireless network technology in IEEE802.11 a, b, point-to-point networks are being constructed in the present study. At OSI level 1, 802.11 g and 802.11 were the best SNR values, while at 802.11 were the lowest point of sound. Investigations at OSI levels 3 and 4 allowed better network usage percentages to be determined under communicational quality parameters. There has been some susceptibility to the AP type. The maximum level of network usage under quality parameters decreased for each standard, with the constant connection speed decreasing. The subnet turnover system is a revolutionary mobile IP system that can move the wireless subnet in its whole with ridiculous speeds. There is a multi-hop separation between both the MN and underground exits. The technology is used to communicate with the public transit system and is prospective for many wireless phone applications, for example, data transfer and a subscription service for train and aviation passengers. PROMES was created by several of the authors of this publication amongst others as a regional atmospheric mesoscale simulation. However, both instances warrant the usage of concurrency due to the long time consumed by the PROMES code and the need for more precise findings.

References

1. Barr, RE, Krueger, TJ, and Aanstoos, TA (2002). The new digital engineering design and graphics process. *Eng. Des. Graphics J.* 66(3), 6–11.
2. Bechthold, M, Griggs, K, Kao, K, and Steinberg, M (2004). Digital design and manufacturing: CAD/CAM. *Appl. Archit.* 9(2), 54–58.
3. Berkun, S (2000). Why good design comes from bad design. *Computer. Aided Des. J.* 9(12), 1312–1316.
4. Caddaz, S and Di Monaco F (2007). The future and the evolution of CAD. *In14th International Research/Expert Conference: Trends in the Development of Machinery and Associated technology. Mediterr. Cruise* 9(3), 108–112.
5. Clark, AC (2005). Technical animation: A new concept for the engineering design graphics discipline. *Eng. Des. Graphics* 69(3), 14–23.
6. Collins, D (2006). Visualizing 3D: Between measurement and illusion; a PowerPoint presentation from Arizona State University about PRISM. Retrieved from the World Wide Web on November 1, 2006: http://vizproto.prism.asu.edu/modeling/visualing3D 2-06.ppt.
7. Evolution Computing Website (2007). Retrieved from the World Wide Web on Jannuary 3, 2007.
8. Fallon, K (1998). Early computer graphics developments in the architecture, engineering, and construction industry. *IEEE Annu. History Comput.* 20(2), 20–29.
9. Fowlkes, WY, Creveling, CM, and Derimiggio, J (1995). *Engineering Methods for Robust Product Design: Using Taguchi Methods in Technology and Product Development.* Reading: Addison-Wesley 10(4), 41–46.
10. Frederick, M (2007). Engineering design graphics. *Eng. Des. Graphics J.* 71(3), 20–25.
11. Gorissen, D, Couckuyt, I, Demeester, P, Dhaene, T, and Crombecq, K (2010). A surrogate modeling and adaptive sampling toolbox for computer-based design. *J. Mach. Learn. Res.* 99:2051–2055.
12. Harris La, VA and Meyers, F (2007). Principles of algebraic geometry. *Eng. Des. Graphics J.* 81(3), 09–23.
13. Harris, LV and Sadowski, MA (2001). Alternatives for saving and viewing CAD graphics for the Web. *Eng. Des. Graphics J.* 65(1, Winter), 14–18.
14. Herrera, R (1998). Problems encountered when substituting the traditional drawing tools for CAD systems in engineering graphics courses. 16(1), 677–680.
15. Hertenstein, JH, Platt, MB, and Veryzer RW (2005). The impact of industrial design effectiveness on corporate financial performance. *J. Prod. Innov. Manage.* 22(1), 3–21. rs of bupivacaine. *Br. J. Clin. Pharmacol.* 6(1), 63–68.
16. Kao, YC and Lin, GC (1998). Development of a collaborative CAD/CAM system. *Robot. Compu. Integr. Manuf.* 14(1), 55–68.
17. Kelly, C (2007). Interview with the regional sales director for CGK & associates and consultant in the emerging 3D and interactive simulation markets. 9(2), 30–35.
18. Kirton, EF and Lavoie SD (2006). Utilizing rapid prototyping for architectural modeling. *Eng. Des. Graphics J.* 70(1), 23–28.
19. Kaswan, KS and Dhatterwal, JS (2020). *Big Data: An Introduction.* Shashwat Publication. ISBN No. 978-93-90290-31-4 (https://shashwatpublication.com/books/big-data).
20. Land, H, Schütz, G, Schmale, H, and Richter, D (1976). Nucleotide sequence of cloned cDNA encoding bovine arginine vasopressin–neurophysin II precursor. *Nature* 295(5847): 299–303.
21. Cheng, MY, Tsai, HC, Hsieh, and WS (2008). Web-based conceptual cost estimates for construction projects using evolutionary Fuzzy neural inference model. Automation in Construction
22. Yu, WD, Lai, CC, and Lee, WI (2008). A WICE approach to real-time construction cost estimation; Moon, SW, Kim, JS, Kwon, KN (2008). Effectiveness of OLAP-based cost data management in construction cost estimate.
23. Shi, H and Li, W (2008). The integrated methodology of rough set theory and artificial neural network for construction project cost prediction. In: *Second International Symposium on Intelligent Information Technology Application*, December 2008, pp. 60–64.
24. Pawlak, Z (1994). *Rough Sets-Theoretical Aspects of Reasoning about Data.* New York: Klystron Academic Publisher.

25. Kennedy, J (1997). The particle swarm: social adaptation of knowledge. In *Proceedings of the 1997 International Conference on Evolutionary Computation*, Indianapolis, pp. 303–308.

26. Ahn, B, Cho, S, and Kim, C (2000). The integrated methodology of rough-set theory and artificial neural-network for business failure prediction. *Expert Syst. Appl.* 18(2), 65–74.

27. Arditi, D and Suh, K (1991). Expert system for cost estimating software selection. *Cost Eng.* 33(6), 9–19.

28. Chau, KW (2007). Application of a PSO-based neural network in analysis of outcomes of construction claims. *Autom. Constr.* 16, 642–646; Martin, D (1977). Early warning of bank failure: A logit regression approach. *J. Banking Finance* 1(3), 249–276.

29. Ling, Z and Jialin, Z (2000). Development of credit risk measurement methodology. *Forecasting* 19, 72–75.

30. Yatao, Z (2002). A comparative analysis of the model for measurement of credit risks. *J. Shanxi Finance Econ. Univ.* 24, 107–108.

31. Kaswan, KS and Dhatterwal, JS (2022). Machine learning and deep learning algorithms for IoD. In: *Internet of Drones: Opportunities and Challenges*. Apple Academic Press (AAP): Canada. ISBN: 9781774639856.

32. Zhengming, Q and Weiyan, C (1999). The appraisal of indicators of industry economic results and a case study in terms of method of principal components. *Stat. Res.* 7, 49–52.

33. Green, PJ and Silverman, BW (1994). *Nonparametric Regression and Generalized Linear Models*, pp. 145–189. Chapman and Hall: London.

34. Fischer, B and Hegland, M (1999). Collocation, filtering and nonparametric regression, part. *ZfV* 1, 17–24.

35. Shi, PD and Tsai, CL (1999). Semiparametric regression model selections. *J. Stati. Plan. Infer.* 77, 119–139.

36. Hong, SY (2005). Normal approximation rate and bias reduction for data-driven kernel smoothing estimator in a semiparametric regression model. *J. Multi. Analy.* 80, 1–20.

37. Sugiyama, M and gawa, HO (2002). A unified method for optimizing linear image restoration filters. *Signal Proce.* 82, 1773–1787.

38. Aerts, M, Claeskens, G, and Wand, MP (2002). Some theory for penalized spline generalized additive models. *J. Stati. Plan. Infer.* 103, 445–470.

39. Wang, QH and Rao, K (2002). Emprirical likelihood-based inference in linear errors-in-covariables models with validation data. *Biometrika* 89, 345–358.

40. Ruppert, D, Wand, MP, and Carroll, RJ (2003). *Semiparametric Regression*, pp. 271–320. Cambridge University Press: Cambridge.

41. Agrawal, R, Imielinski, T, and Swami, A (1993). Mining association rules between sets of items in very large databases. *In Proceedings of the ACM SIGMOD Conference*, pp. 207–216.

42. Kaswan, KS and Dhatterwal, JS (2020). The use of machine learning sustainable and resilient buildings. In: *Digital Cities Roadmap: IoT-Based Architecture and Sustainable Buildings*. John Wiley & Sons: Hoboken, NJ. ISBN: 978-1-119-79159-1.

43. Mannila, H, Toivonen, H, and Verkamo, A (1994). Efficientalgorithm for discovering association rules. *In AAAI Workshop on Knowledge Discovery in Databases*, pp. 181–192.

44. Toivonen, H (1996). Sampling large databases for association rules. *In Proceedings of the 22nd VLDB Conference*, Mumbai (Bombay), India.

45. Park, JS, Chen, MS, and Yu, PS (1995). An effective hash-based algorithm for mining asociation rules. *In Proceedings of the 1995 ACM SIGMOD International Conference*, pp. 175–186.

46. Bida, M and Kreider, JF (1987). Monthly-averaged cooling load calculations-residential and small commercial buildings. *J. Sol. Energy Eng. Trans. ASME* 109(4), 311–320.

47. Al-Rabghi Omar, MA and Al-Johani Khalid, M (1997). Utilizing transfer function method for hourly cooling load calculation. *Energy Convers. Manage.* 38(4), 319–332.

48. Ben-Nakhi Abdullatif, E and Mahmoud Mohamed, A (2004). Cooling load prediction for buildings using general regression neural networks. *Energy Convers. Manage.* 45(13–14), 2127–2141.

49. Mui, KW and Wong, LT (2007). Cooling load calculations in subtropical climate. *Build Environ.* 42(7), 2498–2504.

50. Jorng, TH and Ching, CY (2000). Applying genetic algorithms to query optimization in document retrieval. *Inf. Process. Manage.* 36, 737–759.

51. Punch, WF and Goodman, ED (1993). Further research on feature selection and classification using genetic algorithm. *In Proceedings of the Fifth International Conference on Genetic Algorithm*, Morgan Kaufmann, San Mateo, pp. 557–564.

52. Pietramala, A, Policicchio, VL, Rullo and P, Sidhu, I (2008). A genetic algorithm for text classification rule induction. In: Daelemans, W, Goethals, B, and Morik, K (eds.) *ECML PKDD 2008, Part II. LNCS (LNAI)*, vol. 5212, pp. 188–203. Springer, Heidelberg.

53. Kudo, M and Sklansky, K (2000). Comparison of algorithms that select feature for pattern classifier. *Pattern Recognit.* 33(2), 25–41.

54. Moon, H and Phillips, PJ (2001). Computational and performance aspects of PCA-based face recognition algorithms. *Perception* 30, 303–321.

55. Chen, X, Gu, L, Li, SZ and Zhang, HJ (2001). Learning representative local features for face detection. *In 2001 IEEE Computer Society Conference on Computer Vision and Pattern Recognition*, vol. 1, pp. 1126–1131.

56. van der Schaar, M, Chen, Y, and Radha, H (2000). Embedded DCT and wavelet methods for scalable video: Analysis and comparison. *Visual Communications and Image Processing.*

57. Yang, Y and Xuping, Z (2006). General theory research on morphological correlation for Gray2Scale face recognition. *Acta Photonica Sinica* 35(2), 299–303.

58. Ryu, H, Yoon, JC, Chun, SS, and Sull, S (2006). Coarse-to-fine classification for image-based face detection. In: Sundaram, H, Naphade, M, Smith, JR, and Rui, Y (eds.) *CIVR 2006. LNCS*, vol. 4071, pp. 291–299. Springer, Heidelberg.

59. Zabele, S, Dorsch, M, Ge, Z, et al. (2002). SANDS: Specialized active networking for distributed simulation. *In Proceedings of the 2002 DARPA Active Networks Conference and Exposition*, Washington, DC, pp. 356–365, IEEE Computer Society.

60. Sun, YH, Gong, ZY, Li, H, et al. (2003). Research on scalable active interest management. *J. Image Graphics 8A(SPEC)*, 771–775 (in Chinese with English abstract).

61. Simulation Interoperability Standards Committee (SISC) (2000). *IEEE Computer Society IEEE Standard for Modeling and Simulation (M&S) High Level Architecture (HLA)-IEEE Std 1516.1-2000*. Institute of Electrical and Electronics Engineers, Inc., New York.

62. Chrislip, CA (1995). Level of detail models for dismounted infantry in NPSNET-IV.8.1. Ph.D. Thesis, Naval Postgraduate School, Monterey, California.

63. Carlson, DA and Hodgins, JK (1997). Simulation levels of detail for real-time animation. In: Davis, WA, Mantei, M, and Klassen, RV (eds.) *Proceedings of the Conference on Graphics Interface*, pp. 1–8. Canadian Information Processing Society: Toronto.

64. Pylyshyn, ZW (1984). *Computation and Cognition: Towards a Foundation for Cognitive Science*. MIT Press: Cambridge.

65. Elizabeth, SP, Emma, JH, and Michael, M (2005). Measuring emotional processes in animals: The utility of a cognitive approach. *Neurosci. Biobehav. Rev.* 29, 469–491.

66. Jones, MJ and Rehg, JM (2002). Statistical color models with application to skin detection. *Int. J. Compu. Vision* 46(1), 81–96.

67. Aamodt, A and Plaza, E (1994). Case-based reasoning: Foundational issues, methodological variations and system approaches. *AI Commun. ECCAI* 7(1), 35–39.

68. Simaan, AR (2010). Role of simulation in construction engineering and management. *J Constr. Eng. Manage.* 136(10), S1140–S1153.

69. Bertel S, Barkowsky T, Engel D, and Freksa C (2006). Computational modeling of reasoning with mental images: Basic requirements. *Proceedings of 7th International Conference on Cognitive Modeling, Edizioni Goliardiche, Trieste*, Trieste, Italy, 50–55.

70. Busslinger, M (2009). Landslide time-forecast methods, HSR University of Applied Sciences Institute für Bau und Umwelt. Report, Rapperswil, Switzerland.

71. Bennett, J and Ormerod, RN (1984). Simulation applied to construction projects. *Constr. Manage. Econ.* 2(3), 225–263.

72. Compton, M, Neuhaus, H, Taylor, K, and Tran, K (2009). Reasoning about Sensors and Compositions. *In Proceedings of the 2nd International Workshop on Semantic Sensor Networks (SSN09) at ISWC 2009*, pp. 33–48.

73. Cunningham, P (2008). Dimension reduction. In Cord, M and Cunningham, P (eds.). *Machinel Earning Techniques for Multimedia: Case Studies on Organization and Re-trieval*. Springer: Berlin.

74. De Freitas, S and Oliver, M (2006). How can exploratory learning with games and simulations within the curriculum be most effectively evaluated? *Compu. Educ.* 46, 249–264.

75. Freksa, C (1991). Qualitative spatial reasoning. In: Mark, DM and Frank, AU (eds). *Cognitive and Linguistic Aspects of Geographic Space*, pp. 361–372. Kluwer Academic Publishers: Dordrecht.

76. Fukuzono, T (1985). A new method for predicting the failure time of a slope. *Proceedings of the IVth International Conference and Field Workshop on Landslides*, Tokyo, Japan.

77. Fukuzono, T (1987). Experimental study of slope failure caused by heavy rainfall. *Proceedings of the International Symposium on Erosion and Sedimentation: Pacific Rim*, Oregon, USA.
78. Gruber, TR (1993). A translation approach to portable ontology specifications. Knowledge Creation Diffusion Utilization.
79. Lakoff, G and Johnson, M (1999). *Philosophy in the Flesh: The Embodied Mind and Its Challenge to Western Thought, Basic Books*. Perseus Books Group: New York.
80. Gibson, JJ (1977). The theory of affordances. In: Shaw, R and Brachman, RJ (eds). *Perceiving, Acting, and Knowing: Toward and Ecological Psychology*, p. 492. Lawrence Erlbaum Associates: Hillsdale, NJ.
81. Gaschnig, J. et al. (1981), Development of knowledge -based system for water resources problems, Technical Report SRI project 1619, SRI International.
82. Getchell, K, Miller, A, Nicoll, R, Sweetman, R and Allison, C (2010). Games methodologies and immersive environments for virtual fieldwork. *IEEE Trans. Learn. Tech.* 3(4), 281–293.
83. Hobbs JR (2002). Granularity, Artificial Intelligence Center SRI and Center for the Study of Language and Information. Stanford University, 10.
84. Han, S, Lee, S, and Peña-M ora, F (2011). Application of dimension reduction techniques for motion recognition: Construction worker behavior monitoring. *2011 ASCE International Workshop on Computing in Civil Engineering*, Florida, USA.
85. Ji, SH. et al. (2011). Cost estimation model for building projects using case-based reasoning. *Can. J. Civil Eng. CSCE*, 38(5), 570–581.
86. Jaafari, A, Manivong, KK, and Chaaya, M (2001). VIRCON: Interactive system for teaching construction management. *J. Constr. Eng. Manage.* 127, 66–75.
87. Li, C and Lee, S (2011). Computer vision techniques for worker motion analysis to reduce musculoskeletal disorders in construction. *In 2011 ASCE International Workshop on Computing in Civil Engineering*, Florida, USA.
88. Kugler, M, Kordi, B, Franz, V, and Samkari, K (2011). Linking product and process data in the modeling environment 'CiSmo'. *In Proceedings of the 11th International Conference on Construction Applications of Virtual Reality*.
89. Macal, CM, North, MJ (2011). Introductory tutorial: Agent-based modeling and simulation. *In Proceedings of the 2011 Winter Simulation Conference*.
90. Open Geospatial Consortium (OGC) Inc. (2007). Open GIS® sensor model language (sensor ML) implementation specification.
91. PCI Committee on Tolerance (2000). Tolerance manual for precast and prestressed concrete construction. Precast/Prestressed Concrete Institute.
92. Park, MS, et al. (2010). Schematic cost estimation method using case-based reasoning: Focusing on determining attribute weight. *J Korea Inst. Constr. Eng. Manag. KICEM* 11(4), 22–31.
93. Russomanno, DJ, Kothari, C, and Thomas, O (2005). Sensor ontologies: From shallow to deep models. *Proceedings of the Thirty-Seventh Southeastern Symposium on System Theory*.
94. Rajagopal A, Dembia CL, DeMers MS, Delp DD, Hicks JL, and Delp SL (2016). Full-body musculo skeletal model for muscle-driven simulation of human gait. *IEEE Trans. Biomed. Eng.* 63(10), 2068–2079.
95. Rubin, SH (1996). Computer-assisted instruction in engineering education and training. *Compu. Ind. Eng.* 30(4), 765–779.
96. Sowa, JF (1999). *Knowledge Representation: Logical, Philosophical, and Computational Foundations*. Brooks Cole Publishing Co: Pacific Grove, CA.
97. Kaswan, KS, Dhatterwal, JS, and Preeti, K (2020). Intelligent agent based case base reasoning systems build knowledge representation in COVID-19 analysis of recovery infectious patients. In: *Application of AI in COVID 19*, Medical Virology: From Pathogenesis to Disease Control. Springer. ISBN: 978-981-15-7317-0 (e-Book).
98. Srinivasan, S, Singh, J, and Kumar, V (2011). Multi-agent based decision support system using data mining and case based reasoning. *IJCSI Int. J. Compu. Sci. Issues* 8(4). ISSN (Online): 1694-0814.
99. W3C Incubator Group (2010). Semantic sensor network XG final report.
100. Wojtusch, J, Von Stryk, O, and HuMo, D (2015). A versatile and open database for the investigation, modeling, and simulation of human motion dynamics on actuation level. *In IEEE-RAS International Conference on Humanoid Robots, 2015-DECEM*, IEEE, pp. 74–79. ISBN: 9781479968855.
101. Waterman, D (1986). *A Guide to Expert Systems*. Addison-Wesley: Boston, MA.
102. Wong, JMW, Chan, APC, and Chiang, YH (2010). Modeling construction occupational demand: Case of Hong Kong. *J. Constr. Eng. Manage.*, 991–1002.
103. Wooldridge, M (2002). *An Introduction to Multi Agent Systems*. John Wiley & Sons, Ltd.: West Sussex, England.

104. Ahmed, MT, Dailey, MN, Landabaso, JL, and Herrero, N (2010). Robust key frame extraction for 3D reconstruction from video streams. *Proceedings of the VISAPP*, 231–236.
105. ASHRAE (2005). The Commissioning Process. ASHRAE Guidelines 0-2005, ASHRAE Inc.
106. Anastasiya Yurchyshyna, Alain Zarli (2009). An ontology-based approach for formalisation and semantic organisation of conformance requirements in construction. *Autom. Constr.* 18, 1084–1098.
107. Akcamete, A, Akinci, B, and Garrett, JH, Jr (2010). Potential utilization of building information models for planning maintenance activities. *In Proceedings from The International Conference on Computing in Civil and Building Engineering 2010*, Nottingham, UK, 2010.
108. Andersen, P (1997). A theory of computer semiotics: semiotic approaches to construction and assessment of computer systems. Cambridge series on human computer interaction. Cambridge University Press.
109. Bartoli, A, and Sturm, P (2004). Multiple -view structure and motion from line correspondences. *Procedings of IEEE ICCV*, pp. 207–212.
110. Bay, H, Ferrari, V, and Van Gool, L (2005). Wide-baseline stereo matching with line segments. *Proceedings of IEEE CVPR*, pp. 329–336.
111. Bay, H, Ess, A, Tuytelaars, T, and Gool, LV (2008). Speeded-up robust features (SURF). *Compu. Vision Image Understanding* 110(3), 346–359.
112. BimServer.org (2011). BimServer.org Documentation.
113. Brucker, B, Case, M, East, W, Hustone, B, Nachtighal, S, Shickley, J, Spangler, S, and Wilson, J (2006). Building information modeling (BIM): A roadmap for implementation to support MILCON transformation and civil works projects within the US Army Corps of Engineers. Bureau of Labor Statistics (BLS).
114. Borg, G, and Ottoson, D (1986). The perception of exertion in physical work. *Proceedings of a Symposium at the Wenner-Gren Center, 1985 Macmillan, Computer Integrated Construction (CIC) Research Group*. BIM project execution planning guide, Pennsylvania State University.
115. Cotts, D, Roper, K, and Payant, R (2010). *The Facility Management Handbook*, Third Edition. American Management Association: New York.
116. Chomsky, N (1957). *Syntactic Structures*. The Hague/Paris: Mouton.
117. Chandraker, M, Lim, J, and Kriegman, D (2009). Moving in stereo: efficient structure and motion using lines. *Proceedings of IEEE 12th ICCV*, Kyoto, 1741–1748.
118. Crete, F, Dolmiere, T, Ladret, P, and Nicolas, M (2007). The blur effect: Perception and estimation with a new no- reference perceptual blur metric. In: Rogowitz, BE, Pappas, TN and Daly, SJ (eds). *Proceedings of the SPIE*, p. 64920I. *The VA BIM Guide*. Department of Veterans Affairs, Washingdon, DC.
119. Haynes, D (2009). A tale of two exhibits a comparison of the CD301 and E3202 BIM exhibits. Pepe & Hazaed LLP Construction Watch, No. 3-09.
120. Eastman, CM, Panushev, I, Sacks, R, Venugopal, M, Aram, V, and See, R (2011). A guide for development and preparation of a national BIM exchange standard, building SMART Report.
121. EDM (2009). EXPRESS data manager, EPM Technology.
122. East, E and Nisbet, N (2009). Lightweight capture of as: Build construction information. *Proceedings of the CIB W78 2011: 26th International Conference*.
123. FMI Corporation (2007). *FMI/CMAA Eighth Annual Survey of Owners: The Perfect Storm Construction Style*. FMI Corporation: North Carolina.
124. Groome, C (2007). IFC 2x certification: Agreed procedure, *Building SMART international, IC* 07/002.
125. General Services Administration (GSA) Public Buildings Service Office of the Chief Architect (2006). GSA building information modeling guide series 01- GSA BIM guide overview.
126. General Services Administration (GSA) Public Buildings Service Office of the Chief Architect (2011). GSA building information modeling guide series 08- GSA BIM guide for facilities management.
127. Hartmann, T and Fischer, M (2007). Supporting the constructability review with 3d/4d models. *Build. Res. Inf.* 35(1), 70–80.
128. Hietanen, J (2006). IFC model vie w definition format, Technical Report, Citeseer.
129. ISO (2006). ISO/IEC 19757-3:2006 Information technology: Document Schema Definition Language (DSDL) -- Part 3: Rule-based validation -- Schema Tron, International Organization for Standardization.
130. Kamat, VR, Martinez, JC, Fischer, M, Golparvar- Fard, M, Pena -Mora, F, and Savarese, S (2011). Research in visualization techniques for field construction. *J. Constr. Eng. Manage.* 137(10), 853–862.
131. Lowe, D (2004). Distinctive image features from scale-invariant key points. *IJCV* 60(2), 91–110.
132. Mahalingam, A, Kashyap, R, and Mahajan, C (2010). An evaluation of the applicability of 4D cad on construction projects. *Autom. Constr.* 19(2), 148–159.

133. McGraw Hill Construction (2008). Building information modelling (BIM) transforming design and construction to achieve greater industry productivity, McGraw - Hill Construction Smart Market Report, McGraw Hill: New York.

134. McGraw Hill Construction (2009). The business value of BIM: Getting building information modelling to the bottom line, McGraw -Hill Construction Smart Market Report, McGraw Hill: New York.

135. Nister, D (2004). An efficient solution to the five-point relative pose problem. *IEEE PAMI* 26(6), 756–770.

136. Nisbet, N (2008). COBIE data import/export interoperability with the MAXIMO computerized maintenance management system, US Army Corps of Engineers E RDC/CERL CR-08-1.

137. Oglesby, CH, Parker, HW, and Howell, GA (1989). *Productivity Improvement in Construction*. McGraw-Hill: New York.

138. Pradeep, V, and Lim, J (2010). Egomotion using assorted features. *Proceedings of IEEE C VPR*, 1514–1521.

139. Pollefeys, M, et al. (2008). Detailed real-time urban 3D reconstruction from video.

140. PCI NBIMS (2012). Precast BIM standard project for implementers.

141. Reilly, M (2010). The business of BIM' reviews business challenges, benefits of BIM adoption.

142. Seo, YH, Kim, SH, Doo, KS, and Choi, JS (2008). Optimal key frame selection algorithm for three -dimensional reconstruction in uncelebrated multiple images. *J. Soc. Photo-Opt. Instrum. Eng.* 47(5), 53201–53400.

143. Schmid, C, and Zisserman, A (2000). The geometry and matching of lines and curves over multiple views. *IJCV* 40(3), 199–233.

144. Schindler, G, Krishnamurthy, P, and Dellaert, F (2006). Line-based structure from motion for urban environments. *Proceedings of 3rd Symposium on 3D Data Processing, Visualization, and Transmission*, 846–853.

145. Sowa, SJ (2007). Chapter 2. In: Pietarinen, AV (ed). *Game Theory and Linguistic Meaning*, pp. 17–37. Elsevier: Amsterdam, Netherlands.

146. Sowa, JF (2004). Graphics and languages for the flexible modular framework. In: Wolff, KE, Pfeiffer, HD, and Delugach, HS (eds). *Conceptual Structures at Work*, LNAI 3127, pp. 31–51. Springer-Verlag, Berlin.

147. Tardif, M (2010). Building information modeling: The challenges and opportunities for building owners. Owner's Perspective Summer 2010, 8–11.

148. Tomono, M (2009). Robust 3D SLAM with a stereo camera based on an edge-point ICP algorithm. *Proceedings of IEEE International Conference on Robotics and Automation*, Kobe, Japan, 12–17.

149. Torr, PHS, Fitzgibbon, AW, and Zisserman, A (1998). Maintaining multiple motion model hypotheses over many views to recover matching and structure. In *Proceedings of the 6th International Conference on Computer Vision*, Bombay, India, 485–491.

150. Turkaslan -Bulbul, MT, and Akin, O (2006). Computational support for building evaluation: Embedded commissioning model. *Autom. Constr.* Elsevier, 15(4), 438–447.

151. Venugopal, M, Eastman, CM, Sacks, R, Teizer, J (2012). Semantics of model views for information exchanges using the industry foundation class schema. *Adv Eng Inf.* (in press).

152. Wang, Z, Wu, F, and Hu, Z (2009). MSLD: A robust descriptor for line matching. *Pattern Recognition* 42, 941–953.

153. Young, N, Jones, S, Bernstein, H, and Gudgel, J, (2009). The business value of BIM: Getting building information modelling to the bottom line. Technical Report, The McGraw – Hill Companies, New York.

154. Yee, P, Matta, C, Kam, C Hagan, S, and Valdimarsson, O (2010). The GSA BIM story.

155. Zhu, Z, and Brilakis, I (2009). Comparison of optical-sensor -based spatial data collection techniques for civil infrastructure modelling. *J. Compu. Civil Eng.* 23(3), 170–177; *Int. J. Compu. Vision* 78(2–3), 143–167.

156. Astrand, I (1967). Degree of strain during building work as related to individual aerobic work capacity. *Ergonomics* 10(3), 293–303.

157. Abdelhamid, TS, and Everett, JG (1999). Physiological demands of concrete slab placing and finishing work. *J. Constr. Eng. Manage.* 125(1), 47–52.

158. Ainslie, PN, Reilly, T, and Westerterp, K (2003). Estimating human energy expenditure: A review of techniques with particular reference to doubly labelled water. *Sports Med.* 33(9), 683–698.

159. ASCE (2011). Structural identification of constructed facilities. Structural Identification Committee, American Society of Civil Engineers.

160. Bansal, GD and Saxena, BK (1979). Evaluation of spatial illuminance in buildings. *Energy Build.* 2(3), 179–184.

161. Burns, SA, Liu, L, and Feng, C (1996). The LP/IP hybrid method for construction time -cost trade -off analysis. *Constr. Manage. Econ.* 14, 265–276.

162. Behzadan, AH, Aziz, Z, Anumba, CJ, and Kamat, VR (2008). Ubiquitous location tracking for context-specific information delivery on construction sites. *Autom. Constr.* 17(6), 737–748.

163. Berges, M, Goldman, E, Matthews, HS, and Soibelman, L (2009). Learning systems for electric consumption of buildings. International Workshop on Computing in Civil Engineering 2009, ASCE.

164. Berges, M, Goldman, E, Matthews, HS, Soibelman, L, and Anderson, K (2011). User-centered non-intrusive electricity load monitoring for residential buildings. *J. Comput. Civ. Eng.*

165. Bianchini, A, Bandini, P, and Smith, DW (2010). Interrater reliability of manual pavement distress evaluations. *J. Transp. Eng.* 136(2), 165–172.

166. Chang, KT, Chang, JR, and Liu, JK (2005). Detection of pavement distresses using 3D laser scanning technology. *In Proceedings of ASCE International Conference on Computing in Civil Enginereing*, pp. 105–115.

167. Darby, S (2006). The effectiveness of feedback on energy consumption. Technical Report, Environmental Change Institute, University of Oxford.

168. Eriksson, J, Girod, L, Hull, B, Newton, R, Madden, S, and Balakrishnan, H (2008). The pothole patrol: Using a mobile sensor network for road surface monitoring. *In Proceedings of Mobi Systeam*, 29–39.

169. Federal Highway Administration (2009). LTPP–beyond FY 2009: What needs to be done? Technical Report No. FHWA-HRT-09-052.

170. Fugro Roadware (2011). Application: Pavement condition assessment. Data sheets available at http://www.fugroroadware.com/related/english-alldatasheets (Last Accessed November 2011).

171. Goulet, JA, Kripakaran, P, and Smith, IFC (2010). Multi-model structural performance monitoring. *J. Struct. Eng.* 136(10), 1309–1318; Georgia Department of Transportation (2011). Pavement Preservation in Georgia (Last Accessed July 2011).

172. Heckbert, PS (1990). Adaptive radiosity textures for bidirectional ray tracing. *ACM SIGGRAPH Compu. Graphics* 24(4), 145–154.

173. Hart, GW (1992). Nonintrusive appliance load monitoring. *Proc. IEEE* 80(12), 1870–1891.

174. Huizenga, C (2011). LBNL window and daylighting software--WINDOW 6. http://windows.lbl.gov/software/window/6/index.html.

175. Jin, Y, Telebakemi, E, Berges, M, and Soibelman, L (2011). A time - frequency approach for event detection in non-intrusive load monitoring. *Signal Processing, Sensor Fusion, and Target Recognition XX*, April 25, 2011- April 27, SPIE, Orlando, FL, The Society of Photo- Optical Instrumentation Engineers (SPIE).

176. Jahanshahi, MR and Masri, SF (2012). Adaptive vision-based crack detection using 3D scene reconstruction for condition assessment of structures. *Autom. Constr.* DOI: 10.1016/j.autcon.2011.11.018.

177. Karuppuswamy, J, Selvaraj, V, Ganesh, MM, and Hall, EL (2000). Detection and Avoidance of Simulated Potholes in Autonomous Vehicle Navigation in an Unstructured Environment. *Proc. Intell. Robots Compu. Vision XIX* 4197, 70–80.

178. Kirk, PM, and Sullman, MJ (2001). Heart rate strain in cable hauler choker setters in New Zealand logging operations. *Appl. Ergon.* 32(4), 389–398.

179. Kang, D, Woo, JH, and Shin, YC (2007). Distribution and determinants of maximal physical work capacity of Korean male metal workers. *Ergonomics* 50(12), 2137–2147.

180. Kim, JH (2009). A study on the estimation methodology for the stand -by energy savings of televisions using learning curves and diffusion models. *Trans. Korean Inst. Electr. Eng.* 58(2), 239–241.

181. Kandil, A, El-Rayes, K, and El-Anwar, O (2010). Optimization research: Enhancing the robustness of large-scale multi objective optimization in construction. *J. Constr. Eng. Manage.* 136(1), 17–25.

182. Koch, C, and Brilakis, I (2011). Pothole detection in asphalt pavement images. *J. Adv. Eng. Eng. Inf.* 25(3), 507 –515.

183. Koch, C, and Brilakis, I (2011). Improving pothole detection through vision tracking for automated pavement assessment. *Proceedings of 18th EG-ICE Workshop*, pp. 1–8.

184. Laughman, C, Lee, K, Cox, R, Shaw, S, Leeb, S, Norford, L, and Arm strong, P (2003). Power signature analysis. *IEEE Power Energy Mag.* 1(2), 56–63.

185. Li, Q, Yao, M, and Xu, B (2010). A real -time 3D scanning system for pavement distortion inspection. *J. Meas. Sci. Technol.* 21(015702), 1–8.

186. Li, N and Becerik-Gerber, B (2011). Performance: Based evaluation of RFID-based indoor location sensing solutions for the built environment. *Adv. Eng. Inf.* 25(3), 535–546.

187. Muller, EA (1950). Ein leistungs-pulsindex als mass der laistungsfahigkiet. *Arbeitphysiologie* 14, 271–284.

188. Mardaljevic, J (1995). Validation of a lighting simulation program under real sky conditions. *Light. Res. Technol.* 27(4), 181–188.
189. Myrtek, M, Fichtler, A, Strittmatter, M, and Brügner, G (1999). Stress and strain of blue- and white-collar workers during work and leisure time: Results of psychophysiological and behavioral monitoring. *Appl. Ergon.* 30(4), 341–351.
190. Mardaljevic, J (2000). Simulation of annual daylighting profiles for internal illuminance. *Light. Res. Technol.* 32(3), 111–118.
191. Minnesota Department of Transportation MNDOT (2009). 2009 Pavement Condition Executive Summary. Report No.: MnDOT/OMRR-PM-2009-01.
192. McLauchlan, N, and Bessis, N (2011). Towards remote monitoring of power use: A case for smart meters. *In PARELEC '11: Proceedings of the 2011 Sixth International Symposium on Parallel Computing in Electrical Engineering*, Washingdon, DC, pp. 133–138.
193. Pradhan, A, Ergen, E, and Akinci, B (2009). Technological assessment of radio frequency identification technology for indoor localization. *J. Comp. Civ. Eng.* 23(4), 230–238.
194. P3International (2011). Kill -a-watt. http://www.p3international.com/products/special/p4400/p4400-ce.html.
195. Reinhart, C and Fitz, A (2006). Findings from a survey on the current use of daylight simulations in building design. *Energ Build.* 38(7), 824–835.
196. Snavely, N, Seitz, SM, and Szeliski, R (2006). Photo tourism: Exploring photo collections in 3D, *SIGGRAPH Conference Proceedings*, ACM Press, New York, pp. 835–846.
197. Shaw, SR, Leeb, SB, Norford, LK, and Cox, RW (2008). Nonintrusive load monitoring and diagnostics in power systems. *IEEE Trans Instr Meas.* 57(7), 1445–1454.
198. Sianaki, OA, Hussain, O, Dillon, T, and Tabesh, AR (2010). Intelligent decision support system for including consumer's preferences in residential energy consumption in Smart Grid. *2nd International Conference on Computational Intelligence, Modelling and Simulation, CIMSim 2010*, September 28, 2010-September 30, IEEE Computer Society, Bali, Indonesia, 154–159.
199. Turpin-Legendre, E, and Meyer, JP (2003). Comparison of physiological and subjective strain in workers wearing two different protective coveralls for asbestos abatement tasks. *Appl. Ergon.* 34(6), 551–556.
200. The Energy Detective (2011). TED: The energy detective. http://www.theenergydetective.com/about-ted.
201. Wang, KCP (2004). Challenges and feasibility for comprehensive automated survey of pavement conditions. *Proceedings of Conference on Applications of Advanced Technologies in Transportation Engineering*, pp. 531–536.
202. Wang, J, Ma, S., and Jiang, L (2009). Research on automatic identification method of pavement sag deformation. *Proceedings of ICCTP 2009.*
203. Ward, G (2010). Radiance gen BSDF program. http://radsite.lbl.gov/radiance/man_html/genBSDF.1.html> (October 10, 2011).
204. Ward, G, Mistrick, R, Lee, ES, McNeil, A, and Jonsson, J (2011). Simulating the daylight performance of complex fenestration systems using bidirectional scattering distribution functions within radiance. *LEUKOS* 6(4), 241–261.
205. Yu, BX and Yu, X (2006). Vibration-based system for pavement condition evaluation. Procedings of Conference on *Applications of Advanced Technologies in Transportation Engineering*, 183–189.
206. Yu, YX, Peng, L, and Zhao Chun-liu (2008). Non -intrusive meth od for on -line power load decomposition. *2008 China International Conference on Electricity Distribution (CICED 2008)*, IEEE, Piscataway, NJ.
207. Zack, GW, Rogers, WE, and Latt, SA (1977). Automatic measurement of sister chromatid exchange frequency. *J. Histochem. Cytochem.* 25(7), 741–753.
208. Zhu, Z, German, S, and Brilakis, I (2011). Visual retrieval of concrete crack properties for auto-mated post -earthquake structural safety evaluation. *Auto. Constr.* 20(7), 874–883.
209. BSIM3 Homepage. http://www-device.eecs.berkeley.edu/~bsim3.
210. Pillage, LT, Rohrer, RA, and Visweswariah, C (1994). *Electronic Circuit & System Simulation Methods.* Mcgraw-Hill: New York. ISBN-13: 978-0070501690 (ISBN-10: 0070501696).
211. Hachtel, G, Brayton, R, and Gustavson, F (1971). The sparse tableau approach to network analysis anddesignlation. *IEEE Trans. Circuits Theory* 18(1), 101–113.
212. BSIM4 Homepage. http://www-device.eecs.berkeley.edu/~bsim4.
213. Fan, Z, Qiu, F, Kaufman, A, and Yoakum-Stover, S (2004). GPU cluster for high performance computing. In *SC'04: Proceedings of the 2004 ACM/IEEE conference on Supercomputing* (Washington, DC, USA), p. 47, IEEE Computer Society.

214. Owens, J (2007). GPU architecture overview. *In SIGGRAPH '07: ACM SIGGRAPH 2007 Courses*, New York, p. 2, ACM.

215. Luebke, D, Harris, M, Govindaraju, N, Lefohn, A, Houston, M, Owens, J, Segal, M, Papakipos, M, and Buck, I (2006). GPGPU: General-purpose computation on graphics hardware. *In SC'06: Proceed-Ingsofthe 2006 ACM/IEEE Conference on Supercomputing*, New York, p. 208, ACM.

216. Schive, H-Y, Chien, C-H, Wong, S-K, Tsai, Y-C, and Chiueh, T (2007). Graphic-card cluster for astrophysics (GraCCA) – performance tests. In Submitted to New Astronomy.

217. O megaSim Mixed-Signal Fast-SPICE Simulator. http://www.nascentric.com/product.html.

218. Virtuoso ultrasim full-chip simulator. http://www.cadence.com/products/customic/ultrasim/index.aspx.

219. Fine SIM SPICE. http://www.magmada.com/c/SVX0QdBvGgqX_/Pages/FineSimSPICE_html.

220. Capsim hierarchical spice simulation. http://www.xcad.com/xcad/spicesimulation.html.

221. Dartu, F, and Pileggi, LT (1998). TETA: Transistor-level engine for timing analysis, *In DAC'98: Proceedings of the 35 Thannual Conferenceon Designautomation*, New York, pp. 595–598, ACM.

222. Agrawal, P, Goil, S, Liu, S, and Trotter, J (1994). Parallel model evaluation for circuit simulation on the PACE multiprocessor. *In Proceedings of the Seventh International Conference on VLSI Design*, pp. 45–48.

223. Agrawal, P, Goil, S, Liu, S, and Trotter, JA (1993). PACE: A multiprocessor system for VLSI circuitsimulation. *In Proceedings of SIAM Conference on Parallel Processing*, pp. 573–581.

224. Sadayappan, P, and Visvanathan, V (1988). Circuitsimulation on shared-memory multiprocessors. *IEEE Trans. Comput.* 37(12), 1634–1642.

225. Gulati, K, and Khatri, SP (2008). Towards acceleration of fault simulation using graphics processingunits. *In Proceedings of the 45th Annual Conference on Design Automation*, pp. 822–827.

226. NVIDIA CUDA Introduction, http://www.beyond3d.com/content/articles/12/1.

227. Nagel, L and Rohrer, R (1971). Computer analysis of nonlinear circuits, excluding radiation. *IEEE J. Solid States Circuits* SC-6, 162–182.

228. Amdahl, G (1967). Validity of the single processor approach to achieving large-scale computingcapabilities. *Proc. AFIPS* 30, 483–485.

229. Weiland, T (1977). A discretisation method for the solution of Maxwell's equations for six-component fields. *Int. J. Electron. Commun. AEU* 31, 116–120.

230. Bossavit, A (2001). 'Generalized finite differences' in computational electromagnetics. *In Progress in Electromagnetics Research*, Volume PIER32, 45–64.

231. Weiland, T (1978). On the calculation of eddy currents in arbitrarily shaped, three-dimensional, laminated iron cores. Part I: The method. *Archiv fur Elektrotechnik (AfE)* 60(6), 345–351.

232. Weiland, T (1980). Transient electromagnetic fields excited by bunches of charged particles in cavities of arbitrary shape. *In Proceedings of the XI-th International Conference on High Energy Accelerators*, Geneva, Switzerland, pp. 570–575.

233. Van Rienen, U, and Weiland, T (1985). Triangular discretization method for the evaluation of RF-fields in cylindrically symmetric cavities. *IEEE Trans. Magn.* 21(6), 2317–2320.

234. Klatt, R and Weiland, T (1988). A three-dimensional code BCI that solves Maxwell's equations in the time domain. *In Proceedings of 3rd International IGTE Symposium*, Graz, Austria, pp. 1–8.

235. Thoma, P and Weiland, T (1995). A subgridding method in combination with the finite integration technique. *In Proceedings of the 25th European Microwave Conference*, Vol. 2, pp. 770–774.

236. Schuhmann, R and Weiland, T (1999). FDTD on nonorthogonal grids with triangular fillings. *IEEE Trans. Magn.* 35, 1470–1473.

237. Munteanu, I, Wittig, T, Weiland, T, and Ioan, D (2000). FIT/PVL circuit parameter extraction for general electromagnetic devices. *IEEE Trans. Magn.* 36, 1421–1425.

238. Weiland, T (1996). Time domain electromagnetic field computation with finite difference methods. *Int. J. Num. Modell.* 9, 295–319.

239. Tonti, E (2001). Finite formulation of the electromagnetic field. *In Progress in Electromagnetics Research*. Vol. PIER32, pp. 317–356.

240. Yee, KS (1966). Numerical solution of initial boundary value problems involving Maxwell's equations in isotropic media. *IEEE Trans. Antennas Propagate* AP-14(4), 302–307.

241. Weiland, T (1983). TBCI and URMEL: New computer codes for wake field and cavity mode calculations. *IEEE Trans. Nucl. Sci. NS* 30, 2489–2491.

242. Barts, T, et al. (1986). MAFIA: A three-dimensional electromagnetic CAD system for magnets, RF structures and transient wake field calculations. *In Proceedings of the International Linear Accelerator Conference*, Vol. SLAC-303, Stanford University, pp. 276–278.

243. CST GmbH: CST Design Environmenttm with its modules CST Microwave Studior, CST EM Studiotm, CST Particle Studiotm and CST Design Studiotm. www.cst.com (2006).

244. Munteanu, I and Hirtenfelder, F (2005). Convergence of the finite integration technique on various mesh types. *In Proceedings of Gemic 05*, Ulm, Germany.

245. Krietenstein, B, Schuhmann, R, Thoma, P, and Weiland, T (1998). The perfect boundary approximation technique facing the big challenge of high precision field computation. *In Proceedings of the XIX International Linear Accelerator Conference*, pp. 860–862.

246. Yu, W, Liu, Y, Su, T, Hunag, N, and Mittra, R (2005). A robust parallel conformal finite-difference time-domain processing package using the MPI library. *Ant. Prop. Mag.* 47, 39–59.

247. Schuhmann, R and Weiland, T (1998). Stability of the FDTD algorithm on nonorthogonal grids related to the spatial interpolation scheme. *IEEE Trans. Magn.* 34, 2751–2754.

248. Schuhmann, R, Schmidt, P, and Weiland, T (2001). A new Whitney-based material operator for the finite-integration technique on triangular grids. *In Proceedings of the COMPUMAG 2001*, Vol. 3, pp. 102–103.

249. Schuhmann, R and Weiland, T (2002). Open architecture solves large 3D puzzles. *Microwaves RF* 41, 144–155.

250. Gjonaj, E, Perotoni, M, and Weiland, T (2006). Large scale simulation of an integrated circuit package. *In 16th Conference on Electrical Performance of Electronic Packaging (EPEP)*.

251. Bakr, MH, Bandler, JW, Madsen, K, and Søndergaard, J (2000). Review of the space mapping approach to engineering optimization and modeling. *Optim. Eng.* 1(3), 241–276.

252. Bandler, JW, Cheng, QS, Dakroury, AS, Mohamed, AS, Bakr, MH, Madsen, K, and Søndergaard, J (2004). Space mapping: The state of the art. *IEEE Trans. Microwave Theory Tech.* 52, 337–360.

253. Bohmer, K, Hemker, PW, and Stetter, HJ (1984). The defect correction approach. In Ohmer, KB and Stetter, HJ (eds.) *Defect Correction Methods: Theory and Applications*, vol. 5, Computing Supplies, pp. 1–32. Springer-Verlag, Berlin, Heidelberg, New York, Tokyo.

254. Echeverr´ia, D (2007). Multi-level optimization: Space mapping and manifold mapping. PhD thesis, University of Amsterdam.

255. Echeverr´ia, D and Hemker, PW (2005). Space mapping and defect correction. *Comp. Methods Appl. Math.* 5(2), 107–136.

256. Echeverr´ia, D, Lahaye, D, Encica, L, Hemker, PW, Lomonova, EA, and Vandenput, AJA (2006). Manifold-mapping optimization applied to linear actuator design. *IEEE Trans. Magne.* 42(4), 1183–1186.

257. Hemker, PW and Echeverr´ia, D (2006). On the manifold mapping optimization technique. Technical Report MAS-R0612, CWI, Amsterdam.

258. Hemker, PW and Echeverr´ia, D (2006). A trust-region strategy for manifold mapping optimization. Technical Report MAS-R0617, CWI, Amsterdam.

259. Musumeci, S, Pagano, R, Raciti, A, Buonomo, S, Ronsisvalle, C, and Scollo, R (2003). A new monolithic emitter-switching bipolar trasistor (ESBT) in high voltage converter applications. *In IAS'03*.

260. Miettinen, KM (1998). *Nonlinear Multiobjective Optimization*. Kluwer Academic Publisher: New York.

261. Spinella, S, and Anile, AM (2005). A posteriori multiobjective optimization. *In Applied and Industrial Mathematics*, Italy, pp. 520–529.

262. Jones, DR, Perttunen, CD, and Stuckman, BE (1993). Lipschitzian optimization without the lipschitz constant. *J. Optim. Theory Appl.* 79(1), 157–181.

263. Sawaragi, Y, Nakayama, H, and Tanino, T (1985). *Theory of Multiobjective Optimization*. Academic Press Inc: New York.

264. Borkowski, MJ and Kostamovaara, J (2005). Spurious tone free digital delta-sigma modulator design for dc inputs. *In Proceedings of the IEEE International Symposium on Circuits and Systems*, Kobe, Japan, pp. 5601–5604.

265. Borkowski, MJ, Riley, TAD, Hakkinen, J, and Kostamovaara, J (2005). A practical -† modulator design method based on periodical behavior analysis. *IEEE Trans. Circ. Syst.-II: Express Briefs* 52(10), 626–630.

266. Crandall, RE and Pomerance, C (2001). *Prime Numbers: A Computational Perspective*. Springer, Germany.

267. Gu, R and Ramaswamy, S (2007). Fractional-N phase locked loop design and applications. *In Proceedings of the 7th International Conference on ASIC*, Guilin, China, pp. 327–332.

268. Hosseini, K and Kennedy, MP (2006). Mathematical analysis of digital mash delta-sigma modulator for fractional-N frequency synthesizers. *In Proceedings of the IEEE Ph.D. Research in Microelectronics and Electronics*, Otranto (Lecce), Italy, pp. 309–312.

269. Hosseini, K and Kennedy, MP (2007). Mathematical analysis of a prime modulus quantizer mash digital delta-sigma modulator. *IEEE Trans. Circ. Syst.-II Express Brief* 54(12), 1105–1109.

270. Hosseini, K and Kennedy, MP (2007). Maximum sequence length mash digital delta-sigma modulators. *IEEE Trans. Circ. Syst.-I Regular Papers* 54(12), 2628–2638.

271. Kozak, M and Kale, I (2004). Rigorous analysis of delta-sigma modulators for fractional-n pll frequency synthesis. *IEEE Trans. Circ. Syst.-I Regular Papers* 51(6), 1148–1162.

272. Oppenheim, AV and Schafer, RW (1999). *Discrete-Time Signal Processing.* Prentice-Hall, Upper Saddle River, NJ.

273. Pamarti, S and Galton, I (2007). LSB dithering in mash delta-sigma d/a converters. *IEEE Trans. Circ. Syst.-I Regular Papers* 54(4), 779–790.

274. Pamarti, S, Welz, J, and Galton, I (2007). Statistics of the quantization noise in 1-bit dithered single quantizer digital delta-sigma modulators. *IEEE Trans. Circ. Syst.-I: Regular Papers* 54(3), 492–503.

275. Bush, KG (1998). *Regel bare Elektroantrie be: Antriebs Methoden, Betriebssicherheit, Instandhaltung.* Verlag Pflaum: Munchen.

276. Salon, JS (1996). *Finite Element Analysis of Electrical Machines.* Cambridge University Press, Cambridge.

277. Davat, B, Ren, Z, and Lajoic-Mazenc, M (1985). The movement in field modeling. *IEEE Trans. Magn.* 21(6), 2296–2298.

278. Charusakwong, N, Tangittinunt, K, and Choocharukul, K (2008). Inconsistencies between motorist's perceptions of traffic conditions and color indicators on intelligent traffic signs in Bangkok. *Proceedings of the 13th National Convention on Civil Engineering,* pp. TRP196–TRP202.

279. Choocharukul, K (2005). Congestion measures in Thailand: State of the practice. *Proceedings of the10th National Convention on Civil Engineering,* pp. TRP111–TRP118.

280. Pattara-atikom, W and Peachavanish, R (2007). Estimating road traffic congestion from cell dwell time using neural network. *The 7th International Conference on ITS Telecommunications (ITST 2007),* Sophia Antipolis, France.

281. Pongpaibool, P, Tangamchit, P, and Noodwong, K (2007). Evaluation of road traffic congestion using fuzzy techniques. *Proceedings of IEEE TENCON 2007,* Taipei, Taiwan.

282. Porikli, F, Li, X (2004). Traffic congestion estimation using hmm models without vehicle tracking. *IEEE Intelligent Vehicles Symposium,* pp. 188–193.

283. Lu, J and Cao, L (2003). Congestion evaluation from traffic flow information based on fuzzy logic. *IEEE Intell. Transport. Syst.* 1, 50–33.

284. Krause, B and Altrock, CV (1996). Intelligent highway by fuzzy logic: Congestion detection and traffic control on multi-lane roads with variable road signs. *5th International Conference on Fuzzy Systems* vol. 3, pp. 1832–1837.

285. Alessandri, RBA and Repetto, M (2003). Estimating of freeway traffic variables using information from mobile phones. *IEEE Am. Control Conf.* 5, 4089–4094.

286. Lomax, JTS, Tuner, M, Shunk, G, Levinson, HS, Pratt, RH, Bay, PN, and Douglas, BB (1997). Quantifying congestion. Final Report. National Cooperative Highway Research Program Report 398, TRB, Washington, DC.

287. Bertini, RL (2004). Congestion and its extent. Access to destinations: Rethinking the transportation future of our region, Minneapolis, MN.

288. Dai, HC and Mcbeth, C (1997). Effects of learning parameters on learning procedure and performance of a BPNN. *Neural Network* 10(8), 1505–1521.

289. Quinlan, JR (1993). *C4.5: Programs for Machine Learning.* Morgan Kauffman, San Mateo, CA.

290. Aljawarneh, S and Alkhateeb, F (2009). Design and implementation of new data validation service (NDVS) using semantic web technologies in web applications. *In Proceedings of the World Congress on Engineering 2009: WCE'09,* vol. I, pp. 179–184. London, UK, International Association of Engineering.

291. Aljawarneh, S and Alkhateeb, F (2009). A semantic web technology-based architecture for new server-side data validation in web applications. In Aldawood, A. (ed.) *ICIT'9.* Alzaytoona Univeristy: Amman, Jordan.

292. Sommerville, J (2006). *Software Engineering.* Addison-Wesley, Reading, MA.

293. Sommerville, J and Sawyer, P (1997). Viewpoints: Principles, problems and a practical approach to requirements engineering. *Annal. Softwar. Eng.* 3, 101–130.

294. Clements, P, Bachmann, F, Bass, L, Ivers, J, Garlan, D, Little, R, Nord, R, and Stafford, R (2003). *Documenting Software Architectures: Views and Beyond.* Addison-Wesley, Reading, MA.

295. May, N (2005). A survey of software architecture viewpoint models. *Proceedings of the Sixth Australasian Workshop on Software and System Architectures,* Melbourne, Australia, pp. 13–24.

296. Yamaji, M, Ishii, Y, Shimamura, T, and Yamamoto, S (2008). Wireless sensor network for industrial automation. *5th International Conference on Networked Sensing Systems*, pp. 253–253, 17–19 June 2008.

297. Oesterlind, F, Pramsten, E, Roberthson, D, Eriksson, J, Finne, N, and Voigt, T (2007). Integrating building automation systems and wireless sensor networks. SICS Technical Report T2007.

298. Neil, A: Duffie, challenges in design of heterarchical controls for dynamics logistic systems. First International Conference on Dynamics Logistic, LDIC 2007, pp. 3–24, August 2007.

299. Dressler, F (2007). *Self-Organization in Sensor and Actor Networks*. Wiley: Hoboken, NJ.

300. Tanenbaum, A and Van steen, M (2002). *Distributed Systems Principles and Paradigms*, 1st edn. Prentice-Hall, New York.

301. Elazar, DJ (1987). *Exploring Federalism*. University of Alabama Press, Tuscaloosa.

302. Jie, W (1999). *Distributed System Design*. CRC Press: Boca Raton, FL.

303. Fei-Yue, W and Derong, L (2008). *Networked Control Systems: Theory and Applications*. SpringerVerlag: London.

304. William, S (1999). *Leviene, the Control Handbook*, vol. I. CRC Press & IEEE Press, NewYork.

305. Zhang, P (2008). *Industrial Control Technology*. William Andrew Inc, Norwich.

306. Gregory, K and McMillan, DM (1999). *Considine, Process/Industrial Instruments and Controls Handbook*, 5th edn. McGraw-Hill, New York.

307. Jafari, AM, Sklorz, A, and Lang, W (2009). Target-oriented routing algorithm based on sequential coordinates for autonomous wireless sensor network. *J. Networ. Acad. Publ.* 4(6), 421–427.

308. Jafari, AM, Sklorz, A and Lang, W: Energy consumption comparison between autonomous and central wireless sensor network 6:166–170 (April 2009). In: *Communications of SIWN*, ISSN: 1757-4439 (Print); ISSN: 1757-4447 (CD-ROM).

Index